The Peter Pye Omnibus

The Peter Pye Omnibus

Red Mains'l

The Sea is for Sailing

A Sail in a Forest

Backdoor to Brazil

ASHFORD PRESS PUBLISHING (UK)
1986

Published by ASHFORD PRESS PUBLISHING 1986
1 CHURCH ROAD
SHEDFIELD
HAMPSHIRE
SO3 2HW

Red Mains'l first published 1961
Copyright © A.N. Welsh 1952.

The Sea is for Sailing first published 1957
Copyright © A.N. Welsh 1957.

A Sail in a Forest first published 1961
Copyright © A.N. Welsh 1961.

Back Door to Brazil
Copyright © A.N. Welsh 1986.

This collection published as
The Peter Pye Omnibus
Copyright © A.N. Welsh 1986.

All rights reserved. Except for use in a review, no part of this book may be reproduced or utilised in any form or by any means electronic or mechanical, including photocopying, recording or by any information storage and retrieval system, without written permission from the publisher.

British Library Cataloguing in Publication Data.

Pye, Peter
    Peter Pye omnibus : comprising 4 titles,
    Red Mains'l, The Sea is for Sailing, A Sail in a Forest,
    Back Door to Brazil.
    1. Voyages and travels   2. Sailboats
    I. Title
    910.4'5   G540

    ISBN 0-907069-45-2

Printed in Great Britain by
Butler & Tanner Ltd, Frome and London

Typeset by Solent Design Studio

~~ INTRODUCTION ~~

EDMUND Arthur Pye – always known as "Peter", was born in 1902. His father, Harry Pye, was in the wine trade, but there was a tradition of medicine in the family, and Peter followed this at Cambridge, practising first after qualification in Switzerland. An unhappy first marriage resulted in the birth of Peter's only child, the artist Patrick Pye.

Peter then met my father's younger sister, Annie May Welsh, "Anne", who was starting a career on the stage following attendance at the London School of Dramatic Art. They were made for each other and the close and remarkable relationship which lasted the rest of their lives made possible the adventures described in these pages.

Peter and Anne married in 1936, but they had started sailing together in 1931, and had bought for £25 an old Polperro fishing boat, the *Lily*, which after renovations was renamed *Moonraker* of Fowey, and is the boat they used for all of their cruises. Peter and Anne spent all of their free time sailing and working on *Moonraker*. The family had clubbed together to help in the purchase of a share in a busy West London medical practice, but during and after the war the pressures of being a doctor and anaesthetist became more and more onerous. The National Health Service became a prospect on the horizon, and Peter decided to sell his practice share. His intention was to realize his dream of taking to the sea full time.

Consider them at this point, a middle-aged couple, both slightly built and dogged by ill-health—through most of his sailing Peter had a duodenal ulcer and later a double strangulated hernia, and Anne suffered from terrible sea sickness until she found drugs to control it—giving up a professional situation to embark with extremely limited funds into a most precarious existence. This move into the unknown was considered by the rest of the family as crazy rather than brave!

Moonraker was a strong little boat, and was now equipped for long-distance cruising, but she was still a very old craft. On a summer's evening, with the waters of the Crouch gently lapping the hull, a tot all round and Peter spinning yarns into the night, *Moonraker* was all that could be desired (particularly if you were supple and not too large!)—running in the open sea before a warm breeze she was delightful—but there were long days of scraping and sanding, shellacking painting, cleaning and overhaul of all kinds every winter, cold and chancy dinghy trips, days and nights in open water with cold rain and spray driving in everywhere, and a desperate struggle with wet ropes, sails, faulty bilge pumping against winds and seas which threatened every moment to tear the boat out of control and to its doom.

Peter and Anne loved it all—the challenge was meat and drink to them for they had become creatures of the sea and could think of no other way of living.

As a base they bought a pair of rundown 18th-century cottages in a village on the Crouch. In the fullness of time these cottages were converted into a most interesting and comfortable home, "Mizzen", but during the early cruises they were distinctly spartan. As soon as they could Peter and Anne let the cottages and took to the sea. Peter had a view that you could live for nothing, or next to nothing in your own boat. He had been influenced by Weston Martyr's book, *£200 Millionaire*, and while Peter and Anne never had much money, and never any that was not earmarked for repairs and improvements to *Moonraker*, they managed to live pretty well.

Peter acted as a locum from time to time, he lectured, and it was always part of the grand design to write. He wanted others to share his experiences and love of sailing and cruising. Peter and Anne kept very detailed logs, and out of these were created the books, written in winter evenings at "Mizzen" when work on the boat had to stop.

Red Mains'l was the first, the account of their cruise to the West Indies in 1949/50 which won the Trophy of the Royal Cruising Club in that year. It was first published in 1952 by Herbert Jenkins, and later by Adlard Coles and also appeared in the Mariners Library.

Red Mains'l established Peter as a writer, and although long voyages in small boats are now commonplace, the idea of a twenty-nine foot, nine ton cutter built in 1896 crossing the Atlantic with minimal crew, and scorning to use engine, fired the imagination in 1952.

The Sea is for Sailing followed; it was the story of a voyage across the Panama Canal then to the Galapagos, Marquesas, Tuamotus, Tahiti, Hawaii then up the west coast of America to British Columbia and the Charlotte Islands. This was published by Rupert Hart-Davis in 1957 and 1960, and then by John de Graff in New York in 1961.

A Sail in a Forest described a cruise up the Baltic and into the

Introduction

Gulf of Finland, and it too was published by Rupert Hart-Davis (1961), appearing also in the Mariners Library and in an Adlard Coles edition in 1971.

The last book *Backdoor to Brazil* was never published. The strain of these long voyages and advancing years was taking its toll. In 1966 the Pyes went on what was for them a short cruise round the Mediterranean, a cruise which was, alas, one of those events in which everything went wrong. On leaving, Anne broke her wrist and on the way back, both exhausted, Peter with a damaged arm and in great pain from his hernias, they put into Plymouth. Peter was admitted to the General Hospital for the long overdue operation on his hernias and died there—owing to a tragic mistake in which an anaesthetic cylinder had been supplied wrongly labelled—Peter was gassed to death.

And so passed away a great sailor and a brave man, Commodore of the Royal Cruising Club when he died, but a man who as far as I am aware had only friends not enemies. Peter was charming, genial and kind, the perfect host as was Anne, but more relaxed than she. Tomorrow was never of concern to Peter whereas Anne was the one who set the alarm clock and attended to the details—but wherever either or both were to be found, there too was laughter, interest and friendship.

After Peter's death, Anne (now 62) retired to the seclusion of "Mizzen Cottage"—seldom venturing far afield but visited by a stream of friends and in particular her closest friend, Mrs Barbara Evatt of Southminster, who was with her constantly and at the time of her death in 1983. Anne edited Peter's last book *Backdoor to Brazil* and it is published for the first time in this volume. *Moonraker* herself was exhibited for a while in the Exeter Maritime Museum, but Anne sold her to Jan Steen Eilersen who looks after the boat with loving care in Denmark.

Peter Pye's books need in truth no introduction from me; I was there at the beginning and at the end of it all, and at Plymouth and at "Mizzen", which I had the sad duty of selling. I was not one of the third members they took with them on the epic cruises and I feel I ought to end by paying tribute to these remarkable people, and also to thank the Royal Cruising Club, Jock McLeod and Barbara Evatt for their help. We all miss Peter and Anne very much and their memory will live as long as men shall sail.

ALEXANDER NORTON WELSH
Pendeilo House, Amroth, Pembrokeshire.
29th November, 1985. Copyright.

Contents

Red Mains'l	1
The Sea is for Sailing	155
A Sail in a Forest	319
Backdoor to Brazil	443

Red Mains'L

PETER PYE

For Anne

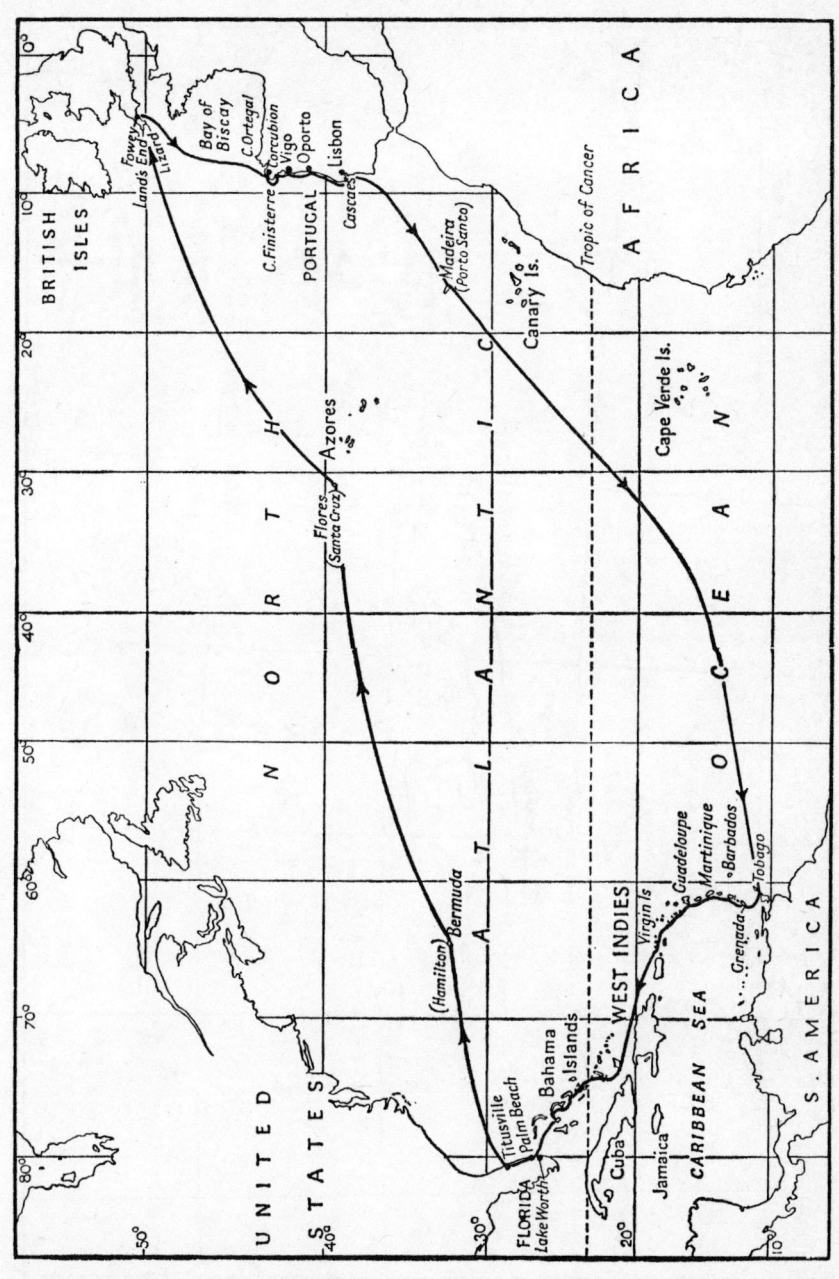

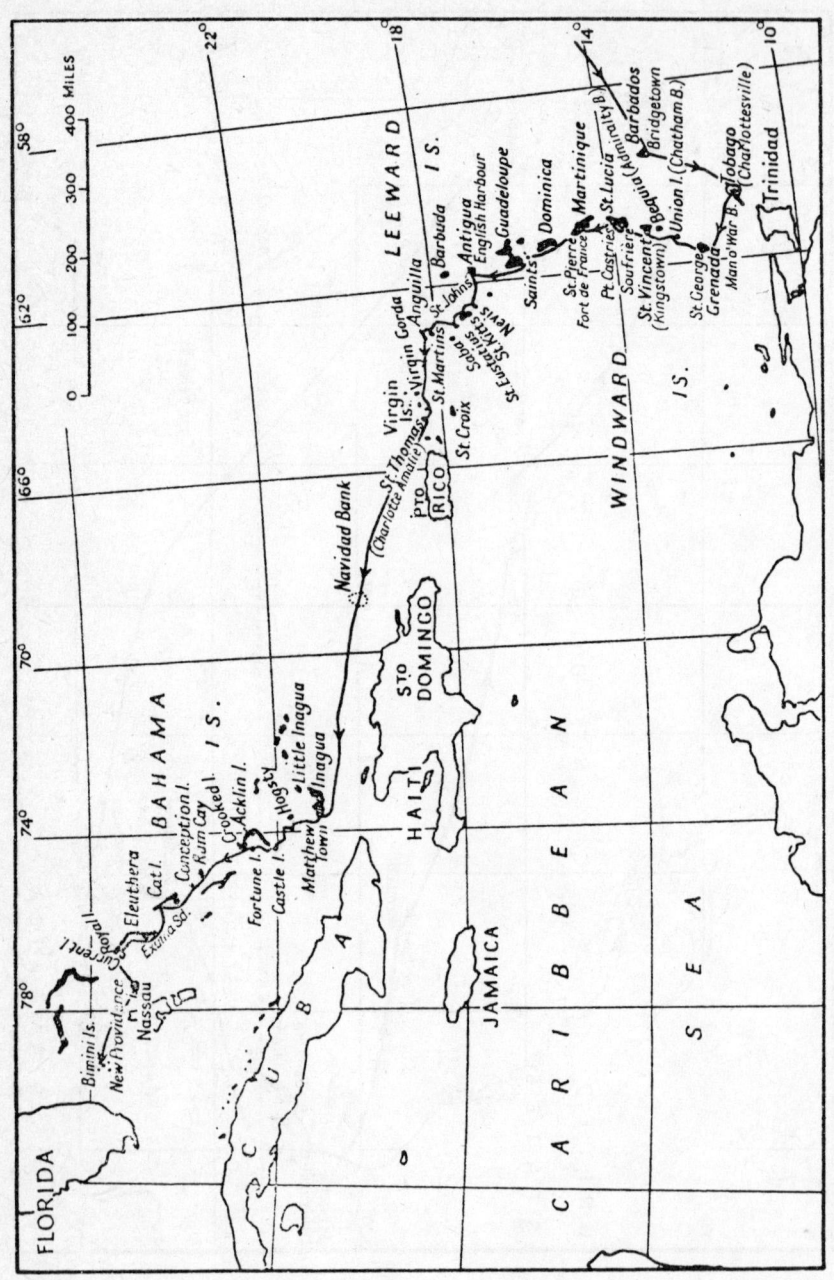

CHAPTER ONE

ONE hot August afternoon I was giving an anaesthetic in an Ealing nursing home. The operation was nearly over when the surgeon asked me whether I had been away for my holiday. I said, "We've been cruising. We went across the channel in a nine-tonner."

A flicker of interest showed in his face. "Fond of sailing?" he asked.

"Very, what little I've done."

The surgeon put a dressing over the wound and a bandage over the dressing. He straightened his back and then turned to me again. "Have you read Weston Martyr's *£200 Millionaire?*"

When I replied that I had never heard of it he told me it was a story of a doctor who found he could live on a small boat for two hundred pounds a year. With his few possessions he sailed through the waterways of Europe, going south in the winter and north in the summer, living the life of a millionaire on his slender income.

There was a pause while the great man took off his gloves and veil and gown. He turned to my senior partner: "Richards," he said, "if I send Pye a copy of this book, sooner or later you'll lose him to the sea. But I shall send it to him, all the same."

My wife's name is Anne. To this day I cannot think why she married me, nor can she. I suppose it is really because she never gives anything up once she has started it. We had a practice, a small house, a smaller car and a large overdraft, and we were as happy as the day was long; we still are.

We had no boat and no money, and Anne had the firm intention of dying at forty, when she thought all life would end. She read the book. She said, "This has given me an idea. If we bought a boat it would be cheaper than hiring one for a month every year."

I shook my head. "The sort of boat we'd want would cost at least a hundred and fifty pounds, and we haven't got that number of shillings."

"But *I* have; I have that amount, and a little more." The look on my face made her laugh. She said, "If I'd told you, we'd have used it for the 'National Debt' [our overdraft], and I was keeping it for something we'd enjoy. I know what that is now. It's a boat."

In the spring of the next year we drove down to Fowey for a few days' holiday and found ourselves one morning in Polperro. The tide was in and fishing-boats lined the quay, their nets drying in the sun. I asked a fisherman if he knew of any for sale, and he pointed to one, lying like an ugly duckling apart from her more attractive sisters. She was too short and stocky for good looks, with not enough rake to her stern, but she had a rather lovely sheer. Her short stumpy masts (she was yawl-rigged like all Polperro boats) were bare of gear and the paint hung in strips from her bulwarks. I would have passed her by without another glance, but Anne looked at her more closely. "A boat with so much draught would be easy to convert," she said, "and the bulwarks would hide the cabin top. Let's go and see her owner."

Our fisherman friend directed us to his cottage. The front door led into a small room full of chairs and brass, with a fire burning in the grate. Before it a man sat in an armchair. He was thick-set, with small eyes in a large round face; his hair was iron grey, and he must have been nearly seventy. He was crippled with rheumatism. His wife said, "Dad, this lady and gentleman have come about the *Lily*."

The *Lily* had been built in the 'nineties by Ferris of Looe, and the story went that the man who had her built paid fifteen pounds more to have her built extra-strong. She was twenty-nine feet long by nearly ten feet beam and she drew six feet aft, when loaded down with gear.

Anne said, "Well, Mr. Curtis, we'll go and have a look at her, if we may. How much do you want for her?"

"I reckon," he said slowly, "she'd be worth all of twenty-five pounds, without the engine."

We borrowed a dinghy and rowed out to the *Lily*. Her plank edges lay smoothly together and there were no short lengths in her topsides—always a good sign, I had been told, in an old boat. She had powerful bows and a broad entrance, and her sheer led down from a freeboard of over four feet at the bows to less than two just aft of the fishwell. She had flush decks, and bulwarks eighteen inches high. Her decks were well worn.

Anne stood by the helm. "I think," she said, "we've found our ship." We scrambled aboard and went below. The fishwell took up the whole of the middle of the ship. We pulled up the floorboards and looked into the bilge. There were firebars, cannonballs, cogwheels and shingle. She was as dry as a bone, but smelt to heaven of fish and tar. In the fo'c'sle was a bogie stove eaten with rust, and a single locker on the starboard side. Aft was a single-cylinder Kelvin, a vast thing, no use to us at all. Anne's face was flushed with excitement. "If she only costs twenty-five pounds, we can afford to have her converted into just what we want. It'll be like buying a new boat." I hadn't the heart to tell her that a surveyor might find she was rotten.

By the time we had finished exploring her the tide had fallen and Anne got tar on her clothes getting back into the boat, but she hardly noticed it in her anxiety to pay Mr. Curtis his deposit. As we rowed away, we admired the *Lily*'s run-aft from her midship section to her stern. She might prove faster than her fat little hull suggested.

After dinner that night we went round to see Mr. Watty, who, many years before, had built a boat for my father. Watty was a man of about fifty-five or so, rather short, with powerful shoulders and long arms. He had fierce little eyes, and his voice had a growl in it like that of a small brown bear. He listened in silence till we had talked ourselves out. Then he said, "The money should cover the work, but most of these old boats aren't worth spending it on." We went back to our hotel, feeling like a dog whose bone had been taken away.

The next morning, we all went over to Polperro, and, after hours of prodding, boring and cutting, Watty looked up and grinned. "If you don't buy her, I will. She's old, but there's nothing wrong with her. The worst job will be getting rid of the smell."

Once more we found ourselves in Curtis's cottage. One of his daughters produced a sheet of notepaper and wrote out a Bill of Sale, to which Curtis put his mark, for he could neither read nor write. "We'll take care of the *Lily*," Anne promised him. "We'll bring her round for you to see what we've done before we take her away."

The *Lily* was towed round to Fowey. Every moment of our last two days was spent aboard with Watty, Anne on the inside and myself on the sails and gear. Everything was to be as simple as possible: lanyards, not rigging screws; paraffin lamps, not electricity; a Primus in gimbals for cooking; the galley aft so that the cook could hand up the food to the helmsman. There was to be no third bunk; we would sail our ship on our own. I chalked out the size of a small self-draining cockpit on the deck and we arranged to have a pole-mast and an all-inboard boom for ease in reefing.

On the day we left, Anne, who had been presenting Watty with a long list of last-minute ideas, suddenly had another one. "Mr. Watty, could you make us a double bed on the port side?"

"What d'you want a double bed on a boat for?" he demanded, his face crinkling at so outrageous a suggestion. "I've never heard of such a thing." I burst out laughing and the poor girl blushed furiously. Watty turned away, muttering something under his breath, but the bed was made.

We changed our ship's name; a dreadful thing to do, as any sailor will tell you, but *Lily* just would not do. We renamed her *Moonraker*, after the romantic vessel owned by a pirate captain, Mary Lovell. The frontispiece of Tennyson Jesse's book shows a woodcut of the brig of that name, with raking masts and a tremendous sheer, as fast and as elegant a vessel as ever you could wish to see. We had her registered *Moonraker* and no one can say that it changed her luck.

On the first day of our holiday we went down again. We looked for her in vain, so we went along to Watty. "Seen her?" he asked. "She's over there," and he pointed to a tall vessel in shiny black paint with a gold band below her rubbing-strake. He was absurdly gratified at our delight and came aboard looking at us, pipe in mouth, while we made pleased sounds at the lightness and breadth of her cabin and the smartness of her varnished spars. He had used his wide experience in carrying out our plans. Mrs. Watty had put a vase of flowers on the cabin table.

Under her new rig she carried six hundred and fifty square feet of canvas in her three lowers, her bowsprit was nine feet outboard, and in a place we called the "engine room" Watty had installed a second-hand 6 horse-power Kelvin. We sailed her round to Polperro as we had promised. Old Curtis met us outside the harbour mouth and took command for the last time. His wife and daughter and two sons came to tea. Their comments were favourable, but Curtis said we hadn't enough ballast for her increased sail. At six o'clock the next morning we were bound away, and as we sailed out with a fair wind the old man stood on the quay and raised his hand in farewell.

In the years that followed we learned to sail our ship, and further improvements were made as the result of our experience. We had stronger shroud-plates, heavier canvas, three-eighths chain instead of five-sixteenths; we added a ton of ballast, putting her down three inches by the stern; we bought a C.Q.R. anchor and a two-speed winch; we added a chart-drawer below the galley, increased the storage-space and bought a carpet for the floor. We learned that she was safe and weatherly and could keep the sea.

Then came the Second World War, and very occasionally we

would go to Fambridge in Essex, where *Moonraker* now lay, and spend a day or two aboard, wondering whether we should ever sail again. But the war ended and she was refitted and refastened by King's of Burnham. Once more we put to sea, but now, when we went to Denmark or Spain, we had a third on board and he or she slept in a built-in bunk in the fo'c'sle. We had a shorter mast and a long topsail-yard, and we bought a new vat-dyed mainsail. When we set it for the first time it took our breath away. It was Turkey-red, and would have made a pillar-box look pale; but it became a distinguishing mark, and people would say, "There's the red mains'l; *Moonraker*'s coming home.

At about this time I had a severe return of duodenal pain, which made work in my practice exhausting. For Anne, too, our situation had lost its charm. Changes were coming, and the thought of State Medicine was depressing. One day a friend came to see us. He had been across the Atlantic in a boat not much bigger than *Moonraker*, and he told us about sailing in the North-East Trades, about tropical islands, waving palms and water so clear that you could see the bottom in full five fathoms. After he had gone, Anne came and stood by my chair. She said, "If we don't go now, we're lost. You'll find you'll have to join the State-service. That means you'll be sixty-five before you retire, and if you work like this you won't reach sixty."

"Shall we give this up and go to the West Indies in *Moonraker*?" I said.

She walked over to the window, watching the steady stream of trams and lorries going down our road. "You mean . . . sell everything we've got and take a chance on what happens if we come back?"

"Yes," I replied.

She sat down in front of the fire, her shoulders against my knees. "It seems a big venture in so small a boat, but it might be a good thing, a complete break from our old life. Let's try it."

The break was not easy to make. It was difficult to abandon the cares and hopes of twenty years of practice. As far as my patients and partners went, my loss would be their gain, as a younger man, keen and tough, would put new life into the job, and such a man was ready to step into my shoes. Then there was my father. He was over ninety, and, although he entered into the spirit of the adventure, he would be pleased to see us back again. There was Benny, Anne's golden retriever, who was as devoted to her as she to him. He, too, was old, and couldn't be left unless we found a temporary home where he would be treated as a member of the family. Finally, there was *Moonraker*. She was fifty-two years old, fastened with iron, her planking unsheathed. To sail in her would be to ask for the attentions of the teredo, an unpleasant worm-creature, which lives in the warm waters of the tropics. On its head is a borer, a replica of a modern drill, and this is so hard that no shipwright will risk his saw upon wood suspected of having the dead worm inside it. The worm enters a plank through a hole the size of a pin's head, turns at right-angles and bores along the length of it. In six weeks the wood will be riddled, and, most treacherously, the damage will not show from the outside. Wood covered with paint is safe, but if the paint is scraped off it is immediately in danger, so that the only safe course is to sheath the underwater hull with copper. If this is done in an iron-fastened ship galvanic action may set up between the copper and the iron. As the iron is destroyed before the copper, there is nothing left to hold the planks to the timbers.

Theoretically, if you separate the copper from the iron there will be no galvanic action, and if the work is really well done this is proved in practice. Winston King, of King's at Burnham, was willing to undertake the job and we had faith in him. *Moonraker* was hauled up on the slip, and they put their best workmen on the job. The bottom was first covered with tar and felt, the iron fittings of the rudder were replaced with phosphor-bronze, and a brass band replaced the iron one at the stem. Then the copper went on. All *Moonraker*'s ballast is inside, so we were not faced with the problem of an iron keel.

Other adjustments were necessary. *Moonraker*'s normal water-supply of sixty gallons might not be sufficient, so we installed a B.O.T. water-producer, which would make about twenty-five gallons of drinking-water for every gallon of fuel (paraffin) used. We put a ventilator in the foredeck and bought a wind-sail for a few shillings. We changed her colour from black to the lightest shade of blue, to counter the heat of the sun. We had twin spinnakers fitted and carried four jibs, apart from the genoa. Then we started looking for a crew.

We spent the winter at Fambridge in a mud-berth, and whenever the weather was fine we scraped, sandpapered and varnished. Just before Christmas we had a letter from Christopher Ellis, a master at Radley College, of whom we had heard before. He was a fellow-member of the Royal Cruising Club, he had sailed with Frank Carr, and had been awarded the George Medal for removing a bomb from St. Paul's Cathedral. He came to see us on his way back from Switzerland, fell asleep in the train and was carried on to Burnham. From there he was lucky enough to find a car to bring him to Fambridge, just as we had given him up and were turning in. He was tired and abrupt and was suffering from asthma, but he thawed out in the warmth of the cabin, while Anne plied him with coffee, biscuits and cake. He was short and thick, just the right build for a sailorman, and when he smiled he lost his disgruntled look and his expression was engaging. He came straight to the point, saying, "I heard of you from Frank Carr and I've read of your cruises in the journal. The best I could do would be to join you in August and leave you at Christmas. I imagine we should have reached the West Indies by then."

"We really wanted someone for the whole year," I said.

We went out into the cold moonlight night and looked at the ship as she lay in her dock. He said, "She looks a bit small. I've been reading about a cruise in which they got winds of gale-force in the North-East Trades. However," he grinned, "the smaller the boat, the better it is for one's soul." Anne and I agreed that our souls wanted no extra torment and we hoped for lighter winds. I tried to persuade him to come for the whole voyage, but he shook his head. "A term away is long enough. Even if they gave me leave, I shouldn't want to stay."

"Would you be willing to join us at Vigo in August? I want to start from Fowey in June."

"Yes, I'd do that willingly."

After an early breakfast we saw him off at the station. As the train pulled out, he leaned out of the window. "I shall be angry if you don't take me," he called. "I want to come very much."

Anne and I walked back down the long, straight road in silence. As we passed the Ferry Boat Inn, she said, "I think Christopher and I would be all right together, and I'm not sure that it wouldn't be a good thing to have a change of crew half-way through the voyage."

"If we can get one, which may not be too easy; but I agree with you about Christopher, I'd like to take him. He's the sort that does well in a tight corner, and I like his smile."

I wrote to Christopher that night.

By the end of February everything seemed set fair for our departure. My father was keeping very well, we had found a home for Benny, and the crew problem had been solved. We bought charts and pilot-books and worked out a plan. To Spain and Portugal in the summer, to Madeira in late September, and across to Barbados, starting in the second week of October when the hurricane season was over. After spending the winter among the islands we would come back across the North Atlantic in June or July. With the North-East Trades to take us over and the westerlies to bring us back, we might have a fair wind for ten thousand miles!

We were just putting the finishing touches to the ship when Anne got an acute appendix. She hadn't been well for a few weeks, and that night I, her doctor-husband, could not fail to diagnose the trouble.

At the end of the week she was out of the home and the surgeon told her that she could sail in a month; but, because of her operation, I insisted that we should take a third to Spain. John Harwood, a young friend of my cousin's whom I had never met, agreed to join us at Fowey the day before we sailed.

Spring gave way to an early summer, and at the end of the first week in June, Anne and I sailed *Moonraker* into Fowey and moored her to two anchors off Mixtoe. We gave her a final coat of paint, and spent hours in the office of Mr. Bennett, the ship chandler, choosing and ordering stores. We had to cater for flagging appetites at the end of a long voyage in the tropics and ravenous ones in the cold of the North Atlantic on the way back. Bennett's weighed each case and nearly a ton of stores came aboard. I threw out half a ton of ballast. Anne sat on the floor and wrote down where everything went and gradually mountains of tins disappeared into lockers, engine-room and bilge. In the locker aft of the cockpit we stored two hundred fathoms of new Italian hemp of different sizes, and the bosun's locker was filled with spare shackles, blocks and wire. There was a gallon tin of methylated spirit, another of sea-water soap (Teepol), sixteen gallons of paraffin (we should have to use this for the water-producer if we needed it), and eight gallons of petrol for the engine. We took out the coal stove and set up the water-producer in its place, leaving our coal with Watty.

The weather remained perfect, with an easterly wind to blow us to Spain. The bonded stores came aboard and the Customs sealed them up in the locker where we had kept coal. Tobacco and cigarettes went into a locker which we had to make specially for them, as there was no more room. I went to the Customs Office and got my Bill of Health, which read,

"To all to whom these Presents shall come.
"I, the undersigned Officer of His Majesty King George the Sixth in the Port of Fowey . . . send greeting . . ."

a document that savoured more of the days of sail than of the era when ships are driven by steam and oil. Fresh provisions, butter, and bacon kept in wooden boxes and packed in salt, fresh meat, twelve loaves of bread, and water for our tanks, were the last things to come aboard. *Moonraker* was so far down by the stern that we emptied half the water out again.

John arrived and we left him to settle in, while we walked over to Pont. The narrow lanes were decked with flowers and the air was still and fragrant. On the way back we sat on a gate at the top of the hill above Mixtoe and looked down on our ship. She looked small, but very trim in her pale-blue paint, her red mainsail neatly stowed and her new burgee faintly stirring in the breeze. We jumped off the gate and ran down the hill to stand for a moment on the quay.

Anne put her arm through mine. "The stage is set," she said. "Let the play begin."

CHAPTER TWO

THE tide came sweeping up the valley in the grey light of dawn. The calm water was full of shadows as it swept past the bend by Wiseman's Stone. *Moonraker* and her crew stirred sleepily and then settled down to two more hours of peace. The sun crept up into the sky, flooding the valley with light, and as the tide turned we hauled our pram on deck and the last link with the land was cut.

The first few minutes of our voyage were busy. A steamer lay moored to two buoys in the middle of the river, and each tack between her tall sides and the steeply wooded bank was so short that we hardly had room to gather way. But the tide was with us and we scraped past her rusty cable, Anne fending off our stern with a boat-hook. A hefty fellow stood in her bows looking down on our anxious faces. "Where are you bound?" he asked. In a sudden fit of bravado, I shouted back, "To the West Indies." He stood there with his hands on his hips, convulsed with derisive laughter.

The breeze freshened and we beat out into the wide, sunlit harbour, where we found a truer breeze. We eased the sheets, the water gurgled past the old ship's stem as the church clock struck the hour. In the narrow entrance, off Ready Money Cove, the breeze deserted us and *Moonraker* lay with her head towards the sea as if hesitating before taking the final plunge. Then an air from astern filled her topsail, she gathered way and sailed out on the sunlit sea towards Dodman Head and the Channel. Away from the land the wind blew freshly, and we soon had the topsail off her. As the sea built up, John's fine tan became like an actor's grease-paint over his yellowing skin. I handed over the helm to him, for there is nothing like steering to take your mind off seasickness. A fine haze spread over land and sea, so that the Dodman was barely visible at noon, when it was two miles on our starboard beam. We streamed the patent log and set the course SW½S. to clear Ushant by some forty miles.

We settled down to our sea-routine of three-hour spells at the helm, arranged so that mealtimes came at the change of watch. In all our passages cooking at sea had devolved on me, for we had never had anyone on board whose stomach would stand up to helping below. This time we carried Dramamine, a new American seasickness remedy, but it hadn't done John much good, so I had scant hope that it would work a miracle on Anne. Today, after a fortnight in harbour and with the swell now running, I expected her to be at her lowest ebb. To my amazement, it was she who went below to get our lunch. I waited for her to come up quicker than she went down, but in triumph she handed out bread and cheese and a glass of beer for me, and for John, poor thing, some water. She stood at the hatchway, grinning all over her face. "This Dramamine has its drawbacks. I shall have to do my share of the cooking," she said. I hardly dared believe it yet. I tried to think what it would mean for her not to spend hours and days feeling so ill that she hardly cared whether she floated or sank. Knowing this possibility, she had still sailed; now, it would be heaven for her.

At four o'clock we caught sight of the Lizard about three miles away. The rest of the land was hidden. I took a bearing on it and wondered when or, indeed, if ever we should see that light again.

As the sun sank straight into the sea, the only clouds in the sky being long streamers from the north-east, the wind dropped a trifle. John had never sailed anything larger than a dinghy, but he could steer a good course and was now feeling slightly better than when he started, although the mention of dinner had turned him green. At ten o'clock he came below for the first time since we left Fowey and tumbled into the lee bunk. I asked him how he felt. He grinned at me wanly. "Fine, skipper, thanks. I'll be all right tomorrow." He was tall and so thin that you could see every bone in his chest. His face was finely moulded almost feminine, and when I first saw him at Fowey I wondered how he would take to the rather strenuous life of a small ship. But I needn't have worried. He was twice as strong as I was, and tremendously keen to learn anything I could teach him.

I dislike the first night at sea. The gathering darkness and the brooding ocean make me long for the land as I long for the sea when I am on land. The unaccustomed motion of the ship, the rattle of a pot or a pan, the swish of the water along the coppered hull, all combine to prevent me from sleeping, and I lie wondering why I am such a fool as to come.

Soon after dawn the wind increased. John hung on to the whole mainsail, but I could tell from the feel of her that *Moonraker* was putting her head down, as she does when she is pressed too far. I waited for an hour and then went on deck. The sky was clear and already the sun was warm. The rolling sea was white-crested with the fine, fair wind, and never in all my life had I seen it so blue. The ship was sailing hard, the bow-wave coming almost to the stemhead as she foamed along. The log-wheel spun at a prodigious rate, and then, as the following crest of the sea flung it from side to side, it would almost stop, only to start again with redoubled vigour. It is no wonder that logs under-register in ocean sailing. I should have to watch young John. He was blissfully ignorant of the strain on mast and gear, and was most indignant when I told him we wanted a reef in the mainsail, as if I did it to spoil his fun.

We hove-to and pulled down two reefs. I came aft to look at the log and found the whole thing gone, sunk without trace! The mainsheet must have fouled it, and the mate had not made fast the lanyard. Fortunately we had a complete spare log, a present from a friend who had given up sailing. I set it at the same reading as the other had been when I came up on deck at morning.

All day the ship ran on. Under shortened sail she was dry and comfortable and, to John's surprise, went faster than before. My noon position put us forty-four miles West of Ushant and we had covered one hundred and thirty-two since noon the previous day, a grand start to our adventure. Cape Ortegal was some three hundred miles away. We altered course to SSW to clear it by ten miles.

In the evening the wind dropped and she was slipping along under all her light-weather canvas. The swell was going down rapidly. The moon came out of the sea and swiftly climbed the sky, throwing shadows of rigging and ratlines on the luff of the mainsail. The topsail and genoa were filled with light, and the murmur of the ship's passing was a most soothing sound.

I was on watch from ten till one. The beauty of the night enchanted me, but in the last hour I looked again and again at the cabin clock, thinking it had stopped. At last it was five to one. I routed out Anne and, without a worry on my mind, slipped into the warm nest she had left and fell instantly asleep. . . .

I seemed to be standing at the bottom of the companion-way gazing at the shadowy hills, the entrance to the harbour, the square, stone keep guarding the Polruan shore, the red light glowing on the Ferry Quay, and the deep note of the church-tower clock striking three. The town of Fowey slept. I looked at Anne, her face pale and serene in the moonlight, sitting with her hand on the helm. Puzzled over this, I said, "Anne, do come to bed; there's no need to sit out there now that the anchor's down." Then I saw her anxious frown and went up the steps to comfort her. From a long way off I heard her voice, "We're not at Fowey, we're crossing the Bay of Biscay." I sat down beside her, and the hills, the harbour, the church and the keep vanished from my sight as if a wand had waved them away. The time was just past three. *It was some years since I had walked in my sleep!*

On the fourth day out from Fowey, at ten o'clock in the morning, we sighted the misty-blue mountains of Spain about twenty miles away. As we came nearer we saw the coast run east and west up to a bold bluff headland and then swing to the south-south-west. Our landfall was on Cape Ortegal. The north-east wind rushed at us from the mountains and we fled down the coast, hard pressed by the double-reefed mainsail. Headlands vanished behind us and we swept past the dark, square shape of the Torre de Hercules, the oldest light-tower in Spain, past Cabo Villano with its jagged spines of rock like a dinosaur's back arching down to the sea, past barren hillsides scorched with the sun, a church in a valley, a monastery on a hill, a wild, cruel coastline that came to a dead end at the light-house on the peninsula of Cabo Finisterra. As we rounded that magnificent headland the north-east wind vanished as if turned off by a tap, and a gentle breeze blew across Corcubion Bay. The sun went down behind the hills and the tracery of Finisterre church was outlined by golden light. We beat towards the dark-green outline of Cabo Cee, then turned northwards up the narrow waterway to the little town of Corcubion, where we dropped anchor as the last of the breeze deserted us.

We stowed the sails and slipped the pram from the cabin-top. A group of men on the quay, the richness of the Spanish tongue, lights appearing in the shaded square, tall unpainted houses leaning on each other for support—we drank it all in until the kindly darkness hid all except the lamps.

By chance I have worked in Switzerland for a time and can speak and read French, but of Spanish, German and Italian I know no more than a word or two, so that, for me, one of the great joys of travelling, meeting people as well as visiting places, is dependent upon the ability of others to speak my language, a degrading restriction. Tonight the Customs, the doctor, the police, and the Guadia Civil came aboard, and, because we could not exchange views, the meeting became irritating to all of us. I like the sound of Spanish; it lacks the delicacy of French, but it is a round, smooth tongue and I wished we had spent time in learning it.

Never did I feel this more than the next morning, when we found three members of the Guardia Civil waiting for us on the quay. They were dark, swarthy men, bristling with weapons.

One of them came forward demanding to see the captain; my crew (the cowards!) went swiftly up the road. The Spaniard made signs for me to row him out to *Moonraker*. He had never seen a pram before, and, as he weighed a good fourteen stone, he nearly drowned himself. The water poured in over the transom, soaking his behind, and when I jumped into the bows to trim the boat he was not even grateful! We rowed out in silence, while I wondered what he wanted. He stood in the middle of the cabin, hurling Spanish at me, the sweat running off his brow. I showed him the ship's papers, the Bill of Health, the passports, but nothing satisfied him. He sat down and groaned. Then his eyes caught sight of an empty cigarette-tin. He jumped up, pointed first to it and then to himself. He pulled out his wallet, showing me a family group of himself, his pretty, dark-haired wife and his daughter, aged two. He rolled the tin along the floor and pointed to the child. I nodded vigorously. "Si, si, señor." We beamed at each other, we bowed, we shook hands, and I rowed him back clasping the empty tin to his ample bosom.

Corcubion is slowly dying. Deep-water ships no longer anchor in the bay to be loaded up with timber; only in the square does the place still live. Black-haired señoritas stride to the well with brass-bound water-casks on their heads, and the market-women sell their produce. By noon the streets are deserted and the little town soaks up the heat.

After dinner that night we set off to climb the hill above Corcubion. Up and up we went until the town lay almost out of sight and the Ria was a silver streak in the moonlight. We panted with the exertion of the climb, but as we came to the top, John, in the lead, stopped in his tracks. "Listen," he said; "I hear the sound of a band."

It came from over the brow of the hill, a little to our left. We walked on quickly to a clearing in front of a wayside chapel. Upon a wooden platform sat the band, their trumpets shining like silver, while around the green were booths and benches where people talked and drank, their eager laughing faces lit up by flares and bonfires. The band struck up, the people danced, the dust rose higher in the air. The fiesta was in full swing.

Spain lay in the grip of a gigantic heat-wave. It drove us out of Corcubion into the wider spaces of Llagosteira Bay, where we simmered on a windless sea by day and strolled through the pine-woods by night. A heavy-oared boat was rowed over by the police, from the village of Finisterre, and after our papers had been thoroughly looked at they mounted a guard, poor fellow, on a sun-baked cliff, to see that we did no harm.

For three days we lay there before a light north-easterly wind came stealing over the water to set us free once more. We sailed for the Ria de Muros and beat in by night, the dark sides of the mountains sweeping down to the sea, while the voices of fishermen called to each other, singing as they hauled their nets. We anchored at midnight off the town.

Compared with Corcubion, Muros was flourishing. It was a fishing-port, and fishing in Spain is a profitable industry. There was a small, stone harbour which dried out at low water, and a sea-wall ran the length of the frontage. We anchored off the wall. Large houses, some of them gaily painted in blues and greens, lay along the water-front. Behind, up cobbled streets, were low doorways leading to interiors whose poverty could scarcely be imagined, but we got used to that in Spain; there is a quality about it that defies meanness, and there is, of course, the sun. In any village along these shores we would come across a courtyard, or a carved granary in a backyard, or a slender cross rising out of an empty square, that took our breath away.

That evening a cool air came in from the east. After the heat of the day it was most refreshing. The glass was steady, the sky clear except for one or two woolly clouds which hung below the tops of the highest mountains. The ship was festooned with awnings which John and I removed, more from fear that if they flapped they would keep us awake than for any other reason. We turned in to sleep in comfort for the first time for a week.

The sound of the chain dragging along the bottom brought me to my senses quicker than a bucket of cold water; it was getting light and I rushed for'ard hardly daring to look at the sea-wall, now less than a hundred yards away, over which the seas were breaking. I let out all the chain there was and watched *Moonraker* drift still nearer, till she swung and snubbed and held. I called the others, casting off the lashings of the mainsail as I did so. The next time she dragged would be the last, and by the wild way she sheered at every squall and dug her bowsprit into each short sea there was no time to spare. Anne whipped round the deck collecting trousers and shirts from the rigging, while John and I heaved down the third-reef-cringle and bowsed down the tack. If we got the mainsail set while the anchor still held, we had a chance; without it there was none. And at the back of my mind was the nagging thought that never had the ship been in such danger, and we were not even at sea, just caught in a trap of our own making. The mainsail was set. Anne brought up the third jib, and both she and John were soaked to the skin (we were still in our pyjamas) before they had it up. Tack by tack we sailed her up to her anchor. The green paint on the chain, the fifteen-fathom mark, came inboard and still she held; one short tack to port, a quick lee-ho, and, with the foresail set, she sailed the anchor out so sweetly that John never felt the jerk on the winch. She beat off that lee-shore like a thoroughbred, and only after the second tack did I dare to look astern to where the wall was fast receding. Anne took over and put her in the wind, while John and I hauled in the rest of the chain and the anchor. We found shelter in the little Ensenada de Bórnalle, a quiet anchorage protected from all winds except the south. We went below to put on some clothes, and Anne lit the stove; the smell of frying bacon filled the cabin. Our day had just begun.

By Jove, how it blew! I never left the ship that day. Squalls off the mountains shook *Moonraker* like a dog shaking a rat, and after this morning's episode I didn't want to see her drift out to sea while we chased her in the pram. After a wretched night we sailed round to a neighbouring inlet, where we found a little circle of shelter tucked up under a cliff, while squalls lashed the water fifty yards away. On the third day the white haze that hung over the mountains lifted. We left with the three reefs still in the mainsail, but we let out two of them as we rounded Cabo Corrubado on the way to Arosa Bay. Arosa is the deepest and widest of the four great Rias between Corcubion and Vigo; its "mountains" are no more than hills, with gentle wooded slopes instead of rock and shale.

The wind hadn't quite finished with us yet; as we beat past Rua light-tower it came roaring down the valley. We put in the second reef on one short tack, but the pilotage was intricate, it was getting dark, and there was neither time nor room to put in another. John and Anne, sitting up to their waists in water on the foredeck, reefed the foresail, and we hoped the gear would stand. There was no sea to speak of, but one squall put her over till her cabin-coaming was under water, a thing I had never seen happen before. The night got very dark. Warm Spain grew cold, and we shivered with the spray, the keen wind and lack of food, for we had had no chance to eat since teatime. Now it was nearly midnight. We saw a white shape and shone a torch on it. It was a fishing-boat at anchor. We dropped ours, stowed the sails and hurried down to eat.

For a fortnight we sailed in sheltered waters. We dined one night at a huge hotel, and the next we sat in a two-roomed cottage drinking new red wine from the grapes that grew on the wall outside.

We sailed to Villagarcia, put aboard stores and water, and ran with a fair wind up the Ria de Rianjo to its very head, where we anchored out of sight of human habitation. The bilges were due for a clean, and Anne had a whole week's washing to do.

By 9 o'clock the work was done. The ship was festooned with drying clothes, dinner was over and the plates were piled for the skipper to wash-up. There was not a breath of wind, and in the still air we heard the chug-chug of a fishing-boat which came nearer and nearer. As we came on deck she circled us; a typical Spanish fishing-vessel with high-flared bows and rounded stern, the blue smoke of her exhaust puffing straight up into the air like smoke-rings from a pipe. A man dressed in city clothes, and older than his three companions, hailed us. He said, "Please, my friend, Emilio Borras"—the young man at the wheel bowed gracefully—"will be honoured if you go to the home of his mother," and he pointed down the Ria to a white house almost hidden by trees. This sentence, unfortunately, exhausted his stock of English.

Side by side, the two boats motored down the Ria, anchoring off punta Capitan as the moon rose over the mountains to the east. Emilio came for us in a dinghy and led Anne across the rocks as delicately as though she were made of porcelain. I saw her puzzled smile at this unusual courtesy, such a contrast to her unromantic skipper bawling at her, "Can't you carry something else?"

We walked up the hill, along a path through a peach-orchard to a gate in a high, stone wall, then through the gate into the court-yard of a house four hundred years old. By the steps leading into the house stood a woman dressed in black, her face pale and smooth in the moonlight. Her voice and the small gestures of her hands welcomed us, although we could only understand a word here and there of her speech. We were taken into a long, cool room, where we sat wrestling with the difficulty of having no common language.

Señora Borras was the widow of a sea-captain who had the deepest respect for the English, a respect shared by his eldest son. He and I sat a little apart from the others until his friend, Ricoy, came over to help us with a few sentences of French. Emilio's questions were about the sea, and as I described our hopes and fears for our voyage and Ricoy translated them back to him his face lit up with enthusiasm. For the moment his mother had forbidden him to take to the sea, but the time might come when the urge would become too strong for him. The long table at one end of the room was laid and we sat down to a supper of oysters, wine and the most delicious peaches that I can remember. Just before midnight we left and walked down the sandy road. The air was still warm and the whitewashed walls of the Ricoys' farmhouse shone in the moonlight.

Beatrice de Bourbon Ricoy was a cousin of the ex-King of Spain. Her fair hair and skin, and the lightness of her humour, made her seem more French than Spanish. She had a flair for decoration. The dark staining of the timbers against the cream walls, the wrought-iron lampstands and the bare simplicity of the furniture gave to the large cool rooms an almost religious austerity. In this setting we were introduced to her eldest daughter, about twelve years old. She greeted us with the grave simplicity of a girl of twice her years and yet was most engagingly young.

Our kind hosts came down to the water's edge. The moon was waning, and as we rowed back to the ship they sang a Spanish song, wishing us well in the long voyage before us. They waved and turned away and we heard the sound of their voices grow fainter as they climbed the hill. Before breakfast, two retainers came out to us. They brought a basket of fruit, fish caught that morning, and two litres of milk. They had orders to wash down our decks.

The evening before we left Arosa Bay, we anchored off Jobre church near Puebla Caraminial. The cabin lamps were lit and were looking at charts for tomorrow's passage. A hoarse sound, prolonged and rasping, came from near by. I went up and saw a fishing-boat so decrepit that I wondered she could float: the light from a lantern lit up the bearded face of a man from whom came this curious sound. Thinking he was drunk or had come to beg tobacco, I shooed him away; but the noise continued, and this time Anne went up on deck. Presently I heard her call, "Peter, this man's deaf and dumb. I think he wants to see our boat." Feeling ashamed, I joined her, and now I saw that there were two boys with him and it was they who had spoken to Anne. They came alongside and fingered the ropes and blocks with many "buenos"; soon boat after boat sailed in till we were the centre of a little fleet, and our decks, gear and spars, were lit by many flares. One or two of the men spoke a little English. They said that *Moonraker* had been recognized as a fishing-boat, but they were all puzzled as to how she had become a yacht. They examined her in every detail and marvelled at her being so strongly built. An old coil of rope gave them pleasure and we exchanged cigarettes for fish. A dozen sails were hoisted to the breeze, a dozen twinkling lights spread out across the bay: a shout, a snatch of song, and they were gone.

From bay to bay, from village to town, we made our way to the south, until on 25th July we sailed into Vigo to find a berth for John in the schooner *Norbar*, homeward-bound. Anne and I left the stuffy heat of the yacht-basin and sailed to the fishing-port of Toralla, which is tucked in behind the island of that name. We lay along the north wall, *Moonraker*'s heel resting lightly on the mud for the last half-hour of the ebb. There we met Agouto, a young Spaniard, broad of shoulder, who spoke American. We dined with him at the local inn, eating fried sardines and drinking a light white wine. With him was a Canary Islander, Niniña, a slender girl with a perfect oval face and black eyes that danced with fun. Later they came aboard. They sat together and Agouto said quite simply, "I love her." Indeed he could do no less; she was such a charming creature. She was leaving the next day for the Islands and he looked at her like a faithful dog who cannot believe that his mistress could be so cruel as to go without him.

In the middle of the night, our last at Toralla, we were woken by the wailing of air-raid sirens echoing up and down the bay. The sound of diesel engines filled the air and fishermen hauled their nets up on the quay, shouting, "Para, Para . . ." After an absence of six years, the sardines had returned that night to Vigo Bay and within the hour the machinery of a great industry was set in motion. Everything that could float, from the largest trawler to the smallest boat, turned out. As they brought in their catch factory hands were summoned by the sirens, for unless sardines are canned within twelve hours the haul is wasted. Millions of fish were caught that night.

The tides were wrong for us that day, but we met a Spanish yachtsman, a navigator of experience, who offered to take us out. There was not enough water over the flats to the east of Toralla, which meant leaving Toralla Island to starboard and sailing between two submerged rocks that lay some thirty feet apart. Our pilot would not at first tell me the leading marks, as if they were some patent of his own, but when I pressed the matter he reluctantly gave way. So we started off, under power, keeping the end of the breakwater in line with a window of a two-storied house on shore. As we drew nearer the crucial spot, the navigator's wife, who had come to keep him company, told her husband that he was too much to the left. This criticism infuriated him. A violent quarrel broke out, and he left the helm the better to argue with his wife. I seized the tiller and kept the marks in line while Anne conned the ship from for'ard. Once through, we dropped the pair into their motor dinghy and ran back to Vigo.

We had enjoyed this short interlude on our own. Tomorrow Christopher would join us from the liner *Highland Princess*.

CHAPTER THREE

THE rain drummed down on the cabin-top and a wet mist drifted across the bay, hiding the opposite shore. A sourness hung over the water of the little yacht-basin. Vigo in the rain was not attractive. For the third time that morning I padded over to the quay where the liner was berthed and looked in vain for Christopher. A very English figure in a raincoat strode past me and then paused.

"Are you Dr. Pye?"

"Yes."

"I'm a friend of Christopher Ellis. He's with the police." Then he smiled reassuringly. "They seem to think it's highly suspicious that he should want to transfer from the *Highland Princess* to *Moonraker*, but he won't be long now."

It was lunchtime before Christopher arrived. He came down the companion-way shaking himself like a dog coming out of a pond. He brought with him an immense canvas hold-all, a suitcase, a duffle-coat, a pair of leather-soled thigh-boots and a drawing-board. He put them on the floor and shut out the rain.

"Heavens!" said Anne. "Where on earth is all that going?"

Christopher grinned at her. "You're lucky," he said. "I nearly brought a cabin-trunk and a shot-gun." Standing there under the skylight, he looked even more tired than he had done at Fambridge in the spring. He said, "Well, how soon before we get under way?"

"You look as if you could do with a day or two's rest," I said.

"Nonsense! That's only because my asthma's been bad. It's better now, but lying here won't help it."

So we sailed that afternoon in the pouring rain up to the Ensenada de San Simon and anchored behind a reef which protected us from the westerly wind. In the morning the sun and north-easter returned. Christopher was enchanted with all he saw as we ran down the lovely fjord which, with the other four Rias, so the legend runs, was made by God's fingers as he rested his hand on this corner of Spain, after finishing the world on the sixth day. We rounded Monte Ferro and anchored beneath the walls of Bayona Castle, while the bells from the great church tower rang out a joyous peal and the little town slept in the heat of the afternoon.

That evening we had a conference about currency.

Christopher's thirty-five pounds was welcome indeed, but we had to budget till October, and to stock up the ship at Madeira for the crossing to Barbados. It was fortunate that he wasn't a second John, who could demolish a pressure-cooker full of potatoes at a sitting, and we hoped that in Portugal, where there is no rationing and therefore no black market, we should be able to buy bread without bankrupting ourselves. Christopher was shocked that we had only bought one meal ashore in six weeks and that it was unlikely that we could afford another. "Why didn't you catch fish?" he asked. We laughed; we hadn't had a bite despite all John's efforts. Besides, as Anne said, they are mostly squid and no one who's seen 'em wants squid.

We planned our route. A friend had made the entrance to Leixoes sound like a sailor's nightmare. "On no account," he insisted, "must you make this harbour at night. They stopped work on the mole before it was half-finished, and it's worse than if they'd never started it." Then he added feelingly, "You won't want much sail running down this coast. It blows up to half a gale."

By leaving Bayona in the evening we should be at Leixoes well before dark the next day, as the distance is little over sixty miles. A light off-shore breeze took us out of the bay. The lower of the two lights, which, if kept in line, guide you clear of all dangers, was so weak that we lost sight of it before we were half-way out. The long westerly swell rolled in; we heard the roar as it broke on the reefs ahead, and in the moonlight we could see the curtain of spray rise into the air and spread like a fan over the thin line of rocks. All down the coast we had been told of a Norwegian yacht which had been caught in this dangerous place by a gale of wind and wrecked with the loss of all her company except for a small girl who was saved by one of the crew. He landed her on a ledge before he was himself swept away, never to be seen again.

The breeze faltered and died away. The ship fell off in the trough of the swell just as the reefs were abeam. A shiver passed down my spine. Christopher swung the starting-handle, and the chug-chug of the engine and the swish of the bow-wave as *Moonraker* headed out to sea were like music to our ears. We made our offing, stopped the engine and waited for wind. I find it hard to possess my soul in patience in a calm, but I had plenty of practice on that passage. The Portuguese Trades were having a holiday, and as we half-sailed, half-drifted down the coast we watched starshells and rockets go up from a dozen villages, for in August nearly every night is a fiesta in Spain. Not once did the wind shift into the north; it was either ahead or on the starboard bow. The land became shrouded in mist, and on the second day out we made a board inshore to find out where we were. A bright-blue fishing-boat came sailing over the swell, her lateen sail sending her shapely hull rippling through the water. I put my pride in my pocket (as I have so often done before) and shouted, "Leixoes?" A babel of sound broke out from four men seated in the stern-sheets, but they all pointed away to the south-east, in which direction we were actually heading. We waved our thanks.

It was not long before we saw the harbour and the tower at the end of the mole. Our friend was right. The swell pours over the submerged breakwater, the high walls of the harbour blanket you, and it wouldn't take much to make the entrance impossible for a small boat under sail. We anchored in the inner basin off the Clube Vela Atlantico. As soon as we had been cleared we went ashore to seek out the international police. The term is misleading, for Portugal is a police-state and we had been told that some of these gentlemen had been trained by the Gestapo during the war. In Leixoes they live in a tower not far from the yacht club. We walked up a spiral staircase into a room where the blinds were drawn against the heat of the sun. There were two desks, with a man sitting at each, writing. Neither looked up, and we stood waiting to be noticed for what seemed a very long time. Then one of them barked something at me in Portuguese and I barked back in English. As we were none of us any the wiser, I tried French, a language I hadn't dared to use in Spain. My interrogator spoke it better than I did, and soon we were chatting like old friends. He gave us yellow slips of paper as receipts for our passports, and when we asked where we could buy milk and bread he came himself to show us.

Although the distance from Bayona to Leixoes is so short, we seemed to have come into a different century. Walking along the street you might almost imagine yourself back in England: red pillar-boxes, English cars, well-made roads and the sort of houses you would see in any of our seaside resorts. There were differences, of course: peasants walking along the road in bare feet, and the strict propriety of the bathing-costumes; while down in the harbour there was no similarity at all. The heat of the day was over; what breeze there had been had vanished. A long, blue boat like a war-canoe paddled across the water till she came alongside the *Jerusalem*, which was landing her catch at the quay. Men and women stood up in the boat, sang and clapped their hands, and the crew of the trawler stopped at times to join in the serenade.

Fogs and calms day after day. One night we dined with friends under a eucalyptus tree and met there a wine-merchant. On hearing my name he said, "Pye? of Reid, Pye, Campbell and Hall?"

"No," I said, "but my father was in the firm."

"You must ring up Maxwell Graham," he suggested, and when I demurred, for Max Graham was a great name in Oporto and my father had retired thirty years ago, he overruled me; so that in the morning I put through a call. Presently a brusque voice barked down the telephone, "Who are you? Harry's son or Burns's?"

"Harry's," I replied.

The voice continued, "My nephew Colin will be out to see you tonight and my car will pick you up in the morning and take you to the Wine Lodge."

The Wine Lodge, when we came to it on that hot stifling day, was on the south bank of the river. It was a long low building in which the light was dim so that you had the impression of walking through catacombs beneath a cathedral, but there the likeness ended, for around the walls and filling the centre of the room were huge barrels filled with port in varying stages of maturity which, we were told, had to be kept at a temperature of 106 degrees. We were shown the processes through which the wine must pass before being bottled, and then we were taken down to the Holy of Holies where great casks (the Ambassador's Vat, the Emperor's Vat) stood round the walls. In the middle of the room was a small wooden cask, unlabelled. Punctually at one o'clock the door was flung open (I caught myself listening for the fanfare of trumpets) and in walked Maxwell Graham followed by two acolytes bearing trays of dry biscuits. He said, "You were ten years old when I last saw you. You have the Pye face."

The bung was then removed from the barrel in the middle of the room, and port was withdrawn by a pipette, so that no hint of wood should mar its exquisite taste.

After lunch Colin drove us over the great bridge which spans the Douro upon which swung three-masted schooners home from the Grand Banks, to the city of Oporto, and we escaped from the heat of the streets and pavements into the cool of the Factory House—British Territory, Colin said, four hundred years. We were shown a small room in which was kept a copy of *The Times* for every day since its publication, and the great dining-room where the beauty of the chairs struck a chord even in my unknowledgeable mind. They were made by Chippendale when he was a young man living in Lisbon. But what struck me most about this place was that it was as much a part of Britain as if it had been built on the banks of the Thames. Christopher and I signed the Visitors' Book, which no woman is allowed to sign. We dined that night with Maxwell Graham, whose surroundings added to his stature: the Georgian House, the high-walled garden, the butler in uniform and the exquisite food and wine. We came away wondering in what part of which century we had spent the day.

Anne went to bed for a few days with a high temperature, and Christopher spent his time hoping for glimpses of a beautiful blonde on the French yacht close by. She was guarded by two young Frenchmen who told us they were bound for Cascaes. One day the hatch burst open and the lovely creature rushed on deck, followed by one of the men. By the forehatch she paused, stamping her feet with rage. "*Alors*," she shouted, "*c'est tout fini!*" It must have been, for the hatch slammed to and we never saw them again.

A light wind blew from the north. This, we said, must surely be the "Nortada." We set sail and started for Cascaes, but, after a heavy thunderstorm in which the wind boxed the compass, calms and head-winds dogged our progress. We passed the Burling Islands, sailing close to Cabo Carvoeiro on the mainland. Long streamers spread over the sky from the north-east, the wind strengthened from the north, and by the time Cabo da Roca was abeam we felt the true weight of the Portuguese Trades. The topsail came off, and Anne and I wrestled with the spinnaker as we rounded Cabo Razo. This sail is a menace unless a line is passed rom the pinrail to control the boom while you unship the jaws and pass it in front of the mast; a thing I never thought of till I saw Christopher do it when furling the sail by himself.

The water smoothed under the lee of the land, and it was not long before the little port of Cascaes opened up and we beat in through the yachts and fishing boats that lay riding to the offshore breeze. The hundred and ninety miles had taken us three and a half days instead of thirty-six hours.

Cascaes was full of colour from the blue shutters of the little white houses on the grey-brown cliffs, the yellow sands and the berets of the fishermen. In the south-west corner of the bay stood the yacht club where the secretary made us feel at home as soon as we set foot in it. He went to endless trouble to get sheepskin for our chafing-gear and took Anne shopping so that she could buy economically. He spoke four languages, was a graduate of

Manchester University (Science), and looked on himself with cynical contempt for accepting his present position. He lived on next to nothing for fear of indigestion and he had lost all confidence as the result of his experiences in Berlin during the last few months of the war. He lived alone.

We sailed into the Tagus and docked at Belem, the better to explore Lisbon. The place was stiflingly hot. We tied up to a seventy-foot ketch, and we had hardly gone below before our neighbour came over to call on us. He wore bathing-trunks from which his stomach rose majestically in well-rounded curves, and his small eyes darted about the cabin like a bird's on the lookout for a cat. He spoke fluent English, with the thick accent of a Dutchman, and he hailed from Rotterdam. I asked him how long he had been here. He said, "One year; and nothing goes right for me. We sail from Holland and I have great trouble with my dents and I must stay here a long time before they are well. Then my wife is ill and one doctor says one thing and another says something else. We stay here month after month and the toredo-worm attacks my ship. I think I must copper her, but I have no money to buy the copper."

"Where are you making for?" I asked him.

His eyes brightened. He said, "If I can go to South America, all will be well, but how can I sail with a sick wife and my ship eaten with worms?"

He was a fine craftsman. He showed us the deckhouse he had built during the long winter months, a major work in a ship of that size. He introduced us to his wife, who lay in her cabin looking pale and ill, with the same restless look in her eyes that her husband had. We met their son, aged ten, and a young man with blond hair and hard eyes, who looked at us with ill-concealed dislike and to whom we were not introduced.

Night fell on Belem. Halliards flapped against masts, and gangplanks creaked as the yachts stirred uneasily in the hot winds. "This," said Anne, "is the home of lost voyagers. Ghosts, not ships, lie here!"

Lisbon is a beautiful city, but I am no sightseer, and the narrow streets thronged with cars exhausted me. We hurried back to Belem and, casting off our warps from the Dutchman, took the last of the flood up to Seixal, a pretty little village that looked more French than Portuguese. Here our friends the Reynolds of Barriero entertained us and advised us that it was our duty to see Arrabaida before we left the coast. They told us about the monastery built in a mountain and the seven chapels that marked the way up, but they did not tell us about the squalls that came hurtling down the side of the mountain or the patches of kelp on the bottom, ready to trip our anchor.

A strong "Trade" took us down to Cape Espichel, and it was evening when we rounded the ancient fort that guards the western side of the bay. The wind had dropped, the squalls being no more violent than we should expect at Cascaes, and we agreed it was not a place to be missed; but as soon as the sun went down the wind rushed at us with the force of a winter's gale. It must have been nearly midnight when I noticed that one set of bearings had altered while the others remained as they were. Christopher came up full of sleep. "But, Peter, we can't be *dragging*."

"Famous last words! For God's sake get some sail on her." We had left the reefs in the mainsail, but the jib went on upside-down, which cost another precious minute. I knew there was a shoal to seaward and the lead showed only nine feet by the time we were under control. We worked the ship back, keeping to the westward of where we were before. Christopher let out a bare five fathoms of chain to see whether that would hold. As the bearing remained unchanged, we let out eighteen and turned in, but I was out more than once before dawn to see if we were still in the same place.

When we sailed back to Cascaes it was time to stock up for the voyage to Maderia. I felt that this would be the turning-point of the adventure. I have no mathematical leanings, and had it not been for the Air Nautical Tables celestial navigation would have remained the stumbling block to my crossing any sea as large as the Atlantic. My cousin, who is in the R.A.F., had devoted three hours or more to teaching me how to use them and then left me to find my way about. I *had* been able to find places like Ireland and a Friesian island, but when it came to an island five miles long, five hundred miles out in the middle of an ocean, it seemed to require a greater accuracy than I could count on. So on that Saturday morning, when the secretary and the President of the club helped to load our last-minute provisions into the pram, it was with some anxiety that I answered their question "Are you sure you can find Madeira?" with a hopeful "I shall do my best!"

CHAPTER FOUR

AS we rowed back to *Moonraker* I noticed that every ship had turned round and was facing out to sea. A light southerly wind ruffled the water, and Cape Espichel, twenty miles away, looked only just across the bay. The glass had fallen a tenth since breakfast-time. Christopher had already set the mainsail, the topsail was sheeted home, and the blocks creaked as she dipped to the swell. Outside the bay we picked up a better breeze from the south-west, pretty well dead in our teeth. *Serica*, our next-door neighbour for several days, came bounding after us, and it was like Alex Symmington to keep to leeward so as not to take our wind. He called out, "Sorry I missed seeing you go. Best of luck for your voyage!"

We thanked him for his kindly gesture. I pointed to windward. "it looks as if we shall have to beat to Madeira."

"No! No!" he cried. "My man says you'll have a north wind before sunset." And *Serica* picked up her dainty skirts and hurried back to Cascaes.

But Symmington's man was wrong. Soon we were pitching into a head-sea, and in the middle of the night a thunderstorm had us all out to shorten sail. It rained for sixteen hours, and it was just like beating down the English Channel, with a short sea and spray and with the same cold wind. We didn't mind; lying at Cascaes wondering whether we should have to run for the Tagus would have been much worse.

In the evening the wind veered and the sky cleared from the north-west. The reefs came out, up went the topsail, and we set course for Porto Santo, the nearest island in the Archipelago of Madeira. There is nothing so satisfactory as being able to lay your course after being chased off it by the wind, and it was in high glee that Anne went up to take over at ten o'clock and Christopher and I turned in.

The moon was still up at four the next morning. A magnificent north-westerly swell rolled up on the starboard beam, and erect little clouds, like soldiers, marched across the sky. The moon went down in the west, but minute by minute the light grew stronger. Soon all the colours of the rainbow were present in the sky. They fused and faded, while over the edge of a low cloud the sun rose like a golden ball and the last star vanished. The wind freshened, and Christopher took the topsail down before he took over from me at seven. I went below to cook breakfast. The cupboard up for'ard was as wet as a grotto, beads of water hanging from the deck-beam and shelfing after yesterday's torrential rain. The Quaker Oats, mildew and all, went into the pan; knives and forks, cups and plates, into the deep trays that we use at sea instead of the table. Christopher sang at the helm. Suddenly the singing stopped. He called, "Peter, something's chafing aloft. It's the peak halliard, I think."

"Can't it chafe a bit longer?" I asked, stirring the porridge bubbling in the pan.

"Mm . . . you know what it is, with a peak halliard."

I knew what it might be, with a peak halliard; so I woke Anne, gave her some porridge, gave Christopher his, and went up to look around. Two strands of the main halliard had parted, chafed by the topsail yard. I came down and finished serving breakfast, giving myself indigestion wondering how long the last strand would last. The sky was rapidly clouding over and I left my scrambled egg to shoot the sun before it went in. Cold egg and lukewarm coffee take the edge off any appetite.

Now for the mainsail. We hove-to, and the moment the sail was off her *Moonraker* did all but stand on her head; the old warning, "one hand for yourself and one for the ship," had a real meaning. The heavy boom swung viciously and I don't think we could have got it into a single crutch without tearing it away from its stanchion. With the permanent gallows and its three notches, the manœuvre was relatively simple.

Somewhere in the ship there was a new halliard ready for reeving, but only after Anne had removed most of the spare rope from the rope locker did she emerge from the depths of the engine-room, dragging the halliard triumphantly after her. Christopher kept the boat dead before the wind, while Anne and I reeved the halliard through the blocks; I hadn't realized how much simpler it was to work aloft when running than when turning to windward—it is the pitch that flings you off—but it was long past the change of watch by the time the sail was set.

The ship ran on. The wind veered to the north-east, the water swilled over the bridge-deck as she scooped it up from the weather - as well as from the lee-side, and the log spun round at a giddy pace. Suddenly at the end of a prodigious roll, the gaff-jaws capsized so that the metal edge cut into the mast at every swing of the gaff. I gybed her over with a crash, waking the others from their afternoon sleep. Anne took the helm while Christopher and I went up to see what could be done. The mast was deeply scored and would have to have a copper band as soon as we made port. For the moment we could think of nothing better than to shorten the parrel line to allow the jaws less play. Christopher lashed himself to the rat-lines, so as to use both hands, and I resumed my watch, fidgeting as I always do when forced to sail off course. When Christopher came down we gybed her back and lessened the swing by keeping the boom in as far as we dared. Then we rigged a boom-guy.

I got in an hour's sleep before helping Anne to prepare the dinner; I would have got more if we hadn't had to pull down a reef and set the spinnaker, but the ship was so much easier for the better distribution of sail that the loss of sleep was worth it. In the middle of doing that we had passed a steamer close by on the opposite course to ourselves and we fervently hoped she was bound from Madeira to Lisbon. By the time the lamps and the navigation lights were filled and lit, the dinner cooked, the helmsman relieved for his meal, the washing-up done and the precious half-hour for spinning a yarn over, it was time to write up the log and the daily journal, set up the bunk-boards and turn in. I looked at the clock and found, without surprise, that I had a quarter of an hour before taking over from Anne at ten. I remembered that a cousin of mine, a mountaineer, once said to me, "What I don't understand is what you do with yourselves all day at sea."

At noon on the fourth day out my sights put me forty-five miles from the island of Porto Santo. A dozen birds wheeled around the ship and a mass of cumulus cloud hung in the sky where I hoped the land might be. The ship ran swiftly before a fresh north-easterly breeze. I said carelessly, "Christopher, you ought to sight land at half-past three. Wake me when you see it."

I went down to sleep, but my eyes kept straying to the clock and it was as much as I could do not to work out my position all over again. What a good thing it is that errors are not cumulative and that the only sights that count are the last you take!

The arms of the clock crept round to half-past three. A shout from Christopher, "Peter, there's your island!" and then, as if to quell my pride, "It's a rotten landfall, quite twenty degrees on the starboard bow."

But I couldn't care less: a landfall at the right time was good enough for me. I woke Anne to tell her the good news, and we both went on deck. Three mountain peaks, a misty blue, rose out of the deep, blue sea. I felt like a million dollars.

The moon shone over mountains and valleys as we passed by

Porto Santo, an island without trees, where they work or fish only to keep starvation at bay. During the war a raft from a torpedoed merchantman drifted along this coast. The two men aboard saw that they would be swept away, so they leapt overboard and one of them sank at once. The other got to within a few hundred yards of the shore, where he, too, went down. "What a pity," said the villagers, as they stood watching from the beach. "He so nearly made it."

This land of lotus-eaters dropped astern. The wind blew and *Moonraker* made short work of the thirty-odd miles to Madeira. The long ocean-swell piled up on the island shelf, the crests of the seas were like pale gold in the light of the yellow moon. Valleys and rocks led up from the sea to be lost in swirling cloud, and over to port lay the brooding shapes of the Ilhas Desertas. The wind dropped and the sea went down as the land cut off the swell. We ghosted along past sleeping villages till the lights of Funchal burst in on my view. It was the hour before dawn. I saw lights in cottages high in the mountains, lights down the twisting roads to the straighter lines of the streets, and by the water's edge the central cluster round the little town. I roused Anne and Christopher . They rubbed their eyes as they came on deck and they were glad I had called them.

In fickle breezes we worked *Moonraker* into the bay and lay becalmed a mile off shore. The pilots got tired of looking at us, or were curious to know who we were, and the Captain of Pilots himself came out in his boat and towed us into the port.

Madeira lives on tourists, and it was unfortunate for us that we were the only attraction. Better a ten-tonner, they seemed to think, than nothing at all. By the time the Customs, the doctor and the international police had finished there was a clutter of bumboats around us, begging custom, bullying us to buy raffia mats, wide straw hats of many colours, avocado pears and bananas, the while they reviled each other's characters and forebears. But Anne was firm. We had, she argued, to be here nearly a month, and the sooner they knew that we couldn't afford to be fleeced the better it would be for us. We bought nothing at all.

As we walked up the pleasant wide streets, lined with palm trees, past flower girls in national costume, we were importuned by beggars, hoteliers and shopkeepers. We refused drives in taxis and meals on shore, and we bought nothing but food. Then, after two days of this, we were left alone, accepted and charged at the same rates as the English colony on the island, about half what was asked from the casual tourist.

Up in the mountains it is like Switzerland just below the snow-line. One day we were up at Balcoës, where Anne made friends with two boys who were busy collecting firewood. They took her to their home, a wooden hut like a Swiss shelter. Inside the one room was a bed of straw, a hen, two broken chairs and a mongrel dog. But from the doorway the view was superb.

As we came down the hillside we saw a file of men and women taking the grapes to the wine-press in baskets upon their heads. From the doorway we watched the tramp-tramp of a peasant as he ground the grapes beneath his bare feet, while the last of the juice was squeezed out of the pulp by a huge stone clamped down by a wooden screw.

We were sitting outside a café in the square one day when an old man walked stiffly by with the aid of a stick. He stopped by my chair. . . . "you are English, sir?" and, before I could reply, "If there is anything I can do to make your stay pleasant, I shall be pleased."

He took us into a wine-cellar, where we sampled different blends of Madeira, and to a factory where they were working designs in lace. We thanked him for spending so much time with us, but he nodded his wrinkled head knowingly.

"You catch flies with honey," he said.

"We are not rich English yachtsmen," we told him. "We have a small boat and sail the sea, as it is the only way we can see the world."

He laughed. "That's the sort of thing all you English say, but you are rich, all the same."

"Come and see our boat," said Anne.

Very slowly we walked down to the quay. In silence he looked at *Moonraker* for a long time. Then he said, "Before you go, you will want many things for the voyage. I will see that no one cheats you," and he hobbled back to the town, a kindly old man at heart.

We were towed into the Pontinha, behind the breakwater, where, so they said, we should be sheltered from any gale that blew. We were surrounded by tugs and barges and our visitors had to walk through a coalyard to get to us, but there was much less swell than off the Cais and we could leave the boat without worrying about her safety.

One day I had finished the washing-up and thrown overboard the dirty water. Looking over the side, I saw the sun glinting on silver and realised I had thrown out three silver teaspoons, mementos of Holland and Spain. Christopher dived, but we were anchored in five fathoms. A boat put out from the shore; her occupant was short and stocky, with an impish face. He said, "My name, Georgie. . . . Good morning." We beamed at him and hurled a spate of English at him, only to find that those five words were the extent of his English vocabulary. By sign-language we told him what we were looking at. He nodded his head vigorously, sprang upon the gunwale of his boat and dived to the bottom, bringing up the three teaspoons in triumph. Georgie was a find. He was mate of the tug *Cory* and kept an eye on *Moonraker* when we were away, scrubbed her bottom and did his best to satisfy his insatiable thirst for gin.

One evening, when we were dining with the Consul and his wife, *Moonraker* was broken into. No articles of great value were taken, but amongst them was a present I had given Anne, to which she was greatly attached. I rowed over to Georgie, who took a tracing of a footprint that had been left on the deck. Christopher drew pictures of the things we had lost and he went off with a knowing look on his face. Back he came next day, like a dog with two tails. He had found a boy whose foot fitted the prints; he had taken him to the police station, where he had been beaten to make him confess. Then the story became slightly confused, but we gathered that our things had been found on a stowaway on the liner that had left the port yesterday and that she had been recalled. We were sorry about the boy being beaten, but we were appalled by the recall of the liner. Fortunately, our friends the Vice-Consul and his wife were dining with us that evening. As soon as they arrived, I hurried over to fetch Georgie and we listened anxiously to his harsh voice and to the questions that the Hutchinsons asked him. Finally Margaret Hutchinson turned to Anne with a smile. "The first part you got right; that's the way things are done here. But the second part of the story was that *if* your things are found after you've gone they will recall you by telegraph." So Georgie was sent away to tell the police to stop beating the boy and that we had no means of receiving a telegram.

We refitted the ship. We led the main halliards away from the mast where they would no longer be chafed by the topsail-yard; Christopher fitted a copper mast-band for the jaws to swing on, and we varnished and painted the ship. As the work progressed, we got more and more in each other's way and a cry would go up, "Who's touched my varnish?" or "Who's trodden on my deck paint?" When we had worked all one Sunday to finish the decks, a Portuguese steamer belched oil-smoke all over the dock. Then it rained! We sulked below. Christopher dropped a pot of varnish from the masthead to the deck and forgot to tell Anne, who walked right through it in new shoes that she had just bought in the town. I couldn't tell you what she said to him!

Shopping was a bugbear; it meant a long walk from the Pontinha to the town, and the market was at the other end. Even the flower-girls and the flowers in the courtyard palled, after a time, in the heat of the day. Once, when the streets were full of passengers from a Dutch liner, Christopher, thinking that a large straw hat and a green frock meant Anne, tapped her on the shoulder and pointed to his shopping-bag. "Two large and one small, all right?" A stolid Dutch face looked at him with alarm. "No, no," its owner cried, "no good!" and hurriedly turned away.

When the devaluation of the pound was announced, it was a bad day for us, because we had just had a bill from the ship-chandler for six hundred escudos—six pounds at the old rate—for a job which Christopher told Anne couldn't be more than fifteen shillings. Sparks flew in the cabin and Christopher stormed into the shipchandler's office and offered him two hundred escudos or he could take his case to the courts. The bluff came off and Christopher swore that he could have got away with even less if he had had the courage to try it. Even so, devaluation cut short our stay and we fixed the ninth of October as our sailing-date.

On the Saturday, one of Blandy's water-barges, containing two hundred tons, gave us our sixty gallons, and a bumboat rowed off with a side of bacon, three hands of bananas, baskets of peaches, passion-fruit, melons, lemons and oranges, one hundred and fifty eggs, potatoes, onions, beans, and fresh and salted butter, which we kept in tins surrounded by fresh water. While Anne and Christopher dealt with these, I made a last bid to get a length of two-inch rope out of the Customs as bonded stores. The rope had been sent from England, and in any other country we had visited they would have let me have it duty-free, provided I took it aboard. The official I saw was bland. "You can have the rope, Captain, if you pay me a hundred and eighty escudos."

"That's as much as the rope is worth. If you send it aboard tomorrow I couldn't possibly sell it ashore, which is what you seem to be afraid of."

"We don't work on Sundays."

"Then we won't go till Monday."

"You can go when you like, Captain. The rope stays here till you pay."

So I paid. He held out his hand, but I asked him for a receipt.

I imagined there was a moment's hesitation. Then he wrote one out. After all, I was tied hand and foot.

By half-past three the rope hadn't come. The office shut at four, so I went along to see Alfonse Quelho, one of the heads of Blandy's. He had shoulders like an ox and his eyes almost diappeared into the wrinkles on his weather-beaten face. He had a skysail-yard voice and had been given the George Cross for rescuing the crew of a torpedoed merchantman at great personal risk. He shouted, "Well, Doctor, what can I do for you?" I told him. He shook his head. "Pity you didn't come to me before." Then he added. "It'll be here in ten minutes; I'll see they bring it out to you." They did, with profuse apologies.

That night we dined with the Hutchinsons at their chalet, fifteen hundred feet above Funchal. The moon shone down from a cloudless sky and circles of light shimmered on the darkened sea. The world looked very wide.

CHAPTER FIVE

BEFORE I went to sleep that night I kept remembering odd scraps of advice and warning which we had been given during the last few months: Weston Martyr's half-jesting remark that he wouldn't put to sea with anyone too big for him to throw overboard; a friend's account of crossing in the Trades which made it look as if, in our puny boat, it would be a test of endurance instead of the pleasure we so hoped it would be, the sailmaker in Funchal who said our shroud-lanyards wouldn't last a week and who wanted to sell us trim brass rigging-screws, the experts who prophesied disaster to our iron fastenings. I thought of the three of us alone on this small boat and the stories I had heard of crews getting on each other's nerves so that not a word would be spoken from one week's end to another. Then I remembered Anne's steadiness and Christopher's resource, and decided that we had a reasonable chance of dealing with whatever might come. I tried to think of all the things I might have forgotten, and in so doing I fell asleep.

I turned out the next morning at seven o'clock to find that Christopher had already stowed his bedding. We took down the windsail and the large awning and had a last look round the gear. By that time Anne had the breakfast ready, a double ration of bacon and eggs to celebrate our last meal in port for a month or more. When that was over, Georgie was alongside to bid us farewell and to drink the last of a bottle of gin. Poor Georgie, to see his puckish face with the mouth turned down at the corners you'd have thought we were sailing to the moon. He looked so comic, sadly shaking his head, that we laughed . . . and had to give him more gin to soothe his wounded feelings.

A taxi arrived with the international police and Georgie brought them out. They gave us our passports and their gracious permission to leave. Much later, we heard they went to the Vice-Consul to claim the fare for the taxi. "You'll have to go and collect it yourselves," he told them, pointing out to sea.

A fresh south-easterly wind furrowed the waters of the harbour. We set the mainsail with a single reef, cast off the moorings, broke out the jib, which had been set in stops, and beat through the crowded anchorage into the open bay. Georgie jumped into his dinghy, shouting, "May the angels guard you!" With this last blessing we came about and cleared the breakwater on the port-tack, waving to a little crowd who had come to see us off. We streamed the log and set the course SW. by S. in search of the North-East Trades.

The wind eased and backed, the reef came out, the topsail was set, and by ten o'clock the loom of Barlavento light was the only sign of where Madeira lay. As I looked I saw the last quick flash before it dropped below the horizon. I went down into the warm lighted cabin, where Anne was already asleep. A stalk of bananas, like a small tree, hung suspended from the table, swaying with the roll of the ship. I turned in on the starboard bunk where I could see the stars through the open hatch and the glow of the binnacle light. The murmur of water slipping past the hull lulled my senses, and for the only time I can remember I fell asleep on the first night at sea.

I woke with a splitting headache, which was not improved when I found that my position lines put me sixty miles north-east of Madeira, when, by dead reckoning, I was ninety miles in exactly the opposite direction. I added and subtracted, I plotted and drew, and under my breath I cursed my crew, who were doing their best to help me. Then it suddenly dawned on me that the sun had a south declination for the first time since I had used the Air Nautical Tables. I looked more closely at the figures to find a minus instead of a plus, and all was made plain. I took over from Anne, who had done an hour of my watch. "You told me," she said, "that you needed four minutes to work out a sight!"

The wind remained light, and on the fourth day a hot wind from Africa ripened every banana in the ship. We held a banana-eating competition, which Christopher won with seventeen at a sitting; Anne was next with seven; and I was out of sight astern with four. Watch succeeded watch, and we congratulated ourselves at having such an easy start to our voyage. Anne wrote in her diary:

"At 4 a.m. Christopher called me and I found him in a duffle-coat, huddled at the helm, the ship barely moving and the air was humid and wretched. No wonder our fruit is rotting! He muttered a warning about everything being guyed and tied in knots to keep things still and quiet, and after an hour at the helm, when the wind came out of the N. or NW. and I had to undo them all, I thought deeply about knots. At 5.30 we were becalmed and I went below and turned in on the outside curve of Peter's bunk. An hour later I just got her going to a light breeze when Peter took over. I turned in and slept and was lazy while Christopher got breakfast, conjuring up toast to enliven the mouldy bread. He refused my offers of washing-up and did it on deck, Peter drying. Then I put the dishes away and stood by for a difficult sight-taking; the sun is shy today. So far we have used one tin of tongue, one of Dorsella and two of condensed milk. We have been five days at sea and come four hundred miles and have about two thousand six hundred to go. Peter has an infected right eye and I have an infected left one, so he is treating both with penicillin drops. I felt sick, but, on Peter's advice to forgo Dramamine and get going, I did so, washed in an inch of rainwater from the deck-bucket, and then prepared the lunch of cold potatoes, avocado pear and tomato mayonnaise. This, with melon and banana and watered wine, I ate at the helm. With spinnaker and topsail set and sailing into the sun, the afternoon watch was delightful. There is a gentle, following breeze and the blue sea is murmuring along with little rushing and splashing noises and tiny white tops. Is this, perhaps, the beginning of the North-East Trades?"

It was. During that day the wind steadily increased and only the boom-guy prevented a gybe in my watch and another in Christopher's, while Anne frankly sailed the wrong course. At seven o'clock the next morning we hove-to, took down all our fore and aft canvas, and set the twin spinnakers. As usual, without the mainsail to steady her, the ship was possessed of the devil and it was nearly three hours before we had the sails up and flying. The boom had to be lashed to the gallows and we bowsed it down with handy-billies to ring-bolts in the deck before it was rigid enough to leave. We tried the spinnakers half a dozen ways before we got them to set moderately free of chafe, and then the after-guys had to be served with greasy rags where they led over the bulwarks. Once this was done, the ship was so light on the helm that a child could have steered her, and what a relief it was not to have to worry about a gybe!

The wind increased to strong, with a big following sea which would rear up above the stern and pass harmlessly beneath us. The movement that night was entered in the log as lively, a plain understatement, for none of us had much sleep. The violent lurches from side to side dislodged the most carefully stowed jug or pan, and, once this had wriggled a little space for itself, the rest followed suit. The rhythmic sound was maddening and I spent quite a time trying to locate a tap . . . tap down below, only to find at last that it was due to the dinghy oars on deck. The wind eased a trifle towards dawn and we gradually became more used to this kind of sailing. By noon we had covered one hundred and fourty four miles in twenty-four hours and I altered course to WSW. From all I had heard, the winds are stronger in the south and we had no desire for more wind than this.

That night Anne called down, "There's a light on the starboard bow."

"Nonsense!" we said. "You're looking at a star."

"It's a funny sort of star; it's waving about in the breeze." So we went on deck, and, sure enough, there was the light, but no navigation-lights or stern-light, which it surely would have had if it had been a steamer. There was no answer to Christopher's repeated signalling. I was on for the dawn-watch, and as the light grew stronger I thought I saw a shadowy mast and the shape of two dark sails. Daylight came, and there, breasting the long swell, was a yawl of eighteen tons under twin staysails, with no one on deck to see us. At that moment our starboard spinnaker came adrift at the tack and wrapped itself round the forestay. I called all hands, and when they had dealt with the sail I showed them what I had found. We saw a man come on deck and look towards us, shading his eyes with his hands. Her course was altered, and as we closed we saw a woman, two children and a kitten walking about her decks. A hail came from over the water, "Are you the Pyes?" It was as if we had met in a street.

Anne goggled with excitement. "These must be the people we heard about in Vigo. They *must* be, because the Dutchman in Belem told me he'd given them a kitten. I can't remember their names."

"What ship is that?" I shouted.

"*Debonair*," was the reply. And then we remembered. They were the Fisks. Pat Fisk had had a job in India and when it had come to an end he had returned to England. He then decided to emigrate to New Zealand, and, as he couldn't get a passage for his family and himself for several months, he had bought a boat, and, without knowing anything about sailing, had set sail. They ran into an easterly gale, lost their bobstay and lay hove-to for five days nearly paralysed with seasickness. After the gale had blown itself out, they had limped back to port. But they didn't give up. On the day that we left Fowey they sailed again from Falmouth, and here we were in mid-Atlantic, nine hundred miles from the nearest land, meeting for the first time.

We took photographs of each other and talked across the water. Then we set our twins and passed *Debonair* to port. As we drew away, I called to Fisk, "What course are you steering?"

"By the wind," he replied.

By tea-time *Debonair*'s mainmast truck had slipped below the horizon.

In the evening the wind dropped, and Anne wrote in her diary:

"This evening was remarkable for the worst rolling we have ever experienced. We were to have a particularly succulent meal of boiled bacon with whole carrots, potatoes and onions, but its creation was hell. Peter peeled the potatoes at the helm; I was cast upon Christopher's recumbent thighs and he remarked that he had no idea how hard I was. I then shot off the port bunk head-first into the galley cupboard and found myself facing the tempo-pressure-cooker with my nose inside the jagged edges of a condensed-milk tin, a bruise on my forehead and the skin off my elbow. I was quite giddy. Christopher said he would eat at the helm. Peter held the pressure-cooker on the Primus for me, and when he left it for a moment it promptly fell on the galley floor and then crashed to the cabin floor, unhurt.

"The fruit salad slopped in and out of its dishes and a jar of dripping lay down and poured itself everywhere it could think of. I climbed into the starboard bunk to dry the dishes, while Peter tackled them from the port bunk. We were both glad, and sweating, when they were finished..."

The next morning Christopher and I hauled the heavy trysail on to the deck, fitted toggles to the luff and sheeted it home to the end of the boom. The effect was instantaneous. The jerk went out of the roll, and life below returned to normal. Later that day Christopher led the afterguys through the quarter-blocks to the helm to see whether she would steer herself, but it was not a success. I gave him no encouragement, because I felt that the extra comfort of having the trysail to steady her was worth the trouble of watch-keeping, and few vessels will self-steer if any fore and aft canvas is set, not even a jib.

The ship sped on. There were days of glorious sunshine when the fleecy Trade-wind clouds drifted across the sky; there were days at a time when we could scarcely see the sun through the grey pall that covered the heavens, when sunrises and sunsets would be full of awful portents of which the wind took not the slightest notice, following its own routine—moderate in the mornings, fresh to strong in the afternoons, and moderate to light in the evening. Whatever the week had been like, Sunday was always nice; the wind decreased, the sun would shine, and we took it in turns to take our ease on the foredeck. I felt at peace up there, detached from everyday happenings. I watched the curve of the twins, taut and straining, pulling the old ship along; I looked at her stern as it rose to the sea, felt her tremble as she hung on the crest, and watched her fling up her nose as she slid down its dark-blue back. Sometimes a shoal of flying-fish would take to the air right under her stem, to swoop and dip in a fairy dance before landing on the water again.

When the vessel's position was fixed at noon, Anne would ask me the day's run and solemnly pencil it on the transom, to add to the growing columns of figures. After a particularly lovely day, the wind increased to strong and for three days it blew hard without the usual respite in the morning and at night. The ship was pressed to her greatest speed, and down in the cabin the noise of her passing played on our nerves like a bow on a fiddle. Anne thought the end of the world had come if I couldn't find a tin or if Christopher cooked one onion too many. I found her wide awake at the end of her watch below. She said, "Peter, d'you think we could heave-to for a night, so that we could really get some sleep?"

"Why, yes, we could. But getting the twins down and taking in the booms makes it hardly worth our while."

She turned away. "I knew it was no good asking you. You'd wear yourself and the rest of us out rather than be a few minutes late."

I went on deck and watched the manful way in which *Moonraker* dealt with the white-crested seas, and at the log which was spinning away the miles. I said, "Anne's badly in need of sleep. *Moonraker* must sail herself tonight, unless we are to heave-to."

Christopher nodded. "I'd thought that, too. We can try the self-steering, but it's really a question of chafe."

"Better chafe the gear than Anne."

So we set to, and it was largely due to Christopher's ingenuity that we got her to sail herself within ten degrees either side of her course. The port spinnaker would lift at times and we chafed a guy right through, but we had plenty of rope, and a cheerful mate was worth all the gear we had. Not that that first night was a quiet one. The wind whining in the rigging and the rain driving it through the open hatch woke us all in the early hours of the morning. Outside it was most uncanny to see the helm going first one way and then the other, steering the ship at least as well as I could have done. After a few minutes I went below and the three of us lay down ready to spring on deck if any of our rather Heath Robinson gear should part. Towards dawn the squall died down and we slept long after our usual breakfast time, but our confidence in the "automatic" was complete. Every morning at seven we un-reeved it, set the trysail, and stood our usual watches. At ten o'clock at night down came the trysail and on went the automatic. In a day or two Anne was as fit as a flea, but I noticed that no one suggested that we should go back to all-night steering.

By 30th October we had completed three weeks at sea and had sailed one thousand six hundred and thirty three miles in a fortnight. Our position that day was 15.69 N., 48.19 W. As we had increased our west longitude, I had put the clock back whenever it got too dark to cook the breakfast by daylight. Our course tended more to the westward and this day it was W. By N. by compass. The eastern sheet of the North Atlantic chart had at last been stowed away and on the western sheet Barbados looked no distance at all, a mere seven hundred and sixty miles.

Christopher and Anne were both a bit off their food and we none of us could look at a tin of milk powder without flinching. I had a slight attack of my duodenal trouble, which I put down to a sauce of Anne's that contained vinegar, while she said it was due to my nearly going overboard yesterday. I had been altering the trim of the sails and had put a turn of the sheet round a pin, without a half-hitch to secure it. The port spinnaker lifted a moment, filled with a bang and whipped the sheet off the pin. Instinctively I hung on for a second and was whisked off my feet into the air. I grabbed the forestay and let the sheet run through my hand, but the fright took my breath away.

30th October being a Sunday was a good day. The Trade-wind blew softly and the ship sailed quietly over an easy sea. We sounded the water-tanks and found we had at least twenty-five gallons left; all the fruit, except a melon, two oranges and a few mouldy lemons had gone and we started on vitamin tablets to keep off the scurvy. We had finished the last of an enormous pumpkin the previous day and the potatoes were growing long shoots, but were still good to eat. We had finished the bacon and were sick of the sight of biscuits. Anne made drop-scones and scone-bread on alternate days, which we regarded as a great treat. Of the tins, corned beef was the favourite meat, with tongue a close second, grapes and peaches the best fruits.

The days had passed all too quickly; the books we had brought remained unread, although Anne would sometimes read poetry at the helm, and Christopher a thriller. I never tired of looking around at the changing sea and the sky.

That night I sat drinking my coffee at the helm. A full moon flooded the world with light, weaving an intricate pattern of ropes upon the dazzling white of the sails. The cabin looked warm and friendly in the yellow light of the lamps and I heard the murmur of voices come up through the open hatch. I remembered how, in Boston Road, I had lain in my bath thinking how wonderful it would be to sail on the boundless sea; how the telephone would jerk me back to the present and I would listen for Anne's knock on the door . . . "Matron at the hospital would like to speak to you" or "Mrs. Smith says would you come and see her baby at once," and the visions of Trade-wind sailing vanished as, in imagination, I ran shivering into the bedroom to answer the telephone. Well, all that was over for the time being and I wondered whether I should want to get back in harness when we got home. But I knew I shouldn't, for the hand of the State had tightened its grip on the doctor's throat, paralysing the good he can do. I took a round turn on my straying thoughts; medicine as an art is lost, clinicians are dead or dying, so up with x-rays and blood-counts and peace to the quiet dead! Thank God I'm here. I never was good at sums.

The Trade-wind gradually died away and we were becalmed. We lay under a great circle of blue sky, while around the horizons were clouds in fantastic shapes like anvils, or great St. Bernard dogs, or snowy mountain peaks. The same clouds, the same shapes, were there last night and, for all we knew, they might be there tomorrow. To the south, rain had been falling steadily from a single black cloud. The heat was terrific. There was no shade on deck and the cabin seemed even hotter. We bathed, but the water was so warm that it felt sticky, like jam. The glass fell and I studied the tracks of hurricanes on the wind-charts. If they occur in November, which is rare, they start in the Eastern Caribbean, hundreds of miles away, so this disturbance is unlikely to grow to serious proportions, we hope.

When the wind did come, it was from the south-west. It came softly at first, as if it might change its mind; but by tea-time it would not be denied, so we took off the spinnakers and the booms, untied all the chafing gear, reeved the mainsheet, rolled up the trysail, and set off on a course south by east, close-hauled on the starboard-tack under all sail to topsail, and with our spirits in the bottom of the bilge.

By next morning the wind had backed and freshened, so we tacked ship, pulled down a reef and sailed almost in the direction of Barbados. There is nothing to recommend beating in the

Trade-wind belt, and Anne wrote in her diary:

"The for'ard hatch is closed, as the foredeck is constantly swept with spray. The temperature, which was eighty, is now oppressive and our clothes are all wet and there is no dry place on deck to hang them, so they decorate the cabin and it looks like a slum. The sea is grey and the sky is grey, but there are only four hundred and twenty miles to go and we are glad. Tea was a filthy meal, as the scone had gone sour and we had biscuits instead. I stumbled through two of them with difficulty and an aching head. Then Peter called all hands as the wind backed suddenly into the east. Tea-things were left on the floor and we put our fore and aft gear to bed and set the twins again. At nine Christopher was still putting the finishing touches to guys and things in the moonlight, while Peter went below to deal with dirty dishes, unfilled lamps, unpeeled potatoes and unmade bunks—a heart-breaking job; but he managed to produce a dinner of tongue, potatoes, spinach and tinned grapes. Except to eat my dinner, I didn't leave the helm till eleven, at which time the others had fixed up the automatic."

Except for one day, when the Trade lived up to its old reputation, the last few days dragged slowly towards the conclusion of our voyage. None of us could get enthusiastic about runs of less than a hundred miles, and no longer did I hear Christopher singing Elizabethan songs at the helm. Anne wrote:

"Sunday again. We have been at sea a month and progress is very slow—only fifteen miles last night. Barbados, if it exists, is less than two hundred miles away, but we are only crawling towards it. I think nostalgically of Fowey and Fambridge, of Benjamin on his farm and the Kings on the water-front at Burnham, with the mist rising from the river and the little streets. Perhaps it is only when we are far away that we see it clearly. I can imagine that the cold wind has reddened my nose, that there is no meat, that Benjamin is dragging behind, and that we have to row out to *Moonraker* in a gale of wind, and yet . . . Here, with my hair unwashed, wearing old pants and a torn pyjama-jacket, lying in a hot bunk; Peter with the washing-up all over the floor, Christopher, bearded and in torn bathing-trunks, reading a novel at the helm; and, since meeting *Debonair* three weeks ago, not a sign of a sail or a distant wisp of smoke. . . . How lovely it will be to sight the shores of England if we ever do, and I hope we will have learned much."

On 7th November, being about one hundred miles from Barbados, we took down our twins and set every stitch of canvas the old ship could carry. The wind improved a trifle and I expected to make my landfall soon after eight o'clock. Eight o'clock came, but no land. Half-past eight, and still no land. I took three position-lines, all putting me within twenty miles of the island as far as longitude went; but there is a north-westerly current here of about a knot, and I was anxious in case I had allowed too much for it and we should pass to the south of the island. Like a fool, I had told all my friends that we were going to Barbados; what was I to say if we landed up at Trinidad? I altered course to the NW., and then, just before nine, there, fine on the starboard bow, was a low line of land. "Land Ho!" I bellowed, and the others came tumbling up to look.

Anne wrote:

"Flying-fish were leaping about as we approached Bridgetown, the breeze bearing us along at a fine pace. I took photographs of a fishing-boat that kept pace with us, three black men as crew, for the fishing-fleet was out and all around as we raced past glittering-white houses, green countryside, and white beaches; then round Needham Point into the most glorious blue-green water, to come to an anchor off the Aquatic Club in four fathoms . . . quite quiet and different from anywhere we have ever been before. Palm trees banked a beach where coloured people in light clothes and big hats were grouped; two silver turrets glittered on a building in the sunshine, and two boatloads of black men hovered near us to help with provisions when we were cleared. We had been at sea for thirty days. The harbour-launch came off, with the harbour-master, Mr. Smith (black), and Dr. Graves (I think his name was). They were charming and took particulars without coming aboard. The two provisioners now leapt on deck and a fierce argument started as to who came first. One was black, the other white. Peter made them toss for it and the white man won. We talked about fruit and meat and milk and bread. They told us that tomorrow was a race-meeting and all the shops would be closed. In the end we were guests of the white provisioner for dinner at the Hastings Hotel, where we dined to the sound of the surf on the beach, glad to sit down because we could hardly walk for the swaling of the land. As we have no money, the young man is paying for our cables and sending them off tonight. We were brought back in the moonlight in the great white be-cushioned boat with its hurricane-lamp hung in the stern, rowed by three black oarsmen over the quiet water to *Moonraker*, bowing gently at anchor off her first tropic island."

CHAPTER SIX

LAST night my thoughts had been so confused by the rush of events, by trying to walk straight on a land which moved from side to side, by the sense of achievement at successfully crossing an ocean, that I had gone to sleep without any clear impression of the place we had reached. It was, therefore, with a feeling of expectancy that I went up on deck in the morning.

Although the sun had not yet risen and the cabin-clock showed that it was only a few minutes past six o'clock, Barbados was wide-awake. Cars travelled swiftly over the smooth road along the shore which led to Bridgetown, and the air was filled with the cries of black men as they swam round the ship in the clear, blue water. Out to sea, against the dark background of a rain-cloud, I could see the white sails of a schooner beating into the bay, while from other vessels anchored not far off came early seafaring noises, and smoke from galley fires blew aft in the off-shore breeze.

These things interested me. I was beginning, after five months of voyaging, to look at things with a seaman's eye. I would find myself thinking, "This is a good place, sheltered from this and that direction; the bottom is clear of dangers." The land, its beauty of line and the grace of its buildings became of secondary importance. True, there were no mountains, such as I had expected; and think of coming all this way to visit an island in which there were places called Worthing and Hastings!

That evening we were invited to the Royal Barbados Yacht Club to meet some of the members, and I remember walking across the lawn in the dark towards a gracious colonial house, listening to the singing frogs and wondering if I should ever be able to enter a strange room full of new faces without an uneasy feeling at the knees; as unnerving as putting to sea from the safety of a harbour. It lasted, on this occasion, for only a very short time, for our host, the Vice-Commodore, came over and made us feel at home on the instant. Within an hour, I had two offers of a crew. One volunteer, Hugh, was short, with a black, pointed beard and a mind as quick as a rapier's thrust. He was mainly interested in an ocean-passage, but his friend Bob was ready to ship on any vessel cruising among the islands. As Christopher said, it looked as if we should want a bigger boat to carry all the applicants.

Invitations to dinner, to drinks and to drives round the island followed thick and fast, and Anne returned to *Moonraker* with her engagement-diary full for the next few days. The ship, with much of her paint rubbed off by the friction of the water, and with numberless small jobs to be done, would have to wait. Stores and water, however, we had to have, so we motored into the careenage next morning in a flat calm. What a place this is to delight the eye of a sailorman! There must have been twenty schooners and sloops, some of them fine ships come down from the Newfoundland Banks to end their days in the gentler waters of the Caribbean. There were the Speightstown schooners that sailed the few miles down the west coast to Bridgetown under the lee of the land. They looked as if they would fall to pieces if you touched them and only the other week one of them had sunk, the cargo falling out of the rotten hull. The crew swam safely ashore.

Away from the waterside the white pavements, the roads and buildings reflected the heat, so that it hurt to keep our eyes open, but there was relief in the reds and greens and yellows of the black women's dresses, and in the stalls of brightly coloured fruit and vegetables in a narrow alley.

Our stores ordered, we strolled towards the outskirts of the town, where a schooner lay hove-down by her fore and main halliards, so that her garboard-strake was exposed to the caulking-mallet of the shipwright as he hammered in the cotton. Two negro women, arms akimbo, laughing fit to burst; a negro with a brutish face, his arm upraised above a woman's frightened eyes; men with brawny arms casting off a schooner's warps as the crew made sail; these things we saw as we walked back to our ship. We were thankful to get in out of the heat and sat down to a lunch of bread and cheese, grapefruit, and the juice of two oranges laced with rum.

Two negroes stood talking on the deck of a Speightstown schooner to which we were made fast. We heard one say to the other, "D'you mean to tell me that li'l' boat come all the way from England?"

"Yeah, she come all the way from England."

There was a moment's pause. "Sure; I'd rather be like Jesus, an' walk."

That night, as I stood on deck before turning in, watching the lights on shore and the brightly lit Canadian *Lady Boat* that had just come in, I felt that I would not willingly be here except in my own boat in which we could go or stay as the spirit moved us. There was a restlessness in the air, too many people, too little room; or was it in ourselves? Was our roving life holding us in so firm a grip that the land irked us?

Hugh and Bob came sailing with us. Hugh had just finished his first novel. He was eager for new experiences, and his training as a pilot in the Fleet Air Arm made him quick to grasp details on board ship. But he was a dominant personality and I wondered whether he was the right person to make a fourth in an ocean-going crew. Bob had come across the Atlantic in a Brixham trawler, and I was surprised he had stayed on her so long. While they had been at Tangier the ship had been up for a scrub. Bob, using a scraper to remove a barnacle, had put the point through a plank. For the next half hour, keeping one eye lifted for the return of the skipper or of the mate, he prodded about the planking with a knife. She was as rotten as an over-ripe plum and at any moment she might have gone to the bottom. When they were half-way across the Atlantic and a thousand miles from land queer things began to happen. Bob said, "One night the skipper woke me up, 'They're coming,' he whispered, 'We've got to get away quick . . .' and then he started to sob, 'No, NO, I didn't tell them anything . . . Nothing at all, I say . . .' as if he were re-living some terrible past experience. I saw little chance of that ship reaching her destination so when we anchored at Bridgetown, I left."

Bob tried his hand at this and that among the islands until he settled down to teaching at Barbados, where he was paid rather less than the doorkeeper at the same establishment. He was the antithesis of Hugh. After a whole day on board, I had no more idea of what he was like than when I first met him. He was a great admirer of Hugh, and I felt he went away with no great opinion of our intelligence, but there was no doubt that he looked like being a first-class crew.

Anne hates committing herself to obligations of this kind, whereas I am the sort of person who would rather have two strings to his bow than be left with none at all. We compromised: Hugh would spend a week with us while we were at Tobago; Bob would join us at Grenada for a fortnight's trial cruise. "But," said Anne warningly, "don't let him think he's coming the rest of the way till we're sure about him."

"Don't you think you'll like him?"

"I haven't an idea. I think he'll be better with you. I am better with Christopher."

One day Pete Brannon, himself a keen small-boat sailor, drove us over the island, up onto the highest hill, from which we should have had a fine view if it hadn't been pouring with rain. He showed us over a primitive pottery-works and then drove us down to the windward coast. For twelve months in the year the wind blows over the ocean from nearly as far as Africa to the east coast of Barbados, with nothing in the way to stop it. Breakers thunder on reef and sand while the Trade wind whistles in the palm trees, bending them always to the west. It is from this coast that the flying-fishermen set out in their boats at dawn, when the wind falls light. They return in the afternoon or evening when it may be blowing anything up to half a gale. As we looked, we saw a sail making for a break in the reef that seemed not more than thirty feet wide. On she came, rolling wildly in the swell, then up on the crest of a tall sea, her bows clear of the water as she was borne through the middle of the pass. A little group of men and women had gathered on the beach; the boat sailed swiftly shorewards in calmer but still broken water. A second before she touched, down came the sail. Then mast, sail, ballast, and everything in the boat except the catch, were thrown into the surf, while all hands rushed her up the beach before the next sea could reach her.

"It's easy in this weather," said Pete, "but when there's half a gale blowing it looks quite hair-raising."

"Do many get lost?" Anne asked.

"A few. The last time I was here, a boat broached-to and rolled on to the reef."

"What happened?"

"Oh, the crew were knocked about a bit by the coral, and they lost their catch."

"What about the boat?" I asked him.

"She looked a wreck, but I expect they got her sailing again in a week or two."

The flying-fishermen are renowned throughout the islands for their courage and skill as seamen, a tradition that must be more important to them than a few flying-fish.

Debonair came in seven days after us. She nodded her head wearily in the swell, as if she were glad to see the land. The children waved, the skipper stood in the bows ready to drop the anchor, the mate was at the helm. Christopher and I got the pram alongside, Anne threw some bread, butter, grapefruit, a few eggs and a bottle of milk into a basket, and we were alongside as the anchor went over the side. Maureen Fisk looked thinner than when we had met in mid-Atlantic, and her eyes bulged like saucers when she saw what Anne had brought. For a moment I thought she was going to cry. She leaned over *Debonair*'s tall sides to take the basket. "How sweet of you!" she said. "If you only knew how sick and tired we are of baked beans."

We hung on for a few minutes, discussing the voyage. They had had the same calm, the same beat to windward, and, as with us, the last few days had seemed endless.

This was the beginning of a friendship that ripened quickly as the days went by. Pat was tall, spare, and immensely strong, one of those people whose movements appear to be slow, but who leave you miles behind if you try to imitate them. He was a man I would have followed anywhere he chose to lead, so perhaps it was not surprising that Maureen felt the same. Beside Pat, Maureen looked smaller than she really was. Her spirit was gay and her laugh infectious, but she could be just as determined as he. Neither of them had the love of the sea in their veins, but that didn't prevent Pat studying the art of sailing and navigation with the seriousness it deserved; but it was a hard road for Maureen. The gear was too heavy, she was tied by the children and the domestic chores, and the only thing about their voyage she would admit to liking was meeting people on shore and in other boats. I don't think she ever learned to read a chart. She was always sea-sick and probably just as frightened as the rest of us, but she wouldn't let Pat go without her. Robin and Carol, aged five and three, had to take their chance, too; like their parents.

At sea the children were harnessed on deck with a bucket of sea-water handy to play with; if the weather got bad, they went below and lay in their bunks or sat on the wooden floor drawing pictures with chalks. They didn't know the meaning of the word "fear." They loved the life. In mid-Atlantic Robin said to his father, "Daddy, I hope I go on sailing until I go up to God." As Pat said, remembering the time his sights were forty miles out, nearly running him on to the island of Fuertaventura in the early morning, that might be sooner than he expected.

Cinderella, the kitten, had joined at Lisbon. She was half-Dutch, half-Portuguese, a proper sea-cat who mewed with terror when she was put ashore. After two or three attempts they gave up trying to acclimatize her to the land and left her to guard the ship. When Robin and Carol got too much for her, she climbed into the rigging, but she was always glad to see them back aboard.

To our great content, "the Debonairs" agreed to meet us at Grenada for Christmas and to sail up the islands in company as far as Antigua. We fixed a sailing-date and told Christopher that if he made any appointments with young women beyond that day he would have to join us at Tobago by air. We felt surfeited by good things, as if we had dined on caviar and champagne when we were used to cheese and beer.

CHAPTER SEVEN

ADMIRAL Goldsmith, writing of *Madalena*'s cruise to the West Indies in 1935, suggested that smaller boats should miss out the southern group of islands and sail straight to St. Lucia. They would save themselves many miles of beating against a strong Trade and the equatorial current that sweeps westwards at a speed of up to seventy miles a day; but they would also miss some of the most beautiful islands, and I noticed without surprise that when he went again in a ten-tonner with a performance no better than *Moonraker*'s he went to Grenada from Barbados. We proposed to sail still farther south to King's Bay, Tobago.

We set out gaily from Carlisle Bay bound for the north-east end of Tobago, 120 miles away, keeping an eye on bearings ashore as we drew away from the land, for the current varies here from five to fifty miles a day.

In sunshine and shadow, before an easterly Trade that capped the seas with white, *Moonraker* ran on in an even unhurried way and in four hours the island was out of sight astern.

What a place of contrasts Barbados is: white sand beaches bordered by palm and manchineel trees swaying in the breeze and streets of overcrowded broken-down shacks; of large houses in ordered gardens, of country clubs and women who might have stepped out of *Vogue* and of little black children in trilby hats and torn shirts (and nothing else), of streamlined American cars and witchcraft, tops'l schooners and airfields, wealth and poverty, all these side by side on an island thirty miles long by ten wide with the highest population per square mile in the British colonies. I wonder the place doesn't blow up. Perhaps one day it will.

The sun went down in a blaze of red and green and gold. As I sat at the tiller, saw the lights in the cabin dim and watched the hands of the clock move towards ten o'clock I thought that the simplicity of life at sea had much to recommend it. Already the small irritations that have their root in too much shore-going were beginning to disappear and Christopher had been wandering round the ship muttering to himself about one small job or another which ought to have been done, cross with me, now, for not having made him do it before. This was the life: it kept you fit, exercised your brain and made you vigilant. Vigilance was the word; to see and to record. Then something else might come out of all this sailing.

Moonraker ran through the warm tropic night till, at eight o'clock, with the patent log reading 110, I expected to see Tobago. There was no land. Sitting at the helm, it suddenly occurred to me that if I was wrong, if we were to the west of the dead reckoning, we should have to get back against the current, so I routed Anne out of her warm bunk to take the helm while I took a mean of three position-lines to find they put me *fifteen miles* to the west of where I thought I was! Duly chastened, we altered course nearly fifty degrees, and a couple of hours later the misty blue mountains of Tobago showed up on the starboard bow.

How different from Barbados! Thickly wooded valleys led down from mountain peaks to small bays and inlets where shadows were cast so deeply that they gave the coast a dark and almost sinister appearance. Not a wisp of smoke or a single hut did we see till we rounded Pedro Point to enter King's Bay on the SE coast. As we beat into this deep inlet against fitful breezes coming down the valley or off the hillsides, we spoke in undertones, not wishing to disturb the solitude around us. High up on a ridge, a man gazed down upon us, his hand shielding his eyes from the evening sun. A pelican soared, circled the ship, then dived with the speed of an arrow into the still water, to emerge a moment later with a fish in its preposterous beak. A quiet "Right, Christopher, drop the hook," and the chain rattled down into the depths leaving *Moonraker* to roll broadside on till we put out a kedge to keep her stern to the swell. The sun sank below the hills, a light appeared in a native hut, and suddenly the forest glowed with millions of pin-point lights, the first fireflies we had ever seen.

Peter Williams was up a coconut tree when we first saw him; Anne and I, exhausted after a long hot walk to Delaford, were at the bottom. It had not really been a long way, but the damp heat—for this is a real tropic island—was something we had not felt before, and Anne, who liked it less than I did, was saying she would give a small fortune for a drink. A voice from above called down, "Yo' like to drink from de coconut?"

At first we could see nothing, so well did Peter fit in with his leafy background, but a moment later he was scrambling down with a cutlass hanging from his belt. His face was so deeply wrinkled that at first I thought he was old, but when he smiled, grinning from ear to ear, he looked young. His cocked hat, set at a rakish angle, his torn shirt and trousers, against the steaming forest, the great black birds with bright yellow tails made me think of Long John Silver and his pirate crew. With a few strokes of his cutlass, Peter cut off the heads of two coconuts and handed them to us to drink. While we drank, he hurled questions at us in the sing-song negro rhythm—where had we come from, how long were we staying, had we any children? "I marry my wife when she is sixteen, she make 'em quick," holding up the fingers of both hands to show how many. He told us that he would bring milk and look after our ship, even pledging his wife to do our washing for us. All these things we accepted politely, wondering, from past experience, whether we should see him again. But Peter Williams was as good as his word: during the week we stayed there he brought us everything we wanted, chickens, eggs, fruit; there was nothing he would not do for us; so unlike Bridgetown, where civility is sold in dollars.

His employer was a busy man, but Peter was most upset that he did not come rushing out to greet us; in the end he wrote to him . . .

Delaford,
Tobago.
4 - 11 - 49.

Dear Sir,
    Concerning the two gentlemen and the Lady at King's Bay, I told them what you said, and they say that they will be very glad to see you on Monday because they will be going away on Tuesday. I also ask them for their names, the Eldest man is Dr. Peter, and the youngest his name is Christopher, the name of the lady is Mrs. Anpy. George also send them some fruit and I carry it for them and they were much thankful for it.

I am yours,
Peter Williams.

But the climax came when we returned, after two days away, to find him sitting by the pram, gazing out towards *Moonraker* with a shotgun in his hand. Anne said, "But, Peter, how long have you been here?"

Peter looked at her reproachfully. "Lady, de captain ask me to look after de ship; he say he be back in the morning, so I wait till he com!" We were a whole day late.

We started work on the ship, replacing the worn-out iron sheathing on the bowsprit with copper, varnishing wire which was already showing signs of rust, repainting the galley and doing many other small jobs that had accumulated. Then came the rain:

not the lighthearted sort that we get in England, but rain so heavy that from our anchorage we could see no land, just a blur of grey. A thin stream ashore became a torrent bearing twigs, small branches and even logs, past our boat in an ever-increasing current. The blue, translucent waters of the bay turned thicker and yellower than those of an Essex creek at low water. For twelve hours we stayed below, listening to the rain rushing off the decks and dripping through the skylights. Then, as suddenly as it had started, it stopped. We surfaced from the stifling cabin to breathe the steaming air outside, but in less than an hour it started all over again. We slept with oilies over our beds; but in the morning the sun had returned to Tobago.

We had an introduction to Captain and Mrs. Short, who lived near the settlement of Richmond. They were a jolly, friendly couple with two charming children. Anna Short insisted that we should leave *Moonraker* and spend the week-end at their house. The house was built of wood and raised above the ground by a strong foundation of wooden piles. Half a dozen steps led up to the front door and we walked from the glaring sun outside into a long, cool room lined in darkly stained cedar-wood. Doors led off to a sun-room which Mayo Short had had built on, and to the bedrooms. How refreshing it was to look out of our window on hills and trees! Not even a pond reminded us of the sea.

Anne and I were enjoying a cold shower when we heard footsteps running outside and Anna's voice, sharp with anxiety, cry, "Christopher, the shed's caught fire at the back, please come quickly." By the time she knocked at our door, we were nearly dressed, hurrying out to the back where an outhouse blazed furiously. Tongues of flame shot into the air and sparks drifted slowly over the house. Anna and Anne disappeared with buckets of water to throw on the roof, while the rest of us shovelled sand on the cause of the trouble, a forty-gallon petrol-drum from which a river of fire flowed along the concrete floor. Christopher hadn't been fire-fighting in the blitz on Plymouth for nothing. He was everywhere at once and it was he who saw the second drum, far too close for comfort, and rolled it down the slope out of harm's way. We were very lucky; if the wind had been a trifle more in the north the Shorts would have been without a home, or if the drum had exploded anything might have happened. The fire burnt itself out just as the fire brigade dashed up the hill.

When it was all over and the mess cleared up, I asked Mayo how it was that the petrol-tap was turned on. He shrugged his shoulders. "Heaven knows," he said. "The houseboy was told to light up, and, by God, he did." Although the shed was burnt to the ground, the lighting-engine next door was untouched and worked at once.

About a quarter of the population, some twenty people in all, came to dinner that night; a pleasant, informal affair where we helped ourselves from a table with a huge dish of island lamb on it and every kind of West Indian vegetable and fruit. We sat around eating off our laps, talking to whoever happened to be next to us. My neighbour was a white-haired sea-captain whose eyes had that clear remote quality that goes with his profession. His face was gentle, but the skin over the bones was crinkly, like fine parchment, and this alone betrayed his age. Anne said afterwards, "His manners are just like something out of Jane Austen: I think he's a darling."

There is an interesting bit of pilotage between Little Tobago and Speyside on the main island if you are bound, as we were, from King's Bay to Man-o'-War Bay round the north-east end of the island. We were warned that the tide kicks up a nasty sea when the Trades blow hard, but the "Winter Trade" had not yet set in. Our trouble came when we were blanketed by Little Tobago island in the narrowest part of the channel. Here the tide swirls round rocks that are just awash, and you are never sure from which direction the next breath of wind is coming. Once, at the end of a very short tack, my cry "Engine, Christopher, quickly!" sent him scuttling below quicker than I had ever seen him move, but before he could swing the handle a lucky puff brought *Moonraker* round.

Beyond the islet, the sea was short and rather confused and I could well imagine that it might be dangerous for small boats in squally winds. We rounded the land, leaving the outlying islands to starboard, and sailed down this magnificent north-west coast to Man-o'-War Bay. Clouds lay over the mountain peaks, making it look hollow and sombre. We beat in, past Pirates' Bay on the port hand, to drop anchor off Charlottesville, a straggling, poor sort of place, whose single street struggled up from the beach to lose itself in the hilly, leafy background. Better huts, built on stout posts, hung precariously from the side of a hill to the left of the village.

And yet in this rather forbidding bay, as yet unpainted by the clusters of red bougainvillaeas that flower in winter months, we had the most carefree week of the whole voyage. The weather was cooler, and Anne shook off the lethargy that had dulled her enjoyment of the land. She is always ready to listen to anyone who wants to talk to her, and I would often find her in the centre of a little group of blacks, trying to answer all the questions she was asked, about the King and Queen, about living in England, and what she was going to do in America. "I don't think we're going there," she would smile. They looked at her aghast. "Yo' com' all dis way in dat li'l' boat an' yo' don' want to go to America?" It was the Mecca to which all West Indian eyes are turned, the home of the mighty dollar.

The people lived on fish and breadfruit, but the baker-woman, who was as broad as she was long, travelled to Trinidad by air! There was no fruit to buy in the village except plantains (like overgrown bananas), which we fried for breakfast, but a mile away we were given eighteen grapefruit from a plantation for the trouble of taking them.

In the afternoons we rowed over to Pirates' Bay, where we lay on the sand listening to the leisurely sound of the swell as it broke, and the swish of the water as it rushed, fan-shaped, up the golden beach. We practised landing in the surf, trimming the pram by the stern and coming in stern-first on the crest of a wave, jumping clear the moment she touched and racing her up the beach. We were in and out of the water like children and only rowed back to the ship when hunger beckoned us.

Hugh flew over from Barbados and joined us in time for dinner on 12th December. We sailed just before midnight, ghosting out of the harbour with the topsail doing all the work, while the mainsail hung in heavy, lifeless folds. Outside we found a light breeze from NNE. The genoa was set and the vessel slipped quietly over the ocean-swell, a creak of a block or the lift of a sail the only sound of her passing. Tobago brooded astern.

I allowed twenty-five miles for the current between here and Grenada, but we couldn't have got lost, for we first sighted the island from fifty miles away. Later, black rain-clouds, each with its attendant squall, put *Moonraker* down till the water bubbled and hissed in the lee-scuppers and the genoa sheet was like a bar of iron. The clouds gathered round Grenada till we saw, through an arch of rain lifting slowly like the curtain of a stage, green land sloping down from heights still hidden to inlets, rocks, and islets, and in the far distance the long, thin finger pointing to the southwest, Point Saline.

The sky cleared, the wind fell light and we sailed slowly past the lighthouse just as the first beam circled above us. We lay becalmed, but there was no peace on board. Quip and jest, point and counter-point were bandied across the sleeping ship. What a difference a fourth makes aboard, especially when the fourth is Hugh! He would make a good crew, I think, and as a third he might absorb enough of our cow-like qualities to be not too agile a companion. But as a fourth, no.

After two hours of drifting northwards on the current, I started the engine and motored across St. George's Bay till the two red lights in line took us past Fort St. George. High above the lights of the town the mountains seemed to hem in the harbour, as if we were entering a huge vault whose roof, the sky, pressed down upon us. As we moved slowly in, looking for a place to lie, the ripple of our wake lapped the paving-stones, so close to the road did the water come. Sleepy, red-roofed houses shared the waterfront with warehouses, and a faint perfume of spice drifted on the midnight air.

CHAPTER EIGHT

SOME days later Anne and I were returning from the market, I with a sack of grapefruit on my back, Anne with fish, bread, and a large pumpkin in her basket. We were walking up the steep hill which cuts off the shopping centre and the meaner streets from the waterside. A young woman crossed the road and addressed Anne. "You are Mrs. Pye? We met at the party last night."

"Yes, indeed," answered Anne, smiling at the recollection of the party at which the lights had failed and we had been introduced to voices without faces.

"I'm Willow Crocker. My husband and I wondered whether you and the Fisks would care to sail round to Calivigny, where we live, and spend New Year there."

"Isn't that Port Egmont?"

"Well, part of it; our particular bit is known as 'Crocker's Rocks.' "

"Someone was telling us about it. Whoever it was said nothing would induce him to go in there."

"John would pilot you in."

"Then we'd love to come."

But Christmas came and went before we escaped from the social round of St. George's and in the intervals Christopher and I painted the bulwarks and topsides so that *Moonraker* looked as smart as the day she left Fowey. There was no wind on Christmas morning. The harbour was as hot as a city office in an August heatwave, but it was gay. Five English yachts lay side by side, their sterns to the quay, outside the neat brick building of the Treasury. There was *Tern III*, Claud Worth's last boat but one, now belonging to Antony Lord and crewed by Walter Fury; *Leander*, a ninety-eight-ton ketch that had followed *Debonair* across from the Canaries; *Keskidee*, a schooner with a history of rum-running in the days of prohibition, now belonging to the Vereckers; *Debonair* and ourselves.

Moonraker went down below her marks when people streamed aboard for a pre-lunch drink, and I wondered what our friends in England would think if they could see the juice of twenty-eight oranges going into fourteen glasses, and rum at three-and-sixpence a gallon! Christmas dinner was on *Debonair*, her cabin decked with flowers, the best silver and china laid out on the polished table, tea on *Keskidee*, drinks in a house looking down on the harbour.

We returned to *Debonair* in the evening, sinking back on to the wide, comfortable berths, exhausted. Commander Newall from *Leander* was with us. He was a fine seaman and looked the part with his grey beard and weatherbeaten face. Only yesterday I had watched him bring his long ship into position between *Tern III* and ourselves as if she had been thirty feet instead of nearly a hundred. Throughout the manœuvre the only command had been to drop the anchor. We all spun yarns that night, but I remember best Newall telling us how when he was a young man, he and a friend had chartered a yacht from Watts of Creeksea on the River Crouch and sailed her to Sheerness. They arrived in the dark and were hailed from the shore: "What yacht is that?"

"Neither of us could remember her name," Newall laughed, "so we hung a lantern over the stern to find out. I never felt so humiliated in all my life." I wondered at Newall, who had been round the Horn in a wind-ship and had sailed with Seligman as third mate in *Cap Pilar*, choosing this little tale from all his vast experience. Perhaps as we get older our memories go back with greater pleasure to early beginnings.

It was some days after Christmas that Anne asked Christopher if he would like her to invite Christine over for a few days from Barbados, where she taught domestic science in a school. He replied, "Do, I'd like it very much." Then, suspiciously, "Did Peter put you up to that?"

When I shook my head he gave me a dirty look and said: "Peter, you're a matchmaker."

Christine came by air. She looked more Swedish than English, with her fair skin and her hair the colour of pale sand. She had merry eyes, a smile that was as disarming as Christopher's, and a fund of good sound sense. Chris and Chris; they were fun together and they laughed at the same things.

So there were five of us aboard when John Crocker joined *Moonraker* after breakfast, while his friend Bacchus boarded *Debonair*, also as pilot. Overhead the clouds were travelling fast, so we put a reef in the mainsail and set the second jib. We squeezed out from under *Leander*'s bowsprit and Newall's eagle eye and ran out of St. George's Bay. By the time we were round Point Saline *Debonair* seemed a long way astern, but, as Willow Crocker would be waiting lunch for us, we hurried on.

It was a stiff turn to windward against a current of nearly two knots. To the east of Calivigny, the only island in the neighbourhood with a house on it, we saw the Crockers' house on Point Egmont and to the left a bluff with dark-green trees on top and brown cliff below. This bluff is the key to the entrance. When it bears 345 degrees, with Adam Island on the mariner's starboard-hand and Calivigny well to port, you can, if you have the courage, run through a gap (about a cable and a half wide) in the reef which stretches from one island to the other. It sounds easy, but we were not used to channels without marks or buoys. Approaching from this angle, it was extraordinarily difficult to see where the sea was breaking and where it wasn't, and it was only when we were inside the gap that I realized I had been holding my breath, and started to breathe normally again: it had been a thrill, tearing through the narrow pass, a boiling cauldron of broken water on each side, a thrill heightened by the peace of the broad lagoon over which we now sailed to drop anchor below the Crockers' house.

Willow Crocket came sailing towards us in an eighteen-foot half-decker with Bacchus, *Debonair*'s pilot, by her side. His right arm was in a sling. "What happened?" I hailed them, thinking, I'm afraid, more of *Debonair* than of Bacchus's arm.

"*Debonair*'s a death-trap," he growled. "If the main-sheet block doesn't knock you out, the vang on the peak wraps itself round your neck and gets you that way. I was lucky to get away with a dislocated shoulder." (The hospital had reduced it without much trouble.)

"But what about *Debonair*?" I asked.

"I thought she'd follow you."

"Well, she hasn't." I felt angry with myself for not having waited for her at Point Saline. There was no possiblity of our returning through the gap against the wind. "She's so slow, she's not likely to be here before dark."

After a late lunch at the Crockers', we stood on the balcony watching *Debonair* making a tack inshore. She was still a long way west of Calivigny.

"Anything we can do?" I asked John.

"We'll go down later on and hang about the reef. If he can see our sail, it will help him find the gap."

Debonair plodded on, but the sun had set behind a bank of cloud before we trooped down the hill to the little jetty. John's little boat was fast, but by the time we had beat out to the reef the landmarks were difficult to see. *Debonair*, outlined against the darkening sky, was running for the gap. John was anxious.

"She'll never make it on that bearing," he said; "she's too far to the west." To and fro we tacked until *Debonair* was very close to the reef, still on her impossible course. If Pat could not see our sail, why on earth didn't he make for the open sea?

Then, with a gasp of relief, we saw her swing to the east and make towards us. She skirted the shoal to head squarely through the pass. We watched her dumbly, without a wave or a shout of welcome, as if she were a ghost-ship, which she soon became against the darker greyness of the land. Night had fallen.

On New Year's Eve the companies of both ships walked up the path to the Crockers'. Islands and bays, headlands and hills, lay in peace round us. Even the reef lay silent. The sea sparkled and danced in the moonlight and the aluminium roof of the bungalow shone like silver. We sat on the veranda, a quiet little party, drinking rum and fruit-juice until it was time to see the New Year in and wish it well.

The next morning, Pat said he had had enough of Crocker's rocks and went firmly back to St. George's. But we wanted to explore the eastern arm of Port Egmont. The lagoon, a real hurricane-hole, at the head of the bay, was absolutely sheltered, but the entrance is only half a cable wide. To get out again, we had a most exciting little beat, *Moonie* taking four of the shortest tacks she had ever made in her life. It was perfect weather for Christine's last sail, and two hours later we brought up within ten yards of *Debonair*, Maureen calling out, "We've got tea ready as soon as the kettle boils," and Anne, holding up our boiling one, "We'll bring this with us."

Christine left the next morning for Barbados. Chris and Chris . . . Well, Christopher was probably right; I was a sentimental old matchmaker and not a successful one, either. Two days later Christopher left for Trinidad and England. Five months is a long time to live in harmony in a boat twenty-nine feet long, in a cabin twelve feet by eight. There was little the three of us did not know about each other.

As Christopher's car turned the corner, I said to Anne, "Well, that's the last we'll hear of him till he comes aboard again. Then he'll sit down in his old place and it'll be just as if he had never left it."

We spent that evening on *Tern III*. She is but a ghost of her former self to look at, as Lord and Fury have cut her down to a ketch and taken away her topmast. But she is still a fine vessel, most suited to keep the sea. The saloon looks bigger than any I've seen in a ship of her size. There are no bulkheads between saloon and fo'c'sle, and there is a large mirror at the forward end. On the port side is a magnificent chart-table, big enough for a managing-director's desk, with drawers at each side above a long shelf filled with finely bound volumes of *Decameron Nights*. There are pilot-books for half the world, and not a single thing out of place: it was cold and immaculate.

As we sat round drinking the inevitable rum I rememberd that Lord and Fury had spent some time in the Mediterranean and I wondered whether they had come across a man whom we had met some years ago on the Spanish coast. I shall call him Jules. We had lain outside his large motor yacht with her tough Breton crew and had met his lovely young wife and their daughter. He had taken Anne to the market and had seen that she had bought the right things at the right prices. He had lived many lives and spoke a dozen languages and could drink a Spaniard under the table. He might be up all night, but at breakfast he was as fresh as the morning dew. He was by no means young.

"Did you meet him?" I asked.

"I did indeed," said Lord. "We met in an evil-smelling wine-shop, the sort of place you instinctively look for a wall to put your back against. I had guessed he was a bit of a racketeer, but when he suggested going into partnership I knew his proposition to be far too dangerous. And so it turned out, for the next thing I heard was that the Syndicate, for which he had been working before starting up on his own, had dropped a hint to the authorities and on his first run in on the coast he was picked up."

"Was that the last you heard of him?"

"Strangely enough it wasn't. I heard in a roundabout way that he had come out of gaol, shot a man for carrying on with his wife and was then languishing in a Sultan's dungeon."

I was sorry. I had like Jules.

One evening, just before turning in, there was a tap on the hull. It was such an un-nautical way of announcing oneself that we knew it must be Pat and Maureen. I went up on deck to find the two of them sitting in their crazy pram with the water nearly up to the thwarts. Maureen looked up. "It's terribly late, but we wondered . . . we think we want a little advice . . . don't we, Pat?" Pat's eyes were firmly fixed on *Debonair* and he made no answer.

"You'd better come aboard, both of you, before you sink." We sat on opposite sides of the table, Anne and I feeling like an elderly aunt and uncle talking to a favourite niece and nephew-in-law. We have no children, but at least we knew what was expected of us: to listen without interrupting while they talked themselves out of their troubles. When they had finished, when their faces were beaming and they were dying to get home to say what people who are fond of each other do say after setting their differences, I disobeyed the rules. I said, "Your trouble, Pat, is that you've got too much to do, both of you. You want a third. After all, you're not doing this for an endurance test."

Anne backed me up. "Look, Maureen, if you got someone, like Peter Mercer from *Leander*, who I know is looking for another ship, you would have help with the children and you could learn about navigation. I know I'd hate not to have a say in running *Moonie*."

Pat shook his head slowly. "I don't think I could get on with anyone else in *Debonair*, not even Peter Mercer."

"You could try."

They baled out the dreadful pram and we watched them paddle back to *Debonair*. Anne murmured, "it was charming of them to come and talk to us like that."

"I wish Pat would take a third," I said, "but I'm sure he won't."

"No, darling; he's almost as obstinate as you are."

Those few days which Anne and I had alone together, the only ones in ten months, passed all too quickly. On Monday, 9th January, the day before Bob came, we stocked up the ship with fruit and vegetables, and Anne said good-bye to the woman at the bakery, who had cooked us a Virginian ham, and to Agatha, the fruit-girl, who burst into tears, crying, "Mistress, send for me when you get to England." She was twenty-four and could neither read nor write, as she had worked for her living since she was a child. We said good-bye to the friends we had made on the island. This morning I suddenly woke up to the fact that we had been out here two months and had visited three islands. The "languor of the tropics" was upon us! It was time to go.

CHAPTER NINE

BETWEEN Grenada and St. Vincent, seventy miles to the north, lie the Grenadines, a chain of islands, about a couple of dozen in all, most of which, we had been told, were worth a visit. But it is collectively that they are so beautiful. When Hugh and Christopher had been with us, we had spent a day or two among them, and I remembered standing on a sandy strip on Mabouya, looking northward to Union and Mayero and Tobago Cays on a perfect morning, watching the seas roll in to break on the reefs in a smother of dazzling foam, the blue peaks on Union contrasting with the small, green humps of the Cays. Where there weren't islands, there were rocks; "Kick 'em Jenny" of fantastic shape, a pointed one, like Cleopatra's Needle, "Sail Rock," looking like a full-rigged ship, and "London Bridge" with a hole through the middle of it.

Now it was quite different. The Winter Trades had set in with a vengeance and squalls of wind and rain swept across the sky. Islands and rocks that had looked so fairy-like were an angry colour, and the spray swept through the hole in London Bridge. We had the strongest winds we had yet experienced, beating up through the islands, and with the current sweeping us down to leeward it took all of a twelve-hour day to make good a distance of twenty miles. It was exhilarating sailing; the helmsman wore bathing-kit and wrung it out over the bridge-deck after coming below to change. We hung on to two reefs in squalls of half a gale, the water cascading over the decks, filling the self-draining cockpit and draining through the skylights that had shrunk with the heat. They soon swelled up again! It was the sort of weather we might have been hove-to in, in the North Sea, where the cold and the grey menace of sea and cloud make it seem worse than it really is. Out here it may blow hard, but the chances of its blowing too hard are rare, and the difference made by the sun and the warm water has to be experienced to be believed.

Even though we drove her hard, we couldn't always make harbour before dark. In all the Grenadines there are only two lights, both visible for a bare five miles, so the choice lies between going in or staying outside, dodging other unlit dangers. We went in, as a rule, with our hearts in our mouths, our eyes glued to the night-glasses trying to see where water ended and land began, or to the compass to take a bearing on a mountain-peak, never very sure that we'd found the right one. The first time is the worst: after that the experience and the confidence you gain make it a little easier. In the end you wonder what all the fuss is about; that is the time the crash may come!

Four days after leaving Grenada we sailed to Union Island on a bright and breezy morning. We anchored in Chatham Bay, which is completely deserted and is shaped like a bowl with a piece bitten out of one side. The wind howls down the sides of the bowl with the force of a winter's gale, and *Debonair* and *Moonraker* tugged and wrenched at their cables like tiger-cubs. In the middle of our first night there a squall hit us broadside on and *Moonraker* heeled till her rubbing-strake was in the water.

Next morning we all set off to walk over a pass nearly a thousand feet high, which, according to the chart, should take us to the settlement of Ashton. The path was difficult to find and very steep, but the view from the top was magnificent, right over to Tobago Cays, where the sea broke along five miles of reef; over the cotton fields rolling down as smooth as the Sussex Downs to the village below. We left Pat and the children on the pass, Pat because he had a broken toe, which I had put in plaster only three days before, and the children to look after Pat. The rest of us set off down the hill with Pat's instructions ringing in our heads, "Don't come back without eggs."

A single street ran down towards the water-front. On each side were five or six rum-shops, a number of wooden shacks and two general stores. Nowhere was there a sign of an egg, for the Grenada Government had fixed the price at five cents (two-pence-halfpenny), a price at which the natives wouldn't sell. Then a small boy came up to Anne. "Eight cents fo' dis egg?" holding out a small, white egg in a small, black hand.

Maureen looked at Anne. "I'm willing to pay eight cents for an egg," she said; "I'm so tired of canned food."

Anne took the egg and gave the boy eight cents. She said, "Tell your mummy we'll buy as many as she can sell us for eight cents." He ran like the wind, his black feet streaking through the dust. Leaving the two of them in the middle of the road, Bob and I walked down to the tiny harbour.

We came back in twenty minutes. The empty street was a milling crowd of children and young women, all trying to force their way towards the centre. I wondered what could have happened, but as we got nearer we saw that each hand held an egg, and in the middle of the crowd were Anne and Maureen. That is the only time, I may say, when we have gone in for the black market in a big way, but the results were most encouraging and we walked up the pass with seven dozen eggs! After that, bread, milk, and chickens were sent over each day, and once a goat was driven over the pass in the vain hope that we might buy it.

The wind blew, the native sloops could not sail and the island ran out of small change so that we had to barter bully-beef for bread. But in the end it was the howl of the wind and the snubbing of the chain at night that drove us from this lovely place.

It was another wild morning when we set off for Tobago Cays, the Debonairs waving to us from the sandy beach where we used to bathe. Outside we found less wind and shook two of the three reefs out. From the chart, the way into the Cays looks more frightening than it is. We had to beat, but the water is clear and we had the light behind us, and Anne and Bob gave me plenty of warning of when to come about. The Horseshoe reef, shaped like its name, protects the three islets of which the Cays consist. The jade-green pools lying on the reef, the dazzling white of the sands and the deep, deep blue of the Atlantic beyond, beggar discription. The air is filled with the dull roar of the breakers and the whine of the Trade wind in the rigging; to the east, the nearest land is Africa. Occasionally a fishing-boat may sail over from Mayero, but, for the rest, we were alone with nature on a grand scale.

We sailed into Admiralty Bay, Bequia, on the last day of Bob's trial-cruise. From the moment he arrived, everything he did had confirmed my opinion of him as a first-rate crew. We had had a hard thrash to windward for his first sail and he had neither punished the ship by driving her too hard nor had he called me for unnecessary sail-changing. The three of us started off with one thing in common—our love of sailing. After a few days he added another—love of the ship. If our common interests seemed to end there, as far as I was concerned it could not matter less.

The weather was like a June day in England, and after breakfast Anne and I set off to walk to Friendship Bay. It became very hot and we sat down at the head of the pass which separates one valley from the other. Below lay the little village of Bequia, red-roofed and tidy at this distance, where men moved like ants about the quay, loading one schooner and working on another. Half a dozen sailing-vessels lay at anchor. Tucked away in a corner, locally known as Hamilton, were *Debonair* and

Moonraker. Bob was at the mast working on the copper band which had started to come adrift.

I said, "Bob told me this morning that he would like to come with us the rest of the voyage."

"What did you say to him?"

"I said I'd like him to."

"Don't you think you might have consulted me first?" she asked quietly.

"Was it necessary? He's a first-rate hand."

"Yes, it was necessary. And I say he can't come." She frowned as she tried to find the right words. She said, "We couldn't ask for a better crew. It's a matter of temperament—his and mine: all the little things . . ."

"Such as?"

"Well, I see that it shocks him when I quibble about your pilotage."

"But you always have."

"Yes, but he's not to know that and when I'm feeling tired and hot and want to be cross with someone, he won't be cross back."

"Is that a good enough reason for not taking him?"

"I think it's one to be considered. I can't promise to be on my best behaviour all the way home."

How well I knew what she meant. It was, as she later was to say, like having a man in our bedroom for months on end giving her no chance to say what was on her mind and any small happening, instead of passing, would grow until the walls of the cabin could no longer contain her pent-up frustration. With Christopher Anne could be as provocative as she liked and receive in return as good as she gave. It did us all good; but Bob was a very different proposition. He was meticulous in his behaviour. He refused to be pushed into argument by anyone and would quietly and efficiently carry on his work in the ship, leaving Anne silently fuming at his refusal to accept a challenge.

There was a pause while I thought things out. Then I said: "If you feel strongly about this, I'll tell Bob that I have changed my mind."

"I shall feel a beast if you do. It isn't his fault that I'm built as I am."

"He'll understand. But before you finally make up your mind, don't forget that there'll be a fortnight's hard work to put in on the ship in English Harbour. With only the two of us to do it, it will take at least three weeks. Remember, too, we have got six thousand miles to sail in the next seven months—too long a passage for enjoyment with only two of us aboard, and from what I have heard the likelihood of getting someone else is small."

"I hadn't forgotten," she said.

We got up and walked down the narrow winding path towards the sea. The water was calm and changed from blue to green as the bottom shelved. The lazy swell broke on the reef outside. Anne was silent all the way down. In the village we met Bob, who had come ashore for some copper tacks.

Anne walked straight up to him. "I hear you've signed on the hell-ship in spite of the blue-nose mate," she said. It was like watching two dogs eyeing each other warily, tails stiff, hackles up. Then they smiled.

There is no doubt that the Grenadines are the pick of the West Indies, not only because of the islands themselves, but because the people who live there are so friendly. True, they are idle and only work to live (who doesn't?), and after that they sit in the sun and talk to anyone who cares to listen. I remember meeting with a wedding-party in Carriacou, a crowd of young men and women, the men in blue suits and straw hats, the girls in frocks of bright red, yellow and green, their faces glistening with excitement and pleasure as they scrambled into a lorry and disappeared down the hill, singing at the tops of their voices like children out for a treat.

They are very poor. Once I was on the point of throwing away a topsail sheet. There was a long splice in it and age had stretched this to half its original diameter, but the skipper of a local sloop shouted, "I'll have dat rope, Cap'n; don' throw it away." He rowed over and fingered it lovingly. He said, "Dat's a lot better'n de main halliard on my ship," and carried it proudly away.

Sunshine and warmth and good teeth make up for a whole heap of money; these folk are contended and happy, as I should be if I had lived in their way from the beginning. They're pretty cut off in some of the smaller places; they get a visit from a doctor once a month, if they're lucky. In an emergency they are taken to St. Vincent in a local sloop. Imagine a twelve-hour beat to windward with a perforated duodenum!

There was a small hospital at Bequia, where there lived a Polish doctor, a man who had served in the R.A.F. during the war. His wife was also Polish. She was quite young, but her eyes were those of a woman twice her age. She had a queer little half-smile, as if she dare not, as yet, let it have full rein. She had been in Poland throughout the war, first under one tyranny and then another. "Give me ten years of German rule for every one of Russia's," was her only comment.

Both Pat and I were grateful to her husband. Pat had developed a dental abscess and the visiting dentist, as black as a bowler-hat, decided to remove the tooth. After an hour or so I went along to the hospital and found Pat looking ill and in great pain, the local anaesthetic having failed to work. The tooth was still *in situ*. I had brought along some evipan, just in case, but the doctor had had no experience with this. He took me aside. "This is no time for red tape," he said. "You give the stuff and I'll stand by just to make things regular." The tooth was immediately and skilfully removed and I went out into the blazing sunshine to find Maureen. She was looking a little worse than Pat for she had been waiting for three hours.

We had been told how roughly the local schooners were built, but I don't think any of us believed they could be as bad as was made out until, on the beach at Bequia, we saw the skeleton of one, started two years previously. We stood and gazed at her in wonder. Her ribs were whole branches of trees with the bark stripped off, but no attempt had been made to square them or to alter the shape that nature had given them. A few planks were in position, joined with ungalvanized fastenings from which brown rust trickled down. I wouldn't have believed that such a ship could float, and yet they say the average age of a schooner is thirty years—a remarkable tribute to West Indian weather! In this particular case the money ran out when she was less than half-completed, so there she lies, being fast devoured by termites.

After that, of course, we could believe anything: how none of them carry compasses, or, if they do, only dry cards which are as useless as no compass at all. How dogs or pigs are carried aboard, so that if a ship gets blown off course and out of sight of land, the animal, suitably starved, is brought on deck to sniff in the direction of the nearest land!

Both *Moonraker* and *Debonair* were short of water. Bequia had no natural springs and the winter had been exceptionally dry. Even the small amount we needed couldn't well be spared. Pat said, "It's about time you came sailing in a proper ship. We'll go to St. Vincent and bring back enough for both of us."

I hadn't the courage to say that we funked that terrible mainsheet block, to say nothing of the vang that dislocated Bacchus's shoulder. We got under way, but Bob was a second late in ducking to avoid the block. It gave him a playful flick and he retired below with blood streaming down his face. Pat swore Bob's blood drowned the sparking-plugs and stopped the engine! Anne and I found plenty to do for'ard of the mainmast.

The tiller was as short as a sailing dinghy's, a piece of iron tubing with relieving tackles to help move it. Even then I've seen Pat put his back up against it, his long legs braced across the cockpit coaming, and heave with all his might, just to keep his ship from coming up into the wind in a squall. She must have a metacentric shelf like a mountain range.

It was blowing a fresh breeze, a one-reef day for *Moonraker*, but *Debonair* was carrying her topsail and breasting her leisurely way over the seas with dry decks. All she needed, I thought, was a different helm, or a wheel, a bit of ballast trimming and a *boom*.

We worked like blacks when we did arrive, after carrying away a cleat on deck and bumping twice on the sand as she surged forward on the swell. I thought how pleasant it was to be a crew for once and able to relax mentally, free from responsibility. Pat said, "I'm not staying here a minute longer than an hour. If you're not back by then," with a meaning look at Anne, "we sail without you."

I rushed about trying to cut through the yards of red tape needed before we could take in water. Bob stayed aboard to help keep *Debonair* off the quay and the bottom, while Anne appeared a minute before the hour was up with a troop of black boys carrying a week's provision for both ships.

We had a fair wind back to Bequia, but if *Debonair* was bad to windward, she was worse when off the wind. As we came in sight of the village the last rays of the evening sun flooded it with a golden light. We beat in against the dying breeze, the shadows lengthened from the opposing hills, and lights appeared on shore and in *Moonraker's* cabin, where Maureen was preparing a late tea for us. It was like coming home.

CHAPTER TEN

TO the north of Bequia lie a series of islands like peaks in a mountain range (which indeed they are) curving in a wide arc, the shape of a crescent moon. They are high islands, from thirty to forty miles long by ten to fifteen wide, and form part of the barrier which divides the Atlantic from the Caribbean Sea. They are evenly spaced, about thirty miles apart, each claiming that its own strait has the strongest winds and the swiftest currents. It is extraordinary, seeing how alike they look on the chart, how different they appear to the eye. Dark Dominica comes after the more rounded, greener Martinique; St. Lucia, the fairest of them all, delights the eye after the grandeur of St. Vincent. They belong to the Windward group, and, as you might expect, their eastern coastlines are iron-bound against the ceaseless battering of the Atlantic, while the western sides are more gentle, with sandy bays where the blue waters of the Caribbean break with a whispering sound upon the beaches. Each island has a port of entry and by law you are not supposed to set foot ashore till you have been cleared at that port, a most annoying rule for yachts if it is at the other end of the island from the anchorage you have chosen. Sometimes we ignored the rule, but we always took the advice of the harbour-master as to whether this could be done with impunity. The harbour-master at these ports is an important man, and if you protest against his moving you from one berth to another it will be you who will suffer; if he likes you, he can be most helpful.

We got a general clearance for all the Grenadines from Mr. Redhead of St. George's, and the harbour-master at St. John's bought eggs for us and allowed us to use his office as a waiting-room.

We were very sorry to leave Bequia. As Anne said, not only was it the perfect size of island, neither so large as to be impersonal nor small enough to be restrictive, but it was also the last place where we could let the days go by without worrying about the tempo of our progress. Now our voyage must be speeded up, or we should never get back to England.

We roared out of Bequia on the last day of January with a reef in the mainsail and the second jib. Although Kingstown, St. Vincent, lies ten miles due north of Bequia, the current sweeps westwards at such a pace that it is impossible to make the port in one tack or half a dozen. Earlier, in *Debonair*, we should have failed to get there without the powerful engine, so this time, instead of going straight across and trying to beat along the coast, we fought it out in the open for five hours till at last we were well to windward. A wet, hard beat with the lee-rail buried all the time.

As we drew nearer, the squalls off the hills whistled down as they did at Union Island, and in one of them the foresail sheet, rope reeved from a new coil last week, parted. Bob made a temporary repair, and we came to anchor off the north-east corner of the bay, which, with the mountains in the background, looked like Madeira. We stowed the sails and heaved the pram into the water; then Bob came aft with the foresheet in his hand. "This is not chafe, Peter; it's rotten." So the three of us sat on the cabin-top with miles of rope around us, examining every inch. It seemed sound, but here and there a few inches of a strand looked furred, like wool. Bob untwisted one of them and broke it in his hands. It was as rotten as an over-ripe pear.

Anne grinned at me. "To think," she said, "that there was I worrying all the afternoon because you'd forgotten to reeve a new bobstay-tackle before we left, and if you had we should have lost the bowsprit!"

We strolled through the streets of the neat little town, looking for bosun's stores. By great good fortune we met the head of a shipchandler's, who gave me some shackles which he had been keeping for his own yacht. We were discussing rust in wire and he sold me some anti-corrosive paint that preserved it for the rest of the voyage.

Along the waterfront they talked of little but the weather. Four schooners, they told us, had been lost and several damaged during the strong winds of January. After the one we saw at Bequia, we were not surprised. A month in the English Channel would sink most of the boats we saw, summer or winter.

In the afternoon of the next day we sailed with a light fair wind which steadily backed to the nor'ard and increased to strong. The mountains frowned on us and the sea looked rough. "We sail for pleasure," we cried, and made for the warm comfort of the land.

By chance we came to the entrance of Cumberland Bay. A brown cliff stood sentinel on the northern shore, the water rustled in the evening light and a valley led up towards clouds which were tinged with rose. On our left a wooden jetty showed the most likely place to anchor and a wisp of smoke drifted into the quiet air.

We entered, and the next morning we walked up the valley past

Spring Village, where new huts stood in neat rows like council-houses, past Spring Garden, a poor relation with huts of mud with straw roofs and boys playing cricket with palm-branches for bats and gru-gru nuts for balls—they are green, about the size of golf balls—up into the hills where the swift-running stream lay far below and Soufrière Mountain reared its ugly head. An old woman with swollen legs passed slowy by, carrying a load of arrowroot upon her bent shoulders. We said, "Can you tell us, please, where this path leads to?"

"Nowhere!" she replied hoarsely. "Only to the mountains." Then, pausing for a moment, she asked, "Where are you from?"

"We come from England."

There was no smile on her aged face. She said, "If your King paid me for my arrowroot I should not be so poor."

We assured her that it was not the King who was dilatory, and Anne slipped a shilling into her hand. She regarded it dispassionately before slipping it into a greasy leather purse; then, without a word, she turned and slowly followed the path which led "only to the mountains." The heat of the noonday sun and the stiff climb had tired us, so we retraced our steps to where the ship waited for us in that enchanting bay.

We left at midnight. There wasn't a breath of wind in this sheltered harbour, but it was blowing half a gale, even more in the squalls, in the St. Lucia channel. We had three reefs in the mainsail, the reefed foresail and the third jib. When the head of this jib blew out we set the fourth. In the early hours of the morning, in my watch, the crest of a sea came aboard by the after-runner and in a second the after-part of the ship was filled with water to the top of the bulwarks. We had the boards in the main hatch and she soon threw the water off, but it was a reminder that you can't drive a small ship too hard with impunity. The incident was nevertheless strangely comforting, so well did *Moonraker* behave. I began to feel that she might even be equal to the return journey across the North Atlantic. You plan a voyage, but you do not believe you will accomplish it when you are measuring distances in thousands of miles instead of the usual hundred or two. I am an optimist about things in general, but I look upon the sea as the ancients viewed their gods, with superstition; and I propitiate the monster in little ways like never filling in my destination in the log-book till I get there. If I ever became sure of myself, I should expect the sea to swallow me up, as, no doubt, it would.

It dismays me to think of the number of times that pure chance, or an Act of God, has rescued *Moonraker* from perilous positions I put her in. Soufrière Bay, St. Lucia (names repeat themselves so often in the West Indies), is well protected. No swell rolls in, it is easy to find with the two Pitons rising, cone-shaped, to over two thousand feet; the difficulty lies below the water, not above. The bay is an old volcanic crater with the five-fathom line so close to the shore that the bowsprit almost overhung the beach before we got soundings. When *Moonraker* drifted back on her cable, her stern might well have been in forty fathoms.

It was on leaving here that we nearly met with disaster. With jib and mainsail set, we had broken out the anchor, but at that moment a puff came from the south. She gathered way, straight for the shore, a few yards away. I lashed the tiller hard up and the three of us seized the boom, trying to haul it to starboard. A breath of wind filled the sail and round she came, and to this day Bob swears that he heard her heel grind upon the beach. Then a cry, "Look out, a reef, just ahead of you!" sent my heart into my mouth, when a strong puff, right off shore, sent her spinning round on her heel and we were away. How many lives, I wondered, had *Moonraker* got left and how pig-headed of me not to use the engine!

St. Lucia meant more to us than just another island whose mountains were low enough to see, instead of always being in the clouds; it was the turning-point of our West Indian sailing, where our course bent more to the west and we no longer had to beat against the Trades. And no day could have been more appropriate, for it was our wedding anniversary, the first we had ever spent at sea. St. Lucia is more French than English; last night the lights of Soufrière had a Gallic twinkle and the metallic jungle rhythm of a Calypso band floated across the water to where we lay. The endless, repetitive notes rose and fell as the breezes blew, quickening the pulse, nagging the brain.

With the genoa set and the topsail drawing for the first time since leaving Grenada, we sailed up the magnificent coast to Port Castries, arriving too late to be cleared. It was a bigger port than we expected; two steamers lay at the quays and we dropped anchor among a cluster of native schooners in the older part of the harbour.

It was dark when I awoke. A cool breeze blew down the windsail and the stars shone brightly through the open skylight. There was movement behind the curtain of the fo'c'sle; that seemed odd, because Bob slept like the dead. The sound moved on to the deck. I slipped out of bed without waking Anne and went up on deck.

I don't know which of us was the more startled, the negro sitting on the bulwarks just for'ard of the shrouds or myself, but he was first off the mark. In a second, he had doubled up like a watch-spring, leapt backwards into the water and had swum for the shore. He was as big as an ox and I was glad to see him go.

Bob's shorts, his cigarette-case and lighter were still lying on the cabin-top. When I woke him he didn't seem at all worried: "I never carry more than a couple of pounds in my pockets," he said; but later he discovered that twenty pounds had been taken from under his mattress while he slept. He said, "I can hardly grudge it to such an enterprising thief," but the mate had different ideas. "It would have been better in the coffers of the ship," she said.

Port Castries, although an excellent place to restock with tinned food, is a blot upon a fair land. Most of the town was destroyed by fire some years ago and no one has done more than put corrugated iron on the less burned buildings. We sailed to Vigie Cove, a mile away, where *Debonair* was anchored near another West-country boat of twenty tons. Three young men had sailed her out and hoped to work their way across the Pacific. There was a dampness about her as if the water was seeping into her bones that made us think that her sailing days were nearly done. We liked the young men; they were full of initiative, but the ship needed a shipyard and a cheque for a thousand pounds.

A general strike threatened. Instead of the usual negro smile, men went about with surly, discontented faces. At night, dark shapes flitted among the ruins or stood about the waterside. At the last moment, the strike was averted and the air lifted as after a summer's storm. Bob stayed to look after the children, while Pat and Maureen and the harbour-master, Commander Milbourne, came sailing with us down to Marigot. "The Debonairs" fought over *Moonraker*'s tiller, they found her such a joy to steer. Pat caught a barracuda which Anne fried for lunch, and we were so carefree that we overshot Marigot Harbour and had to beat back again. Pat climbed a coco-nut-tree, but when he came down the skin of his legs stayed on the tree.

In my journal, to commemorate that happy day, I have a photograph of Pat and Maureen sitting under a notice-board nailed to a tree upon which is written:

NOTICE

TRESPRESS WILL
BE PERCUITED.

BY ORDER.

On the way to Martinique, with the sheets eased and the ship going like a train, we saw coming towards us sixteen small sail turning to windward, like butterflies in a field. Each boat looked long and narrow, like a dug-out canoe, with a short mast and a sprit-sail, a sort of Thames-barge sail in miniature, without the gaff. Each canoe carried three men: one to steer, one to bale (a hard job this), and one to lean well out to windward to prevent her from turning turtle. They went like the wind and were already far from from the nearest land. I heard later that most of these boats were built by the Caribs in Dominica. A V-shaped block of wood is cut from a tree, hollowed, and set up on a block over a smouldering fire on the beach. The hull is partly filled with water, and the wood, softened by the boiling water and the steam, is shaped by the weight of large round stones placed inside the hull in the right positions. A top strake is added to give more freeboard.

We passed close to "The Diamond," a rock nearly six hundred feet high, up whose precipitous sides the Royal Navy hauled guns and stores from the decks of a "seventy-four" (the *Diamond*) that was courageously laid alongside. For a year they harassed French shipping until lack of water forced them to surrender.

Sailing into Fort de France Bay, with its wide expanse of sheltered water and the green hills around it, was like coming into Falmouth, but there the likeness ended, for a smellier, dirtier harbour it would be hard to find. We tied up in a corner near the Yacht Club, where a tug shunted lighters across our bows every half-hour, missing us by feet. Ashore it was delightful, just like any little town in the South of France on a hot summer's night. We made our way to Chez Étienne, where we ate Omelettes aux Champignons off thick, white plates and drank red wine from a large carafe. The chairs at the tables were full of men and women of all colours from white to the deepest shade of brown. Near to us was a young woman whose face and colouring were like that of a Gaugin. She wore a white flower behind her ear. Her man had a heavy, smooth face, the skin faintly tinged with yellow. His eyes brooded on her.

After dinner we walked up the narrow street towards the river.

The crowds had gone and the silence was only broken by the tinkling of a piano and by a man's voice, singing. There were lights in windows and quiet interiors, a corner "Pavilion" with a child's dress in an upper window, a ragged shirt in another, pictures glowing on the walls in the light, and, below, a dim bar with huddled figures.

At the Yacht club, M. Figuères was big and jolly, with a proper appreciation of his own skill as a helmsman. "What is the use of my racing," he asked, "when I always come in first?" He was an excellent host and took a morning off to drive us round the island. We drove to St. Pierre, which was destroyed in 1902 by the eruption of Mont Pelée. Nearly three thousand people were killed, only one being saved, a prisoner in the dungeon. In the museum were bent and broken watches, their hands pointing to eight o'clock, stacks of nails melted into a single block, photographs of the lava coming down the mountainside and of the ships in the harbour, all of which were burnt to the water's edge except one small steamer. The story is told how, with most of the crew ashore and the burning lava falling on deck, the mate succeeded in knocking out the pawl on the windlass before he was burned to death. The captain rang for full speed astern, tearing the shackle from the ring-bolt as the last of the cable went overboard. Badly burned, the captain sailed her to St. Lucia.

We left at one in the morning, sailing up the coast close-hauled to the steady off-shore breeze which left us becalmed under the lee of Mont Pelée. The sun rose behind the mountain, streaks of gold and pink shooting up into the sky behind the mass of cumulus that hung over the mountain top. Two broad streaks of brown descended from the crater and Anne shivered in the morning air. Then a north-easterly breeze filled our light-weather sails, bearing us quietly over the Dominica channel, which, for weather, has the worst reputation of them all. Ahead, mountains rose up out of the sea, mysterious and forbidding. There is nothing pretty about the south coast of Dominica, a fitting place for the Caribs to choose for their last stand against the invader. Sailing close to the south-west corner of the island, we stood away on the starboard tack as the wind drew into the north, then picked up the sea-breeze in the afternoon, which carried us past tumbling waterfalls and deep ravines, to leave us becalmed four miles off Barber's Block, a rock like a Chinaman's hat.

The sails hung motionless and we sat on deck watching the light fade from land and sea. Bob said, "It's funny coming back to

Dominica like this. At one time I thought I'd spend the rest of my life here." Anne looked up from peeling the potatoes. "D'you mean," she asked with interest, "that you wouldn't have gone back to England at all?"

"I don't think so; there didn't seem any reason for my doing so. I couldn't settle down at Oxford and I couldn't get the sort of job I wanted."

"But you're going back there now."

"I know, but I shall take the first berth I can get in a boat that's leaving for somewhere else."

Anne shook her head uncomprehendingly. Bob's mind was something she would never understand.

The night was as black as ink; no light on the water, no silhouette of land against the sky, no stars and not a breath of wind. The creak of a block, the snatch of the boom as the ship rolled in the slight swell, were the only signs that we were still afloat.

It must have been ten o'clock when the wind came, hard off the land so that we had to get the topsail and genoa down as soon as we could. How typical of sailing—hours of calm, then a tearing wind, sailing blind, looking for an opening in a coast we couldn't see, for a light that might or might not be lit! Through the night-glasses I saw the line of demarcation where the sea joined the land, when we were about a quarter of a mile away. We came about and beat up the coast. It was still so dark that we could not see the smallest indentation and we actually crossed Prince Rupert Bay, which we were looking for, without seeing it. It was the bluff at the farthest end, against a clearing sky, that showed us where we were. We worked our way in by short tacks; a riding light appeared, then another, and we found ourselves among a fleet of schooners anchored off the settlement of Portsmouth. Of a light on the jetty there was no sign. It was four o'clock in the morning.

When the Customs came aboard before breakfast, they told us that the light had been destroyed three times by hooligans and now no one had the spirit to put it up again, that a government launch had been wrecked because the crew had been unable to see the light; and the bell which now was tolling was for the three victims who had lost their lives. To our great regret, we had no time to explore this wild and rugged place. Nothing less than a fortnight would be the slightest use, so we filled the ship with fruit (grapefruit at a penny, limes a present from a friend of Bob's), and sailed away, hoping to return another day. The wind was free and *Moonraker* smoked along. From astern came a sloop, a rakish vessel with her great flowing mainsail and long boom, the water foaming at her pretty bow. As she romped past us, her crew lined the bulwarks, holding aloft a rope's end mocking our puny speed. Clumsy she may have been, but she was most satisfying to the eye.

We sighted the group of rocks which are the Saints against the background of gloomy Guadeloupe and entered by the south-west pass, sailing close to the needle-like Les Augustines, upon the nearest of which stood a leafless tree like a gibbet without a skeleton. We anchored off Bourg des Saintes, which might have been a Breton fishing-village, surrounded by islands and rocks and the white sails of fishing-boats upon the quiet water. The Customs officer at first refused to let us land without a clearance, but he had a "*froid dans l'estomac*," and when I sympathized with him medically we became good friends. Later I heard him talking to the master-shipwright upon the quay, grumbling about foreigners who wanted to land without papers. "*Pourquoi pas?*" replied the man. "*Le pays est libre.*"

The Trades were gradually losing their robustness as February drew to its close. The wind was light from the east as we left the Saints, the old ship gurgling through the water under mainsail, topsail and genoa, to cross the channel towards Guadeloupe; the decks were dry, Anne was sunbathing on the foredeck, Bob had a finger on the helm and I was nearly asleep on the starboard bunk.

Suddenly I heard Anne call, "Peter, I believe this is *Mollihawk* coming towards us." I scrambled up through the open forehatch to see a tower of sail bearing down upon us; we saw the pretty schooner-bow and the long squaresail yard on the foremast and then her signal letters mounted to the starboard crosstrees . . . M.N.S.R. it *was Mollihawk*.

We first met Commander Nicholson, her owner, at Terschelling in the Friesian islands in 1937. Nearly ten years later we were introduced as strangers at a club dinner where we talked for quite ten minutes before we realised that we had met before (that's what the years do to you). Then the following year on the Dart, when he was up the foremast on *Mollihawk*, I hailed him from the deck, but he took not the slightest notice, not even glancing down. I stood gaping at him as he was gently lowered in the bosun's chair. He climbed out, grinning at me and shaking my hand in his enormous fist. He said, "I'd just put my knife right through the mast, like cutting butter. I didn't dare call out, as even that might have snapped the thing!" And now we met in the

Caribbean.

Nicholson, looking rather more burly than when last we met, left the wheel and stood at the rail. "Good to see you, Pyes," he called, "can you wait at English Harbour till the second of March?"

"We shall be there till the tenth. Where are you bound?"

"To Barbados." Then, with a wave of his hand, "Give my love to the family when you see them."

Mollihawk, with her charter-party of Americans, stood away towards the Saints until we could no longer see her tall spars against the land.

Guadeloupe looked a dull, heavy sort of island, and we did not propose to call there, but our leisurely progress up the coast was enlivened by meeting another yacht, a slight, blue hull with a tall Bermudan sail and a tiny mizzen, a very modern-looking yawl. She took not the slightest notice of our waving until she saw that hallmark of respectability, the Blue Ensign; then she turned towards us. Both ships hove-to; and to our query, "What ship is that?" came the answer, "*Galway Blazer*, from England and Antigua. Is that *Moonraker*?"

Galway Blazer had sailed from England with a crew of two: Commander King, her owner, and Guy Cole, a cripple. His wife had joined him at Antigua, and now they were sailing down the islands with their baby, who was a few weeks old. We hoped to meet at Bermuda in June, but we never did.

While sailing between the islands, we kept hourly watches during the day and our usual three-hourly ones at night. I took the first, from ten o'clock till one, when we were off the northern end of Guadaloupe. We could sail our course to English Harbour with the wind a point free, and the old ship slipped through the water with scarcely a sound, a fitting end to the first half of our voyage.

The crew problem which Anne had foreseen flared up at intervals. On deck I could wish for no better crew, but when we were in harbour there were occasional clashes. The day we left Portsmouth I had come aboard after getting the ship's clearance to find Bob depressed and miserable.

"What's the matter?" I asked him.

He sighed. "I can't do anything right where Anne's concerned. It might be better for me to pack it up and for you to get someone else."

"Don't be an ass," I told him, and called Anne down from the deck where she was taking the tyers off the mainsail.

It was something about a picture which Anne wanted to hang in the fo'c'sle and Bob didn't. I would rather deal with a coral-reef than with two egos that don't fit. "Listen," I said desperately, "For the sake of a bloody picture, which neither of you cares tuppence about, you are prepared to wreck the whole voyage. For God's sake, kiss and be friends!"

"*Kiss?*" they both cried, aghast, and then, thank heavens, laughed.

Well, a lot of sailing lay ahead of us, and difficult navigation. The low, reefy islands of the Bahamas with their unpredictable currents, and the final test, the crossing of the Atlantic. If anything could cure differences of opinion, these would.

At dawn we were to windward of Antigua.

CHAPTER ELEVEN

THERE is some difficulty in finding English Harbour from the south-west; but coming from the south, the dark green, almost black outline of Fort Charlotte Point is the landmark to look for. It is exactly like the sketch at the top of the chart, and as you get nearer the giant columns sculpted by nature on the face of the point (the Pillars of Hercules) clinch the matter. The wind always comes off-shore, and we had Bob at the crosstrees on the look-out for the reefs that extend from each side, and Anne up forward, ready to back the jib if we were left without sufficient way to come about. We entered, and at one moment the ship was rolling in the long ocean swell; in the next, even the sound of the sea was a distant murmur and we were sailing up a winding channel as smooth as an inland lake. This was no offshore anchorage or harbour open to the west; the wind and the sea could do what they liked for a whole fortnight, and we could forget about them.

In front of us lay Nelson's old dockyard, the weathered brick and the grey roofs of the buildings looking strangely spick and span in the sunlight till we saw the ruins behind. *Debonair* and *Palmosa* were there and an American diesel yacht whose name I have forgotten, but whose claim to immortality rested on her deep-freeze, big enough to hold a year's meat. All had come to greet us; Pat and Maureen, Mrs. Nicholson, Robin, Carol and Captain Hudson looking every inch a naval officer. It is pleasant to take your ship alongside a quay with every stitch of canvas set, and pleasanter still if you have an audience. I brought her round in a wide sweep to come in head to wind, behind *Debonair*. Then we saw the bottom shoaling quickly to starboard. I called to Anne to let go the peak and main. Bob rushed forward with fenders, and Pat, Captain Hudson, and half a dozen native policemen seized the bowsprit. Thanks to their combined efforts no damage was done to the ship. But I'd forgotten the topsail. The main was half-way down the mast, the peak held up by the topsail sheet; as pretty a mess as you could see. In the eyes of the Captain (R.N.) I caught a look of pained surprise.

And, after all that, we had to go straight out again to clear at St. John's, twenty miles away, with a beat back tomorrow, which was Anne's birthday. Captain Hudson said, "You can take the short cut inside the reef on the way there, but"—and he looked at the hamstrung peak—"I think I should go outside it on the way back. It's rather narrow for beating."

The Cade reef, which looks on the chart rather like a crocodile's head, a sinister likeness in view of its fangs of coral, lies west of Old Head Bluff. The excitement of the pilotage, and the many bays and inlets we passed on the way, made the journey pleasant enough. St. John's is a new, raw-looking place like a town in a wild-west movie, and the harbour is shallow. With our six-foot draught, we lay half a mile from the jetty, yet if the wind had come from the sea we would have been aground. We collected our mail from the bank, Anne had a quick look round the shops, and we were away before dawn the next morning, for Anne was determined to get back for her party. We were on our mettle to beat through inside the reef, apart from the miles it saved. There is little swell and the water is crystal-clear. One of us stood up in the bows at the end of each tack to watch the coral, and we came through uneventfully.

A crowd had gathered to fend us off from the quay, but I remembered my topsail this time and took it off before coming alongside. Anne was in time for her party, and ten people squeezed themselves into *Moonraker*'s cabin for the occasion.

Against a background of ruined buildings, of careening-capstans for heaving down men-o'-war, of gun-barrels driven into the ground for bollards, and the austere solitude of the Admiral's house where Nelson lived when in command of H.M.S. *Boreas*, we settled down to a fortnight's work. Bob found a cracked manifold when he overhauled the engine, which we were able to have welded in St. John's; he devised a plan to prevent our losing the first few gallons of water whenever we put to sea, and he made and calibrated a water-gauge. Anne had all the sand-papering, varnishing, and the painting of the tins in which we kept biscuits, cakes, flour and sugar, while I painted the ship, reeved new gear, painted wire rigging with anti-corrosive paint, and all three of us cleaned and chipped the two thirty-fathom lengths of cable. We started at eight and worked till one, slept in the afternoon when it was too hot to do anything else, and were at it again till dark.

Every night at seven o'clock the dockyard gates were locked, although the police, who lived just inside, would always open them if we wanted to go out. It gave us a feeling of being shut off from the rest of the world except on Wednesdays, when floods of Americans drove up in cars to "do" the dockyard. Sometimes they would give us the remains of their sandwiches, as visitors do at the zoo; we were jolly glad of them, as fresh food was hard to come by at times. The Nicholsons went into St. John's once a week, and we took it in turns for one or other of us from *Debonair* or *Moonraker* to go in with them and bring back provisions for both ships. It was like living in a large family, and if you wanted anyone after working hours you had to hunt round till you found them in someone's cabin, or in the paymaster's house, where the Nicholsons lived. Except Anne. If Anne disappeared, I usually found her in the Admiral's house, where she would be writing letters or her diary, or be there just because she wanted to be quiet. The dockyard was her house and she could escape from *Moonraker*'s small cabin by just stepping on the quay. She was very happy at English Harbour. When *Mollihawk* came in, the family got bigger and there was another place to hunt for people, while in the middle of the lawn in front of the paymaster's house Amber of *Mollihawk* would be telling Cinderella of *Debonair* all about her hundred-and-eighth kitten.

As in all families, things didn't always go right. Maureen came home from a shopping expedition to find that Pat had covered their evening clothes, which she had laid out to air, with a fine coating of soot from the exhaust of his charging-plant; Vernon Nicholson returned to be told that his son Desmond had driven the car back from St. John's with a broken spring; and I ruined my crew's afternoon sleep by turning the cabin upside-down looking for a filter for my camera, only to find it was over the lens all the time. But these things only added to the gossip of our little world.

We listened to the results of the General Election, a fairly satisfactory one, I thought, as the Government's small majority would slow 'em down a bit, but Pat was wild. "I'm glad I'm going to New Zealand," he growled; "the lousy beggars have made the place unfit to live in."

"What nonsense you talk, Pat!" said Anne, who always got impatient with anyone who said things about England, even if they were only aimed at the Labour Party. "If you feel that way about it, why don't you stay and help get rid of them?"

"You'd do the same, if you had children, Anne," said Maureen, quick in Pat's defence. Anne shook her head, then laughed. "It's too hot to argue," she said. "If you two want to go to New Zealand, good luck to you, but if you think you'll get away from red tape, Pat, you'll have to find a south-sea atoll."

"He may find one all too easily," murmured Bob.

We made a determind war on cockroaches. The first had come

aboard at King's Bay, Tobago, on a leg of lamb. It raced for the shelter of the engine-room and reached it half an inch ahead of the hammer with which Christopher had tried to kill it. It looked a huge beast, nearly three inches long and full of babies. It was disconcerting to know that a female could have thirty thousand children in its normal sex-life.

By diligently clearing out the potato-box, and killing up to a couple of dozen at a time, we rarely saw them walking about the cabin, but when we spent an evening on *Debonair* we would see them running in and out of the lockers like ants in an antheap. Maureen sprayed them with insecticide, but she was too tender-hearted to see whether they were more than stunned, which they never were, so in the end she had to do something more drastic. One morning she came round looking pale and feeling rather sick. She had killed "thousands" in one locker alone! Poor Maureen was always having shocks. One day, when I was talking to Pat, she came up with two empty buckets in her hands. "You'll have to get the water this morning, Pat," she announced firmly.

"Why must I?"

"Because there's a policeman under the tap having a bath. With nothing on!"

Emmie Nicholson, who was standing by, smiled at Maureen's consternation. "That does happen sometimes," she said, "but I never think it matters so much if they're black, do you?"

Nothing mattered in English Harbour, not even the water. Having looked inside one of the local tanks, I rushed off and bought some chlorine. A quarter of a teaspoonful of this in our tanks (sixty gallons) would keep us safe, I hoped.

Harvey Conover's *Revonoc* came in, the first real American yacht we had seen. On board was Rod Stephens, Commodore of the Cruising Club of America, whom I had always wanted to meet. They took us for a sail one day. *Revonoc* was the last thing in ocean racers, and sailed into the eye of the wind in a way which was a revelation. She was beautifully kept and handled. When she was under way there wasn't a thing on deck to get in the way. For a moment I had an urge to take all *Moonraker*'s rope away and fit her up with wire, but only for a moment. They used nylon rope instead of chain for the main cable, and the yacht would go back and back as the rope stretched, without a suspicion of a snub.

While Anne was at the tiller, she was horrified to hear the command, "Keep her at six and three-quarter knots," until I showed her a speedometer thing—whatever they might call it.

Rod was magnificent; the care he took in navigating through the Cade reef was truly professional and a lesson to me, with what my friends call my "fine free style" of pilotage. For two or three days they were absorbed into our family of vagabonds and then they were gone.

The time fled all too quickly. *Debonair* and *Moonraker* shone in their new paint and varnish; even Captain Hudson approved of our handiwork. I was glad of that, because I'm not a good yachtsman. I don't put a white top on my cap on May the first, nor do I bother very much with flags. I am so proud of my club burgee that it goes up on the first day of the cruise and comes down on the last. One day Captain Hudson said to me, "You know, Pye, I've known men keep their ensigns up *all night*!"

"Shocking, sir," I agreed. Did we, or did we not, haul ours down last night?

Far worse than that were the grapefruit. Every day something like seven grapefruit and fourteen orange-skins were thrown overboard from the two ships. As the wind was always in the north-east, they collected astern of *Moonraker*. We looked at them sadly, but the disgusting pile got bigger. Then one day it disappeared. Emmie Nicholson said in an awed voice, "He *paid* a black boy to take them away!" We grovelled. After that, Anne trotted across the dockyard every night, her string bag full of fruit-skins. On the last night Pat and Maureen came to dinner and the Nicholsons came in afterwards. Emmie's soft Irish lilt was soothing to listen to, and she told us how, when they were living on *Mollihawk* at Galmpton, they got their milk from a farmer's wife who was something of a Tartar. One day Emmie was late in collecting the milk, a horrid offence. She began to apologize, but the farmer's wife silenced her with a wave of the hand. "I don't mind youse," she volunteered; "youse don't lead a normal life."

"And me," said Emmie indignantly, "with a husband and two children."

The next morning *Mollihawk* left at seven, *Debonair* at ten, and ourselves at eleven. Cinderella had fallen in love with Dicky Dockyard and had twice to be put back aboard. The children were strangely silent. They looked rather pathetic with their arms and legs done up in Elastoplast where they had cut themselves while fishing, and the four of us stood awkwardly for the first time since we met. Then it was time for them to go, and everyone came out to wave good-bye and wish them well.

I can still see, so plainly, *Debonair* belching clouds of smoke from her exhaust, making towards the Pillars of Hercules and this may be an opportunity to tell you what happened to the Fisks after they left English Harbour behind them. After sailing through the Panama Canal they missed the Galapagos, ran out of fuel and into fourteen days of calm and contrary current, sighted Hiva Oa in the Marquesas with two gallons of water left in their tanks and reached New Zealand after weathering a gale so severe that Maureen wrote to Anne saying that she now knew the meaning of "being snatched from the Jaws of Death" (her capitals). Pat's temperament which had prevented him from accepting a farm under his father's supervision must have also made it impossible for him to learn sheep-farming from his aunt, so when next we heard from them, before we left for the Pacific, Pat had gone into the local Income Tax office. I think he must have done well because he became a Tax Investigator (on the strength of his police service in India) and we gathered from the yearly letters that things were a little easier for them. Then, three years ago, almost to the day, we learnt from a cutting in a New Zealand paper that Pat had "disappeared." Gradually the story unfolded itself: Pat had left home on a week's tour of duty to visit a number of villages in a very mountainous part of the country and had not returned. Maureen at once sounded the alarm and police, trackers and, I believe a helicopter, combed this wild and difficult country. Only his car was found with one door flung open, half a cup of tea still left and a sandwich half-eaten, but of Pat himself there was no more trace than if he had been kidnapped by a Flying Saucer and taken to the moon.

Nevis, St. Kitts and St. Eustatius lie in a row, with Saba to the north of them. We had a perfect day and a fair wind for Nevis, but it was slightly marred by my finding the Primus empty at tea-time. I seized a can from the engine room to fill it while Anne, who was sitting on the bridge-deck, watched me with a lazy eye. Suddenly she yelled, "Look out, that's fish-oil." I knocked the filler out of the Primus and the oil trickled on to the cabin floor and down towards the bilge. Fish-oil, fourteen years old at least!

We did not go to Saba and we would not now return to the other three. Not that we shall forget St. Kitts; it blew great guns while we were looking for an anchorage, and someone, probably the skipper, left the calabash on the cabin-top and it slid into the sea, right side up. We went after it. One moment we'd be bolt upright, almost becalmed under our shortened canvas, and hove right down to the cabin-coaming by a squall in the next. With all our efforts in trying not to hit it yet to get near enough to pick the calabash up, more than a little time went by before we got it aboard. Anne grinned at me as she fished it up. "That's a lesson not to go overboard in this ship."

At St. Eustatius we were told that a schooner had rolled her main top-mast overboard off Orangetown. We were only surprised that her mainmast didn't follow it. How we rolled! A dory came out to us, the sort of boat they use on the Newfoundland Banks. We were just getting in when Anne asked them what they charged.

"Five dollars, lady."

"But that's a pound," we gasped; "that's impossible."

The negro looked contemptuously at our pram. "You'd be drowned in that," he said, spitting over the side.

"Possibly," I answered, "but we can stay aboard. I'm sorry you've had your journey for nothing."

"Take you for ten shillings."

"Nothing more than five, or we stay here." There was a pause, then, "Take you for five."

But we need not have paid them a cent. They had been sent out by the Acting Governor, the senior schoolmaster, to fetch us. We were shown over the neat little town and the fort with its cannon pointing out to sea; we signed the visitors' book in the library and drank fizzy burgundy at his house. He gave us our clearance and we took off as the light left the land.

Anne and Bob had been debating for days whether we should keep the reef pennants rove. Bob maintained that they were chafing the mainsail, as they were; Anne said that it was safer to leave them in case we should need to reef in a hurry. Now that the weather was fining up, I decided that the mainsail must have priority, but the discomfort of last night at St. Eustatius had made me forget all about it. We had a fresh breeze as we sailed to St. Martin's, close-hauled on the starboard tack. Just as we rounded the outlying rocks of Groote Bay, the clew-cringle of the mainsail parted, but, instead of the horrible noise of flogging canvas, nothing happened at all as the first reef-pennant took the strain. I looked thoughtfully at those rocks about a cable down to leeward.

Anguilla, a few miles to the north, we loved. It is a low island, the first we'd seen for a long time, and it has a funny little islet, little more than a sandbank, with eight palm trees on it. As we came up the coast we saw the trees apparently growing out of the sea. The village of Sandy Ground consists of a few wooden houses and huts, but the anchorage is nearly always full of fine sloops engaged in the salt-trade; they get the salt from a pond behind the village.

Major Crear was in charge of the administration. He was a real "Outpost of Empire" figure. His wife, small and very alert, worked with him to improve the island, which has no natural resources except salt, and no desire for any change at all.

I remember the long trumpet-like note of the conch-shell which the fishermen blew as they tacked towards the land in the early morning; and how Bob or I would drop what we were doing and row off in the pram, trying to get there by the time the boats were beached, as the catch would be sold in a matter of minutes. Then there were the Lakes, a family who had been out here for eighty years with their fleet of trading sloops and their flocks of sheep. We sat in the quaint Victorian parlour of their house, with its rocking-chairs, texts, and pictures of Highland cattle, and listened to a long account of their efforts to catch the thief who was stealing their sheep on Dog Island.

We were so hemmed in by vessels the evening we left that I wasn't sure we could get out, but I wasn't going to use my engine in this stronghold of sail. It was blowing hard. We put a couple of reefs in the mainsail, hove up the anchor, missed the bowsprit of *Fair Toil* by inches, slipped under the stern of the *Sunbeam R.*, tacked by the jetty where the Lakes had come to see us off, and made for the open sea. At least, that is what I wrote in my Daily Journal. But it was really more like this: "Back the jib, Bob. My God, she's not coming round! Yes, she is. . . . Anne, pull in the lee sheet. . . . Stand by to go about . . . Lee. . . . Oh. . . . Stand by to fend off that chap's stern. . . . Hell, that was a close shave. . . ." When we were clear we thanked our stars that we had emerged successfully and unscathed.

We streamed the log for the first time in three months as we passed Sandy Island and set the course, W. by N½N., for Round Rock passage in the Virgin Islands, eighty miles away. I had quite forgotten how peaceful sailing was once there was no land about. At dawn the high land of Virgin Gorda lay on the starboard bow and Fallen Jerusalem ahead, its pink boulders like the tumbled minarets of an eastern city. To port, Virgins of all shapes and sizes stretched away as far as the eye could see. We sailed between Round Rock and Ginger Island into water as sheltered as the Solent, crossed Sir Francis Drake's Channel, saw two people running out of a white house on the point above Brandy Wine Bay, waving as they recognized our burgee (Geoffrey Owen, who lives there, is a fellow member of the R.C.C.), and stood into Road

Harbour.

Half a dozen sloops were rolling their scuppers under in the swell, so we tucked ourselves in behind the mangrove trees in the mouth of the Careening Cove. There was hardly enough water for us according to the chart, but Anne swung the lead as if her life depended upon it and we found nearly three feet more than we expected.

Road Town is a single street winding along from the quay towards a valley. Apart from the post office and treasury, where we exchanged our currency, there seemed to be nothing at all except a store which sold bread and tinned goods, but Anne accepts this sort of place as a challenge. She found a dress-maker, bought half a pound of coffee in a blue-painted cottage, a pineapple from a woman on an upstairs balcony, and left our sea-water-kettle to be repaired at a carpenter's shop outside which they were building a boat on a plot of grass. On Saturday mornings, when the boat comes in from St. Thomas, Road Town springs into life. Fishing boats creak and groan against the jetty, their holds filled with blue and gold and silver fish; fruit and stores of all kinds line the quay, and white men exchange the gossip of the week. By noon the boats, the crowds, the white men and all the food have gone and the little place falls fast asleep once more.

For eleven days we were entertained by the Owens and sailed from island to island, dropping anchor at a different one each night; not once did we have the pram on deck. On the day before we left we visited Little Harbour, Peter Island. The bay is shaped like a horseshoe, the water smooth and blue, with here and there a catspaw of wind upon it. From the veranda of the low, stone house, high up on the point above us, a man in a wide straw hat, like that of a witch or a Texas rancher, looked down. This was Brudenell Bruce, about whom we had heard so much—that he was the brother of a marquess; that we should be shot at if we landed, if not by Brudenell Bruce himself, then by his children, who were as wild as leprechauns; that they were fabulously rich; that they were poor to the point of starvation. We went ashore and bathed where a blue fishing-boat lay tethered to a small jetty. A little girl ran down the path from the house and contemplated us in silence. At last she found her tongue, and said, "Father says will you come up to the house?" But Brudenell Bruce came down to greet us. His belly drooped and flesh hung in folds about his face. His voice filled the still air of the little bay with its high-pitched note.

In the evening we walked up to the house in the moonlight. The main block consisted of schoolroom, bedrooms and a graceful living-room with a great fireplace, built in home-sickness, not for use. There were pictures of Brudenell Bruces in armour, on horseback, and reclining on chairs in robes; there were Danish grilles with ships inset. The dining-room, with the kitchen leading out of it, was in a separate building, the oven in another, and the little stone keep over the water was the lavatory; no plumbing, nothing to go wrong. Indeed there was nothing to go wrong in this sanctuary except the home-made electricity—which *had* gone wrong. We sat talking on the veranda, drinking coffee and eating sandwiches that must have taken Mrs. Brudenell Bruce hours to prepare. She said, "I had a shock when you came in; you all looked so fair, I thought you must have come from my country, from Denmark."

Anne did her best to answer all the questions that were showered upon her, about Denmark, where we had been in 1948, about life in England, about clothes and what people were talking of. Diana, who looked older than her fifteen years, sat shy and silent, listening to a glimpse of the outside world. But there was nothing shy about the ten-year-old Arabella, once she got used to our being there. She was gay and irrepressible, loving this social occasion. Bob and I listened to a tale of changing fortune, of many things tried, not always a success. Recently the sheep had been doing better and the devaluation of the pound had helped to sell them at St. Thomas. Simon, the only son remaining at home, was twenty. Having failed to draw him into the conversation, I went and sat beside him. When I asked about the future, he replied: "I'm going to Australia to farm."

Before we left they gave us a case of books and a leg of lamb. We were very touched by their hospitality, but the thing I shall remember is the mother's face when she said good-bye. It was as if her last hope of escaping to the outside world was being torn away from her.

On 3rd April we sailed into Charlotte Amélie in St. Thomas and saw the Stars and Stripes flying over the Customs buildings. The place had become a legend to us. All through the islands they had said, "You can get it at St. Thomas." After the small towns of the British West Indies, Charlotte Amélie looked to us as New York might appear at first glance to a backwoodsman. Many of the working girls were dressed up as if they were going to a cocktail party, in long frocks, very high-heeled shoes, and nylons. One or two of the shops put one in mind of Bond Street. But apart from these and the self-help stores, with their wire perambulators and adding machines, the town was much the same as Bridgetown, Barbados.

As soon as we had finished with the formalities and had a quick look round, we sailed to Long Bay, a little to the east of the town. There was quite a fleet of yachts, and the one next to us, *Lang Syne*, we had seen before. We had crossed her bows on the way to Necker Island. Rigged as a modern staysail schooner, her double-ended hull with tremendous beam and sheer was the kind of thing you see in an engraving of ships of Nelson's time. It was not long before we met her owners, the Crows. Unaided, they had built their ship (she must have been all of twenty tons) in four years. Mrs. Crow had caulked the hull and had done much of the inside decoration. They had built her in Honolulu and went for their trial sail to the Marquesas, two thousand miles away. When they reached there, it had not been worth going back, so they had sailed round the world, and here they were, nearly home, at the end of a three-year voyage. They were simple folk, who did not look in any way remarkable; yet they must have had something most of us haven't got. We asked them how they liked the West Indies. "Fine," they said. Anne asked them which islands they had called at. "We didn't exactly call at any," said Mrs. Crow; "we sailed here from Trinidad, but we saw quite a few in daylight. I guess," she added, "that all islands look much the same after a three-year voyage!"

We met the Wagners in *Rubicon*, a sixty-eight ton ketch. It must have been quite like home for Anne to hear Mrs. Wagner's delightful Scottish accent. Wagner himself spent most of the time between the wars going round and round the world. I asked him what sort of trip he had had out from England this time. "Not good," he said, "not good at all. I had ten people on board, but not one of them knew a thing. I tried to teach them, but they wouldn't learn, so I gave up; after all, it is not far to Trinidad!"

During the afternoon the Norwegian ketch *Stavanger* came in, and we quickly made contact with her ship's company. The "Stavangers," as we called them, were terrific. At first glance Jul Neilsen, the skipper (he was a dentist in Oslo) was the least impressive but that was, I think, because everything about him was restrained, as if there was so much power behind him that he had to hold himself in. He had a quality about him—like Rod Stephens. Kaarl Hemson was a cameraman, working in the United States. His jet-black beard was as thick as a hearthrug, covering most of his face. The rest of it was tanned the colour of mahogany. And there was Lilliruth, his sister. She looked older than her years—as you might expect of anyone who for years was carrying hand-grenades about in suitcases in occupied Norway—but she was tremendously alive.

They had sailed from Oslo to New York: there they had worked, Jul as a dentist, Lilliruth as his assistant, till they could stand it no longer. It was dollars, dollars, dollars, till they hated the word, so they set off for Barbados in the middle of December, one of the worst months for crossing the Gulf Stream. They ran into a storm in which the winds reached hurricane force. For fifteen hours they ran before it under bare poles, trailing two sea anchors and four warps astern. Lilliruth, describing the experience, said, "I was a little frightened, but there was much to do. My poor brother was very sick, Jul must stay at the helm, and the ship was leaking, so I pump the water out very often and I became quite tired. But it was a north-east gale and it blew us away from New York. When it was over, I enjoy it very much." Her eyes danced with merriment at the recollection of hours of desperate work in a leaking ship.

Stavanger was worthy of her crew. She was an old Norwegian rescue ship and everything about her was on a grand scale. Her mizzen-gaff was thicker than our mast, and Bob and I fingered her flax sails with awe. Down below you could hold a dance in the saloon and we envied them being able to eat in the fo'c'sle where the galley was, so that the cabin did not always smell of food.

Five days passed like an afternoon in this pleasant place and in such good company.

CHAPTER TWELVE

IT was barely six o'clock when I came on deck on Saturday morning. The clouds were motionless and there wasn't a breath of wind. The island of St. Croix, nearly thirty miles away, stood out as if it was only ten, and the glass had fallen two-tenths since noon of yesterday. From now on we were within the range of "Northers," extensions of North Atlantic depressions which invade the Trade-wind belt; and the fickle breezes of the last twelve hours made me think one of these was not far away. They do not, however, last long, and at this time of the year they rarely reach gale-force. There was no reason, I decided, to postpone our departure for Inagua.

We nearly disgraced ourselves in that distinguished company of ships by getting away on the wrong tack. We missed colliding with *Lang Syne* by a hair's breadth, but the Crows, sheltering in the doghouse from the rain, never raised an eyebrow. As a start of a five-hundred-and-forty-mile passage, it was disappointing; we lay rolling outside the harbour in a calm and it was not till eight o'clock that evening that we streamed the log off the southern end of Savannah Island and sailed NW½W. through Virgin Passage to the open sea. The wind veered to NNE. and *Moonraker* longed to get into her stride, but every now and then she would go wallop into a head-sea that attacked her from the north-west, jarring her from stem to stern. As the wind rose, topsail and genoa came off, but the motion was as bad as it could be. I turned in to get a couple of hours' sleep before relieving Anne at one in the morning.

"Peter... Peter..."

I stumbled out of my warm bunk and staggered to the companion-way. "What's the matter?"

"Sorry, darling, but I'm sure we're being taken too far inshore."

I looked out over a confusion of tumbling sea, and ill-chosen words rose to my lips, the sort of irritation a skipper must never give way to, not even to his wife. Instead, I said, "Can you see any lights?"

"Yes, the one to port which must be San Juan, and I can still see Culebra."

"Right; I'll take a fix and we'll see where we are."

I took bearings with the hand bearing-compass, and as I did so I noticed a ragged bank of cloud low on the port bow; at least I *hoped* it was cloud, but was careful not to mention it till I was sure of my position. Then I said, "We're twelve miles north-east of Cap San Juan and our course is taking us right away from the land."

Anne's voice was no longer anxious as she said, "So that *was* cloud, after all. I'd been watching it, but it didn't seem to move." She added, "Thank you for not being cross."

I turned into my bunk, but could not fall asleep. I dislike myself when I become bad-tempered.

The wind rose steadily all day. Before noon the foresail had to come off; by tea-time there were two reefs in the mainsail and the wind was shifting between north-by-east and north-east in squalls which may have been moderate gale-force. At seven o'clock it was pouring with rain, with every possibility of a dirty night. I backed the foresail and went below. Bob said to Anne, "Now we know what to do when it rains—we heave-to and come below."

We set about preparing "tiller soup," the standard dinner on *Moonraker* in winds of force six and over. Two tins of meat soup, slices of cold ham and potatoes, either cooked in the pressure-cooker or used up from a previous meal. The whole panful is heated until the ham is hot and served in the largest bowls we have. After that, mugs of steaming coffee. As soon as I had finished eating, I let draw the foresheet as far as the mast, eased the mainsheet, and let her romp along at five knots, while we turned in below. I dreamt I was riding a camel across the Sahara desert and a huge bird like a vulture kept flapping its wings in my face. I woke; the wings of the bird were the foresail, flogging itself to bits. What a filthy night it was! I got soaked to the skin with spray and rain before the sheet was repaired and the sail set to weather again.

There are certain conditions of sea and wind and sky that will turn even a diehard cruising man with a gentle disposition like mine into a veritable tyrant of a bluenose skipper. This happened the next day. The wind blew hard from the ENE., the sea was big and regular, and the sun shone from an almost cloudless sky. Bob and I set the spinnaker and altered course to the west soon after noon. *Moonraker* leapt like a stag when she felt the weight of the wind in the curving sail, but Anne humoured her, countering each twist and turn with just the right amount of helm. The mast whipped alarmingly; the preventer-backstay was set up and the boom-guy rigged in case of a gybe. For four hours she was logging seven knots; never before or since has she sailed as she did that day. Just before tea-time we passed a tanker, a sizeable ship, at a distance of about three cables. The smoke from her funnel blew straight down to leeward and the swell was running high enough to hide her completely when we were down in the trough of the sea. *Moonraker* must have looked a fine sight, with her bow-wave up to the top of her stern. Then, with a noise like the crack of a whip, she rolled the last two feet of her boom under. I didn't know which would go first, the guy, the boom, or the bulwark where the guy led through the fairlead. But nothing broke adrift. Bob and Anne rushed forward to take off the guy, and we carried on. Anne sat behind me, wedged in a coil of rope. She said she couldn't bear being below, listening to the noise of water rushing past the coppered hull, the creaking and groaning of timbers, and the violence of the ship's motion. I marvelled at Anne; a year ago she would have been furious with me for driving the ship like this, but now she sat there, looking at the straining gear, her mouth a little drawn, but with the light of battle in her eye.

In the end the spinnaker had to come in; and to make the decision easier, the wind freshened again as night drew in. Anne took over the helm while Bob and I lowered the sail, ascertaining in advance that the strap around the spinnaker-boom was secure before we started the halliard. Our course took us over the Navidad Bank, where the soundings rise from five hundred fathoms to twelve. I was not quite sure what the effect would be, with the big sea then running, but I needn't have worried; the long swell became a confused popple for a minute, then we were on the bank and it was like sailing down the Wallet from Burnham to Harwich. An hour went by; the seas started to build up, our nerves tautened and the ship continued her wild rush. Towards dawn the wind eased and I was the only one who failed to record twenty miles logged in a watch, in spite of setting the spinnaker. By noon we had covered one hundred and fifty miles, the best run we had ever had; but it wasn't finished yet. Anne hung grimly on to the whole mainsail for the afternoon watch, but blotted her copybook by gybing at the end of it, carrying away the after-runner cleat on the bulwark stanchion. We took this as a sign that we were trusting our luck too far, so pulled down a reef. By the next morning it was all over. Only an occasional wave-crest gleamed whitely in the sunlight as *Moonraker* travelled swiftly over the long swell with all her finery aloft. "That was the best sail I ever remember," Bob said, "but it lasted quite long enough." For all our driving we failed to make land that night.

From the chart, Inagua looks like a seal balancing a ball

(Little Inagua) on its nose. It is as flat as a pancake except for three low hills, and is about forty-five miles from nose to tail. A single lighthouse guards the island at the south-western end, by the tail. Our first sight of the place, a timely warning of our approach to the Bahamas, was the wreck of a steamer, cast up on the reefs off the south-east corner. Low mounds of land, with small mirages between, like those you see in the Zuider Zee, appeared behind, while to the south'ard we saw *Stavanger* on a course that converged with our own. All day, before a light easterly wind, we sailed along the barren coast without a sign of a house or hut or human being till we rounded South West Point in the evening to drop anchor off Matthew Town, thirty seconds before *Stavanger*. A wharf with a crane on it, a large shed with a corrugated-iron roof, a jetty, a well-built house where the Commissioner lived, a few huts; that was all we could see of the "town" from the sea.

Before turning in that night we went aboard *Stavanger* to compare notes. They had left St. Thomas twelve hours after us, had had the same strong wind (Jul had logged it at force 7 at times) and were delighted to see us, a delight only slightly tempered by disappointment that we were not far astern of them. They had aboard another crew, a man who had tried to take passage with us back to England and of whom Lilliruth's only comment was "He is good at sleeping." She was, I thought, looking thinner and very tired and she confessed to Anne, while they were making coffee in the galley, that all the cooking and washing-up on top of the deck work and standing of watches, was beginning to get her down. Anne was horrified. She said, "Don't the others take their turn? On *Moonie* I only cook the dinner one night in three, at sea, and we have a rule that the cook never washes up."

"That is splendid," cried Lilliruth, "we shall start tonight."

In the morning Matthew Town took on a different character. Small high-powered lorries rushed from point to point, leaving a trail of dust in the air. Americans in shorts and singlets strode along, talking in crisp phrases, and even the blacks had a purposeful look about them. This was not the Inagua we had read about in Gilbert Kringel's book and Mr. Commissioner Burrows smiled when we told him how surprised we were. He had a broad, flat face and a voice most striking in its softness. He said, "Ah, that was before the Eriksons came. They have brought much good to the island." Inagua is still a British colony, but we felt that we were the foreigners.

After tea we sat on a plank in the after-end of a lorry and were driven over to the saltpans to see the pink flamingoes. The evening was very quiet and a thundery mass of cloud was reflected in the miles of smooth, shallow water in which the birds were walking. It was, indeed, a symphony in pink: pink flamingoes, pink water and pink-edged cloud in the light of the setting sun.

We met two of the Erikson brothers, their wives and the wife of a third who was away in Japan, on board *Stavanger* that evening. They were real pioneering folk, content to live hard and to take nothing out of the salt business till it was running like clockwork. They were hospitable and friendly as Americans know how to be so well. The three brothers were third-generation, hundred-per-cent Americans, built up on the natural toughness of the Danes, brought up in the Puritan atmosphere of New England, educated at home (with the help of a tutor) by a mother whose resemblance to Queen Mary was startling. No wonder they had a way with them. Success was paramount; nothing must stand in its way. Nothing has.

We were dining with the Bill Eriksons. As we were having coffee, I heard the wind sighing in the branches of the trees. I slipped outside and stood for a moment on the beach. A cool breeze blew straight on shore and I knew that the sooner we got back aboard the better. We said good-bye and raced to the pram. On the first journey to the ship I put Anne aboard fairly dry, but Bob and I had a tough pull. Lights appeared on *Stavanger* and I saw the four of them standing in the bows. We listened to the sound of the surf upon the beach. I shouted to Jul Neilsen, "I'm getting out for the night," and Jul called, "I've put out another anchor. I shall wait till dawn."

We got the anchor, broke out the jib and made an offing of about five miles, where we hove-to on the off-shore tack and slept till dawn. Then Bob and I started beating towards Hogsty Reef, fifty miles dead in the teeth of a fresh wind with lots of squally showers. This seemed a poor way to enjoy ourselves, so we gave it up just as Anne put her head out of the open hatch. "I thought we were going to Hogsty?" she said. At that moment we crossed tacks with *Stavanger*, who was plodding northwards towards our common destination. We talked together and I gathered that Lilliruth was angry with Jul for not following our example last night, and now Anne would be cross with me for not following *Stavanger*'s.

Molasses Reef, behind which we anchored, was not quite the

restful place I had hoped for. We dropped anchor in the only small patch of sand (surrounded by miles of coral heads) that I could find but later I became worried about this and sent Bob down to have a look. He reported that the chain was wrapped round three coral heads like a warp round a bollard and that the anchor was lying useless on its side. With Bob under the water and Anne in the bows directing me by signals I managed, with the engine, to extricate us. Relieved at this I looked round and saw that we were no longer alone. A large American ketch had come in quite close and her crew were standing at her rail gaping at us like men at monkeys in the zoo. "What the hell are you playing at?" shouted her captain, to which Bob, who had been more or less under the water for a couple of hours, replied with some asperity, "If you look where you've dropped your hook, you'll soon find out." They stood and stared at their luckless chain for a long, long time. The Captain said, "I guess we'll sort that out in the morning. If you care to take this warp you can lie to us for the night and save yourselves from getting into another mess," which helpful offer we were not slow to accept.

It was hardly light when we cast off their warp and started beating up the coast. I have often thought about that ketch and wondered whether she was still there.

The wind was from the NNE., a little better than yesterday, but there was plenty of it and we drove the ship in a most unkind way, hoping to get to Hogsty before night. The reef here is nearly circular, with the highest rock three feet above the water. Inside the lagoon (five miles wide) is an anchorage; the Eriksons did not recommend it, but the name attracted us. As it grew dusk we left the ship to herself and climbed aloft on the ratlines. We all thought we saw broken water about a mile on the starboard bow, but ships have been lost on evidence like that, so we came about, made an offing of several miles and again hove-to till dawn. Then we set off again. My morning sight, taken in the middle of breakfast and not worked out till later, put me to the west of Hogsty instead of to the east. As a current might easily have put us fifteen miles in this direction, I was not unduly worried. We could not make Hogsty, which now lay to windward, so we made for Castle Island. I became really worried when my dead-reckoning put me on top of a hill a hundred feet high, and there was no land in sight!

Was the compass bewitched, or the chronometer wrong? I pulled myself together as I remembered I had taken only a single position-line that morning because I had wanted my breakfast.

My noon sight I felt sure was right, so an hour later, when the sun's azimuth was right for a longitude sight, I took four more, which sat each upon the other. They showed my morning effort to be twenty-five miles out to the east! The lesson was cheap at the price.

It was daybreak before we rounded Castle Island. Under the lee of the land, on a sea as calm as a millpond and with a fine beam wind, we sped past cays and sand-bores, past Acklin, past the post office marked on Fortune Island and the place where *Tai-mo-Shan* stranded on Crooked Island in 1934. We entered Portland Harbour with a dying wind, to find it a great expanse of water protected by a reef we could hardly see. We couldn't land at Bird Rock Lighthouse because of the swell and we had to set the mainsail to steady the ship, so that we could dine in passable comfort off the cabin table. We lay becalmed all the following day.

Our feckless journey continued. We were swept past Rum Cay by a north-westerly current; we found Conception Island uninhabited. We were out of bread, fruit and potatoes, so that Anne insisted we must make Cat Island. As we altered course for Cat, the glass fell, gusts of wind came from the south-east and a huge grey cloud enveloped the sky. Down came the rain, such rain as we had never seen before, not even at Tobago. We shivered with the cold and drank hot soup instead of eating the usual bread and cheese, while the wind went round in circles. It steadied in the north and blew half a gale, while we tore along the coast of Cat with three reefs in the mainsail, Anne kneeling on the bridge-deck with the soaking charts in her hand. Suddenly she yelled. "There are reefs *outside us*, and ahead!" We gybed all standing. Thank heavens we'd put that third reef in!

At Hawksnest Point the coast bends to the north-east for ten miles before turning to the north for forty. The wind whipped the short seas into foaming white and our anchorage lay eleven miles dead to windward. I said, "We can't make it before dark."

"Another night hove-to?" asked Anne. She collected a bucket half-full of rainwater and took it below. "Bob, if you get tea, I'll do the washing."

In the meantime I backed the foresail to the mast and let her jog along, back the way we had come. I scanned the shore for a possible anchorage and thought I saw one. I called down, "Can you come up?"

"Can't you wait? I can't leave these drop-scones."

"O.K.," I said, "if you prefer being hove-to to anchoring."

Two heads appeared at the hatchway as if by magic. "Anchor?" they said. "Where?"

I showed them where, behind a reef on a sandy bottom. That night we listened to the wind and the driving rain and were lulled to sleep by the rolling ship. We should have grumbled in harbour, but as an alternative to dodging about Exuma Sound it was heaven.

The weather cleared next day and we had a pleasant sail to Bight. There was no jetty where one should have been, and a conspicuous white tower on a hill was not marked on the chart at all. We dropped anchor and Bob rowed ashore for information. It was Sunday. He came back with the news that it was Bight, and that a missionary named Hall, who had lived on the island for twenty years, had taken him to his house, given him three of their four potatoes, their only loaf, and two tins of pineapple canned on the island. Later, Anne and I accompanied Bob ashore to visit him. Mr. Hall met us at the water's edge. He had a great flowing beard like a prophet and a jolly laugh. He was immensely round amidships and embellished his conversation with proverbs and biblical quotations. He was the unofficial doctor to the community, a position he filled with enthusiasm and no little skill. We asked him what had become of the jetty marked on the chart. "That went in the 1941 hurricane," he told us. "I shall never forget that storm: I was out helping people whose houses were being washed away, when I was caught by a gust of wind which rolled me over like a barrel. I thought I was never going to stop rolling." He roared with laughter at this recollection. His wife, who beside her fat and cheerful husband looked frail and tired, took up the story: ". . . and when he came home he found me sitting on a packing-case with the water lapping over my feet!"

"But you weren't hurt?" asked Anne.

"No, no, lady," roared Mr. Hall. " 'When the whirlwind passeth, the wicked is no more, but the righteous is an everlasting foundation.' "

We walked along the hot, shadeless road in search of fruit. We passed a Roman Catholic church, an awkward home-made sort of building with stiff, unhappy murals in the porch; and then past the chapel belonging to the Plymough Brethren, which was where the Halls had worked so long. We went past houses which had been wrecked by the hurricane and others whose walls were unfinished for lack of money. Only a few were sound and lived-in. But we saw no fruit anywhere. I said to Anne, "This heat is the last word; let's go back. It's no good going any farther."

"No," said Anne, firmly, "you both grumbled because there was no fruit aboard. They can it here, so there must be some." So on we went, Anne marching ahead, while Bob and I trotted behind, commiserating with each other about the heat and the determination of women when they have once made up their minds. The success of the expedition is perpetuated in a photograph I have in my log-book showing Anne and Bob with a basket between them containing eighteen grapefruit, a hand of bananas and two pineapples. They are sitting on a bench outside a whitewashed shack with a slate roof, on which there is a notice, "Gilbert's Drug Store." Mr. Gilbert, standing stiffly to attention, is there, too, as well as the large fat woman who went to find Mr. Gilbert to open his store for us.

In the evening we walked towards the tower, which was not marked on the chart, along a narrow path and through scrub, till we came to a gateway and a shrine. From here we climbed steeply, past seven shrines (numbered in Roman numerals), representing the Stations of the Cross, until we came to the top, where the white tower stood like a lighthouse, but with only a bell to toll. A tiny chapel hardly bigger than a cell, and living quarters on the same small scale, stood near by. We wondered what brought Mr. Jerome, an Englishman and a retired Roman Catholic priest, to Cat Island, though he could hardly have found a place more suited to meditation and prayer. To the east the great Atlantic thundered on the shore below and the Trade wind blew like a cleansing spirit. To the west the placid waters of the Bight lay sparkling in the sunlight. . . . A skilled man, Mr. Jerome, he laid every brick and stone of this tiny monastery himself. There is an atmosphere about the place which made us reflect on many things . . . and on God.

Little more than twenty-four hours after we came in we were off again, sailing west for ten miles to clear an area on the chart marked "Numerous coral heads reported," then north-northwest towards Eleuthera and one of the more exciting adventures of our voyage.

Eleuthera is shaped like Cat and is a hundred miles long from end to end. As on Cat, the main settlements are in the bight, but in this case the western part is very shallow and filled with sandbores. In 1934 Geoffrey Owen found a way in round Powell Point, but the channel is reported to have changed since then. In December, as we were leaving Barbados, a man who had done survey work at the northern end of Eleuthera came aboard. He looked at the chart and said, "I'm afraid you'll have to find your way in as best you can. That chart is quite useless, the banks change every year. The tides run hard. Go in on the flood, but don't stick as you won't find anyone to help you. No one goes that way; they use the northern end." His information gave the place a background, but little else.

We arrived at Powell Point at four o'clock in the afternoon, with the light behind us but with the tide ebbing. We should have to wait four or five days before the combination of light and tide was right, and the light was the most important. We were all keyed up as I went up to the crosstrees to spy out the best course. Should we go south or north of the long sandbank over which the water was a vivid green? I made up my mind to give up the attempt if we found less than eight feet of water under our heel. Near to Powell Point we found the edge of a definite channel and decided to follow, wherever it led. I never looked at the chart once. We had some anxious moments, but after two hours of sailing we came out into the deeper waters of the bight and altered course for Hatchet Bay, twenty-five miles away. Moonlight danced on the wavelets; a single light showed up against the low hills of the long thin island. We waited for dawn to go through the eighty-foot-wide entrance to Hatchet Bay, which, with our boom squared off, looked more like forty. Inside lay a landlocked lagoon, the most sheltered anchorage since English Harbour. Bob missed our rather dramatic entrance and not even the chain rattling down woke him up. I was more tired than at any time during the whole voyage. We slept.

CHAPTER THIRTEEN

THE Hatchet Bay Company was something like the Erikson Company at Inagua but with a difference: here the pioneering stage was over. The whole concern moved with the precision of a machine after its teething troubles are forgotten. Each employee has his own little bungalow in its own little garden, a tropical garden city. At the store were pyramids of shining tins, a deep-freeze, cut bread and tenderized meat. As Bob said, they did everything but chew it for you, and he wouldn't put it past them to do that. Every day a seventy-foot M.L. left the bay with farm produce for Nassau, returning in the early morning of the following day. The company is run by Mr. Austin Levy, an American millionaire, and it is the pride and joy of his wife's heart. We were in a dilemma about the Levys; we had earlier been given an introduction to them, but we couldn't remember by whom. We had mislaid the letter. As the name meant nothing to Bob, it was most likely to be someone at Grenada or Barbados.

The Levys did not live at Hatchet Bay, although they had a house there. We had been told that Mrs. Levy was quite a person, so that when Anne and I set out to find her it was with more than usual interest. By mistake we went to the wrong house and by chance found her sitting on the veranda. I said, "Our name is Pye and we have an introduction to you; but we've lost the letter and can't remember who it was who gave it to us." Mrs. Levy smiled, a friendly, welcoming smile. She said, "Come and sit down. They told me there was an English yacht in the harbour; you must be from her." My heart warmed to her. She must be nice if she alluded to a ship as "she" instead of the awful "it."

Anne said, "We think it was someone in Barbados. Do you know anyone there?"

"Barbados? Let's see. Why, yes, of course, the Graves's."

"That's right," we cried, "the Graves's."

I then remembered what Mrs. Graves had said to us. How for years fresh food at Nassau was so expensive that the poorer people could not afford milk, eggs or vegetables, and how Mrs. Levy had persuaded her husband to start a farming scheme to provide food for them. Before we left, Mrs. Levy promised to drive us round the farm that afternoon and invited us to a barbecue which they were holding for the employees and their wives on the South Beach that evening. "I hope my husband will be there," she added; "he would be sorry to miss you."

We don't know much about farms, but this one certainly seemed up to date; the "mooternity ward" was a lot cleaner than some places I produced babies in when I was in practice. The young calves, two to a cubicle, had a cement trough for their measured milk and meal, and a bar on which to cut their teeth. There were massive bulls, thousands of hens like Rhode Islands, only sturdier, and millions of eggs which we watched being candled and sorted by machines that did everything but talk. We saw the pigs on Wallowing Hill, their dinner being cooked in barrels on an open fire. No doubt one of them was at that moment roasting on a grid for us to enjoy that evening. There wasn't a single thing that Mrs. Levy didn't know, from the family history of the newest of the staff to the workings of the latest type of incubator.

The barbecue was a joyless affair. Some of the men played sporadically with a ball, the children played by themselves, and the women sat languidly on the beach. No one made the slightest attempt to hide their boredom, but the "barbecue," pork roasted for six to seven hours on a grid over an open fire, was delicious, and the sauce, which had a piquant flavour and was spread over the meat with a large brush, was something I still dream about.

In the middle of the meal we saw Mr. Levy's plane circling overhead, and after what seemed only a few minutes he was sitting by my side. He looked pale compared with the rest of us. His face was thin and lined, as if the cares of wealth sat heavily on his shoulders, but his eyes were keen and very intelligent. He said, "What do your patients think about your being away all this time?" I told him briefly and rather diffidently what we had done, fearing that any American would think we were just plain crazy. When I had finished, he said rather sadly, "I envy you the peace of mind such a voyage must bring to you, although I should not want to do it myself." Then he added, "But there are other things I enjoy doing. I like quietly sitting at home or playing in a small orchestra—not that I get much chance to indulge them. It seems I'm at the beck and call of everyone except myself."

"Would you like to come and see our ship, sir?" I asked him.

He shook his head. "I'm due in Washington tomorrow afternoon and there is a lot to do before I leave. I'm sorry." He got up, and as we shook hands he said, "How wise you are to give yourself a break! Good-bye and good luck." We watched him hurry off to his car beside the burly figure of his manager.

The party broke up soon afterwards and we were driven back

to the quay. We found the crew of the *America* having coffee in their cockpit and joined them at their invitation. The *America* was a fifty-fifty ketch, about forty-five feet long, and gave Bob and me the willies every time we saw her. Her engine was, I hope, a powerful one, for her sails and gear were like toys. Her mainsheet was inch manilla, thinner than any purchase we had on *Moonraker*. However, we liked her owner, Ed., a cheerful, hearty guy who had sailed his ship from Chicago down the Mississippi to the Gulf of Mexico and thence to the Bahamas. So far they had been eighteen months from home.

With our ship looking smart in a new coat of paint, we left Hatchet Bay the next morning; but for unavoidable reasons we were two hours late. I was furious, because it meant that instead of going through Current Cut we should have to go round by the Fleeming Channel, twenty-five miles out of our way, and spend the night behind a rock if we could find one. Current Cut is a narrow channel between Northern Eleuthera and Current Island. The *Pilot Book* says of it, ". . . a narrow channel through which the tidal streams rush with the force of a rapid, but which is used by small craft with local knowledge at slack water." As we had missed slack water by two hours and had no local knowledge, anyway, we were hardly justified in attempting it. We shaped our course for the Fleeming Channel, but it was galling to see the Cut across the way, looking so simple at this distance.

Anne said, "Which way will the stream be running?"

"Against us," I answered; "we'd never get through against the tide."

"Couldn't we go and have a look at it?" she asked. "After all, we could always turn back."

The Cut looked tempting and we were not likely to come to any harm. I said, "Right, we'll try it," and put down the helm. As the ship increased her speed with the wind abeam, eating up the distance between us and the Cut, my confidence began to melt. The chart was on too small a scale to be of any use, and the word "rapid" had an ominous ring. Then Bob from his usual perch called down, "There's a shoal across our bows, no, two shoals, with what looks like a channel between."

I thought hard. Now was the time to turn back, before it was too late. On the other hand we ought, with this commanding breeze, to be able to control the ship. I called to Bob to con us through the channel and with Anne in the chains sounding all the way we roared through. Now we were face to face with the Cut, through which the water boiled and whirled. At first we made some progress close to the left bank, but the tide soon brought us to a halt. We sailed crabwise across the stream and the rate at which we were carried back was a grim warning of what would happen if we got into the tide-rip in the narrows.

We found a narrow lane of smooth water where we crawled forward, so close that we could have touched the bank with a boat-hook, but even here the current became too strong and as we began to slip backwards we called up our last reserve, the engine. Inch by inch we crept over the water. The narrowest part couldn't have been more than two hundred feet wide and our hearts sank when we saw a wedge-shaped strip of pale green water extending from the bank nearly to the centre of the rapid, where the race ripped itself into angry seas. Over that shoal we had to chance our luck, sailing as close to the rapid as we dared. The wind freshened, heeling the ship, reducing our draught and with the one-fathom mark on the lead-line just below the water, we slipped through, sailing over a sunlit estuary with the growling monster of a current behind us.

Anne started to go below. "How long d'you think it's taken us?"

I thought back quickly. "Forty minutes?"

"One hour and three-quarters," she said, with a laugh.

Pleased that we had made the Cut despite all the *Pilot Book* said about it, I was relaxed and off my guard. I had studied the entrance to Royal Island Harbour; it was narrow and there were two rocks, one big, the other small; both of them, I thought above the water. As we drew near, I saw two rocks. They looked closer to each other than they appeared on the chart, but I was not particularly concerned as we should be coming in close to the eastern side, away from both of them. As we sailed in, the wind came more off the land and I paid-off to keep way on her to bring her to an anchor. Anne and Bob took in the headsails. There was a sudden cry from Anne as she glanced over the side, then a grinding, jarring sound as *Moonraker* struck the reef, listing over to port, her stern nearly two feet above its normal level. For a moment time stood still. I saw *Moonraker* wrecked on this lonely island and our venture ended in ignominy, and all for lack of that extra care. I never knew till then how much I loved our ship.

It was easy to see what had happened: the two rocks I had seen were one, separated by a few feet of water at high tide. The second reef, which we were now on, had its ugly head just hidden below our starboard bilge. If we had come in at any time except high water, the mistake couldn't have been made. Bad luck, perhaps, but no excuse. We set the genoa, which heeled

Moonraker over a little further, but achieved no more. We were lowering the dinghy to take out an anchor, when a motor boat left a little jetty which I hadn't even noticed. She came alongside. The man in her said, "You'll fall right over when the tide goes down. We've got twenty minutes to get you off." He took our grass warp and the little boat tugged and strained without effect. And then, as if in answer to our prayer, a more powerful boat came round the corner. Bob said urgently, "Peter, We'll never get her off by towing ahead. Get this boat to take a line from the masthead and pull at right angles, so as to reduce our draught still more." I took his advice. Even if we tore off all our copper sheathing, it was better than losing the ship.

The two motor boats pulled for all they were worth, an extra puff of wind heeled us still further, there was a shudder, then three bumps, and *Moonraker* was off. The scene ended on a note of comedy. The old ship, with five tons of inside ballast, takes some stopping once she starts; and now she was waltzing round the harbour towing her rescuers stern-first, one from the masthead and one from the bows. We dropped anchor and hauled our friends alongside.

To every skipper the word "salvage" is a nightmare, and at the moment the word loomed large in my mind. I said, "We cannot tell you how grateful we are to you." The skipper of the second boat laughed. "You were lucky. We'd all but left when we saw you sailing in. Couldn't place you, with that hull and rig. Then we saw you run aground. Otherwise . . ." and he shrugged his shoulders expressively. "Where are you from?" he asked. We told him. "Looks a good sea-boat," he said appreciatively. "Well, we must be off, we're late already."

"But look here," I said, "surely . . ."

Towing *Moonraker* off the sunken rock. Royal Island

He shook his head. "No, no, skipper, thanks all the same. We're only too pleased to help. Never know when we may need it ourselves." With a smile and a wave, he started his engine and made for the harbour-mouth. The other man, who had his two little girls with him, came aboard for a drink. He was caretaker of the "big house" among the trees and lived on the island with his family. "The life suits me," he said, "but what the boss wants to keep such a place for, when he only comes for a week or two in the year, I don't know." When he had gone, Bob went over the side to inspect below the water-line. We can still hardly believe his report—which was later confirmed—that *Moonraker* had suffered no more damage than surface scratches to her copper sheathing.

In the evening Anne and I went for a walk on this long, thin island which looks, on the chart, like a crown. All Anne said about this afternoon was, "You poor darling, I felt so sorry for you, I could have cried," which shows that no husband ever knows what to expect from his wife.

The next morning we beat up the narrow channel to Spanish Wells, anchoring in midstream and rowing in behind Charles Island to find a narrow inlet packed with small craft like a backwater on the Thames. On one side was the village, on the other a belt of mangrove trees. When a hurricane threatens they run the boats in among the mangrove trees, where they're safer than the houses. I have never seen such a place for flowers and paint, flowers in window-boxes and gardens, brightly painted doors and windows, and beautifully painted boats. The villagers are descendants of the Eleutheran Adventurers who came out from England four hundred years ago. There is a law which forbids any black man or woman from spending the night in the village.

In the evening we returned to Royal Island in company with a small American yacht with a paid skipper. A young woman aboard called on us later and asked where we had come from. We told her.

"From England?" she replied, her eyes round with wonder. "You crossed the Atlantic in *that*?"

"Yes," we said modestly.

She looked at us with new respect until suddenly a bewildering thought struck her. "But, say," she demanded, "what did you do for *ice*?"

We left before sunrise and sailed out into the New Providence Channel. Long before we saw New Providence Island, Nassau water-tower stood up out of the sea like a signpost pointing the way. As we approached the harbour, Anne called me. "Peter, come up and look at this craft. I think she's broken down." About two miles on our starboard beam was a motor boat, and through the glasses I could see two men working a large sweep. We altered course, threw them a line and towed them into Nassau under sail, a thing I've always longed to do. But what pleased us most was that we were able to repay, to some small extent, the debt we had incurred two days before.

CHAPTER FOURTEEN

AND there, between Hog and Nassau, was *Stavanger* who had arrived two hours ahead of us. It was quite extraordinary how the two ships had missed each other at so many places. They had seen us sailing past them as they lay at Fortune Island, we had seen them off Portland; they had seen our lights as we drifted past Rum Cay in the dark. They went outside Cat and Eleuthera while we went inside; and last night they had anchored off Pimlico Island, no distance at all from Royal Island. Things were different aboard *Stavanger*. Lilliruth was radiant. "It is wonderful," she said, "Every day a new cook, and every dinner better than the last." Now they wanted us to sail with them to Bermuda and start the voyage back to England together.

It was a tempting proposition, but for a long time we had had our eyes on Florida. The idea had been mooted in a Berkshire cottage as the result of a chance remark by a friend. He had been looking idly at a chart spread out on the dining-room table. "See this place. Titusville, on the Indian river?" he said. We looked. The scale was very small, showing the Indian river as a thin line winding down inside the east coast of Florida parallel with the sea, with the town of Titusville marked small. "I have a cousin there who has an orange-grove. I'm sure he would be delighted to put you up if ever you get there. Not that there's much to see," he added, "only swamps and forest and alligators."

"You've been there?"

"Yes; but it was a long time ago, nearly twenty years. I enjoyed it."

That was how it began. We found from the *Pilot Book* that we could sail up the Intracoastal Canal which linked up with the Indian river, so all that remained were ways and means. The "means" had proved possible. The "ways"—whether we could get visas for the States—we should find out now that we were at Nassau. Above all, it seemed a pity to be within a couple of hundred miles of another continent without going there.

The next morning we went to collect our mail from the bank. It was a tall, imposing building with a black and white stone floor. There was a bunch of letters for us, the accumulation of nearly a month's post. I started in on mine and then looked up to say some trivial thing to Anne. She was staring out of the doorway, with a letter in her hand from our friends in Essex who were looking after Benny. She looked at me, her eyes blurred with tears. She said, "I ought never to have left him. He died thinking I deserted him." She picked up her letters, put them carefully in her basket and walked, very upright, out into the sunlight. My eyes followed her but I knew it would be better for her to be alone. Anne loved Benny in a way that did not blind her to the fact that he was not human, but she felt more responsible for him than she would have felt for anyone but her own child. When it seemed unlikely that we should have children of our own, some of the love that would have gone to them went, quite naturally, to him. I, too, was fond of Benny, but what I liked best about him was his devotion to Anne. It was the big thing we had in common.

I must have been standing there some time when Bob came in. He said, "I've just seen Anne. She wants us to go over to the Consulate. She'll be there in a few minutes."

"Did she tell you about Benny?"

"Yes, Peter, she did."

We must have spent nearly two days at the Consulate, where the Consul, an understanding person, waived a point of technical importance which would have prevented us from getting our visas. After having our fingerprints taken like criminals, we were free to go when we liked.

On the morning of the second day I heard a hail, "*Moonraker*, ahoy! Is Dr. Pye aboard?" I went on deck and there was Etheridge sailing past in *Grabe*, which was looking as pretty as a picture. We had last seen Etheridge in Brest in 1947, and as *Moonraker* now had a shorter mast and was pale-green instead of black, and as he had no idea we were out here, it was quick of him to recognize her. He dropped anchor and came aboard. Then we took him over to *Stavanger*, where they were delighted to see another ship so like their own so far from home.

That evening we foregathered on *Grabe*. Hers was a spacious cabin, with the table tucked away to one side, and pleasant with the warm colour of the cushions, and Kedge, the Irish terrier, curled up in his basket on the rug. There were eight of us: an artist, a dentist, a doctor, a sheep-farmer (Peter Mercer), two shipwives and a schoolmaster; all with a common interest, a love of boats and far voyaging. As happens on these occasions, the talk turned to other men and ships. Jul told a story of two Norwegians in the *Hoo Hoo*, a ship of twenty tons, about the size of *Grabe*; they sailed down to the "Roaring Forties" to look for traces of the *Kobenhavn*, a four-masted barque which had vanished without a trace, and with more than a hundred cadets aboard. Jul told his story in dry, laconic style. "They hit a very strong gale with tremendous seas, and one sea, bigger than the others, caught them on the beam and rolled them right over and up the other side. Everything was swept off the decks, the mizzen mast was broken and they sustained much damage. And so they reached Australia . . ." and the rest of us conjured up just what "and so they reached Australia" might mean down in those regions where gales blow month in, month out, and lines of marching seas tramp around the world.

Jul gave a little chuckle. He said, "They sailed back to Norway and the Mayor of their home-town was to hold a reception. But they were so excited at coming home and in such high spirits that they fought each other during the morning so that not even their own families recognized them, they were so battered."

Etheridge lit his pipe and looked at us over its smoking bowl. He said, "I had a curious experience, coming down from the Great Lakes this year. I was alone and the weather had been bad, so by the end of four days I was pretty tired, for I had had no sleep. The wind dropped that evening and I went below to cook myself a hot meal. When I came on deck, there was land ahead and the entrance to a small inlet with a black conical buoy on the starboard hand. I sailed past the buoy and entered the harbour, using the lead, as I hadn't any idea of where I was. When I got eight fathoms, I dropped anchor. There was a cottage close by, with a little jetty down by the water's edge and a man standing looking towards me. The lights went up in the cottage windows. I called to the man, asking him where I was, but he turned his back and walked into the cottage, shutting the door. In the meantime two men had come down to the jetty and boarded a launch. They started the engine and passed me close by on their way seawards. I called to them, asking what place it was, but they looked away without answering. I thought what curious people they were. Then I went below and turned in. In the morning the sun woke me, streaming in through the hatchway. I stretched myself pleasantly, thinking of the eggs and milk I should get for breakfast. I went up on deck. I looked around. There was no cottage, no harbour, no buoy and no land, but the ship was anchored in eight fathoms!"

As Etheridge ended his story you could have heard a pin drop on the cabin floor.

Mrs. Levy drove us round Nassau one afternoon, and the one thing we shall remember is the beauty of the gardens and the flowers and the dazzling white of the houses. Her own house is

coloured with a faint pink wash which is most restful to the eyes.
    On the last day we were there the "Stavangers" called to take us ashore. Bob said, "If you leave me the pram, I can finish scrubbing the bottom at high water and join you at the bank at twelve." He had been cleaning the copper sheathing by going down a rope slung round the ship and getting as much done as he could while his breath lasted. To this we agreed, and at twelve o'clock we were at the meeting-place. But no Bob. The minutes went by and still he did not come. Anne looked at the clock. She said, "It's not like Bob to be late. I hope nothing's happened. . . ." Another ten minutes passed before he turned up, looking as if he had seen a ghost.
    "What's happened?" we asked anxiously.
    "Nothing much," he answered a little breathlessly. "Caught my foot in the prop and couldn't get it out."
    "My God!" I said. I felt a little sick as I remembered that there had been not a soul to help him. I said, "How did you get it out?"
    "God knows; it's hard to think when you're drowning. I suppose I must have kicked the blade round with my other foot."
    "You'd better have a drink, Bob," said Anne.
    "Don't worry, I've already raided the brandy bottle."
    The key to our next passage was a thin, iron structure called the North-West Channel light-tower. This flimsy construction stood at the top end of a bight which the sea has driven like a wedge into the northern part of the Great Bahama Bank. To cross this was one of the reasons of our voyage. The bank extends for hundreds of square miles, the depths upon it varying from practically no water at all to over three fathoms. Rocks, sand-bores and coral heads lie within its boundaries, but there are routes which avoid them. The one we had chosen led from the North-West Channel light-tower to South Riding Rock, a distance of about sixty miles.
    On 6th May we left Nassau at half-past five, just as it was getting light. As our mainsail flapped in the breeze, the "Stavangers" came pouring out of the hatches and waved us good-bye. We gybed round their stern, a curtsy to an elder sister, and streamed the log off the entrance to the harbour. By ten o'clock we had entered the bight in the bank and were sailing towards the tower, watching the numerous cays and reefs as they hemmed us in more closely. On the chart was a profusion of black crosses, denoting rocks around the light-tower, but not a single rock or coral patch did we see that might have been a danger. We left the tower to port and sailed thirteen miles due west before

altering course for the light on Riding Rock. We hung over the side and watched the bed of the sea go by; long stretches of clear sand, flat slabs of coral, long streamers of dark-green weed like grass, and schools of fish as they scuttled away from our shadow.

We meant to anchor for the night, just for the sake of talking about it, but the wind piped up, so we carried on, only heaving to for three hours for some sleep near the eastern end of the bank. An hour before dawn I gave Bob a course that should have taken us clear of all dangers and settled down in my bunk again. I was almost asleep when I heard his hail, "Rocks ahead, Peter, quick." I was out of my bunk in a flash, colliding with Anne as she leapt from hers. Bob was hauling in the mainsheet for all he was worth and I tailed on behind him, while Anne pulled in the headsail sheets. The fresh wind on the full sail made the water swirl in the scuppers and *Moonraker* tore through the water close-hauled on the port tack. I went for'ard and stood in the lee rigging, watching the line of evil reef and the growing distance between us. It was a lonely place in the moonlight, the unwatched tower on the treeless cay and the swirling, eddying tide that had brought us so close to disaster. A bad place to be wrecked. It might have been a day, a week, or a month before another boat went by. I joined the others in the cockpit. I said, "There must be a terrific set to the nor'ard, but the chart shows the arrows pointing on and off the bank."

"The tide doesn't always look at the chart," said Anne.

We raced past cays and rocks with a fine beam wind until a white tower with a broad red band hove in sight and thoroughly upset our enjoyment. It shouldn't have had a broad red band. To have assumed that the band had been painted since the issue of the Light-List would have been to ask for trouble, so Anne looked all through the *Pilot Book* till she confronted me with a perfect replica of the tower, but on an island which I had hoped was a hundred miles away. It took me ten minutes to convince her that her tower was not the one we saw; even then I don't think she really believed me until the next land-mark came along, proving that this was the exception to the rule and that someone *had* added the broad red band.

Our wild rush came to an end when we dropped anchor off the western shore of South Bimini. The Bimini Islands are flat and desolate, with small, green trees bent by the eternal Trade wind, but the dazzling white of the sands and the pale-green water give you the feeling of having come to an oasis in the middle of a desert of ocean.

As the sun went down the air was filled with the roar of high-powered motor boats from Florida, their tunny-rods protruding like the antennae of cockroaches as they returned from the fishing grounds to Bimini Harbour. Invitations to "come on in" did not tempt us, and as soon as our meal was over we prepared the ship for sea.

At a quarter-past ten we were off, skirting the shoal to seaward of our anchorage before setting course for Lake Worth Inlet, seventy miles away. Between us and the coast of Florida lay the Gulf Stream, pouring out of the Florida Strait from the Gulf of Mexico and the Caribbean Sea. I allowed three knots for the current assuming the ship sailed five. I was very tired that night, yet I could not sleep. The last five days had been difficult for Anne and me. Benjamin stood between us. I comforted myself that it would not be long, but the first move had to come from Anne. I rolled out of my bunk and went up on deck. The moon was so bright that the stars were pale and infinitely far away. I said, "I'm wide-awake, and I'd just as soon take her. Go down and get some sleep."

She put out her hand. She said, "I'm so sorry, my dear...." We talked together for a long time and then I went below to fall asleep on the instant. Bless her heart, she took an hour of my watch that night.

When I came up before breakfast, there was the New World, five miles away on the port beam. I gazed expectantly upon this straight, tree-lined coast. Coming northwards through the Bahamas, we had met more and more Americans; their vitality and the way in which they search after new things had excited our imagination as to what their country was like.

The wind had gone down since I had last been on deck and no white crests ornamented the Gulf Stream seas. They tumbled playfully in little pyramids of blue water, their slopes patterned with dark squares like a Charles Pears painting of a quiet sea. I wondered, idly, what they would be like in a full gale.

Bob and I were washing up when Anne called out, "Come and look at this." Far away on the port bow, rising out of the sea with its lower edge distorted by a mirage, was a great square mass which reflected the sunlight from a hundred different points. It might have been anything, from a huge liner to a dream which had its origin in too much wine. I studied it through the glasses and even then I did not at first tumble to the fact that these were the skyscrapers of Palm Beach.

So fast did the Stream take us up to and past the city that we looked anxiously at the featureless coast. If we missed our mark we should never get back. We saw the Light and Whistle buoy first, then the narrow opening against the dark line of trees. We crawled crabwise through the channel, stemming the tidal set, to be faced with a profusion of buoys where the sea-channel met that of the Intracoastal Waterway. We missed the shoals and found a quay upon which was painted PORT OF PALM BEACH. We brought *Moonraker* alongside under engine and made fast to America.

CHAPTER FIFTEEN

IT was a day of bright sunshine and strong light, reflected from white buildings, from the shining bodies of a hundred cars parked upon the quayside, and from the little sparkling waves on the canal. The Customs, the immigration officer and the doctor came aboard. They were polite and efficient. I went to the Customs House and asked for a cruising licence.[1]

The young man across the counter stared at me. He said, "A what?"

"A Cruising Licence," I repeated.

As he continued to stare, I pushed across a letter I had had from Washington, telling me to get one at my port of entry. He read it carefully and then fetched a large book of forms from another part of the office. He said regretfully, "This'll save you a hell of a lot of trouble."

I grinned at him, "And money, too," and carried it triumphantly from the building, wondering whether he'd have given it me without the letter.

We had just finished lunch when a hail came from the quay. "*Moonraker*, ahoy!" I went up on deck. On the wall above me was a biggish man with a square, bronzed face, looking at the ship. He went down on his haunches and extended a huge hand. "I'm Bill Elmslie," he announced. "I met Henry Denham of your club in Villefranche this year. D'you know him?"

"Indeed I do," I replied. "Come aboard."

Bill Elmslie had lived in the States for forty years, only coming back to England to help fight in her two wars. He had an American accent and spoke in the style of an American. He said, "When you folks are ready, we'll move your little ship round the corner where she'll be out of the way. Then I'll drive you round Palm Beach, you'll dine with me at the Taboo, and spend the night at my house. I'm sorry my wife's away, but that can't be helped."

I said tentatively, "We were thinking of making an early start tomorrow."

He shook his head firmly. "Tide's wrong till after nine. I'll

---

[1] A document given to bona-fide yachtsmen of foreign countries which saves them harbour dues and pilotage fees and makes it unnecessary to put down a sum of money in bond to ensure that they take their yacht out of the country. It is available for six months and can then be renewed.

return you aboard in good order after breakfast."

He drove us off in his Buick. We came to the outskirts of West Palm Beach and drove down a tree-lined avenue of single-storey houses (it gives a wrong impression to call them bungalows), with not a single hedge or a wall between them. I said, "It's funny seeing nothing to separate one house from another. You wouldn't get much privacy in your garden."

Elmslie looked at me quizzically. "Americans don't like privacy; it worries them."

We came to the centre of the little town with its wide streets, electric signs, and car-parks crammed with cars; more cars, in fact, than people, in appearance the same kind of people you would see on any day in a seaside town in England in the summer. Then there were the drug stores, where you can buy penicillin or a hot dog or an ice-cream-sundae or a fountain pen, and can go on buying them till eleven o'clock at night if you wish.

We bought a few things: shoes for Anne, a shirt for me, trousers for Bob. "Finished?" asked Elmslie, as we returned to the car. "Now you've seen West Palm Beach," he went on, "you've seen every town in Florida. Some are bigger and some are smaller, but they're all the same. That's why people here like going to England, where each town has its own character." He slowed the car as we crossed the Intracoastal Waterway. He went on, "You have to be well off to live this side of the water. Not that that means me," he laughed; "we rent a small house in a back street." Then he took us round showing us the houses belonging to people whose names are known by the cars they make or the soap they sell or whose faces are seen on the films. But the season was over in Florida. The great had departed and it was like a gilded set on an empty stage.

He drove us down a long, quiet road and stopped the car in front of a tall house built in the Renaissance style. This was the "small house in the back street." It stood in a courtyard of trees and we walked through a wrought-iron gate into an austere and graceful hall and up a winding staircase to our rooms which overlooked the canal. The walls were a dusty pink with blue-grey furniture; over the enormous bed was a spread the colour of gold. We bathed in a blue bath in a pale-blue bathroom. We joined our host in the hall, and sat back in deep, comfortable chairs with drinks at our sides.

Elmslie owned a schooner and the pilotage of the Bahamas fascinated him. He said, "Pye, did you ever read that book by a young American couple who sailed those waters? Say, what was it called?"

"I know the one you mean," I said. "I remember it because there was an episode in it which has always stuck in my mind."

"What was that?"

"You remember the day before they set out from Miami? The wife comes up on deck and tells her husband the Japs have bombed Pearl Harbour and America is in the war. The husband is doing something up the mast. He stops, and stares out over the sea for a long time without saying a word. You think he's saying to himself, 'Blast this war! That's dished our cruise.' But not a bit of it; he's wondering how to get out of the country before the authorities stop him, and the next morning off they go."

Elmslie said quietly, "I never even noticed that." He went over to the table and poured himself out a drink. "I agree," he said, "no Englishman would write that, even if he felt it. But I don't think it's unusual in an American. You see, they're brought up to do what they want to do, to make a success as individuals. They've never had to leave their farms and jobs to defend their homes as you've done in Europe for the past thousand years, and they resent any interference with their plans. They'll fight all right, as they've shown in two wars, but not by instinct. They take time to adjust themselves to that sort of discipline."

What a difference it makes, having three thousand miles between you and the enemy, instead of thirty!

"Are you not an American yourself now?" Anne asked.

"No, I'm still British," Elmslie smiled. "It never seemed to me that you could change your nationality by signing a piece of paper. But my roots are here. It's a fine country."

We dined at the Taboo. The *filet mignon* was a dream; the chef brought our steaks round for inspection and then scorched them carefully over a fire, the heat from which could be felt at our table. M. Boulestin himself could have done no better. Later we stood on the Florida beach and watched the moon rise over a quiet sea. Then, tired with excitement from all we had seen, we tumbled into bed and slept dreamlessly.

The Intracoastal Waterway runs for two thousand miles up the east coast of America, its course following, where possible, the natural direction of rivers and lakes. In places it is as narrow as the upper reaches of the Thames and in others you can hardly see one bank from the other. In the spring, high-powered motor boats roar along its entire length from Miami to New York, and in the autumn they all roar back again. From Lake Worth to Jacksonville the narrow, well-buoyed channel is dredged to eight feet. Etheridge had told us in Nassau, "Don't sail at night, don't try to beat, and don't get into a line between buoys on the same side of the channel. If you do, you'll go aground." We thought it might take us a long time to do the one hundred and twenty miles to Titusville, being dragged off first one bank and then the other. On the chart we owned the channel between *pecked* lines was no thicker than the lead of a good thick pencil.

Bob put the chart in the folder we kept on deck and said, "Let's make Anne steer all the way to Titusville. By the time she gets there, she'll never take her eyes off where she's going for the rest of her life."

Anne said, "That's O.K. by me; I should like to spend a year in the States."

We set off very carefully under power with not a rag of canvas set, and ran aground not half a mile from where we started, but we were going so slowly we soon got off again. As we progressed we gained courage. We set the mainsail, and sailed through our first bridge (canal traffic takes precedence over road traffic). Then, greatly daring, we set topsail and genoa and raced across Lake Worth, passing a dozen little islets on the way. There is something very satisfying about sailing a ship along a narrow inland waterway. *Moonraker* seemed enormous when we got to the stage of hauling in the mainsheet to prevent it getting entangled in the mangrove trees! That first day we were seldom away from the sound of the sea as it thundered upon the beach, but it couldn't get at us as we meandered safely through the countryside. Every now and then we would look back and see a small speck in the distance, with a fleck of white in front. The speck would grow into a powerful motor craft, but as they passed us they all slowed down so that their wash should not disturb us. One particularly flashy vessel was very intrigued. Her skipper pointed to us and shouted to his mate below decks, "Take a look at this, Homer. Like something out of Mark Twain." Indeed, we became quite famous. As we sailed slowly through an open bridge, people would get out of their cars and line the road. A man turned to his wife and said, "That's the English sailboat; I heard about her two days ago." They never seemed to mind our keeping them waiting. When the canal became the Indian river, it broadened out and at times you could scarcely see one bank from the other. The way ahead was lost in the distance except occasionally where a bridge lay suspended in the air by a mirage, while cars, like insects on a thread, moved slowly across, dignified in their remoteness. Then a line of trees might seem to block our way, to become, as we approached, small islands with quiet backwaters, tiny creeks, and elegant houses with gardens coming down to the water's edge. The towns were few and far apart; they were small and neat, each being the counterpart of the next, as Elmslie had said they would be.

On the third day out from Lake Worth Inlet we came to Titusville and tied up in the little dock above the bridge. It was too late to telephone our friends, so we turned in early. What a night it was! Mosquitoes in scores zoomed to the attack, and for every one we slew a dozen more flew in, attracted by the light. We longed for the daylight. When it came, we were a sorry sight, with swollen arms and faces. On my way to get the milk, I met the manager of the shipyard to which the dock belonged. "Mosquitoes?" he said with surprise. "There shouldn't be many about yet." I showed him my arms and face. "Oh, that's nothing. In another month there wouldn't be anywhere between bites!"

We hadn't finished breakfast when Irving Holder, "Dook" to Titusville and cousin of our friends in Berkshire, came aboard, and took the ship by storm. He was small and very thin and his brown eyes were never still. He talked at great speed, and, like anything else which gathers momentum as it travels, he was hard to stop. He said, without drawing breath, "Why didn't you phone me last night we had a room booked for you at the Dixie as soon as you arrived. I'm afraid I can't put you up, as my wife isn't very well, but I've fixed up for a car to bring you down to your ship each morning. When you're ready I'll take you up to the hotel and then out to Mims for lunch."

I took a deep breath, but Dook started again before I could open my mouth, "Will you give us a talk at the Kiwanis' Club next Tuesday?"

"Of course I will," I replied, "but I really don't think we ought to stay at an hotel..."

Dook interrupted me, "Now look here, Doc, this is all tied up and nothing you or I can do will stop it. You sit back and relax." That, from Dook, was good!

Anne said, "It's really lovely of you, but surely we can walk down from the hotel."

Dook was most distressed. "I can't let you do that," he cried. "Why, it's nearly half a mile away, and besides, it isn't hospitable."

I grinned at him and said, "It's my job to keep the crew fit. If they get too fat they'll be no good at sea; they *must* have that morning walk."

Dook whirled us out to his ranch, which lay two miles beyond the village of Mims. It was a backwards sort of place, a wooden bungalow that he had built twenty years ago and to which he had added a kitchen, another bedroom and a veranda. He introduced us to his wife and to his daughter Anne, aged twelve. She had the eager face of a child, but she was dressed in the teen-age fashion with reddened lips, stylish clothes and the latest hair-do. For ten minutes she kept up a stilted, adult conversation, then she threw it to the winds and rushed about showing her dolls to Anne.

They showed us the orange groves, but the sturdy trees were almost bare of fruit, as the season was over. Dook told us that a frost had killed the trees some years ago and for a long time they had no fruit. But now, with better forecasting, they could light fires among the trees to save them. They took us over an orange-packing station where we saw a negro nailing boxes together with sixteen nails in under half a minute. His whole body danced with a savage rhythm, vibrating with the blows upon the nails. The muscles of his arms and neck rippled in a beam of sunlight and the sweat ran off his body on to the wooden floor as box after box came off the line.

Each morning we walked across the street from our mosquito-proofed hotel to a restaurant for breakfast, then down the long, white road, where no one ever walked but ourselves, to the dock. One afternoon we were driven along the smooth, straight road that ran between the marshes and prairie-lands of the St. John's river to Orlando in the interior. The city was laid out on a broad and generous plan and the lakes around which it was built made it almost beautiful. We visited a branch of the Sears-Roebuck Stores. As we approached, the doors swung open silently, a touch of magic provided by a photo-electric cell. It was like a Woolworth's on a grand scale, where you could buy anything from a motor mower to an evening-gown. President Roosevelt, when asked how Communism could be destroyed, said, "Send Russia a million copies of the Sears-Roebuck catalogue."

We saw, by request, a street of single-storied frame-houses where the lower-income groups lived. Each house had four or five rooms and all were fitted with refrigerators, self-operating electric stoves, and washing-machines. Anne said, "Surely, Dook, a labourer couldn't afford a house like this?"

"He could! by the time he wanted to get married, he could pay a deposit and the rest would be on 'time.' "

We were introduced to the judge, the district attorney, lawyers, doctors and business men. As we met more and more people we gradually became used to the form of their speaking. It was short and direct; they never wasted time in introducing a subject or rounding it off, and if you couldn't grip their attention they turned away. Knowing this, my knees felt extremely weak as we walked along to the Kiwanis' Club on Tuesday morning. At the last moment Dook hurried up to me. "Look, Peter, will you say something to them about State Medicine?"

I said, "I gave up my practice before State Medicine started."

Dook laughed. "Forget it. As long as you say how dreadful it is, they'll love it!" Although this was an all-male gathering, they invited Anne and asked a woman doctor to keep her company, but Anne was nearly as dithery as I was, and we neither of us ate more than a morsel of food. However, it went off a great deal better than I had dared to hope. After it was over my first questioner asked me if it was true that England was a Communist state, and the second, did I think war was likely to break out this year. My answer to the first seemed to lay their worst fears at rest and to the second I replied, "The sea protects you Americans but it seems to act like a sounding box; I've heard more about war in the last fortnight than I have in four years in England."

Nearly all the Kiwanis' Club came down to see our ship that afternoon, but what surprised us most of all was the interest the man in the street showed in her. They were most apologetic if we broke off work to talk to them and they would never come aboard. It was just a friendly curiosity and we did nothing to discourage it. There were few ways in which we could express our appreciation of the kindness we were shown, and this was one of them.

Anne and I took five days off to visit some friends in North Carolina. This is the real South, not like Florida where everyone we met seemed to come from the North in search of a more tranquil life.

On our return we found that Bob had repainted the decks and the inside of the fo'c'sle. On how he had spent the rest of the time he was more reticent, but we gathered that the young women of Titusville had not entirely neglected him. I think he would have liked to stay in Florida. He fitted in with the temperament of the place, and Anne and I were touched that he never came and asked us to get a substitute.

Our next concern was where to leave the Intracoastal Waterway for the open sea. The nearest inlet was at Ponce de Leon with not more than nine feet on the bar. Dook took us over there by car. It was a bare, windswept place and the tall lighthouse looked too slender for its grim surroundings. The entrance lay between sand-dunes. The ebb was running hard and angry seas broke upon the hidden banks of sand. A narrow line of port and starboard buoys tossed restlessly in the channel and the swell broke on the bar. We walked across to the coastguard station and went to see the captain. I explained that we wanted to leave for Bermuda as soon as we could, but that if there was any unreasonable risk I would rather go to Jacksonville, seventy miles to the north. I asked him whether he could give me a tow. He said, "O.K., berth by the quay here the night before and we'll take you out in the early morning, when it's quiet."

The tides would be right in two days' time, so we arranged to be there on Saturday evening. As we walked back to the car and heard the roar of the sea, Anne shivered in the evening breeze.

On Friday evening Dook came down with four dozen eggs, two hundred oranges, a hundred grapefruit and a couple of baby alligators, these last a present for our friends in Essex. When they looked at you, they hissed, so Bob and I voted Anne to be their keeper. They were known as Port and Starboard, and Dook had lined a box with tin so that they could lie in water. We were sorry to say good-bye to Dook. He had spoilt us dreadfully and we had qualms, occasionally, in case we showed it.

That night I went to see the manager of the yard to pay him our berthing-fee, a cent a foot waterline per day. He said, "There's no charge to you, Doctor. We're glad to have had you here and sorry you have to go." That was the sort of hospitality we got from Titusville in Florida.

At a quarter to seven the next morning we cast off our mooring lines. Bob swung the starting-handle, the engine coughed into life, the little group on the dock waved and we chugged out between the tall beacons marking the channel to the fairway. There was not a ripple on the water. At breakfast-time a light air came over the marshes from the east, we set all sail and Titusville disappeared astern.

That afternoon we ran so hard aground I thought we should be there for ever. It was most humiliating, as I was at the helm and could blame no one except myself. A power-boat pulled us off, but a few minutes later we met a tug coming to our assistance, telephoned for by a friendly watcher from a house on shore. The evening light was beginning to fade as we rounded the last corner of our inland journey and there were the lighthouse and the broken waters of the inlet. Our spirits soared as the evening breeze bore the sound of the ocean upon its salty breath.

We made fast to the quay and the captain of the coastguards

came striding down the path. He was a tall, handsome chap, loose-limbed and strong, his face crinkling in a circular movement as he chewed gum. He went for'ard and eyed the winch. "Well bolted down?" he asked. I nodded. "Good," he said. "We'll be towing you through two lines of breakers in the morning." He grinned like a schoolboy at the look on our faces. He said, "You'll be O.K." He came below, examined our papers, had a drink and left us. "Sleep well," he called to us over his shoulder.

After dinner we screwed the table down athwartships and prepared the bunks for sea; then Bob went ashore with his pyjamas under his arm. His bunk was full of fruit and he'd been offered a bed at the coastguard station; I went with him to look at the sea. The light and whistle buoy winked away in the darkness and the ocean slept. Only on the shoals was there a snarling. I walked back slowly, thinking of the bar and of the four thousand miles between here and England, to find Anne in her bunk nearly asleep and the drone of many mosquitoes in the air. I "flitted" round the skylights and the hatches with D.D.T. in oil without apparent effect, but the insect repellant lotion on our hands and faces kept us free from their attentions.

It was still dark when I turned out in the morning. I tidied my bunk, put the kettle on, woke Anne, and then walked across the sand-dunes. There was not a breath of wind, and in the grey light the sea was the colour of steel. I could not see the swell breaking upon the bar. On the way back I met Bob. "Had a good night?" I asked him.

"Awful. They kept me awake telling me about all the wrecks they'd had in the last few weeks."

The coastguards came for us in a powerful twin-engined, flat-bottomed craft, and they made the three-and-a-half-inch manilla warp fast upon the winch themselves. "O.K.?" they asked. We hauled our warps aboard and off we went with an hour of flood still to go. They towed us slowly, but the ship wanted careful watching in the tide rips and eddies of the entrance. Out between the sand-dunes we went, and I noticed that a brisk breeze had sprung up, blowing right on shore. Anne and Bob hoisted the mainsail and set up the jib in stops, but it was only a gesture and to stop the rolling; our safety depended entirely upon our tow. Anne was on the fo'c'sle head with Bob. She turned to me and said with some astonishment, "Surely they're not taking us through that?" I looked and saw first one, and then another line of breakers. "I shouldn't think so," I said encouragingly. But, indeed, there was nowhere else for us to go.

As we came to the breakers, our tow slowed down until we had steerage way and no more. *Moonraker* rose almost to the top of the first one, but even then it jarred her. I shouted to Anne, "Shut the skylights, quick." Then the second line was on us. The launch went up on end, the ship started to climb and Bob jumped for the rigging. The crest of the wave curled over the bow and swept the ship from end to end. Standing in the cockpit, I was up to my waist in water, and the decks were full to the level of the rail. The drum of the winch was twisted and useless, but we were so glad to have the ship afloat that it seemed a small price to pay . . . until we had to pay it at Bermuda.

Never again shall I go out through Ponce de Leon Inlet.

CHAPTER SIXTEEN

THE sea was very quiet that afternoon as I took over from Anne after lunch. The log rotated in little bursts of movement and then was still. The boom jerked from time to time as the ship rolled and shook the light air from the sail. Below all was quiet. Bob was fast asleep and I could see the book that Anne had been reading lying open and neglected in the corner of the bunk; and, if I knew anything about it, she would be asleep as well. Presently a dark-blue line crept across the even swell. The ship heeled and her noises, the creaking of blocks, the slat of sails, were stilled. I trimmed the genoa sheet and eased the mainsheet a trifle. I watched her sailing on her course for a minute or two and then lay down on the bridge-deck. I must have dozed off a little, for when I next looked up she was smoking through the water, the leech of the genoa shaking as she nosed into the wind. The sun had gone behind a dark cloud and caps of white sat upon the little waves. A basinful of spray came over the weather-bow and a few drops trickled along the bottom of the cabin-coaming and down across the bridge-deck. I hauled in the mainsheet, and as I did so a pain around my middle started gnawing in the silly nagging way it had been doing for the last few days. My pain and I had been such close companions for the last fifteen years that we took little notice of each other as a rule, but after ten months' freedom from it I was now inclined to make more fuss than before. It was my own fault; rich food, and a drink which Dook had said was used by the G.I.s to clean their buttons, had brought the trouble back again. I didn't think Anne had spotted it yet, but if it got any worse it wouldn't be long before she did.

I looked astern to where America lay just below the horizon, and I hoped that the simpler life aboard and freedom from worry, now that the land was behind us, would give me a chance to recover. The clouds passed, the sun came out and the breeze died to a gentle air. I went below, opened the galley-doors and put on the kettle.

Waking Bob was an art that had to be learnt; the trick was to tickle his nose until he opened his eyes. He never smiled, as Christopher did, but got straight up, swinging his legs to the ground. I went on deck till he joined me. It amused me to see how Bob and Anne used to come up time after time, going through the same small actions peculiar to each. Bob always looked at the compass and asked me the course. He then settled himself comfortably in the well and looked to windward. Anne's first glance would be at the hounds. Having seen that there were no ropes foul of blocks and that the gaff-jaws were swinging as they should, she would look all round the horizon. Finally she would ask the course and sometimes look at the compass. As to the skipper, the crew swore that he had eyes in the back of his head and had been born saying, "You're off your course!"

The weather remained fine and the glass was as steady as a rock. The wind veered to SSW. and we left the warm, crinkly, blue waters of the Gulf Stream behind us, after they had carried us fifty miles to the NNE. Apart from one or two squalls, when we had to hand the genoa and topsail for an hour or two, we hardly touched a sheet for days on end. Anne sunbathed, Bob did things with wood and tools, and I lay on the fo'c'sle with my head on a sail, trying to forget my aches.

One morning when I took over from Anne at breakfast-time she was more than usually wide-awake. She said, "How's your stomach this morning?"

"All right, why?"

"Only that you've been going about with that sour look on your face, and you haven't been smoking your pipe."

I got Bob working on the Air Nautical Tables and the sextant. He was very quick at picking things up, and in a day or two his sights were as good as mine. He had an accurate mind and didn't make the stupid mistakes that I had made at this stage. Anne hadn't got the hang of it yet. If *Moonraker* was lively, she found the sextant heavy to hold as she tried to steady the sun upon the horizon. Once or twice she spent the whole of her watch below, working out her sums. It made her tired, but it was fun teaching her. She took four times as long to learn as anyone else would have done, but she never said "I see" when she didn't, and she never forgot, once she learnt.

On the fifth day out the wind veered into the north-west in a squall and we gybed the boom over to port for the first time for nearly three thousand miles. It was no wonder that there was a fifteen-degree twist in the mast at the hounds and twenty-five degrees at the topsail sheave. After an hour or two, the wind went back again. By noon that day we were five hundred and forty miles from Ponce de Leon with only three hundred and sixty to go for Bermuda. It happened to be the day for pumping-out. *Moonraker* had always been a dry ship till she was coppered. Winston King had warned us that she might make more water, but it was very little and throughout the voyage she had taken only twelve or thirteen strokes of the pump to empty the bilges after each three days at sea. But this time I pumped and pumped until she sucked at the eighty-sixth stroke. I called to Bob, "Someone's left the lavatory on. She was half-full of water."

"Wasn't me," he answered. "Nor me," said Anne.

"Have either of you seen the pan full, the last two days?"

"Definitely not," they chorused.

"Well, she's leaking somewhere. Bob, you'd better have a look at the drain-pipes below the cockpit."

I heard the sound of things coming out of the engine-room, and then Bob's voice calling, "Nothing there, Peter. Both sides are all right."

I thought of all the other places where leaking might start. There might be a weak place in her port quarter, where I had dug some sap out of a timber, and the shipwright at Fowey had poured cement into the cavity. But there was no leak there. I took up the linoleum and prized up the boards in the fo'c'sle floor. There was a little water on the cement flooring, but when I sponged it out none reappeared, so there was no leak there.

By that time I was in a filthy state and smelt to high heaven of bilge. I said, "Well, one of you two must have left the lavatory on. We've got enough to do without pumping-out the Atlantic every day." Wisely, they let this remark go unchallenged. "We'll pump her out each day till we get to Bermuda," I growled and stumped back on deck.

The next day we were almost becalmed. Five strokes of the pump cleared the bilge, so my theory that the lavatory had been left without being screwed down seemed to me to be the most likely one. I felt much happier, and by the time we made our landfall I had forgotten it.

It is curious how some places have the reputation for being difficult to find. We met a man at dinner one night in Florida who, when he heard we were sailing to Bermuda, said, "I hope you find it. Half the fleet used to miss it in the Bermuda race and had to have a Navy ship to shepherd them back to the fold." From the chart you can see for yourself that it's no place to make in thick weather. It looks like a South Sea atoll cast up in the region of the North Atlantic westerlies by mistake. On the south-east corner of the atoll lie five islands, of which Hamilton is the only one of any size, being fifteen miles long and less than a mile wide for most of its length. The highest hill is less than two hundred feet high. There are a number of little islands inside Hamilton

Sound itself, but the danger lies to the north where the Great Bermuda Reef spreads, like a coral fan, northwards from the islands for a distance of more than seven miles. The currents are uncertain and our friend warned us not to trust our dead-reckoning for longer than twenty-four hours from our last celestial fix. We were, therefore, more than pleased when, on the morning we were due to make our landfall, we found a clearing sky and a brisk westerly breeze. All three of us spent a good deal of time fixing the ship's position, and, as the results agreed, we were not altogether surprised when land showed up dead-ahead soon after three o'clock.

The wind fell light and we ghosted along the south-east coast of Hamilton. Darkness fell, and the moon was put out of countenance by thousands of lights from huge hotels; large houses, lighthouses, aerial beacons and motor-cars. We looked at it with disappointment; we could have seen that sort of thing any evening off Brighton beach.

It took us all the next day to reach through the Narrows, beat through South Channel and run through Two Rock Passage. The houses looked naked in their whiteness, and Anne who had been studying the scene intently, suddenly said, "Look! All the trees are dead. That's why the houses stand out like that." And so seemed to be the case. Although there were a few places where the trees still thrived they served to make the tracery of other trees even more dead.

Tired with the heat and with the slowness of our passage, we turned at last into Dundonald Channel which leads to Hamilton Harbour. I was looking at the town when part of it seemed to move away from the rest! Three large funnels appeared upon the mass, which quickly gathered way. Anne's reaction was quick as she steered *Moonraker* the wrong side of the port-hand buoys where, fortunately, there was water enough for us. The *Queen of Bermuda* swept past, her beautiful proportions making her seem smaller than she really was. She had been built, we were told later, to fit Two Rock Passage, with a yard to spare on either side. We sailed through, past little islands with here and there the white sail of a dinghy and people bathing; we thought how lovely it would have been but for those pathetic trees. In front of us lay the harbour, and to starboard was White Island, where we had been advised to anchor. A black schooner, *Pinta*, a lovely vessel, lay close by.

Anne and Bob got down the topsail, and I was about to swing her into the wind when a woman on *Pinta* said in a level, unemotional voice, "Can you help me, please? My father has fallen over the side, and I can't get him into the dinghy." I at once prepared to lay *Moonraker* along the schooner's port side, but as we rounded her bow we saw the old man struggling over the gunwale of the dinghy. He waved to us triumphantly.

As we stowed our gear, the woman rowed over to us, resting on her oars a few yards away. She was dressed in an old pair of slacks and an open-necked shirt. "You're the Pyes of *Moonraker*, aren't you?" she said. "The 'Stavangers' waited for you till yesterday. They were sorry to miss you. If you give me a list of what you want ashore, I'll get it. The shops will shut in half an hour." We watched her row across to Hamilton with her shopping basket and our list. Hardly had she left when a cluster of motor boats came out, bringing a letter and a chart from *Stavanger*, fruit, potatoes, and so much bread that we didn't know what to do with it. In return Anne showed them our alligators. She took them out of their box by the backs of their necks and they hissed at all the right things.

The next day we were taken to see the "Fitted Dinghy" racing. These boats are fourteen feet long, with deep fin-keels, and carry almost as much sail as the famous Sydney Harbour boats. Each has three suits of sails, but once the race is started, they cannot change them, and none of the suits have reefs. These races are held only three or four times a season and there is tremendous excitement among the onlookers. The waterway to Somerset, where the races were being held, was like the roads to Epsom on Derby Day. Our motor boat was a Mark Boat, a grandstand seat for the entertainment which was a trifle less exciting than it might have been through lack of wind. Each boat was jeered at or encouraged as she passed by. The barracking was not without results, as was shown when a boat, whose crew, according to our crowd, were "the very end," was becalmed close by. The abuse so touched them on the raw that they failed to see a breeze coming from ahead. They were caught aback with their spinnaker boom out and were quickly in a pretty mess. Most boats started with four men aboard, but one by one the men would leap overboard, to lighten her, leaving the helmsman to finish the race on his own. The most popular win of the afternoon was when the *Victory*, fifty-five years old and skippered by a man of seventy, beat the *H.D.F.C.* (whatever that stands for) by half a length.

At this stage I had a letter from home making it important for me to return as soon as I could. Maddeningly, my pain had recently become worse. I managed to keep about for a day or two;

then Anne took charge and made up a bed for me on the starboard bunk, where I lapped milk like a cat. I had plenty of visitors. There was Mike, a thin young man with charming manners and a twinkle in his eye, who told us how much he would like to make an ocean passage in a small boat; and Wallace, short and fat and shy, with a heavy face, but with a humour as dry as a Tio Pepe. There was "J.C.," with his gammy knee and language the colour of a beef-steak, as hard as nails but very kind. Both he and Wallace offered me a bed and the doctor from H.M.S. *Sparrow* came to see that I was treating myself in the right way. But at the back of my mind was the recurrent thought that we must get away at the earliest possible moment and it worried me that in my present condition I should not be able to do my full share of work at sea. Then I had an idea. "We might ask Mike if he'd like to come," I suggested.

"He'd jump at it," Bob said, but Anne was more cautious.

"It's a big responsibility," she said. "He's only a boy. We'd have to talk to his mother first."

Mike's mother seemed content that he should accompany us and the young man himself was delighted. I tried to tell him what it would be like, but he'd already made up his own mind about that. It was arranged, however, that we would await the return from England of his father in two days' time for final consent. But in the interval somebody looked across from Hamilton and expressed the opinion that a ship of *Moonraker*'s size had little hope of crossing the Atlantic in safety, an opinion which naturally upset Mike's mother who had no desire to see her son go to a watery grave. In view of her fears we offered to call the whole thing off, but Mike wouldn't hear of it.

We were in this state of indecision when Mike's father came aboard. He was a dapper little man, with quick, darting eyes; he came straight to the point. "I hear you've asked my boy to go back to England with you," he barked. "Do the scamp good, instead of kicking his heels about on the beaches here. The trouble is, someone's upset my wife, so I told her I'd come and see the boat. I can't say I know a lot about boats, but this one looks all right to me."

Anne said, "I don't think Mike should come unless your wife feels happy about it."

He nodded his head. "I appreciate that, but she won't worry now that I've been aboard and seen the ship. Besides, can't let the boy down; he's very anxious to come."

I said, "I have told him that if life at sea doesn't come up to his expectations we will put him ashore at Flores and let him find his own way home."

"Excellent. Then we will leave it at that. Come and see me tomorrow and we'll fix the other details."

Rest and proper diet were having their effect and I was beginning to feel a good deal better. One afternoon I returned aboard to find Anne reading a letter from our friends in Essex. She said, "They want the alligators sent by air. They don't think *Moonraker*'s safe enough."

"What *is* all this?" I demanded in some exasperation. "Everyone seems to think this darned ship is going to sink." But I was glad to be rid of the alligators. They lived in their container under the pram which is kept upside down on the cabin-top. The thought of getting the pram unlashed in a gale of wind in order to attend to the alligators was not a comforting one. Neither did I look forward to housing them below decks should Anne decide they were cold. I was all for sending them by air, so Bob and I went at once to the B.O.A.C. to arrange their passage. We learned that some interval must elapse before they could be accommodated. This was a little awkward, because by law they could not be landed other than for immediate trans-shipment, and we wanted to leave almost at once. However, Anne called on *Pinta* and they agreed to take care of them until they could be taken to the aircraft.

Tuesday was fine, with a light south-west wind, and we sailed round to St. George's, ready to start the next morning. Breakfast that day was not a happy meal. Anne was not convinced that Mrs. Darling's fears were dispelled, and she was angry with me for putting to sea when I was hardly convalescent after an ulcer. I took her ashore and walked her up the street, both of us arguing fiercely while tears of rage rolled down her cheeks. At last, seeing that I was determined to sail, she gave a sniff and took me by the hand into a shop where Indians sold charms. She bought one for seven-and-sixpence. I hoped it would work.

Back on board Anne finished the stowing, including a supply of special bread that had been baked for us which we were told would stay fresh for a fortnight. Mike and I painted the inside of the pram; Bob brushed the slime off the copper. Wallace and his daughter came to see us off, while crowds of people lined the cliffs to wait for the finish of the ocean race from Newport. At two o'clock we pushed off from the quay, set the genoa, mainsail and topsail, rounded the last buoy in the narrows and stood away to the NNE. On the skyline we could see a tower of sail, the first of the Bermuda fleet. We saw her alter course and break out a vast blue spinnaker.

By dusk the land had faded from sight and *Moonraker* was sailing over a quiet sea. Mike already was seasick.

CHAPTER SEVENTEEN

NOW that there were four of us, we rearranged the watches. Anne, Bob and Mike stood the usual three-hour trick, while I took the afternoon watch from one till four. This meant that each of the others had fifteen hours off watch one day in three. It became known as "My day off," although Mike called it "My double-duty day," as, in turn with the others, he became responsible for organizing dinner on that day. I did the navigation, as usual, and was called for any sail-changing that might be necessary at night.

When we left Bermuda, we decided to sail, as near as the wind would allow, a great circle course to Flores. Originally we had meant to explore all the Azores, but that was now out of the question. The water situation for the four of us, and the uncertainty of knowing how Mike would make out, made it advisable to touch at Flores, which lies a hundred and twenty miles to the west and north of the other islands. In laying my course, I kept midway between the advice of Nicholson of Antigua, who had warned me to keep to the south, and the Bermudans, who advised making for the Gulf Stream as soon as possible, even though it meant more miles to cover.

Mike could not have had a better introduction to passage-making. The weather was perfect, the sea slight, and there was plenty of time to sleep and rest. He was bound to take a day or two to settle down, and, apart from his watches which he always took no matter how ill he felt, he had no fixed jobs on board for the first week.

Dramamine kept him from being sick most of the time, but it did not have the beneficial effect it had on most people and it worried me a little to see how tired the motion of the ship made him when conditions could hardly have been better.

On the second night out, the glass fell sharply, the wind backed to the south-east and squalls of wind and rain drove at us out of the darkness. Soon after midnight, Bob called urgently for less sail. The wind had veered to the SW. and it was blowing hard, too hard for the whole mainsail. *Moonraker* was steering wildly and running down by the head. Anne, in long oilskins and sou'wester, was close on my heels, but I sent her back to call Mike, for this was an occasion when he would learn more in ten minutes than in a week of good weather. Up for'ard there was the utmost confusion; the genoa and spinnaker were lying in a sodden, shapeless mass, a coil of rope had come adrift from its pin and the end had washed through the scuppers. It took the three of us quite a time to sort things out, while the ship was doing her best to roll her decks under and the mast bent alarmingly. Once Bob at the tiller called out that he couldn't hold out much longer, and Anne, who was laboriously coiling miles of peak-halliard that had kinked itself in every fathom, muttered: "That'll larn him to hang on to his whole mainsail!" But in the end we got the tangle straight. We took in the jib and set the foresail, backed the sheet, and while Bob put down the helm we sweated the mainsheet in. Once hove-to, she lay like a duck, falling and rising as each sea swept past, while the wind hummed disconsolately in the rigging. We put two reefs in the mainsail and resumed our course; now the ship ran easily over the rising sea. I stayed aft for a while, talking to Bob. After a while, it seemed to me that she might just take the spinnaker, so once more Mike and I went forward, got out the boom, slung it across the ship, shackled on the guys, and the tack of the sail, and bent on the halliard to its head. With a crack like a whip, the sail filled. As we made our way aft, I said, "What's she like, Bob?"

"She'll start planing soon," he grinned.

Mike went below. The sky was now clearing to windward and the wind would veer still further. I got out the two-inch boom-guy and led it from the end of the boom through the fair-lead in the eyes of the ship. This was not the sort of weather to gybe all standing. By 5 a.m. the wind had veered to NW., so we gybed, resetting the spinnaker to starboard. In another hour the wind had fallen light, and we let out the reefs, set the topsail, and finally, as it went into the north, replaced the spinnaker with the genoa. If sail-changing was going on at this rate, I, for one, was glad we had a fourth.

Poor Mike, this was a bad day for him. By ten o'clock we were becalmed in as bad a swell as I have ever experienced. Waves seemed to rush at us from south, west and north, and all we could do was to sheet the mainsail hard in, take the topsail off, and wait. The sun burned down from an almost cloudless sky and thin wisps of steam rose from drying decks, sails and clothes. Mike lay suffering on the port bunk, Anne read on the starboard one, and Bob, who is as case-hardened against sea-sickness as myself, lay in his bunk in the eyes of the ship, reading the Saturday *Evening Post*. I mooched about the deck doing odd jobs, cursing the lack of wind and worrying about Mike. I remembered how Admiral

Goldsmith, also bound from Bermuda, had to sail a hundred miles out of his way to land a sick member of his crew, who lay as if dead until the sight of land miraculously restored him to health. The calm lasted all day, and the ship gradually turned herself round until she faced the way she had come. It required quite a little strength of mind not to try to turn her back again.

Mike made a heroic effort to eat dinner that night, but he fell asleep in the middle of it, his body swaying gently as the ship rolled. The glass fell steadily and the sky became overcast and greasy. As night fell, Bob hung the riding-light up on the gallows, and before we turned in we double-reefed the mainsail and set the foresail aback.

I woke suddenly. I looked out and saw the riding-light swinging on the gallows and, in its yellow beam, thundery rain fell vertically. The time was a quarter to three. I let down the canvas side to my bunk and rolled out, but as I put on my oily, a squall struck the ship, putting her hard over on the port side. I switched on the binnacle-light, saw that she was heading south and went up to take over. *Moonraker* paid off slowly, but as soon as she got round to her course she ran like a scalded cat. The others emerged from the cabin, hooded figures like monks from a cell, and I only realised the severity of the squall when I heard it had woken Bob up by pitching him out of his bunk. But, as he said, that should not have been enough to wake *him*! The squall passed, and before Bob took over to finish his watch the spinnaker was set to port.

I was deeply asleep when I heard Anne's voice repeated, as in a nagging sort of dream which wouldn't leave me alone. I opened my eyes and saw it was light and from the feel of the ship there was more wind than we had had for some time. The sky was leaden and the grey seas which rushed up astern looked angry and remorseless. Anne did not smile as she saw me at the hatch, she was too busy at the helm. She said, "She wants a third reef." As Mike had had a good spell in, I turned him out and together we got in the spinnaker. He went forward to smother the sail as if he meant it, and he got it under control before it could tear itself on the winch or wrap itself round the forestay.

"Feeling your feet, Mike?"

"Think so, skipper, but why you do this sort of thing for pleasure beats me."

I sat with Anne for a few minutes. In fine weather she can be an irritating helmsman, but when *Moonraker* is running before a big sea none of us are a patch on her. She seems to know what is going to happen a second before *Moonraker* herself does, as I imagine a good horsewoman does when riding a favourite horse. It was lovely to watch. By teatime we were becalmed under a sky that looked as if it had never heard of a breath of wind! So it went on. Calms succeeded squalls and our daily runs fell to forty and then twenty. Mike was not the only one who felt that it was a long way to Flores. However, once we were north of the thirty-sixth parallel, the calms were over and the first week ended with a glorious sail before a south-westerly breeze in which each watch-keeper added twenty miles to the score for a whole twelve hours. I worked out my position and found that the week's total was four hundred and eighty-nine miles, the worst record of the voyage by a long way. We read the water-gauge and found we'd used so little that we could have gone straight to England. The mainsail began to look in poor shape. The day before I had noticed the stitching of the reinforcement-cloth to the clew had carried away. To test whether it was likely to go further, I gave it a pull and the cloth tore in my hands. It was as ripe as a pear. From now on all depended on the cloth that was left, and I wasn't going to test that by pulling! I was further worried by the fact that *Moonraker* was starting to leak again. I talked it over with Bob, who maintained that it was a general seepage, due to the working of the boat in the seaway. Apparently he had always sailed in ships that leaked, and it worried him not a scrap. He said, "Wait till you have to pump her out every watch for half an hour, like we had to in the old 'So and so,' then you can start worrying." That was all very well, but, if he was right the most likely conclusion was that galvanic action had attacked her fastenings and she might at any time spring a butt. And if *that* happened in a place where we couldn't get a sail round it we should have a long, long row!

The next morning we were still running well before the fine west wind. The sea had built up into a long easy swell and the old ship rolled contentedly along, putting her decks under at the end of any roll heavier than usual. I went into the engine-room for a bit of gear and found the water swishing about only an inch below the flywheel. The ship was nearly half-full. I glanced at Mike, who was asleep on the port bunk. I would have given a good deal not to have had him on board at that moment. Bob was on watch. I took the pump-plunger up with me and told him, "The bilge is full of water and everything's coming out of this ship till we've found the leak." I pumped for over a hundred strokes and still she didn't suck; even Bob raised his eyebrows at that. I left the plunger in and started taking things out of the engine-room and piling them on to the cabin floor. Bob leaned down. "It's not in there, Peter; I had a look yesterday." I crawled in with the torch. Almost at once I saw it; water pouring in through a three-inch crack in the starboard drain pipe of the cockpit. No sight could have filled me with such joy as did that dirty trickle. I noticed that when the ship rolled to port the water stopped as if turned off by a tap. She must have been heeled to port whenever Bob had looked.

I went up on deck, and stood on the bridge-deck for a moment, noticing that the heaving rolling had not been due to the sea but to the amount of water she had had in her. I turned to Bob. "There's a job for you. You'll want a cork!"

We hove to on the starboard tack, and Bob went over the side to put a cork in the end of the pipe. Then he bound up the crack with insulating tape, went over again and took the cork out. I watched for results. No water came in. Looking back, there can be no doubt that the pipe started to crack when we were towed through the breakers at Ponce De Leon Inlet, and as she had so often been on the starboard gybe or tack, it had taken us an extraordinary length of time to find it.

From now on our daily runs were good. We drove the ship as hard as we could, and I was often fetched from my bunk at night by a cry for more sail. Mike had become a capable crew although he still insisted that only fools could *enjoy* themselves at sea. On Monday 3rd July my noon sight gave us a run of a hundred and fifty-five miles for the previous twenty-four hours, of which twenty-five must have been due to the Gulf Stream. In the afternoon the wind increased to a fresh breeze and we pulled down a reef but kept up the spinnaker. That morning we had been round with the paint-pot and no stains of rust marred the brightness of the ship's appearance. At seven-fifteen I came up to relieve Mike to have his dinner. Close astern of us, and coming up fast, was a "Liberty ship." She was in ballast and looked enormous. Mike's eyes were on the compass. I said, "Well, Mike, where did she come from?" He looked astern and shot from his seat as if he had seen a ghost.

"My God!" he cried, "Does she want to run us down?" It was the first steamer we had seen for many days and she was certainly close. For a long time after that I would see Mike giving quick looks astern!

As the vessel came up with us we could see the captain standing by with his megaphone. The crew were leaning over the bulwarks. As they towered above us, *Moonraker* must have looked very small. The captain shouted, "Are you all right?" I shouted, "Yes, thank you." "Do you want your position?" It sounded ungrateful to say "no" and I was sure he had it ready on his tongue. He had. "You are eleven hundred and seventy miles east by south of Boston!" We were sailing at about six knots at the time and the S.S. *Tini* kept perfect station on us.

The captain called, "Where are you bound?"

The meeting of S.S. *Tini* and *Moonraker*

"The Azores," I shouted, but in America they call them the A-zores and he couldn't get it. "Flores," I tried; but that was no good either. The next time I shouted, "England." Unfortunately we had reached the peak of our great circle course, and our nose was pointing somewhere towards Lisbon. This apparently gave the captain renewed concern. He raised his megaphone again and repeated: "Are you all right?" As we reassured him a squall came down with a flurry of wind and rain and, to our astonishment, the S.S. *Tini* of Delaware turned right round through one hundred and eighty degrees and sailed away to the west.

We talked about it for hours; where they had come from, whither they were bound and what a delightful gesture it was to have come out of their way to see that all was well with us!

Several weeks later I wrote to the captain of the S.S. *Tini* to thank him for his kindness, and incidentally to tell him where we *were* bound! I had a letter back, a most charming letter, of which I quote a part: "It makes us happy to think that you felt our slight deviation from our course merited a word of thanks. However, since you have so thoroughly proven yourself as a 'blue-water sailor,' there is little need to remind you that tradition centuries-old dictated our action. We were naturally especially pleased that you needed no assistance. Possibly, too, in addition to the impelling force of tradition, we were motivated somewhat by a latent urge to abandon the relative comfort and security of a ship's bridge to solicit a berth with you on a real ship, which your *Moonraker* definitely is. . . ."

We were lucky that night. The glass fell and the wind increased to strong. We pulled down another reef and at three o'clock in the morning Mike called me. The wind was veering, he said, and he thought we ought to gybe. I took the spinnaker off her, using the strap by means of which one man can manage the sail in anything less than a gale; by the time I'd finished, the wind had backed again. There didn't seem any point in gybing at the moment, but before going below I housed the preventer backstay. An hour later the wind whipped round to the NE. in a squall, the boom-guy snapped and the mainsail came over in the most almighty gybe. It was a nasty moment for Mike, but if the preventer backstay had been set up it would have been worse. The mast would have gone by the board!

It was a vile morning. The wind settled in the ENE. and the rain came down in bucketfulls, so hard that it helped to keep down the sea. Under one reef, the number two jib and the foresail, *Moonraker* plunged solemnly along while her crew reacted each in their own way, Anne outwardly cheerful, Bob laconic, and the skipper more sour-faced! Poor old Mike went down into the depths, sick with the change of motion. The weather relented; at the end of my afternoon watch the rain stopped, the wind veered quickly, we tacked the ship and set off once more, sailing a little more to the north to compensate for having been driven to the south.

For the next three days the weather remained unsettled, but the wind continued in the south-west. Drive, drive, watch after watch; down topsail, in reefs; out reefs, up topsail; spinnaker for genoa, genoa for spinnaker; nothing must be left undone to keep the log spinning as fast as the ship could turn it. It was terrific fun.

On 10th July the ship was tearing along at nearly seven knots before a southerly wind with every stitch of sail we could carry. A week before we had started a sweepstake on the date of our landfall and already Bob and I were out of it. If we sighted Flores before dark, it was Anne's, after that it was Mike's. At noon our position was sixty miles from Flores. The highest point of the island is three thousand feet, so I reckoned we ought to see it about five o'clock. Mike laughed. "I can't believe it. For twenty days nothing but sea and you say we shall sight *land* in just over four hours!"

The others were on deck and Mike and I went down to get lunch.

"You know, skipper," Mike volunteered, "there were times in the early days of this trip when I thought I'd have to ask you to put me ashore at Flores. I honestly didn't think I'd survive, but now I want to stay with the ship until we reach Fowey, if you'll have me."

I was glad of this. Not only was he becoming a useful crew, but the idea of putting a man ashore at Flores, where he might have to wait weeks for a boat, did not appeal to me.

I said: "That's great, Mike. We shall be pleased to have you with us."

He said; "I doubt if you'll ever make a sailor of me, but I should like you to have a try."

I forgot whose watch it was after tea, but I was at the helm. The other three were up the ratlines, and just at five o'clock (this is the Gospel truth) Bob saw Flores on the port bow, a lump of an island with clouds obscuring the higher land.

We pressed on. The wind fell lighter as the day drew to a close. The sky brooded over us and we imagined Flores as the only land in a world of sea. Night fell and we heard the thunder of the ocean against the iron-bound coast which we could no longer see. Only the flash of Lagen's Light proclaimed the land at all. Presently we took down the topsail and genoa, backed the foresail and left the ship to sleep.

When I came up, before the sun, Flores lay to the north-west and nothing I had ever seen looked half so lovely. A scattered hamlet lay around the lighthouse, and, as the light grew stronger and the sun arose, it shone on blue hydrangeas which grew in ordered lines like walls, marking one man's land from another's. The island was green; not the dull green of a land that is parched by the sun, not the lush, sensuous green of the tropics, but the green of Old Ireland, nurtured by mist and rain. I called the crew, for this was no morning to lie abed. We set the genoa and sailed up the coast while the off-shore breeze came to us, bearing the smell of flowers and fields. Eight miles to the north, the white church-tower and the cluster of buildings told us that we had come to the principal village, Santa Cruz. There is, as far as I know, no chart of the entrance to this place, because there is no harbour to enter. We saw, however, a boat-quay, many dangerous rocks, and a crowd of people. There were boats lying to moorings off the quay, but the reef protecting the anchorage, if you could call it such, looked so dangerous that we hove to and waited for something to happen. The crowd grew. An official came down the steps and stepped into a long double-ended boat pulled by many oars. She pushed off, came through a gap in the rocks, and made towards us. In silence we waited for her.

CHAPTER EIGHTEEN

WE had not long to wait. The oarsmen brought the heavy boat alongside and the captain of the port stepped aboard. He spoke no English, and Anne's Portuguese was not exactly fluent. He pointed to our sails and dropped his hands; we dropped our sails. By signs he inquired our draught, and by signs we gave it. He then directed us to follow a motor fishing-vessel that lay hard by; she took us towards a gap, a hole in the wall which I would never have dared go through. It looked about three times the width of our vessel, between a rock awash and a reef which lay, green and hungry, three feet below the water. We turned sharply to starboard and my first impression of this backwater among rocks was better than it might have been.

They brought us alongside the quay, which was thronged with fishermen and peasants in rough clothes, while high above, on top of a great wall of concrete, women and girls looked down, waving and throwing flowers to us. Portuguese small boys were everywhere.

The four of us were busy fixing springs and warps when a dapper little man in a light-grey suit darted out from behind two policemen and hooked Anne round the leg with the crook of his umbrella. "Tell the captain," he hissed at her, as she recovered her balance with the help of a backstay, "tell him I will speak to all people for you. I live in America many years."

After the authorities had finished with us he came aboard. He told us he had stowed away on a sailing ship some forty years ago, and had made good in America. Now he and his wife had returned to help his innumerable nephews and nieces. We gathered that any luxuries Flores enjoyed depended upon such benefactors as Da Silveiro. I was a little suprised that he had remained so definitely Portuguese.

He was invaluable to us. He fetched a sailmaker and explained what we wanted done; he saw the captain of the port and told him that I was not willing to lie against the quay all night because there was too much scend rolling into the bay; and he escorted Anne and me up the narrow street to the little square where we sat on a bench under the trees. It was very quiet. The sun shone on clean white walls and red roofs, on the corn drying in back gardens, and on two small oxen standing patiently between the shafts of a cart like a Roman chariot. I asked, "Do you have hotels here for visitors? What do the people do for entertainment?"

Da Silveiro smiled courteously and said, "You are our only entertainment. When they see your little boat this morning, everyone has a holiday, same with the children in the school. You are the first yacht to come in and lie in the harbour." I thought how pleasant it was to be the cause of a public holiday.

Our guide took us into the biggest store and with his help we ordered all we needed. "If you were many persons, we could not have fed you. We kill only to feed our own people, about one steer a month, and the boat from Horta is not expected for three more weeks." We bought butter (Flores butter is as good as French), we ordered two chickens, enough bread for the voyage and some excellent cheese. The water we should have to carry ourselves from the quay, to which it would be brought by cart from the square.

When we got back, Bob and Mike went off to explore. They climbed the hill above the town, they were introduced to some prisoners in the gaol, which was without lock or key, and they visited a wineshop, where they drank the harsh red wine of the country. They came back to a lot of hard work. We did what we were told and moored the ship athwart the harbour, taking twenty fathoms of chain in the pram over to the rocks on the east side and putting two kedges out astern, with warps to each quarter. The weather turned nasty with some rain, and a swell rolled in from the north, making *Moonraker* roll abominably and putting her stern almost on to a rock over which there was five feet of water. I went in search of our friend, and when I found him we went to see the captain. Da Silveiro translated, "The captain says you move to the northern end of the harbour, because the wind it comes from the north." I forbore to ask what happened if it then came from the east. I knew the answer to that: Get out!

So we weighed the kedges, dragged in the chain, and towed *Moonraker* to the northern side, where we moored her to her anchor and chain out for'ard, with a warp from each bow to a pinnacle of rock, covered with cloth to prevent chafe, another from the port quarter to the quay, and a line to a buoy from the starboard quarter. We then had several feet in which to swing before we hit anything. More important still, we were lying head-on to the swell. It was getting dark, but we were helped by a powerful lamp which flooded the ship with light. This was not to help us, but to allow those who could not come to see *Moonraker* by day to see her by night.

The next afternoon the mayor took us for a ride in his car, one of two on the island. The road led upwards and round hairpin bends, ending abruptly on the side of a gorge where the mountain air was like wine. Men with pickaxes and shovels were slowly advancing towards a buttress of rock. We retraced our way northwards towards Deshayes Bay, where Sir Richard Grenville lay before his famous battle. The sea looked rough between Flores and its appendage, Corvo; the wind was NW., and, if the speed of the dark squalls hurrying away from the land was anything to go by, it was strong. Again the road came to an end. In time it would encircle the island, though not for many years, for there is no money to pay for modern equipment.

At eleven o'clock the next morning, Thursday, 13th July, we were ready for sea. The sailmaker had made a fine job of the clew of the mainsail and this morning he brought back the spinnaker on which he had been working for half the night. We started to undo ourselves from the various rocks to which we were attached, we warped the vessel round, started the engine and, with the sailmaker as pilot, we motored through the gap in the reef. As soon as we were clear of all dangers, we dropped him into his dinghy, hoisted the one-reefed mainsail and set the course NE.

In light airs and squalls we drew away from the land. Flores now looked cold and forbidding, with dark clouds hanging low over her fair countenance. Each squall increased in vigour, and then, with a growl, the strong NW. wind was upon us, making us take in the second, then the third, reef in quick succession, setting the third jib in place of the second. By the time Corvo was abeam, the weather was so thick that that high little island was completely lost to view. The sea built up quickly. It was the biggest we had yet seen, wide valleys flecked with milky white between dark hills of water, whose crests were like mountain plumes. There was no vice in them, but they were big and strong and to make a beam wind of it meant a strain on the rudder that was not quite justified; so we altered course to ENE. This in itself was a good course for the English Channel, but we had been warned by many to make north until reaching the 45th parallel, in order to avoid the NE. winds which blow to the eastwards of the Azores.

The ship drove on; every now and then the top of a crest would hurl itself against her broadside, and burst in a fan of sparkling light, the water cascading over the closed skylights, forcing itself through cracks and spraying the indignant forms of the watch below. The sound of her advance, the whine of the wind, filled the cabin with a volume of sound, a sort of Hallelujah Chorus to the finale of our voyage.

Mike was sick again; but now he no longer slumped down like a sack of flour. He remained alert and was absorbed into the family, rejoicing in this fine, strong wind that was carrying us back to England and Home.

The sunset was a violent colour and portents of wind were in the sky, but the glass, after a slight fall, remained steady. I went up at each change of watch, but, apart from one rather sharper squall, the weather gradually improved so that the third reef was out before daylight. By noon we had put one hundred and thirty miles between us and Flores. Towards evening the squalls grew heavier, but before the night was over *Moonraker* was gliding over a truly magnificent swell, close-hauled on the port tack under all her light weather canvas. By the evening we were becalmed.

I turned out the next morning at five o'clock. The sky was flat and grey. The northerly swell had disappeared and a westerly one, just as impressive, was rolling up astern. The upper part of each wave was roughened with little ripples, like a pond on an open common, but the troughs were smooth and oily. The ship rose and fell like a bird asleep on the water. By the time I had taken the riding-light off the gallows and stowed it in the fo'c'sle, there was enough air from the west to pull the foresheet a-lee, let out the mainsail and proceed upon our course, NE.

During the day the glass fell slowly. The sun came out, the wind freshened to a whole-sail breeze, and gradually backed through south to SSE. It was cosy in *Moonraker*'s cabin that night. We had eaten the last of our Flores chickens as a pilaff with rice and raisin and egg, the soft light of the cabin lamps fell on cream paint and on polished brass. Mike was sound asleep on a mattress on the cabin floor, Anne was writing up her diary and I the ship's Daily Journal. Outside, Bob was enjoying the last of his after-dinner pipe, the wind came in fitful gusts, and there was a fine drizzle of rain. Soon Anne put the books away, and I turned out the starboard lamp, trimming the one above my head, so that the helmsman could, by leaning down, see the clock and the barometer. I put up my canvas bunk-board, and turned in.

In my sleep I was aware of the increasing wind and sea, so that it was difficult to know whether I was awake or not. Then I heard Anne calling me just before midnight. The wind had veered to the SSW. and was blowing a fresh breeze. The glass was going down. We pulled down two reefs, put the ship back on her course, and Bob and I went thankfully out of the pouring rain into the warmth of the cabin, leaving Anne sitting up to windward, her eye on the lighted compass-card.

I woke at half-past four. A grey light filtered into the cabin from under the pram and I noticed that someone had put two boards in the hatchway. Through the remaining gap the rain drove horizontally into the cabin. The glass had fallen four-tenths since noon of yesterday, and as I reset it the needle moved another quarter of a tenth downhill. *Moonraker* was running heavily; the sky was full of rain and wind, and to windward it was a darker grey from an advancing squall. Rain dripped from Bob's red beard and the creases of his bronzed face were rimed with salt.

It was five o'clock when Bob called, and I hardly heard his shout. It took three of us to haul down the third reef-cringle and we put an extra lashing through the cringle and round the boom; it was blowing hard. When *Moonraker* was back on her course, we set the third jib and took the foresail down. By noon it was blowing a moderate gale and the glass still fell. For the first time we pulled down the fourth reef, and Bob, standing on the cabin top, could reach the level of the gaff-jaws with his hand. By dead-reckoning from yesterday's noon position, we had reached the 45th degree of latitude, so we gybed her over and set course E. by N. for the English Channel.

When the others went below, they found that Mike had made a panful of scalding soup of which I drank my share before it became too full of cold salt water. The sky darkened, the pall of cloud came lower, so low that the racing clouds seemed to skim the masthead. I shouted to the others to put in the third board, cutting me off from below except for a string attached to the ship's bell in the cabin. The air was filled with spray from the blown-off tops of the seas and the surface smoked with spume; the rain and the wind flattened the seas and the ship sheered wildly. More than once I nearly pulled the string to summon the crew to heave her to, but the squall passed. For the rest of my watch the wind varied between force six and seven on the Beaufort scale and by the end of the three hours I felt I had been on watch for days and I ached in every limb. Below, no one slept. The noise, the violent lurching, the howl of the wind and the darkness of the cabin, kept them on the alert. Towards four o'clock Anne got up to open the galley; she forgot the string and tolled the bell. The others, who were beginning to relax, jumped out of their skins and were not a little peevish to see Anne laughing at them!

She opened the hatch a little, then took out a board. Later she told me that, from down below, the seas, as they towered above the stern, looked terrifying, and she half hoped that I would have to heave to before she came on watch.

By six o'clock the glass reached its lowest reading, six-tenths in thirty hours. Dinner that night was "Tiller Soup" and I took my hat off to Bob, who was in charge, for cooking potatoes in the pressure-cooker to thicken it up. We finished with a tin of peaches and mugs of steaming coffee. By eleven the glass started to rise. I went on deck. It had stopped raining and the moon, showing through a gap in the torn sky, lit a tumultuous scene. The wind had backed and I set the reefed foresail to give her a little more sail. Then I went below and fell sound asleep.

"Peter; wake up, wake up, wake up. . . ." Anne was bending over me, already dressed in oilskins and sou'wester. I was suddenly very wide-awake. I felt the ship go up on the back of a sea and shudder from stem to stern as if all her planks and timbers were coming apart. I was very angry at not being called before.

I said, "Hell, she'll break up, like this. We must heave to." I flung on an oilskin and went up, followed by Anne. The sky was as black as the Styx, the sea a cauldron of white. I shouted in Bob's ear, "How long . . .?"

"About half an hour ago . . ."

I took over the helm, but at that moment there seemed to be a lessening in the weight of wind. We waited. The sky lightened to windward and in another ten minutes it was obvious that the squall was over. Anne took the helm, as it was now her watch, and Bob and I went below. The time was a quarter-past one. Bob looked tired out. When the squall had struck, he had hung on for a bit, hoping it would blow over. Then he couldn't find the string to the bell. He had shouted, but his voice was torn away by the wind. Anne, lying in her bunk, wondering why he didn't ring the bell. Finally she had got up and opened the hatch. In a single glance she had seen enough to waken me.

Bob explained, "I was afraid she'd broach to. It was blowing harder than I've ever known it."

It was still dark when a different movement awoke me. *Moonraker* was being tossed like a cork. I went on deck and found Anne sitting nodding over the tiller, while less than a moderate wind filled our rag of sail. The motion on deck was indescribable. The moon was out, shining down from a large circle of clear sky.

I said, crossly, "You'll have the mast out of her like this. For God's sake, let's get some sail on her." Anne was almost dropping with sleep. "Mast's all right," she murmured. "I was waiting for the change of watch."

I called Bob and we shook the reefs out. We were very tired and the ropes were as hard as iron. It took us hours, or seemed to, but the steady stride of the ship as she felt the extra canvas was a joy. We set the spinnaker.

The barometer rose in a slow, even curve, the wind was steady from the NW. and the sun shone down from a fine-weather sky. Under topsail, whole mainsail and spinnaker, *Moonraker* sailed swiftly over the heaving swell left from yesterday's blow. The decks were covered with drying blankets, coats, clothes and sails, the hatches were open, and I could see Bob and Mike polishing the brass, while Anne washed out the galley. My noon sight put us seven hundred and fifty miles from Fowey, but Anne was three miles nearer! In sunshine and rain, in squall and lull, we drove the old ship home. Day by day the line of our advance swept across the chart at one hundred and twenty-five miles a day. We put the clock on for the last time, and now ship's time was G.M.T. We sewed our ageing sails.

Then, on the morning of 22nd July, the glass fell and the wind freshened from the south. Rain slanted down from a grey sky, and Mike did his best to hang on to the whole mainsail till Bob and I had prepared breakfast. I mixed a saucepan full of porridge, handed it him to put on the Primus. He took it and the handle broke! As a substitute for watery glue, I can thoroughly recommend the mixture. Anne opened an eye to survey the scene. She closed it again and turned over. Bob threw down a couple of swabs from the cockpit and I sponged up the porridge, while he wring out the swabs. By the time that was over, the ship was doing her best to dive under the sea for good and all, so we put in a reef. Then more porridge, a bite of scrambled egg, and another call from Mike. My sea-booted leg caught the coffee-pot fair and square and over went the coffee to join what was left of the porridge. The ship came first, so in went another reef, but the chaos below was too much even for Anne. When we came down, she had cleared up the mess and made fresh coffee.

The sky cleared, but there was a surprising amount of weight in the wind and a really big sea. I went up to take a noon sight, when suddenly *Moonraker* side-slipped down the back of a wave against the helm, which Bob kept hard up. The strain on the rudder must have been terrific; indeed some weeks later we found that three of the fastenings round the rudder-cheeks had snapped off inside the wood. As she lifted to the next sea, the crest hit her like a sledgehammer just forward of the shrouds, flooding the decks, the sails and the crew with half a ton of water. It took me hours to clean the sextant! Somewhat chastened by this example of broaching-to, we pulled down the third reef. The afternoon was sunny and she ran on before the strong, fair wind. Anne came up to take over before tea. She stood looking astern at the great rolling seas and ahead at the empty ocean. She said, "what a pity it is that there is any land, for then we could go on sailing for ever."

The Home Service of the B.B.C. grew ever louder and that night we came into soundings on to the European shelf, and the ocean swell died down. We caught sight of a trawler on the Sole Bank at the break of day, and the night of the 23rd saw us with our navigation lights lit for the first time since we left Bermuda. The wind fell light and steamers appeared from nowhere. All next day we sailed quietly on under one-reefed mainsail and topsail. The cloth which chafed against the after-shroud when the full sail was set was a line of pin-point holes, and Anne swore that she could put her finger in and rip it from top to bottom.

At two o'clock the next morning, 25th July, Bob woke me to say that he had picked up the Lizard Light. I followed him up on deck and went for'ard. The ship was ghosting over the quiet sea with scarcely a murmur of sound. I stood for a long time looking at the light, winking away in the darkness. It was thirteen months and three days since I had seen the Lizard disappear into the haze astern, and now there it was again, that outpost of Old England to which we were so glad to return. I used to feel that it was by accident that I sailed upon the sea; that what fascinated me most was seeing new countries and new people, and that sailing was just a better way of doing so than walking, or driving a car, but now I knew that that was no longer so. Long after tropic islands and coral beaches had faded from my memory, I should remember the thrill of this homeward passage, best of all, these last twelve days from Flores. The wide loneliness of a great ocean breeds a humility that is good for the soul.

England's shores were enveloped in mist and rain when I turned out before breakfast, hoping to see the land. In drizzle, we rounded the head where the lighthouse was, guided by the mournful blast of her foghorn. Aboard, the ship quivered with activity. The cabin had a major spring-clean. Bob went about seeing that all the coils of halliards were neatly stowed, and we let the reef out of the mainsail, for it didn't matter if there was a rent in our sail as long as we reached Fowey that night. The wind backed to the south and freshened, and the ship heeled to her press of sail. The mist thinned and then broke up, clearing from the west, showing the whole lovely coast from the Lizard to the Rame. The wind veered to the NW. and then to the north. Down came the genoa and up went the number-one jib, and we beat towards Gribbin Head. Mike brought the chain up from the locker, and Bob shackled it on to the anchor; the small waves smoothed under the lee of the land. We saw the entrance to Fowey harbour and the Troy Class out for an evening sail. We sent up the Yellow Jack. As my watch ended I handed over to Bob, but he shook his head. "This, Peter, is your moment; it must be rather fun."

A little white motor boat put out from the harbour, coming in our direciton; she rounded-to and slowed to our gentle pace. Friends waved, gazing at us as if we were ghosts. Above the noise of their engine, they shouted. "Welcome back to Fowey! The cut of your topsail looked familiar, but when we saw your red mainsail, we knew it *must* be you."

In light airs we worked our way into the calm of the harbour. There were the grey-stone houses, terrace upon terrace, climbing up the hill to the west. There was the ferryboat putting out from Polruan. The clock struck the hour as it had done when we sailed away.

A gentle breeze came from the north and *Moonraker* slipped through the water towards the mouth of the Pont. The sea-gulls wheeled and cried, and from up the river came the deep note of a ship's siren echoing among the hills. *Moonraker* swung into wind and tide. Down came the jib and foresail. Over the side went the anchor. *Moonraker* of Fowey was home.

The Sea is for Sailing

PETER PYE

THIS BOOK IS DEDICATED TO

all those whose hands worked on the ship, to the doors which opened in welcome from Spain to Polynesia, from Alaskan cold to the sun of Mexico, to the 'simpatico' of many lands, to the names and stories still untold

CHAPTER ONE

ANNE once said that we sail with one hand in God's pocket. I think we live our lives that way, too, for this story would never have been told if the long arm of coincidence had not sent the Smeetons striding down the sea wall at Farnbridge in Essex at the same time that it sent me up it.

The wind was from the north and there was snow in the air. Miles was six foot six, with a face whose form suggested that it had been sparingly carved from teak, a Roman nose and a look of the mountains in his stride; Beryl walked behind him. They were laughing as they hurried down the path, no overcoats, no scarves, no hats... the hairs on Miles's chest peeping through his half-buttoned shirt.

A few yards later I stopped in my tracks. There was something in the air.... With a prickly feeling running up my neck I turned and followed them down to the shed. Pausing a moment to think up an excuse for such unwarrantable curiosity, I opened the door and walked in.

Mick the boatman said, "Ah, here's Dr Pye. He might be able to help. He's just come back from the West Indies."

Miles looked down. "Pye... Pye... where have I heard that name? I know; you met a friend of mine, Dick Goss, at Tobago. He said if that man could cross the Atlantic in a boat like his, he was sure I could."

A most engaging smile spread over Miles's face, "I hope he's right," he said. "I am looking for a boat to sail back to British Columbia."

The Smeetons found *Tzu Hang* at Dover. She was a forty-five-foot ketch, built at Hong Kong of teak on the lines of *Tai-Mo-Shan*. They had never sailed before, but they took her across the Thames Estuary at night and made the entrance to the Crouch on the morning tide.

At that time we were settling into our cottage at Steeple, and often, when we went over to Burnham, Beryl would be swinging at the masthead from a bos'n's chair. I remember her as a small, brown person, as sure-footed as a mountain goat, a woman who had walked across Turkestan, ventured alone into Tibet, ridden up the Andes, and with Miles, reached 22,000 feet on Tirich Mir.

Whenever I think of Miles I remember a morning on the Crouch when *Tzu Hang* and *Moonraker* were anchored side by side. It was one of those slightly misty days, and Miles was standing by the mast looking down the river to where the low banks seemed to run into space, so that if you were to set sail your course would take you at once into strange, uncharted seas.

"The world would be intolerable," he said, "if adventure were not just around the corner."

One way and another we saw a good deal of the Smeetons that spring. Clio came back from school. She was tall and thin, a child of ten with a puckish face who was always reading books. By the time they reached Victoria, Clio would have lived in half the countries in the world and crossed a couple of oceans.

I heard a grown-up say to her once, "How wonderful to have had all those experiences," to which Clio replied in a small serious voice, "I've had too many experiences."

Just before they left we were having dinner aboard. We were talking about the Galapagos Islands and of the families that inhabit those remote places, when Miles suddenly said, "Why don't you come out to British Columbia and spend the winter with us?"

On the way back to our cottage that night the smell of the countryside, the fields and the view from Steeple Hill over the River Blackwater, a ribbon in the moonlight, made the idea of leaving it seem the most foolish thing we could do. We spoke no words, but instead of going upstairs Anne pulled out an atlas.

Atlases are no cure for pipe-dreams. With a hand-span you can reach out half across the largest ocean, and the sea is a delicate blue without a single wave.

Anne said, "Look; we can go to the South Sea Islands, up to Hawaii and then to Victoria."

Her finger travelled down the west side of America.

"I've always wanted to go to Mexico, and then we can come back through the Panama Canal and the West Indies."

"That'll be fun, beating against the winter Trades."

She looked at me scornfully, "*Tai-Mo-Shan* did it, so why can't you?"

If you look at *Moonraker* with an unbiased eye (a thing neither Anne nor I can do) you will see a short-ended (one might almost say no-ended) cutter with great freeboard for'ard, very little aft, a tremendous sheer, high bulwarks, a transom stern and a long bowsprit. A ship that looks like a box and sails like a witch, built in the year 1896 by the eye of a craftsman, in a shape that might bring tears to the eyes of Mr. Jack Giles but would please those of Captain Joshua Slocum.

Twenty-nine feet long, drawing six feet and over and with a foot more beam than *Wanderer III*, she is built of pitch-pine planking on oak frames. She is a happy ship; sea-kindly and safe when running before a strong wind, capable of inspiring the utmost loyalty in all her crew. I suspect she is extremely jealous, for if ever Anne and I go sailing in another boat, she lets things fall off her or sails like a pig until we beg her forgiveness. If she thought we were going to sell her, she'd drown us.

Such was the ship that Anne and I left a year later as we rowed down the Fowey river to meet Christopher, our crew, at the station. It was pouring with rain.

Christopher had the same name as our previous crew; he was x, the unknown quantity. He was twenty; he had been to Eton, had sailed as a boy and mate in a Thames barge, had a commission in the Twelfth Lancers during his National Service, had spent a week of still autumn weather with us, had rung up from Switzerland to put off helping us to fit out the ship and was now coming straight from Henley. His father had said, "I'm sending him with you instead of to a university."

We loaded his kit-bag, his suitcase, his bowler hat and his gun into the pram and set off up the winding river. On the one hand a rather gorgeous young man in an exquisite reefer jacket, on the other, two oil-skinned figures with rivers of rain running off their crumpled sou'westers.

An idea came into my head.

"Have you got a dinner jacket in that case?" I asked.

"Yes, of course I have," he said.

CHAPTER TWO

CLOSE-HAULED to a fine north-westerly breeze we said goodbye to the shores of England early in July, gave Ushant a berth of thirty miles, nearly missed Spain by a gross navigational error, flew down the coast with a strong fair wind and, off the entrance to Camarinas, gybed to make into the bay.

There was a sudden crack up aloft. "Oh, look, Peter, look!" wailed Christopher. "There's something wrong."

There was indeed. The gaff had broken off at the gooseneck and Anne and I clawed down the sail.

Christopher stopped biting his nails. "If that had happened outside," he said, "I suppose we'd have had it."

"Not at all," said Anne equably, "you would have mended it."

We had come this way before when coming to Barbados in 1949. Then we had sailed through the West Indies by way of Bermuda. This time we planned to revisit English Harbour in Antigua before going through the Panama Canal and for this reason we didn't linger on the Spanish coast.

Our last port of call in Spain was Bayona. We had not meant to stay there for more than a night, but Anne and Christopher were ashore shopping when a Spaniard, in a rich Scottish accent, asked whether he could help with a little interpreting.

Miguel became our friend. He showed us where to eat oysters by the hour instead of by the dozen, he took us up a mountain to the remains of a pre-Roman village, the foundations of each little round dwelling still standing with a place for the pole to keep up the thatched roof, and to a restaurant overlooking the Minho which divides Spain from Portugal.

Over the very river above which we were now sitting he had, during the war, helped to smuggle Allied airmen until a friend at the Foreign Office warned him that he had been discovered and unless he left the country within forty-eight hours he would most certainly be put in prison.

His wedding was in two days' time. "But," said Miguel, pointing down the hill to an inconspicuous barn, "I spent a very pleasant honeymoon, waiting for a moonless night."

His escape to England was uneventful, and as he was a doctor of some note in his own country he was given a post at a famous London hospital. After the war he returned to Spain and became the leading specialist in his own line.

One day an influential acquaintance of his asked him to take a young man on as his assistant. A year or two later this young man told Miguel that he was engaged to be married.

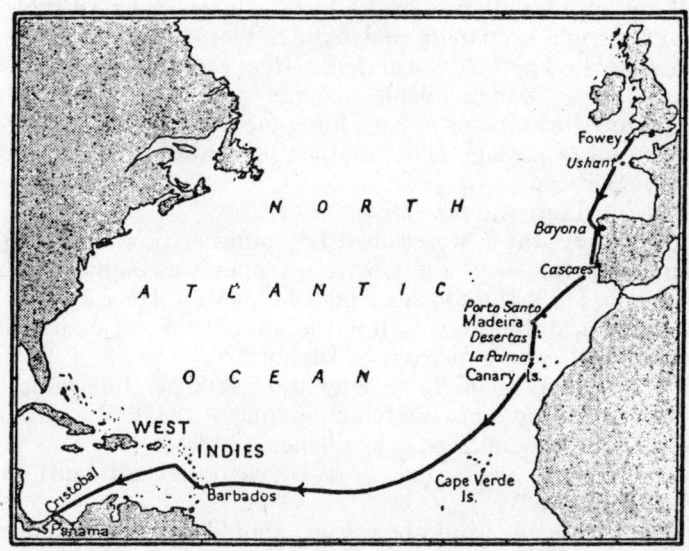

Fowey to Panama

"Splendid," said Miguel. "Who are you marrying?" The young man mentioned an illustrious name.

"I do indeed congratulate you. I suppose, now that your work will be more political than medical, you will be giving up your appointment here?"

The young man smiled at him thinly. "I shall be giving up my post," he agreed. "I have been given yours."

Cascaes, 320 miles to the south, lies at the entrance to the Tagus. We ghosted in, the genoa and topsail doing all the work. A voice, made raucous by the loud hailer, called, "Would the English boat with the red sails now entering the harbour please keep outside the racing marks?"

That is the trouble with Portugal. The fishermen and the peasants are much like their Spanish neighbours, a little more dour, perhaps, and much more ironic; but this place, for all its Moorish look, the hills of Sintra and the rakish trawlers with their high, flared bows, might almost as well be Cowes.

Among the fleet of chromium-plated yachts, tucked away in a

quiet corner, were three craft of a different sort. The *Viking*, a double-ended Swedish boat, was a bermudian ketch. Sten and Brita Homdahl, blond and strong, had made their small cabin themselves. It smelt of pine woods, and above the stove was a painting of a little house in the forest, all covered with snow. I hoped it would keep them cool in the tropics.

Behind the *Viking* was *Wanderer III*, as English as her crew, so workmanlike, so dependable that the success of their voyage round the world was as much a foregone conclusion (to us if not to them) as a passage from Southampton to Cherbourg in the *Queen Mary*.

The third ship was the *Harry*.

The *Harry* was a Morecambe Bay prawner now owned by a Dutchman who, with a fellow countryman, was bound for San Francisco. He had a touching faith in his ship. He said, "She is much older and more versed in the ways of the sea than I. She can find her own way across the Atlantic."

I agreed that she might be older and even wiser, but was it fair to ask her to find an island ten miles long, three thousand miles away, without so much as an astrolabe?

"Ah," replied her skipper, "I may have no sextant, but I have four compasses."

Now in case any would-be voyager should think this a sensible thing to do, I will tell you what happened. They set out from one of the Canary Islands bound for Barbados but the *Harry* ran ashore on a beach in Brazil!

Viking, *Wanderer III* and ourselves were bound for the Madeiras and La Palma but I had met a man in Funchal who had been to the Salvages, a deserted group of rocks only visited by fishermen.

He said, "They're more like the Galapagos than anything this side of the Pacific." He added, "Don't run on a reef, there's no water."

A hundred miles from anywhere! The web was spun.

On the way we ran into a patch of bad weather and for the first time the third reef was tucked into the mainsail.

There was a bit of a sea running and the wind was dead astern. Christopher took over from Anne at ten o'clock that night, and I pottered about the deck inspecting gear and watching Christopher's face peering anxiously into the binnacle and eyeing the lifting boom.

"All right?" I asked.

"Y-es, I think so."

I went below and slept with one ear open.

At the change of watch he called me. The look of strain had gone.

"Twenty miles on the log," he said. "Jolly good show!"

Porto Santo and Madeira, a night in the Ilhas Desertas: the ship sailed south....

An island of laval rock mounting to a peak, a hollow bay with steep sides like a cavern, seas breaking green over a shelf, cries of shearwaters, thin and weak, shouts of wild-looking men, a longboat rolling in the swell; Anne's cry, "Less than three fathoms," paying out the chain till the anchor held, that is what entering the Ensenda de Cangarras on Selvagem Grande was like, just as darkness fell.

"A tierra...!" shouted the wild men. We obeyed.

Thick Porto Santo vowels echoing round the walls, barrels on the rocks, the hoarse commands of Paulo de Caries (a Rudolf Valentino, bearded and in rags), the stink of fish, the cauldron of soup bubbling on the brazier, flares lighting up the caves where men lived among the rats.

This was their last night here. Their water catchment was empty, the last shearwaters were being rammed into the last barrels, the long staves with their barbs for hooking the birds our of their holes were being stacked in the caves, and by this time tomorrow the island would no longer ring to the cries of men for many months to come.

Loaded down with three eggs, a present from their meagre store, the back end of a tunny fish and twelve salted shearwaters, none of which we dared to refuse, we departed. For two nights we ate those birds . . . a cross between a duck and a sardine and far, far richer than either. I was on watch. Ahead were lights that were half-way up a mountain on La Palma thirty miles away. There were six shearwaters left. Making sure that Anne was sound asleep, I dropped them overboard.

La Palma stands like a sentry looking over the Atlantic Ocean, and, like all sentries, it seems very much alone. Its people are tough and independent, poor and proud. A thousand feet above the little town is a church built in 1704. Around the walls are silver ships presented by princely merchants in thanksgiving to God for saving their lives, lanterns of ship-wrecked vessels, paintings of heroic deeds at sea. We look down over terraces of vineyards, orange trees with round, bright fruit and in the distance Pico de Tenerife rises out of the sea like a benevolent Mount Everest.

We get to know the shape of that mountain well for we are in sight of it for three days after leaving Santa Cruz de La Palma. From La Palma to Barbados is a distance of two thousand seven hundred miles. We pick up the Trades in 24°N. and sail within a hundred miles of the Cape Verdes.

A ship is a little world. Ours contains three people. Out of the hatch, overheated by oven and tropic sun bursts the mate with a sudden cry, "The damn' bread won't rise," and rushes to sit on the foredeck under the swelling sails.

Christopher pokes out a hopeful head, "Should my intercept be nearer the sun, or farther away?", sighs, and goes back to his plotting.

Washing your face in an inch of water, feeling the salt in your flying hair, the warmth of the sun through an ancient shirt, turning out in the night to silence a tin that rolls with the rolling ship, seeing the same faces from four feet across the cabin sole day after day, week after week, if these things don't seem worth while, give up your dream of the southern seas and take Mr Weston Martyr's advice and catch the nine-fifteen.

The ship sails on under her Trade Wind rig. The swoop of the frigate bird, the flash of dolphin, the scatter of flying-fish, taking the ship's position, comparing the last day's run, the smell of coffee brewing, landfall after twenty-eight days.

Barbados lies ahead. We round Needham Point and the day and the wind go out like a light. *Moonraker* pauses reluctant to leave the peace of the ocean for the worries of the land. A boat puts out from the bay.

Breathless as if he had been rowing a race, Sten clutches our bulwarks: "How many days? How many days? Today we too come in."

The customs has come and gone, our friend has rowed back to his ship. Christopher has already turned in and Anne is making our bed. The green light of a schooner stealing into the bay, the ragged sail of a fishing boat caught in the gleam of the riding light,

> Up in the mornin', out on the job,
> Work like the devil fo' me pay,
> While tha' lucky ol' sun has nothin' to do
> But roam about heav'n all day.

The West Indies—again.
Christopher has jaundice in Barbados, I at English Harbour.

I fret over the weeks of delay, and it is not until towards the end of January that we set sail for the Panama Canal. We take a slight risk letting her sail herself at night in these waters. I see a steamer alter course having seen our sails in the moonlight. I sleep better for this.

It is a curious thing that each of us goes up at least twice every night, and yet none of us meet: a subconscious watch-keeping, or a deep-rooted instinct for self-preservation.

The winter Trade Winds blew freshly, the spinnakers strained at their poles like greyhounds on the leash, but I was desperately weary and very glad when we sighted the light on Isola Grande at ten o'clock one night. The aerial beacons, the loom of lights contrasted strangely with the savage jungle half seen beneath the moon.

Relaxed and pleased as I always am when the ship swings to her anchor, I found that a busy day lay in front of us. Being measured for the canal, forms, questions, answers and a long row to the Port Captain's Office without delay. A pleasant young man, the Measurer, said, "We'll give you a pluck in there."

"It'll cost 'em seven bucks," growled his chief.

We rowed.

The Zone at Cristobal is a narrow strip of land running along the waterside between it and the Panama Railway. In it are the offices, clubs, commissaries and houses belonging to the Company. The houses are mostly two-storied frame buildings all very much alike with only a lick of paint and the termites holding hands to keep them up. On the other side of the railway lies the Panamanian town of Colon, a place of mean streets, of rather ugly houses; an unfortunate town, we felt, because it is too near civilization to drift into the slovenliness which seems its natural bent. A nearness that gives it traffic lights, drugstores and Bay Street where passengers from "cruise ships" buy Guatemala homespuns and Hindu curios.

But if, after a little while in the Zone, you get tired of seeing too many large and open-hearted men, so alike that you have to look twice to recognize your friends, too many well-turned-out women wearing the same sort of clothes; shoes and lipstick, all tanned to the same shade of brown, their shapely heads shown to the best advantage by the newest style of hair-cut, then cross the line and rest the eye upon a motley scene of many colours, blacks, whites and yellows, some fat, some thin, some with slanting eyes, others with eyes that sparkle with life, faces creased with laughter, faces sullen, faces kind and faces cruel; but different, as different one from the other as their cousins across the railway are alike.

The Yacht Club is a ramshackle looking place with a restaurant, hot and cold showers and a bar which is rarely empty. Scattered around are various sheds, a patch of grass where sails can be laid out to dry, a slip for vessels drawing six feet or less and a large open building in which members build their own boats.

Outside is a notice which reads:

This space is reserved for Naval Architects and their critics.

A casual "Hi-ya" or "Hallo" may come your way; then someone comes along and looks at your boat and steps aboard for a drink. Very soon he is telling you that he, too, is going to the South Sea Islands, only he came in a year ago meaning to stay a week. But the Zone is short of men, the pay is good and his pal landed a job before the week was up and as he couldn't go on alone he got a job too. Then he met a girl and the months slipped by and the worm got into his ship. Presently he takes you along and shows you what had once been a live and sentient thing, a ship of grace and beauty with a few bits of running gear hanging from her masts and that dusty look that ships, like women, get when they are no longer cared for.

You walk back with him to your own ship more determined than ever not to let her stay here too long. He puts his hand on your shoulder, for by now you are on intimate terms, and says, "Say, Peter, you don't want a crew, do you? It's time I got out of this joint."

You explain that you haven't got room for a fourth, and then you realize he never thought for one moment you would. It was a gesture . . . and he strolls back to the Club and goes into the bar for a whisky.

After a few days the place starts to grow on you. People help you to store up the ship, they drive you around and it is pleasant, after the drenching heat of the day, to sit on the Club veranda in the cool of the evening.

Someone says to Anne. "You can't go next week; we have friends coming in from Nassau, and I want you to meet with them."

And you say to yourself. "Why not do some of the work which has been so long postponed and stay here a little longer."

On just such an evening a big man with a square head and fleshy face came over to our table. Pointing to *Moonraker* he barked, "That yours?" We admitted it. He held out a large and flabby hand; "Name's Sam Brown, Assistant Port Captin. . . . Glad to know you, folks, and if there's anything I can do, I'm your man." We thanked him and I explained our lack of power and the awkwardness of our nine-foot bowsprit.

"For goodness sakes," he roared. "We'll have to tow you through behind a banana-boat. Against the rules, but rules don't matter to me. I'm retiring this year." Then he added, "What day d'you go through?"

"On Thursday!" I cried, at random.

The walls of the Gatun locks frowned down upon us from an immense height. We looked to our lines and fenders. The gates shut, and in a moment the whole placid surface of the water became a boiling cauldron. *Moonraker* surged and heeled and groaned but the *Real* (our banana-boat) took all the knocks against the wall and we came up, unscathed. Three times this happened, and then from a great height we looked our last upon the Atlantic and set off, with Captain Wilder, our pilot, across Gatun Lake.

Across wide spaces of rain-swept water, through narrow, swampy cuts, close to islands where alligators swam, the *Real's* diesel thumped its monotonous note. We slowed through the Gaillard Cut where, if she gets too close, the muddy bank may slew a big ship's stern round (and ruin the pilot); we were lowered a little at Pedro Miguel, crossed the Miraflores Lake to enter the locks which dropped us down to the sea. There is not much that is cheap left in the world of today but our transit, tow, pilot (paid £3,000 a year) and two long stalks of bananas, a present from the skipper of the banana-boat, cost five dollars and fifty cents.

At the watershed the rain had ceased and now, as the last great gates opened we saw for the first time the Pacific, shimmering like an inland lake in the afternoon sun.

CHAPTER THREE

AMERICAN yachtsmen have a word for the Pacific; they call it "The Mean Sea". Islands disappear, new ones arise, tidal waves, tornadoes and waterspouts range across its waters like wolves over the Siberian plains. It is a vast sea, covering a third of the world and from here to the Marquesas, the first of the South Sea Islands, is not much more than half-way. Between Panama and the Marquesas are the Galapagos (Spanish for freshwater tortoise), islands that have been surrounded by mystery and on which strange things happen. They belong to Ecuador and we had been told that it would take more dollars and more time to get a visa than we could willingly spare.

"Don't go there without permission," said Captain Baverstock. "Yachts have been impounded and some have never been seen again."

The battle for our visa began next morning. I was told to be at the Consulate at ten o'clock. After waiting several hours I met the Consul. He was a short, dapper little man with an olive skin, faintly tinged with yellow. His English was much on a level with my Spanish but I understood I could have a visa for thirty dollars.

"How long will it take?"

"A month, perhaps."

I shook my head. The Consul said, "If you pay me fifteen dollars I send a cable to Quito."

"How long will that take?"

He shrugged his shoulders, "A week, perhaps."

We parted with expressions of mutual esteem.

That evening, two things happened. We met Señora de Sosa who had a friend in the Foreign Office, and we met Lee and Ann Gregg of the ketch *Novia*, bound for the Galapagos. So far, Lee said, his visa had cost him sixty dollars. He had applied for it three weeks ago, paid the fifteen dollars for the cable to Quito, but after a fortnight there was still no visa. So he had rung up the State Department in Washington, paid for them to ring up Quito and now, after paying another fifteen dollars to the Consul, he was expecting his visa on Thursday, the day before he sailed.

I went to the appointment with the friend in the Foreign Office, and after the week-end lull I returned to the Consul. He was more affable. A cable had been sent to Quito, my visa would cost me twenty dollars and no extras.

I was profuse in my thanks.

"When shall I get the visa?" I asked.

He shrugged his shoulders, "Perhaps Thursday, but if not I regret I am called away for a week."

The day before we left the anchorage frizzled under a burning heat, unrelieved by the usual Trade Wind. Inside air-conditioned offices (where I spent a good part of the day) it was pleasant enough, but as I sallied forth the heat hit the back of my neck like a sledgehammer and I arrived back on board peevish and thirsty.

There was no sign of tea. In a scattered heap on either bunk were seventy pounds of flour, cartons of cigarettes, cereals, wire trace, fish hooks and copper nails, while Christopher was cutting up a yard of bacon and Anne was stowing a mountain of fruit into boxes that I feared would be stowed on the cabin floor. The sweat dripping from their faces made me thirstier than ever, but it occurred to me that this was the moment to make myself as inconspicuous as possible. Delicately, like Agag, I abstracted a ball of marline from under a pile of toilet rolls and disappeared up the mast to reseize a thimble.

We dined that night with Señora de Sosa. We sat in a courtyard, open to the stars, in which palm trees and tropical plants in tubs and green things hung down from a balcony above. The house, nearly three hundred years old, stood four square about the courtyard, and the thickness of the stone of which it was built kept out the noise and stress of the city. We dined on Panamanian food at a Spanish hour and drank a Chilean wine. Towards the end of the meal one of the guests, the Chief of the Canal Personnel, said he thought that in ten years many of the executive posts in the canal would be held by Panamanians.

Señora de Sosa, who had been talking to me about Ecuador, broke off to flash a smile at him.

"Dear John," she said. "In ten years' time, there won't be any of you left at all."

Next morning I went ashore to ring up the Ecuadorian Consulate. At the head of the long concrete pier I met Ann Gregg of the *Novia* sitting on a couple of wooden cases.

"Has Lee got his visa?" I asked.

She nodded. Ann is a dark, neat little person with, I should have said, some Spanish in her blood, but this morning her usually animated face looked vexed and worried.

Suddenly she burst into tears.

"I don't care who knows it . . . I'm just plain scared of this goddam ocean, and if Lee doesn't come soon he'll find me gone."

I knew so well how she felt, and I remembered having to comfort Anne for hours, only that was a long time ago. So I told her this, and how, one evening when I was rowing the late Admiral Goldsmith (surely one of our most joyous small-boat voyagers) back to his ship in Dartmouth, he suddenly leant towards me and in a stage whisper that must have carried miles:

"I say, old boy," he said, "d'you ever get frightened when you put to sea?"

"Every time, sir," I said.

"So do I, old boy—so do I!"

I saw Lee put off from his ship and when it no longer looked as if Ann would run away, I went about my telephoning.

There was, of course, no visa.

I rang Señora de Sosa to thank her for our delightful evening.

"Did you get your visa?"

I told her we had not.

"You are going without?"

There was, although I may have been mistaken, a challenge in her voice and I, having almost made up my mind to miss the islands out, replied, "Of course."

When I got back to the ship she was ready for sea. The topsail had been bent on to the yard, and I noticed that she was lower in the water than she had ever been before. The only thing my crew had left for me to do was to sort the charts, and in case I should forget this they had placed them in a pile, with Chart No. 786 on top. This chart, from Cabo Corrientes to Cape Horn, displays a largish slice of the world. In the upper half is the great bight betwen Cabo Corrientes in Mexico to Punta Ajuta in Ecuador (a distance of 2,160 miles) at the head of which lies the Gulf of Panama looking, on this small scale, like an off-shore anchorage. The sea enclosed within this bight is notorious for its calms.

As I looked at this I though of the Fisks whom we had met on our voyage to the West Indies. Now Pat, when I last saw him, had every intention of following the golden rule (for sailing ships) of making south to the Equator before sailing west to the Galapagos. But I think the people here, unused to English boats that rely on sail instead of power, must have persuaded him (as they tried to persuade me) to make straight to the islands. To give himself a greater range Pat lashed two extra drums of petrol on deck.

The Fisks carried a moderate wind out of the Gulf, and for one more day they were able to sail. Then it fell calm. Day followed day without a catspaw of wind to ruffle the surface of this silent sea and even the swell went down.

Pat motored on until, with his drums of petrol empty and his tank almost dry he had to stop his engine. The ship, like that of the ancient mariner, lay motionless on the painted ocean. The Humboldt current, welling up from the stormy wastes around the Horn, began to carry them north-westwards of the islands, and light airs pushed them slowly and inexorably into the counter-equatorial current which, clasping the ample *Debonair* in a fast embrace, took her backwards towards the American continent from which, with so much labour, she had just come.

While the children played with chalks on the cabin floor Pat and Maureen scraped and varnished to prevent themselves thinking of the future. They rationed water, but as Maureen said, it was difficult to tell children of four and six, when they were thirsty, that they must not drink.

For fourteen days they drifted backwards. Then Providence, not for the first time, intervened and as if to emphasize its bounty, sent them a black squall from the north-east in the middle of the night, almost dismasting them! Slowly, for other squalls followed, they worked their way southwards and, thanking God, they picked up the South-East Trades, driving their ship across three thousand miles of ocean to race their rapidly diminishing water supply. By the time they sighted the mountains of Hiva Oa in the Marquesas, one tank only held two gallons.

Remembering this, I saw that in the broad sea between the mainland and the Galapagos there was only a lane, a relatively narrow one, down which a sailor could steer his ship. If he strayed to the left he would run into the current coming up from the south, if to the right the same fate that overtook Pat might overtake him. Three hundred miles off the coast of Ecuador lay the islet of Malpelo standing like a signpost in the middle of the lane. For that island I should have to steer.

With Pat's story and that of the sailing ship that went round and round in the middle of the Gulf until her planking rotted and she fell apart, we sailed out into this strange sea, and before night was upon us it blew like smoke! That, of course, is a relative term, but it blew hard enough for me to take the topsail down, for Anne to mutter at me for not putting a reef in our brand new light-weight mainsail, and for the boom guy to part in the middle of the night causing her to gybe all standing and carry away the after runner cleat.

Christopher and I, arriving simultaneously on deck, disentangled Anne from the mainsheet which had nearly carried her

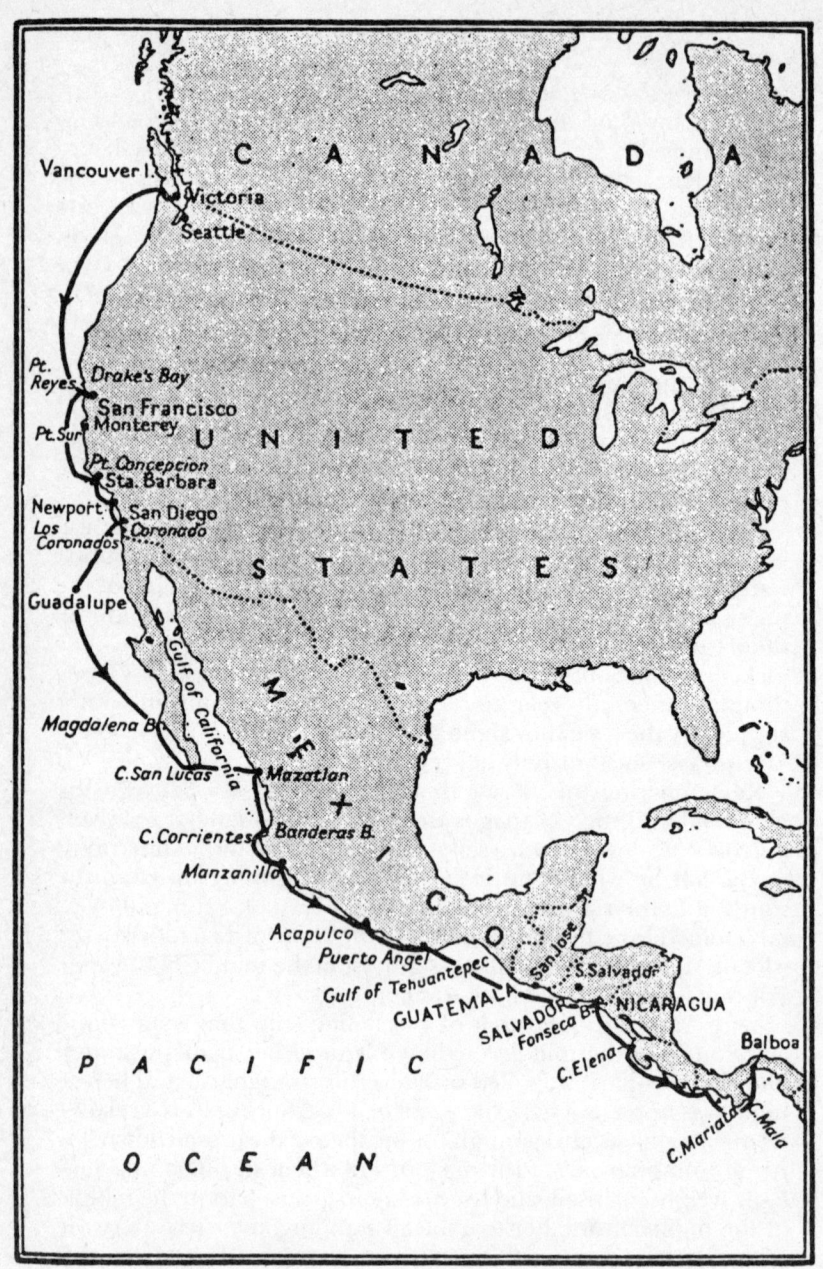

British Columbia to Panama

overboard, hove-to and pulled down that reef. By noon we had sailed right out of the Gulf, a hundred and twenty miles in twenty hours.

On the morning we sighted Malpelo we were virtually becalmed. This lonely rock, covered with bird droppings and without a vestige of scrub on its rounded sides, looked very much like a sketch that Anne made of it; the head between the paws, the arched back, the tail (a group of rocks) . . . Pluto, to the life.

As the short twilight faded into night the air was filled with the beat of wings and a thousand birds flew in low above the water to their roost, and at that moment the gurgle round the stem, the creaking of the blocks as they took the strain and the curving of the sails proclaimed a breeze. That breeze became our friend; it rose and fell, backed and veered, but not for a moment did it leave us. Each night the Pole Star crept lower in the sky, the Southern Cross rose higher, and then one morning we breakfasted in mid-winter and lunched in summer. That night the Plough was upside down. We had crossed the line.

But we were anything but idle. Anne wrote, "Peter and Christopher spend most of the day sail changing", and "I was hot and sticky on watch but there was no peace for me as I had to gybe three times. There is so little wind I would haul in the sails and let us sleep but Peter says no—"

A few nights later, in a different mood, she wrote, "the moon is up, catching a gleam from the varnish of the boom, playing chequers on sails and spars, a night of tropic beauty. As I see it, we are in the late afternoon of life. It has been a long morning. In the cool hours, the growing up, the studying, the fun of being young and keen and gay; then, as the sun rose we settled down to work, to build a practice and to watch it grow. In the afternoon we set off to sail the waters of the world and see what we had been missing, shut up in our suburb. All the hours are good if we do not grow too tired, too soon."

At dawn on the eleventh morning out from Panama we came out of a rain squall to see a green island of middle height fine on the port bow. The island is uninhabited, although two wireless masts, relics of the American station built there during the war, make us hesitate for a moment before anchoring in Gardner Bay on Hood Island. It is covered with a thick green scrub and cactus from which grows a yellowish sort of fruit. Up the coral beach the sea rushes in long fan-shaped curves, and in the cool green water, clear as crystal, are the bronze shapes of sharks. The sea is alive with them, and we nose our pram into the water gingerly. They take no notice and, gaining courage, we row off to the beach, but I am *very* careful to choose the right wave to carry us in; nor do we waste any time in dragging the pram up the fine white sand. The island has been silent, but now the air is filled with the barking sea-lions (oddly human in this deserted place), and black heads come swimming towards us. They land, bark genially, rub themselves in the sand and bathe in the surf. We bathe too but keep a wary eye open for sharks.

There is, we think, no water on this island. A flightless cormorant with a red bill follows Anne about like a tiny dog, pelicans swoop into the water after fish, red crabs spreadeagle themselves on black rocks, and a flock of black iguanas, under the charge of a large green one hurry away at our approach. The green one turns on us balefully. His scaly back and rudimentary spines suggest a resemblance to a prehistoric monster.

Floreana, thirty-seven miles to the west of Hood Island, is bigger and higher, having a mountain, an exstinct volcano, of seventeen hundred feet. After the first war the Wittmers and the Ritters came out from Germany to settle here, the Ritters having first had all their teeth extracted and one pair of false teeth made out of steel which they wore on alternate days. Both the farms were in a valley on the west side of the island, they grew fruit, coffee beans and vegetables, and they never ran short of meat, for wild cattle roamed the island, left from some previous occupation.

Into this seemingly idyllic existence came the Baroness and her lovers and all the passions of a Grand Guignol unfolded on this remote island. One day this South Sea bubble burst; Ritter was found murdered, the Baroness escaped with some of her lovers in a boat which was eventually found on a neighbouring island. Their bodies were never identified.

It was off the north coast of this island that we found ourselves at dawn. A breeze, a gift of the early morning, hurried us along past age-old cliffs, grey and black, past Onslow Island whose centre had fallen in to make a small lagoon and around whose perimeter cacti stood like skeletons. We stood in to Post Office Bay.

No longer do outward bound sailing ships put in to post letters in the barrel on the beach for other ships home from the whaling grounds to take back to the mainland, but less than a year ago a yacht came in for a day on passage from Holland to Tahiti. She had as crew a Dutchman, a Belgian and a German and her master, also Dutch, had the reputation of being a driver of men.

Already Lamberty had had trouble with the German and the Belgian, and against his better judgment he put in so that these two could pay a visit to the Wittmers.

He said, "If you are not back by sunset, I sail without you."

The two men walked up to the Wittmers' farm, five miles and a thousand feet up, found the Wittmers out, removed some of their possessions (as souvenirs, they said) and returned to Post Office Bay. On the beach was a bundle containing their clothes and papers, but the ship had gone! They wrote letters in four languages begging the next ship to sail round to Black Beach and rescue them, put them into the barrel and started off on the long trail up to the farm only to meet the outraged Wittmers coming down.

We found the barrel on its side in a clearing behind the beach; empty. On the rotting post were nailed boards with the names of ships, the most recent being *Tzu Hang*, to which we added *Moonraker*, posted three letters in the box with money for stamps (all arrived a few months later) and rowed back to the ship. The only sound was the braying of wild donkeys.

There were soldiers, we had been told, at Black Beach, in the charge of a sergeant. I was unwilling to risk any chance of having the ship impounded; Anne said it was ridiculous to suppose they wouldn't let us call in for water, even if they didn't allow us to land, and Christopher backed her up, so we bearded Black Beach.

After mistaking a rock for a man-o'-war (so jittery was this Gilbertian crew), we arrived to find the soldiers had gone, the wireless station had not functioned for two years, and the Port Captain most amiable as long as we stayed only for a short time. We had missed the Government boat by two days!

It so happened that the Wittmer family were down at the beach in their little two-storied house they had built in three days from wood brought over from Seymour Island (ex-U.S.A. base) by Irving Johnson in the brigantine *Yankee*. Of the four Frau Wittmer was the only one who could speak English. They let us fill up our tanks from their water catchment, gave us bananas and pineapples; we had supper with them and they accepted the small things we had brought them most graciously. It was so like calling on someone in a distant suburb, an event of so little importance in their lives, that it made me realize how completely self-contained you become if you live in a place where it takes a year and a day for a book to come from London by air mail.

We were just turning in that night when I thought I heard the creak of an oar very close to the ship. A bearded figure rose as if from the surface of the water, so loaded down was the dory in which he and his companion stood. In a voice so soft that it might have sprung from the Hebrides, he said, "Buenas noches, señor, ¿Quiere estas naranjas?"

While Christopher and I heaved three sacks, made of hide and full of firm green fruit, on to the deck, they and Anne settled down in an unhurried, tribal way to barter. Eleazer Cruz had bought the Ritters' farm which, being lower, produces fruit earlier than the Wittmers'. He had learned that a ship had come in from the mainland and needed oranges, so he picked all he could, loaded them on to a mule and had come down to look for the ship. When he saw *Moonraker* he almost turned back again, for how could such a cockleshell need so much fruit? When Anne explained that we should be at sea for a month he became most anxious. He was a man of the mountains and the valleys, he said, but he hoped, and I could see he thought it almost too much to ask, that God would watch over us. In the meantime there were things he would like to have for his children in exchange.

Anne, explaining carefully that in such a small boat our resources were very limited, offered him two cartons of cigarettes, three tins of porridge (a great delicacy this) and, best of all, a jar of bacon fat that our visitor saw standing in the galley.

The deal was confirmed over a glass of aguardiente and they clambered back into their dory and paddled silently away until their shadows were lost against those of the land.

CHAPTER FOUR

FROM Floreana to Hiva Oa in the Marquesas is 3,180 miles as we sailed it. As Anne saw it, it was thirty-eight days:

1st day. New baked bread from the Wittmers and a hot cooked lobster. Handkerchiefs flutter form the house with the narrow, lidded eyes. The sea before us is a vast heaving field of sparkling blue, the furrows many ships' lengths apart, and it looks as if it had no more land to offer.

2nd day. The little awning is rigged to make a tent for the helmsman. A short square whale sleeps with a little fountain spraying as he breathes. A red moon rises. I hand the Southern Cross in the port ratlines and the Plough upside down on the starboard quarter.

3rd day. The log line entangles in the night so fishing is frowned on. Galapagos tree tomato chopped as a flavouring is scented like juniper.

4th day. A hot ship, a glassy sea. The air is wet.

5th day. Hot, long, windless. The four-days'-old cake has a bloom of mould over it.

6th day. A sea of lumps and hollows. We fall and pound. We are right under the sun, and the sun's angle is 92 and cannot be subtracted from 90. After fruitless thought by us all C. suggests shooting from the east instead of the west. It is then too late.

7th day. Morning comes with a bang! All hands! *Moonraker* tries to push her way *through* the waves. C. is too asleep to tell topsail halyard from spinnaker. The breeze changes its mind a dozen times and we return to the rig we started with until tea-time when a North Sea mist and rain makes me suggest less sail, so Peter sends me below to make a fresh fruit salad and takes the helm till he fills the cockpit, floods the engine room (the porthole wide open) and decides to take in sail. Wet sails, wet crew, wet rugs. Rain. We rig the twins.

8th day. Tumbly seas, rain and squalls. I notice how large Christopher is. He shuts out the light.

9th day. Lustreless; when the after guy parts and the port boom leaps forward Christopher, shaking himself like a shaggy dog in the afternoon sun, wakes and says, "Can I help?" This makes Peter laugh. Little holes appear in the sails.

10th day. The spinnaker boom is lost as no one bothered to lash it on deck when changing to fore and aft rig. We hunt for it from dawn till lunch-time. Wretched day.
11th day. No comment.
12th day. Another reef earing gives. Peter burns his foot against the hot kettle, stubs his toe under the bulwark. He thinks he has broken it. A strand parted in a shroud lanyard. We heave to on the other tack and I hold the light while the others renew the lanyard using the after-runner tackle to bowse it down tight. The wind moans; they are up to their knees in water. The weather is bewitched; as fast as the eye can turn from compass to sky a squall is on us, from the side, the back and even from above. The wind and water hiss; stars are blotted out.
13th day. Fish jump and flying-fish fly. I am weary and lunch is of old biscuit. The sunset is a flood of amber beauty, and we let the ship sail herself all night with the foresail a little backed.
14th day. Sleep was wonderful, the day a delight. Porpoises snort and sharks glitter. Peter fits a new nipple to the Primus and cleans the galley while I bake bread and scone. Christopher renews a line on the gaff and greases the jaws. The potato locker is in his charge and he has not sorted it and half are rotten. I see a dirty ship, neglected gear, greasy topsides, unsorted onions, unwashed clothes and all of us lethargic. I say so. Peter snaps, C. is silent and I sulk.
15th day. The main halyard gives and a new one is rove. Peter sorts the onions and C. say, "Jolly good show." There is a quiet sky but an enormous sun halo. Steering is quiet peace.
16th day. The sun is warm. Christopher cleans the fo'c'sle and splices a new spinnaker sheet. Peter makes a complicated strop so that we can use the topsail yard for a spinnaker boom. There is a new young moon.
17th day. We go back to twins. Half the new rope is rotten with lying in the locker (in spite of airing it in port).
18th day. I darn the little holes in the mainsail and *Moonie* does her best to roll me off. Tonight we are rested; only 1,490 miles to go.
19th day. I feel stiff and sick. Peter wants something different to eat and has lost his pen and a screw from the mirror rolls into the bilge.
20th day. Blue sea and a smoky sky and a white bird hovers. I bake a good loaf at last! It takes 2¾ hours. I think of Liverpool Street Station and the London tube and the blue waves rolling along look good. Chicken soup (special) and pancake tonight.

I go on watch and let Christopher enjoy it hot. Suddenly all hell is let loose. The port boom rises in the air and the spinnaker disappears in the night. It is retrieved. The cringle has gone. Sleep is uneasy as all our ears are waiting.

21st day. A ragged day with water slopping over the decks. We find uncooked pudding (crumble) not unpleasant.

22nd day. The spotlight is knocked over and won't work. Great seas are rolling along but the wind is light. A wisp of smoke or a steamer's bridge would be a welcome sight. My sole contribution to life today was to wash the tea-towel.

23rd day. The world is fresh; dark blue seas marching and a happy rushing sound. The newly-made cake is all right until Peter stands on it. He has a cupful of crumbs and we finish the ginger cake. An odd uneven sea, and one stood on end and poured itself down the open fo'c'sle hatch. Cries of rage below.

24th day. Peter's birthday. It takes an hour to change into fore and aft rig so that I can mend the spinnaker. After chicken, asparagus, chocolate mousse and Martinique wine we leave Peter with Venus and the moon.

25th day. I invent a switch for the binnacle with a cork, two aerial wires and a match. It works. The afternoon sun is before the mast and throws shadows on the rigging. The cabin is quiet but a different set of dishes is rattling.

26th day. Rain, and I am dreaming of hot soup when cold biscuits are thrust through the hatch. Into the peace of the afternoon, a cry . . . the boom and sail flail and our port spinnaker is gone. The waves to port are dashed flat and the tops blown. P. and C. retrieve the ruins and I go below to make scones. Weevils in the rice.

27th day. Wet and squally and Christopher glancing often behind him after yesterday's catastrophe. I examine the ravished spinnaker and with Peter's help cut a strip of new canvas 3½ inches wide and 125 inches long. Reefed the main after dinner.

28th day. Sewing spinnaker. The others take my watches and make drop scones for tea.

29th day. Christopher reports the loss of the log spinner, the last. No one says very much.

30th day. While I am sitting on the foredeck mending the spinnaker Peter comes up to make a strop. He half lowers the sail in my face and it takes off my hat. I protest. It flops off my only pair of glasses into the sea. Peter is so sorry that he drops my last marline spike overboard. I am very full of rage and quite sad.

31st day. The gaff jaws give where they were welded in

Camarinas. We sail under trysail and one spinnaker and later add the genoa. Peter chisels at the gaff all day to make it fit an old boom fitting. Christopher, helping him, talks about drinking port at Barreiro and makes P. cross. The work is heavy but he fits the metal on and screws it in. C. files off the nut holding the bolt. Not having caught a fish since leaving England we had to catch one today. It was a shark. We haul it alongside and lasso its tail and Christopher shoots it. It tastes like cotton wool.

32nd day. The fitting doesn't work. Experiments with reversed bolts and filed pins. Christopher pours water over himself and his mouth is too dry to eat.

33rd day. As the sky lightens we turned out. I left my bunk ready for my promised return but it stayed till night. The sail was hoisted; Peter, aloft, watched it. Trouble. . . . Brass screws were replaced by old steel ones. Supports are filed to fit. I clean the galley and paintwork, take the helm for trial and error of sail setting, carry up grape juice and a late lunch. By evening we are under one reefed main, topsail and spinnaker. Peter is queer and trembly and I fall into a drugged sleep. Waking is unpleasant but my night watch is cool and tranquil. An empty tin glittered for an hour in our wake.

34th day. The spinnaker is now sewn and ready for an emergency setting. Thunder and lightning in the night.

35th day. Peter comes up in the night, the light gone from his eyes. "A coral patch," he mutters; then he wakes and goes back to bed.

36th day. The breeze is unhappy, trying to pry under the sail and tossing the topsail like a blown leaf. My patch in the old spinnaker is giving where the forestay rubs. Peter is reading *The Chinese Room* but he puts the cringle in the head of my spinnaker and sets it. I mend the other. My eyes are fuzzy with sewing, the dim compass and the sea.

37th day. The moon rose behind a bank of floating figures. All the clouds today turn to islands, but it is Christopher who sees Fatu Hiva first and we turn towards it, not sure which it is until P.'s noon sight tells us the way to Hiva Oa. I wash my hair and itch less. Christopher shaves and smells of scented soap.

38th day. I wake to the sound of Christopher's voice offering me porridge and go up on deck. The whole beauty of the island bursts upon me in glistening green; coconut palms on the shore, steep, furrowed slopes rising to the peak of a great mountain in a wispy nest of cloud. Waves pound on the rocks, white streaks turn into waterfalls, Hanake Island stands like a silhouette in the sunlight, the white and red of the little light structure peeps through the trees and out of the bay comes a schooner with men, bananas and copra. A man in a white helmet raises his hand in greeting.

Under Black point and into Taa Huku bay we sailed with a dying breeze. A horseman, bronzed, with his hand shading his eyes, gazed down upon us. With a great shout, "Teei-oo" ringing round the steep walls of this narrow place he turned his horse and galloped down the path towards the village.

As the mainsail was lowered our Heath Robinson gaff collapsed and it was with some surprise that we turned to a greeting at our side. A tall blond young man gripped our rail.

"My name," he said, "is Lamberty."

CHAPTER FIVE

INTO the very bay where we now were anchored Lamberty had sailed his converted lifeboat *Kroja* from Holland three years before. He had walked up the shady path, over Black Point and down into Atuona and there he had met Rebecca the chief's daughter. All sense of time and of the safety of the ship seemed to desert him until late that evening a horseman galloped down the road with the news that *Kroja* had dragged on to the beach and was now being pounded by the waves. The whole village turned out to try and save her but it was too late. *Kroja* was a total loss. Lamberty stayed on.

One day a Belgian yacht bound for Hawaii came into Taa Huku bay. Seeing a chance of returning to Holland to find another boat Lamberty rowed out and offered himself as crew.

"Wait for me, Rebecca, for one year," he told her, and sailed.

They put into Caroline Island for water, found none, ran the ship on a coral head, and pumping her watch and watch, sailed on to Christmas Island, six hundred miles away.

Back in Holland, Lamberty found a publisher for the book he had been writing, became master of the *Anna Elizabeth* and set sail to keep his tryst with Rebecca. His long forced passage with an untried crew may well have been the reason for the events in Post Office Bay.

When I first saw Rebecca she was like an untamed gazelle, wary and still but when she smiled it was as sun chasing shadow. They made a handsome pair but a man whose ambition it was to sail round the world non-stop, might, we thought, be a difficult person to follow for a girl with only one sound lung, and almost prostrate with seasickness. They were planning to sail back to Holland, but we wondered what would happen if they got so far and Rebecca could go no farther. I could see that Rebecca, from the way she looked at him, wondered that too.

R. L. Stevenson once said that the view from Black Point was the finest in the world. The sweep of the bay, the Pacific rollers thundering on the curving beach a hundred feet below, the sultry valley, the red roofs peeping through the palm trees, the heavy scented air of an island sleeping off the excesses of its turbulent past; an island now inhabited by a dispirited and listless people, we had been told, forlorn remnant of its savage healthy tribes. But the French have a cure for this which is saving the

Marquesans from the Carib's fate. Mixed blood is producing a stronger race and for the first time the population is on the increase.

At the hospital, small framed buildings in the same compound as the doctor's bungalow and shaded by trees and bougainvillea, Dr Stern never knew when he did his round what patients he was likely to see. Some might have gone home for the day, or have changed places with others who needed a rest. "They are half wild," he said, "and if you were to treat them like Europeans they'd die. We try and make them so happy they'll want to come back." He had been most impressed by the results of streptomycin and thought that the battle against tubercle had been almost won.

Once every six weeks, sometimes twice, the island schooner *Vaitere* (Running Water) sails into the bay. There is mail, a new face or two; there are stores, pigs and wine; and that night no light will shine from Black Point, for there will be no one capable of walking up the path to put a match to it. A benevolent government, which rations wine to the Marquesans at two litres a month, says nothing about not drinking it in one night.

For three weeks we sailed among the islands. *La poste* (three letters) had to be delivered to Ua Pu and the doctor's family were badly in need of vegetables that only grew at Nukuhiva. A three-quarter-inch bolt and stronger plates from poor *Kroja's* remains now held our gaff aloft and we sailed for Hanamanu on the north coast. We arrived at night; a huge buttress of rock dividing the bay in two and standing like a medieval fortress against the sky was our only guide.

If ever I were to be shipwrecked I would pray that it might be at Hanamanu. I could live on bananas big and small, yellow and pink, on coconuts and lemons, breadfruit and taro, all in great profusion and growing wild. There is a trail, now overgrown but still possible to follow, lined by purple flowers and orange blooms like orchids that leads towards the mountains and a great plateau where game runs wild.

In a clearing behind the foreshore lived a handful of copra pickers. When we asked for some drinking nuts they mistook our meaning and offered us spirit distilled from the flower of coconuts. It had a kick that made absinthe seem like water. We had stumbled on an illicit still.

The village of Hakahetau on the island of Ua Pu is some sixty miles to the north-west and has the reputation of being hard to find. The only chart I had was a drawing of its salient features and a lifelike picture of a cave, by the doctor, on the back of an envelope. This cave, he said, was important because by the time you saw it you had passed the village. I saw the cave all right, and then looked back through the glasses and found the village tucked right into the head of a bay within a bay, dwarfed behind by pinnacles of rock which would have made a perfect setting for a story by Poe and illustrated by Rackham.

We dropped anchor on the place marked on the envelope, watched the seas tumbling on the pebble beach and swirling over the peninsula of rock where the doctor had told us to land. Soon a pirogue, manned by a tall Marquesan (the bluer the blood the taller the man) came out to welcome us with bananas and a couple of fish caught that morning. Haki then explained, in excellent French, what we ourselves could see, that it would be wiser if he took us ashore and so avoided *l'ecrasement du canot*. Choosing the largest wave to sweep him up that stony shore he landed us with great skill and directed us to the Valots' house.

Under scattered palm trees, past native huts roofed with pandanus leaves, with coconut matting on the earthen floor for beds, and both ends open to the winds of heaven, at the head of a procession of children, women and men, we ended up at the schoolhouse where the Valots stood to welcome us.

Claude Valot was a pale young man with limpid eyes who had been a chartered accountant, an instructor of parachute troops, a *Directeur de banque de l'Indo-Chine à Tahiti* before renouncing the world, as he put it, to come and teach the French language to the inhabitants of this island, who had had to manage up to now without this inestimable benefit. His house, built of wood and not unlike a suburban bungalow, was neat and trim and very hot, and he and his charming wife showed us over this and the school with as much enthusiasm as their singular detachment allowed.

That night we dined with them. Quantities of raw fish soaked in *citron* and served with coconut cream were followed by sucking-pig, with a hibiscus flower in its ear, roasted whole with baked breadfruit, sweet potatoes, poi and a bottle of Burgundy. The great meal, the wine, the scented night, Claude's slow didactic speech, produced in me a philosophic mood, and I thought what an introvert one would have to be to live contently alone with one's wife and with only books and a gramophone as contact with what we call civilization. To have lived within the boundaries of a great city, to have seen the world at war at your very doorstep, to have made close friends; these things, I thought would prevent me from ever wanting to live in a South Sea island where the talk

The Sea is for Sailing

of fish and coconuts and the daily village life would be the only stimulus to existence. I was full of admiration for the Valots, but I could not envy them.

After dinner Haki came to tell us there was a swell rolling in and that we must not delay. Our host took his paraffin lamp to light the scene, and we walked down to the landing, where a small crowd, not wishing to miss the fun, had collected. Haki got his outrigger away and then paddled round to the rocky peninsula upon which we were standing. Riding a long sea, using his paddle as helm and backing water at the same time, Haki brought his outrigger in, level with our feet. "Jump," he shouted to Anne who did so and the next moment the canoe was five feet down. Christopher and I followed each in turn.

The next day Haki made us a present of a *tiki*. It was of flint and had a long, sharp leading edge. Valot told us that it was a tool used by the natives in the time of Captain Cook. He also told us that Haki had once swum six miles out to sea in rough weather to rescue a man from a sailing canoe. Before we sailed we gave him wire trace, hooks and a lure, and he in turn tried to tell us how to catch fish, but that, we thought, was beyond even the powers of Haki.

A fresh trade wind bore us swiftly over the twenty miles of sea between Ua Pu and Nuku Hiva, and it was noon when we made in between the Sentinels lying guard at each side of Tai O Hae just over a hundred years after Herman Melville so entered in the whaler *Dolly*, and here is how he describes (in *Typee*) the welcome accorded to that tired ship:

We were still some distance from the beach and under slow headway, when we sailed into the midst of these swimming nymphs, and they boarded us at every quarter; many seizing hold of the chain plates and springing into the chains; others, at the peril of being run over by the vessel in her course, catching at the bob-stays, and wreathing their slender forms about the ropes, hung suspended in the air. All of them at length succeeded in getting up the ship's sides, where they clung dripping with the brine, and glowing from the bath, their jet black tresses streaming over their shoulders, and half enveloping their otherwise naked forms. There they hung, sparkling with savage vivacity, laughing gaily at one another, and chattering away with infinite glee. Nor were they idle the while, for each performed the simple offices of the toilet for the other. Their luxuriant locks, wound up and twisted into the smallest possible compass, were freed from the briny element; the whole person carefully dried and from a little round shell that passed from hand to hand, anointed with a fragrant oil; their adornments were completed by passing a few loose folds of white tappa, in a modest cincture, around the waist. Thus arrayed, they no longer hesitated but flung themselves lightly over the bulwarks, and were quickly frollicking about the decks. Many of them went forward, perched upon the head-rails, or running out upon the bowsprit, while others seated themselves upon the taffrail, or reclined at full length upon the boats. What a sight for us sailors!

How avoid so dire a temptation? For who could think of tumbling these artless creatures overboard, when they had swum miles to welcome us?

Where were these maidens now? The port was deserted and a group of Marquesans stood forlornly upon the beach. Black clouds lay heavily on the mountain peaks and there was a feeling of gloom that was in keeping with the rain that now fell in torrents.

Arming ourselves with "insect repellent" against the ravages of the nau-nau fly, so different from the "fragrant oils" of Melville's maidens, we went ashore to find Bob McKitterick, the trader, playing patience with his Marquesan wife. For forty years Bob, from Yorkshire, had lived among these islands. He was getting old. We chatted over a bottle of beer and a plate of mangoes of all the people whom we had read about and he had known; Muhlhauser and Robinson, Temple Utley who had been at St. George's Hospital when I was there and Commander Graham and his daughter Margaret and, more recently, the Crowes, the Hiscocks, and the Greggs of *Novia* who had sailed less than a week ago. Just before that, said Bob, a ketch flying the Swedish flag, had worked her way into the bay and then, to his amazement, had worn ship and sailed out again. Since the time they were nearly cast upon the breakwater at La Palma and Sten had discovered that he couldn't tow her with the outboard, the Homdahls had taken a wary view of landlocked anchorages with feckless puffs of wind inside them.

As soon as we had read our mail, cashed a cheque with Bob, given him some copper nails for his sloop, walked up a brown and yellow stream to look at the bay from above, filled our water-tanks, bought a few tins (at forty per cent over their price at Tahiti for freightage), we said good-bye to him and his family and left him staring out to sea. Bob had a growing conviction, he told us, that soon, in a week or a month, his son, whom he had not heard of for fifteen years would be sailing into this bay.

But if Nuku Hiva had been rather disappointing we were to see a glimpse of the old Marquesas reflected in the new.

Following the *Anna Elizabeth* we sailed into Hanehavane on the island of Tahu Ata; a difficult bit of pilotage without an engine, involving two right-angle bends, a passage forty feet wide and two hundred yards long between two underwater banks of coral and the entrance to the lagoon itself marked by two stakes twenty feet apart with a rock in the middle, over which there might, we hoped, be six feet of water. Inside the lagoon as if to welcome us to the gates of heaven, or to bury us if we failed to make it, stood a priest in a long canoe manned by many dusky paddlers.

We had come for a scrub, for this is the only place, we had been told, where there was a rise and fall of five feet. We put an anchor out astern, ran the ship ashore on the sandy beach and tied her up to a palm tree. *Ffavoa*, the doctor's boat, came tearing in, swaying from side to side as her crew of Marquesan girls crowded the rails first on one side and then the other. The tide receded, each mast took on its own peculiar angle, the girls, their bright pareus streaming away from their bodies, swam, like schools of dolphin, from ship to ship till the copper shone like warming pans. They swarmed aboard sitting, on the bulwarks like Melville's nymphs "sparkling with savage vivacity and chattering with infinite glee".

The sun went down, a fire was lit, the circle grew as each ship's company joined it. The crackling flames, the murmur of voices, a note of song, the dim shape of Hiva Oa across the moonlit water, suddenly made me wonder if life in the South Sea Islands would in fact be as insupportable as I had thought.

CHAPTER SIX

BETWEEN the Marquesas and the Societies lie the Atolls, known to the early Polynesians as the Paumotus, or "Cloud of Islands". To navigators they have another name, the low archipelago, for few of them (none in the north-west sector) are more than a few feet above the water. Some are circles of coral with lagoons inside looking on the chart like wedding-rings, some have lyrical names like Mangareva and one of them, Anaa, whose lagoon is shallow, reflects an image of itself into the sky in a beautiful pale green colour to be seen from a great distance. But in thick weather, the currents unpredictable, the Trade Wind blowing at half a gale, they earn other names, the Isles of Disappointment and the Dangerous Archipelago.

For these islands we set sail, the wind being fair and light. On the first night when I went up to relieve Christopher for his dinner I noticed that the gaff jaws had capsized and were tearing at the copper sheathing round the mast. "Good God!" I cried. "How long has that been going on?"

"Not long, Peter. I noticed it after you'd gone below but I didn't want to disturb your dinner."

Our new bolt was badly bent. Using the Primus as a forge I made half a dozen not altogether successful attempts to straighten it in the vice, then took the helm and gave Christopher the job of setting all sail. He came aft looking as our Benjamin used to after chasing a chicken. "I'm terribly sorry," he said. "I think you'd better try and get someone else at Tahiti."

"Go on down and get your dinner," I growled.

I lit my pipe and my sharpened senses relaxed. The moon flooded the ship with a strong, clear light.

"Thought you said we were a university," groaned the gaff jaws. "Your job is to teach ... to *teach* ... " squeaked the blocks.

I called Christopher.

"If I haven't made a seaman of you by the time we get to British Columbia, you'd better go home. It'll be my fault," I said.

Five days out from Tahuata I took my sight at noon and, on working out my position, found we were only seven miles from Takaroa. There had been nothing to be seen from the deck. Anne clambered up the ratlines.

"Come and see," she called. "It looks like grass growing out of a blue lawn."

All that afternoon we half drifted, half sailed down the western shore of the atoll. It was made up of small islets, some grey, some pink, and in between were gaps where green water lay in pools on the reef. Through these gaps the eye caught glimpses of a lagoon so wide that the distant shore could not be seen. By nightfall we were still a few miles off the pass into the lagoon. Banks of cloud piled high above the island, rain came down in torrents and the wind boxed the compass. It was most difficult to judge our position for one lot of trees looked exactly like another. Anne kept the ship off and on, while Christopher and I, fearing we should want to use the engine to get through the pass, bent double beside its silent body trying, by unsticking both exhaust valves, making a new carbon brush out of Anne's drawing pencil, clearing the jet and doing half a dozen other things whose nature I have now forgotten, to coax it into life.

I straightened my back and looked out to find the moon was up, the sea calm and Anne asleep against the bulwarks. Feeling aggrieved I nearly woke her up, but on second thoughts Christopher and I turned in, the less anxious for knowing that if there was any danger she would immediately wake up.

At dawn Anne was taking out the kinks induced by cramp. On shore a black, forlorn shape resolved itself into the wreck of the *County of Roxburgh*, once a four-masted barque, lying high and dry on the coral sand. Christopher swung the heavy fly-wheel, the engine burst into life and we motored down the coast until huts, bungalows and a tiny church revealed the village, and the swirling outcoming tide, the pass. By keeping within a few feet of a coral bank we edged in inch by inch to come alongside the stone quay within a few feet of *Novia*.

When two voyagers meet again everything must wait until the insatiable curiosity of each for the other's adventures (and the pleasure of recounting his own) is satisfied. With a single mind we leapt aboard *Novia* to sit in her capacious cabin and without pausing for breath we each recounted our adventures. *Novia* had left Panama two hours before we did, had anchored at Gardner Bay twelve hours before we got there and slipped out at dawn, had visited the Wittmers' the day we left and had made a fast passage to Ua Huka in the Marquesas in twenty-seven days before a fine steady Trade; which shows how very different two voyages across the same bit of ocean at the same time of the year can be. This encounter was providential, because Lee had a bronze bolt with which we replaced our bent one, and not until that was done did we step ashore.

The village was almost deserted, only an old, old woman with eyes aglow and a spring in her walk as if she might break into a hula gave us the native greeting, "*Ia ora na*", and a thin black dog which walked slowly out into the lagoon to search on the drying reefs for fish. If times were hard, Lee said, the natives eat the dogs. At slack water he and Christopher went swimming, Lee scanning the depths through his underwater goggles. Suddenly he scrambled out on to the reef.

"Chris!" he shouted. "There's three sharks down there. Let's go scare them away."

Without waiting for a reply, he dived. Christopher, after a fraction of a second, followed him. Knowing how he dreaded these brutes, I thought he must have felt a little like Sir Arthur Grimble when he was offered, with truly Polynesian hospitality, the opportunity to become human bait for octopus.

In the evening a canoe came over from the pearl diving village. Lines were baited and flung into the pass as the flood came in, and within a few minutes a shark was hauled triumphantly ashore. Seven feet of snapping, fighting fish, thrashing in the dust while Tiariki, long-handled knife in hand, waited like a matador for the kill. In a flash he was on to the shark's back, the knife plunged in below the head and out of reach again almost before our eyes had registered the attack.

Tiariki, like most of the young Tahitians, spoke fluent French, and he offered to pilot us in to the lagoon, an offer we gladly accepted for we had been warned by the *Pacific Island Pilot*, Vol. III, that "the eastern end of the pass is barred by a coral reef except for a small channel through its northern end, with a rectangular bend in it, which gives access to the lagoon; the currents in this channel are very strong, local knowledge is essential and it should be used only in the case of necessity."

Under Tiariki's eye *Moonraker* swept safely through at slack water, her decks crowded with men and girls, and towing three pirogues. Distant trees grew larger as we ploughed our way over the mirrored lake, huts appeared, and a procession of young girls dressed in white (for it was Sunday) walked into the Mormon Church from which came the lively, rhythmic singing of Tahitian songs. Tiariki grinned.

"They sing in church," he said, "but they sing of love."

Scarcely had our passengers gone when the gendarme came out.

"Where is your permit to land on this island?" he asked; and when I told him that I had none because I was told that none was necessary, he said, "You are the third yacht in three years to come here without a permit. You must leave at once."

I asked him aboard, gave him a glass of Dubonnet, a little cognac and a large dose of my most persuasive French. We could stay, he told us, till morning.

That night he came again. He said, "I understand you are a doctor of medicine, Monsieur?"

"That is so."

"My little boy has a fever and is sick. Would Monsieur come and see him?"

The gendarme's hut was at the end of what might be called the village street. The glare from an Alladin lamp fell on the plaited walls of coconut fronds, the roof of pandanus leaves and on the pale, worried face of his young wife who had only just come out from Paris to "this savage island". The child was sick, but I was more relieved than I care to admit when I found that I was not faced with an acute appendix. In a day or two, I reassured the mother, her boy would be well again.

By the time I got back to the shore a wind had sprung up. The trees swayed like ships under sail, and now and then a coconut fell with a thud upon the ground. I walked to the windward side and watched the seas marching against the island like Roman cohorts. My face was whipped by spray. It was nothing more than a strong breeze, but I remembered the wreck of the sailing ship on the reef outside. Hurricanes are not common in this part of the Pacific, but it would be a little like living in a great industrial city in the Atomic Age. One would never quite know.

My patient improved and, as you can imagine, I heard no more about permits, but news in such a village does not take long to travel, and when the natives found that he had indeed recovered, they suddenly remembered they had seen no doctor for at least three years and all their half-forgotten pains came back to them with redoubled vigour. A practice was born overnight.

Lee has described this place as a boom village, a sort of Tuamotuan counterpart of the Californian gold rush, for men came here from Manihi and Ahe, from Arutua and Rangiroa for the pearl diving. A good diver might well earn fifteen hundred dollars in a season. A bicycle, an outboard motor for his pirogue, a coloured American shirt and tins of bully beef from Australia bought from the Chinese storekeeper where he banks his pearl shell, are the measure of his wealth. At the end of the season he sells all and has one glorious fling at Carnival time at Tahiti, and two months later works his passage back to his own island, broke.

The day we rowed out to watch the pearl diving, sound carried over the water like an echo in a valley. The cries of the divers extending their lungs before *la plongée*, a yodelling sound and a curious whistling shriek, mingled with the chatter of the boat crews across the placid water. We found Tiariki with his head just above the water, his goggles on and about to dive. A boy of fifteen stood in the stern with a coil of light line at his feet attached to a twenty-five-pound weight which Tiariki held in his hand while making the descent. Another, thicker rope led down into the depths and was attached to the basket into which Tiariki put the shells a hundred and twenty feet below. Through a wooden box with a glass bottom I watched him go. It was like a slow-motion film, smooth and effortless and from the time he started to the time he came back was a few seconds under three minutes.

In Polynesia it is easier to arrive than to depart. At the time we were due to leave canoes put out from the shore, headed by the Chief, who put aboard a sack of oranges and his hat band that Anne had admired for the lovely colouring of the tiny shells from which it was made. An old man whose grandson I had treated for fluid on the lung and arranged (I hope) for transfer to hospital at Tahiti, gave me a basketful of the most delicate cowrie shells. Girls with flowers behind their ears put *leis* round our necks and it was with the greatest difficulty that I persuaded our pilot to start. I knew that the tide would already be racing out through the channel into the pass. Our pilot was very old, could speak no French and, I discovered soon after leaving the village, was almost blind.

We were three-quarters of the way across the lagoon when we overtook a couple in a pirogue. In answer to our pilot's shout the girl jumped aboard. She turned to me, "*Monsieur, le vieux demande que la machine va beaucoup plus vite.*" I went up the ratlines. The current, I could see, was sweeping through the channel at a good ten knots, the water, as black and smooth as tar, poured round the bend, while an eddy, pale green over sand, ran in the reverse direction.

The reef, drying out in places, was at the turn knife-edged, but as long as the ship could be controlled by her helm she should be able to negotiate that turn. Christopher and Anne were standing by the mast, silent.

"We'll try it," I said.

Moonraker gathered way with incredible velocity, heading straight for the reef. Our pilot struggled to put the helm up for the bend, but *Moonie* had the bit between her teeth and to this day Anne swears that our bowsprit overhung that coral. I sprang at the tiller, the old man's belly between it and the bulwarks, squeezing until he grunted for breath. The ship came round. Our pilot's face was running with sweat, not all of which, I thought, was due to exertion. Thank God for a night at sea!

I don't quite know how we ever got into Ahé; the sun was already in the west when I saw that violent tide boiling out of the twenty-five-yard-wide pass, forcing its way far out to sea. But there was a fine beam wind, we set the genoa, the ship heeled far over, and inch by inch we overcame it until we got to the trees where the wind was cut off. We started the engine and were still taken back, we sailed first to one side and then to the other, but that tide had us beaten. And then, without warning, the wind switched, and for about ten minutes blew hard into the pass, and by the time it changed we were through the worst and sailing into the lagoon. But this had taken time and the sun was getting low, nor was there a ghost of a sign of a village. That there was a village at all was only by word of mouth; none was marked on the chart.

Suddenly to the north-west a column of smoke rose into the air. Piloted by two young men each with a flower behind his right ear we came to an anchorage behind a reef. The village gathered on the beach. They led us to a long bench on which we sat drinking green drinking-nuts, the women plaited poinsettias and a white flower like the Tiara Tahiti into leis, they took us by the hand to their fishing pool where bright green parrot-fish swam over the pink coral bottom and to the water hole through which clear water welled. It tasted only slightly brackish.

That night as we sat at dinner we became aware that our ship was full of people. Brown faces looked down upon us, through the hatch and the skylights, and a girl's voice whispered, "*Anne, Anne, du vin, s'il vous plaît!*" Tiahe seized our Madiera *machete*, an instrument with five strings, found two of them broken and sent Horu, his wife, for catgut. As the moon rose over the trees our company started to sing. The rhythm is as bold and accurate as that of a Calypso, but it has a haunting quality that the Calypso lacks. Tiahe, who had had more than one glass of wine, suddenly burst into a savage tune, summoning Horu to dance. Slim, very dark, her mouth turned down at the corners, Horu rose; her face was a mask, her movements sensual, provoking and utterly primitive. Cassimi, Head Man, joined her. Faster and faster grew the tempo of the music, the more savage the movements within the tiny compass of the bridge-deck while the onlookers stamped their feet in unison. And then, as tension mounted to a peak, Tiahe stopped and the dancers sank to the deck.

Four days later they accompanied us to the pass, a large pirogue towing behind; Tiahe, a ruff of poinsettias round his neck, a flower behind his ear, one brown foot on the tiller, his voice in full song, while Cassimi stood by the mast, a bronze statue in a straw hat. He pointed up at our spread of canvas, swelling before the breeze.

"Too much sail," he cried, "so soon will you be gone."

The pass was upon us. We watched them set their sail and wave and wave and finally turn away. I watched Horu stow her trophy in the bottom of the boat. She had carried away my favourite hat.

CHAPTER SEVEN

OUR course through the main chain of atolls lay between Rangiroa and Arutua. Towards this gap, no more than a gate in a hedge of atolls, we ran before a fresh southeasterly breeze. The night was dark and overcast, and with no observations to check the uncertainty of the currents I stood on the upper ratlines trying vainly to enlarge my horizon.

Anne's shout came from the deck, "Copra! Can you smell it?"

I could indeed, and over the port quarter was a thin line of trees and the white of broken water. Ahead the gate lay open and with the lightness of spirit that every navigator feels when the most recent danger lies astern, I worked out a course for Venus Point on Tahiti.

Papeete, the capital of Tahiti, has been called the Paris of the South Seas. The uneven houses along the waterfront, the honking of horns, the ringing of bicycle bells, the smell of garlic. And when it rained, and the water rattled down on the iron roofs of the Chinese restaurants and ran down the yellow gutters, and bent old women stood in doorways, and canned music blared out from lighted windows, it was so like a scene from a Rene Clair film that I half expected Jean Gabin to come strolling down the pavement.

The Americans had their own idea of what life should be like in the South Seas; barbecues on the beach, a vahine or two and all the modern conveniences of the U.S.A. In the background is the island itself, for which Papeete is but a mask. Valleys and mountains as yet unexplored, great peaks each inhabited by its own familiar spirit and unclimbable by man, a lake which legend has it is inhabited by eels with ears; where natives live very much as they did two hundred years ago, and where strange things still happen. There was the Tahitian schoolmaster who went to teach on a Tuamotuan atoll, fell in love with an island girl and had two sons. When the time came for him to return he told his vahine that he must leave her but that the two boys must go with him to Papeete to be taught. Prostrate with grief she swore that she would lay a curse on the children if he left without her, but, deaf to all her entreaties, he sailed. Some months later the elder boy fell sick, was taken to hospital, grew rapidly worse and within a week was dead. No medical evidence for his illness could be found. Then the second boy fell sick, but again the doctors could give no diagnosis or offer any hope. In desperation the schoolmaster took the dying boy in his arms and walked to a far valley where there lived an old woman of whom he had heard in his childhood as an exorciser of evil spirits. He came to her hut at night and implored her help. The old woman laid the boy on a bed of leaves and touched his eyes.

"You are in time," she said, "come for him in seven days. He will be well."

Our lives, for the short time we were there, were closely bound up with the waterfront, our friends among the New Zealand and American yachtsmen, but even here the spell of the island was disturbing, and I remember at a party one night after Ross Norgrove had been singing Maori songs on *White Squall*, he suddenly turned and said, "You don't want to go to British Columbia among all that snow and ice. Come to New Zealand with us." And almost before we knew what we were saying our plans had been changed.

Then in the morning some incident, so small that I have completely forgotten it, changed them back again. Anne was on deck at the time and what I call the "Look" came into her face. I have only seen it twice, but I know better than to challenge it. She said that to change our whole voyage at this stage was ridiculous, that she was doubtful if we could finish the voyage in less than three years, and that this would be adding a fourth, and that it was too long to be "scattered about the world in a boat" and that the crew you knew was better than the crew you didn't and that she for one had no wish "to change horses in midstream". What had threatened to become a tense situation ended in a roar of laughter at this agile mixing of metaphor and rather to our relief our brief madness was over.

One morning I was walking along the quay with the head customs officer. He pointed to a small boat tied to an enormous buoy in the middle of the harbour. She looked a mere toy.

He said, "D'you know where she's come from?"

I shook my head.

"Her last port was Valparaiso and she has come round the Horn from east to west in winter."

M. Bardieu had been a punt-builder on the Seine and had taken seven years to build his sloop (she was nineteen feet on the waterline). He made her as indestructible as it was possible to do with so small a vessel. He could steer from inside the cabin, and there was an almost waterproof cover over most of the cockpit to protect him from the weather.

Marcel Bardieu was a stocky little Frenchman who had a charmingly naïve way of minimizing the obvious dangers of such a voyage. He had had, he said, no intention of rounding the Horn in winter, but he was knocked overboard by the boom when some six hundred miles north of this region and had to spend many weeks in hospital. By the time he came out the summer was over, so what could he do but go on? As he was beating down Lemaire Strait between Staten Island and Tierra del Fuego a gale blew up which, with a nine-knot tide running against it, caused a "confused" sea. His vessel capsized twice in the same morning, and a fifty-pound anchor lashed to the cabin floor broke adrift. (I have seen the mark on the cabin roof) and damaged both the vessel and himself. He carried on, but after rounding Cape Horn the weather became so bad that he ran for one of the fiords where a small vessel can take shelter. Ross was with us at the time and I remember his rugged face suddenly wrinkling into a great grin, "Doc!" he cried, "I guess this guy is made of something different to you and me!" I guess Ross is right.

Among the many fine vessels in Papeete harbour was William Albert Robinson's brigantine. I cherished a very faint hope that we might meet him and we nearly did. A friend of ours had driven us round the island, and on the way home we saw a tall white-haired figure with stooping shoulders and rather protruding lips. Our friend was about to apply his brakes when he changed his mind. "That's Robinson of *Svaap*," he said, "but I can see from his back (Robinson was earnestly contemplating a ditch) that this is not one of his days for being interested in other people."

Complete with our new gaff fitting, loaded down with two months' stores, we sailed from Tahiti on a Monday. The scent of Tiara Tahiti was born on the off-shore breeze as we sailed slowly towards the pass. We threw overboard our leis. And then, suddenly, the wind changed, blowing briskly from the sea, so perhaps our leis did drift back to the shore and will compel us, in the tradition of the island, to return before we die.

CHAPTER EIGHT

FROM its appearance on the chart Moorea is shaped like a heart with its apex facing south. It is, like Tahiti, entirely surrounded by a reef, and between this and the shore are deep lagoons and narrow channels, scattered coral heads and shallows. On the northern side, along which we were now sailing, two passes, only to be identified by the absence of broken water, led into two deep indentations which seemed to penetrate to the very heart of the mountains, whose splintered outlines give to the island its look of fantasy. We chose the second of these, and as we beat in a little wind came rustling down the valley.

During the night I woke with a start. I went up on deck. The bay was filled with stippled light from the moon that hung suspended from a cloudless sky, and silvery shadows danced upon the water.

The stillness was absolute.

There was something very queer about that valley—as if the outraged gods were contemplating violence on this unwelcome intruder; nor would my heightened senses have been surprised to hear the beat of drums or to see a long canoe pulling out from the darkened shore. Gradually the sense of danger lessened and I cast about for some explanation of my curious state. It might, of course, have been the moon but I am not usually moon-struck, I am not psychic, nor do I usually imagine things that do not exist. All I know was that I felt like a dog whose hairs bristled with apprehension. Then it passed and I have never felt it again.

Along the sandy path to the village those passers-by that we met seemed strangely silent after the people of Tahiti. We had the same impression of the village, a straggling place, until we came to a store owned by a Tahitian woman married to a Chinese. Her laughing toothless face seemed to infect all her customers. She found mangoes and the island pamplemousse—a fruit half orange, half grapefruit, and better than either—and she hustled a small boy into shinning up a coconut tree for nuts; she even hinted at eggs. She took our air mail letters to give to the captain of the island boat who would post them at Tahiti. The money? "Oh, leave that till next week," she cried, "the captain will tell me how much."

We became known as *"le petit bateau anglais d'Urofara"*. Our bread and stores arrived by mule ridden by the boy-friend of the girl in the hut behind the cove; a girl whose face and form seemed made for a painting by Gauguin. But when I went for fish I had to go early. It would still be dark, and the sound of the conch shells echoed round the hills as each little canoe with its flare in the stern like a glow-worm, crept up the bay. At the village shadowy figures came stealing out of the huts, and in a few minutes all the catch would be sold and the canoes hauled up on the beach.

Farther up the bay lived Mr Kellum the planter whose house, built on stilts, overlooked Robinson Cove. It was at his suggestion that we went round to Paopao to see MacDonald the painter. "He's been here for nearly forty years and knows more about the islands than anyone."

We paid several visits to Mr MacDonald's hut, right on the water's edge but never found him in till the night before we left, when we went at dusk. The door was open, but no sound came from the darkened room.

"Is anyone in?" called Anne.

"Who's that?" came a voice.

"A fellow Scot to see you."

"You'd better come in, all the same."

Our host lit a candle, stuck it in the mouth of a bottle and glared at us with the aid of its light.

"Aren't you off the yacht? Is one of you a doctor? I loathe yachtsmen and hate doctors. I hear the government has put you in your place and you'll soon be let in by the back door; where you belong."

Nettled by this sudden attack on a profession I have no reason to despise (and wondering if it had anything to do with an ulcer half hidden behind a pad of cotton wool), I said "You seem to share the views of Mr Bernard Shaw."

"Shaw? Yes, I knew Shaw well; we were contemporaries. He wrote a few good plays but he never had any ideas. He borrowed those from James Joyce."

The room was full of shadows. Our host sat on an upturned packing case while Christopher leaned against the wall, and Anne and I sat on the only two chairs. He opened a bottle of wine.

Whatever he thought of doctors (or yachtsmen) MacDonald loved the Tahitians.

"Damn fools, the French," he exclaimed, "they call 'em lazy but they're nothing of the sort. They've found the right way to live and they've the guts not to be stampeded out of it. I've seen 'em after a hurricane's wiped out all they've got. They'll work like niggers and laugh while they're doing it. Children? They're the most adult people in the world."

He strode round the tiny room.

"You must go now. I go to bed when the sun sets, and it's long past that now."

He shepherded us towards the door, and as we walked away from that lonely place his harsh voice followed us into the night, "Come and see me again."

The passage on which we now embarked was rather less than a hundred miles. The wind was fair, and during the night (under the light of a waning moon) I sighted the mountains of Huahine fine on the starboard bow. The aura of mystery with which I endowed it took my mind back to a book by Peter Buck about the migration of the Polynesian race. Here, we were right in the heart of what he calls the "Polynesian Triangle" and ahead, although not yet in sight, was the island of Raiatea, the "Sacred Island" to which came fleets of Polynesian vessels to join in the religious festivals, not only from Tahiti and nearby Moorea, but from the distant islands of Hawaii, the Gilberts, Marquesas and a dozen others. On such a night as this it was not difficult to imagine this fleet treading the same waters as those through which we were now passing; great ships of up to a hundred feet with one or more masts each rigged with its tall spritsail, the twin hulls (hewn from the trunks of great trees and planked up to increase their freeboard) and on the deck between them the women and children asleep, the warriors eager for the first sight of land but with implicit faith in their navigators: navigators who were able to make a landfall after a voyage of two thousand miles at a time when Europe was only beginning to see the light of the Middle Ages.

It was in this mood that we first sighted Raiatea looking much bigger than it really is, with little Tahaa to the north of it. These two islands are in fact connected by a reef which encircles both as a placenta encircles twins. The wind freshened considerably and for the first time we experienced the sensation of sailing for a lee shore and a reef over which the sea tosses the spray as it breaks. We could hardly have chosen a better place on which to practise this art for not only has nature arranged two small *motus*, or islets, to flank the pass but the French have built two stone towers which, when kept in line, lead safely into the lagoon. We rounded to and made fast to the quay at the village of Uturoa.

This happy place was full of light and movement. Swift sailing pirogues (Robinson says they are the fastest in the world) sped

The Sea is for Sailing

across the lagoon, their outriggers lifting to windward in the sharper squalls, larger craft came in from Tahaa laden with fruit, the women in bright dresses, the sun shining on the greens and purples of the shallows, and at no great distance the Pacific breaking on the endless reef that keeps the water between the islands smooth.

Over this paradise presides the French Administrator M. René Charnay, and it was to his house that we went that afternoon. He came to the door. At first he seemed far from cordial, but this was due to a misunderstanding about our nationality. He showed us into a spacious room overlooking the harbour, and at once my eye was caught by the head of a Tahitian girl superbly sculpted in stone; the work of his wife, who was now waiting at Papeete for the birth of her child.

At first René Charnay's sidewhiskers and fringe of beard round the perimeter of his chin, together with his signature "rené charnay" gave him rather a precious look, but this was an impression that was soon forgotten when he started to speak. Although he was still a young man his life had been more adventuresome than many. He had finished reading Law at the Sorbonne (paying for it by working at night at an abattoir) and during the War he had been extremely active in the Resistance. He entered the Colonial Service and was sent as District Commissioner to French Gambier. From his description this sounded as primitive a place as you could find in the world of today, and he had had the unusual experience of having to shoot three of his natives for eating their wives. He must have won their confidence before he left, because he was made a member of a secret society to which no white man had been previously admitted. At his initiation he was given a small, beautifully carved box that contained a red, odourless powder. This he was told to guard with his life, because it killed without leaving a trace. Later he had it anlaysed by a friend in Paris who confirmed that it was extremely lethal, nor could he say what the poison was.

"Did you keep it?" I asked.

"Of course," he replied. "After all, one never knows."

There was a little restaurant near the quay owned by a Marseillais to which he took us for dinner. There were benches round wooden tables, and on these we sat eating Polynesian food garnished by the resources of the Midi and washed down by a wine of Burgundy. Our conversation, I kept thinking, was the sort of talk which you might listen to anywhere in France, with its peculiar detachment towards the disasters, the history and the future of their country that only Frenchmen acquire. In the background came the haunting note of Tahitian songs, the soft shuffle of bare feet dancing. For a moment M. Charnay listened; then, with a little grimace, half comic, half sad, he cried, "Why should we be so cruel and want to make these children grow up?"

The day we left Raiatea there occurred one of those small happenings which only take on their proper significance when viewed in the light of later events. The channel across the lagoon splits round Le Banc Central. The tide was low and the wind ahead. Anne went up to con the ship, for in places there would be little room for the short tacks we should have to make.

We had covered only a short distance when she called down, "I don't see a way through. We must turn back."

Knowing the place only from the chart I started to reassure her, but she climbed down and came aft.

"It's too far from home to take risks," she said.

It was so unlike her not to enjoy such a simple puzzle for so experienced a pilot that for a moment her words disturbed me, but later she seemed to have recovered, and I put off trying, as I so often do, to answer such awkward questions.

That evening we sailed into Apu Bay on Tahaa, and in the short dusk we rowed into a sort of inland lake. The woods, the smoke curling up into the still air from the native huts, reminded us of Friday Street near Leith Hill.

"I wish we were there," said Anne. "I wonder whether I shall ever see it again."

To Borabora or as it was once known "Porapora of the muffled paddles" was a matter of sixteen miles, but it was a sail to remember. The reef off the south-western aspect of the island is a mile wide. A low muttering, like thunder over distant hills, only continuous and infinitely sinister, great seas rising like lions to the kill, their white manes toppling, the green shallow water over the reef, the whole scene dominated by Temanu whose rocky slabs look like an old time locomotive in a wild west film. We raced in through Teavanui (the only pass in this immense barrier) under a press of sail. As Anne stood on the ratlines conning her in I was reminded of Mr Charles Pears's painting, *The Clerk's Dream*. It was all here in front of my eyes, with us in place of the schooner.

A passing pirogue pointed us round to Faanui bay to tie up alongside a concrete wall built by the Americans during the war. We had had a full day, so it seemed to us, but it was by no means over. By the time we had finished our meal a little crowd had collected and, curious at the sight of a man doing the washing-up, they had come aboard to investigate more closely; then, taking us lightly by the hand, girls for the men and a man for Anne, they led us through the forest towards the beat of drums. We came to a clearing lit by flares, and there were two lines of women sitting on their haunches performing the breadfruit dance under the *Chef de hula*. No conductor could have expressed more clearly what he thought of his orchestra than did this man of his pupils. His eyes flashed at a break in the rhythm, he danced with rage at a careless movement, he clapped at a graceful gesture, taking his class back and over till their movements were all but perfect. This team, at the Carnival, carried all before them. Well done, *Chef de hula*!

By the quay at the little village of Vaitape stands, on a plinth, the bust of Alain Gerbault. No man since Paul Gauguin died had so goaded and jibed at authority for its exploitation of the natives, nor had anyone more enjoyed the goading. Alain Gerbault, after his world voyage in *Firecrest*, had become a national figure and on his return to Tahiti the Governor with his retinue came down to the quay to welcome him. Gerbault was on deck. He waited till the Governor started his speech and then deliberately turned his back and disappeared down the hatch, slamming it after him. The bust shows an arrogant, sensitive face, more artist than seaman.

The days passed quickly. Taihuto lent us bicycles when we wanted to go to the village, we rowed round the southern end of the island where the colours on the reef and on the *motus* are beyond my powers to describe, and we had a visit from François Sandford, the schoolmaster. François' grandfather came from Boston, his mother was half French, half Tahitian, but he himself is passionately Tahitian.

"What is the good of my teaching these children French history?" he asked, "when all they want to know about is their own country. If I taught them how to be better fishermen, or to grow more taro and breadfruit, I should be doing something useful."

He had started a pamplemousse plantation and children took cuttings from his trees so that one day they would have plantations of their own.

We were asked to dinner with the Sandfords one night. The weather was stormy and the rain came down in sheets. As we were gloomily contemplating the mile-long walk there was a sound of an engine, and there was François in a battered old truck, the only vehicle we ever saw on the island. He drove us through the steaming forest over a road that was now a lake while the rain drummed down on the roof as it did in the story by Mr Somerset Maugham. Lysa Sandford stood on her veranda to welcome us. The mother of six children, she had a slender and willowy figure, and her head reminded me of the sculptured girl in M. Charnay's drawing-room. Lysa, like her husband, had the blood of more than one race in her veins, but was as proudly Tahitian as he.

After dinner I was looking through their scrap-book when I came across a letter from President Roosevelt thanking François, as *Agent français* for his discretion and tact during the occupation of the island by six thousand American troops. It had not been easy.

One night, at a dinner party to which the Sandfords had been invited, a Colonel, who had looked on the wine when it was red, insisted that Lysa should drink from his glass. She refused. The Colonel rose to his feet and hurled the glass out of the open window. Lysa, shaking with fury, stood facing him and a sudden hush fell on the noisy scene. Slowly a smile crept over the Colonel's face.

"Guess I made a fool of myself, Lysa. Let's sit down and forget it."

François liked the Americans. He could appreciate their big-heartedness and the way they wrote to him year after year at Christmas, as if the friendship formed during those years mattered to them.

Sometimes when we were shifting stores or working on the rigging or touching up paintwork I would find that Anne had slipped away for a little to talk to Mati, Taihuto's wife, while she prepared the huge bowl of manioc and taro on which the family seemed to live, or busied herself making grass skirts and costumes for the Carnival at Tahiti. She and Taihuto used to come and sit in our cabin bringing an egg or a papaw, and I treated Taihuto's leg. After a week we felt we could have stayed there for ever. There was a tranquillity about it, a restfulness of spirit like the Peace of God.

CHAPTER NINE

HONOLULU, to which port we were now bound, lies a little west of Borabora and not much more than two thousand two hundred miles to the north of it, but to get there in a sailing ship the *Ocean-Passages of the World* (as inspiring to me as the *Odyssey* to the ancient Greeks), suggests making to the eastward to cross the "Line" on the hundred and forty-seventh meridian of longitude. This deviation, adding several hundred miles to a voyage that is already long enough, is necessary for two distinct and separate reasons; the adverse direction of the North Pacific Trade Wind and the westward-flowing equatorial currents.

There is, it is true, a ribbon of east-going current between the broad layers of the north and south equatorial streams but this counter-current, as it is called, is unreliable and has even been known not to flow at all. So the thing to do, I thought, was to sail a point free while we were still within the influence of the South-East Trades, keeping the wind on the starboard bow as the Hawaiians had done when returning from the festivals and feasts at Raiatea nearly a thousand years ago.

Although the morning of our departure was ushered in by rain and by wind blowing at nearly gale force, the weather cleared during the day, and, by the time we were ready to be cast off from the quay by the little group of people who had come to say good-bye, it could hardly have been more fair. Sailing along the outside of the reef in smooth water, with the sun shining on the *motus*, the beaches, the verdant forest and the chuckling sea, it would have taken little to make us turn back; but then who could tell if we should ever be able to bring ourselves to leave again?

By the time we had rounded the northern end of the island the past had slipped away like a dream and we were pitching into a head sea, leaning over at the uncomfortable angle of a ship hard on the wind. Having sailed downhill, so to speak, for ten thousand miles none of us was looking forward to the sudden lurch, the buffeting, the quick cling with the hand, the crazy angle of the drinking mug and, worse than all, the damp, stifling heat below when the forehatch has to be kept tightly shut. In a big sea we either stuff a sail between the pram and the cabin top and cut down the light or else run the risk of spray coming in through the closed skylight as if it wasn't there. As we are more cheerful in the light we usually wait until one bunk or the other is soaked through before applying the remedy, as with the horse and the stable door. And all this we had exchanged for the long, easy roll with the steady Trade Wind blowing through the cabin and the forehatch open to the sky. No wonder people run round the world!

By the time dinner was over it looked as if we were in for a dirty night. The washing-up bowl, canted to stop most of the greasy water from slopping on to the floor, was between my feet, the plates stacked in one deep tray ready to be put into the other when they were dry. Every now and then a bucketful of water would come down the hawse-pipe for as yet Anne had been unable to find the tennis ball with which she usually plugged it up. Plasticine, her second line of defence, had not proved entirely efficient, for half-an-inch of water was lapping over the fo'c'sle floor. Tennis balls and plasticine! Shades of Gilbert's First Sea Lord!

I looked out into the inky blackness of the night to where the binnacle light shone dimly on Christopher's face, and even as I looked he called for a second reef. I waved my hand to show I'd heard, but I went on with the washing-up hoping I'd finish it like Drake his rubber of bowls, but a moment later we must have dived into quite a biggish sea, for a large part of it, so it seemed to me, came through the closed skylight as I knew it would if we waited long enough. I handed the mop to Anne and went up to help Christopher reef.

When I came down again the floor was washed, everything stowed away, the bunks smoothed under the waterproof covers that we clip on over our harbour ones, the tennis ball found and Anne sitting curled up in her corner writing her diary as if this was the most natural way to make a journey. By now it was almost ten o'clock. Backing the foresail a little towards the mast we left *Moonraker* to plunge through the night while we slept uneasily below. So adaptable are even the more frail of the human race that after a couple of days of this we had almost forgotten what running before the wind was like.

Fourteen days and eleven hundred miles after leaving Borabora we crossed the "Line" on the meridian of 145° 30°W. I had had a bad throat, and it was unfortunate that this coincided with the worst night of the passage. Sweating with fever and aching from head to foot I listened to the creaking and groaning of the labouring ship and the note of the wind in the rigging. She wanted another reef. Was Anne asleep? Ought I to call her or was the weather not as bad as I thought?

Then I saw her get up, wake Christopher, heard the sounds of their going on deck, the wild flapping of the mainsail until they pulled down the clue, Anne's voice, shrill against the wind, Christopher's answering shout. In the morning Anne said, "We had quite a night; finished up with three reefs and the small jib."

"I didn't hear a thing," I said.

The wind, after heading us for several days, had again settled in the south-east and on the night in question (we were due to cross the "Line" at midnight) the ship was running with the sheets well eased for the first time on this voyage, course having been altered to north after noon that day. The night was very fine, the moon was up, the sea smooth and small Trade Wind clouds drifted across the sky. I was writing up my log before relieving Christopher, when he called down:

"Peter! There's a flare on the starboard bow!"

By the time I was up it had gone.

"What was its bearing?"

"About north by east."

"Was it going up when you first saw it, or down?"

"I think up, but I can't be sure."

"How far away?"

"I've no idea, but not close."

From the crosstrees I looked out on the blue-black ocean, the silvery bow wave as *Moonraker* sailed through the night, and from a few feet below Anne watched too. Could it have been a flare from a boat? It was more likely, I thought, for it to have some from an aircraft a hundred miles away, but always at the back of one's mind was the thought of some ship's boat or a yacht with no more flares to send.

Three days later the South-East Trades left us at the southern edge of the Doldrums as if the wind had come to a fence beyond which it dare not blow. This belt of squalls, calms and torrential rains lies between the South-East and the North-East Trades and varies in width from a hundred and fifty miles to several hundred according to the longitude you are in, the season of the year and even the year itself. Huge rain-filled clouds hung in the sky, winds came from all points of the compass, and for hours we lay on a glassy sea. To catch every breath, each sail had to be constantly trimmed, and we hung grimly on to the topsail and genoa even when a squall hummed in the rigging and water hissed over the lee deck. We shivered with cold in the rain and steamed in the pitiless sun.

After three days Anne's throat became so painful with a double quinsy that she couldn't swallow at all. I put her to bed and started her on penicillin, but she got worse instead of better. Before my eyes she developed signs of blood-poisoning, and in the middle of that night the wind struck from the north-north-east with a whoop of glee. Have you ever tried to nurse a patient with a temperature of 104° in a small boat close-hauled to a Force 5 wind?

In time, that seemed like years, her temperature started to fall, and with another half-dozen injections she should be well. I went to my case for my last box. Instead of twelve doses, there were three! But in a sailing ship you must either be dead or well and it was only five days later that Anne crept back on watch.

The rest of our passage to Oahu, the island on which Honolulu stands, was pure joy. The wind went round to east-north-east and our course trended more to the west. The bracing wind, the perfect weather put colour in Anne's cheeks. We sailed to windward of the island of Hawaii with its tremendous mountain (they say it blankets the Trade for a hundred miles) and it was a poor day when the ship's run was less than 125 miles.

On the thirtieth day out, soon after dark, we saw the lights of Hilo twenty miles to the south. The wind increased and in the morning Maui was abeam. As we ran into the Palolo Channel the wind became much stronger. I was on deck at the time, partly because I like looking at the land after a month at sea and partly because of the weather, when behind Christopher's back I saw a cloud, yellowy white, a twisting, writhing thing, advance with the speed of an express train, turning the water to steam. Thank heavens for our small spinnaker! I lowered the halyard a couple of feet, jerked the jaws of the spar away from the mast, and in ten seconds the sail was down, blanketed by the mainsail. The squall struck; the mast bent, the bows went down and down until the bow-wave came over the stem, the gear creaked and groaned but, much to my surprise, it held. Five minutes later the worst was over. We tucked in another reef.

Squalls of gale force, calms, light airs and a pitch dark night under the lee of Molokai, great tugs towing huge pineapple barges (some trick of the light made them look like railway carriages), and just before dawn out into the Kaiwi Channel with the island of Cahu dimly visible in the lightening sky, its roughened peaks running down the northern side like the spines of a prehistoric monster.

At close quarters all semblance to a South Sea island vanished.

Masses of low-slung bungalows, never-ending processions of cars (like torpedoes in cream and red and green), huge pink palaces in which no prince would ever reign, tall, modern buildings, funfairs and enormous flags proclaimed the might of the U.S.A. which has swept the Polynesian race from off the face of this island all for the sake of "progress".

As we beat into the narrow entrance of the main harbour a ketch overhauled us, her crew waving and shouting to attract our attention. At last, for our thoughts were far away, we recognized the crew of *Ghost* (whom we had met at Tahiti) among the crowd on deck.

We were, apparently, going into quite the wrong place and they had most kindly come out to put us right, piloting us into the Alomoana Yacht Basin. Here we were manœuvred into a pen (like one of those double-ended cars) and left to the Customs and Immigration. The Harbour Master came to welcome us. "Say, Captain," he said, "I'm sure glad to know you. Would you like for me to plug in the power and the telephone?"

Before we could step ashore the Ghosts came back. *Ghost* was much slighter than *Moonie*, although she was a foot or two longer. She had been designed by a well-known Auckland yachtdesigner and had done extremely well in some of the Tasman races. There were four Ghosts, the owner Ken, a stevedore and a racing bicyclist, Neil the navigator, and his elder brother Keith, a truck-driver, and Arnold, who was a fireman in Auckland. After eighteen months' work (or was it two years?) these four had saved up enough money to take six months off and see something of the world. This sort of thing is by no means exceptional in New Zealand, although *Ghost* was smaller than most of the boats that set out on the edge of the Roaring Forties to make their easting before sailing north to the South Sea Islands. What seemed remarkable to us was that four men, none of them small, were able to live at peace with each other in such very confined quarters. Perhaps it was because they did not make the mistake of staying too long in port, and while at sea they drove their ship to the limit as if they were in an ocean race.

While we had been at Papeete, Neil and I, as navigators will, had been discussing our routes across the oceans, and Neil had seen my track (of which I was not in the least proud) across the South Pacific.

He said, "Good Lord, Peter, surely you don't bother to take sights every day when you're in the middle of the ocean?"

I murmured that I indeed did do so, not only to find the ship's position at least once in the twenty-four hours, but because knowing a day's run was good for the ship's morale; it made each man do his best to make the next one better.

"Oh," said Neil, "I only take mine once a week until I get near my landfall."

We asked what sort of a trip they'd had coming up from the Marquesas and how long had it taken.

Ken, in an off-hand sort of way said, "It took us thirty-two days."

The others laughed.

"Come on, Neil," said Arnold. "Spill the beans."

And, with a rueful grin Neil began his story. They had made good time, he said, up to the "Line" and through the Doldrum belt. He had been taking the ship's position once a week as was his custom until within three hundred miles of Hawaii, when he had intended to take it every day. It was most unfortunate (but just the sort of thing that happens) that the weather at this time was unusually bad for these parts and that the sun's angle at midday was over 80°, so that he had to take the sun's meridian altitude exactly at noon to find his latitude. But the sun did not come out at noon. And on the second and third days the sun did not come out at noon. By now he was getting a little worried. He had been able to get a longitude position line that put him on the longitude of Oahu and he was still sure that he was south of the island. "There's nothing to worry about," he said to Ken. "Steer north and you'll sight the island in the morning." When morning came there was no island but that day the sun came out at noon and Neil took his sight. They were two hundred miles north of Oahu still steering north, and the next land ahead was the Alaskan Peninsula!

∽∽ CHAPTER TEN ∽∽

HONOLULU . . . a vast hotel, a crowd of smart women, men with open-necked shirts imprinted with the forty-eight States of the Union, attentive waiters, a lift soaring to unknown heights, an endless corridor with doors discreetly labelled: doctors, attorneys-at-law, real estate and the British Consulate (like cells in some Utopian prison): a friendly drugstore (air-conditioned like the rest), where people understand the problems of small boats, a place to linger over a malted milk shake; a window where native carving is beautifully displayed and costs the earth; streets jammed with cars (more cars than people), and red and cream buses tearing up the long, straight, hot road back to the Alamoana Yacht basin, a road along which no bicycle and no pedestrian ever passes. An island thick with wealth and the high standard of living, where *hula* dances are organized by kind permission of Kodak; an island with the most perfect climate in the world, on whose northern coast the Pacific thunders in almost primeval state, whose coral sands still lie virgin on Sunset Beach, whose every available acre is used for the growing of pineapple, whose mountain ridge (sharp as a razor's edge) is pierced by a narrow gap through which the Trade Wind roars with such violence that it blows a waterfall upwards: an island possessing the finest museum of Polynesian art and history in the Pacific, through whose doors we dare not penetrate, for it is easier for us to enjoy this place if we think of it as pure American.

We had introductions to several families living here, and the first one we made contact with asked us to a party two days later.

Our hostess graciously agreed to come and see our ship before driving us back to the house, and we were at some pains to be sure we recognized her before she should get lost among the vast numbers of vessels in the basin. We had no difficulty. As she advanced along the wooden staging, her stately bearing, the small parasol above her head, her daughter and two grand-children walking just the right distance behind her, removed all doubts from our minds that this was our distinguished visitor. Tall, and with a face not unlike that of the late Queen Mary, she stood looking at our boat, and I could see that she was filled with wonderment that any friend of hers could have written introducing such a vessel's complement. She accepted the situation and summoned sufficient courage to climb down the companionway into the cabin. Here she refused an invitation to sit down, but remained standing under the skylight (the only place where this was possible), her eyes wandering shrewdly from corner to crevice, and we were thankful to have had time to make the place as presentable as any cabin in a small ship engaged on a deep-water voyage can look. Anne showed her the galley (her face relaxed a little and broke into a half smile) and after that, to the disgust of her grand-children who were just starting to enjoy themselves, she said, "Now I'll take you home. There's a little more room, where we can talk."

The house was built in the Italian style, with large rooms of good height, like some of the villas I had seen overlooking Lago Maggiore. It seemed to fit in so well with the climate, the superb view over Waikiki beach and the bay beyond, that you did not question the appropriation from another country of a style so essentially traditional to it.

Our host the Senator (whose grandparents had sailed round Cape Horn and had landed on these islands among the first missionaries to come from the United States) suggested a swim in their outdoor swimming-pool and by the time we had changed back again other guests had started to arrive. This was the first American cocktail party I had ever been to, and it was a revelation after the easy, "leave you to get on with it" attitude of those in England. As far as I could see our hostess introduced everybody to everyone else with a word to explain the reason for their being there. Nor was there any need, so Christopher and I agreed, to have any dinner afterwards, for tiny steaks were provided on a spit to be dipped in delicious sauces, there were sea-foods that I had never heard about, as well as the usual sausages and whirled slivers of bacon, eggs in every form and any sort of drink you cared to ask for. Anne, poor girl, did not manage quite so well. "How can I enjoy these glorious things," she mocked, "if I have to talk to a complete stranger with my mouth full of meat and with grease on my chin?"

The party was in full swing when I noticed a small group of people coming in late. Presently I felt my arm gripped as if by a vice and, half turning, I found myself looking into a pair of sharp, bright eyes set in a pale face, of which the other remarkable feature was a thin, very firm, mouth.

"Are you Dr Pye?" and as I moved my lips, he went on, "I'm Dick Rheem of the *Morning Star* (an ocean racer, not a newspaper). You gave me the shock of my life."

The Sea is for Sailing

Seeing the puzzled look on my face he laughed. "There was I, last Thursday, rounding into the Kaiwi Channel, knowing I was first or second boat in (and we'd done pretty well, I figured) when what d'you think I saw, fine on my port bow? A miserable little reefed down gaff cutter!"

We had, I remembered, glimpsed a large ocean racer coming in from the sea, and we'd wondered whether she was one of the Trans-Pacific fleet on the last lap of their 2,150-mile passage from San Pedro. But she'd passed us long before we came to Diamond Head.

I said, "She looked a beauty."

"No good trying to talk about boats here," he said with a wry grin. "Come aboard tomorrow morning."

And at that moment we both became involved once more in the meshes of conviviality.

The *Morning Star* was a bermudian ketch ninety-eight feet long. Her sheer was a delight to a sailor's eye and, unusual in a modern yacht, she was distinctly rakish. She had been rigged as a schooner and had established an all-time record from San Pedro to Diamond Head of nine-and-a-half knots. After an accidental gybe in the middle of a wildish night Dick Rheem could never quite forget how much worse it might have been and had her converted into a ketch at the cost, it was confidently rumoured, of a hundred "grand". Now ships, like women, sometimes have an aura round them; some are just plain dull, others have the spice of life, while some you take your cap off to and offer up a silent prayer, but if Dick had said, "What about a voyage around the Horn?" I'd have left with him that morning.

Our host appeared on deck. He was an American version of an Elizabethan and his voice (I only heard him raise it once) could put a "jump into a wooden dog". *Morning Star* carried a racing crew of sixteen men. Dick said, "I don't ever have any trouble with 'em. If they can't discipline themselves they don't come aboard twice."

Before we left he said, "Connie and I (Connie, his wife had, like most of the other wives, flown over to join her husband) want you all to come to the *Morning Star* party on Wednesday."

That very day Anne went down with a bad throat and a temperature. Feeling anything but in the right sort of party mind I followed Christopher into the Royal Hawaiian Hotel. I had heard so much about this place that I probably expected a carpet of gold to be surrounded by the spices of the Orient, so I was faintly disappointed to find that it was nothing more than a good, high-class hotel. We gathered for the cocktail party in a large private room which was soon crammed with people. Andy, a sailor and a composer of songs, made a speech and handed round copies of a song that he had written especially for the occasion. I sing it still for it has a catchy little tune.

We went in to lunch. I can recollect little of the conversation between my neighbours and myself for its details were lost in a background of tremendous sound, of enormous, exuberant vitality against which the songs of three Hawaiian minstrels were submerged, their mouths moving to inaudible words. Facing me, between the pillars of the building, was the beach and the reef beyond which the jade seas rolled in, the spray whipped from their crests by the off-shore wind like snow from the ridge of a mountain. I gazed at this scene in all its brilliant colouring, my mind puzzled by the feeling that there was something missing. Then my fuddled brain woke up. There was no sound as the breakers fell; their roar was drowned by the clamour within.

Dick Rheem drove me back to the Yacht Basin, and as we said good-bye (he and Connie were leaving in the morning by air for San Francisco) he handed me a deep red *lei* for Anne. He said, "You're doing what I should like to do but it looks as if time will never let me catch up with it. Good sailing, and come and see us in San Francisco."

I found Anne's temperature higher and her throat worse. Although massive doses of penicillin soon put her right, I made up my mind from this moment that we must spend the winter in British Columbia. It was not only that by the time we reached Victoria we should have sailed twelve thousand miles in seven months, but it was the constant change of scene, meeting new people and absorbing so many different impressions that had worn Anne out. Once again we had received a warm invitation from Beryl Smeeton, and even if we didn't spend the winter in her house we could always live on the boat.

When I talked to Christopher he said, "Apart from Anne's illness I don't think we could have gone on. I feel, quite badly, that I need a spell ashore. I'll write to my parents; they may want me to go home."

We had meant to spend only a week at Honolulu, but when Anne was better one party led so easily to another, and Christopher was having the time of his life. There was a great deal to do to the ship. We changed over from our light tropical mainsail to our 18-oz. northern waters sail, and we renewed the running gear that we had been unable to replace at Tahiti because it was so expensive and of such poor quality. Here, it was cheaper than in England. The copper on the starboard side at the waterline was as thin as paper and was peeling off a foot at a time between the bows and the shrouds. Ernie Simmerer, who was a naval architect as well as doing shipwright work, said he thought he could find some copper that wouldn't cost much and that he would help me to put it on. But by then I had come to know Ernie fairly well. He had made a ratline for me, and when I went to pay for it he said, "Someone gave me this bit of oak and I made it while I was talking business to a client. It hasn't cost me a cent, so it won't cost you anything, either."

Rumour had it that Ernie wasn't doing very well, which is hardly to be wondered at, for he rebuilt a mast for an Australian ketch that had been dismasted three hundred miles to the south of Oahu, where her owner and his wife, both past middle age, rigged a jury one and made port. He refused to let them have a bill "because they did such a fine job."

I said firmly, "Ernie, there's another layer of copper under that one and it's going to last us back to England."

We had been in the basin only a very short time when the Crowes came to see us. We had met them in their schooner *Lang Syne* in 1950 sailing down Sir Francis Drake's Channel in the Virgin Islands; and later in the island of St. Thomas. They had completed their three-year circumnavigation of the world and were now living on their ship in the basin. Bill ran the slipway, and Billie his wife, worked in a store; one day, when they had gathered together a sufficient reserve, they hoped to sail again. *Lang Syne* was stripped of gear and sails, but her great beam gave the impression below that you were in a small house. When I came into the saloon (Billie now called it the "living-room") three things caught my eye. A carved spear from the Marquesas, given them by Bob McKitterick when they beat back eight hundred miles with something he badly needed from Tahiti, the carved head of a girl from Bali and a painting by Le Tec, a Frenchman who had been killed in an accident shortly before we arrived at Papeete, a man who used black velvet instead of canvas. René Charnay dubbed him a charlatan, the Americans raved about him. This was a painting of a Tahitian drummer. His head was thrown back and his face was alight with a pagan ecstasy. It reminded me of the sketch of the head of "the Soldier" by Leonardo da Vinci and the sheen on that native's arms shone like the painting of a velvet gown by David Jagger.

Bill said, "I knew Le Tec (he pronounced it Lee Tagg) quite

well. He was down and out and wanted money to buy more drink. I gave him sixty dollars. A guy offered me six thousand the other day, but I wouldn't part with it, not for all the tea in China."

Bill and I discussed our passage to Victoria. He said, "The rule is, make easting if you can and northing if you must"; but I had noticed from the American wind charts that north of 45°N. the winds were north of north-west, so I proposed to sail due north for 1,500 miles before turning towards the east. By doing this I hoped (I might almost say I prayed) that the worst of the Pacific "High" (where we might be becalmed for days or weeks) would lie on my starboard hand.

On the Canadian yacht Dragoon (fifty-nine feet long and the only British entry in the Trans-Pacific race) the "High" was plotted every day and, as their departure, and ours, grew nearer, they plotted it every hour. As the centre may move to a spot five hundred miles away as easily as a flea jumps into a bed, all this seemed to us to be only faintly profitable to a vessel sailing a hundred miles a day. When we left Captain Holmes, R.C.N., wished us good-bye.

"We leave tomorrow," he said. "I'll give you a bottle of whisky if you get there first."

CHAPTER ELEVEN

NORTH of 45°N. the Pacific is a gloomy sea, said to be the most sunless of the oceans of the world. The crew of *Gemini* (an American couple who roam the world as Arabs roam the desert) told us that we would have the utmost difficulty in getting sights and that during the summer months the coastline of Vancouver Island and the State of Washington to the south of it were usually enshrouded in mist or fog. The winds, we hoped, would be fresh and aft of the beam, for the stronger they were the quicker should we arrive at our destination.

Towards this sunless sea we sailed from Honolulu on a Thursday in July making our way to the westward under the lee of the land. It was almost dark by the time Point Kaena came in sight but fierce squalls already warned us of what lay ahead. Dinner was eaten hurriedly, the dishes stowed away, and a second reef tucked in the mainsail. Taking a deep breath, we rounded the Point.

Bill Crowe, when talking of our departure had said, "Oh, boy; oh, boy, those first three hundred miles will sure be rugged." And Bill was right. In a matter of a minute or two we were soaked to the skin by the sheets of spray driven across our decks from the steep and vicious seas. Slamming the hatch behind us, we went below leaving old *Moonie* to fight this battle on her own, close-hauled on the starboard tack.

Blear-eyed and weary, for it had been almost as wet and wild below as above, I went up on deck at six o'clock the next morning. It was still blowing hard, but the seas had lengthened out, and a glance aloft showed that all was well. Oahu was out of sight astern, and the discomforts of such a night had, I thought, one compensation. If the ship had survived them she was unlikely to fall apart in the immediate future; for she was then fifty-eight years old, eighteen years beyond the age when Mr Humphrey Barton thinks that a yacht has finished her ocean-going days. Althought we had kept her up to the best of our (and King's) ability, her underwater body was as it had been when we bought her twenty-two years ago, except for some added fastenings.

Weeks afterwards, we were told that *Dragoon* sailing twenty-four hours after us, had had her troubles too. Driving through the darkness she had carried away a forestay, lost a sail and had had to be pumped out in the middle of the night. The crew had said, "What about poor old *Moonie*; d'you think she's still afloat?"

Sailing six points off the wind we covered 312 miles in three days, and on the fourth we shot out of the Trade Wind belt as if it were a line of demarcation across the ocean. Lying idly upon the sea waiting for a breeze we saw a steamer hull down on the southern horizon. To our astonishment she turned and headed in our direction and presently came abreast of us. Her captain, using the loud hailer, called:

"Are you all right?" in a thick Norwegian accent.

"Yes," I answered and then thanked him for coming all this way to find out. Without another word, the captain swung her round and continued on his way. So odd was this abrupt breaking off of relations (for ship's masters are seldom businesslike when talking to small boats in the middle of large oceans) that we cast about for some explanation. Christopher, I think, found the most likely one. "Our mainsail is red," he argued, "the same colour as that of a ship's lifeboat. I suppose he was upset when he found she was only a miserable yacht in no trouble at all."

Followed a week of perfect sailing, seven hundred miles in seven days with hardly a sheet started except to follow the wind as it veered from east to south. On the twelfth night out a sub-tropical sunset of unusual warmth seemed to promise that these conditions would hold, but by morning the scene had changed with the speed of a moving picture. The temperature dropped like a stone; two jerseys, a flannel shirt, heavy sea-trousers and long sea-boots replaced the shorts and singlet. The veiled sky and the long brownish wisps of cloud (my "cohorts" of an advancing depression) were there waiting for me.

From that moment we became alert, hard and compact; determined to drive the ship to the limit but to take no chances with this cold grey waste of sea, pitiless, watchful and waiting, so it seemed, for us to make some fatal error. The days pass. Wind and rain with scarcely a glimpse of the sun, three blankets over the watch below and plenty of good days' runs. A north-westerly gale. We heave to and sleep. I look out on a wild scene; a clearing sky, great crested seas, emerald green before they break, cold as if they'd come from the Bering Sea. A cloud advances with the speed of a train, a cloud like the hand of a man; its fingers furred by wind and stretched across the sky; a squall that makes us heave to again and drives us below to have breakfast standing within the small comfort of the Primus stove. All day we run before this strong, fair wind, the decks awash, judging the weight behind each squall. This is what we sail for, to pit our puny strength

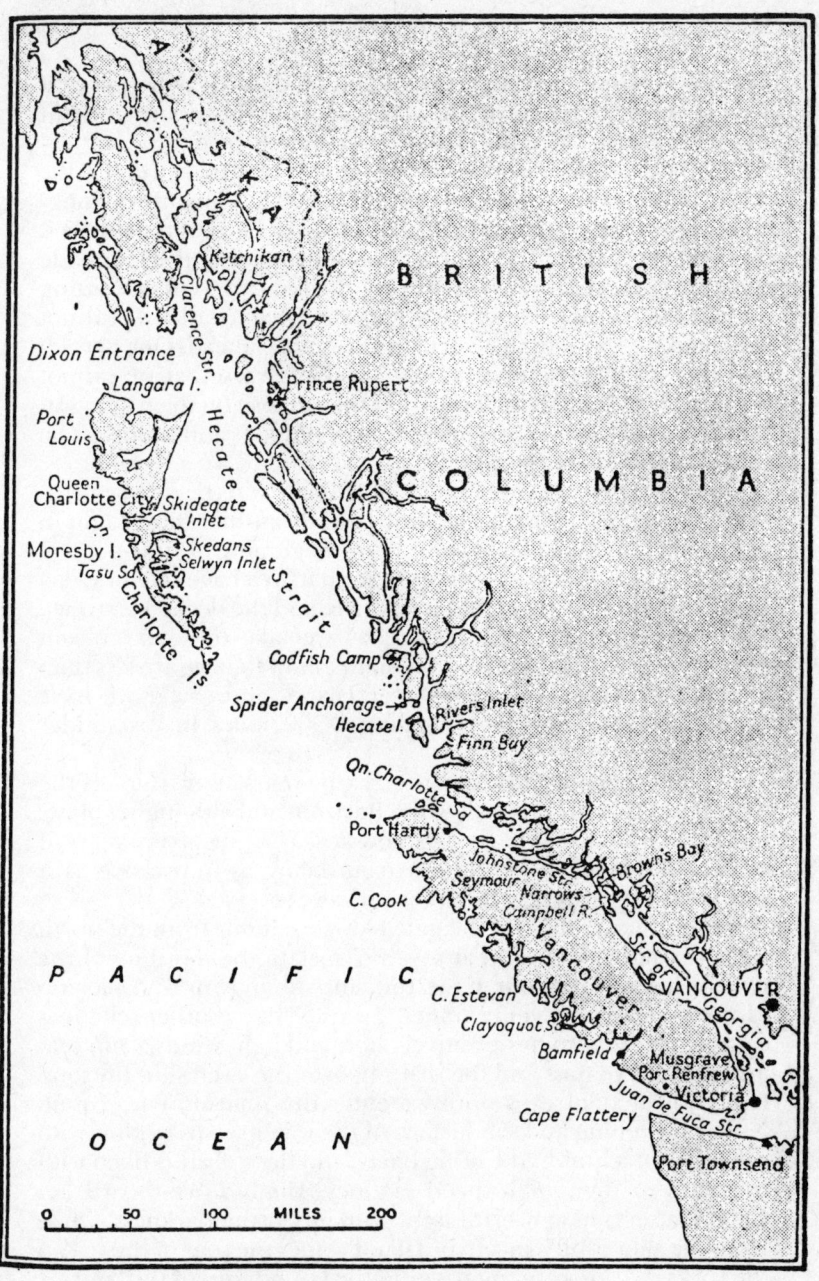

British Columbia to the Charlotte Islands

against an ocean that can crush us and send us to the bottom if it feels so inclined. Gone are the warm seas and the drying sun, but in a week we are twice the crew that we were before.

We have an air escort, self-appointed, of two North Pacific Albatrosses, locally known as Goney birds. They are brown, long-beaked and have a wing-span that looks to be about eight feet. They have been with us for a thousand miles and have made themselves extremely useful during the last two weeks by sitting on logs the size of trees which are so water-logged that we cannot see them for more than a very short distance ahead. One at each end they sit like two towers on a breakwater, so that we cannot possibly miss them. For all we know they may sit on them at night, but in the dark we can see neither birds nor logs and simply hope that they will not lie in our path.

Our course trends away to the north-east and then east-north-east and we reach 49°N., the same latitude as the Lizard Light in Cornwall, but more like Norway at the beginning of June—now I come to think of it, even colder than that. We have one fine day when the sun comes out and it is warm, and the decks are strewn with rugs and sails and clothes, as we take this heaven-sent opportunity to dry them out. My sights show that we are less than a hundred miles from Vancouver Island, and so far we have beaten our own record by sailing 2,500 miles in just under twenty-five days.

But luck is against us. An easterly gale roars at us from off the mountains that are still below the horizon, and although it blows harder than I have known it to blow at sea during all my years of sailing, the land keeps the sea from being as impressive as it would be if the direction of the wind were reversed.

Rather to my surprise the gale blows itself out from the north thirty-six hours later and at seven o'clock in the morning of the twenty-seventh day out I see the sun shining on a glacier on Mount Victoria seventy miles away. The weather changes completely. It becomes positively hot; and light winds, calm seas and wreaths of mist and fog drifting over the swell shut the land from our anxious eyes until we enter the Juan de Fuca Strait. Now it is evening and the surface of the water seems to glow with the lights of a hundred fishing boats, and the still air is filled with the hum of their high-speed engines. Dimly to starboard lies Cape Flattery, its powerful light winking in the darkness, while from the shores of Vancouver Island comes the roar of the sea on the rocks. We are contained within the boundaries of the land.

To the early explorers this strait must have seemed like the mouth of some vast whale. Seventy miles of dark and gloomy water between the Olympian range on the one hand (up to six thousand feet high) and the virgin forests and hills of Vancouver Island on the other. Where, they must have wondered, did it lead to? To the "Strait of Annan" and the "North-West Sea" or to a vortex (for the currents run strong) like a gigantic Corrievrechan from which there would be no return?

It was too much for poor Juan de Fuca, a Greek in Spanish pay, for although he probably saw the opening, the account he gave was proved so false that he could never have explored inside.

We made slow progress during the night, and in the morning wet clouds hung above the bluff to the east of Port San Juan, and only a darker grey betrayed the presence of the other side. We felt hemmed in, and the ten-mile width seemed considerably foreshortened. What a place for calms! Later, the clouds lifted and the Olympians, clear and god-like in their mantle of snow, looked down upon us, making the strait look narrower still. We were proceeding at the rate of a knot, when a ketch appeared ahead. She looked to be a vessel of about twenty tons with no sails on either mast, and with long trolling poles, like the antennae of cockroaches, lashed to her rigging. A man stepped out of the wheelhouse and joined the woman who was already standing by the rail.

"Are you the *Moonraker*?" he called. "The Smeetons have been expecting you for some days. You're late."

Although our paths did not cross again for some months this couple's story is so typical of what people do in this young and exciting country that I shall relate it as we drift, or kedge for adverse tide, on our way up the Juan de Fuca Strait. Tony was a young Canadian when war broke out. He worked his passage to England, joined the R.A.F. and, after much frustration, trained as a fighter pilot. This alone is rather surprising, for Tony is built on a massive scale, and the way he speaks and his slow and deliberate movements make you think he would be more at home in bombers. He finished up as a Squadron-Leader in night-fighters. After the war he and Bridget (a Southampton girl) married and went to Grand Cayman, where they sank all their money in having a boat built at a local yard from designs by John Alden. Her hull was hardly planked up when labour troubles broke out, so they finished the essentials themselves and sailed her up to British Columbia. The *White Hart* is what we in England call a fifty-fifty, with a small sail-plan and a large engine, but she is a superb sea-boat.

In four years of fishing they saved enough money to convert *White Hart* into a yacht and to take six months' holiday on the Californian coast. Two years later they planned a trip to New Zealand. They have a small son whose play-pen is the deck and Tony and Bridget run that ship without any help. It is a tough life; Bridget herself has caught up to three hundred fish in a day, as well as looking after her child and doing the domestic chores of a twenty-tonner. I think, too, that Tony must be an unusually good fisherman, because our friends at Fisherman's Wharf said, "All we have to do is to find Tony. That's where the fish'll be."

Only a few days ago I had a letter from Miles Smeeton saying they had met *White Hart* in mid-ocean three hundred miles south of Norfolk Island in the Tasman Sea. Tony and Bridget had loved the South Seas. Tahiti, New Zealand, British Columbia—as long as they can catch fish the world is theirs.

Three days of light airs and calms . . . but when at last we had passed Sooke Harbour a fine southerly breeze sprang up with the young spring flood. Ahead and within sight were Race Rocks and the Race Rocks Lighthouse. The Channel between the rocks and the shore is nearly a mile wide and is deep, but the surface of the water is torn by tide rips and eddies, for the current runs up to nine knots with a set towards the rocks on the flood. With this commanding wind, and with the thought in my mind that we must get used to such places I steered for the Race Rocks Passage. My crew raised their eyebrows. They did more than that; they pointed out to me that the whole of Juan de Fuca Strait lay on my starboard hand.

The ship sailed on.

We were doing twelve knots over the ground when the wind dropped. It was as if a hand seized her, dragging her unprotesting towards those waiting fangs. Christopher went down to try the engine because, in a case like this, you must try everything. It went.

Round Williams Head we beat into the Quarantine Anchorage and came to an anchor, thirty days out from Honolulu. We should have liked to have lingered, but the doctor would have none of us. "You must be cleared by Customs tonight," he said firmly; so up went the sails once more and, like a cur chivied from one side of the street to the other, we crossed the eight-mile bay to Victoria. The sun went down lighting Mount Baker, rising above lesser peaks to a height of nearly eleven thousand feet, with alpenblum. So clear was the air that it appeared not seventy miles away as on our chart, but twenty.

It was almost dark. Fish-boats, tugs, lighters, a ferry and a forest of masts confronted us, as, half blinded by the lights of harbour, ships and town, we searched for a place to lie.

Out of the maze there came a voice, "Is that *Moonraker*?" and to our despairing answer, the unknown voice shouted, "Come along in here!"

Sails came down, the ship lost way, Christopher jumped into the pram and towed us down a narrow lane between a dozen boats. Dim figures on the quay made us fast. They had seen our sails across the bay, had rung the Customs and were waiting to take us to the Harbour Office where we had to report that night. Before they left they pressed a dollar into our hands to ring the Smeetons in the morning because, they said, "You won't have any of these!"

CHAPTER TWELVE

THERE must have been a hundred fish-boats at the wharf; large and small, with high, flaring bows and low, flat sterns, marked sheers and tall superstructures so tall as to look almost like the bridge of some larger ship, pulleys and drums, miles of wire, trolling poles slung along stumpy masts and, on the big seiners, acres of nets. Their crews were small; two men (or man and wife) to a forty-footer, and only the seiners carried more than three. Ship-to-shore radios, automatic pilots, fathometers and direction finders were standard equipment on all but the smallest.

Most of the men, it seemed, came along to look at us. Dressed in "logger's shirts" in patterns of red or yellow squares, or in thick Indian sweaters with strange birds across the front, their seaman's gait, their slow speech softened by wind and sea, nothing could have been more different from the Alamoana Basin at Honolulu.

Many of these men had emigrated, and there were others whose fathers or grandfathers had come out from the "Old Country" and were anxious to know if Bristol or Huddersfield still looked the same. Ed, who kept a bos'n's store at the head of our dock, "fixed" our broken exhaust and, on looking round, trotted back to his shop for a brand-new shackle for the bobstay.

"That 'un you've got there looks a bit thin, Doc," he said. "You put this 'un in his place."

And then a fisherman came strolling along with a twenty-two-inch salmon dangling from his hand.

"Guess this is too small to be of any use to me," he said. "It might make a bit of a meal for you."

All this with such unconscious grace.

We rang the Smeetons. We walked along to the telephone box by Ed's shed arguing as to who should speak first because, suddenly, it had become enormously important to hear their voices.

I used the instrument.

"Hullo!" came B.'s clear voice.

"This is Peter, from Victoria."

"Peter—Peter who?"

I tried to hide my anxiety, "From England."

"Oh! Peter! Oh, my dear, where are you speaking from? When did you get in? How's Anne? What sort of a passage? Wait; I'll go and fetch Miles."

I handed over the receiver to Anne and moved around to stop my knees from shaking. By the time we'd used up the dollar we'd arranged to meet between James and Sidney Islands in the Strait of Georgia in two days' time.

From a casual acquaintance at Honolulu we had been given an introduction to a gentleman who lived outside Victoria. Very kindly, on hearing that we also knew the Smeetons, he invited us up for lunch. He was small, very light on his feet with pale eyes and a high, penetrating voice. It became obvious that he had a very full acquaintance with what might be called England's Upper Crust, and I had the impression, perhaps erroneously, that as friends of the Smeetons, we were a little undersized.

He said, sharply, "The Smeetons, although they've only been here for three or four years, have become a legend. Beryl is as tough as leather and neither of them feels the cold. The last time I was at Musgrave there were no doors or windows and I don't suppose there are any now. They probably wouldn't be considered necessary. Do you think," he questioned, "that you will be able to live that sort of life?"

"Perhaps not," I agreed, "but we can always try."

On the Wednesday morning we sailed from Victoria, negotiating the channel between Trial Island and the shore, which is less than a cable wide and where the current boils and whirls. Out in the Gulf of Georgia the wind deserted us and we settled down to a long, hot drift. A blue day; blue hills, blue mountains, blue sky, dark blue lines of breeze that never moved in our direction, so blue indeed that even the pines seemed no longer green. We lay in this idle fashion until it was borne in upon us that soon the tide would turn, so we coaxed our reluctant engine into a semblance of life (two-and-a-half knots flat out) and proceeded towards our rendezvous.

We were, of course, late; so late that *Tzu Hang* had almost given us up when she descried her long-lost sister and came bounding to meet her. The dinghy shot off her deck and B., rowing as if her life depended on it, came alongside.

"Oh, well done, well done," she cried. "I just can't believe it."

She handed us a packet of mail, and then the two ships made their way northwards, while a steady flow of talk and news crossed and re-crossed the intervening water.

Presently Miles sang out. "We'll have to go on. I'll milk the cows and come down and put a light on Musgrave Point. You might miss it in the dark."

So they left us to thread the narrow channel of the Iroquois Pass, dodging rocky islets covered with a growth of pines, past Canoe Cove, up into Saanich Inlet and under the great bare brow of the mountain on Salt Spring Island that we were to get to know so well. A light breeze followed astern, but our thoughts, released by a temporary easing in the pilotage, took wings towards the house (marked Conspic. Ho. on the chart) which we were now approaching and to the story of how B. had found it.

Back in 1945 B., having been shown a photograph of the place, had bought it across a dinner table in India. Eighteen months later she and Clio (aged five) arrived in Eastern Canada, bought an old Canadian army truck and drove three thousand miles across Canada to Vancouver City. Taking the ferry to Salt Spring Island she covered the last four miles in as many hours over the mountain track to Musgrave.

The place was in ruins. The roof sagged, wind and weather came through the walls, the floor gave beneath their feet. B. looked round; two hundred feet below, the smooth dark water flowed towards the Sansum Narrows; across the strait rose the hills and mountains of Vancouver Island. She thought to herself, "This land, once it has been cleared, should be good for sheep and cows. Thank God Miles isn't here. He wouldn't be able to see it as I can. This is going to be worth while."

She set to work to rebuild the house, reinforced by Miles, once he had got his discharge from the Army, and then, because they were at that time unable to get their capital out of England, they ran out of money. So Miles joined the Canadian Army, was posted within the Arctic Circle in mid-winter from where he wrote letters to B. about the cold to which she replied (with undoubted truth) that she was colder than he.

In the end the Canadian Army (or the Arctic cold) gave Miles a duodenal ulcer and he returned to Musgrave and in time (a remarkably short time, it seemed to us) they had a house with a roof and walls, "country sheep" which Miles picked up cheap and left to fend for themselves in the bush, "town sheep" for which he expressed the utmost scorn (because they had to be looked after). A bull, a cow, hens, pigs, ducks, geese, guinea-fowl and a goat completed their livestock. Certain changes had been made when they came over to England to buy *Tzu Hang*; and the bull was disposed of, I had been relieved to hear, because I am not good with bulls.

It grew dark. Miles had been right about the difficulty of finding Musgrave at night. So black were the trees, and so foreshortened was the width of the water by the high ground, that I was thankful when a light, like a candle in a window, appeared from the level of the water. There was B. in a dinghy.

"Miles is standing by the buoy," she called. "Pick it up and come ashore."

By the light of a lantern we pile into the truck with a couple of kitbags with our things for the night. Then we are off. The engine roars, the wheels bite into the deep dry ruts and we head up a narrow track winding through the forest. Bumping and swaying, twigs snapping, brambles and branches brushing our faces, the warm still air, the smell of the exhaust, the scent of pines, all excite our senses. We cross a bridge over the now dry bed of a stream, a light appears among the trees, a gate that Christopher jumps down to open, the shadowy form of a house in a wide clearing. The truck turns into a shed. B. leads us through the dairy into a workroom with a high wood ceiling. Electric saws, drills, planes, benches, an old iron stove that once heated a church, a kitchen and dining-room easy to live in and as practical as B. herself, a dishwasher, a stove that turns itself on and off, windows and doors are everywhere. The living-room is three sides of a square and in the western wing, so to speak, is the sort of fireplace you might expect in a Tudor house in England. Tibetan stirrups of carved wood, a Persian carpet found by B. on her travels, a tiger shot by Miles and a fine broad staircase leading to the bedrooms. Primitive! Why, the place is more highly mechanized than anything I'd dreamed of. We sit down to eat. I remember being surprised that five people all talking at once managed to eat so much in so short a time.

For the next three weeks we worked hard on the ship. We put her ashore and renewed the copper round the waterline, stripped her of gear and sails, scraped, varnished, painted, patched sails and counted all the tins left in our lockers of which, to our surprise, there were four hundred and seventy-five. The weather was glorious, like an Indian summer at home, and our daily walks led through the pine-woods. The forest came to the water's edge, and the cove was only open to the north, from which quarter the wind never blew with any strength.

Coming round a bend in the path we would see the masts of the two ships, the clear blue water, the Government wharf and the shed, the float and Roy's boat beside it. Fourteen feet long, beamy and flat-bottomed, I wouldn't have set foot in it on the Round Pond. Over the middle half Roy had built a high cabin to protect the tiny engine, the mail and himself, and on the front of this he had painted, in large red letters, THE ROYAL MAIL. Roy himself was thickset with a round, red face and placid eyes. He had been taught to read by one of his many uncles, had never been to school nor spent a single night away from Salt Spring Island. He spoke as his people did, with a strong Yorkshire accent. He carried the mail twice a week to and from Burgoyne Bay three miles up the coast with the determination of a King's Messenger riding across Hounslow Heath in the days of Dick Turpin. There was little he did not know about forestry and carpentry, and he adored the Smeetons, who in turn said they could overcome any catastrophe except that of losing Roy.

One morning towards the end of our refit we were working on the boat when there came the sound of a hunting horn and when we looked up we saw a ship that was suddenly familiar to us. She was the *Tara*. She belonged to an engineer from San Pedro and it was he who had taken us through the passage in the reef to the Alamoana basin in Honolulu. At the time Bill had said he might be going to Alaska and we had suggested he should call in on his way south. They had come down from Ketchikan by the "Inside Passage" delighted with their ship and excited at the success of their voyage. Miles was down in the cove that afternoon and we all went aboard. *Tara* was about thirty-six feet along, very beamy and of moderate draught, and it was astonishing to me that Bill could have built her himself in four years working only during holidays and at week-ends. There was, however, one thing we didn't quite like. The main gaff went up and down on a steel jack-stay. It seemed to us to be not quite strong enough to take the strain of that swinging spar.

Bill and his wife and their two friends were invited up to baths and dinner at the house and we sat yarning over the fire as sailors will.

Miles asked Bill if he had had any trouble with his gaff, to which Bill replied, "None at all. If it comes on to blow I lower my main and turn on the engine."

I must have murmured something about a lee-shore for I remember Bill saying, "I can't imagine a sea so big that I couldn't motor into it."

Tara left the next morning bound for Seattle and then for San Francisco. Two weeks later we heard there had been bad weather on the west coast, and we wondered how *Tara* had fared, but it was a long time before we were to hear what happened.

The work on *Moonraker* finished, Christopher went off to Victoria to become a plumber's mate in a shipyard at seventy dollars a week. Before he went he drew me aside to tell me he'd heard from his people (as we had done) that they were anxious for him to finish the voyage back to England.

"And of course," he added, "I want to, too."

Until that moment I had been almost certain that he would leave us, and I wondered at what stage during the passage north he had changed his mind. And how like him not to come bursting down with the news at the end of some nautical crisis (as I should have done), but to have waited patiently until he was absolutely certain. Well; we should be delighted.

So Christopher went off to live at Fisherman's Wharf, and before we laid the ship up for the winter we sailed down to find him living on tins of Chuck Waggon Dinner and Pacific Milk and sharing a houseboat, sleeping in the owner's bunk by day and working by night.

It was blowing hard, very hard in the Juan de Fuca Strait the day we said good-bye to him, but under the lee of Vancouver Island we had no more difficulty than tying several reefs in the mainsail. We arrived so late at Musgrave that we spent the night aboard and walked up to Conspic. Ho. in the morning.

Beryl said; "Christopher rang twice last night to ask whether you were back. He sounded as anxious as if he'd been your son."

Looking back on the six months that we spent at Musgrave it seems to fall into two parts like the two acts of a short play; the autumn and the winter. Part of the plan for the autumn was that we should look after the farm whenever the Smeetons went away for a few days, so Anne and I were shown how to milk. We started by milking one cow between us, for Anne's hands being smaller she found it easier to milk from the front teats while I tried the back. Our wrists ached, Folly put her foot in the bucket and Molly seemed to have dried right up.

Miles, when asked how we were getting on, said, "Peter gets the best results but Anne has the better style."

At the end of a week Anne headed her diary, "I Milk a Whole Cow". Miles showed me how to split logs, to use the machinery in the workroom, and Anne was taken along by B. to feed the animals, but most of the day I spent writing down on the boat trying to earn some dollars before starting off in the spring.

Anne worked at the house in the mornings, came down to the boat to help me in the afternoons and cooked the dinner at the house in the evenings. When the Smeetons were away I usually milked the cows and she fed the animals.

B. ran her house as Anne runs *Moonraker* on a long sea

voyage—no waste, no frills but plenty of the essentials. One plate, one knife and two hot meals a day. To this sort of thing we took like ducks to water, for we were used to it. Nothing but flour, sugar and rice was brought in from the outside world except a sack of potatoes which, in a weak moment, B. got for the Pyes, when their faces fell at the thought of six months of rice. The day started with porridge cooked with milk instead of water in a double saucepan. I asked B. where whe had learned to make it that way.

"I was living on a ranch in Patagonia," she said, "and one day I stupidly got lost whilst out riding. After a day and a night I came on an Indian family camping and they fed me on this. It tasted like ambrosia, and I've made it this way ever since."

Porridge and cream and eggs, and cup after cup of coffee; but how B. mattocked all day in the bush on two slices of charred toast (for that was all she ever had) I cannot think. It was her boast that she could sit down and eat for an hour or two on end and last the next thirty-six without another bite. I can believe her.

If you felt weak in the middle of the day you could always gnaw bread and drink milk, and while we were there tea and cake round the workroom fire after dark became an institution that even B. recognized. Twice a week she baked bread, delicious brown loaves, the best I've ever tasted, but once when she and Anne were gossiping away together she forgot to put in the yeast. Thinking that yeast late was better than never she threw some in, with the result that each loaf could have replaced a sizeable pig of our ballast. Those loaves looked like lasting a long time, until I hit on the idea of taking a new one down to the boat each day. None came back, and B. only got wise to my sudden extravagance after I had put the last of them into my bag. I fled down the path.

I became the unofficial doctor to the few inhabitants on that part of the island, a Dutch family near the Smeetons and the various branches of the Smith family of which Roy was one. Koos and his wife had spent their early married life on a barge on a Dutch canal. His prospects of getting on, said Koos, seemed nil when he received a letter from America offering him (through a Dutch friend) the job of caretaker to the American's house above Musgrave Cove. Koos was the right man for the post; a tremendous worker and always good-tempered, he had saved money, had a little farm of his own and two children one of whom I had to see fairly often. As often as not I returned to Musgrave with a bagful of greenstuff that was a welcome addition to carrots. When we left they loaded us down with all kinds of provisions quite out of proportion to anything that I had been able to do for them.

We had imagined that once we got to Musgrave we should be completely isolated, but during the early autumn ships came into the cove and people came for the week-ends. One Sunday we walked down through the woods to the Mitchells whose house overlooked the Sansum Narrows for a "whisky-drinking and hymn-singing party". The house was robustly and expensively simple, and as the Mitchells only lived there for three summer months the gloomy darkness which enveloped it during the winter did not affect them. Although most of the party came form Chicago they sang hymns with some of the fervour of frontiersmen, holding their tall glasses full of "whisky-on-the-rocks" and downing them like men. It was like watching the drinking scene in *The Beggar's Opera* become suddenly and sternly Calvinist.

In November the rain started. It rained every day for six weeks punctuated by occasional gales, and it rained all day and all night for a good deal of that time. The bed of the stream became a babbling brook and grew into a foaming torrent. It rose to within a few inches of the bridge and a large section of the path lay under water. The dark pines dripped and dripped.

Before Christmas Clio came back from boarding school with a school friend. Clio was nearly thirteen now and was five foot ten-and-a-half inches tall. She was very slender with the manner of a frisky colt. It was a busy time for presents *had* to be made on the spot, and when I came home in the evening I would find people bent over the workroom benches, others crawling about the floor cutting out designs for penguins, cows or boats. On Christmas Eve Koos and Corrie, with Bertie their kaishond, two yachtsmen who had come into the cove, and all of us from Conspic. Ho. scrambled into the truck with Minnie the goat and Pooh-Bah the Canary Island dog and rumbled down past the cove and up eight hundred feet to the Post Office where Roy lived with his people, and to the various log-cabins of his uncles, all of whom were called Smith. Accompanied by Koos on his accordion we sang both lustily and loud (if not always in tune) all the Christmas carols we could remember. We sang them to each other on the way back, as the truck swayed from side to side and the trees flickered in the glow of the lantern that Clio held on high.

Our last visitors before the winter clamped down were the Sykeses. Vivie and Raith ran a chicken-farm; that is they fattened birds with concentrated feeding, and as long as the birds didn't get some fatal disease during the six weeks that this process took they sold them at a profit. They were considerably younger than either the Smeetons or ourselves and Raith was almost as tall as Miles and considerably broader. They joined in our entertainments with the same abandon as they rounded up a thousand chickens in a night, and I can see Raith now, dressed in a frock made out of two sugar bags, holding Anne, wrapped in a blanket and screaming lustily with tears streaming from her eyes. By his side stood B. the perfect picture of an embarrassed husband, in Miles's only pin-stripe suit, the trousers turned up to the knees, while Miles, looking benignly over his spectacles and dressed in impromptu cassock and surplice, baptized her with rum. I can even remember the word, of two syllables: Churchill.

We loved guests at Conspic. Ho. They were bound to be the right sort, for the wrong would never have stayed. The best bits of Molly (who had been shot and put in the deep freeze) came out, and coffee was allowed after dinner. As we stood on the Government wharf to see the Sykeses off, Vivie kissed Anne, and said, laughing, "Now, don't forget. Call me and say 'Guests' and those food parcels will be right along."

The curtain rang down on Act I.

A howling south-easterly gale roared round the house, and the temperature dropped like a stone. Snow drove over the tops of the trees and piled against the barn and the sheds in deep drifts. The wind dropped, and now the flakes fell softly and relentlessly. In peaked cap and oily, with the collar turned up and wearing my sea-boots, I took my can of milk and trudged down the path. From behind me B. flung open the kitchen window.

"You look like the Retreat from Moscow," she shouted gleefully.

The pram was half full of snow and *Moonraker* seemed buried. I went below and lit the wood stove which the Smeetons had lent us for our stay in B.C. and soon *Moonraker* and I were a lot warmer than Conspic. Ho. That evening, when Anne and I walked up through this strange white world, there was no light shining from Koos's cottage. The power had gone. And when we got to the house, so had the water.

Miles and B. were bubbling. Crisis! The very spice of life. No stove, no baths, melted snow in a bucket to drink, and a good chance that a year's food would go bad in the deep freeze before the electricity came back. Miles came back from milking Folly with a broad grin on his face.

"Ha! No logs! All hands tomorrow, Peter."

While Miles, Roy and Koos went off into the woods to look

for frozen sections of pipe, B. and I sawed logs all morning, and Anne wheeled them in. In the afternoon we took the long double-ended saw and attacked a tree that had fallen some months ago. By the time we had made two cuts through that trunk it appeared to be twelve feet thick, but B. went calmly on, so I had to, too. I had always felt that Anne was the only woman I should ever want to sail with on a long sea passage, but now I would have added another.

When it became too dark to see, we stopped, but by then a goodly pile had been stacked under the roof of the veranda, and after they had had time to dry out (if they ever did) we should have something to keep us warm. Back at the house the water was on, and dinner was cooking away on *Tzu Hang's* old Taylor paraffin stove. Conspic. Ho. was under way.

It took ten days and three hours for the deep freeze to rise to melting point and it took ten men ten days and four hours to reach and repair the electric cables that had been twisted and torn by falling trees in the five miles of forest between here and Burgoyne Bay!

For six weeks it snowed and rained and froze and thawed, but never again with the ferocity of that first fall. It was weather for wolves and bears, but wolves kept to the remoter valleys on Vancouver Island, and bears had never been seen on the island, althouth an occasional cougar swam the Sansum Narrows and plagued the farms. More than once I heard the hoot of an Arctic owl, big enough, Miles said, to carry off a chicken. In the middle of February the sheep started to lamb, and Anne helped to look for lost lambs and to transfer those whose mothers didn't want them to others whose lambs had been lost. Rocky the ram, four-square and with contemplative eyes, seemed enormously proud of his large family. Anne used to take him an apple-core, but if she forgot to keep her eyes on his he'd be waiting to catch her off-balance, and once down she came, much to Rocky's content and Anne's discomfort. It never happened again!

Minnie the goat broke into Folly's bin of oats and ate so much she nearly died, and now B. and Miles couldn't make up their minds whether Folly wanted a bull. Miles was all for taking her to Ganges by sea and B. was for crossing the hill. The snow had almost left Musgrave but at a thousand feet it might still be several feet deep.. The glass was tumbling down, and rain was on its way when at last Folly was coaxed into the truck.

Of their adventures Anne wrote in doggerel and Miles illustrated it for Clio.

We ran into snow that was two feet deep
And trees that had fallen and lay in a heap.
With the winch on the truck we moved them away,
But it took us, you know, the best of the day;
And when to the foot of the hill we came,
We thought some giant had been playing a game,
The trees like Spillikins lay on the ground,
As high as a house and all in a mound,
The road was blocked for half a mile
"Now this," they said, "will take a while."

They'd had no lunch, and they'd had no tea
The trip had been "ill conceived by B."
Miles took his axe and started to hack,
He disregarded the pain in his back,
Into a culvert he staggered and stumbled,
"How unconsidered!" B. thought he mumbled.
After a night tied up to a tree
Alone, deserted by Miles and by B.,
Folly just felt it was meant as a hoax
When B. brought food in a pail to coax.
She stood and shivered and turned away,
"I won't eat oats nor even hay."
I really think she was hurt to the core
"I simply cannot," she said, "stand more,
If this is what cows must do to be mated,
I think that love is over-rated."

Looking back on those lengthening days of late winter the memory that will stay with me longest is coming down in the morning before the sun was up and gazing through the drawing-room windows at the land and water that lay spread before my eyes. Not a thing, I thought, could have changed in a thousand years except for growth and decay under the hand of nature; a scene devoid of colour, the grey sky blending with the distant snows, the dark headland across the straight . . . all shades from black to white. But this very lack of colour gave the place a mantle that enhanced its immensity and emphasized the loneliness.

About the middle of March the sun came out and the world seemed to burst into life. The trees threw off the last traces of snow, lambs cavorted, hens laid, ducks mated, and Minnie forced an entrance in the middle of the night covering the house in dottles. But, as Miles remarked, "Thank goodness, goats are constipated."

There was work at the house and work on the ship. And then

one day Roy took all our sails down to the cove in his truck, and I felt the threads of Musgrave begin to stretch and break.

Miles looked round at the evidence of our departure. "We're not coming to see you off," he said. "You're not guests. If we miss you when you come south, we'll see you in England. Good luck!"

And so with a couple of kit-bags slung over our shoulders we walked down the path to where *Moonraker* was lying waiting for us in the cove and I don't believe we exchanged one word until we came aboard.

The other day while I was writing this account a letter came from the Smeetons from Australia. It was from B. and showed a photograph of their Siamese cat sitting on *Tzu Hang's* rail with that watchful look that I have seen in B. herself, wishing us a Happy New Year, and with a brief note saying she would see us in August of this year.

It was as laconic a way as I know of telling us they were bound round Cape Horn from Melbourne, for by no other route could *Tzu Hang* reach England at that time. We had, of course, received a hint of this because, once you have sailed the seven seas, or some of them, you become a member of a "bush telegraph" that is both swift and accurate. We knew that they had a third hand aboard, and a good sailorman at that, and for this we were frankly grateful. The Smeetons, as you may have gathered, are man-sized people, but Cape Horn has a distinctly evil reputation and I for one will be glad when we hear that they have safely weathered it.

CHAPTER THIRTEEN

OUR first sail of the season was a short one of only sixteen miles, but it was a foretaste of what it might be like in the spring. We left the cove with the topsail up, pulled down one and then two reefs and contemplated a third, while squalls of the violence of a gale came tearing off the mountains, driving before them a mist like a plume of smoke. Only the fact that we were sailing in sheltered water prevented us from being hove-to. The spray had the quality of ice, sleet drove against our sodden faces, and we arrived within the shelter of Canoe Cove feeling as if we had done a hard day's work.

The Scott-Moncrieffs came over from Victoria to fetch us. Ronnie Scott-Moncrieff was slightly shorter than I was and when he smiled his whole face wrinkled as if he really meant it. To see him dancing an eightsome reel in the kilt and tartan of his clan reminded me irresistibly of a Scottish chieftain who would defend his castle to the last man and let the enemy in only over his dead body. Lois, his wife, cannot really be described as being passionately fond of boats or the sea, and it would be hard to imagine a worse introduction than hers to *Moonraker*. She had come down with Ronnie on the second morning after our arrival in B.C. Christopher and I, emerging from the engine-room were covered in oil and grease; bits of magneto, valves and spanners lay on the cabin floor, and Ronnie had to sit on the table. But, leading the life we do, it seemed outrageously inhospitable not to ask anyone aboard just because there was no room for them. My wild appearance and the marks of dirt where I had rubbed my nose or an ear may have given me an intimidating appearance, but whatever the cause Lois stepped meekly aboard and sat down on the last inch of settee available. I myself was fascinated (I was leaning on the engine-room doors behind her), for every time I closed my eyes I could hear Marjorie Fielding in *Quiet Week-End*.

The Scott-Moncrieffs' house overlooks Trial Island, and from the drawing-room windows mountains and water vie with each other, so that it is difficult to keep your eyes for long on either. To me it is a more beautiful view than Robert Louis Stevenson's from Black Point in Hiva Oa. The house is so near the water's edge that part of it is bolted down on to a rock, and on a still, misty day the beat of a tanker's diesels coming up the Juan de

Fuca Strait is communicated to you as if you were in the cabin of your ship.

It is an open, friendly house and there was much coming and going, for two of their children were still at day schools in Victoria. It became a second home to us.

For our summer cruise we might have been tempted to do nothing more than sail from cove to bay, from one fiord to the next, for it is a curious thing that where inside waters are available the sea takes on a more sinister reputation than it does when you must either face it or give up sailing. Few yachtsmen go to sea in Holland, and during our year's stay in B.C. we met only two that had sailed round Vancouver Island. We received no encouragement to go north from any of our friends except Dave Rogers.

We had first met Dave at Honolulu as a member of the crew of *Dragoon*, from whom we had failed to win a bottle of whisky. He had been a chartered accountant in Vancouver City, had tired of an office life and had bought a fish-boat. For several years he had fished the waters between the Hecate Strait and Cape Flattery, and if he hadn't lost his ship by fire he might well have been there now.

Dave began talking almost at once about the Queen Charlotte Islands, which lie a hundred and twenty miles north-north-west of Vancouver and stretch for two hundred miles north-west of that. He spoke of a place called Two Mountain Bay in Tasu Sound on the West Coast in a slightly lower key, telling us he had weathered the worst sou'-easter he had ever known tied up to half a dozen trees. He compared it to the country round the Magellan Straits and declared there was a saying in these parts that "Men sail the seven seas *and* the Hecate Strait". It seemed a pity now that we were so near not to go and have a look at it, and when Ronnie said he would come with us we based our adventure on the Queen Charlotte Islands. Now the north coast of the Charlottes is only thirty miles from the shores of Alaska. Althouth no one in B.C. thinks anything of going there (by the Inside Passage) those in England might think of Eskimos and Polar Bears. So Ketchikan was added to our list.

One evening Dave and Willi, his wife, came up to the Scott-Moncrieffs and four heads were bent in earnest concentration over a mass of charts and sailing directions. Chairs and sofas had been pushed away and Lois and Willi held a watching brief. It was a little hard on Lois, I thought, that Dave had to develop some sort of conscience that very night about sending us up to those bleak and inhospitable shores.

He told us, as others had, that we shouldn't leave the inland waters until the beginning of June, that sou'easters in the Hecate Strait were dangerous not only by reason of the shallow waters, the unpredictable currents and the unlit dangers, but also the heavy rain, which invariably accompanies these storms and cuts visibility to a mile. He gave instances of strandings and shipwrecks, of fishermen who had lost their lives off Rose Spit. Ronnie was as enthralled as we were, but it might, I thought, be a different matter for his wife to listen to what must sound like the measured tread of a pavane with death. Lois is a quiet person. I watched her sitting there without a movement of her hands, a little smile playing round her mouth at some of Dave's more dramatic moments. Finally she spoke:

"Mr Rogers, surely in summer the weather is not as bad as all that?"

"You never know," answered Dave. "The worst gale I was out in was in August. It blew the best part of a hundred knots and I remember a large American boat, not fifty yards away, trying to make for shelter. One moment she was there and the next she'd gone, without a trace."

Lois laughed a little uncertainly. "Put it this way," she said. "If Peter and Anne asked you to go on *Moonraker*, would you go to the west coast of the Charlottes with them?"

"Of course. It's only that I want Peter to know what sort of place he's going to."

Anne and I took *Moonraker* up to the Gulf of Georgia, in and out of islands, through the Porlier Pass where the pram half filled in the tide rips, sailed across the Georgia Strait (the width of the Straits of Dover) with a topsail breeze and came in the evening into Burrard Inlet, where the wind dropped. I towed our old ship into Star Boat Cove just to the east of Point Atkinson. The lights came out in tall buildings and were reflected in the glassy waters of the inlet, and the last rays of the sun glowed on the snows of the higher peaks that surround Vancouver to the north and east. The roar of a great city came to our ears blurred by the blessed distance of five miles that lay between it and us.

I have often wondered what the place looks like from the air. It is built, of course, in squares and blocks like all North American cities but it may easily seem more compact than it appears from the ground. We were told that the first baby ever to be registered within the city precincts was still alive; and now 700,000 people live here.

Bob Harlow lives, like a hawk in its eyrie, at the very top of the

Vancouver Hotel and directs the talks side of the C.B.U. He speaks very rapidly, and he had made it quite plain (on our first visit) that he was interested neither in boats nor in the people who sailed them.

"But write a few scripts if you like," he said, "and I'll look at them."

It was to record these and to spend some time with friends in the city that we were now here. One day I had a telephone message from Bob saying that he wanted to come down and see us. He sat in the cabin, looking a little lost carrying an umbrella and in his town clothes. I gave him a drink.

"I don't know what you folks have done to me," he said, "but I've bought a boat."

On a golden day in May Ronnie and Lois picked us up and drove us along the Fraser Valley, up the Fraser Canyon to Ashcroft and Kamloops, to the Selkirks and then down the Okenagen Valley. We spent the nights in log cabins and slept to the sound of rushing mountain streams or to the stillness of a lake.

Ronnie took things quietly, driving a hundred and fifty miles a day, and the only disappointment was that the road to the Rockies was still blocked by snow. One of the great disadvantages in travelling in your own boat is that there is so rarely a chance to know more than the watery edge of the country in which you find yourself, but this expedition gave us at least an idea of what B.C. was like behind the great barrier of the Coastal Range. We thought it wonderful.

Back on the ship we made ready for Dave and Willi to join us for the first week of our trip towards the north. This first part of our voyage lay through broad stretches of water, past clusters of islands, across the mouths of deep fiords; good sailing if only there had been enough wind. He took us into coves, gorges and sounds that we might never have discovered for ourselves.

At one settlement, Whaletown, where there was a float to which you could tie up, a store with a deep-freeze and any provisions you liked to buy, we walked up the road to find a little church built very simply of wood, painted white and shining in the afternoon sun. It had been built as a memorial to John Ansel who had been the first man to found a mission on this lonely coast which, for weeks at a time, is cut off in the winter. He spent most of his life among the islands and on the west coast of Vancouver Island using his own ship as headquarters until missions could be established ashore. After he retired (he must have been well over seventy) he sailed his vessel, a gaff-rigged ketch rather like a small Brixham trawler, down to Panama with the help of two girls. From there they set off to Jamaica and had a rough passage, we heard, and then, just as they sighted the island Father Ansel had a stroke. It must have been a hard decision to make, but those girls thought it would take longer to reach the island, some fifty or sixty miles to windward, than to run back the four hundred miles to Colon. With the current against them, I'm sure they were right, and John Ansel was still alive when they sailed in between the breakwaters.

Every ship that sails north inside Vancouver Island must pass through either the Seymour Narrows or the Yaculta Rapids. The tide runs through the Narrows up to seventeen knots although the more usual rate is twelve to fourteen. In the middle of the narrowest part lies the Ripple Rock over which there is nine feet of water at low water springs. At various times people have tried to blow it up to reduce the tremendous eddies that it causes, and once a barge sixty feet long with eight men aboard was moored to the rock. In the heavy overfalls of a particularly strong flood the barge capsized and all eight men were drowned. When we heard this story we thought we'd try the Yaculta Rapids but, unfortunately, we met a man who had been through the Yaculta Rapids. His vessel was a Tahiti ketch and however much you may dislike this type of craft she is at least buoyant. Coming through on the flood he had the unusual experience of watching his stern disappear in a whirlpool. It came up again, of course, but he had never felt quite the same person since.

We chose the Seymour Narrows. The tides are worked out to the nearest minute with the rates of the stream for every hour. Slack water lasts for twelve minutes. With Ted Rose, a doctor friend of Ronnie's who had come (he said) to see how to sail in these waters without an engine, we left Campbell River, six miles to the south, at what we thought was the right time. The wind was light ahead, and as soon as I felt the force of the stream I knew we should arrive far too early. There seemed only one thing to do; we swung the ship round till she faced the way she had come, set the spinnaker, and continued towards the narrows backwards at about the pace we wanted. The wind died away. Overshadowed by high, pine-covered hills black under a lowering sky the dominant note was of gloom, a gloom that was deepened on our ship by one of our engine's two cylinders taking a day off. With lifeless sails we were drifting through the water when a ten-thousand-ton steamer that had been waiting at anchor got under way. Right between Ripple Rock and the mainland we were caught in the grip of an eddy and swept across her bows. I saw Anne's white face looking up at the advancing bows and I knew she knew that the steamer had to keep straight on no matter what lay in her path.

"Fools rush in . . ." I muttered, when a smart breeze swept down a valley and filled our sails. In a moment the steamer was past, a group of men standing on her bridge, as if turned to stone, looking down upon us.*

There were now ten minutes to go before the tide was due to turn. The breeze faltered. With our eyes on the clock we crawled like an injured snail towards Brown's Bay and on the tenth minute (this is God's truth) we slipped into the quiet water of that cove. Ted broke the silence as we stood watching the flood sweeping down Discovery Passage.

"You two do take your pleasures in a most peculiar way," he said, mopping his brow, and I thought I heard Anne murmur, "With one hand in God's pocket and very tightly clenched."

Up the interminable Johnstone Strait, as long as that of Juan de Fuca, we beat and beat against a fresh west wind, while high mountains gave place to lower ones, and the pine trees grew shorter, until one morning we were shot out into the broad expanse of Queen Charlotte Sound. Sea and sky were a uniform grey with islands like humps on camel's backs, indescribably lonely and forbidding. For the first time the ship stirred to the ocean swell and the glass fell, slowly and steadily.

Opposite the northern end of Vancouver Island the mainland is outflanked by rocks and reefs, by sounds and inlets, while to the north-west islands large and small give protection to deep channels that wind towards Alaska. Outside these islands the coast is fringed by groups of islets, passages marked "unexamined" and the whole coast is wide open to the Pacific Ocean.

It was to explore this coast that we set out with Ronnie Scott-Moncrieff who flew up (there is no road north of Campbell River) to take Ted's place at Port Hardy. Our first day ended at Finn Bay at the mouth of Rivers Inlet. The weather had behaved much as Dave had said it might, the bright morning giving way to a threatening sky, a rising wind and squalls of rain which blotted

---

* In case anyone should be deterred by our experiences it is only fair to add that navigation is safe enough through the Seymour Narrows if carried out within an hour either side of slack water *provided* that the vessel is equipped with an adequate engine. Without this it is a hazardous proceeding.

out the landmarks in a most disconcerting way. It was dusk by the time we reached shelter and shook out the reefs, and so narrow was the entrance to Finn Bay that we nearly missed it—a tiny gap in a forest of pines through which we half drifted towards a cluster of lights on the starboard hand. This turned out to be a fish camp; a scow moored to the bank with chains. There was a store, ice for keeping fish (hardly necessary, we felt), two tanks of "gas" and half a dozen fish-boats.

Unseen voices asked us where we'd come from and who we were and when we'd told them we'd crossed Queen Charlotte Sound one of them said, "Didn't you listen to the forecast? It's blowing fifty knots."

Looking back on the short time we spent on that bit of coast I can't remember anything I have enjoyed more. "Local knowledge is essential," is how the *Pilot* would describe some of the places we poked our noses into, and I must admit there were times when a little would have come in handy. A snap decision of mine to take the Kwakshua Channel (marked "unexamined") nearly landed us in trouble, but it was cool and quiet as a cave when we turned to starboard down a narrow gully that cuts Hecate Island in half, passed between two islets and out into Hakai Pass.

The great Pacific rollers came tramping in on the winds of a fresh breeze, columns of spray like depth charges rose in all directions and we looked in vain for an expected light tower.* For a moment I could see no way out. The sea, however, was breaking on anything we were likely to hit, and by a process of elimination and a determined will to survive we mastered the intricacies of this unpleasant situation and shaped a course to clear all visible dangers.

Old *Moonie* went like a train, breasting the seas with that surprising power that she packs into her short little body, and I found myself falling in love with her all over again. The fresh wind, the big sea, the brassy glare of the sun as it sank towards the west gave that touch of anxiety which makes it so much more fun (and the more advisable) to find an anchorage for the night.

We were bound for Spider Anchorage, where several narrow entrances led to a landlocked lagoon. In the circumstances only one was possible. I identified Spider Island, the key to the spider's web, and we came tearing in with seas breaking on either side and it was at that moment that Anne cast doubt into my mind. There were no marks or lights or buoys, of course, and one islet looks

---

*It had been destroyed in the recent winter gales.

very like another. Point and counter point flew across the deck till Anne herself solved the problem by climbing up to the crosstrees and seeing in front of her, through a passage in a wall of rock, the lagoon itself. I relaxed, but Ronnie was not used to this.

"You're like a couple of children," he muttered. "Why can't you make up your minds and stick to it?"

Why not, indeed; but suppose I had been wrong?

In time we acquired some sort of local knowledge ourselves. A fisherman came aboard at Spider bringing a present of a salmon.

"You folks should visit Codfish Camp," he said, "they'd sure be glad to see you." He put a horny hand on a dozen islands (so small a scale are the only charts available): "The camp's in there. You want to look out for a rock off that point and there's a shoal in here ... turn in and you'll find the scow moored there."

They were certainly pleased to see us. At every camp there would be some story of the life along the coast; we were told of the seiner which, a hundred miles off-shore, dropped her propeller into the drink. Her skipper hewed down the bulkheads, made two paddle-wheels of them, rigged his mast athwartship and drove the paddles with his winch engine. By the time they made port the pole had eaten right through his bulwarks and through half the deck as well. There wasn't a smear of grease or butter left on that ship!

And then there was the ship that steered herself.... We heard that one from Jim, the storekeeper at Codfish. Jim and his brother left Vancouver City bound for Selwyn Inlet on the Charlottes in their salmon troller. The weather was thick all the way up and when they got into the Hecate Strait it was so thick that you couldn't see the bow from the wheelhouse. They had been doing watch and watch for two days and a night and Jim said he was pretty tired as he took over at midnight. About six that morning, just as it was getting light but just as thick as ever, Jim peered into the compass bowl in a dazed sort of a way and suddenly realized he'd been standing there for his whole watch, sound asleep! In something near a panic, he called his brother. He said, "Look, Ed, I've been asleep the whole of my blessed watch."

"No, you wasn't," replied his brother, " 'cos I came up about two hours ago and you talked to me. You was on course too."

Jim scratched his head, "Darn that," he said, "I know I been asleep. We may have been waltzin' about all over the blinkin' Strait."

And at that moment the curtain lifted a trifle and there they were steaming up Selwyn Inlet!

We ourselves were bound there a few days later from Camano Sound, ninety miles across the Hecate Strait.

I went on watch at four in the morning. We should, I thought, be approaching Selwyn Inlet. A fine drizzle drove through the air on a rising southerly wind, the ceiling was down to a hundred feet, and visibility was under a mile. Ronnie, blue with cold, was at the helm. I fussed over the chart. There should be an off-lying island, the only distinctive one on the coast. Suddenly Ronnie's shout:

"Land," he cried, "above us!"

And out of the mist, like the long edge of a saw, cut Reef Island, dead ahead.

CHAPTER FOURTEEN

FROM the chart the Queen Charlotte Islands look like a great kite, flown on a hundred and twenty miles of string from the top of Vancouver Island. When I first bought a general chart I thought they'd made a mistake and given me a map, so empty of figures were the sounds and fiords that penetrate their rugged coastline. Although there are reputed to be two hundred islands in all, there are two main ones, Graham in the North and Moresby in the South. Our first introduction to them, Selwyn Inlet on Moresby, was typical. Dark pines clung to almost impossible slopes which rose into mist and cloud. Cold, bleak and wet.

And yet to me, as we sailed into this deep fiord, it was more exciting than anything I had seen before. It was the remoteness, the savagery of the place, a thing I cannot do justice to in words. There should by rights have been nothing there at all, so that it came as something of an anti-climax to turn a corner and find, facing us, a logging camp and people.

The camp consisted of a long green building with an out-house for the plant, which made the electricity. The bunk-house, for that was the name they gave to their living quarters, was kept scrupulously clean, and the long deal tables were laid for supper; clean white plates, white cups, tablecloths and large white notices which read, "Please after your meal put your silverware into the pail. Thank you."

We met the High Rigger, paid at twenty dollars a day, whose job it was to rig the "skyline", a mast with pulleys, blocks and cables for shifting trees from where they were cut down to the "coal deck"; the "Fallers" who were paid by piece work. "They either get rich or get killed" we were told and we gathered the odds were little better than even. The loggers were a young, tough crowd, but work kept them out of mischief, and no drink was allowed in the camp. The Superintendent was new. He had been sent out to replace one who had not been able to keep harmony, for the men's isolation is complete: no roads, no outside entertainments, no women (except for a single wife who looked as if she found her position to be not altogether without strain), mail once a week by bush plane, casualties evacuated by seaplane.

These islands were, and are, inhabited by Haida Indians, a tribe lighter in colour than the coastal Indians and, except for their more oriental eyes, remarkably like the Polynesians. Some were tall and of fine physique and they had had the reputation of being the fiercest warriors along a thousand miles of coast. Legend has it that they came across the Bering Strait while it was still land and settled in the Queen Charlotte Islands. Constant raids on the mainland kept them free from too much in-breeding and preserved the race.

A little to the north of Selwyn Inlet lies the deserted village of Skedans. We arrived off the peninsula on which the village was built in the early evening. It was open to the Hecate Strait and not a place that a prudent mariner chooses to spend the night in, but the glass was high and what breeze there was came off the land.

What a perfect place to defend! To landward a steep and rocky bluff, to seaward a small hill that had been fortified and could be defended to the last man. On each side of the peninsula was a beach, so that the returning warriors could use either side according to the wind and I could imagine the victorious fleet sailing in after carrying the war into the enemy's country as far south as Discovery Island in Vancouver harbour four hundred miles away, whose name in Indian days, after the Haidas had been there, was Dead Man's Island.

Totem poles, magnificently carved, but bare of paint and rotting fast, stood among the trees and the long grass, some straight, others at a drunken angle. The archway of a meeting house was entwined by undergrowth; and we found, in what must have been the tribal burial ground, the bleached skulls and bones of children. Sixty years ago seven thousand Haidas lived in the valleys near Skedans when, with the suddenness of the plague, smallpox wiped out all but two hundred. No Haida has ever spent a night there since.

It was getting dark when Anne almost stepped on a day-old fawn. Its body was beautifully marked with spots and stripes of white against its warm brown coat. Her hand went down.

Ronnie said, quickly, "Don't touch it. If you do the mother will never come back. She's probably watching you."

Twenty miles north of Skedans Point lies Sand Spit and the entrance to Skidegate Inlet. It is, from a pilot's point of view, a remarkable place, for right across the entrance to the Inlet and for seven miles to the north runs a sand bar too shallow to cross with six-foot draught at low water. The wind had freshened and we were making for Dead Tree Point, sounding furiously with the lead while the ship buried her lee rail under a press of canvas.

There was, we found, more water than the chart marked, and we were soon easing sheets for the run up the inlet. Broad and well protected by the bar, dotted with islands and fair of face, this fiord bends to starboard, and round the corner we were confronted with the snows of the Slatechuck Mountain and the buildings of Queen Charlotte City, all twenty-four houses of it, which with a church, three stores and a hospital, go to make this northern metropolis. We entered the tiny harbour under sail, clawed down the canvas, let the halyards run and came alongside the float. A little group of people had gathered to take our lines, and a thin, gaunt man with blue eyes and a brogue, whom men called Paddy, leaned over our bulwarks and said in a hoarse whisper, "Sure, an' you're the first boat to sail in here from England in a hundred years."

We stayed for three days. We had been warned that you must never ask anyone in Queen Charlotte City why he lived there.

"There is always some very good reason," we were told, "but not one they like to talk about."

They took us over the hospital, the little church, the school, (for Haidas and whites) where I showed some coloured slides of the South Sea Islands. They fed us, they washed our clothes and offered us baths. No community ever did more to give strangers a free run of their little town.

Our last day we spent at the Haida village three miles down the Inlet. The houses were a little bare of paint, and inside they were as empty of anything but the essentials as a Tahitian's hut, and just as clean. We talked to fishermen, one of whom had lost his big seiner off Rose Spit a month or two ago, and to the Old Men of the Tribe who spend their time making models of totem poles in the Slatechuck stone which, when polished, resembles ebony. One man had a face like our pilot who had so hazardously taken us out of the lagoon at Takaroa. He was working on a medallion on which he had carved a vigorous-looking raven in relief. While he worked away with a minute chisel he started to tell us the story of the Raven and the Moon:

Long, long ago a raven killed the child of the owner of the moon, climbed into his skin, cried until the parents gave him the moon to play with, and then, when no one was looking, slipped out of the baby's skin and flew up through the smoke hole with the moon tucked under his wing. He flew to Nass River where he came upon some Oolaken fishermen who refused him fish unless he gave them light. Much to their delight he pulled out the moon and, tearing bits off with his powerful beak, he threw the pieces into the sky to make the stars, the sun and the moon. Although it was a little difficult to understand this rambling tale (which I have considerably shortened) it does explain why, on their totem poles, the raven is displayed in such a prominent position.

That evening we sailed across the sound to Alliford bay, making fast to a disused R.C.A.F. buoy. There wasn't a breath of wind and the bay was as still as a pond. I told Anne and Ronnie to make fast with an old coir rope. We turned in.

I was dimly aware of a shattering noise going on all too close to my ear. It was no human sound, nor had it anything to do with the sea. I opened my eyes. Halfway between a squawk and a screech, that's what it was. I turned out of our warm bunk to see a raven striding round the bulwarks. But when he saw me, instead of flying away, his eyes glowed with fury, he flapped his wings and intensified the squawking. I went up on deck, and with one last baleful look he flew away. I looked ahead. *Moonie*, under bare poles, was sailing herself towards the rockstrewn entrance to the bay.

By mid-day the old ship, under main, topsail and spinnaker, was out in the Hecate Strait. At its southern end it is a hundred miles across, a width it maintains for two hundred miles until the northern end is reached. Here the navigable width is limited by the overfalls off Rose Spit and the reefs off the B.C. coast to less than twenty miles. As it trends to the north-north-west the bottom shelves from fifty fathoms to nine. The south-easters, for which it is notorious, as Dave had said, funnel up the narrowing seaway with increasing strength and fury.

On this lovely day, with a steady glass and an off-shore wind, I went below without a care in the world. I think it was the feeling of strain that woke me a bare two hours later, and never have I seen weather change in so short a time or in so sinister a manner. A pall of light brown cloud covered the entire sky, and small wet cotton-wool clouds hung in the mountain valleys. To port the low coastline of Graham Island was all too close. By five o'clock we had two reefs in the mainsail, by six, three; by seven, four. We hove her to.

Wet, cold and anxious, I took a last look round and followed the others below. From time to time I cast a glance at Ronnie, for this was his first real gale, but from the quiet way he was chopping sticks with our blunt axe and gathering brickettes and bark for the fire it worried him as little as it would have done a fish.

The Hecate Strait was living up to its reputation: the wind howling out of the sou'-east, the smoking sea, steep and ugly as if it was scooping the very mud off the bottom, the ship blinded by the fury of the elements. Sail had to come off. With infinite care, for our lives depended upon it, we got the mainsail down, lashing gaff and boom to gallows. Turning, we ran under bare poles towards the Dixon Entrance. She was running too fast. I think Anne and I must have thought of the warps at the same moment, for without a word I saw her and Ronnie paying out the two thirty-fathom warps astern and after that I knew that if I could keep the vessel off the rocks she would still be afloat in the morning.

So successful had Ronnie been with the fire that the whole stove glowed. Between our one-hour watches (so bitterly cold was it on deck that we could stand no more) I sat over it warming my frozen hands. I remembered the story of Conrad's, it may have been his own, of how, as mate, he went up for his master's ticket. He was asked what he would do if his ship was driving down on the North German coast and as fast as he tried to extricate his hapless vessel, the examiner removed the means by which he attempted to do so.

At last he said, "I'm sorry, sir, but there's nothing more that I can do."

"Dammit, man," cried the examiner, "can't you pray?"

Soon after dawn I must have dozed for a few minutes. Anne was asleep in her bunk in her oily and sea-boots, and I heard Ronnie's shout.

I looked out on that waste of water. It was still blowing hard, but the rain had stopped and three islands to starboard gave us our position. The shores of Alaska were dimly visible ahead.

The glass, which had fallen rather more than half an inch, still fell, and as we entered Clarence Strait heavy squalls fell upon us. In thirty hours, I see from my log, we reefed and un-reefed that main eleven times. We tore up Nicholls Passage. Black mountains whose tops were white with fresh snow frowned down upon us, as if unwilling to welcome such an insignificant intruder to so wild a land. We shot into the Tongass Narrows—it was the 14th of June.

The neat, white little town of Ketchikan appeared ahead, a kindly fish-boat told us where to berth. We ran into the small boat harbour and let everything go with a run, only to haul all up again as the ship was gripped in a strong current that threatened to throw her out. It took us thirty mintues to sail thirty yards, and by that time we were being cheered from the bank like a football team.

We were, as you can imagine, pretty tired. The Customs came to clear us. They asked us many questions about the voyage and then they left. As they walked up the float I heard one of them say:

"Two of those guys are M.D.s. You'da' thought they'da' had more sense!"

CHAPTER FIFTEEN

RAIN. Drizzle or downpour from racing clouds and a pall overhanging the mountains, people striding from street to street taking as much notice of the wet as an African does of the sun, a river running past Indian huts built on stilts against the spring floods, a harbour full of fish-boats, for they said this was the worst spring they could remember. And then, one morning, sun shining from a pale blue sky. The whole face of the little town changed. The vivid greens of the hemlock, the dazzling snows that seemed to come right down almost to the town itself, the white buildings washed by the rains and the wooden roads supported by long piles like trellis-work, scrubbed and weathered to a pale grey.

Although Ketchikan is no longer a frontier town it has a pioneering air. People are far too busy making money to have time for the pursuits of leisure, but they have one fixed and common purpose, to leave Ketchikan as soon as they are able; the young to go on, the more mellow to go back, if possible to somewhere warmer like Honolulu. All, that is, except the fishermen. But fishermen are like farmers; they grumble but they never quit.

All this abominable weather began to make us feel we might have to beat back to Victoria, so we cut short our stay and on an afternoon of no wind we left under engine (our engine liked Ronnie and had allowed him to coax it into action) bound for Prince Rupert to "clear" for Canada. Our course never took us out of sight of land and we were now well stocked with American charts. That night we put into Hasler Harbour, a misleading name for what is no more than a bay protected from Revillagigedo Channel by an island whose shores seemed to be covered with green sand. I meant to go and have a look at that sand, but a fisherman came chugging in round the other side of the island and her owner held up a salmon.

"This any good to you?" he called.

To which Ronnie promptly answered, "Is it not!" and rowed off to collect the fish and ask our friend to share it.

His name was Jim Gordon, for fourteen years a radio-operator in Pan-American Airways.

"The pay-cheque was good," he said, "but when they grounded me I quit."

He came to the north-west, bought a fish-boat in Seattle and fished the Alaskan waters in the summer. So far he'd been able to keep himself during the winter, run a car and go down Mexico way for a bit of sun. No, he'd never had anyone else aboard and never missed the company that another would have given him. He'd been out for the last two weeks and was returning to Ketchikan with a boat full of fish. But Jim was more than a fisherman, he was a born seaman. In this short time he had acquired a mass of information about coves and holes among the rocks where he had weathered severe storms, and he talked as a man who has spent his life on the coast. He had a voice rather like Raymond Gram Swing to whom we used to listen so intently during the war.

It was still light when he left us, around eleven, but now the cove was quiet. The golden eagles, of which we had seen at least a dozen when we first arrived, had stopped talking to each other, and the clouds had lifted revealing a cold northern sky. It was strangely colourless, for it was almost time for the sun to go to bed.

Our last night in Alaska was spent tucked up in one of Jim's holes behind Cape Fox. The glass was falling, but we were wet, cold and very tired; nor was it prudent to sail these waters at night because of the danger of hitting logs. So we dropped anchor and set the alarm for three o'clock. It needed no alarm to wake me. A fresh east wind blew straight in and one look at the sky and the glass warned us that another sou'-easter was on its way. We beat out and soon we were at it again shortening sail, reef after reef, while endless rain went through our oilskins like water through a sieve. It must be quite a time, I thought, since there had been anything dry aboard. We reached the Metlakatla channel, a short cut to Prince Rupert, but so narrow and winding did it appear on our chart that I should not have had the courage to attempt it had it not been for Jim. It meandered past an Indian village, past sandy bays where for once hills and mountains seemed pushed away. Above all, it was smooth and quiet after the turmoil outside.

Prince Rupert did not look attractive. It is an untidy, top-heavy sort of place, the skeleton of a businessman's dream of a great city, a future golden gateway to the Orient. Unfortunately the businessman went down with the *Titanic* forty years ago, since when no one has thought Prince Rupert to be worth while. The town is some distance from the dock, and not for a minute, not for a second, did it stop raining.

But there is something I like to remember. We were tied up to the Prince Rupert Yacht and Rowing Club. We had by this time exhausted our supply of "gas" (most of it had gone on priming) so I took our three two-gallon cans to the man who looked after the gas station. I pulled out a five-dollar bill but he firmly shook his head.

"I read in some newspaper you'd sailed from England to Victoria on twelve gallons," he laughed, "I guess I'd like to give you this to get you home."

The west coast of the Queen Charlotte Islands where we were now bound is as wild and rugged, so we had been told, as the Magellan country. Inhabited by bears, eagles and deer but not by man, it is indented by inlets and fiords and visited by fishermen during the summer; and by one other sailorman. He was the sort about whom legends grow up overnight. Some said he was an ex-Royal Navy man, others that his sister owned a great house in Mayfair (and a Rolls-Royce) but the men in the Charlottes knew him for a superb seaman to whom the whole coast from Cape St. James to Dutch Harbour in the Aleutian Islands was an open book. Before I had heard anything about him I came down one morning to Musgrave Cove to find a stranger lying at anchor. She was a gaff cutter with an enormous exhaust pipe coming out of the after end of the cabin and she looked so weathered that she fitted into her bleak surroundings (it was snowing and bitterly cold) as a thrush into a hedge. She had an air about her that dissuaded me from immediately calling on her owner, and by the time I next looked out she had gone.

We saw her only once more, in the spring, running before half a gale of wind down an inside passage. Her owner, bearded, blended with the appearance of his ship and looked as silent and as taciturn as he was in fact reputed to be. We half hoped to see him on this coast where he had made his name.

We slipped out of Brown's Passage on the tail of the last sou'-easter. We crossed the Hecate Strait making for the west coast of the Queen Charlottes. By the afternoon of the following day we were within five miles of Langara Island, off the north-western tip of Graham Island. "So near," Ronnie was to say, "and yet so far away . . ." For within the hour the wind had switched from east to west bringing with it a thin, tenuous mist from the cold Pacific.

The uncertain currents, the light head-wind, the unreliable log, after five hours of beating to and fro all I knew was that I had no idea where I was. And then, just before I handed the ship over to Ronnie the mist lifted to port, and there was a small square of land like a window in a wall, bearing south-east. But what land was it?

Anne, pouring the water from the pressure cooker into a basin on deck, gave it a glance. "Langara Island?" she asked.

"Good Lord," I said. "Perhaps it is."

Although it disappeared almost immediately, the more I thought of it the more determined I became that it must be the west coast of Langara, and I worked out a course for Ronnie that would take him down to Port Louis.

I was not asleep when Ronnie called me. "Peter, come up a moment, will you?"

He said, "I can hear birds twittering, land birds, to starboard."

I looked at him blankly.

"That means there's land to starboard," he explained patiently.

"The nearest land," I muttered, "should be a thousand miles away."

Ronnie's face sharpened. "Can't you hear them?"

"Yes, but one bird is the same as another to me."

And at that moment I heard another sound, one that I knew only too well: breakers. Even then I didn't stumble on what we'd done. We hauled our wind making north of west and still the land, now dimly seen as a darker grey, clung to us like a limpet, and then the mist cleared for a moment and I saw the light in Parry Passage, bearing south. We'd come right down the wrong side of Langara Island.

But I knew where I was now, in a tideless backwater, Nigeria Bay, and there we stayed all night, *Moonraker* lying like a dog at her master's feet; for there wasn't a breath of wind, and it was too deep to anchor.

The sound of a high-speed engine brought me on deck at dawn to see a fish-boat circling round and round us.

Her owner hailed me: "Why don't you come into Henslung Camp?"

"No wind," I shrugged, "and our engine's broken down."

"Aw, there's no fish in the sea this morning," he said. "Throw me a line and I'll tow you in."

The radio and a Prince Rupert newspaper had mentioned our appearance on the coast, and curiosity was rife. The fish-camp (there were really two, one where the men owned their own boats, the other in which the Company owned the boats and hired the men) was the largest we had seen. It was like a little floating town, and there were few things that a seaman might want that could not be had at the store: our petrol pipe was mended within the hour. Some of the men fished alone, others with their wives. There was a girl from Liverpool, a man from Devon, a private secretary to one of the heads of the C.P.R. who preferred the sea to the office, and a chief of the Eagle tribe whose grandfather had owned the last three-masted schooner on the coast. The talk was of fish and boats, of the seiners (like the wicked uncles) who netted fish in the rivers (for this was a camp of trollers) and the paucity of salmon. A halibut was plopped on our deck and out of courtesy Anne saw no alternative to cooking all forty pounds of it on her single Primus!

By the time we were up next morning there wasn't a boat in the place, so we followed their example and put to sea, a calm, smiling sea and a light following wind and *sun*! At first the coast resembled that of Cornwall, but before we came to Port Louis in the evening sombre snow-clad mountains appeared to the south. Port Louis is supposed to be the one harbour on the west coast that is safe to run for if caught by bad weather, but to us, that evening, it looked inexpressibly gloomy. The fresh wind astern, the clusters of islands in the deep and frowning bay, the sea breaking on reefs, no lights, no marks and two islets that we had to identify, one of two hundred feet and one of one hundred and fifty, made a little more difficult by the taller of the two having recently lost its trees!

At the entrance to the bay in which we hoped to anchor the wind was cut off, and we half drifted, half carried our way into this silent pool whose name was Kialthli Inlet. There was not a sound . . . not a cry of a bird, not a whisper of the sea on a beach, not a stir in the forest. A blood-red sunset bathed the trees in a gory light. It would have been a good place for Miss Greta Garbo.

From here to Tasu Sound is the finest coast, if you like your coasts to look like this, that I have ever seen: high mountains, precipitous ravines, black forests, desolate and forbidding; a coast to make you ponder on the insignificance of man. A fair wind had taken us south-eastwards all day, but in the evening it fell too light for us to make Tasu before nightfall. What a place, I kept telling myself, to be hove to. But the night was short, and by four o'clock we were under way to a freshening onshore breeze and a falling glass. The sea was a bottle green. The wind backed, and it became a race between us and the weather, with the odds increasingly against us.

Grey cliffs, their tops lost in the gathering clouds, fell sheer into the sea, a great wall of rock through which, at two hundred yards from the entrance, no hole oculd be seen. Clouds swirled down from the heights above, and if they blocked the entrance before we found it we were due for a nice long wait on a cold and angry sea. But we beat 'em! On the next board there was the opening and, like a glimpse of a promised land, we saw the sun still shining on a blue and glittering lake.

"Down topsail," I shouted, as the ship, with the sheets just started, raced for the narrow opening, and as we entered this rocky gorge the clouds came down to the level of the sea and it was like running into a tunnel full of smoke. Squalls from either side, water the colour of ink flecked with white where the wind whipped it round; then we were out on the other side, the sou'-easter still held at mountain level from breaking in.

We spent three days in Tasu Sound. Most of the time it rained and blew, but even a hurricane could not have hurt us in such a sheltered place and the stove burned merrily day and night. We had heard that a trail once led over the mountains from Two Mountain Bay to Selwyn Inlet but we found no tracks except those made by bear and deer. Anne saw a cub run up a tree and was quietly going to talk to it when Ronnie pulled her away. His sharp eyes had seen the mother sitting at the bottom! A trail led us to a waterfall. The pool into which the fall cascaded was brown, for this was cedar water, poisonous to most people, and we had been told that fishermen wrecked on this coast had died of thirst. This we found hard to believe, for all we would have had to have done was to open our mouths and lift them up.

Ronnie took a rifle ashore to shoot deer but he went alone, for Anne and I are not at our best in undergrowth, and as Ronnie so rightly said, "How can I stalk deer with you crashing through the forest like a herd of elephants."

We sailed into Wright's Inlet. This, to our minds, was the finest anchorage of them all. It was a little unfortunate that on that very day the Baby Blake got blocked. Ronnie and I spent the whole afternoon in the fo'c'sle bent double over it but in the end we carried it triumphantly through the cabin and hoisted it on deck. Ronnie said firmly, "I'm going ashore to get a stick to clean the outlet pipe." It occured to me, after an hour had passed, that he was finding it extremely difficult.

There were now eight days of Ronnie's leave to go. The distance to Victoria was 473 miles and there was time enough, I thought, to visit at least one inlet on the west coast of Vancouver. Ronnie, who has lived on Vancouver Island most of his life, did not share my view. Head winds, moderate to strong, prevailed until we sighted Cape Cook; followed by calms. Fourteen hours here, seventeen hours off Cape Estevan. I saw what Ronnie meant.

We could not land him, as there are no roads across Vancouver Island, no roads, indeed, of any sort until you get down to Bamfield where there is a boat to Alberni. This, then, was the position at noon on July 5th. The ship was becalmed off Clayoquot Sound, and Bamfield lay forty miles to the south-east; Ronnie's leave was up in two days. In the evening a northerly wind sprang up, freshened, and veered to the north-east. That ancient rhyme:

> Last night the sun went pale to bed
> The moon in haloes hid her head

fitted the portents perfectly, and during my watch the glass dropped like a stone. Driving rain, two reefs in the main, followed by three and then four, a short steep sea—how sick we were of these sou'-easters!

We plunged on, for I was determined to land Ronnie if it was humanly possible. The wind, I argued, was along the coast, I should recognize Cape Beale if I saw it; but what if I could not find it? We stood in for the land. Two hours later, with the tension mounting, minute by minute, I caught through the murk what I took to be a high bluff of land. Wherever that bluff was, it wasn't Cape Beale, and at that moment it really started to blow. We got the ship about at the third attempt, and for half an hour we ran with the sea and wind abeam to make a much-needed offing. It was a most exciting sail, but in the end, as I was afraid it might, a sea swept ship.

Ronnie, who was for'ard lashing down a coil of rope, jumped for the ratlines, Anne and I were lifted right off the deck, clinging to the gallows, and, like the owner of the Tahiti ketch in the Yaculta Rapids, we watched the after end of our ship disappear below the sea. The oars were swept from under the pram, the pram shifted but did not break its lashings, a sail lashed down on the foredeck was lost overboard. But by the time the next sea arrived, *Moonraker* had thrown the first one out, and we took the hint and hove to.

Rather dazed by all this battering we went below. The stove was out, the bunks were soaked, and while Ronnie was re-lighting the fire he was thrown violently against the wireless set, bruising a rib.

The whine of the wind, the crash of the seas, the rattle of spray like a distant burst of machine-gun fire, the concentration of thought, the physical force of moving uphill from the starboard side to the port, squatting on the slippery floor with a couple of tins and a pan, having forgotten to get the opener, hoping that someone filled the Primus after breakfast, but guessing they didn't and finding your guess was right.

The dim cabin (for a sail had been lashed between the pram and the cabin top to prevent more water coming through the skylights), the smell of wet clothes swinging in time to the ship's motion in front of the smoking fire, the knowledge that the gale is blowing you back the way you'd fought to come and that Ronnie's leave is up tomorrow night.

But the sea is for sailing, and this is a sailor's life. Hot stew and mugs of coffee are heartening things, and we turn in to get what sleep we can.

The blow was as short as it was fierce. A day later found us just inside the Juan de Fuca Strait becalmed on a long swell left over from the gale, and wishing for a friendly fishing-boat bound for Victoria that would take Ronnie home. Ronnie was working at the engine, when I saw *White Hart* making towards us. Never have the "Watch dogs of the Juan de Fuca Strait" as Tony and Bridget style themselves, been such a welcome sight, for Ronnie would be in Victoria that night.

Tony came out of his deckhouse.

"Where were you in that blow?" he hailed. "It blew sixty knots and eighty in the Hecate Strait, and it's the worst they've had on the coast in July for fifty years."

CHAPTER SIXTEEN

DURING the winter Christopher had earned enough to travel across the United States by Greyhound bus, had worked his way back to England, spent a couple of months at home, booked a passage to Hudson Bay in a cargo steamer and had come down from Churchill by train.

He arrived at Victoria in August laden with ship's gear from King's at Burnham and a couple of jibs from Sadler's, which he managed to put through the Customs as ship's stores, and just in time to help put the finishing touches to the ship before the start of her long voyage home.

Moonraker had not been out of the water for eleven months and I suspected her bottom was a trifle dirty. Round the waterline the copper was riddled with pin-point holes and was thin as a sheet of paper. We had just decided to scrub at the Royal Victoria Yacht Club, when *Aura*, a small American sloop, sailed in. This in iteslf was so rare an event, for few Americans have the patience to sail in light winds or in a restricted anchorage, that I asked them aboard. Before they left Norman Blanchard said:

"You folks must come and visit with us at Seattle."

I explained that we should be on our way south in a few days.

"Look, Peter," said Norman, "I heard you say you had to scrub the bottom, why not haul her out at my yard on Union Lake? It won't cost you a dime."

I hesitated; not because all this might delay our departure but because, after less than two hours' acquaintance, Norman was offering me such a golden opportunity.

He said, "You can give a talk to the Seattle Yacht Club, and if there's work to be done you can pay me out of that. Call me before you leave Victoria."

In light winds and in thick weather we sailed across the Juan de Fuca Strait to Port Townsend, arriving at midnight. At eight o'clock the next morning I went along to clear for the U.S.A., and to my astonishment was hailed by a familiar voice. *Aura* had come to meet us. More than that, a motor-vessel had come to help to tow us. It was a triumphal procession that steamed all the thirty-eight miles up Puget Sound and locked into the Union Lake around which the city of Seattle is built.

Norman said he'd never seen anything like *Moonraker* in his life. Her full bilges, her fine run and her deep draught, her massive rudder fittings, all intrigued him.

He said, "I wouldn't have credited that a ship of her age could have kept her shape so well."

Nor could we understand how she could have sailed at all, so thick were the barnacles on her bottom.

Never have we scrubbed in such comfort. We scraped off the barnacles and washed her down with a hose. Norman came along with a huge tin of grease.

"Here, Peter, rub this all over her and she'll stay cleaner a bit longer. Now, what about this copper? Friend of mine at Pacific Marine said if I cared to come along he had some lying around the yard he didn't want. Now I come to look at it, there's enough for your waterline."

The week we stayed at Seattle it rained most of the time, making the city look a little drab. I was taken over the Medico-Dental building that had just been added to the University of Washington. It is built in the contemporary style and is not without a certain practical beauty of its own, and it is, as you can imagine, magnificently equipped. The young professor who showed me round took me into the students' common-room, spacious and restful. I congratulated him on having such a pleasant place to relax.

"Relax!" he cried. "Our stoodents don't relax, Doctor, they work. We reckon we have five per cent of nervous breakdowns in a year."

One night the Blanchards asked us up to dinner on our own. There was a sensibility about Norman that does not often sit hand in hand with the feverish life of an American businessman, and we enjoyed that evening more than most, but when we left Eunice said to Anne:

"We feel so selfish not sharing you, but for just this once we wanted to have you to ourselves."

I went to see Norman in his office next day with my pockets full of dollars from the talk. I asked him for his bill.

He said, "My directors (I didn't know he had any) tell me that we've had so much publicity over you with the radio and T.V. that it's going down on the expense sheet. I'm not sure we shouldn't pay you!"

It was a wonderful feeling having a clean ship. We left Port Townsend on the beginning of the ebb and slipped out over the smooth sea with wraiths of fog drifting in from the strait until it became impossible to see the bowsprit end from the helm. The diaphone on New Dungeness Point brought back memories of the Sunk on a hot misty day in the Thames Estuary (how far away that seemed!) and we groped our way in behind a low spit of land which does in fact recall to mind Dungeness itself.

What a sail we had that night! The wind fresh from the west, the tide pouring down the Strait deceiving me by the pace it carried us up to windward, Anne's brilliant notion of counting the sequence of the red light for which I was so boldly steering to find it was Albert Head, a full eight miles to the west, the wild rush into the calm waters of the harbour nearly missing Fisherman's Wharf altogether, so unusual an appearance did it present. It was empty!

One or two of the seiners fishing off Active Pass (in the Gulf Islands) had intercepted a run of salmon making for the Fraser River. Within a very short time eighteen boats were hauling in fish as fast as it was humanly possible to do so. The Victoria to Vancouver steamer was confronted by a mass of lights, nets across the pass and a bunch of fishermen too busy to curse them as they tried to hoot their way through.

"This is our night, pal," they said. "You'll have to wait."

By breakfast time a million salmon had been caught, and as salmon was retailing at two dollars fifty a fish a few men had made a large number of dollars in a night.

There was, as you may well imagine, considerable rejoicing at Victoria that night. We had been out to dinner and were walking down the float when we noticed an Indian weaving uncertainly about the dock. By law no Indian is allowed to be served with alcohol, but this one had obviously been able to get around this tiresome regulation. As he was carrying a rifle under his shoulders we made a hasty retreat to our ship having, we hoped, escaped his notice.

We slipped below, drawing the curtain. The next thing I knew was that the curtain was thrust aside and the muzzle of a rifle was pointing at my middle.

A voice whispered, "White man come out."

The others, not in a direct line of fire, crept forward on a plan of their own, while I stayed there hoping that either the rifle was not loaded or that the Indian's fingers would not fumble too closely with the trigger. I thought I heard Anne slip out of the fo'c'sle and at that moment the barrel wandered away.

What happened next was a sort of anti-climax. I jerked the barrel to one side, Christopher joined me, Anne took the Indian in the rear but there was nothing there to fight. He was just like a dish of jelly, limp and cold. We took the bolt out of the rifle (it was not loaded) and dragged him back to his seiner. In the morning I went round to return the bolt to the skipper but the ship had gone so when he next takes that rifle out of the rack to shoot a deer, he'll get a surprise!

Before we sailed I had a letter from Bill Priest of *Tara*. You may remember that we had last seen him steaming out of Musgrave Cove on his way south to Seattle and then to San Francisco. Some months later we had heard through the ocean voyager's grapevine that *Tara* had been lost, a rumour that was afterwards contradicted but, as there is rarely smoke without a fire, we had wondered what had given rise to it. In this letter Bill told us his story:

They had left the Juan de Fuca Strait rather later than he had intended and had been caught in a sou'-easter in which the main gaff and the steel jackstay had carried away, the mizzen sail split and *Tara* was driven many miles off her course. That the gale blew along the coast and not on to it undoubtedly saved their lives.

The gale blew itself out and, as so often happens in these waters, was succeeded by days of calm. They motored down the Oregon coast and arrived off Gray's Harbour at night. *Tara's* people were desperately tired and the one thing they wanted was to set foot on dry land; but Bill had no large-scale charts of the harbour or of the river beyond. He rang up the coastguards on the ship-to-shore radio and was told that it was safe to come in as it was nearly high water, so he negotiated the entrance and motored up the river. Unfortunately he mistook a light that was in the middle of a rocky patch for that on a lighted buoy and at five knots with the flood-tide under him he ran *Tara* right up on the rocks, ripping a considerable part of her port side out of her. To most of us *Tara* would have appeared a total loss, but not to Bill. With the help of the coast-guards he got hold of some empty oil-drums and, as the tide went down and the water poured out of her hull, they cut down the bulkheads with axes, enlarged the opening to the hatch and packed the hull with empty drums. They tacked a sail over the torn hull and arranged for a launch to stand by as the flood returned.

Tara floated. The launch took her in tow, but on their way up to the shipyard the pressure of air below started to lift the cabin top so there were Bill and his crew hammering in nails for all they were worth to prevent the sea from wresting victory from their grasp—and they won! But, as Bill said in his letter, how much less exhausted they would have been if they had spent one night more at sea.

Some weeks later I met Bill at Newport, California. He looked, although this may have been my imagination, an older man.

He said, "You know, Peter, there's still a lot I've got to learn about the sea."

CHAPTER SEVENTEEN

PROFITING by Bill's unfortunate experience in *Tara* we made up our minds to keep a hundred miles off the coast of Oregon on our way to San Francisco. By doing so we should avoid the constant north-westerly current running up the coast and gain some advantage, perhaps, from the warm Japanese current running in the opposite direction.

With this plan in mind we left Port Renfrew (a pub and a dozen houses climbing up a hill), and as the ship rose to the swell our hearts rose too, for we were homeward bound after two years. The day was fine and sunny, and as we reached the Light and Whistle buoy a salmon troller, a stranger to us, came up at high speed. While her owner kept the boat a few feet away his wife threw a prince of fish upon our decks.

"Good luck," she cried. "Give my love to the Old Country when you get back!"

The wind fell light, and all night we sailed or drifted over a quiet sea, and at dawn we were only just outside the strait, it was as if *Moonraker* was reluctant to leave.

Light head winds, sudden squalls and torrential rain were our lot until we were within three hundred miles of San Francisco. Here we were so utterly becalmed that it seemed as if the world had run out of wind. The sun beat down upon our decks from a cloudless sky.

The following afternoon I came up on deck, sleepy-eyed, and at first I could see nothing except the long north-westerly swell, until I noticed a few pale blue whorls like the paws of a cat spreading away from the ship in an ever-widening circle. A faint air came from the north-west, the ship stirred, and before I had time to guy the boom and set the spinnaker (the others were deep in their afternoon sleep) the circle had grown till its form was lost and a breeze had been born again. It grew into a healthy child that night and into a lustier one next day. On the following morning my meridian sight gave me rather a shock. We were too far to the west. How humiliating it would be if the current and the surface drift from this fine wind whisked us past San Francisco before we could make in to the land! The breeze, now two days old, was Force 7 on the Beaufort scale and under reefed staysail and four-reefed main we hauled in the sheets and made for the land. It was Anne's watch and if she did not complain it was from

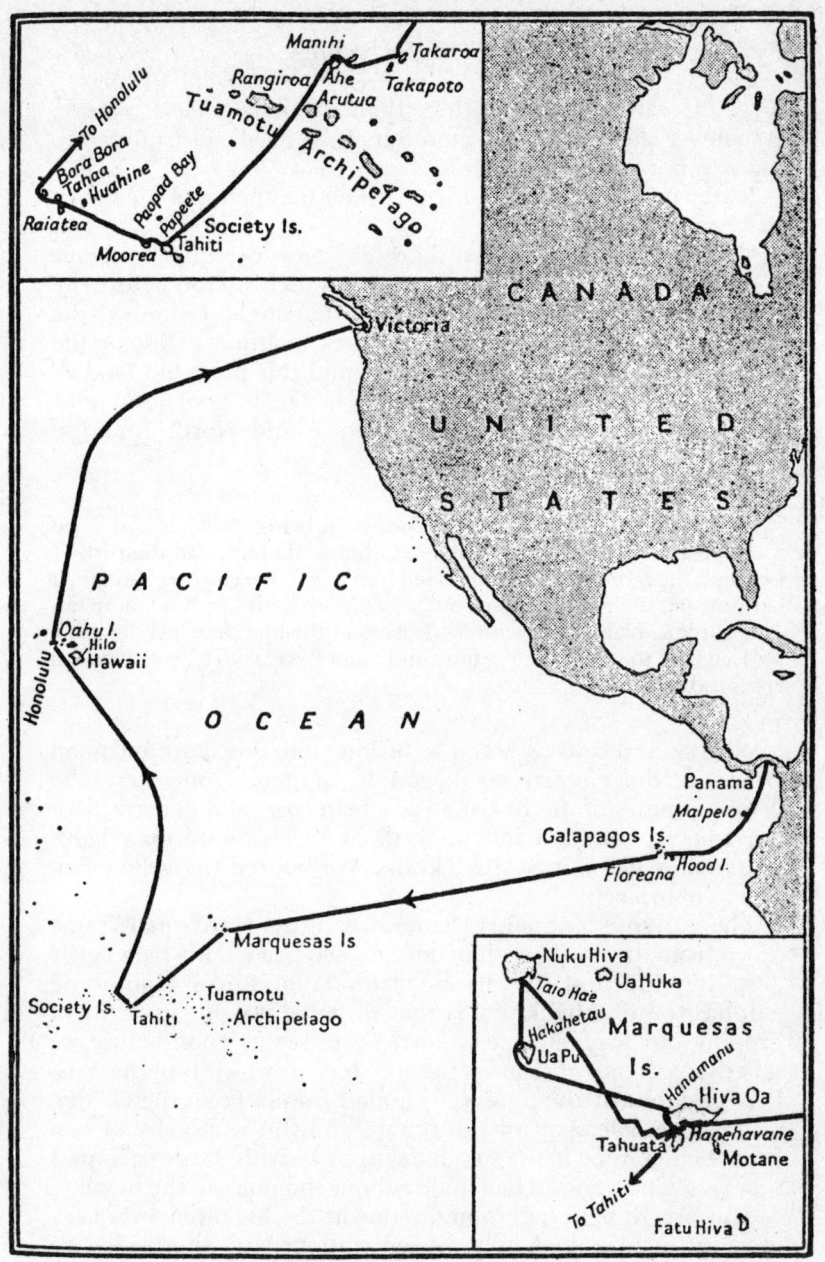

Panama to British Columbia

force of circumstance rather than from a stoical nature. Whenever she opened her mouth half the Pacific Ocean tried to slip past her throat.

"Good practice," I told her from under the shelter of the hatch, "for crossing the Caribbean."

My noon position showed there was little need for my panic and as soon as it was my turn to go on watch we ran before the wind with dry decks. At ten o'clock that night I climbed the ratlines and saw the flash of Point Reyes Lighthouse fine on the port bow twenty-five miles away. Behind this point lies Drake's Bay where Sir Francis came to an anchor in June of 1580 after giving up his attempt to find a way round North America. Hakluyt records.:

> We found the ayre so cold, that our men being grievously pinched with the same, complained of the extremities thereof, and the further we went, the more the colde increased upon us. Wherefore we thought it best for that time to seeke the land, and did so, finding it not mountainous, but low, plaine land with 38 degrees of the line. In which height it pleased God to send us into a faire and good Baye, with a good winde to enter the same.

We followed Drake's example, beating into this "faire and good Baye" as the eastern sky began to lighten. Gone were the dripping pines of the British Columbian coast and in their place the smooth rounded hills looked, in that pre-morning light, remarkably like our Sussex Downs. We hoisted the yellow flag and went to sleep.

The ship snubbing at her chain woke me up. Hard squalls came down from the north, a white mist, as cold as a wraith, blew eerily past the ship and the diaphone on Point Reyes Lighthouse emphasized my thankfulness that we were not at this moment groping our way into the Golden Gate. It was noon before we sailed. In patches of clearing mist the red-brown cliffs of the coast flew past, but by the time we rounded Bonita Point the Golden Gate, the noble span of the bridge and the white city of San Francisco, shining in the sun, burst upon us with the same impact that Desolation Sound had done a thousand miles to the north.

This was to be, I had thought, one of the big moments of my life, but if an onlooker had been stationed on the bridge he would, alas, have seen no stately sailing ship winging in from sea but a reefed-down gaff-cutter that appeared to tack downwind. For one of these disagreements which break out in the best regulated yachts (forgive me if I am wrong, but I think they probably do) was in full swing. Christopher had friends at Sausalito on the north side of the bay; I maintained we should "clear" at San Francisco on the south side, and Anne, who has never had the slightest reverence for authority, said that was silly. As arguments were hurled across the decks so did the ship point first to San Francisco and then to Sausalito.

Of course we went to Sausalito, and naturally no one took the slightest notice of our yellow flag. The U.S.A. officials are not always partial to yachtsmen, and I dared not go ashore; so in desperation I rowed into the Yacht Basin, looking lost, until the master of a motor yacht asked what I wanted.

I told him.

"I can get the Customs on my 'phone," he said. "I'll speak to the boss."

In a moment or two I was speaking to the boss myself.

"I hear you've come a long way to see us," said a pleasant voice. "I'll send a man over to clear you in the morning."

I rowed back to the ship. Christopher and Anne had dinner waiting for me. Not by so much as a flicker of an eyelid did they betray their evident content. Afterwards, being well fed, I went up on deck. There was a flat calm and a thousand lights were reflected upon the water. Our breeze, just over three days old, had died.

Americans say that there are three cities in their country that are worth a visit, New York, New Orleans and San Francisco. San Francisco is built, like Rome, on many hills, up and down which we rode, like children out on a treat, on cable cars. In the evening, as we walked along the almost deserted business section, the narrow streets, the massive stone buildings, reminded us of Leadenhall Street on a Sunday afternoon.

It has the largest Chinatown outside China and, like all great cities, its slums and hide-outs, but the sad part of San Francisco is the harbour.

In the museum there are photographs of the bay studded with full-rigged ships waiting to load, but from Telegraph Hill this morning we saw, in all these miles of docks, two ships; both of them sound asleep. Strikes and lock-outs were responsible for this; the work, we were told, of one man who had successfully driven the trade southwards to San Pedro, the port for Los Angeles. It was to be hoped, they said, that he would go there too and drive it back again.

Down in the fish harbour at night the place still comes alive.

The garish lights, the honky-tonks, the canned music and the rattle of plates bring to mind what San Francisco must have been like at the turn of this century. Here the spirit of the sea still lives; in the sturdy lines of the fishing craft, in the men who sail out in search of salmon or who hunt the albacore down to the coast of Mexico. Mr Gann, in *Fiddler's Green*, gives you the feeling of the waterfront, or what is left of it, far better than I can.

Facing you, as you come in from the Golden Gate, is the Island of Alcatraz. It is small and is almost entirely covered by the huge stone buildings of the prison. On the chart it is surrounded by red lines inside which no vessel may penetrate. When fog comes rolling in through the Golden Gate (as it does four days out of seven at this time of the year) you can hear the horn on the lighthouse sounding its dismal warning to the free and its chance of freedom to the prisoner; but it is the boast of the authorities that no man has ever escaped from Alcatraz and lived.

While San Francisco hides her head in fog Sausalito basks in the sun. It is small, and the buildings straggling up the street reminded us of Sesimbra in Portugal. Christopher's friends, whose house overlooked the harbour, drove us up the Napa Valley where grow the finest grapes, according to the San Franciscans, in California. We visited an American wine lodge. A rather bored middle-aged man took us round. From his remarks I gathered they had no time to waste in letting wine mature so they first extracted the elements of natural processes, "hotted 'em up" and finally re-injected them. We tasted but saw no reason to buy.

We went on to an Italian wine lodge. It was a family affair. A man with the look of a Lombardy peasant in his eye introduced us to others of his family (first-generation Americans), discoursed about wines, comparing theirs with those of Italy, and told us that here there was little difference in their methods. The grapes were crushed by machines (no peasants' feet allowed in this asceptic country) but otherwise the juices were allowed to ferment in their natural way. The wine tasted good, and we bought as much as we could conveniently stow aboard our ship.

On the only afternoon that we had set aside for work on the ship (for San Franciscans are a hospitable lot) a man came hobbling down the float on crutches, his right foot so swathed in bandages that I took this, quite wrongly, to be a case of gout. He was short and stocky with a pointed grey beard. Hilary Belloc described himself as a "Mender of Roads" but in a less mechanical age he might have been one of the great entertainers like the late

Mr Percy French.

A few days ago Hilary had been inspecting a manhole. As he lifted a heavy cover he said to himself, "Now, don't drop this on your foot."

"Blow me," said Hilary, "I forgot all about the bloody thing and dropped it on my foot."

Hilary and Nevil Shute who was over from Australia, were thinking of going down to the Big Sur country in a few days, and they asked us to come with them. Hilary's entire luggage for the three days consisted of a case of red wine and two straw hats.

The road kept close to the coast with occasional detours round hills while the Pacific thundered on rocks or surged into sandy bays.

We lunched at Monterey. Cannery Row was deserted. Where was the Palace Flop House, the Bear Flag, Suzy's Boiler and Western Biological? I do not know, for I had not the courage to go and find out.

Farther south we had a look at Carmel Mission, the oldest on the Coast, but Carmel had been "hotted up" like the American wine, and retained about as much feeling as a downtown drugstore. Only the tower and the belfry had been left alone.

When we had disentangled ourselves from curios, mementoes and hordes of automobiles, we drove to Point Lobos, watching the famous cypress trees waving in the breeze, drove down the "Seventeen Mile Drive" (where people build houses on the same scale as Palm Beach) and had tea in Pebble Beach. The village is "cute"; Olde Worlde Shoppes, and a house, so Hilary said, that had all its plumbing done in gold. On the walls of the Bank there is a plaque showing Friar Sierra running through a wrought-iron grille with the worried expression of a client that has been refused an overdraft.

We headed south to the Big Sur Country. It used to be a haunt for people who wanted to get as close to nature and as far from their fellow men as possible, but since the highway has been built it is on its way to becoming California's greatest "Back to Nature" attraction. It has fluted mountain ridges, deep valleys and a climate as good as most. We left the highway and drove up a narrow dirt track which rose in spirals until we looked down upon the Pacific from a great height. The noise of the engine disturbed young deer which bounded in great leaps into the bush, and we came in time to the bungalow of Henry Miller, the author. He was out. A soft wind blew in from the Pacific Ocean sixteen hundred feet below, and the heat haze that had given this rugged coastline an ethereal look slowly disappeared. Mountains, valleys and sea became hard and real and there was no trace of a human hand.

We never met Mr Miller, but I read an article of his quite recently on the Big Sur Country. He writes:

> I have come to take a different view of it however . . . Yes, I can visualize vast multitudes living where there are now only a few scattered families. There is room for thousands upon thousands to come . . . There will be airplanes, seaplanes, helicopters . . . An isolated Paradise may be good for the soul but the Paradise which belongs to all because it is made by all is the one we long to inherit . . .

A brave New World, in fact?

We got back into the car and climbed still higher till we came to a wood on the summit of a ridge. Here we were met by eight horses and a veritable giant of a man whose pale face was framed in a long black beard. His stare was neither hostile nor friendly but wary, as Man Friday's might have been till he got to know Crusoe better. To Hilary's questions he returned monosyllabic answers, allowing us to pass on our way to his cottage with a nod of his head. This cottage had been built by a Spanish gynaecologist, a friend of Hilary's, who had subsequently died of drink. Everything was of concrete, walls, floor, a great fireplace and a huge double bed where the gynaecologist slept on straw. He was a mystic who was given to fits of violent remorse, and in one of these he had lit a fire in the middle of the room and then had torn a hole in the ceiling to let out the smoke. He was a man of great personal charm when he was sober and was most attractive to women. The fact that none of them lasted very long may have had something to do with the bed. Hilary, striding about this large, untidy room, talked about the place in Jaime's time while a woman, silently and efficiently, fried hamburgers for her son. At length he decided that his hostess, whose guests were none of her choosing, might have other things to do, so we took our leave.

Of the man we had met at the gate there was no sign.

Our way home took us through a redwood grove and we got out to see the trees; but the thing I remember is Hilary tramping down a sunlit path declaiming Housman in his strong, clear voice. He took the Highway Number One back to San Francisco, past artichoke fields, lettuces in orderly rows in gargantuan flat fields where packing vans and men were almost unseen in all this distance.

Every few miles there were vast hoardings on which were pictured a happy American family with the words YOU ARE LUCKY TO LIVE IN AMERICA underneath it. It was, I think, part of an advertisement for someone's beer, but it seemed to me it might serve a double purpose. If I had to look at that month after month, year after year, it might almost make me believe it.

CHAPTER EIGHTEEN

A SPARKLING wind filled our sails as we sped down the coast from San Francisco at a greater speed, so it seemed to us, than that at which we had motored down it a few days ago. Measuring our runs in days instead of hours we were content to let the roaring bow wave and the curving mast seduce our senses into thinking that time was relative, and at dawn on our first morning out the Big Sur Country looked strangely mysterious, for the tops of the highest mountains, hard and brown like a distant ridge in the Sahara desert, stood out above a veil of mist as though it were a mirage a hundred miles away.

If we had known that this was to be the last good breeze we should have for the next three months our high spirits, as we rounded Point Concepcion (two hundred miles to the south and locally and grandiloquently known as the Cape Horn of the North Pacific owing to the difficulty of rounding it against the fresh north-west wind and the current) would have been more than an octave lower.

At dawn we lay a mile or so off Santa Barbara harbour becalmed in a thick fog. Christopher, for about the twentieth time, suggested it was time to start the engine, but since we had unseized it with infinite trouble at Port Renfrew without finding out why it had seized up, I was determined to use it only for an emergency. But Christopher's doleful expression (he had a girl friend waiting for him here) was too much for me. We cranked it up, the breakwater and the buoys marking the sand spit to port came into view, but within two hundred yards of our berth the poor thing developed a rattle in its throat that was all too realistic and died.

Poor Christopher! There was no shore leave. With blood and sweat, amid oil and filth, we levered the heavy engine out, rigged a sling and with a handy billy guided it on to the deck. Even to my unmechanical eye there was something very definitely wrong. A neighbouring yachtsman who had given us a hand and much good advice told us nonchalantly that to put in a new front bearing, which was the cause of the trouble, would cost not less than two hundred and fifty dollars; a hundred pounds!

We were given an introduction to Mr G. In his spare time G. was a big-game hunter. He had the shoulders of an ox, a great square head, a lined and pitted skin rather like the rhinos he may have chased, but in amongst the folds of flesh two merry eyes shone out and belied his otherwise ferocious aspect. He listened to our story in an amused, off-hand sort of a way:

"I've no time to do your engine," he said, "but I'll come and see your boat." In silence he looked at our spars and gear and took in the small, untidy cabin with a wry smile. He said, "If you're so crazy as to come out from England in this I guess I'd better fix your engine."

I explained our predicament more fully: "We've only got a small dollar reserve but the Bank of England will send yachtsmen money for repairs, up to a certain amount, if they get an estimate of the work involved."

He nodded. "Come and see me around noon, to-morrow."

The next morning we met him over the body of our engine.

"Fifty dollars too much for you?" he asked, and when I started to speak he went on, "Pays my man's wages, that's all I want."

The work was to be completed by Saturday, and on that day we all trooped down to fetch it. Along with the new main-bearing, new big-ends and other improvements G. had thrown in a gallon of oil and a bagful of handsome rags, the sort of rags Anne and I could dress ourselves in!

He said, "Jim, here (Jim was his mechanic), wants to help you put it in."

When we protested that this was entirely unnecessary, he smiled. "He doesn't want to be paid for it, he just wants to see it running. He can do what he wants with his week-end."

This, indeed, was providential, for as soon as we had bedded the monster down (it is only six-horsepower, but it feels like a ton weight) Jim clutched the exhaust-pipe a shade too tightly so that it crumpled to rust in his hand. From somewhere he found another for three dollars; and on Sunday night it ran with more sweetness than it had for several years. Jim did not drink, neither did he smoke, and it was as much as we could do to feed him, so anxious was he not to denude our ship of stores, of which he thought we might be in need.

I said, "Jim, you've been very good to us, surely there's something we can do for you in return."

"There sure is," he replied. "Send me a postcard when you get back."

Now it was not only on account of Christopher that we had come to Santa Barbara. While at Honolulu we had met the Kelloggs who had invited us to stay at their ranch on our way south. Although we were a year late and Irma was now in

Arizona, she had repeated this offer, insisting that we stayed at the ranch until she could join us.

The Rancho Monte Alegre lies behind Carpentaria, some twelve miles to the east of Santa Barbara in the foothills of the mountains. Under a cloudless sky the place lives in a little world of its own among acres of lemon trees worked by Mexicans. Beneath a row of tall palm trees stands the graceful one-storeyed ranch house and the guest cottage where Ian and Betty Dewar live and where we lived too until Irma arrived. Farther down the slope was the bunkhouse. This had been converted by Pete (Irma's son-in-law) who lived there and kept a watchful eye on the Mexican workers, while Joan, for whose sake Christopher had begged me to start the engine, lived opposite in what had once been the office. She shared this with seven (or was it seventeen?) cats.

While in Santa Barbara the white buildings and the broad streets swam in the heat of the noon-day sun, and at night the restaurants reverberated to the shouts of Mexican singers and American saxophones, we lay in Betty's garden, or by the shores of a tiny lake at the upper end of the ranch. We came to know them well.

Both Pete and Ian had been fliers, Pete in the last and Ian in the first war. Seeing little future in the R.A.F. in the late twenties Ian had taken a job with a Canadian air-line and come out with his wife and two children, but before he arrived the air-line had gone bankrupt.

He told me how he had joined a charter firm, and for the next year and a half he flew people from province to province, from town to town.

"Talking to you like this," he remarked, "has reminded me of a queer little incident just before the Wall Street crash. A client of ours approached me personally to fly him on a special mission because, he said, I knew how to keep my mouth shut. Although this was against the regulations the boss suggested that for such an excellent client (he was a doctor who was reputed to have made a fortune out of performing illegal operations) I should fall in with his wishes. We set off about mid-day and he told me to follow the Red River up into the mountains behind. The country was wild and rugged, but the doctor indicated to me a valley at the head of which was a grassy plateau where we landed without difficulty.

"We walked to a clearing where there were buildings, but what puzzled me more than these—and how they could have got there—was the low continuous roar of machines. It was a noise faintly familiar, but before I could think what it reminded me of the doctor had hustled me into an office, where I was introduced to one of the most powerful men I have ever seen. Hirsute, I suppose you'd call him; his face was covered in black beard and under his open shirt was a growth like the Black Forest. He spoke to me in execrable French, but when he and the doctor conversed I couldn't understand a word they were saying although, again, the sound was vaguely familiar.

"After the doctor had finished his business he said, 'I shan't be coming back tonight, but this gentleman's son wishes to travel with you.' The young man was nearly as big as his father, but spoke good English. I told him he'd freeze to death in his shirt sitting in an open cockpit but he refused to put on as much as an overcoat. He never turned a hair."

I said, "And the noise?"

"A printing press."

"The language?"

"Russian."

Pete drove us down to Hollywood in the station-wagon, and we had the experience of being driven on the Los Angeles Freeway, where cars fly in and out like tracer bullets, and the minimum speed is 55 m.p.h.

Pete says it is the safest road in the U.S.A., but Pete is used to battles in the air and we are not. We dined at Don the Beachcomber's under three paintings by Le Tec lit by coloured lights in blown-out porcupine-fish, eating delicate Chinese food and drinking Barbados rum. We were back in bed on the ranch before dawn.

In the meantime gangs of painters, decorators and Mexican women were busy preparing the ranch house for Irma's arrival. Long-distance telephones, telegrams and letters changed and counter-changed the moment of her coming. Then one day she just appeared.

Descended from a Norwich sea-captain and a Spanish señorita, Irma is a remarkable woman with a low, husky voice. In spite of being a grandmother, she has the grace of a Spanish dancing-girl, her long black hair falling over her shoulders. She hides an acute business sense behind a façade of girlishness, but she is one of the most generous people we have ever met.

Irma spared us a week.

Thinking we could do some little thing in return for her hospitality, we asked her whether she would like to see our colour slides and hear something of our travels.

"That would be lovely," she said, "I'll ask some friends in after dinner and share the pleasure with them."

She asked about thirty and it was nearly midnight by the time the party was over. Irma came up to Anne and me. She said, "My friends were so delighted they wished me to give you this small token to show their appreciation." The "token" covered the cost of the engine, and this reversal of my intentions made me blush to the roots of my hair.

On the day she left she made two appointments in the town, and not one of the twenty-five people who had come to see her off (so unerring is her instinct for collecting round her devotees of both sexes) would have given any odds on her catching that train. The great engine puffed into the station, Ian rushed off to try and bribe the guard to wait a little longer when Irma stepped radiantly on to the platform with hatboxes, trunks and several minor slaves to carry her things. She kissed the womenfolk, accepted our trifling gifts as if they were myrrh and incense and was wafted away towards Arizona.

The passage to Newport, California, is a distance of only a hundred and twenty miles, but it took us three days. The mist hung on, and for a day and a night we navigated by the sound of the traffic along the coast road, coming about, for the wind was ahead, when the roar grew too loud, and again when it had almost ceased. But we kept an eye on a motoring map, for at times the road went inland behind hills!

An acquaintance of ours had had an accident in this very part of the world. He was an Australian whom we had met at Honolulu and again, much to our surprise, in Vancouver City. He had, he told us, been given the job of taking one of the ocean racers back to San Pedro. They had made their landfall at Santa Barbara and a day or two later they had left, as we had done, in mist and with only the lightest of airs. They set off under power, adjusted the automatic pilot to a course that would take them between Anacapa and the mainland and retired below. Some hours later our friend came up on deck with a bowl of soup in his hands and there, right in front of his nose, were the cliffs of Anacapa. Before he could put down his soup they hit the beach.

"Coo," he said. "Sixty thousand dollars down the drain."

Not having an automatic pilot, we negotiated the channel successfully, but the passage was not without its perils. Between Point Huamine and Point Dune was a guided-missile range which extended an unspecified depth to seaward (probably about sixteen miles) from a mile offshore. It was, however, never used at night. We took no chances and navigated this sheet of water within half a mile of the shore and at night. Again, crossing San Pedro bay all the tuna clippers in the world seemed to be homeward bound from the fishing grounds off Peru. One of them came so close that we could see a small sea-plane, like a crouching insect, on her afterdeck. The thump of their powerful engines, the cluster of lights about their enormous superstructures and the hiss of their bow waves kept us on the look-out until just before dawn. Then there was fog.

Entering Newport was like sailing into a Dutch canal, with houses right down to the waterside and creeks winding into the flat and featureless shore. Yachts by the thousand lay at anchor, but in spite of this gross overcrowding there was a peace about the place that appealed to our imagination. As we drew alongside the Newport Harbor Yacht Club somone came running out of the Clubhouse and said that Dr. Pye was wanted on the telephone and was I he? Peggy Slater had seen our sails from a friend's house as we beat up the channel. Could we, she asked, come and have dinner at their house? We most certainly could.

Peggy is a yacht broker from San Pedro whom we had seen in Barbados, met in Honolulu and again in Santa Barbara. She lives in a bungalow at San Pedro right on top of a cliff, and a single plate-glass window runs the whole length of the living room overlooking the Pacific Ocean. A ship's wheel for a table, coral shells and fans round the walls, the model of a four-masted barque and a glorious divan where Anne and I once spent a blissful night watching the firelight on the redwood ceiling and listening to the murmur of the sea on the beach two hundred feet below.

Peggy was one of the few women we met on this coast who was a seaman in her own right. She took us sailing one day in her K.38. Anne was at the helm and Peggy and I were below talking about the ships we had known and heard about. Suddenly she broke off in the middle of a sentence and glanced out of the hatch at a vessel tearing down under a press of engine.

"Give this thing a wide berth, Anne," she said. "There's an awful lot of inexperience on that ship."

But it is as an ocean-racing skipper that Peggy is best known. Some years ago she was sailing master of *Apache* in the Trans-Pacific race. The *Apache* was running with her whole mainsail and a web spinnaker before half a gale of wind when the cry went up: "Man overboard!"

Peggy was on deck in a flash. Someone had thrown the man

a lifebuoy with a smoke attachment, but the seas were so big that in this short time all sight of him had been lost. Peggy came to the conclusion that to gybe with that spinnaker set would dismast the vessel, so down it had to come, and by that time they had run a mile.

Peggy said, "I needed all my know-how. I had a man on the lower spreaders, and I could hear the screams from the poor guy's sister, who had to be held down in her bunk by more men than I could willingly spare from the deck. At one time we were less than two hundred yards away, but in the sea then running we failed to see him. It must have seemed incredible to him when we turned away."

They searched for twenty-nine hours. At the end of that time the captain of the escort ship that had joined in the search said he had orders to proceed with the rest of the fleet and that *Apache* must also continue. Peggy refused. Backwards and forwards went the argument (for by now the sea was smooth), and at last the captain agreed to search for another two hours farther to the east, where Peggy's navigator thought the missing man might now be. An hour later he was found, alive!

Lying in the harbour of Newport was the schooner *Vega* which we had last seen at Papeete. She was being entirely re-fitted for a passenger service from Honolulu to Tahiti, and her crew were from the South Seas: from Atuona, the Paumotus and the Societies. We brought wine, someone produced a guitar, and in a moment houses, yachts, cars, dollars and even the American language vanished, and we were back among the waving palms, the dusky maidens and the murmur of the sea upon the reef.

As we walked back that night we believed more strongly than ever that MacDonald the painter had been right: these were no children who, if given the chance, would reach out for the benefits of a Western State. They were as adult as we were, loving their way of life.

We sailed in company with Hale Field and his wife in their gaff-topsail cutter *Renegade* in the usual mist and light winds. On Saturday night a fog came down. I woke to hear Anne talking in a conversational manner to Hale. I was out in a moment. Although I could see nothing at all, I could hear the crash of *Renegade's* boom as she rolled in the swell. Both ships were becalmed, and as there was nothing to be done I went below. The desultory conversation went on and on and on, and I hoped Hale's crew were better at sleeping than I was.

Christopher had a smart breeze from ahead in his watch, but in

The Sea is for Sailing

mine it petered out. When that happens I curl up on the cabin floor and snatch some sleep. It is not a thing I encourage in the others, and my excuse is that at the slightest change in the weather or at the beat of a steamer's engines I shall wake up. But on this occasion a breeze sprang up unannounced; and with a feeling of guilt I found the ship sailing merrily back the way she had come, while *Renegade*, whose crew had stuck to their duty, was almost out of sight. Now in all the years that I have indulged in this unorthodox practice I have never been caught by my crew, but I had more than a little difficulty in explaining to Christopher why *Renegade*, which had been well astern when he went off watch, was now so far ahead.

At San Diego, big, noisy, and rather inaccessible from the harbour, there lay in a neglected corner of the dockyard half a dozen boats and a band of sea adventurers who had founded the first international cruising association. The only qualification is that you must live aboard a sea-going vessel and cruise when you are able. You might describe them as the core of those Americans, some of whom we had already met in the South Pacific, who sail from country to country, from continent to continent, turning their hands to any job until their finances recover sufficiently to continue their marine prowling about the world. They came from a cross-section of the population, they were individualists scorning what they called the "rat-race", bound to each other by the ties of the sea, independent, self-reliant, abhorred by the bureaucrats but the cream of the earth, no doubt, to Mr Geoffrey Household. They were the nearest thing to the Westerner's conception of South Sea Island life.

After a few days we went round and joined them. At the issue of the monthly bulletin we sat crowded into *Black Dolphin's* spacious cabin and fittingly enough there were letters from *Wanderer III* from Capetown and from *Yankee* from the New Hebrides.

It was while we were at San Diego that the Los Angeles Yacht Club did me the honour of asking me to give them a talk at one of their lunches. Peggy drove us up to the city where we met a number of the Trans-Pacific ocean racing men and Dwight Long (of *Idle Hour* fame) who had recently been making a film in the South Sea Islands.

He was feeling depressed.

He said, "If I'd taken the advice of my friends and used professional actors instead of spending months trying to train the Tahitians it might have been a success."

After the talk a member got up and said, "Now we would like to hear something from Mrs Pye."

Anne, who hates talking because she says she never knows what her tongue is going to say next, stood up.

Someone asked, "Mrs Pye, can you tell us how we can get our wives to go to sea with us?"

Anne said, "Oh yes, I can tell you that at once. Don't keep them in the galley."

There was an awkward silence, and the meeting broke up in disorder. The word has evidently gone round, for Anne has never been asked to speak since!

No foreign yachtsman could, I think, come down this coast without being interviewed by television, by radio and the press; nor could he escape being visited by a great many people whose only interest in the ship is curiosity and to have something to talk to their friends about. It gave us quite a lot of amusement, and Anne one day heard a woman in our cabin say to a friend, "I saw Mrs Pye on T.V. She looked so tall and graceful and lovely, but of course T.V. is *so* deceptive, isn't it?"

CHAPTER NINETEEN

WE sailed on a Sunday in November. The breeze was light from the north-west, tempting us out. Night descended upon us, a Joseph Conrad sort of night, dark and mysterious. Behind were the neon lights, the flashing lights, the roar of jets, seaplanes and air-liners, while on the beam was the silence of Mexico; nothing but the dim shapes of mountains, as remote as Mars. To seaward a single light flickered, for it was Mexican and therefore temperamental, on the Islas Coronados.

In her early morning watch Anne had cleared Los Coronados—"round dry humps sticking steeply out of the water"—and was steering for Isla Guadalupe, unlit and uninhabited, a hundred and fifty miles away. I first saw it two days later in the pre-dawn light. The precipitous cliffs of its northern end rose out of a veil of mist, softening their bold and rugged outlines; and once more it came upon me that there can be no more exciting thing than making a landfall in the middle of the sea. The wind piped up, and I had to call the others to shorten sail. The anchorage was in a small cove, a mile and a half from North Point, and was hardly big enough to swing a cat in, and our bowsprit was almost over the beach before we found the bottom with the lead.

There was someone there after all; a fisherman poaching lobsters for bait. He thought we were Mexicans and took to the bush, but when we ran up our colours he came out with half a dozen lobsters.

He said, "This is a goddam awful place. You roll like hell, and if a sou'-easter comes up you have to get out at once."

Warming to his subject, he went on, "Looks a bit like that now. I've seen a *chubasco* (Spanish for surprise storm) roll a tuna boat over and drown her crew."

He downed a pint of beer.

He said, "Last year a boat got wrecked over on the west coast. Took 'em fouteen days to scale the cliffs and walk seven miles to this bay. Blow me, when they got to the top of that ridge over there they saw a tuna boat from San Pedro anchored right here. They got most of the way down when the fish-boat up-anchors and steams out. They were half-dying of thirst and lack of food and that kinda made 'em mad. They yelled and waved, and then one of 'em set fire to the bush. The skipper saw the smoke and picked 'em up. Were they lucky!"

To the south a long curving beach was occupied by giant elephant-seals, slimy and repulsive with red, open mouths and hooked noses. On a bluff were the ruins of a penal settlement. The silence was absolute except for the whoof of the seals.

As I look back on the weeks we spent off the Mexican coast, my recollections are of constantly searching the horizon for wind. Our standards fell so low that steerage way was dubbed "not too bad", and a light breeze became like a Trade Wind. There is a note in my journal that for nineteen hours the log spinner had not rotated for so much as half a turn, and we looked upon our topsail with the greatest affection.

But if the voyage was slow and irksome because we were pressed for time there were compensations. The unruffled sea, the warmth of the sun, putting the world to rights beneath a shining moon and over an after-dinner cup of coffee, and making a landfall so beautiful that the memory of it still sends a little prickle of appreciation down my spine. It appeared at dawn. A high mackerel sky, suffused with bands of brilliant red and mauve and purple, held my attention until my eyes dropped to the level of the horizon where, as in a fairy tale, I saw two distant mountains sitting on the very rim of the world. They were part of the outer ramparts that enclose Magdalena Bay, a peninsula composed of sand-dunes and low, flat country that divorces the place from its more fortunate neighbours.

The bay is an inland sea eighteen miles long by ten wide approached through a narrow opening; and on the sands of this lagoon are bones of dead whales bleached by the sun, for here they come to die. Round a point we came upon our first Mexican village, a collection of adobe huts covered with corrugated roofs, around which we could see no living thing.

Doffing his wide sombrero the Captain of the Port welcomed us to his puebla and started to bake us *tortillas* with his own hands. A pile of maize, a hollow in the middle of the pile, a little water in the hollow, the whole kneaded by strong, stubby fingers, flicked from hand to hand like cards by a conjuror, thinned and flattened, the while he beamed with pleasure at the rapt attention of his pupils; he then baked the *tortillas* on a griddle made of tin and previously heated in a kerosene can used as an oven. It looked so simple, but when Anne tried her hand, amid grins and "*buenas,*" her *tortillas* bore no resemblance to the master's.

The great delicacy was tinned shark-meat in oil, and a tin was opened for us. Never have we had to work so hard to show a proper appreciation of such an honour.

The people had to fetch every drop of water from the waterhole half a mile to the northward, and if it hadn't been for the fish in the sea they would have starved. The only money they had was spent on beer, and by five o'clock most of the village was insensible, a thing you could hardly blame them for because there was nothing else to do.

Our voyage continued. The rocks off Cabo San Lucas at the tip of the Bahia California reminded us of the Needles as they had done the Worshipful Thomas Cavendish of Trimly in Suffolk when he lay in wait for the yearly arrival of the Manila galleon in the *Desire* with the *Content* in close attendance. Thus he captured the *Santa Maria* and took her into Aguada in Bahia San Lucas where he put his prisoners ashore:

> They were set ashore where they had a fayre river of fresh water, with great store of fresh fish, foule, and wood and also many hares and connies upon the maine land.

But the place seemed to have changed in the last four hundred years, for there was no "fayre river", no fish or hares or connies, but a canning factory and a temporary butcher's shop beneath a tree from which hung the remains of a slaughtered bullock. Children and dogs carried away the entrails under the predatory eyes of huge buzzards with great red heads waiting for the remains.

Anne took her shopping basket, and we walked along the long hot road to the puebla, a more modern affair than Puerta Magdalena, with a village square, a church, two shops and a profusion of red bougainvillea. A shy, gentle population, many of them lighter in colour because of the mingling with Nordic blood from shipwrecked mariners, stood about the doors of their adobe huts hoping that we would talk to them. Giant cacti gave the rounded hills and the dry, open valleys the prickly look of avocado pears.

After making our official entry into Mexico (it is cheaper to do this here than in any other port in the country) we set sail across the mouth of the Gulf of California. The first night out we were, as so often happened, becalmed. There was little swell, the night was overcast and the stillness was intensified by the creaking of the mainsheet blocks as the mainsail, hauled in tight to prevent its slatting, tried in vain to free itself. Below us the inky water was alive. A huge manta ray glided by, its enormous fins, like the wings of a delta jet, outlined by the phosphorescent water; there were dolphin and porpoises, sea-snakes and a slim, good-looking young shark that rubbed himself for hours against our copper to our mutual advantage. A breeze sprang up from the south-west and landed us off the entrance to Mazatlan twenty-four hours later. Creston Island, shaped like a hound resting its head between its paws, plays the devil with the wind, and a backlash put us almost on top of a reef. Christopher jumped for the engine, Anne ran forward to back the jib, and another puff from the opposite direction, thank God, blew us off again.

A little later Christopher's worried face appeared at the hatch, "I can't get this damned engine to go," he said.

I had been so busy I had quite forgotten him.

In the port no one noticed our presence, so the next day we went along to the Port Captain's office. We waited an hour. He was a big man for a Mexican, his face hidden in rolls of fat, and a large cigar rotating between his lips. Our few formalities were soon concluded and we were about to leave when a clerk with padded shoulders and eyes as cold as granite whispered, "Dues for pilotage."

The Captain frowned, "This is an English yacht," he said.

"No matter," said Granite Eyes. "All ships must pay."

I waved my cruising permit in front of him but this he ignored.

He said, "That has nothing to do with us. At Mazatlan, all ships pay."

I said, "But we had no pilot."

"That makes no difference, Captain."

"How much do we owe?"

The Port Captain looked at our register. "Sixty-three pesos."

Granite Eyes took him up at once. "This yacht came in on Sunday. One hundred and twenty-six pesos for overtime."

I said, "How can there be overtime if no one comes out to our ship?"

Granite Eyes shrugged his shoulders. The heat of the noon-day sun, the difficulty of understanding what they said made my head reel, but Anne looked cooler than ever. Her Spanish is basic.

She said, "Si conocer el reglemente aqui, Capitan, restamos un otra dia y noche al mar."

The Captain rose to his feet. He took his cigar from his mouth and bowed to her. "There has been a mistake." He glared at Granite Eyes in a way which made that very unpleasant young man grow paler still. "This yacht, this English yacht, came in today. I saw her myself." He turned to me. "That will be sixty-three pesos, Captain, thank you."

The town is very Spanish, with its streets dreamy and quiet during the hour of the siesta, the blue and gold cathedral, the glimpse through an open window of a child kneeling before an altar, for it wanted less than a fortnight to Christmas, and each little house had its shrine.

Behind and to the north is Indian country; hundreds of square miles, we were told, where the rites of the witch-doctors and the distilling of *peyotl* from the cactus root are still carried on much as they were in Cortez's time. If a white man strays too far he may be warned off and allowed to return or on the other hand he may disappear like D. H. Lawrence's *Woman that Rode Away*.

The season was now far advanced and any moment, they said, we could expect a brave north wind, but our luck was out and our slow progress down the coast continued. We put into Banderas Bay because, on our chart, there was a place with the name of Santa Cruz de Juan de Costello; such a place, we felt, ought to be worth a visit, but all we could see was a deserted lime-kiln, a dug-out canoe with a mast and sail, and two small huts. As we were learning fast, the poorer the community the more truly hospitable it is to the passing stranger. We were met by a deputation, and to our surprise a well-dressed young woman spoke to us in slow and urgent tones about a child whom she thought might be having pneumonia. On hearing that I was a doctor she hurried me away to an adobe hut with a few broken slats on the outer wall and a roof of thatch with a hole to let out the smoke from the fire. The child was wrapped in sacking, and I had to do as the French country doctors do, listen to the child's chest with my ear, an indignity to which the baby naturally objected in the strongest possible terms. Thanks to antibiotics, it made a quick recovery.

Señora Beatriz, who came from Mexico City, was staying with her brother Pedro round whose ranch the village revolved. His hut was larger than the others and was supported by a great brazil nut tree, which grew in the middle of the room. A stove built of lime had an ingenious device for making *tortillas* easily and an oven for cooking. Beatriz, her two young daughters, her brother and another young woman who may have been a sister, all lived in this room, but they did have beds which were frames of wood with rope netting (like our bowsprit shrouds) and supported at each end on empty oil-drums. The estate lay behind the village in a broad valley and here pumpkin, frijoles, callabasos, maize and trees of papayas grew. Loaded with papayas for our voyage Pedro chose for us an enormous pumpkin which he said would last for weeks. Beatriz, without a thought, whipped off her outer skirt, rolled it up into a small cushion, put it on her head and carried the pumpkin home.

As it grew dark I noticed that none of the peasants were conscious. They lay about in a sort of stupor, and if one got in the way Pedro, not urgently, put him on one side like a child. Was this the result of *peyotl*, or an unusual reaction to alcohol? I should have like to have asked him.

As there were no roads the products of the rancho had to go by sea to Puerta Vallerta, a place we had been warned against visiting because of the violent swell upon the beach. We saw the canoe sail that night. Her sail was mast-headed and her skipper, a young lad, wedged himself in between the sacks of maize and fruit. There could have been no more than six inches of freeboard by the time everything was in, and I was glad that the night was calm.

We put into Manzanillo for Christmas and were at sea for New Year's Eve, and how we longed for wind down that bare and arid coast. Off Cabo Corrientes a contrary current held us up for three days, and after that we changed our tactics, following the bays round at night, keeping close to the shore as Bill Phillips suggested we should.

Bill was one of those people who kept turning up in unexpected places. We had met him at Balboa in the ketch *Blue Peter*, and then he had dropped casually in to see us at the Royal Victoria Yacht Club having bicycled over from the Empress Hotel. We got to know him better still at San Diego where he lived. I think Bill was in the advertising business, but it was as an explorer and a cruising man that he was known among his friends. He knew the coast from San Diego to Panama better than most, and had once sailed his ship far up the Chiriqui River before taking a canoe into the interior where no white man had ever penetrated. The natives were unclothed and resembled those that Slocum described in his passage through the Magellan Straits. It was this, Bill said, that gave him the idea of modernizing Slocum's methods by using an electrified fence instead of the Captain's tin-tacks.

Bill's words to us were "Keep just outside the breakers." And I'm sure Bill was right, for more than once I remember going up the ratlines while the ship was slipping bravely through the water to find that a mile to seaward there was not so much as a ripple on the moonlit sea. Although we lived with the roar of the breakers in our ears night after night and week after week, I must confess that I felt the strain, for I am not one of those iron-nerved men who take such things philosophically. Even now on a quiet night in an Essex creek I can still hear those breakers.

A mile off-shore . . . those were the instructions; but the interpretation of what a mile might be was left to the watch. Mine, Anne used to say when she came up to peer at a rugged cliff, was definitely short and hers, I know, was long; while Christopher's (he was short-sighted) was a little uncertain. Before dawn on 3rd January the loom from the lights of Acapulco showed up on the port bow, and in the morning we sailed past sheer precipices of rock with tiny houses hanging in the clefts, through the Boca Chica and into what must be one of the finest harbours in the world, like a sapphire set in a dark green bowl of hills. Bodies bronzing on the beach, old men paddling rafts with awnings to protect you from the sun, dark young men on skis twisting, jumping, turning behind foaming speed boats, smart yachts, coloured beach umbrellas, dance-bands, enormous hotels and the deep Mediterranean blue of the sky made one realize that Cannes or Acapulco, Honolulu or Blackpool, all are very much the same.

On land the tremendous noise and bustle in the market, the deserted streets behind, the little restaurant in a corner of a square belonging to two matadors (man and wife) great pans with lids that you lifted to inspect each dish simmering on the stove, the strumming of a guitar, the swirl of a flowing skirt, the clicking of the fingers, the swaying of a figure, all these brought back to us the earthy smell of Spain.

That flavour of Spain followed us when we took a bus inland; the dry hills, the peasants walking by the side of the road as the first light flooded the valleys, the two dusty little towns at which we stopped for refreshments, the thin, emaciated cattle, the goats on a high plateau and then at the end of the two-hundred-mile drive to the mountain town of Taxco, six thousand feet up, older than Mexico City itself, a fairy place with the twin brown towers of its Cathedral, the streets and houses straggling up a hill, the shady square on the brow, the shops filled with silver from the silver mines, and the advertisements for a bullfight to take place in the capital that week.

At Taxco we stayed with a Saxon baron and his wife who lived in Humboldt House. Their dining-room had been a Chinese Trading Post in 1593 where silks and spices from the Orient were stored when they were brought overland by mule-train from

Acapulco, the port of disembarkation for the manila galleons. The Baron, a friend of Count Von Luckner of *Seeadler* fame and an anti-Nazi, is an architect but is probably better known as an archaeologist, although he says that this is only his hobby.

His first wife was the great-niece of Franz Joseph, Archduke of Austria, whose murder at Sarajevo was the spark that kindled the first war. In the second war the feeling against Germany was so high in Mexico that when she was desperately ill at her last childbirth no doctor could be found to attend her and she died. Later the Baron married her niece, a tall slender girl with a sweet face. Between them they have eight children ranging from one year to seventeen. The passion with which they conducted their arguments in German, Spanish and English, and their flair for stage effect made me think I was watching a performance of *The Constant Nymph*.

The Baron was at that moment making a model of a tomb that he had found in which were the remains of the last Emperor of the Aztecs, Coatemo. Coatemo had surrendered the city of Mexico to Cortez, on condition that Cortez spared his life, only to be murdered by him shortly afterwards. The Aztec's family were most anxious that his body should be buried on sacred ground (for Coatemo was a Christian) and the priest who lived in his mother's village agreed to do this under a vow of secrecy. The secret was kept for four hundred years until, the last direct descendent having died, it passed into the hands of a distant cousin, the owner of a drugstore. He, after consulting the local priest, told the authorities in Mexico City, and they asked the Baron to investigate the story. He found no signs of the tomb beneath the church but discovered a record that the original church had been burned down and the present one built on top of it. Below the site of the original altar, and so well concealed that it took the Baron and his assistants weeks to unearth it, they came at last upon Coatemo. The emperor had had a fitting burial, for he lay in a hexagonal tomb surmounted by a dome and lacquered a deep red inside.

Our last port in Mexico was Puerto Angel, the Port of the Angel. Remembering our experiences at Mazatlan we trod delicately up the steps of the Port Captain's office, for we had failed to make our entry before noon that Saturday, and felt the threat of "overtime" hanging over our heads. The Port Captain was a jolly fellow. He greeted us warmly, showed us the view from his window looking over this enchanting bay, the Government wharf where a coaster called once a month, the winding path up to the scattered village, the fishing canoes drawn up on the beach, the whole place hushed and asleep in the afternoon sun.

He said, "It is good that you go now while there is no sign of one of those storms that come at this time of the year."

He gave us a clearance direct for the Canal Zone for which he charged us twenty-three pesos instead of the three hundred and sixty we should have had to pay for the same thing at Acapulco. He shook hands.

"Go tomorrow, while the weather is good. Buen viaje!"

But this place was so lovely that we could not tear ourselves away quite so easily. We shifted our berth to the other side of the bay where the sea whispered on a golden beach, and we spent one glorious day bathing and lying in the sun. A tiny lamp burned all night in a shrine in the burial ground which lay unobtrusively above our anchorage.

Puerto Angel is, however, a difficult place to lay in a stock of fresh food. The neighbouring town of Pochutla, said Claudia who did our washing, was *muy bien*, and her brother offered to take Christopher there by bus. They would be back, he said, by five o'clock.

By seven it was dark and there was no sign of Christopher, and I was just pulling the pram up to go ashore when I saw through the night glasses a small canoe approaching. Christopher and Glycerio tumbled aboard in the last stages of exhaustion: they had walked the ten miles back!

Pochulta, Christopher said, was a broken-down place like Corcubion in Spain. They had found little in the market, and Glycerio had gone from stall to stall muttering, "*Chyotes, no hay, papayas, no hay,*" in evident distress. When they got back to the bus the driver was tired and would not leave for the port before morning.

Christopher had declined his companion's suggestion that he should wrap himself up in a *serape* and sleep in the street and had managed to goad him into walking home.

"I enjoyed my walk back," he said, "we had to wait to let two bulls finish a fight in the road, we met lines of *burros* each with its driver under impossible Mexican hats, a man with a string of iguanas hanging from his belt, two serpents, and a vulture picking at a dead dog."

CHAPTER TWENTY

JUST as an American yacht bound for England would almost certainly have heard of the Portland Race so had we been warned of the Golfo de Tehuantepec before arriving in Mexico. With barely concealed relish they told us of what had happened to coasters and steamers caught in a bad "Tehuantepecer" and of the yacht coming up the coast with a broken tail-shaft which had taken twenty-eight days to sail across the Gulf of Puerto Angel, and of how the water at the head of the bay is forced out by the strength of the wind causing the current to flow in along both sides of the gulf at the rate of two knots.

"The only way," they said, "is to follow the coast right round, because, the wind being off shore, the sea is smooth."

With a powerful engine and with no sails set I am sure this is the wisest course to pursue, but the risk of being dismasted by the first onslaught of the gale if it arrived in the dark was too great to take and as an ancient knight might walk delicately across the mouth of the dragon's lair, so did we set off from Puerto Angel with a light fair wind bound for the shores of Guatemala three hundred miles away. As it grew dark, low, flat clouds hid the darkening mountains, and the wind died. The world was stilled.

In the tension of its coming the Tehuantepecer was like a flying-bomb. At one o'clock in the morning a slow westerly swell was the only sign of movement on the sea. When Anne relieved me there was a light air from the north, and I went forward to set the genoa, but in the short time it took me to do this I noticed the ship was starting to pitch into a little swell coming from the northeast.

An hour later Anne woke me. She said, "There's no wind to speak of, but I'd like you to come and look at this sea."

I went up on deck. All around were seas with breaking crests toppling aimlessly as if waiting for the wind to direct them. Only a whisper of a breeze filled our sails and the motion was like that of a toy boat in an agitated bath. On this occasion the wind came gradually; Force 3 to 4, Force 5 to 6, Force 6 to 7. Topsail and genoa had long since come down, and three reefs had been put in the main. Now, in the half-light of the dawn we pulled down the fourth and ran with the wind on the quarter. The sun came up like a ball of brass into a sky that was hard and white. The sea was becoming dangerous, and the wind was blowing a gale. We hove to and went below; all we could do was to wait. Of this waiting Anne wrote:

> I am among wet pillows and blankets feeling seasick and unable to make Dramamine fight it. All day we lie in our bunks but get little sleep, and the wind and the sea throw us about. The motion is intense, the sea magnificent. Nothing is in sight, but we cannot see beyond our immediate wave, and Peter climbs the ratlines before dark with the riding light in case we should be blown across the steamer track during the night. I get out a tin of soup and one of corned beef but feel too sick so C. and P. deal with them, and later I sip half a basin of tepid asparagus soup with disaster. I rush to the hatch clutching my oily in my hand, just in time to hang my head over the top board. I go up after this unfortunate episode, and see a coil of rope has come adrift in the scuppers and go forward to see to it. Peter, who doesn't know I have left the after-deck, comes up and his voice is raised in a great cry: "*Where are you?*" All desolation was in those words, and I answer quickly and come down to lie again damply and suck a slice of pineapple.

About ten o'clock that night the whine of the wind rose several notes. Soon the mainsail would have to come down, as the ship was badly pressed at the top of every sea. For an hour we hung on till we could not bear the strain on hull and gear, even if *Moonie* could.

But, as we rolled out of our bunks, there was the faintest lessening of the wind. We stood huddled by the companionway half in and half out of our oilskins, and I thought how tired the others looked.

Slowly the wind came down the scale.

"Definitely less," we said, and turned into our bunks and slept.

By six o'clock that morning the wind had dropped to Force 6. I called the others without the slightest hesitation, for after the gale was over was the time when we must use the wind, for, according to Bill, the calm which follows a Tehuantepecer is only a precursor of another.

While they were shaking out some of the reefs I went up to take down the riding light. When I got to the hounds the motion was so violent I found that all I could do was to cling on with both hands and both feet. I let go the lashings, all but the last one, shouted to Christopher to man the spinnaker halyard, to which the head of the lamp was attached, and let go the last lashing. At that precise moment *Moonie* bucked like a mule and the lamp was torn from my fingers.

It flung itself against the mast, smashing the glass, swung

forward and with long splinters like icicles hanging from a coping, it came straight for my head.

I caught it.

Glad that I was still alive and still aloft, and thinking that the seas would soon wash the blood from the decks, I guided it triumphantly below, to find that all this had not escaped the attention of the mate, but she was so angry that she forgot to ask me why I had not rigged a downhaul on it.

She said, "Where the hell d'you think you're going to get a new riding light!"

CHAPTER TWENTY-ONE

TWENTY-FOUR hours later we were becalmed. The surface of the ocean, which should have been as smooth as the Serpentine on a summer's day, was wrinkled with tide-rips, and the air was filled with a sibilant hiss as if thousands of sardines were under way. This was not fish but current. The Tehuantepecer was over, and now all this sea was rushing back into the middle of the gulf to replace the water which had been blown out. It was an awe-inspiring thought.

The turtle was swimming towards us at about the same pace as we were sailing towards him. Almost without thinking I grabbed a gaff and hooked him under the armpit and hauled him up the topsides. I called for help, for he weighed all of a hundred pounds and Christopher left the helm and Anne woke up. Remembering our shark in the South Pacific I turned to Christopher:

"Get your gun and shoot him."

That turtle's innocent, almost trusting expression left a memory that was only just surpassed by the excellence of his steaks and the taste of his soup. After talking to a number of ocean voyagers and reading the accounts of many others, it seems that unless you live among the fish like the Norwegians of *Kontiki* or Dr Bombard in his raft, catching them is a chancy business. Only Anne refused to be defeated, and it was not till we reached the shores of Mexico that her persistence won. On one of those rare days when the sea breeze attained Force 4 she threw the fishing-line overboard. That a salmon plug, reminder of our unsuccessful British Columbian days, was still attached to it did nothing to dismay her. She ran it over a cleat on the boom to keep it away from the log line, holding it in her hand. Suddenly I saw her stiffen, and without a word she began to haul it in hand over hand.

Looking back along the ship's wake I saw the gleaming underbody of an albacore swaying from side to side in a despairing effort to escape. As well it might, for behind it there was something else.

"Oh, Peter . . . quick! There's a shark after my fish!"

Christopher came running up with a hammer, and between them they landed the albacore, cheating the shark, enraged at the sudden loss of his meal, by inches. From that day on, from the coast of Mexico to the Gulf of Panama, all we had to do if there was enough wind, was to stream the fishing-line at half past six to catch a fish for dinner.

Guatemala, whose mountains we sighted seven days after leaving Puerto Angel, had for its principal port the open roadstead of San Jose, but the sight of the breakers upon that beach frightened us off and we passed it by. The coast is low, and the mountains, nearly thirty miles away, look deceptively close, so that if you approach them, as we did, towards evening it is as well to know exactly where you are. And all down this rather featureless coast with its infrequent lights and uncertain currents, I fixed the ship's position by celestial navigation as a check to dead reckoning.

Almost without knowing it we had passed from sub-tropical Mexico into the lush jungle of the Tropics, the huts and little beehive dwellings of Indians replacing the compact little towns that we had occasionally seen along the shores of Mexico. Presently the plain gave way to foothills, the foothills to mountains. Many were cone shaped, but one, as we approached it with the aid of a fine sea breeze and more than a half knot of favourable current, seemed to have a cloud permanently above it. Rumblings like those from a distant thunderstorm grew louder, and soon there could be no doubt that one of these innocent peaks was erupting. We passed it at night. It looked like a flower-pot glowing with inner fires, and every now and then a river of molten lava would pour down the valley. I broke my rule about keeping a mile off shore and increased it to three, but the dry, rending sound of those subterranean explosions made it difficult to sleep, and once during Anne's watch a "red ball of fire like a trailing flare" fell into the water not far to the west of us.

With a fine offshore breeze we sailed past La Libertad in El Salvador where *Tai-Mo-Shan* once lay. So bad was the surf that her crew, who wanted to visit the town of San Salvador, were taken off by a motor-boat and hoisted ashore by a crane. We passed it by, but the glare from the lights of a modern town, for that is how they speak of the place, two thousand feet up and in the middle of this wild and lonely country, struck us as a little odd.

Two days later we anchored off the Island of Meanguera in Fonseca Bay. Eleven days had passed since we had set foot on dry land; tantalizing when you are so near that you could almost jump on to it. We were within three miles of Amapala, and in the morning we went up on deck to see what sort of place it was. Anne wrote in her diary:

"The day is happy and alive with colour, yellow and gold flowers on the island astern, with its blown, dry trees and slashes of red and gold earth. On Conchaginta Island there is a bay and a little village. The sails of native boats glimmer in La Union channel, and a steamer lies off Amapala. We think we will sail up on the flood this afternoon."

But Anne was wrong. Christopher, buried deep in the fo'c'sle, was hunting cockroaches. I was trying to mend the riding light. The ship heeled suddenly and steeply; a bowl of dirty water catapulted, in company with a half decarbonized Primus and a tin of Vim, on to the starboard bunk. By the time we came on deck, it was blowing half a gale across seven miles of open water, and it would not be long before we started to drag towards the island.

How curious it is that, when every moment counts, one's mind has time, without impairing its efficiency, to turn back a page or two of memories, and I saw, quite clearly, the sea-wall at Muros Bay in Spain. That I had once again anchored in a place vulnerable to the only wind that was likely to blow with any violence seemed so criminally negligent that I dared not contemplate it, but Providence, aided by my crew, who without speaking a word, got sail upon the ship quicker than I would have believed possible, intervened and with twenty yards of grace, it looked no more, we sailed the anchor out and made an offing.

As we gybed and ran for the open sea Christopher, still a little out of breath, wailed, "Peter! Surely you're going to Amapala?"

"And miss this wind?" I exclaimed.

But I must confess, in all the hurry, I had forgotten the place!

Like the proverbial scalded cat, *Moonraker* raced out of the Gulf of Fonseca with the northern hard on her tail. The sun went down, and the moon came up, and the ship stormed along the dark and deserted coast of Nicaragua. At the change of watch I went up to relieve Christopher and saw to my astonishment the lights of a town fine on the port bow.

We had, up to this moment, been keeping two miles off shore to avoid Speck Reef but if this were Corinto, Speck Reef lay miles astern.

I studied the chart. It was possible, I supposed, that with the norther still blowing as hard as ever and the increased rate of current caused by the magnificent offshore breeze, this might indeed be Corinto for it seemed unlikely that a new town should have sprung up where the chart, corrected to two years earlier, showed not even the presence of a village. The place was nearly abeam; we could see no flashing light although, if it were weak, which was more than likely, it would be hard to see against this blaze of light. Instinctively I had been edging closer in while Christopher and Anne peered anxiously ahead.

Suddenly I heard Anne cry out. "Someone's flashing a light at us. There it is again! Two short and a long . . . Peter, you're too far in. *Get out!*"

And as the words died on her lips a roar filled the air. Less than fifty yards away a great sea had reared its noble head and broken upon Speck Reef!

No sooner had we passed this upstart place than the loom of Corinto's light was seen ahead.

For two days and two nights that norther blew. It was as heady as a new wine; the speed of the ship, the astonishing way in which the coast fled by, helped by the prodigious current, made me light-headed, daring me to chance my hand through the Murcielago Channel. My excuse to my crew, who were frankly horrified, was that it would make it easier to fetch Culebra Bay without a tack, as if one tack, or even two, would make the slightest difference, a point they vainly made in argument.

As we approached Cabo Elena, a long, narrow peninsula jutting far out into the sea, I must admit that qualms of conscience assailed me, for it was blowing Force 6, the ship was pressed, and this remarkable coastline is forbidding in the extreme. Off the Cape is a rock like Cleopatra's Needle and all round were the rugged Bat Islands through which this passage led.

"There can be no sea in there," I reassured myself, "and therefore no danger."

We rounded the corner. It was like entering a witch's cauldron. The wind tore down the hills and rebounded from the other side, and in the middle was *Moonraker*, buffeted and bruised like a mouse by an angry cat! A small incident, as is any mouse in a cat's life. But if ever you come down this coast don't go through the Murcielago Channel if a *Papagayo* is blowing.

Out of the witch's cauldron, we streaked across the bay to enter what the *Pilot* calls the "finest harbour in Central America". But in all this vast natural basin there was only the howl of a dog and a light gleaming yellowly from the top of a small cliff.

We went ashore in the morning. As there was a slight swell running we employed our usual technique, backing the pram in stern first and, when I gave the word, the others jumped out and pulled the pram (and me) up the beach. Unfortunately I misjudged the depth, and to my surprise, and very much to theirs, they disappeared below the water. Three men, swarthy and cutlassed, were coming down the hill. With not even a smile but with perfect old-world courtesy they greeted Anne and Christopher as they came up.

Señor Contreras invited us up to his rancho, where brothers and sisters, nephews and aunts, gathered on a low, cool veranda. Hens and geese, dogs and pigs ran through the open house: at the back a blaze of red bougainvillea, carts with wooden wheels, a plough that would have looked old-fashioned to a Roman peasant, and a long flat stone with holes for gourds of water.

When Señor Contreras rode back from the nearest puebla where he'd gone to buy fruit and bread for us, he brought us the news that Costa Rica had been at war with Nicaragua for the past week!

Although we had sailed only eight hundred miles since we had last been ashore, the land being continuously in sight had made the mate less strict with water, and now we were running short. Our friends told us they had water to spare, and took us down through a banana grove to a stream, a stagnant pool covered with green slime, over which hovered a million flies. I was about to decline their kindly offer when they showed me a small circular hole through which welled comparatively clear water. This, they indicated, was *muy benito*. We filled our water-bags and carefully poured into each the right amount of Chlorox before taking them back to the ship. As none of us was any the worse, this speaks volumes for Chlorox.

The long straight coast down which we had been sailing for so long now changed its character. There had of course been something to watch; a bird of prey falling upon another bird, a manta ray, weighing a ton or more, leaping into the air to fall back with a splash that could be heard for a mile, a native village by a stream, a fishing boat on passage. But from Culebra to the Gulf of Panama, deep indentations like those of Nicoya and Dulce penetrate far inland.

Between Cabo Blanco and Punta Burica lightning played in the east, rain-filled clouds, the first for many months, cast their shadows upon the forests. We were chased all night by a thunderstorm. When I took over from Christopher at four o'clock the thing was gathering speed. I was running before a brisk wind with everything set, when I became aware of a noise like steam escaping from a safety valve. It grew louder and louder and nearer and nearer, and then I saw it; a column of water as high as the mast, swaying like the stem of a flower bowing to a gentle breeze, a thing of grace and form, travelling straight towards me.

I gybed all standing.

The water-spout passed harmlessly by, watched by my disgruntled crew, who seemed to think I'd gybed for the pleasure of waking them up.

At the coming of the day the Cordillera Salamanca (12,000 feet), remote and unchallenged, looked down upon me.

In Bahia Honda in the Republic of Panama (like a bowl with serrated edges and green with jungle) we towed a native and his canoe to the village. It gave us an *entrée* and we were given, as a great delicacy, *conejo*, an animal half-way between a rat and a rabbit, and much tougher, I imagine, than either, and long strings of dried *tortuga* which hung from our ratlines like streamers.

It was blowing a norther the day we left, and outside the shelter of the land the sea was rough and wet. On rounding the Pilar Del Sal (it was covered with bird droppings and the colour of the salt we keep our bacon in) at the southern end of Isla Cibaco, we saw the most enchanting bay. It was small, yet deep; it was protected from the north, with a wide and curving beach, the shape of a half-moon upon which sat a hundred pelicans. A stream cascaded down the hillside and its solitude was undisturbed by man. It beckoned to us, like Eve to Adam.

The norther blew itself out, and reluctantly we tore ourselves away from the diving pelicans and the bubbling stream to battle our way along that particularly unpleasant bit of coast between Cabo Mariata and Cabo Mala where the wind is always ahead and the current against you. Then we stood close-hauled across the Gulf of Panama, found the current running up the south-east shore, and anchored off the Balboa Yacht Club three months to the day after leaving San Diego.

CHAPTER TWENTY-TWO

TO go through the Canal from the Pacific side was more difficult to arrange, and I made the bad mistake, urged on me by an acquaintance, of trying to arrange a tow with a banana-boat without the permission of the Chief Dispatcher. I am no good at concealing truth, and it took him less than a minute to discover it. His face looked pained and grim and he suggested the only way was to be towed by a Canal launch at the estimated cost of over a hundred pounds. Even when I said I thought Cape Horn might be cheaper there was no answering smile.

He said, "I shall have to report this to the Assistant Port Captain. Be here tomorrow at ten."

I brought Anne with me. The Captain, she discovered, had been born in Aalborg in the Limfjord and was a friend of Captain Petersen who had been so kind to us at Skagen when we had been run into by a Danish fishing boat. She produced a photograph of *Moonraker* taken in Moorea, and he delighted us by recognizing her at once for a west country fishing boat.

Then he turned to me. "They tell me you wanted to be towed through by a banana-boat. You know that's against the rules?"

I said I did, but explained the smallness of our engine and the difficulty, of which he was fully aware, of beating through the Canal.

He smiled, "By the time you get down to the Magellan Straits it will be winter. I think we'd better relax the regulations."

He shook us by the hand. "Leave it to me," he said. "I'll fix it."

Our interest had been roused by a particularly fine vessel in Balboa anchorage. The *Chiriqui*, a famous ocean racer, which under her late owner had many fine passages including a voyage to Easter Island, had now been sold to someone at Los Angeles and was being delivered by an amateur crew. Although I never counted them all at once there must have been at least seven of them.

She left the day after we arrived with a fine fair wind, her engine going full blast and the sail covers on. That night she returned.

I rowed over and asked what had happened. Her mate said, "Only the dynamo. We'll fix that in a day or two."

Again she set out with the same fine breeze, but this time she came back under sail, neatly handled, and picked up her buoy. I rowed over. No one came to the side, but one of the crew threw over his shoulder, "The engine's packed up."

On the day before our "transit" she set out for the third time, and believe it or not, that evening there she was again. And what d'you think was the matter now? With a crew of seven aboard she had put back because the automatic pilot had gone wrong!

During our stay at this end of the Canal the *Faith*, an American ketch, came in. Larry and Babe, with their son Bill, were fellow members of the Seven Seas Cruising Association, and we had met at Acapulco. Like so many Americans, Larry had built his own boat in his spare time (she is thirty-six feet long and of generous beam) and her after end was a conglomeration of switches, dials and cables to control the various instruments, automatic pilot, radio telephones, fathometer, direction finder and power winch, without which, Larry maintained, no sensible man would put to sea.

Although *Faith* was a little down by the head due to extra fuel tanks for her powerful engine and the charging plant, protected by a wooden cover, on the foredeck, Larry did in fact use his sails more than you would have expected.

They, like us, had had their share of "northers" and calms while coming down the coast and it was during one of these calms that an American steamer stopped and hailed them, asking them if there was anything they wanted. At first they said, "No." But Babe had a brainwave. "Captain!" Babe's voice rang out loud and clear, "have you any ice-cream?"

"Sure we have," was the Captain's answer. "How much d'you want? A bucketful?"

So a bucket of ice-cream was handed down.

Then Babe, bless her, had another idea. "Captain!" she sang out, "if you meet an English sailboat with a green hull and a red mainsail, would you give her some ice-cream too?"

"O.K.!" called the Captain, his voice a shade less enthusiastic, Babe admitted.

As at that time we were a week ahead of them we never met that steamer; but I could not help smiling at the thought of our surprise, and delight, if she had suddenly dumped upon our deck a gallon of ice-cream!

Wishing to see for themselves what the transit was like, the "Faiths" came aboard with the Pilot.

By an unavoidable chance we arrived at the lock at dead low water springs, and at the third locking of the day when the sluice operators were thirsting for their lunch and one could abandon all hope of the sluices being opened at anything but full pressure.

Now this, of course, being our second passage through the canal, I thought I knew what to expect. There were two springs, two bow lines, two stern lines and four motor-tyres along the starboard side and one of us with a roving commission to put a fifth at any point where he thought fit. As I glanced round at the Pilot's "Stand by, now," the ship seemed trussed as tightly as Gulliver had been by the Lilliputians; but the next moment proved me wrong. Fighting like a cat, *Moonraker* stretched herself several feet away from her protector (the banana-boat) and, with a sickening lurch, hurled herself at the bigger ship, the top of the bulwarks taking all the weight of the blow. If Larry hadn't whipped the spare fender in at the most dangerous place our bulwarks might have presented a very curious appearance. As we reached the top the Pilot mopped his brow—because of the heat, no doubt—and said, "I wouldn't have thought those bulwarks were all that strong." Nor, to be quite honest, would I.

Our day was not yet over. The banana-boat, as if incensed at having this upstart mongrel tied to her tail, chirrumped along at a good seven knots, and the wind across Gatun Lake blew at twenty-five knots in our teeth. Tired, wet and depressed still further by watching the seas breaking right over the breakwater, we secured our ship with her stern to a float and strolled over to the restaurant in search of a meal. The covered veranda, the people standing and sitting in groups or strolling on the dock, put Anne in mind of a crowd of passengers waiting at a station for a train that never comes. Our depression didn't last long. Roy and Carol Rice came over to our table bringing with them their guest. "Meet Peggy," they said.

Peggy was a compact little person with eyes that were very much alive. A journalist by profession, she had roamed the world; but the most remarkable thing about her (we got to know her well) was her ability to promote an aura of suppressed excitement wherever she happened to be.

Not so long ago she had bought a fifty-three-foot schooner and sailed her from Florida through the Yucatan Channel to the Cayman Islands. As these islands are low and there was no one on board who could take sights, Peggy, not unnaturally, became anxious about her position. One of the crew, however, was a Cayman Islander and while Peggy was fussing with her charts (her words, not mine) he called her on deck.

"Captain!" he cried. "See those birds?" and Peggy looked up at a flock of birds that were flying off in different directions.

"Now, Captain," he said, pointing to each group in turn, "these are going to Grand Cayman . . . and those to Little Cayman . . . and those over there to Cayman Brac. Now bring me the charts and I'll show you where we are." As Peggy said, when they sighted the island the next morning, it was a perfect example of "position by triangulation of birds."

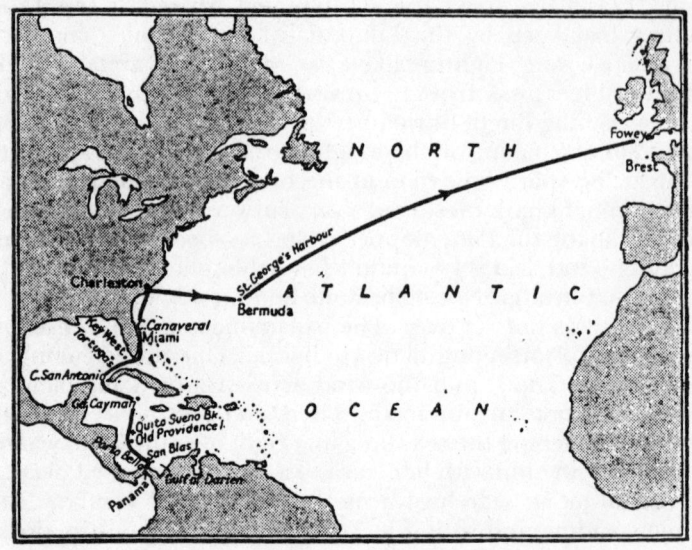

Panama to Fowey

Her voyage continued: she had, she said, to leave Jamaica under a cloud and she had been in Old Providence Island only a week when a friend warned her that a gunboat had been dispatched from Colombia to order her arrest. I don't think for one moment that Peggy had done anything wrong; it was just that "authority" to Peggy was anathema, worse than a sea-lawyer to a bucko mate.

I, too, had made up my mind to sail by the Yucatan Channel and Peggy inspired us to call in at Old Providence; so on 16th March, gilded with fresh paint and gleaming with varnish and resplendent in our new turkey-red mainsail straight from Sadlers at Burnham, we set sail in the evening and beat out of the incredibly narrow passage between the submarine nets guarding the entrance to the harbour and beat eastwards until Porto Bello lay abeam.

Carol Rice had told us that Porto Bello depressed her; nothing there, she said, but impenetrable jungle, buzzards, thin, ravenous dogs and tin shacks. But to us it had a different aspect; the old fortifications, destroyed by Drake and again by Morgan, still stand as grim reminders of those boisterous days, and the only way to reach the place is by the track the old mule trains used four hundred years ago across the Isthmus from Old Panama.

Near the site of the ancient church is the more recent one, remarkable for the fact that it contains the image of the Black Christ. The image is striking. The figure, crowned by thorns, leans forward as if in anticipation of great events; the face is dark, the eyes piercing, and the wood of which it is made is almost black and *does not float*.

The story begins with the foundering of a Spanish galleon off the coast and the image being washed up on the shore. It was treated with great reverence, but three times it was pillaged, and on each occasion the marauding vessel sank and the image *floated* back into the harbour. A three-day festival is held every October to commemorate this astonishing legend.

The people, a mixture of Negro and Indian blood with a touch of Spanish here and there, were friendly enough and showed us their dummy turtles realistically executed in wood and stained to the right shade of brown with which they lured the genuine ones into the waiting trap.

For the rest Porto Bello is much as Carol described it, but it has a sheltered harbour, good holding ground, no swell and little sun, for along this coast there drifts a thin layer of vapour, giving it rather a sinister appearance which fits well the denseness of the jungle.

From here to the Gulf of Darien an easterly current, of which we were able to take full advantage, sets along the coast. We spent a night in the lee of Isla Grande that we might look across to where Drake lay . . .

> Slung atween the round shot in Nombre Dios Bay
> An' dreamin' arl the time o' Plymouth Hoe.

We hove to the next morning off the island of Porvenir. There are three hundred islets in the Gulf of San Blas, so that what we saw that morning were groups of palm trees scattered about the water, protected by long reefs, upon which the sea broke with an impressive roar. Indeed, so frightened was I of making a mistake, and not living to make another, that we ran back the way we'd come for a couple of miles to make absolutely certain of our position.

On this island of Porvenir, less than a mile long and a few hundred yards wide, lived the Acting Intendiente, Señor Hector Castillo; a youngish man with a cherubic face and humorous mouth turned down at the ends as if in ironic contemplation of his own misfortunes. Señor Castillo had broken his leg some years ago, and there was so much shortening that he was unable to walk a step without crutches, an accident, he feared, which would prevent him from ever rising in his profession.

He could now only look forward to ruling over several hundred islands inhabited here and there by small, long-haired men, dark brown in colour, whose women wore gold rings through their noses as a sign of individual wealth. The presence of two Panamanian sergeants, the Panamanian baker and his wife, the only woman on the island, only accentuated his isolation and increased his longing to return to his family in Panama on his yearly leave.

We dined with him that night, and our fellow guest was the captain of a copra schooner from Cartagena. I had wandered over to have a look at her as she lay against the primitive jetty. She was V-shaped, incredibly narrow, drew less than four feet and had no more freeboard than a long canoe. She was rigged as a gaff schooner with tall masts and on top of these they had fitted topmasts! She must go like the wind, I thought, but the seamanship to sail such a vessel in the rough winter seas of the Caribbean made me see myself as a very indifferent mariner.

The captain was a Colombian, soft of voice, a handsome man with the hallmark of a sailor. I had been able to do him some slight service in looking after one of his crew who had an abscess in the palm of his hand, for which he was quite unnecessarily grateful. I remember we talked about England, and I was amazed that in such a remote place they seemed to know exactly how our country was run (which is more than we do) and to follow the opinions of our statesmen as if the world's peace depended upon them. It was odd to us as Englishmen to find two men of different nationalities who thought so highly of our own.

We spent five days among the islands. Native huts with thatched roofs of palm fronds nestled under trees, and in some of the larger islands near the mainland, we were told, were communiities living so equable a life that they could well be an example to other countries who might at first sight think themselves superior.

Rarely were we out of sight of a sailing *caraqua* off to the fishing grounds or to collect copra or to transport a family from one island to another. The San Blas Indians are a reticent people, nor could we understand a word of their dialect. They were as fierce in battle as they are at home on the sea, and a generation or two ago they defeated the Panamanian army that was sent to suppress them.

The evening before we left the shores of South America we dropped anchor in an enchanted bay of pale green water with foreshores of the palest sand, which, when you strode into the water for a swim, stirred up into a thick precipitate, like milk. I woke before dawn and rowed myself ashore, walking across to the windward side. In the growing light dark clouds came sweeping in from the sea on the wings of a fresh Trade Wind and from the barrier reef the ocean looked far from inviting. It suddenly occurred to me how far we were from England, a thought which might not have occurred if the wind had been reversed.

I was walking back to the pram trying to think of an excuse for delaying our departure when I thought of that Colombian copra schooner making her way back to Cartagena. Within an hour or two we were beating out of the channel on our way to Old Providence Island, a hundred miles off the east coast of Nicaragua and two hundred and seventy miles to windward.

Our voyage was blessed by good fortune; the North-East Trades were moderate to fresh and only for twenty-four hours did they blow hard enough to bring home how unpleasant the passage might have been.

Old Providence is a mountainous island which, like those of the Societies, has a reef extending some distance from the coast, enclosing lagoons of quiet water and with passes in and out. It is said to have been inhabited by Morgan's buccaneers, and its inhabitants now claim this distinction with the pride we all feel in our forbears if only they are bad enough. The island belonged to Great Britain, but Queen Victoria gave it away to Colombia, an action that made the island violently pro-British. Indeed, when we anchored off a tiny village and broke out the Blue Ensign (a flag they'd never seen but whose nationality they guessed by the Union Jack in the corner), the coloured people came out in boats bringing presents of oranges, white bread and coconuts.

The clean, bracing air, the lovely wind, the jib-headed fishing boats, as crazy as those of Barbados, brought back to us the smell of the West Indies. I was out of action at that time, running a temperature and with an ankle so swollen and painful that I could not put my foot to the ground, but I enjoyed the sail to Catalina Harbour sitting on the foredeck with my leg propped up while Christopher and Anne did all the work, their faces instead of mine frowning in concentration over the pilotage.

A mile or so from our destination a native boat roared down under a press of sail.

"Captain, we pilot yo' into de harbour . . . very dangerous . . . ten dollars."

Ten dollars! Did they think we were flying the Stars and Stripes?

"Five dollars, then."

But Anne shook her head, and side by side the boats sailed along.

"Captain, if yo' won't take de pilot, we'll race you!"

Much to their astonishment, and to ours, we beat them to it handsomely.

The Port doctor was a Turk, educated in Colombia. He had a look at my ankle and suggested cortisone. I had been used in American to seeing this rather dangerous stuff handed out like aspirin, and I concurred. I think it did my ankle quite a lot of good, but it woke my duodenum up to such an extent that the discomfort accompanied me back across the Atlantic to the shores of England. And the doctor was not even qualified!

Ashore, the island is a curious mixture of English and Spanish; English spoken in the streets and stores, but when the sun goes down Spanish sung to a guitar instead of negro songs to a Calypso band.

Our friends the Faiths came in, and a few days later we sailed in company for the Quito Sueno Bank. This reef runs north and south for twenty miles, submerged along its entire length except for the last hundred yards, upon which has been built a light tower with a weak light (unwatched).

In the centre, on the leeward side, are two underwater crops of coral heads running to the westward for six miles and in between these, for those who could find it, was a sheltered anchorage. There we could lie out in the middle of the ocean with nothing but water to look at and no sound but the cry of a passing bird.

Now we made it quite clear, Larry and I, that we wouldn't attempt it in the dark. About five in the afternoon Larry came close alongside:

"Peter," he shouted. "D'you think it's safe?"

And I replied, "No, it's too risky."

So Larry started his powerful engine and drew ahead on his

Moonraker at Fowey

The Cabin looking forward

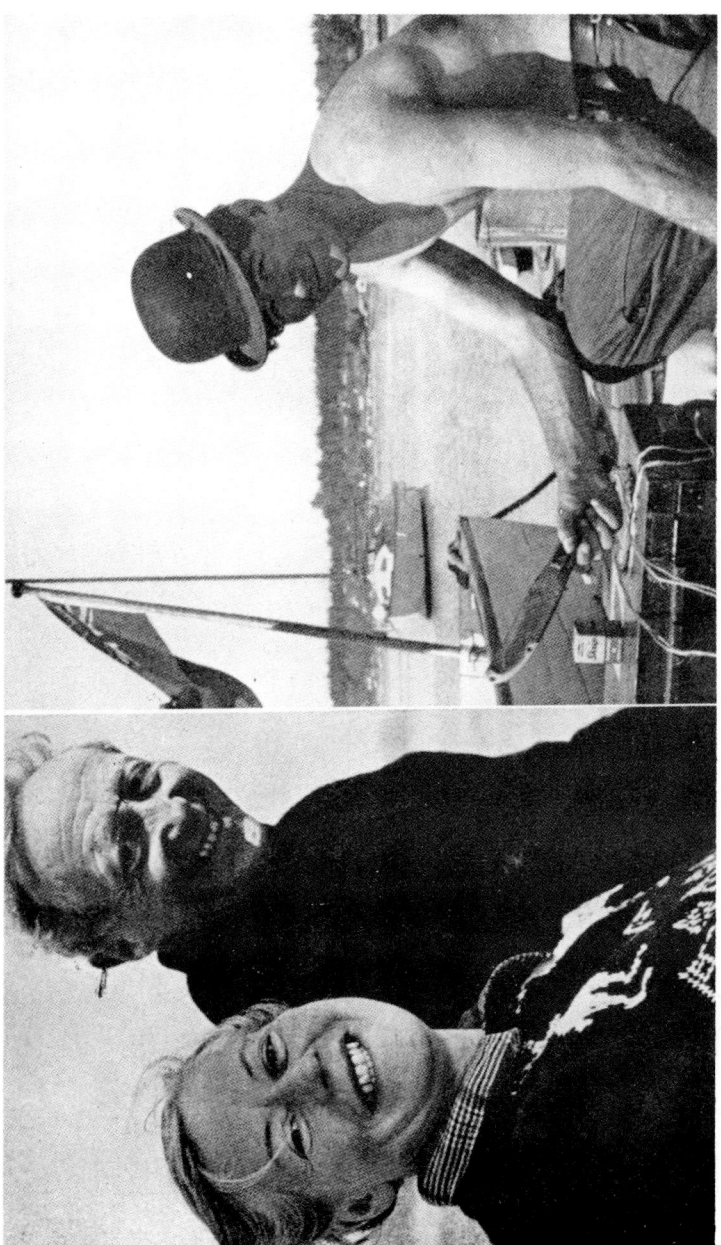

Skipper and Master

Will Christopher pad about the streets in bare feet and bowler hat?

The Barrel at Post Office Bay

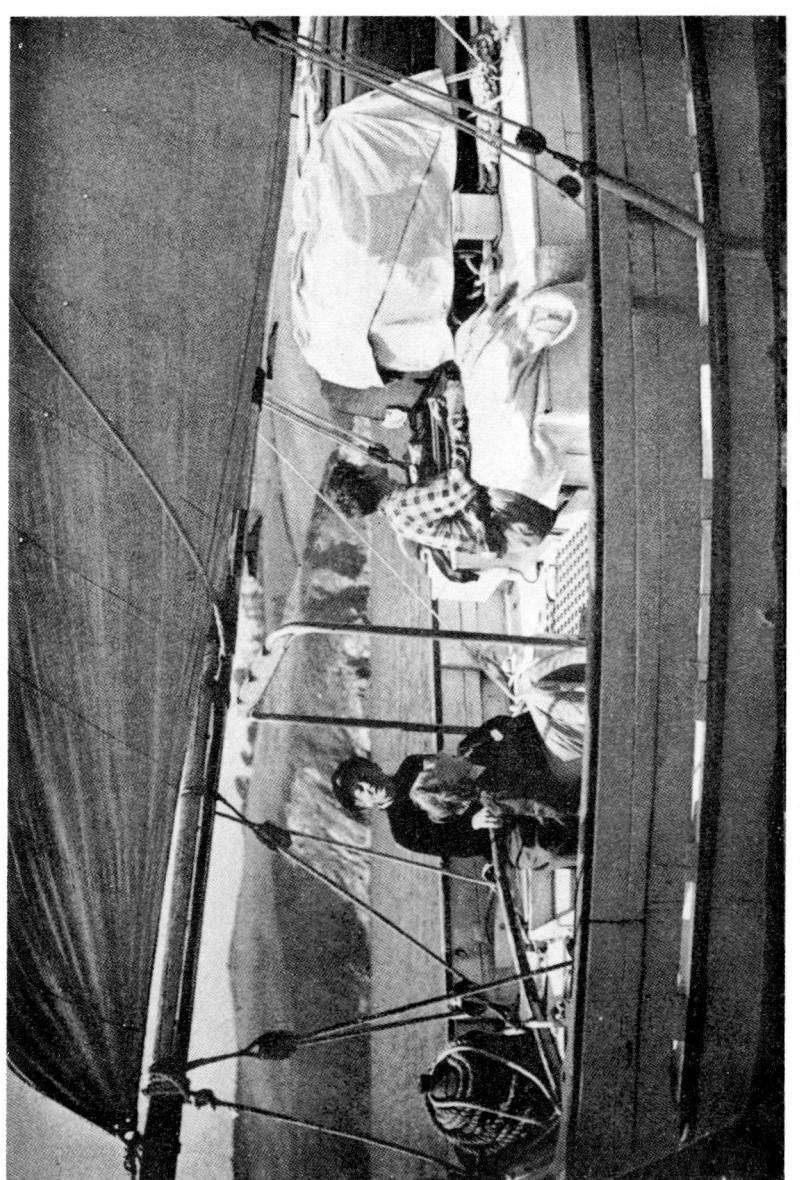

In an hour or two, or three or four, a breeze will come

Peter Pye making sail on *Moonraker*, Rio de Janeiro, 1962

Anne Pye handing the mainsail on *Moonraker*, Rio de Janeiro, 1962

Moonraker off the Sugar Loaf Mountain, Rio de Janeiro, 1962

course for Jamaica. When he was safely out of sight we tacked towards where we thought the southern end of the reef might be.

It grew dark before we got there and, as I sat up on the crosstrees staring ahead I was reminded of that time five years ago when I tried to find Hogsty Reef at the same time of day. I had had the feeling, as I had now, that I was playing a dangerous game and that the only prudent thing was to clear out. But I didn't.

Anne and I were below finishing our dinner when Christopher called out, "Peter! What about those rocks you were worrying about?"

"We've passed them some time ago," I replied.

And at that moment she struck!

CHAPTER TWENTY-THREE

THE impact knocked *Moonraker* over on to the other tack, and in a scene of the utmost confusion we dropped anchor on the first patch of sand that we could see, shimmering palely in the moonlight.

Ten minutes later the bilges were still dry. We lay all night to the full scope of our chain, and the drone of the wind and the chop of the sea seemed to emphasize the precariousness of our position. I slept little.

At first light Christopher went down with his underwater goggles and reported that the copper was torn in four places and that in at least one the wood was badly scored. As the sun rose higher we could see the fantastic growths coming up from the bottom, some thick and tough, others not so strong. Our coral head must have been one of the slender kind and broken off at the impact. We winched in the chain and under shortened sail we wove our way by eye through this prickly maze. We set course for the island of Grand Cayman three hundred miles to the north.

I was on watch when we expected to make our landfall, soon after dawn on the third day out. It was still dark, the moon was high, the sea smooth and the topsail had already been taken down to prevent a premature arrival off this low and ill-lit southern shore. Suddenly, something like panic overtook me; I became quite sure that land was dead ahead and at no great distance.

Leaving the ship to sail herself I climbed the ratlines and peered through the night glasses. No dark line appeared ahead, no smell of land, no sound of breakers. I checked the log; only the current was in doubt. Still with this sense of danger ringing in my head, I got the jib off her and was about to heave to, when I caught sight of a glow no bigger than a man's cigarette *broad on the port bow*! The Light! The current must indeed have been doing overtime. A small incident, but one that illustrates how unreliable moonlight is; that shore for which I had been so diligently searching could not have been more than half a mile away.

It was broad daylight when I worked the ship into Georgetown Bay, shaped like a wide V with the little town at its apex. To port was a white coral beach; the water, sky and land dazzled the cold eyes of a northerner with the intensity of light. The place was an open anchorage with a bad reputation for north-westerly winds. Speed was the thing if anything was to be done to *Moonraker*;

and this was Easter Sunday.

Scarcely had we stowed the sails when a motor-boat put out from the shore. Papers . . . ? We showed our clearance from the Canal to Port Everglades in Florida, and in a moment official business was over. Was there anything, the harbour master asked, that he could do for us?

There was indeed; we were towed towards the shore through a narrow passage between rocks into a pool with a bottom of fine sand. Here we were made fast to half a dozen rocks. The ship was careened as far over as she would go, and within an hour "underwater shipwrights" (our term for men who hammer nails in under water) were working on the hull, encouraged, no doubt, by the singing of hymns across the road from the House of God. They reported the planks to be badly scored, that in two places the wood had been penetrated to an unspecified depth, but that copper tingles should prevent the ship from leaking.

By four o'clock that afternoon, she was anchored off.

That evening a swell, slight but enough to have made such an operation as this quite impossible, rolled into the bay and did not cease while we were there.

The island is windswept, reminding us of Inagua in the Bahamas. There are houses without roofs, houses with only one wall still standing, evidence of the fearful hurricanes which have in the past devastated this low-lying land and drowned so many of its population. The Cayman islanders, as you might expect, are a race of seamen. As soon as a boy is old enough he will leave the land and ship aboard a turtle schooner or one of the deep-sea fishing-boats that work off the coast of Cuba.

We paid a call on Captain Benny Boden to whom we had an introduction from Bridget and Tony Reeves. When we arrived, the Captain, his wife, daughter and son, were busy sewing a huge expanse of canvas that would one day be *Yankee's* staysail. Anne, our sailmaker, had brought along the genoa which, in a Force 3 wind, had split from luff to leech, for it was as rotten as a pear. She asked the Captain, with a glance at me to silence any protest, how long it would take to make a new one.

The Captain asked, "When are you leaving?"

"Tomorrow," I said.

"Give me another day and I'll have it ready."

They finished that sail in less than the promised time and for half its cost in England.

The Trade Wind had settled in the south-east, and it was a topsail and spinnaker run to Cape San Antonio. We picked up the low hills of Cuba in the morning of the fourth day out, and late that night (so strong was the current against us) we were once more pitching into a steep sea heading for the Gulf of Mexico. I had wanted to explore the waters enclosed by the numerous cays that line the north-west coast of Cuba but having been warned at Grand Cayman that several fishing boats had been fired upon when approaching this coast we decided to keep the sea.

At dawn a cry of, "Sail on the starboard bow!" brought me on deck to find a Cuban schooner, a rakish-looking craft with the name of *Domingo Despues* (Next Sunday) bearing down upon us. She was almost bare of paint, her foresail a thing of patches, and her crew, dark and swarthy or as black as pitch, of the kind that might well have raised the Jolly Roger a century ago. Without a wave of the hand they circled us twice and then with vociferous shouts beckoned us to turn and follow them into some hole in the wall of Cuba. We declined their invitation and watched them disappear to the south-west with a feeling of relief.

Against a short, steep sea, and with a fine current, growing stronger every day, we pitched our way to the Dry Tortugas; but from Key West to Fowey Rocks we were rarely out of sight of the tall buildings and huge oil storage tanks that now deface what must at one time have been a paradise of islands. As we worked to the eastward the wind fell light and veered to the south, and the stream began to race.

I said, "We'll get to Port Everglades in the middle of the night. Let's anchor behind Fowey Rocks."

"There's no anchorage there," said Anne.

"If you go here . . . and here . . . and in behind that bank you'll be able to lie in comfort," I told her.

Christopher chewed his nails.

"As on Quito Sueno Bank, I suppose?" he said.

The low coastline slipped past at the rate of knots, and, marked by a haze of heat, the skyscrapers of Miami appeared to port like giant liners in a mist. We anchored off Miami Beach.

The dark sea, the gently rolling ship, the red, green and mauve neon lights lining the waterfront, the lighted windows reaching up to the stars and the roar of the traffic: it was all very exciting, as if you were sitting in the stalls watching a ballet (the dancing lights) illustrating the Tower of Babel.

In the grey light of dawn Miami took on that used look of a proscenium after the show was over, and we hurried on to Port Everglades to "clear" for the U.S.A.

From Port Everglades to Bahia Mar is a distance of about two miles, along the Intercoastal Waterway. We set off under sail, avoiding the innumerable power boats that dashed at speed in a north and south direction. It was rather like driving a farm cart across Piccadilly regardless of the traffic lights, and by the time we got there we were hot, exhausted and more than a little dishevelled. I am, however, an opportunist and I quickly pointed out to my crew who, for different reasons, wanted to sail to Charleston by the waterway instead of taking the outside route, that this would prolong our voyage for another year and probably for ever. Without a single word of protest, they agreed.

I don't know how many millions of dollars the Americans have spent on Bahia Mar Marina, but they are not a race to do things by halves, and there is everything here that the heart of an American yachtsman can desire: stores, Post Office, swimming-pool, bars, restaurant, dance bands and a glossy ship-chandler's that outshines Captain O. M. Watts's.

It was not the sort of place you would expect to find the Hiscocks or ourselves, but we had come here to see Ann Davison, about whom we had heard and read so much (she was the first woman to cross the Atlantic single-handed).

There is a quality about men and women who sail the high seas that is hard to define and even to detect if you meet them ashore, but the moment they come aboard they seem to fit into the atmosphere of the ship as if they belonged; nothing obtrudes, nothing jars. So it was with Ann Davison. "Steadiness" is the word I think I want to describe her presence.

The day before we were due to leave we were looking out over the Canal, when round the corner came a rather battered-looking ketch in search of a night's rest. Suddenly one of her crew waved vigorously in our direction, and then we recognized her. She was the *Zaira* and we had first met her at San Diego more than five months ago.

Zaira had left San Diego Yacht Club on her way to New York the day after we arrived there. She was spick and span, her spars shone with varnish and her crew, large and tough, were justly proud of her. She must have been about the same length as *Faith* but of narrower beam, she was bermudian-rigged on both masts, and had an echo sounder, an automatic pilot, a radio-telephone, a large and powerful engine and a charging plant. She was, in a word, well-found and looked a fast vessel. Before they left, we met her owner; rather small for an American, with bright blue eyes, a freckled skin, red hair and a chin like the Cabo de Roca.

Passing the time of day I said we hoped to be in Acapulco for Christmas, but by then, he said, they would be in Panama as he had to get to New York in the spring.

To our surprise we saw her the moment we got to Acapulco. They had, the owner said, run into trouble at Mazatlan, had escaped to Manzanillo where they were hauled before the authorities, but had been rescued by an understanding Port Captain. This had meant delay and frustration, and the crew had left the ship as soon as she put into Acapulco. Now he was searching for another and soon after we left he signed on Olie Hall. Hall was a wiry South African who had the reputation of being a tremendous worker. He had come out with the Warrs in the *Muriel Stevens* from Capetown and was looking for just such an opportunity. They set off immediately, put into Corinto in Nicaragua for petrol and were charged a hundred and fifty dollars for harbour dues alone. They passed through the Canal ahead of us and had left Cristobal the day we arrived there.

Their passage to Jamaica had not been an easy one. The wind had risen to gale force and they had been driven through the channel between Rosalind and Mosquito banks and had even sighted Cape San Antonio, over four hundred miles to leeward of their destination.

Nor was this all. Their sails blew out, two main halyards parted, and the three of them, for the owner's young brother had joined them in Panama, sewed sails day and night. Then the ship started to leak. The engine packed up, the charging plant was flooded, no lights, no echo-sounder, no ship-to-shore telephone, no automatic pilot. There must have been times, with the water over the cabin sole, when it might have seemed wiser to run down wind to the nearest port, but this did not seem to occur to the owner. He said he was going to Jamaica and to Jamaica he went. It must have been something to do with that chin!

From Jamaica they sailed through the windward passage, and while they were close-hauled under the lee of the land they went ashore on Crooked Island very near the place where the *Tai-Mo-Shan* stranded. After three back-breaking days of hard work they got her off without help and reached Nassau, where they were at last able to get the engine repaired; and now they were here on their way to New York.

The owner looked at *Moonraker* with a rueful grin. "You might think, Doc., that this was a case of the tortoise and the hare!"

CHAPTER TWENTY-FOUR

HOPING for a fast passage with a fair wind and the Gulf Stream under us we set off for Charleston four hundred miles to the north. It was not exactly a coastwise passage, for north of Cape Canaveral the land trends to the west of north, forming a great bay a hundred miles deep between here and Hatteras.

In the afternoon a thunderstorm of great intensity gathered over the land and over the sea astern. Flashes of lightning, peals of thunder and torn clouds travelling at great speed made us take the topsail down, but nothing more came to us than a fresh breeze. Later, a heavy northerly swell came rolling down from the wastes of the North Atlantic.

Followed four days of head winds, thunderstorms, gusts of nearly gale force and the filthiest sea (the current being against the wind) that I have ever tried to drive a boat to windward in.

The rest of the voyage was uneventful, and on the seventh morning out the coastline south of Charleston was in sight. With a fine fair wind and a sluicing tide we roared through the narrow entrance leaving the mellowed buildings, the cannon on the Battery and the slender spire by Wren to starboard and entered the Intercoastal Waterway to find a berth in Wappoo Basin, a muddy creek where tiers of elderly boats are made fast to wooden stages with rotting posts.

I can think of no better American land fall than Charleston for an Englishman; the quiet houses with walled gardens, the air of leisure, the sense of the importance of the past.

Hardly had we secured our ship to the posts when a girl came out of the office of the small boatyard and summoned me to the telephone.

"Hurry," she said, "they're calling you from New York State." Over the wire, as clear as if she were speaking in the same room, I heard Bee Hodge's voice (Bee was a friend we'd met in Lauderdale).

"Peter! Are you all right?"

"Why, of course."

"But that thunderstorm on the day you left. Didn't you get caught in that?"

And when I explained that it had passed harmlessly astern, she continued, "That storm did two million dollars' worth of damage at Fort Lauderdale and they had winds of a hundred and twenty miles an hour at the airport."

As I walked back to the ship it seemed to me that the times that Providence had intervened were mounting up.

Christopher went off to stay with friends at Greenville while friends of ours from North Carolina came down to take us back to Fuquay Springs.

They drove us through the Smokey Mountains and we spent a Sunday at Chapel Hill. The orchestra playing on the campus, the attentive audience in a circle on the grass, the tall trees, the red brick college buildings in the distance, the quiet little town under the hot Carolina sun: the South, little different from that of Scarlett O'Hara.

On the way back our friends drove us to Fayetteville to catch the Atlantic Coast Express. I had stupidly misread the time-table and we arrived one minute before the train was due to draw out. Leaving the others to carry a mountain of gear (Anne and I take as much for a fortnight as most people do for a year) I raced on to the platform and went straight to the "fountain head".

Panting, I said, "Look, we've *got* to catch this train. Can you wait?"

To which the driver, leaning down from the cab of the enormous diesel-electric locomotive, replied, "O.K. I can hold her."

In all the bustle of getting aboard, I still had time to wonder what would happen if an American, vivid in a shirt of many colours, rushed up the platform at Paddington and tried to stop the Cornish Riviera Express.

Out of the wide estuary and between the stone breakwaters where the hustling seas, sharp and prickly with tide-rips make *Moonie* watch her step, out through the buoyed channel beyond which they break in anger on the shallow sands and into the wide Atlantic where the wind, now unfettered, falls light and leaves us time to contemplate our departure from the Promised Land.

How can we give a proper impression of so vast a continent from six months' sailing round her coasts, or an unbiased one when we are leaving so many friends behind us? But, as you were so insistent, Carol, I will try.

Your country glitters and you forget, being used to all these brassy lights, that our eyes are not accustomed to it and you forget, or perhaps you have never realised, that we English are so very different, a difference that is made more difficult to understand by having a common language; although you are doing your best to remedy that defect. Englishmen as a race are what you call in America, "sales-resistant". If you come to our country, which I hope you will, no Britisher will try and "sell" it you, because his love for it is deep. He will grumble at its fogs, its climate, its taxes, its government and almost anything, except perhaps, the English spring.

And when he returns your visit he may be embarrassed by the enthusiasm of your welcome and unable to swallow America when you push it down his throat. He may go even further and think you are trying to persuade yourselves that you are "God's Own Country" because in your hearts you have your doubts about it. May I make a suggestion?

Let him open his eyes on it and absorb it for a little and then he, like us, will go back to Britain and tell his friends that you are indeed as fabulous as you think you are.

It is rather less than eight hundred miles from Charleston to Bermuda. On the eighth day out the glass was falling, the weather threatening, and there was no chance of getting a sight. Dark before its time, the night came on, and I was reminded of Ed Ayres's remark made to me five years ago when leaving Ponce de Leon Inlet.

"Good sailing to Bermuda," he had said, "if you can find it."

We should, if my reckoning was right, have sighted land an hour ago. The three of us on deck, the rain, long foretold, slanting down; the ship under shortened sail; how long could I safely carry on? Better be sure than sorry, on such a night . . . and then Christopher's great shout:

"Peter! Quick! The Light; right above you!"

Like a street-lamp in a London mist, Gibb's Hill Light flashed out.

It is a wise skipper that never lets a fair wind run to waste. Day after day it blew fresh from the west while I fretted in St. George's Harbour; but Christopher had never been to the island, and we had friends to see again. Five days went by before we let go our lines and sailed through the Town Cut bound for Fowey in Cornwall.

Three hundred miles later I was at the helm. It was a blue, sparkling day, Christopher and Anne were asleep in the cabin, and I was easing the old ship over a cross swell which at times made her roll the last two feet of her boom under the crest of a sea. My mind, except for watching the swell, was a thousand miles away, when suddenly, right in the middle of this great sea, there was a crash!

I was amused at the bewilderment and alarm in Christopher's

face as it appeared in the hatchway, because it must so closely have mirrored my own. Both he and Anne thought the mast was coming down, and I that the bottom was falling out!

Three chastened mariners, a broken bobstay-tackle, a bent stem-plate, a thrashing tail a few feet from our planking, green slime spreading like oil upon the waters, marked the end of this encounter.

Perhaps it was as well; for the whale cleaned off our barnacles and we cleaned up the whale.

I was interested, some months later, to hear Peter Scott, in a broadcast, say that whales are soft. Soft is a relative word.

The days passed pleasantly enough. We crossed the broad band of the Gulf Stream, and once we had left it to the south we had real passage-making weather, the stuff I'd dreamed about down the windless coast of Mexico. Our hopes were high and our spirits soared, a hundred and forty-five miles on the clock; and then came a change. The glass fell, and great black clouds hung menacingly astern.

In the middle of the night, Anne recorded, they decided to advance. Long flashes of forked lightning, thunder and torrential rain, calms and catspaws kept her standing there "like a patient cow in a rain-soaked field". Right in the middle of all that blackness she suddenly saw a star, as if nailed to the masthead. Puzzled, she altered course wishing to throw it off, but the star, now more like a thin bar of fire, kept wandering up and down the top three feet of the mast. Softly she called me, but I was sound asleep and Christopher (who was very wide awake) went up instead. "Good heavens," he exclaimed, "you've caught St. Elmo's fire."

After the last peal of thunder, the last vivid flash of lightning, the last squall, all the wind, so it seemd to us, vanished from the face of the North Atlantic. My log, of course, does not confirm this.

There were periods of calm lasting twelve hours or more, there were days when the wind, mostly ahead, reached Force 1 to 2, but there were others when we ran before a gentle breeze, and once we covered a hundred miles. Christopher became more like a shaggy dog than ever, his trusting eyes resting upon me confidently to find a breeze from somewhere, myself irritable and cross partly because I still cannot take calms equably, and partly on account of the effect of the cortisone the Turkish doctor gave me; while Anne wrote:

"I don't feel as if I ever lived anywhere but on the sea, and the days go by all too quickly, even the damp and misty ones."

The S.S. *Gardenia* of South Shields (looking like Masefield's poem) steamed sedately by; a happy ship, we thought, and her north country skipper paid me the compliment of not giving me her position. The S.S. *Empire Merchant*, on the other hand, left us alarmed and despondent for we disagreed by a whole degree of longitude!

It took me the rest of the day to make sure that this had been due to our mis-hearing, for at that time I had been thirteen days without a time signal.

One night the ship was becalmed, and I noticed the masthead lights of a steamer in line a long way astern of us; but steamers move fast these days. I once met a man, an Englishman, who had found himself as lighthouse-keeper on Race Rocks which, you may remember, is a focal point to traffic coming up the Juan de Fuca Strait. Before dawn on a February morning he noticed the masthead lights of a steamer dead in line coming up the Strait, about five miles away. The weather was clear and the sea was smooth. My fiend, who had the instincts of a seaman, kept his weather eye lifting and when the steamer was less than a mile away he suddenly realized that she had not yet seen the light and was heading straight for disaster. Fortunately, he and his colleague had been overhauling the fog-signal the previous evening and the airtanks for starting the fog-horn engine were full. He blew him a U. Two short blasts and a long. You can imagine that skipper's feelings. It must, to him, have sounded like the trump of doom. The steamer, steaming at fifteen knots and helped by a strong flood-tide, heeled violently to starboard, passing *inside* a buoy that was anchored on a reef.

These masthead lights were rapidly getting nearer and it seemed to me that if a brand-new steamer of a well-run line could not see the light from a tower eighty-six feet high, this one might well not be able to see me.

Quietly, so as not to wake the others, I started the engine, and not till the ship's red light glowed at me unwinkingly did I stop it again.

Five hundred miles from Fowey the wind came in from the north-east. As the weather was pleasant our progress, though slow, was not too disagreeable. We crawled over the banks which lie across the mouth of the English Channel, and here it blew hard for a day, forcing us towards the French coast. Brest lay temptingly close, but what, after all, did a few days matter? The wind, seeing that it could not now deflect us from our purpose, kindly backed to north.

We picked up the Lizard Light as it winked out at the beginning of the night, twisted our way through two lines of steamers and in the early morning of the fortieth day out from Bermuda, lay becalmed three miles from the Dodman.

The sun soaked up the haze, and the town of Fowey was just out of sight. In an hour or two, or three or four, a breeze would come and we should sail in through the Heads into the harbour from which we had set out three years ago. What changes should we find, I wondered, and how should we take to living on the land? Would Christopher pad about the city in bare feet and a bowler hat, and should we be content with creeks?

My thoughts were disturbed by the sound of a vessel's engine and a boat came up that was familiar. She stopped, her sails casting their shadows upon the water. Her people welcomed us.

"Come aboard," I said, "and have some coffee."

And I hurried down to start the Primus.

Presently Anne looked out.

"Hullo," she said, "where have they gone to?"

"They wanted to get in," said Christopher. "They've already been two nights at sea."

A Sail in a Forest

PETER PYE

To The Little Birchwood

ACKNOWLEDGEMENTS

I would like to thank the Editors of the *Yachting World, Yachting Monthly* and the *Royal Cruising Club Journal* for their kind permission to reprint some of the material which appeared originally in those magazines

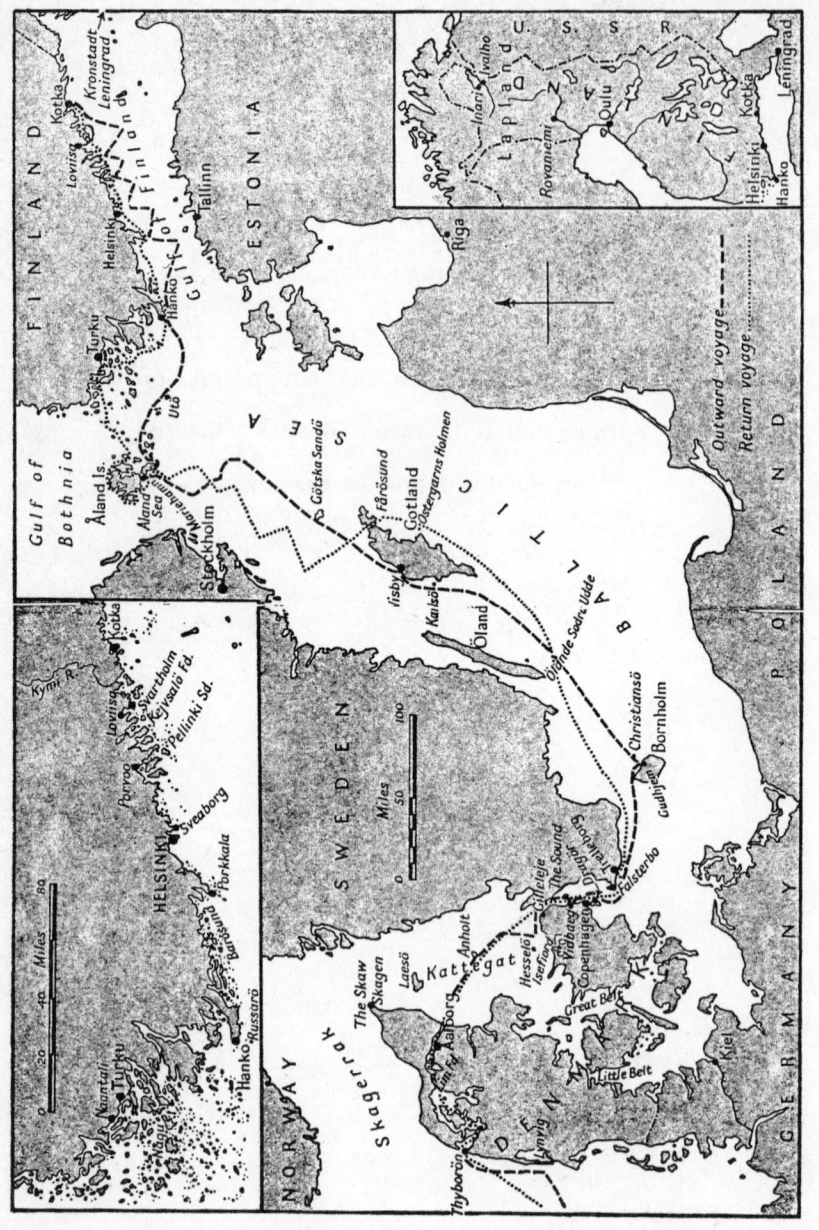

CHAPTER ONE

"THOUSANDS of miles of forest, tens of thousands of islands set in a tideless sea," my friend's voice was almost lyrical and the room suddenly filled with sound, Sibelius' tones of light and shade painting a picture in my mind of the land of the Kalevala legend: a rough-hewn land where men with axes attacked the endless trees and rode logs down swift-flowing rivers: a northern land where the summer sun dipped briefly below the horizon and rose immediately to start another day. His voice went on as I rose to take my leave. "Go now, before it is too late," he said, but whether he referred to Finland's precarious history or to my own advancing years I had no means of finding out. And then I ran into another man who is half Finn and half English, and who offered to put me in touch with friends of his in Finland, so that one day a letter with a stamp bearing the inscription "Suomi-Finland" dropped into our letter-box: an air-mail letter on the back of which was the name of the sender, Captain Eino Koivistoinen with an address at Kotka, a place I have never heard of.

He wrote:

Dear Dr Pye,
    I have been told that you may be visiting us next summer in your good ship the *Moonraker*. It would please me very much if you could sail to Kotka as soon as possible after arriving in this country as I would like to show you not only the beauty of our countryside but how our people live. I do not mean in the cities, there it is the same over the world, but in the small places, on the lakes and by the sea. That is where you may learn something about Finland. . . .

The letter was so *simpatico* that I felt the Captain himself might be worth a voyage of over a thousand miles to meet, but it was Anne who put the seal on it. One day in March when two feet of snow lay on the ground and the sky was black with more to come, she burst into my study in the morning, a thing she never does, and, almost stuttering with excitement, she said, "I've let the cottage for six months."

"You've *what*?"

"They want to take over in a month's time," she said, "so now we'll have to go to Finland."

CHAPTER TWO

WHEN Anne had left me I found I was unable to concentrate on what I had been doing. I pulled out a general chart of the North Sea and studied the three ways by which a ship may reach the Baltic Sea: by the river Elbe and the Kiel canal (like going in by the back-door), a route I have not liked since Anne and I walked by mistake into the local Gestapo Headquarters at Kiel before the War; by the middle way which cuts through the heart of Jutland's farm country on the Limfiord; or to the north, the way the big ships go through the Skagerrak to reach Kattegat round the Skaw. There is, I feel, a marked difference between the polite and gentle southern part of Denmark and the harsh northern Jutland, from whose harbours, which face the North Sea or Kattegat, put out the toughest seamen in Scandinavia to fish the Dogger Bank the year round, playing cards in the fo'c'sle in front of a red-hot stove while a full winter's gale is howling up above. These Jutlanders speak with a rough clipped tongue, and more than once Anne has gone up on deck thinking a boat from Glasgow has just come in. The farther north you go the hardier do these men become, until Jutland narrows to a long strip of land like the spur on the head of a unicorn: the Skaw. And whenever I see that place with the village of Skagen tucked up near the tip of the spur it brings back memories, not all of them agreeable, although ten years have somewhat softened their impact. Our introduction could hardly have been worse. We came tearing into the outer harbour in the middle of a stormy night, turned unwittingly to starboard into a part of the harbour reserved for fishing boats and, while we were getting sail off, we were cut down to the waterline by a sixty-foot fishing boat that came chirrumping out of an inner basin at a rate of knots. Her master went hard astern, threw us a line and towed us to the nearest quay, for he, like I, thought we might sink before we got there. Three timbers, three planks and a part of the covering board would have to be replaced and an informal court of enquiry was held next morning at the Harbour Master's office. We arrived sleepless and anxious, my cousin Joan, who had joined to gain cruising experience, still shaken after the collision, to be met by the Harbour Master (heavily built with a smooth round face and an appraising eye), who sat us down at a long table opposite the skipper of the fishing boat, a lean blue-eyed northener, tough as nails.

Captain Petersen said: "The fisherman says you had no lights." To which I replied that at least two men on the quayside had seen our lights as we entered the harbour and the lamps were still warm when I felt them after the collision which obviously had put them out.

"Besides," said Anne, "he could not have seen them. The dinghy in the bows of his ship completely blocked his view."

"Did you see a man in the bows while the ship was coming at you?" asked Captain Petersen.

"No."

The Captain said: "There is a rule that all ships under way at night inside the harbour must have a look-out in the bows. The fisherman says his mate was there, you say he wasn't." The Captain shrugged his shoulders and dismissed the fisherman.

I stood at the window, worried about the ship, angry at the fisherman for not admitting he had no one in the bows and puzzled by the undercurrent of hostility towards us among the men in the harbour.

The view from the window matched the bleakness of my mind. The cold grey sky from which the rain slanted down, the mounds of empty fish trays stacked by the auction rooms, the trucks standing on rusty lines, the forest of masts lying five or six deep against the quays in this great harbour in and out of which (even in those days) four hundred vessels sailed each twenty-four hours. Only one thing, at the moment, pleased me: a bronze statue of the coxswain of the lifeboat in oilskins, sea-boots and life-jacket, holding in his right hand a heaving-line. The rain trickling off his sou'wester seemed to make him so much more real. I gave a start when a large hand gripped my arm. "If you claim damages for this collision, doctor, it will mean going to court and I do not think you will win. I have little doubt that there was no look-out and I quite believe your lights were burning, but those men who saw them will not come forward; you turned into the wrong part of the harbour and in Skagen the fisherman's word is worth more than yours." The Captain offered me a cigar and then lit his own. He said, "Have your ship made safe for the passage back to England and then let her be properly overhauled by your own shipyard."

Joan stayed with the Petersens while the fo'c's'le in which she slept was being repaired and we had time to explore the little village (for that was all Skagen was in those days) and to wander through the flat open country, past sand dunes and reeds waving in the breeze, silent but for the birds and the roar of the sea on the windward coast. In places the sand had collected into drifts like snow, its yellow surface furrowed like waves upon a pond by the furious gales of winter that blow first from one side of the isthmus and then from the other. Below these drifts lies the old village of Skagen, buried alive in one night of storm over two hundred years ago. Only the top of the old church tower can still be seen, a mile from its more fortunate successor. But it was to the museum that we went most often. At the turn of the century a group of artists led by Mickel Anker came to work and live among the fishermen, painting scenes from their daily life: the manning of the lifeboat, families sitting through the long night waiting for their men to return. After twenty years they left, but their paintings remained as a gift to the fishermen at Skagen. What men they were! There is a painting by Anker of a gathering round the bonfire which is lit each year on Midsummer's Eve in which Drachmann, better known for his poems than his painting, stands apart from the rest, his huge frame, his Viking head with its red pointed beard, his fierce eyes lit by the flames of the bonfire, while he holds forth, one feels, to lesser folk.

But my favourite, also by Anker, is of two fishermen standing by a lifeboat looking out towards Skagens Rev and some luckless vessel (unseen in the picture) which is driving helplessly towards it. The painting is called "Can they make it?" and in the stern unyielding faces of those two men is the very meaning of the sea.

One night before we left it blew a gale from the south-east, a rare event in summer, and I turned out at first light to look to our lines. The rain had stopped, but it was still blowing great guns and a tremendous sea rolled into the outer harbour. About a mile away was a trading ketch with a trysail set on her mainmast, making for the entrance. I was not the only one out at that early hour. Not fifty feet away stood Captain Petersen, like the master on his bridge, his feet apart, his body balanced against the wind, his eyes fixed on the sea, the harbour and the ship like the men in Mickel Anker's painting.

In the frame of mind into which I had now worked myself, as I pored over one chart after another, one of those faces in that picture had much in common with that of a friend of mine, another Dane, whom we had met in Arendal in Norway some years ago: the same piercing blue eyes, the heavy lines and crows' feet under the lower lids that seem to come from looking at far horizons. He had shown us over his remarkable vessel, *Sol-Lys*,

A Sail in a Forest

a bluff-bowed beamy cutter designed by him on the exact lines of a trading vessel of a hundred years ago: dead-eyes and lanyards, ratlines, long squaresail-yard, a captain's cabin in the stern with two small square windows (like the windows in the stern of a miniature galleon) peeping out from the transom. The only light he allowed was a copper lantern with a candle in it. He was a man inspired by the sea. This in itself is not uncommon, but sailing before the mast in four-masted barques had made a difference to Knud (as it does to every square-rig sailor) giving him a grasp of the immense forces involved when a big ship is running before a gale and a respect for the sea that only this experience can teach.

At that time we were making plans for a voyage to the Pacific, so that it was some years before we again visited Scandinavia. This time we were lying beneath Kronborg's castle when a long thin and vaguely remembered figure leaned over the quay above our ship and reminded us that we had met in Norway.

He said: "A friend told me you were lying here so I have come up to take you to my home in Skodsborg."

And when I made some slight protest, for we had been in the act of getting under way, he said with a charming smile: "If you look over the wall, doctor, you will see that I have ordered the north-west wind and already it has come, so now you can wait till tomorrow with an easy mind."

Knud is a naval architect. For some years he worked for a firm of shipbuilders at Helsingör, but in the late thirties he set up on his own as a consultant. It was a lean time. His wife, a doctor, did his typing at night after she had finished seeing her patients, and just when things were beginning to get a little easier the War broke out. I did not like to ask him much about that, but I do know that several of the small vessels he designed turned up in some mysterious way in Scottish ports many months later. After the War he started to get a number of inquiries from Norwegian firms.

He said: "They told me they had no money, but if I could wait for my payment they would like me to design their ships. I, too, had no money but I had the greatest admiration for the Norwegian people and the fight they had put up during the Nazi occupation, and for that alone I ought to help them."

The Norwegians, I have been told, have long memories. Knud now employed a staff of seventy men and women, and although he has designed many ships in many countries, including Britain, the people he liked working for best are the Norwegians.

Before he drove us back to the ship he gave us advice about our route up Kattegat to Skagen and in particular to give the islands a wide berth. Two days later, in the early hours of the morning our young crew, his hands full with a ship now running by the lee, too proud to call his skipper, forgot to look at a rapidly approaching island and the more rapidly shallowing water and ran the ship ashore off the southern coast of Laesö. For an hour we bumped over those iron-hard sands and not since a dark night among the coral heads on the Quito Sueno Bank have I been so filled with the fear that I had lost my ship. But by some miracle she survived that terrible bumping and by sheer luck, for at the time she was hardly answering the helm, she sailed through a twenty-five-foot gap in a line of boulders to reach deeper water.

Once more we arrived at Skagen with our spirits at the lowest ebb. As we turned to port into the main harbour (now greatly enlarged) the fuel launch whose crew in the old days had been more than taciturn now waved enthusiastically before coming alongside to take us in tow. Captain Petersen himself came out of his office and as soon as we were moored he stepped aboard and handed us a letter from Knud. He wrote:

> There was something I forgot to tell you last night. . . . If you leave the island of Laesö to starboard be very careful of the current. Often it runs to the north-east instead of to the north, setting you on to the shoals. I once went ashore there myself. . . .

Somehow I felt a little better after that.

Ashore houses were springing up like blades of grass and hotels were going up like mushrooms. We were still the only yacht in the harbour, but there were no black looks from the fishermen and the place was crowded with tourists and the shops with souvenirs. Skagen had a new look but we were not at all sure that we did not prefer the old.

CHAPTER THREE

MARCH went out like a lamb. Friends came down to Lawling Creek and we swarmed over the ship with pots of paint and varnish. Dear *Moonie*, each spring I look at her with increasing delight, her planks are smooth in spite of her sixty-three years; and I think with the greatest affection of Ferris of Looe, that old rascal of whom it was said that the more he drank the better he built. Perhaps it was during some particularly magnificent orgy that he first thought of the *Lily*, as she was then called. Her dimensions are just figures: 29 feet long, 9 feet 7 inches beam, 6 feet draft, but she has crossed the Caribbean from west to east in the teeth of the North-East Trades, sailed 2,500 miles in twenty-five days and once she has logged a hundred and fifty miles in twenty-four hours. These things are little in themselves and other ships of her size may have done better, but there is one thing in which it would be difficult for her to be surpassed: her luck. I will not tell you her other qualities because I love her, and to do so would be like discussing your wife with your friends. She is, after all, my ship and not yours, or rather she is Anne's and mine, for Anne owns sixty-three sixty-fourths and I own one, which means that we shall never sell her, for it would be impossible for us both to be angry with her on the same day. So we have her for better or for worse.

She is a gaff-cutter and carries a tops'l. With all her kites aloft she sets 800 square feet of canvas, and one of the few rules that a new crew has to learn is that he is not allowed to take in sail without calling the skipper. The cabin is wide, its coamings and ceiling are painted in light colours and the galley can be shut off from the rest of the living-room, so to speak, by closing a couple of doors. Brass, mahogany lockers and brightly coloured cushions make it seem, we have been told, more like a country cottage than the inside of a London tube, which is how a modern cruiser-racer sometimes looks to me. We have, too, a double bed and when Hammond Innes first saw this it so tickled his fancy that he said *The Sea is for Sailing* should have been called *Thirty Thousand Miles in a Double Bed*. I have no doubt he was right.

In that cabin, twelve feet by eight, three of us lived for three years and came back better friends than when we started; and I still think that the only absolutely necessary quality that a crew need have is that he should be easy to live with. For this voyage, which could not last more than five months, we had chosen our crew with care: a Dutchman whose name was David. He was the son of the doctor at Terschelling who had looked after me while I was ill, and David had sailed across the Waddenzee to Den Helder with us. He was young, strong and willing, but what clinched it was something he said before we started. We were looking at charts and he pointed to a buoy. He said: "I know the channels up to this buoy. Beyond that buoy I only think I know them."

May came in with a cold east wind. A week before we were ready to sail I had a letter from David. It brought bad news. His father was desperately ill and David could not come.

Although this was a voyage that Anne and I would have tackled on our own, a third, we think, makes the difference between pleasure and hard work, so we flung wide our net out of which came three very different fish. The first, little more than a boy, took one look at *Moonraker*'s gear and fled up stream as fast as his young arms could work the oars, the second, a dark young man with Teddy-boy hair, tried to persuade us to make for Tahiti instead of Helsinki, and the third, a nephew of friends of ours and a member of a sailing family, passed the only test that we had time to give him, a sail in the river Blackwater. He was leaving for Italy for two weeks holiday and would join us in Denmark and Anne and I would take the ship over on our own. Then I had an idea. I rang up Joan. I did so with some misgiving because she has never forgotten that passage back from Skagen when we had to pump the North Sea out of the ship every day for a week and faced more than our fair share of bad weather. I never heard her grumble once but what she found hard to forgive was that on her return home, she had to go straight from the office to bed every day for a week.

Since those days Joan has become a person of some consequence and I do not disturb her at the office unless I must. At last I was put through.

I said: "Would you like to come to Denmark with us next week?"

"Not if it was like last time."

"The ship's as tight as a drum."

There was the briefest of pauses.

"Where do I join?" she asked.

On the day we left a friend came over by car to bring us some last-minute stores. She stood on the bank as the breeze filled our sails. She said to herself, "They're mad. A puff of wind would blow Joan over: Peter's sick and surely Anne can't sail that hulking ship and look after the other two as well." But before we reached the North Sea, before, indeed, our voyage could be said to have begun, we suffered a brief encounter that gave us a glimpse, like a glance through a lighted window from a passing train, of quite a different point of view.

The day was done: the Naze Tower of Walton cliff was slowly fading into the night. The lightest of airs still held from the south, and for the last hour or two a small open boat, not more than sixteen foot, had slowly crept up on us until she was only a few yards away, so close that we clearly heard the chuckle of the water round her bows.

"Where are you bound?" I asked, without raising my voice.

"Wherever the wind blows me: the same as you," came the answer. The voice was not young. With no cabin and no stove to warm himself by he must be cold.

"Come aboard," I suggested, "and have some coffee."

"I'll stay where I am," he said. "I've coffee in a Thermos, and I'm quite happy where I am."

Soon a strengthening wind drew *Moonraker* ahead. We were bound for Denmark but it was getting late, the night was dark and the river Orwell was nicely under our lee so that I was not surprised to find us anchored under the shelter of Shotley. By the time we had stowed the gear a small riding light was bobbing up and down inshore of us. Our friend was right. The wind had blown us into the same place.

The weather remained fine, the wind fair and before our neighbour awoke we set course for the Limfiord (or the Skagerrak) some three hundred and fifty miles away. Two nights later I relieved Joan at ten o'clock. I found myself becalmed on a sullen sea and a swell rolling up from ahead. The sky looked as if it might be conjuring up some devilry, and at midnight it occurred to me to listen to the forecast. I returned to the helm with plenty to think about. A depression was moving east. There were warnings of gales from Finisterre to Thames, severe (Force 9) in Portland and Wight; and in Fisher and German Bight (in which areas we should be for the next few days) strong north-east winds, with the obvious inference that soon they would be worse.

Astern lay the Texel Light-vessel, its three flashes stabbing the sky, while on the starboard beam were the Frisian Islands with two channels through which I could safely enter sheltered water. I am not fond of gales, but whenever I think of turning back I remember something that happened many years ago. Anne and

I had been beating up channel in the spring. It was cold, wet and windy and the sea was rough. While Anne was fast asleep I put up the helm and ran back the way we'd come and Anne woke up as we were entering a West-Country port on a sunny morning. She was not cross: she simply said, "I don't understand: if we had gone on we should have been almost there. Now we have to start all over again."

I looked around. Perhaps the weather did not look as threatening as I had thought and the fishing fleet to the south-east (probably from Urk) went contentedly about their work, their engines muffled by distance to a drone like bees in a summer garden. If these men did not give a thought to the weather, why should I? A light breeze came rustling over the sleeping sea from the east and *Moonraker* woke up. I should have enjoyed myself immensely for the rest of my watch if only that wind had not had the breath of ice. After two days of rain, thunderstorms and bitter east winds (I had no idea that the North Sea could be so cold in May) we made our landfall on Lynvig sixty miles to the south of Thyborön. The wind dropped completely. The lighthouse, perched on its little cliff hung suspended in mirage. In such conditions sound travels a long way and somewhere out to sea and getting closer was the chirrump... chirrump... chirrump... of an enormous single-cylinder diesel, a sound that no one who has visited Denmark's shores will ever forget. Out of the haze comes the familiar ice-blue hull, the masts, the riding sail of a trawler from the Dogger Bank. She turns towards us and her diesel slows to what seems to us like one explosion a minute. She loses way until hands can bridge the gap between us, but in spite of the long North Sea swell she doesn't touch us. The skipper comes out of his wheelhouse, the crew line the deck and a wooden tray piled high with plaice, mackerel, blocks of ice and innumerable claws of crab is handed over. Cigarettes pass the other way.

The skipper says: "There's no wind, why not come in to Ringkjöbing? I'll tow you in."

If only Finland were not so far away! They left us to prepare a gargantuan meal of fried plaice with crab sauce that Boulestin himself could hardly have bettered. If only I had been content with less!

Anne wrote in her diary:

Sixth day at sea.... I took over from Peter, still looking pale, at 4 a.m. and heard growls of thunder, sharp and sudden claps and bursts right overhead and a breeze that threatened the tops'l. In as many hours the glass falls four-tenths and we are hove-to under two reefs and clouds of water. There is a little brown bird under the dinghy and a dank heap of feathers glares at me. This I pick up and carry below to make it a nest (ill chosen idea) in Joan's woollen scarf. Sleep, breakfast, lunch and the storm is over. The bird becomes a dove and the scarf unspeakable and we are left with a lumpy sea and a N.W. wind too light to still the boom. The dove sits in the sun and makes experimental flights but land is out of sight and neither he nor we can make it so he retires to a place of his own choosing and closes his red eyes....

Even now I had not yet made up my mind whether to enter the Limfiord or Skagerrak, partly because I still remember Knud's scornful remark, "There is only one way a seaman can reach the Baltic from the English Channel: by rounding the Skaw." But I like the entrance to the Lim and the little town sheltering behind the ramparts of the harbour, the low windswept peninsula of sand that runs from here to Bovbjerg. That morning in May any landfall would have been difficult. Low clouds, almost mist, swept in on a south-west wind, Force 6 on the Beaufort scale, and there was something about that sea that made it look awfully shallow. Suddenly Anne shouted: "Fish markers!" and then, right ahead of us was a sandy, shingly beach with nothing to tell us whether we were to the north or south of Thyborön until I saw a shed that looks like a hangar, but is, I recollected, a fish factory three miles south of the town. By the time we were off the entrance the weather had cleared and it was, as I had feared, quite irresistible: those long spits of golden sand, the narrow channel winding towards Nissum Bredning, the hills beyond; and so once more we failed to round the Skaw. Thyborön was left astern, we crossed the Bredning and ran aground trying to beat up the channel to Lemvig and "in a cloud of steamy language" came off again. Anne's diary ran on:

    We browse in the sunshine, dry sails, oilies, sweep the fluff and crumbs from the cabin floor, eat our third breakfast and let sleep creep in on us. In the evening we enter Lemvig: we tie up alongside a tarred catwalk and the harbour master chats over a cigar. We are the first yacht of the season. In the little town strange words fall off our tongues; a butcher slices veal and, knife in hand, points up a street where we may find milk and spinach. By 9.30 we are in bed and asleep. Peter dimly hears a voice from above which says in English, "Oh dear: too late."

CHAPTER FOUR

TO sail through the Limfiord is to draw breath between two seas. On every side is rolling farmland into which penetrate branches from the Lim to encircle islands, to end at a little town or at a quay at the foot of a country lane. Through these inland waterways, past patchwork, quilt fields and sleepy villages we sailed, not lingering, for Joan's time was getting short. This was our third passage through this place in which there are no tides but where currents are sometimes strong and not once have I escaped running aground. Now, I thought, I knew it—which, no doubt, was the reason why we rounded the last corner before Aalborg, pink in the setting sun, only to be set hard and truly on a mudbank by the current. In silence we went through the motions every sailor knows: the warp paid out from the bow as the anchor is taken out into deeper water, the heaving in of the slack, the manning of the winch as the warp is led to the drum and the moment of disillusion when the anchor comes home while the ship stays still and you start all over again.

"DAMN *Moonie*!" gasped Joan as she fell on her knees. "Last time the pump: now the winch!"

At eleven o'clock that night we went below, defeated. The water had dropped a foot. During the night the wind fell and the water came back. Before dawn we were on deck, numb after yesterday's toil. The lights of a large coaster came swiftly down the channel, her wash curling like small breakers.

"Wait for it," I cried, "then heave till you break!"

Moonraker stirred and then with as sweet a sound as a cork coming out of a bottle she withdrew herself from the mud.

So Joan left, and her place was taken by John. He also looked tired, for he had come overland from Italy.

"Well," he said, "do we sail at once?"

But when we assured him we were not leaving till the morning he curled up in his bunk and slept for several hours, after which I told him a little about Kattegat and what to expect from her....

From the Skaw, Kattegat runs south for a little more than a hundred miles to join the Baltic through the Belts and the Sound. Her waters are plagued by sudden storms, by unpredictable currents set up by winds and by the raising or lowering of barometric pressure, by melting snow and rain in Lapland a thousand miles away and by gales in the North Atlantic: by the uneven nature of the bottom and by the islands that lie within. I can pay her no higher compliment than to say that Knud treats her with the greatest respect, although at the moment he seems to have mastered her.

But that day at the beginning of June, Kattegat's face was fair. She blew us southwards and if only John had remembered to take his avomine he would have enjoyed it too. The sun went down, the moon came up and the cliffs of Anholt took on an air of mystery that they do not wear in daylight. To starboard, a long way out of sight, were the Big and Little Belts and the tree-covered islands and fiords to which we had sailed last year with so much enthusiasm. There are bits that we liked but Anne wrote in her diary, "it is like sailing among fields and farms, more suitable for a ploughman than a seaman." No: although I am frankly afraid of Kattegat it would be to her that I would return. She is a challenge, with all her nasty tricks, to any sailor and I like, too, the islands she hides in her bosom: the flat and windswept Laesö, the Danish Desert, Anholt, which in the height of the August season is as empty as the Qu'amiyat.

The wind had dropped to a whisper. The sun was not yet up but the light was good, and in the distance I could see, like an island in a boundless sea, the Kullens, those remarkable hills on the Swedish coast that make the best landmark for entering the Sound. Away over to starboard was a light-vessel (that would be the "Kattegat"), and on the bow a headland which I immediately identified as Gilleleje. I was a little puzzled, I remember, by the relative positions of these things and the hills had looked a little vague (I put this down to haze) but I was drowsy after three hours on watch and at that moment Anne appeared at the hatchway rubbing the sleep from her eyes.

"Good morning, my love," she said. "Where are we?"

I showed her the salient points. She took the glasses off their hook, gazed at the light-vessel, examined the cliffs and went below to look at the chart. Now if you have sailed with anyone as long as I have sailed with Anne you can tell, from the look in her eye or from some slight movement of her body, what she is thinking about and I had a growing suspicion that she had discovered something. Those Kullens were a very long way off and when I looked at the compass... But I was too late. In a voice like a cat that has finished the cream, she said, "That light-vessel has painted upon its sides the words 'South Kattegat': that headland looks remarkably like the island of Hesselö, and are you by chance making not for the Sound but for the Isefiord?"

That woke me up completely.

Our passage down the Sound was one of calms and headwinds. Hamlet's castle, the freighters and tankers passing to and fro from Kattegat to Baltic, the almost Caribbean blue of its waters scattered with the coloured sails of yachts where once sailed barques and schooners. Even now, if you wait long enough, you may see, as I did, a stately square-rigged ship passing from one sea to the other without noise or smoke, looking as strange as a Manila galleon would have appeared to one of Nelson's captains.

It was breakfast time before we worked our ship close inshore under the lee of the hill on which stands Knud and Helga's house, but long before we anchored the family was out on the terrace waving with handkerchiefs, scarves and tea-towels while Brogie (their son) stood by to hoist the ensign: but their ship, *Sol-Lys*, had gone.

CHAPTER FIVE

LONG and low, built in a rather Canadian style, the house overlooks the Sound, the island of Ven and the Swedish hills behind. The garden falls steeply to the beach where a boathouse, a quay and a mast (complete with topmast, gaff and ratlines) from an old English cutter provide a nautical flavour without which, I suspect, Knud would be unable to breathe. Up this path we climbed to be greeted by Helga, who was more moved than I had ever seen her. She said: "Knud left a week ago for Viana do Castelo where he has some trawlers building, but he was so tired and ill that I wished I had gone with him."

"Where is he now?"

"I had news of him from a Danish fisher-boat on the Dogger Bank, from the Tongue 'Lightning ship' and from Dungerness. Since then, nothing. . . . You know what he is: he won't put in anywhere till he gets to Portugal."

"He's done well. Don't worry, Helga, this will do him good."

"I know," she said with a doubtful smile, "but there are so many things: steamers, fog . . . but when I saw *Moonraker* come sailing in I felt so much better. She has survived, so why not Knud?"

The odd thing about Knud and Helga is that they are so alike. Both have this hard core of inspiration running through their lives; for Knud, the sea: for Helga, the North. She is, as I have told you, a doctor running her own practice, but when she was young she spent a year at the little hospital at Jakobshavn on the west coast of Greeenland, the first woman doctor to work so far to the north in that barren land. It made a great impression on her, as Knud's experiences in a windjammer had on him, and she returned to Denmark with every intention of going back. What stopped her was Knud, and I don't imagine that even he found that particularly easy. Hanging on a wall in their drawing-room is a painting of an icy mountain, a fiord and a small settlement with a Danish schooner in the foreground painted by an artist from photographs that Helga took while she was out there. It looks a bleak place, but there is something about it that makes you realize what it was that got inside her soul. On her desk, second in place only to Knud and the children, is a picture of two huskies, the leaders of a team on an expedition which must have been gravely hazardous. . . .

Spring had come to Jakobshavn when she was sent for urgently. A man was reported to be dying on the other side of the estuary. There was as yet no sign of a breakup in the ice and she and her guide crossed the fifty or sixty miles without great difficulty. It was a fortnight before she dared to leave him, and by that time the sun was warm, the air almost balmy. On that very morning the Eskimo guide told her that the ice was no longer safe and they would have to wait until they could go by boat.

"But that may be weeks; and I must return to the hospital."

The Eskimo shrugged his shoulders. "It is not safe," he said, "and I will not take you."

She stood there trying to think—a difficult confinement due any day, a case in the wards about which she was far from happy and her only colleague not expected back for a fortnight; and that other voice, perhaps, whispering in her ear, "A live doctor is better than a dead one: and are you capable of driving a sleigh in the sort of conditions with which you may be faced?"

She thought she probably was not.

"Very well," she said to her guide, "if you will not take me, make ready the sleigh and the dogs. I leave in an hour."

But this was too much for him, and when Helga left he went with her, a circumstance that proved fortunate for Helga.

"Peter," she told me, "that was a terrible journey: the grinding of the ice, the crash of great blocks of ice falling one on the other . . ." In her effort to find a word or a phrase her voice became almost incoherent . . . and then the telephone rang. I tried very hard to get Helga to pick up the threads of her story, but the moment had gone and her answer was always the same: "No: Peter, it was really nothing because we got through all right."

The House on the Hill is a happy house: by day a cacophany of sound, Masta's music pupils (Masta is Helga's sister), Helga's telephone, the tramp of Girl Guides, the drone of an electric floor-polisher, the ringing blows of Brogie's hammer as he repairs a strake in his dinghy down by the water. At half-past five, when Knud returns from the office it is as if the captain is back on the bridge, and the day ends round the log fire with a murmur of voices as soothing and as satisfying as one of Masta's incomparable soufflés.

Skodsborg, their nearest village, is six miles from the heart of Copenhagen: a Hans Andersen city of tall houses leaning one against the other like old men, of fantastic copper spires, the copper green with verdigris, where the yards of sailing ships tower over grey walls and ocean-going freighters lie within a few moments' walk from green lawns. Through the echoing corridors of a museum we found in a quiet room a Viking ship so old that the temperature must not be varied by so much as one degree, for if it did she would disappear like 'She' in Rider Haggard's famous book, and in the evening we watched at the Royal Opera House a Verdi opera transformed into a Danish saga (grey battlements and Scandinavian armour) without loss of face. But Copenhagen has something more than this: it has Tivoli. You may know the story: how the people of Denmark were growing restive under the misrule of their king, of how the king sent for his counsellors and said, "What shall I do to keep them contented?" To which one of them replied, "Build them a pleasure garden where they can walk and play in the evenings. They will then think no more about things that do not concern them."

So a pleasure garden was made, the people were happy and the king, no doubt, went on ruling as badly as before. We, too, walked in Tivoli. There were amusements, a large concert-hall, a puppet-show, a street of a hundred years ago: but the feel of the place was best expressed by a Dane, who said to me, "Here, the people are never drunk, for they love their gardens so much that they would not dare to bring them into disrepute."

We walked with Helga past the famous Mermaid to gaze at the Gefion fountain, at the massive shoulders of the leading bull, at the grim unyielding face of Gefion herself, while Helga told us the legend which many of you may know. Gefion, who found favour with King Gylfe of Sweden, was promised as much land as she could circle with a plough in a day. She turned her four sons into bulls and ploughed with such ferocity and success that a large slice of land fell into the sea to make the island of Zealand on which Copenhagen stands.

How else, indeed, could it have come about, when the shape of Zealand so closely resembles that of Lake Väner in Sweden?

Our minds filled with legends, our hold with Masta's "Cake for Kattegat" (without which Knud never left the Sound) and with a soft west wind allowing us to sail a point or two free, we sailed out of the Sound and rounded the southern point of Sweden. For the first time we entered the Baltic Sea.

CHAPTER SIX

THE night was dark: the sort of night when the loom of a light can be seen at twice the distance you have any right to expect. Our course was east and the ship ran easily over the quiet sea, the spinnaker out to starboard, the heavy boom guyed to port with two-inch hemp that had started life as a main-sheet. There had been no need for John to call me at the change of watch, for I had been in that semi-conscious state from which I can be roused by the throb of a screw, the feel of a lifting boom or a change in the note of the wind. I stuffed three biscuits and a bar of chocolate into my jacket pocket, glanced at the barometer (as steady as the proverbial rock) and went up on deck.

"Good morning, Peter," said John. "Steamer route to starboard, coast of Sweden to port and Smyghuk Light bears north by east." It came so glibly off his tongue that I knew he'd been rehearsing it. The passage down Kettegat had done John good. He had felt so ill that I had had to steel myself to call him out on watch or to change a sail, and now it would be some time before he again forgot to take his avomine. But sailing is in his blood and if he survives us and we him, by the time we get back to England he will have the makings of a seaman. On such a night my mind is free to contemplate the sea upon which we are now sailing: an inland sea, in spite of its thirteen hundred miles of length, if you include the Gulfs of Bothnia and Finland: a restricted sea, Knud calls it, into which he has never yet thrust his bowsprit. Well: he now must be in his element running down the Portuguese Trades with four thousand miles of open Atlantic on his starboard hand. My own feelings are somewhat different, for I have to return from Finland before the autumn gales, a voyage, our friends tell us with ill-concealed zest, that will be a dead beat to windward all the way. So, good Baltic, I will say nothing about you that would tend to raise your seas in anger, at least till I have reached my native shores. But you must admit, dear Baltic, that you are a trifle on the narrow side. The Swedish coast is close aboard, Bornholm lies just below the horizon; and less than sixty miles to starboard is land which we have become accustomed to look upon as red.

When we first thought of sailing to the Gulf of Finland I wanted to explore the coast round Riga and Tallinn about which Dr Arthur Ransome wrote in *Racundra's First Cruise*. I even hoped to be able to pull a string or two, but after some delay a friend wrote:

> Their refusal can be best put this way: having read *The Riddle of the Sands* they have been so impressed by what could be done by one small boat that they have no intention of allowing such a hornet within twelve miles of their peace-loving Republic.

Nor is the Baltic without its natural dangers: its seas, though short, can be extremely steep and it is notorious, like Kattegat, for the suddenness of its summer storms. Tonight she is in a peaceful mood: although the wind is about Force 4 on the Beaufort scale there is no more sea than in the Thames Estuary at slack water. At five minutes to four I go down and call Anne, make an entry in the log and climb into her vacant berth. In five minutes I am asleep.

The wind held fair and at noon we rounded Hammerodde on Bornholm and raced down the north-east coast looking for Gudhjem. The entrance is on a Lilliputian scale, being no more than thirty-six feet wide and flanked by rocks upon which the swell breaks. The houses, their roofs, like red hats, pulled well down over their ears, climb down the hill to the fish quays on which are men packing their silvery catch into boxes between layers of ice. As at Polperro, of which this place reminds me, huge baulks of timber are placed across the entrance at the threat of an on-shore gale, but it needs only a small wind to raise a lop that sets the boats inside dancing like marionettes on strings. So it was with us: at half-past two in the morning I was wakened by the ship grinding her fenders against the wall. I looked at the cold east wind, decided the risk of waiting to be too great, woke the others and shifted, under power, into the inner basin, where we were safe but far from comfortable. We breakfasted, I remember, on the cabin floor as if we were hove-to in a gale. Then we made a dive for the shore and scrambled up the hill behind the village.

It was good country for tramping, said Anne and John, so off they went while I settled myself down behind a rock. Two hundred feet below lay the little harbour and I could see the island of Christiansö twelve miles away, framed in the Mediterranean blue of the Baltic Sea. It looked such a perfect size, like a child's model of a medieval castle with the Fortress on the Hill, the Watch Tower and the sun glinting on red roofs within the walls. Mr Eilersen, a friend of Knud's, had said, "If you go there you may never come back. I know a man who went for a few days fishing and stayed for thirty years. He has found the perfect life: when there is fish, he fishes, and when there is none he is content with nothing."

When Anne and John came back, brim full of health and vigour, they woke me up. Anne said, "It's pleasant country, but why the Danes think it is like Scotland I cannot imagine. Perhaps it's because of the heather."

The wind backed in the night and we went off on a cloudless morning. Christiansö is in fact a group of islands of which only two are inhabited.

Between these two runs an arm of the sea, and at either end of this ships can shelter, according to the wind. Because the wind was in the west we chose the northern end. The *Baltic Pilot* still gives instructions as to how a sailing ship should be berthed, but as we hauled our wind and came in sight of the breakwater, the white warping bollard and the tiny space in which to bring the vessel head to wind to stop her; as our sails came fluttering down like leaves from a tree and the anchor went over the side, the chain checking when there was but two feet of water under our keel, my mind boggled at the degree of seamanship needed to bring a brig or a small barque safely to rest in such a place. It is an art that must be almost dead.

From where we lay under the shadow of the Watch Tower our thoughts were intent upon Christiansö across the water, the island from which, Mr Eilersen had said, we might never return. The round walls of the Fortress, now a lighthouse, the wall, six feet thick, which still encircles the island, the ancient cannon pointing in our direction as if we were a menace to its solitude, brought to mind the days when it was the scene of many a bloody battle between the pirates who used it as a base for attacking the Baltic trade and the Danes who came to throw them out.

We landed on Fredriksö, a bare windswept islet of sand, stones and a few cottages with the washing flying in the breeze, to make our way to Christiansö across the flimsy single file affair, like the bridge of San Louis Rey, which was opened, if a boat wanted to go through, by anyone passing pulling on wires. Christiansö is rocky with clumps of pine trees and ponds so thick with water lilies that they look like fields. If you stay there quietly for a time you will hear frogs begin to bark like dogs. From the highest point we looked down upon the scattered cottages, each with its own garden in which grow figs and peaches and flowers. In the west Bornholm lay like a cloud upon the sea. The tranquility of the place has been fostered by the Danes who allow only artists, pilots and fishermen to live there; we were shown over a small house,

A Sail in a Forest

beautifully fitted up, where members of the Press may rest from their efforts to put the world to rights or to help destroy it. I loved the place. I could walk round it in no more than twenty minutes.

Almost the first person we met when we got back to the village was Johannes Jensen, a great barrel of a man with pale plump cheeks and a gold-toothed smile. Fishing, it seemed, had been good since Mr Eilersen had been here, for Johannes exuded an air not altogether compatible with "when there is none, he is content with nothing." Maybe it has something to do with the tourists which swarm over the island from noon till four every day of the "season," when most of the other inhabitants stay indoors and go to sleep. Over this island, said Johannes, ruled the Governor, as much an autocrat as the master of a sailing ship. With the post of Governorship he combines eighteen others: Lighthouse-keeper, Chief of Police, Chief Justice, Chief of Customs, Chief Magistrate, Registrar with authority to marry people—and others I can no longer remember—all of which gave it an air of fantasy like Mr Gilbert's First Sea Lord.

Down in the South Harbour were a few fishing vessels, women washing clothes in sea water (already so fresh is the Baltic) and the ketch *Biscaya*, a typical Swedish rescue ship. She had been converted into a Sea Scout training vessel with bunks for twelve boys and cabins for master and mate. The boys each had a fortnight on board and they cruised between Stockholm and the Naze. After supper the mate brought two of the senior boys aboard *Moonraker*, and later we were joined by the Captain, whom Anne described in her diary as a "swift light person with an air of danger as though he were constantly showing a red light." He spoke perfect English and was tremendously keen on his job. He said, "I try and teach my boys the first principles of seamanship and to observe the sea and the sky and the barometer as well as to listen to the meteorologists. You remember the gale at the end of July two years ago? I was lying in the Elbe in company with another Swedish yacht, bound for England. It was obvious from the sky that bad weather was in the offing and the barometer was already going down. My friend came aboard to tell me he was leaving in an hour. I pointed to the track of my barograph but my friend only laughed. He said, 'You can do without those sort of things nowadays. All I do is to listen to the forecasts.' Two days later his ship was driven ashore on the Horns Rev, and he was fortunate to escape with his life."

The Captain rose to his feet. He said, "Well, we must be going. We are off early in the morning."

"On Friday the thirteenth, Captain?" asked Anne with a smile. For a moment he stared at her and at the clock on the cabin bulkhead which showed twenty-five minutes to midnight.

"By heaven, Mrs Pye, you're right. Mr Mate! Rouse out the crew. We sail in twenty minutes."

And, by heaven, they did!

CHAPTER SEVEN

WE sailed before dawn two days later and at noon the ship lay becalmed. Anne wrote:

The glass is almost as high as we have ever known it and the evening has the texture of a ripe peach and the log has ceased to record our progress.

Sunday, June 15. Night was spent in a vacuum between steamers with the air like ice and ramparts of steamers criss-crossing the steely water. At 2.30 I set the log and an hour later the spinnaker to a growing air from the S.W. About three the sun rises red. John cooks breakfast and the day is a rush of water under a great blue dome of sky. We expect to see Ölande Sodra Udde to port but so swift is the current setting us to the east (towards the shoals off Öland) that it appears to starboard.

Monday, June 16 finds us creeping up the west coast of Gotland, a light haze hiding and teasing us and a fog horn faintly blowing. The islands Karlsö (Great and Small) are with us ahead and during the day we come to know them well. The outer one is like a crocodile awash and without a tail: the inner more like a frog. The skin of the crocodile is nobbly and at his waist line there is a line of cupressus. As I sail on, a band of people appear on his head and run down his flank and round the high point of his rump into another world. On the inner island John sees caves and all about us eider ducks sit in groups. Peter comes up at tea-time surprised to see the islands still close, although astern. Gradually Visby peeps round the corner with her crooked night-caps darkly above each tower. A yacht coming in points our way. The yacht club bears the notice ADGANG FORBUDT and we are waved to come up behind the ketch *Baltica* in the outer harbour among rotting cabbages and other less reputable things.

Night, I always think, is kind to towns, heightening the romance of the old, softening the rectangular glassiness of the new, but in spite of the ancient wall that surrounds this city, the noble gate, the narrow streets, Visby, with its black-topped towers and red roofs climbing up the hill, looked to me better from the water. We half-sailed, half-drifted up the coast of Gotland the following afternoon, intending to make a landfall on the Svenska Björn light-vessel (marking the southern end of the channel into the Åland Sea) one hundred and thirty miles away, but at dawn next morning my plan was changed. Something nasty was brewing: you could smell it in the damp, cold air, the backing wind (just north of east), see it in the tumbling glass and in the brassy sun now rising above the trees on lonely Götska Sandö. Up the middle of the Baltic we sailed, away from the Swedish shore. We drove her hard: seven knots hour after hour, water creaming over the decks, spray flying. Grand sailing in a race against time to make our landfall on the Bogskär rocks, for this was no place to be caught in a gale I then could have sworn was coming. To starboard was the Gulf of Finland, to port the entrance to the Åland Sea and ahead the rocks, islets and shoals that run for a hundred miles from Hanko in Finland to Flotjan Tower in the west, of which Bogkskär was the outpost which we now must find.

A grey pall, like London in November, settled over the sea. Visibility was down to a mile, rain spattering on the upturned pram, less wind (the calm before the storm?) and somewhere in all that murk our landfall. A motor ship, rust-stained by wind and weather, appeared on a converging course. Within her protected bridge paced the officer of the watch, warm and dry, a man who knew not only where he was but where he now was going. And then, when she was no more than a ghostly shape, we suddenly saw her turn four points to starboard and fifteen minutes later there was a weather-beaten tower standing firmly on those lonely rocks—Bogkskär.

We altered course for Flotjan, keystone to the approach to the Åland archipelago, twenty-six miles to the west-north-west, and Anne, now that land was imminent, took over the pilotage. The northern night, not black but too dark to see, replaced the gloom of evening, and with it came lights along the coast not one of which, not a single one, agreed with our current light list.

Of the events that now took place I have found it difficult to write because this story ends in anti-climax. We were not wrecked, we did find the Flotjan Tower, there was no gale but the tension in ourselves was no less than if the ending had been less fortunate, so I will content myself with describing, as briefly as possible, the facts. After timing and re-timing the lights Anne and I stood over the chart in argument, of which only the last sentences need to be recorded. She said, "Don't, please, say you know where you are. You don't, not for certain. I agree the lights are in their right positions, but we didn't even get near enough to Bogskär to see the colour of its tower."

The rain came down in sheets, the wind whistled in the rigging. This, I thought, was it. We shortened sail, but just before John and I went below we heard a light-and-whistle buoy. The light was wrong, but there was no getting away from the whistle and its position on the chart, and I turned in leaving Anne less anxious,

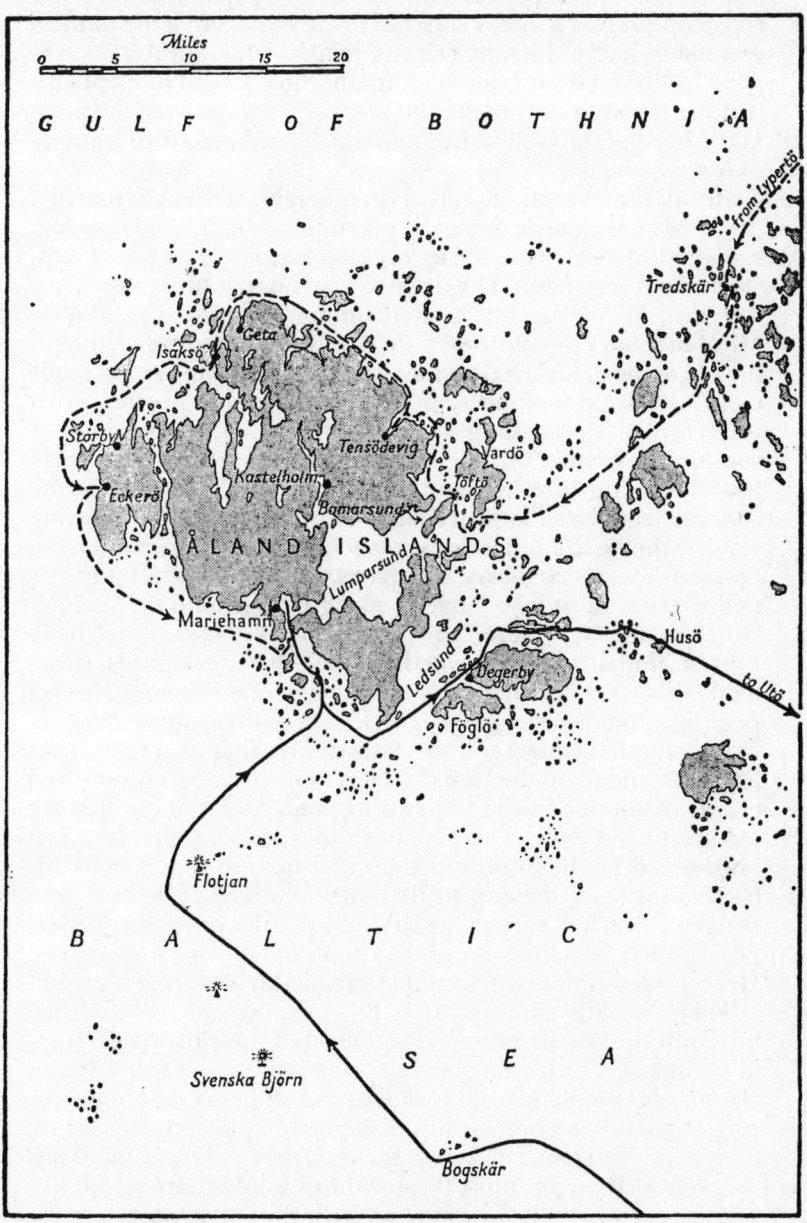

but still half blinded by rain, on course for Flotjan. An hour later the deep siren of a motor ship nearly blew me out of my bunk: a great ship half hidden in swirling banks of fog not thirty yards away, followed by another and another like a herd of elephants trotting through the jungle: the first timber ships from the ports at the head of the Gulf of Bothnia which had been freed from ice only ten days ago.

Steamers to the left of us, reefs to the right, and a glass that had dropped an inch since dawn the previous morning. And now fog: it was as difficult a situation as any with which we had been faced. We ran our distance to Flotjan; no siren, no roar of breakers; just the hiss of waves, the rain drumming down as it did in Mr Maugham's famous story; and the wind, now slowly fading. I hauled in the mainsheet, and we stood to the north-east for a mile before heaving to. John slept, Anne was brewing coffee when suddenly an ear-splitting roar brought us all out on deck. A coaster, the captain hurling curses on us, slipped past our stern. We let draw the foresheet and headed away to the north-east, tail between legs like a motorist caught overtaking at a bend. Leaving John at the helm I followed Anne below. Rain dripped from the hood of her oilskin jacket, her face blue, her hands numb. She said, "There must be a current taking us back into the steamer lane. I'm sure we're here," she put her finger on the chart, "to the west of Flotjan." So we groped our way slowly eastwards, close-hauled in what was now less than a moderate breeze, all eyes peering into the mist, lighter now, for the day had already begun. Everything happened at once: the sea breaking on a reef, rocks like teeth and upon the base of a larger one the lonely unwatched tower, its top hidden in the swirling mist and quite unlike the picture in the *Pilot*. This scene, so inexpressibly desolate, was heightened by the appearance on that bare rock of a man, his back towards us, moving stiffly down to a boat pulled up on a fringe of beach. Tempted as we were to call out to him, "What place is this?" we closed the useless book and opened the light list. Here the description fitted, and I bore silently away into the mist.

There is little more to tell. By the time we had finished breakfast the rain had stopped and the mist was clearing. In front of us, in an ever widening horizon were islands: not half a dozen, but in scores looking as like, one to the other, as sapphires in a ring. A tall tower where no tower should be appeared on what we took to be Nyhamn, the key to the channel to Mariehamn. How excellent, I thought, must those *Notices to Mariners* be (all five years of them) if only they were aboard. Eventually we found the old mark, a beacon that looked like a beetle on tall legs, which allowed us to proceed in safety. The sun came out and with all her finery aloft the old ship sped past bare skerries of red rock worn smooth by countless years of ice, past islets with pine and birch, past islands with small red houses and boats moored in coves, past little light-towers like dolls' houses. Into the straight wide lead that ends at the town itself we sailed where, had we been twenty years earlier, tall ships would have swung to their cables.

After making fast to the yacht club staging I learned three things. The lights on this part of the coast had been changed during the last two years; the tower on Nyhamn had been built two years ago by a company mining ore under the sea; and the glass, whose antics had so alarmed me, had not fallen without reason. A gale had swept up the Baltic and into the Gulf of Finland while the centre had passed harmlessly over our heads into the Gulf of Bothnia, the man on Flotjan had gone there to see to the light. On the night in question it had been out.

CHAPTER EIGHT

THE town of Mariehamn is built on a peninsula running southwards from the province of Jomala so that there is water on both sides of it; and when you walk up the hill, as we did, it was like coming upon a town in a forest: avenues of linden trees, young and green after their long winter's sleep, with somewhere behind those dancing leaves, large white houses built of wood, standing in their own grounds. In our walk to the eastern harbour, a distance of rather less than a mile, we saw one car, half a dozen bicycles and perhaps twice that number of people walking leisurely along the path, their faces not town faces all screwed up with worry, but relaxed and open, glad to see the sun and breathe the air which carried the scent of pine and birch and the smell of wood-smoke. And yet its appearance is deceptive, for this town of between four and five thousand people controls two hundred thousand tons deadweight of shipping, shared by ten companies which have their headquarters here, a fifth of Finland's merchant navy; and it is to the sea that it owes its wealth, its navigation school (the best in Finland, the Ålannings say), the fine Town Hall, the modern Church. At the eastern end, overlooking a wide and shallow bay, is the small, compact shopping centre. We had arrived on the eve of the summer festival and the shops were closing for three days. The bread had gone, except for six dark, flat loaves with holes as if to let out the air. When Anne produced her purse the baker waved it away. "I shouldn't have sold them anyway," he said, and with this doubtful recommendation we returned to the ship. On the hill above our berth stands the Nautical Club and the Museum overlooking the decks of the *Pommern*, once the fastest of Gustav Erikson's sailing ships but now part of the Museum, given to the town by the firm. In front of the Museum, dedicated to the men who lost their lives in sail, is a bronze statue of the Man at the Wheel. The steadfast look, the power behind those shoulders, reminded me of the statue outside the Harbour Master's office at Skagen. In the Museum was the saloon and the Captain's cabin salvaged from the wreck of the *Herzogin Cecilie* off Bolt Head. On the table was an old log book and as I thumbed the pages the shriek of a Cape Horn gale, the thunder of torn canvas, the faces of the three helmsmen upon whom the lives of the crew so largely depended, filled that silent room.

A Sail in a Forest

It was Midsummer Eve. On a grassy space on the hill preparations were far advanced for the ceremony of the Raising of the Pole, as a thanksgiving for the coming of summer. The Pole is garlanded with flowers and far away up at the top is a figure of the Toiling Man, whose arms and legs are made to work as he is blown round and round by the wind. Below him are ships with sails that voyage on endless journeys, and as the year goes by the arms and legs of the little man come off and the sails of the ships disintegrate; but that is what happens to men and ships and the Pole stays up until the same time next year. This ceremony is carried out throughout the hamlets and villages of Åland.

That afternoon we had a visitor: Captain Gunnar Bowman, ex-master of the four masted barque *Moshulu*, a little man with a thin angular face and gimlet eyes which bored into John as they must have done into other young men whom he was thinking of signing on as apprentices. I had been told that he was Gustav Erikson's white-headed boy, "because he was so economical: never lost a sail in a gale because he never set one."

He said, "It's good to be on a ship again. When the war ended Captain Gustav said to me, 'If you will take command of the *Moshulu* I will buy her back again.' But what was the good? I said to him, 'Where are the officers to man the watches? Gone,' I said, 'left the sea, gone into steam or dead. Sail is finished,' I said, 'and so am I.' So now I look after the Museum and am as much a part of it as poor old *Pommern*.

The talk turned, as it so often does, to other ships and the Captain spoke of the loss of the *Pamir*, then very much in the minds of ex-masters of sailing ships. He said, "I do not understand how this thing could have happened. The sudden shift of wind ... I have seen it so often and always the signs are there ..." and I had a mental picture of this careful master shortened down to his topsails, every man waiting for his next command.

When the Captain had gone we went up the hill to see the raising of the Midsummer Pole, but the evening was damp and a cold mist crept up the Sound. Even the songs and the faces of the people failed to dispel the gloom that ushered in the worst summer in Finland since the War. Depressed, we returned on board and set about cooking supper. Anne at the table washing meat, John and me, each with a basin, preparing potatoes and greens, arguing hotly as to whether the fire should be lit. . . . John and me for: Anne against because, as she so rightly said, we had only ten days' Coalite to last us back to England. In the middle of all this the hatch was pushed back and a face appeared at the opening. I asked it to come down and Ingemar Palmar delicately insinuated his length into the crowded cabin. He had, he said, seen our ship while watching the Raising of the Pole and had come down to invite us up to his house. "This is a night of celebration," he said. "You must spend it among friends." So the meat was put in the galley, the vegetables in a pot and we accompanied Ingemar to his home.

On the way there John asked, "What is that flag flying at *Pommern*'s peak?"

"That is the flag of Åland. This is one of the days we are allowed to fly it."

"But I thought you were Finnish."

"Not by choice," replied Ingemar with a scornful glance. "Ninety-nine per cent of the people voted to belong to Sweden where most of our people come from, but your League of Nations put us under the Finns."

I said, "I thought you were an autonomous state."

"Well, I suppose we are."

"Are your young men conscripted into the Finnish services?"

"No: but we pay taxes to the Finns."

"Wouldn't you have had to pay taxes to the Swedes?"

"I suppose we should: perhaps bigger ones."

"Then you haven't done too badly."

"Perhaps not," replied Ingemar with a grin, "but it's just as well if you come to Mariehamn as a stranger not to call it Maarianhamina."

When we came to his house, not far from the Town Hall, his wife came down the stairs to greet us in a marked Australian accent. These two had met in the Spencer Gulf while Ingemar had been serving his apprenticeship about the *Viking*. Fortunately for Ingemar, Jocelyn had fallen in love with the *Viking* (she was not, she said, entirely indifferent to one of the members of her crew) and when *Viking* sailed Jocelyn sailed with her to study art, so the papers said, in England. Before they reached Cape Horn the third mate fell from a yard and Ingemar took his place. I imagine a sailing ship running down her easting is as good a place as any for a girl to find out what her man is like, and when they reached England Jocelyn paid but a fleeting visit to her relatives, forgot her art and followed Ingemar to Mariehamn.

The house was of wood, of course, centrally heated by an enormous wood stove in the basement and the windows were doubled against the cold and the snow. We dined off Baltic herring soaked in vinegar and spices, veal, and a fine grain porridge, smooth and thin, served with lingenberry jam. Over coffee, served from an old Åland copper pot, we spoke of Gustav Erikson, whose name is so closely associated in Englishmen's minds with Mariehamn. I knew, of course, from books that he had built up the largest commercial fleet in the world of sailing ships, I had listened to sailor's talk which praised and damned him in equal parts, and I had met an old Danish sea captain who had known him when he was still a shipmaster.

"Close as hell," was his verdict, "and not popular with his fellow captains: but what a man for work! The last time I met him was just before the War. One of his ships was docked in Copenhagen and the Old Man happened to be in the city on business. I heard he'd gone aboard, so I went along to see him. There he was sitting on a bench in the sailmaker's locker busy with palm and needle repairing an old to'gallant sail and making a better job of it than the sailmaker."

He said, "You won't find many shipowners doing that."

"How did he make his ships pay?" I asked Ingemar, "when no one else could."

"Because he wouldn't insure them and supervised all the fitting out himself. My father always said there was no one who knew as much about square-rig as he did."

"I wonder what he was really like," I mused.

Ingemar said, "My father could tell you. He was apprentice, second mate and mate to Captain Gustav for six years. When the Old Man changed ships, he changed with him, but since the day my father left to take command of his first ship he has never spoken of his former master."

He gave me a quizzical look. He said, "Go and see him in Eckerö. You might succeed where others have failed."

Before we left that night Ingemar told me a rather heart-breaking little story. The Old Man's health was slowly fading when one day he demanded to be taken aboard one of his ships. They took him down on a stretcher and hoisted him over the side and a light came into his eyes at the sweep of a big ship's decks and the beauty of her spars: at the tang of paint and tar.

He gripped the shrouds and tried to hoist himself up but he was too weak and fell back, exhausted.

A few days later he died.

∾∾ CHAPTER NINE ∾∾

IF you look at the map of Åland opp. page 346 you will see that the mainland (if you can call it by such an earthy name) is invaded by long arms of the sea from all points of the compass, so that even in the middle there seems to be as much water as land. To see something of this Edgar Erikson, Gustav Erikson's son, drove us round by car one afternoon. We had been given an introduction to him and had called on him at his office in the grounds of what was once his father's house in Mariehamn's principal street. It was a busy place: telephones ringing, people striding from room to room on the business of the sea, and around the walls pictures of sailing ships having a hard struggle, one felt, to hold their own with the new oil-burning vessels with which the son has replaced his father's fleet. There was only one thing out of place. Edgar Erikson, with his Viking head and his calm level voice, looked as if he would have been more at home on his father's poop.

Our road led through woods of birch and pine, across open spaces where every inch of the shallow soil was tilled in farms that would in Essex have been considered extremely small. We stopped to admire the crumbling walls of Kastelholm and stared at the lancet window through which a Swedish king of long ago had looked with longing on the outside world, in which he never again was destined to live, for he was poisoned by his brother: a fate, our host said, that was so common that it was scarce worth remarking on. We drove on towards Bomarsund until we came to a bridge from which we looked over on to the blue waters of Lumparsund where, during the Crimean War, the British and French fleets fought a strange battle with the Russians: strange not only because at first glance the Åland islands seem a long way from the Black Sea but because this battle was watched by an English yacht, the *Pet*, which had sailed from Lowestoft with two hands for'ard and two gentlemen aft. The *Pet* is listed as eight tons, and is described by her owner as a "very small cutter yacht, about as long as a moderate sized drawing-room and as wide as a four poster bed . . .", but from the frontispiece at the beginning of the book (*Two Cruises with the Baltic Fleet* by R. H. Hughes) she looks a trifle bigger due, perhaps, to her long counter, her boom which overhangs her counter by several yards and an enormous topsail set on a yard as long again as her topmast. On

A Sail in a Forest

her arrival at Ledsund (to the east of Lumparsund) she was greeted enthusiastically by the officers and men of the combined fleets and was promised a ringside seat for the battle. Of the scene, the Rev. Mr Hughes writes:

> Nearly in the centre of the group [the Åland archipelago] is a fine sheltered roadstead called Lumpar bay, communicating with the sea to the northward by Bomarsund, a narrow strait between the islands of Bomar and Prestö. This strait was strongly fortified on the Bomar side by a large half-moon battery, close to the water's edge ... on the eastern, or Prestö side, another martello tower, Fort Prestö, guarded the passage. The narrow strait might be considered perfectly impassable, and consequently Lumpar bay, with its villages, and the barracks and stores which were being accumulated, were considered safe from a hostile fleet.
>
> It was, however, I believe, Captain Sullivan of the *Lightning* who discovered and buoyed out a south passage from Led Sund to Lumpar bay; a passage so narrow and intricate, that the Russians had entirely neglected to fortify it but so deep and so judiciously marked, that our line of battle ships steamed up and down, without, I believe, one accident of consequence. It was by this passage that the *Cuckoo* towed us up to the scene of action. . . . The dark pines threw their branches over the sea on either side, and now and then, as the strait wound among the woods, a taunt topmast with a blue ensign or blazing tricolour might be seen, like some interloping tree of strange outlandish growth, towering over the sombre pines. Villages and fishermen's huts appeared here and there: but war had already stretched out his desolating hand, and no human form, divine or otherwise, could be discovered.
>
> It was still early when we cleared the narrow creek, and the magnificent panorama in Lumpar bay burst upon us; the Russian forts, glistening white in the sun's glare, straight before us; to the westward, little scattered islands and dark peaceful woods; and in the foreground, some thirty sail of different sizes in all the pomp and circumstance of war. . . .

Slowly the fire-power of the fleet reduced the Russian defences and the ships moved up, followed by the *Pet*, and,

> heaving the *Pet* to, with Mr Peter to attend her, we rowed ashore with Ned—and a splendid scene of havoc we found. The mud embankment (of the fort) was ripped up, torn, and almost levelled by the frigates' fire. The guns upset and dismounted: one with its great thirsty throat gaping upwards at the sky, another in shame and confusion nozzling its head into the dirt. In one of them the shot was not rammed home, but remained as the terrified gunner left it in his haste, about half way down the barrel. With some difficulty we got it out and brought it home as a momento. . . .

And so the book goes on, Mr Hughes enjoying his war with gusto, remaining till the end, when the Russians had at last been driven out of this part of the world and the *Pet* sailed for home not without a few scornful comments appearing in her log about the tactics of the C.-in-C.

His voyage prospered until he had left the Sound for Kattegat. She treated him roughly but what she did to him was nothing to what was to follow from the North Sea. For nine days this stouthearted clergyman drove his ship across the angry waste of waters, being thrice hove-to and himself at the helm for an unbroken stretch of nineteen hours in weather that caused the loss of five sailing vessels and sent a French frigate hurrying back for shelter after her bulwarks had been washed away. Mr Hughes wrote: "So we had every reason to feel well satisfied and thankful at the safe termination of our cruise."

So we left the bridge from which, if we had lived a hundred years ago, we might have watched the stirring events so pungently described in Mr Hughes' book, and followed the road which turned and doubled back upon itself to avoid the inlets which interfere so frequently with the continuity of the land. I cannot remember passing a single car, and our host had time to comment upon the scene through which we passed: the windmills, their sails broken or dishevelled by the Finns during the War in case the millers hoarded flour; a house standing at the edge of a wood, of which he said, "There lives a newly married couple," and when Anne asked him how he knew this, he stopped the car and said, "Do you see those two tall poles in front of the house? Young peeled trees with the tuft of leaves at the top? That means in Åland that they are newly-wed."

"And how long do they remain newly-wed?"

"Until their first child is born."

"They would have been up a long time with us," said Anne.

In a flat plain of farm land stood the village of Saltvig. Edgar Erikson pointed to a house which stood some way from the road. He said, "The last time I came through here I watched that house moving across the field. It was being shifted bodily on a trailer to its new bed of bricks. Houses are so scarce and so expensive that it is easier to take them with you if you are moving to another part of the islands. It is wonderful what you can do with a house as long as it is made of wood."

In time we came to the village of Geta and started to climb into the "mountains" three hundred metres high. The sun was now in the west and a haze spread over land and sea turning the fiords to silver and softening the edges of this wild and barren coast which faces the Gulf of Bothnia. "Of all the waters in Finland," he said, "this is my favourite cruising ground." A tourist inn had been built near the highest point. The place was empty and we sat at the windows eating a Danish sandwich and drinking the delicious coffee which they serve you in this country. Our host drank tea. He said, with a smile, "I have never been able to face coffee since I had to drink it in England."

On our way home we drove through Findström, right in the heart of the mainland, and stopped to look at the Church. It had been built in the fourteenth century and stood apart from the village, surrounded by trees and fields fenced by laying whole saplings slantwise in the old Åland way. Erikson said, "Wood was so cheap there that it was not worth the labour of cutting." Inside the Church the light was beginning to fade but there was enough to see the paintings of saints and scenes from daily life that covered the walls, and there was one of a Hansa *kogg*, a small high-prowed vessel with a single square sail and two tiers of oars, a type of ship that was used in the earliest days of the Baltic timber trade. These paintings had only recently been discovered after being hidden under layers of plaster by the Lutherans, who, no doubt, thought that such frivolities were no proper decoration for such a stern and rigid faith.

Edgar Erikson took us back to his father's old home, now his own. It was the sort of house that a man might dream about while sailing the seven seas: as immovable as a rock. The well-proportioned rooms, the unbroken length, where the Captain could still pace the deck: chairs so deep that three small Britishers disappeared from sight, a wall lined to the ceiling with books, and an enormous fireplace with a mantel of dark wood in the centre of which was a painting of the *Lawhill* running under double topsails down in the roaring forties.

In the dining-room there was a picture of Gustav Erikson's youngest son, extraordinarly like his brother, standing on the foredeck of one of his father's ships. He had shared his father's almost fanatical love of sailing ships and had been first mate of a barque that was sunk with all hands by a Russian submarine in the Gulf of Bothnia.

CHAPTER TEN

THERE are six thousand six hundred and fifty-four islands in the Åland archipelago and among these we had to find our way to Utö, the Outer Isle, before making up the Gulf of Finland to Kotka, from where, you may remember, Captain Koivistoinen had sent us his letter many months ago. As we turned down the sound against the light southerly wind my mind was occupied by the very number of islands with which we might be confronted, making pilotage an almost impossible task without Finnish charts. These had been given to us by the Sea Bears, an association very similar to that which has its headquarters in Baker Street. They are a joy to read, the colours giving an immediate visual picture of the whole, white for depths over ten metres, yellow for under and a dull grey (or brown) for the land. Between the islands, which lie as thickly upon the charts as weevils in a jar of tropical rice, run the black lines of the recommended routes with the least depth of each route marked in brackets. The dangers are marked by sparbuoys whose names indicate the direction of the danger in relation to the mark. There are four to learn and, like the Rule of the Road, they must be learned by heart. The north mark is a red inverted cone: the south a black cone: the east a black cone above an inverted black cone and the west a red inverted cone above a red cone. It is no unusual thing for the tops of these buoys to be knocked off by passing vessels, and then you are left with a red spar for the north mark, black for south, black and white for east and red and white for west. There is a fifth mark which is placed on a rock itself: a cross whose shaft is painted in red and white stripes. This is called a "tacking mark," and can be left on either hand.

If you come tearing round a bend to be suddenly faced with a mark whose presence catches you completely by surprise you can tell at a glance without reference to the chart to which side the danger lies *if you know your marks*. If you don't, God help you.

Two hours after leaving Mariehamn we anchored in a half-moon bay. Like so many of these anchorages it was almost landlocked by other islets and reefs and no sound broke the stillness of this pretty place. Indeed the only sign of habitation was the wood-smoke from a shack which, we guessed was the *sauna*, or Finnish bath, belonging to some dwelling at present out of sight. Two cows, full of milk, stood knee-deep in water. We rowed ashore to find the farm that owned the cows. At the top of a small rise we came across it, the usual white wooden building with a red roof, the breeze blowing the curtains through open windows: flowers in a bowl, the washing-up of the last meal half done but no sign of anyone at home. Milkless, we walked home, pausing by the *sauna* door at which stood a man, relaxed after his bath. To our question he replied, "The farmer died and now is buried at Mariehamn and the family are not yet back."

"Are there sons to take his place?" asked Anne.

"Not one," was the reply. "The sons have left, one to Sweden, another to Helsingfors; but that is happening in all these islands. The old people die and the farm will be sold as a summer cottage to townsfolk."

As night fell—a mere darkening of the scene as if a shade were drawn over a lamp—we met for the first time the Åland mosquito.

Although Jungle Oil (a Swedish remedy) prevented our being bitten to pieces it did nothing to deaden the noise of their wings, and it was a heavy-eyed company that next morning hauled on ropes and chain.

The lane of water banked by islands down which we had sailed from Mariehamn now opened out and we crossed two wide bays with more islands of all shapes and sizes to the left of us, bare skerries to the right, and turned into Ledsund in the wake of the yacht *Pet*. As a mountaineer is lured by each succeeding peak we were tempted by a thread of water running inside the eastern shore. This thread coiled like a serpent under dark pines and rustling birch whose branches bent before the strong north wind which now hurtled down this gorge-like place. The red roofs of Degerby village were growing clearer with each short tack. We passed so close that the sound of a hammer on iron rang out above our heads from a shipyard but the narrow channel ahead wash halved by a shoal, our eyes were on sparbuoys, the woods closed in on us; the village with its sudden burst of life now lay behind. Our tacks grew even shorter until, round another bend, we came to a wide fiord. Therein lies the charm of this sort of sailing: one moment you would be beating in open water with the ice-cold spray flying over the heeling ship, the next, almost upright, it would be like sailing down a forest path, so near are the trees to each other across the narrow strip of quiet blue water. But all this tacking and doubling back along the winding tracks of the prescribed routes took longer than I expected and there was now no hope of making Utö tonight. Already the islands were thinning out and to starboard was Husö, with a bay on its leeward side into which I thought we might venture. It was marked on the chart with a single sounding, while round the edges were a lot of angry dots which indicated rocks.

With the utmost circumspection (for these soundings are unreliable) we beat in and came to an anchor in three metres with plenty of rocks to be seen lying about on the bottom through the clear water.

The island was composed of granite, in the crevices of which grew stunted trees gnarled by wind and weather; and in the middle, on a small flat plain, miniature fields had been laid out with such care that you felt that each ear of corn, each rather sad-looking cabbage, was of the utmost importance to the man whose house was so well concealed that we found it only by accident. From the highest point we looked out towards where Utö must lie some twenty miles to the south-east; over a sea like a desert on which each smooth-bellied rock, like a camel's hump, lay down to rest. It was difficult to imagine that a few months ago it had been too dark to read except by artificial light, that snowstorms had driven across the cruel sky and the sea been full of ice.

We woke to find that the north wind had deserted us. The sea shimmered under a hot sun and all day our sails hung lifeless between the passing of one zephyr and the advent of another, our blocks groaning and creaking like the joints of an ancient horse whose strength is insufficient to reach the next milestone from the last.

As the sun went down a breeze crept over the sea. At long last the Outer Isle lay ahead, as lonely as a Foreign Legion outpost in the centre of Morocco. Lights flashed out from towers on outlying rocks and through the glasses houses seemed to rise out of the water. We beat up the winding channel (reading the chart by the glow in the northern sky) past buoys and beacons into a land-locked anchorage as sheltered as the courtyard of a castle.

Although by now it was little short of midnight by the time we landed a sort of reception committee was waiting for us: three soldiers, a young man from Kotka and two fair-haired girls. "Come and see our lighthouse," they said. It was a military area, we were told, but one of the girls borrowed the key from her father, the lighthouse-keeper, and with our soldier escort, they said, all would be in order.

Half-way to the top of the rectangular tower we came to a chapel which, until a few years ago, had been the only church on the island. Planks laid on trestles served as pews, a tiny pulpit stood close by a painted cross and two angels' wings supporting a harp, all painted in gold, hung on the wall behind, a present from Sweden for the rescue of a Swedish ship. As I stood there contemplating this simple room a picture came into my mind of how it might have looked, packed to suffocation with as many of the inhabitants who could climb those awkward stairs listening to the preacher, his voice half drowned by the roar of a winter's gale, while thirty feet above him the light flashed out its silent warning.

Below the lantern a small gallery encircled the tower. Leaning on the substantial iron railing I looked out towards the Baltic, lit by the weak light from a moon which, at its zenith, scarcely climbed above the horizon. The sea looked innocent, as a meadow misted with dew, but out of it rose a jagged line of reefs upon which was the bridge, still awash, of a German motor ship which had gone ashore in a full December gale in the middle of a snowstorm, and while listening to her story from my companion I thought how true it was that in spite of radio beacons, radar, ship-to-shore telephones and all that science has brought to navigation, the old Law of the Sea that a ship is safer at sea in bad weather still holds good. The master had reached the age of retirement on that very day (his birthday) and this was to have been his last voyage. When the breeches buoy into which he had climbed reached safety he was already dead: from the bitter cold, or from a broken heart.

On the leeward side of the island upon which this lighthouse stands is the little village and in the middle of it stands the well. It is both wide and deep and to the side is a post to act as a fulcrum for a long weighted pole, at the other end of which is a bucket on a rope. So efficient is this simple device that you can raise and lower the bucket full of water with two fingers. As we were studying this a man came out of the house beside it. He walked with the aid of a stick and introduced himself as the lighthouse-keeper. He said, "Come inside and drink coffee."

We followed him up the stairs to an upper room overlooking the lagoon, the long coarse grass (well laced with stones and boulders) with which this bleak island is covered, the fish sheds built well out on to the water so that the boats can be kept afloat under cover, and a man sitting in the sun on a wooden quay gutting fish, the blood dripping off the wood into the dark clear water.

Our host told us that he had lost his leg on his first day as mate in a steamer, when a wire hawser had snaked across the foredeck and removed his foot. "It seved me right," he said, "for leaving sail for steam." He stumped over to the window and looked out over the treeless waste. "All this," he said, "happened a long time ago. Already I have been lighthouse-keeper for twenty years."

A sudden thought came into my mind. I said, "This lighthouse, I noticed, was built in 1814, but the light was first established, according to the British Light List, in 1753. What happened to the first?"

"It was burnt to the ground when the Russians chased the Swedes out of Finland. It looked like this," and with firm skilful strokes he drew a rough stone tower, not square like the present one but round, with a candle room not unlike the top of a modern lighthouse and small lancet windows peeping out from the body of the tower like those in a mediaeval castle. "It was fitted," related my host, "with a parabolic reflector . . . so."

From the small yard-arm hung a pot, like a charcoal burner's, in which a coal fire was kept burning all night in case the candles were blown out.

"Once every hour," said our artist, "the keeper had to go aloft and turn the reflector so as to give some change in the light. Thank goodness," he added with a smile, "I was not then its keeper. But I like it here and sometimes when I look out to sea I feel I am master of a sea-going vessel on which live eighty people."

CHAPTER ELEVEN

WE sailed from Utö in the afternoon, the wind a little east of north. Ten miles and three hours later (so light was the wind) the last of the shoals, the last outcrop of rocks over which the sea broke with a sibilant whisper, were astern, and once more we found ourselves in the Baltic Sea. We hauled our wind for the Gulf of Finland and the town of Kotka one hundred and seventy-five miles away. When John called me at four o'clock in the morning I did not have to glance at the water streaming off his oilskin jacket to know the picture had changed. The ship was pitching into a steep sea, short, bad-tempered, vicious: lacking salt to give it buoyancy and depth to give it length, as wicked as the English Channel would be if it were married to the Zuider Zee.

This wind was from ahead; no land was in sight and a high thundery cloud, like the famous mushroom, hung over the Estonian coast. I did not care for what I saw. The topsail came down with a run and by eight o'clock Hanko was not more than two miles away. Anne woke up. She came up on deck and faced the wind and the grey sullen sea, and I recalled those forebears of hers who had fished out of some God-forsaken Scottish port and to whom, it would seem, the weather hardly mattered. She said, "I thought you were going to Kotka," and without comment went below to study the pilotage into the port of Hanko. By the time the wind had reached Force 6 we were safely tucked up along the wall in Hanko's southern harbour.

When we first stepped ashore (before breakfast, for we were in need of milk) we heard for the first time Finnish spoken in the shops and in the streets. It was a melodious sound after the harsh Scandinavian languages, a Latin sound whose roots sprang in some roundabout way from the Magyar, but so difficult is its grammar and composition that it would, for us, be quite impossible to learn. Hanko was, we had been told by our half-Finnish friend, Finland's only pleasure resort. To the east stood large houses in their own grounds where Russian nobles had once spent the summer, a casino and a long curving beach where old and young pedal rafts, paddle canoes, sun-bathe, laugh and make love. The sun, the sheltered coves, the sails of racing yachts, put me in mind of the south of France, a thought that was instantly dismissed by the bite in the wind and the chill of the water. From this playground we tramped westwards through streets of well-filled shops, past timbered cottages, by the shores of a wooded lake, over lichen-covered rocks (covered also with hundreds of broken bottles left over from the Midsummer Eve celebrations) to the docks in the western harbour, in which not a single ship was berthed, and along miles of rusty railway lines to a station that was deserted except for one wood-burning locomotive, the tender piled high with logs, beside two empty trucks.

Over this heterogeneous mixture stands the water-tower up which rise eager sightseers in lifts at one hundred and fifty Finnmarks (2s. 6d.) a time to look over fifteen miles of empty sea. A little below the tower is the church whose outer walls of granite reflect back the light in a hard white glare and whose inner pale blue walls and high ceiling breathe a cold austerity.

The weather broke that afternoon. Thunder cracked overhead, rain fell, dirt from the quay blew across our decks and in the middle of all this we had a visitor, Captain Saarinen, the Harbour Master. He had a flat even voice that neither rose nor fell but held a certain fascination, like water falling drop by drop on a stone. He remembered the Dixons in *Dusmarie* on their way to spend a winter in Lapland and thought he had met Adlard Coles. He told us that when the ports in the Gulf of Bothnia were once more filled with ice the commercial harbour here would be crammed with shipping and the railway lines with trucks. Before he left I remembered to hand him the Visitor's Book to sign. Idly he thumbed the pages. "You've been about a bit, I see," he said. "I myself sailed through the Golden Gate as a ship's boy, after beating round the Horn.

"Things are different to what they were in those days," he said with a sad smile. "I was once bosun on an American five-masted schooner bound from Sidney Heads to Callao. Two weeks out the Captain died and it turned out that the mate couldn't even navigate. God knows where we went: blown far to the south'ard by a north-east gale, then too far to the nor'ard where we were beset by calms and headwinds. He daren't close the South American coast because he couldn't even find his latitude and was frightened of getting too near a lee-shore. The crew reckoned we were lost for good, and so did I."

"You got there in the end?"

"Aye, ninety days it took us, instead of the usual forty: we were out of food and short of water when we first sighted land."

He said, "That voyage taught me a lesson. I came back to Finland, went to navigation school and finished up with my master's ticket. I spent the next few years in the coastal trade before becoming master of my own vessel [he pronounced it 'wessel']. She was a three-masted schooner with the lines of a clipper and I was the happiest man afloat. Then, one autumn, I sailed from Portugal homeward bound with salt. We met with headwinds and it was the middle of December before we entered the Gulf of Finland to meet a full gale from the south-east, putting me on a lee-shore . . ." The Captain held his large egg-shaped head in his hands, as if it was almost more than he could bear to continue his narrative.

He said, "I picked up the light on Utö just before the snow . . . snow is like fog . . . you see nothing. Two men in the bows to listen for breakers. I took the wheel myself . . . *'Breakers ahead!'* a moment before she struck. The masts went over the side: a great sea broke over the stern sweeping one man overboard: the rest climbed over the bows on to the reef. . . . I can see it now: the ship breaking up before my eyes, nine of us without shelter or food . . . soon our clothes freeze to our bodies. Then the snow stops and I can see Utö light so near I can almost touch it. We fire rockets, but no answer comes. All next day we wait . . . between snow showers we see the island, less than two miles away and I think of the people, warm in their houses and how we shall soon be there . . . but no lifeboat comes . . . only the snow, the sleet and the bitter cold. By nightfall three of my crew are dead. The others no longer speak. I thump them with my fists to keep them moving, but exhaustion is on them and they lie huddled in the lee of a rock soaked with spray which freezes. Only anger keeps me alive. Why should men die when one lifeboat at Utö would save them? The gale runs into another day: no boat could live in the seas. I fight to keep awake and make the others move. Two more have died, and tonight will be the last, I think. In the night there is sudden shift of wind, to the north. The wind dies away but now the cold is like a pain. But the men of Utö are not asleep. Lights are moving on the island and the navigation lights of a boat are coming down the channel. I hear the beat of her engine and a ringing shout. . . ."

The wind moaned in the rigging but inside the cabin no one spoke. Presently the Captain raised his head. He said, "You must forgive me for wearying you; I have not spoken of this for years, but seeing the names in your book brought it all back and once I had started I did not seem able to stop."

I re-filled his glass with whisky. I said, "What happened then?"

"It is only when bad things happen to yourself," he said with a charming diffident smile, "that you try to put them right. I had known there was no organized rescue work on this part of the coast but as long as I was all right it did not worry me. Now that I had lost half my crew, and my ship, it was time it did.

"I went to England and studied the work of your lifeboat service and came back here with many facts and figures: but I had much difficulty in interesting the people who had to spend the money and who had not had the advantages of my experiences."

I would have said, however, that it was quiet persistence, rather than the figures and facts he brought back from England, that won the day. That soft melancholy voice, those brown pleading eyes would wear down or melt the heart of the staunchest bureaucrat. They gave him all he wanted, made him Inspector of Lifeboats and now, in a few days, he was setting out in his new ship to visit the fifteen stations for which he was personally responsible.

The rain had stopped and our guest rose to take his leave. He said, "Now you must come and see my new ship, the *Isakari*." We followed him aboard. She was about seventy feet long, double-skinned, double-framed, double-decked and fitted with radar, depth-recorder, automatic compass, two 120-h.p. diesel engines and ten watertight bulkheads; as unsinkable as the Germans thought the *Bismarck*. She was planked with an Argentine hardwood, Perope, which is impervious to drift ice and "so full of fat that it cannot rot." Nor did I fail to notice that this high-powered vessel was rigged as a ketch with two sturdy pole masts carrying gaff sails, and a staysail stowed under a stout flax cover at the foot of the forestay.

As we got to know him better two things in the Captain's character stood out. His love for the sea and a passionate love of his country; and when I say his love of the sea that is misleading; he loves the ships that sail upon it. It came out in little things: in the two ship's portholes let in to the massive oak door of his house, in the chairs that he himself had made in the shape of half-dinghies, in the paintings round the walls, some of them by an English artist called Woods who had once sailed with him.

As for his patriotism, it was bound to surface before long. He said, "Neither Britain nor America understand the Russian people. The Russians respect one thing: force. Look what happened to the Baltic States. We fought the Russians, the Estonians and Latvians threw themselves on the Russians' mercy. The Russians have no mercy. Even in these days an attitude of mind is important. The Russians know we should fight their tanks with clubs if we had nothing better and that is what they understand."

We spent the last night at his red brick house which had been built on the site of the previous one, destroyed by a Russian bomb. In the background flitted his wife, a dark, small woman with whom conversation was difficult, for we had no common tongue. When the Captain said goodbye at the door he took me aside and put his hand on my shoulder. He said, "Be sure not to get inside the twelve-mile limit on the Russian side. When they were at Porkkala they seized Finnish yachts and kept them for a month before sending them back. They fed their crews on porridge. But if they caught an Englishman he would, I think, be lucky to get porridge and he would never see his ship again."

CHAPTER TWELVE

FROM Hanko the Gulf of Finland runs east-north-easterly for a hundred and forty miles before curving to the east for another seventy to end at Kronstadt, the naval base of Leningard. Along the Finnish shore, at intervals of between twenty and twenty-five miles are light-towers on off-shore rocks or small islets: Russarö, Jussarö, Porkkala, Kalbådagrund and Tisk Digskär which, with the Helsinki light-vessel, form a chain of lights like milestones along a highway. Throughout most of its length the Gulf is not more than forty miles wide and at Porkkala, where both Finland and Estonia reach out to each other as if trying to shake hands, the distance is no more than twenty-five. Less than that: for an offshore island on the Red side subtracts six miles, and if the Russians take their limit from its northern tip instead of from the coast the navigable width becomes seven miles. I was a little anxious, after the Captain's warning, not to make too close an acquaintance with our friends of the Hammer and Sickle.

We sailed out of Hanko on the very day I had said I would meet Captain Koivistoinen at Kotka, a hundred and thirty-five miles away. The wind was moderate from the east, dead in our teeth, and we made short tacks, clinging to Finland like a child to its mother's apron-strings. In the afternoon the wind fell light and the land became lost in haze, but at tea-time I picked up a black square tower on a small skerry that we identified as Jussarö. I came about, the wind backed, and I was able to sail my course for Porkkala Light (twenty-four miles away).

I still am not sure what went wrong. In such conditions it is easy to think you are doing better than in fact you are.

The luff of the genoa shakes, you pay off to get way on the ship, you edge into the wind till the sail flutters again, and all the time the vessel sags away to leeward because not once has she been boldly and properly handled. Perhaps, too, the anticyclone which now had established itself, caused a south-westerly current for which I never thought of allowing. The sun went down: the great red glow that lasts from dusk till dawn filled the northern sky but no light from Porkkala's tower appeared. I left the ship to sail herself and went for'ard to study the horizon. I saw it at once. A powerful light fine on the starboard bow, high up as if it was extremely close, and to the south'ard, another.... These lights must be Russian. A glance was enough to make me realize that we were well within the twelve-mile limit, but long before Anne confirmed our position I had come about and was heading for Finland at a pace, it seemed to my fevered imagination, that would make a snail seem fast. The night was quiet, not a single steamer light appeared on the deserted sea, but for the last few minutes I had been aware of a low muttering like waves surging into a distant cavern. The muttering grew to a roar. Out of the south-east came a wicked-looking corvette with four motor-torpedo-boats cavorting round her heels like hounds round a huntsman. Signals flashed, guns fired. Not a navigation light between the lot of them. They passed a mile to the south.

Had they seen us against the glow of the northern sky, or were they bent on ploys of their own? The flotilla wheeled: the corvette to the north-west, the motor-torpedo-boats to the north, as if to head us off. The sound of engines died. Our ensign fluttered in the breeze, the lights burned steadily, the topsail showed white against the dome of the sky. The three of us stood on deck, not speaking, but each picturing to himself the inside of a Russian prison. A signal flashed out from the parent ship and with a bellow they came at us. We rolled in the foam of their passing. Again their engines died and now the four boats lay poised: one ahead, one astern and one on each side, so close that we could see the silhouettes of men on their tiny bridges. Anne said, quietly, "Look, the escort ship. . . . She's coming."

This, then, was the end.

Signals flashed out from the corvette's bridge like tongues of lightning. At the same instant the four motor-torpedo-boats opened up their throttles. It was like the bursting of a dam. We waited for the flood to submerge us, but instead of advancing it receded, growing fainter and fainter as the flotilla made off to the south-east and the passing of that sound was the sweetest music to our ears.

The breeze freshened and *Moonraker* curtseyed to the dancing waves. In an hour, or perhaps two, for we were not yet quite ourselves, a tree-covered peninsula showed up on the horizon and Porkkala light winked at us in a friendly mocking way. Some time after dawn (it is light soon after one o'clock) Anne passed the lighthouse, describing it as "a pink lighthouse that looked like part of a dwelling, with a green roof, built in the middle of the sea. . . ." She sailed as close as she dared to get the best of the offshore breeze which came and went as the sun climbed high in the sky, and by the afternoon factory chimneys, storage tanks, high buildings, the copper dome of a great church and ships making in and out marked the presence of Helsinki. Tantalizingly close but never seeming to come nearer was the Helsinki Light-vessel, swung to the west-bound stream, and so still was the air that the throb of a coaster's engines could be heard as she negotiated the inside channels.

At ten o'clock we passed the light-vessel. The yellowing sun threw long shadows upon her decks and her crew waved as they lined the bulwarks, puzzled by the blue of our ensign instead of the usual red. We beat slowly eastwards until, the following evening, we slipped past the outer approaches of Öregrund, behind which island we hoped to find an anchorage for the night before proceeding to Kotka in the morning. A little red motor boat put out from behind the island with figures in blue and gold standing in her cockpit. She rounded under our stern, came alongside and a young man jumped aboard, stepped into the cockpit, took the helm from Anne, sat down and said, "You're two days late." As nobody is in the habit of caring whether I am two days late or twenty, I swallowed my surprise and gave him some coffee, but when I saw him leave the well-marked channel and head towards a maze of rocks I thought, like Mr Belloc, that I should enjoy his company the better for knowing just how long it would last.

"Who knows?" was the reply; then, glancing at the gear-lever he said, "You have an engine?"

"Yes," I agreed, "but only one gallon of petrol."

The pilot shrugged his shoulders. He said, "The current is against us, the wind will drop but it should not take more than a week"—he grinned—"to sail the sixteen miles to Kotka." My heart warmed to him.

He was taking us this more intricate way, he said, "because I do not trust my fellow-pilots to remember that steam gives way to sail."

It became quite obvious that no one else would be required to take the helm, so Anne and John turned in and I lay down on the grid in front of the hatch between working the sheets whenever our pilot came about. I complimented him on his handling of a vessel, which at least must have been a little strange to him. He said, "I find her a little small. The last sailing vessel I steered was the four-masted barque *Olivebank*." The pilot yawned and stroked his stubbly chin. He had, he said, trained in sail, taken his master's ticket and served in ocean-going freighters before joining the Pilot Service. "It's a good life," he said. "One week on a rota living on Öregrund, and one week at home with my family." There was a story which, later, I was told of how he led a rescue party to save the lives of the crew of a British freighter last December. Time after time he had boarded her at the risk of his life. A full gale had been blowing and the sea had been strewn with ice but when I had tried to get the details from the Captain of Pilots all he would say was "The Captain did his duty."

The night was over. We had reached a part of the channel that was broad and free from dangers and the smell of frying bacon drifted up from the galley. "I like your English breakfasts," said our pilot, "so I'll take your advice and have mine in comfort below."

The country, now that I had time to study it, looked different. The trees seemed darker, grew more thickly and there was a primeval look that made me think of wolves. Nor could it have altered much since the day when the yacht *Pet*, whose path we had crossed in Ledsund, had followed the Anglo-French fleet to watch the attack on Kotka.

A fine seaman, Mr Hughes. Undaunted by the rough handling he had received at the hands of the North Sea the previous autumn, he was obviously delighted to be back at the scene of conflict. This time, however, he was sadly disappointed, for the Russians had abandoned Kotka and were now out of range of the Navy's guns. Mr Hughes and his friends wandered round the deserted village. He writes: "The houses, with their windows and doors loosely barricaded as the peasants had left them in their flight, the traces in the better houses of comfort or little home luxuries, a pretty fuchsia tree in a flower pot, a little bird cage with the door open, just as some poor girl had snatched away her pet bird and left the cage in her haste; all these things told their little tale of the tears and terrors which war brings with it." Not even these were left because when the stores and barracks were set on fire the wind changed and destroyed the entire village.

The pilot finished his breakfast. In the distance loomed the slender chimneys of pulp mills, and borne on the northerly air was the smell of pulp which brought back memories of Nanaimo in the Gulf of Georgia, but not even there had I seen such acres of wood as were now drying in the sun on the outskirts of Kotka. In the lee of the island we were becalmed. Anxious not to keep our pilot from more useful duties, I started the engine and with sails furled we motored past docks and steamers to the islet on which stands the Kotka Yacht Club. In spite of the early hour Captain Koivistoinen had come in to greet us from his island home where the family had been spending their holiday. He said, "I was worried. I thought you might have fallen into the hands of the Russians."

It seemed so long ago that I had begun to wonder whether we had not exaggerated our danger. I told him our story and asked him whether after all this might have been the Finnish Navy.

He said, "I think you have been very fortunate. There is now no Finnish Navy."

CHAPTER THIRTEEN

IT might seem strange that a foreign yachtsman should want to visit Kotka: the smell of pulp, the factory chimneys, the railway lines, the trucks and trains, the ships following each other up the channel as they do in the London river. But we were here as the result of Captain Koivistoinen's letter and now he was sitting by my side as curious, he told me later, about me as I was about him. At first he was a little shy, reserving judgment until he had had time to find some mutual background. Like so many professional seamen, to whom the sea has taught a sense of truth, he gave the impression that he could see right through your outer covering into the works inside and after talking with him for a while I was anxiously hoping (without being too sanguine about it) that my "works" would win his approval. He had been a seaman all his life: sail, steam, the Finnish Navy (in which he had been the Commander of a submarine during the War), and was now Head of Navigation for Eastern Finland. He had had nine books published, had translated some of Cook's Voyages and that of Slocum, and his first play had recently been accepted by the National Theatre at Helsinki.

I was deep in some nautical discussion when John handed me a note from a pilot launch. It was an account for several thousand Finnmarks for the assistance of a pilot for whom I had never asked. I said, "This is the first time we have been boarded by a pilot since entering Papeete, where pilotage is compulsory."

Captin Koivistoinen looked up quickly. "You needn't have taken a pilot if you didn't want him," he said, sharply. So I told him how he had come aboard off Öregrund. "Surely," I said, "it would have been a difficult and an unfriendly act to have thrown him overboard."

The Captain laughed. "That one might have been very difficult to throw overboard," he agreed, and then he added, "If you will please give me that slip of paper I will make some enquiries."

I never heard what happened, but I was distressed that I should so soon have caused him embarrassment.

The Captain took us along to his flat for breakfast. As we had had ours some five hours ago a second was more than welcome. The street in which he lived was in the old part of the town near the docks, and the flat occupied the first floor of Number 12. Like most Finnish houses we were to visit, the rooms were large and airy and uncluttered by inessentials so that they looked bigger than they were. One side of the hall, which ran the length of the flat, was lined with books and there were books, too, in their living-room and bedroom.

I remember a fine reproduction of "The Defence of the Sampo," a scene from Kalevala (the Finnish Legend), an ivory carving of a Chinese street with thirty-seven figures which the Captain had found in the Far East, and a portrait of his daughter that reminded me of a wood-carving of a girl's head with which Miles Smeeton (of *Tzu Hang* fame) had been presented in Hawaii. We were introduced to Salme, his wife, one of those warm, happy people who was so eager to make herself understood that the meaning of what she said came through to you. After we had done justice to a meal of ham, fresh salad, sweet rolls (eaten without butter) and delicious cups of black coffee which the English contingent laced with cream and the others didn't, the Captain said, "Here is the key to the flat. We hope you will stay here while you remain in Kotka. Salme will show Anne how to use the stove, the beds are made up and John can use the maiden's room: and I hope you will spend the week-end with us at our cottage on Net Island."

Having thanked him for this charming offer I said, "Neither Anne nor I like leaving the ship. I know she's safe but it upsets routine and makes it harder to go back."

The Captain smiled, "No master likes leaving his ship," he agreed, "but I insist you come to Net Island," an invitation we gladly accepted. He said, "Use the flat as you would your home. I have put out some records of Beethoven and Sibelius [how could he have known how much pleasure this would give me?] and I'll show you how to use the radiogram."

That afternoon we tamed the great wood-burning stove (not unlike an Aga) but I could hardly believe it was as efficient as Salme claimed. From the time John put a light to this cold monster to the moment the kettle boiled was exactly ten minutes. While he and Anne used the washing machine I wandered through the rooms picking out a book here and there, listening to the haunting tunes that Sibelius used in his symphonies now echoing through the flat. Many of the books about the sea were in English. Naval history, voyages of discovery, Conrad, Lubbock, Villiers, Slocum, Robinson and a dozen others, but I noticed that a whole section had been devoted to Tahiti. Later the Captain spoke about this. He said, "I have never been there but it has become almost an obsession. I have read all the books

I can find, memorized the reefs and the lagoons and the leading marks for entering them, studied Gauguin's paintings. Sometimes I feel that I know the life of the island so well I could write a novel about it. Perhaps one day I will."

But Kotka, too, has romance. In the years that followed the Anglo-French attack in 1855 (watched by *Pet*) Kotka returned to normal. Peasants rebuilt their small wooden houses, farmed the shallow soil, fished in the sea in summer. The great Kymi river roared seawards from the forests in central Finland, a huge field of potential wealth as yet untapped by the timber merchants; for transport was too difficult. One day a Finn named Ahlqvist, with a few companions, dismantled a disused *sauna* in the heart of a forest many miles from Kotka, tossed the logs into the mighty river, watched them on their headlong race through rapids, guided them between shallows and over rocks and collected them at their journey's end at Kotka. Ahlqvist, by this simple experiment, had solved the transport problem. Millions of logs were towed through the frozen forests by horse and left on the Kymijoki until in the spring the sun melted the ice and the river once more was open. A steam saw-mill was built: then another and another. Then a pulp-mill, a paper-mill. Finns, Norwegians, Swedes poured into the towns. Houses sprang up, docks were built and within ten years eighty ships could be counted at one time waiting their turn to come alongside. I cannot say it is a beautiful town: it does not pretend to be. Its job is to house and feed the workers upon whose efforts it depends. It does this in huge rectangular blocks of flats, centrally heated and with acres of glass to let in what light there is during the long dark winters, which is little enough. In the summer many of the workers live in small country cottages and go daily to their work in town. There is about it the robustness of a frontier town (which at one time it was) with a liveliness of spirit that grew upon us slowly as we watched men, and women, loading fresh clean planks on to the decks of a coaster or bales of paper into the holds of an ocean freighter or people just sitting on a bench in the sun for a mid-day break. There were no sullen faces, no anxious glances: a family content with itself and its job but with a keen eye for the stirring events which soon might follow.

We were taken over a mill that made paper for cement bags by the owner's brother one afternoon. The Managing Director met us at the gate, a young man who looked as if he had come straight from Michigan, crew-cut and all. He said, "Glad to know you, doctor, and glad to know you, Mrs Pye. Here we have the most up-to-date mill in Scandinavia completed less than two years ago: the most important mill in Kotka, the biggest export town in Finland. That little old-fashioned building over there is where the old mill was started. It's real quaint. . . ." His patter learned during six months in the U.S.A. studying American methods went in at one ear and out at the other, for I am not statistically minded and my wayward thoughts were suddenly back in a London cinema long before the war watching the opening scene in *The Testament of Dr Mabuse*, in which a crouching figure creeps along a wall like the one beside which we were now walking. And all the time a deep-throated roar, sinister in its expression of power, came from inside the building, as it did now.

Our guide, walking with short quick steps that went so well with his sentences, took us in through a small door and up a flight of steps down which came a blast of air that might have come from a *sauna*. We were ushered into an enormous room with a central aisle running the length of the factory and reaching up to the roof. On each side were the great presses and rollers revolving at enormous speeds squeezing the water out of the pulp which was fed into them, drying it and turning it out at the far end of the room in rolls of paper each weighing one ton and a quarter. The predominant factor was noise. There were two distinct notes, a rumbling bass that was not without a soothing charm and a whistling scream almost above the pitch of the human ear, the sort of note that would send a dog round the bend. My second impression, standing there in the middle of the aisle, was of being alone. There were men about, of course, but so vast was the stage, so compelling the parts of the actors (the vast machines) that human beings became dwarfed to the role of stage-hands, unwanted till the play was over. We had nearly concluded our tour of inspection when suddenly there was a break in a roll. Clouds of paper were hurled into the air and lengths of torn strips wound themselves round nearby machines. A man leapt for the switchboard but before he reached it two others had seized knives and slit the roll (travelling at thousands of revolutions a minute) with the swift skill of Mexicans cutting the throats of others. The whole incident must have lasted less than a minute but the feeling of all that power suddenly unleashed, the tenseness in the faces of the men, the Managing Director standing quietly by, his eyes watchful, his hands clenched, made it for me a moment I shall never forget.

At the end of our tour we were taken to the "little old-fashioned mill." It was like a veteran car to a new Bentley, clanking and snorting happily away, steam hissing from its leaking joints; but there is, we were told, one sort of paper it makes better than its modern sister, so its life is spared.

Our host stood at the gate. He said, "The Pyes would like to see something of interest in Kotka. Where shall I take them?"

"To the Tzar's fishing lodge," replied the Managing Director, "and as the mill seems capable of running itself in my absence I would like to join you."

More than a little flattered, we piled into the large American car, myself and the Managing Director sharing the front seat with the driver. As we drove along the road with glimpses of quiet water peeping through the trees he told me something of the turbulent history of his people and as I listened I felt I was beside a different person: no longer the Executive with the racy style but a man whose brown eyes glowed with some inner fire. He spoke of the Russians and Swedes fighting each other over Finland's devastated land, of the Russians playing for a hundred years a cat-and-mouse game with the Finns, a little freedom there, a little encouragement here, to clamp down once more with an iron claw.

He finished by saying, "Do you not think it remarkable that after being enslaved for six hundred years we are now free and have remained so after two wars?"

"It is more than remarkable," I answered. "It is like a fairy story in which the beggar girl becomes the princess. I would have said it was against the Law of the Political Jungle, as improbable as the story of the Jews."

By this time we had arrived at Langikoski. In a glade of spruce and pine and overlooking a tributary of the Kymi river that frothed and foamed over rocks and shallows, stood the Tsar's fishing lodge built for Alexander III and kept as a memorial to him and his Tsarina (the beautiful Princess Dagmar of Denmark) because, explained our host, Alexander had happened to be in charge of the Cat when the Mouse had been allowed some liberty. On the veranda was a pile of felt overshoes which we slipped on over our own before entering the large downstairs rooms in which the furniture had been kept as in the days of the Royal Family. The walls and floors were the natural light colour of the wood: there was a dining table of birch and two chairs of the same wood made like small thrones; a silver samovar, Russian hand-woven curtains and a great stove with an ornate iron door. Upstairs in the Royal Chamber there had been recent changes, for the King and Queen of Denmark had spent a night here, but in the children's room and in that of the Royal Guard the beds were simply slats of wood upon which were laid straw mattresses. Fifty yards away and hidden in the wood was a private chapel so small that it would have been impossible for more than two people to worship there at the same time before the single ikon.

Alexander III, my host said, was a simple man fond of chopping firewood (the axe he used was predominantly displayed), and fishing for trout and salmon, but it was only for a few days in each year that the royal couple could escape to this quiet place and I hoped that here at least his mind had been free from the fear of assassination.

We dined that night at the yacht club with these two men who had explained so patiently all they had shown us. The evening was fine and through the open windows we looked out over the sheds and the ships lying at the quays, asleep and silent at this late hour. I am not sure whether our host had been to England but the Managing Director had. He commented on the English stage and drew comparisons (not always complimentary) with what he had seen in America. I remember, too, that there was not a book that we mentioned of which he had not heard and few he had not read, but in the end we returned to the subject next his heart, the problems of industry.

He said, "There was one impression I came away with from England. Your workmen and the staffs of your factories are not friends with each other as we are here. Maybe this is a legacy of the past, but it must be changed, not in some vague future time but now, before it is too late." He rose from his chair. He said, "You must excuse me but I have some things to finish at the office." He shook hands with us. He said, "I enjoyed myself in England. It is a wonderful country to live in, but to work I should go to America."

CHAPTER FOURTEEN

THERE was little doubt in my mind that as guests in Finland we should be unable to avoid the Finnish bath. I looked forward to it like a young sailor to his first gale: with a reluctant determination because there is nothing that can be done to prevent it. People embroider these things: they describe how you will be roasted in a blackened room and then made to roll in the snow. Our initiation took place on our first evening at Kotka. We had gone ashore to the yacht club where we were held in conversation by a Finn who had come to take *sauna* and would we like to join him? I could see there could be no refusal.

"But not you, madame," he said to Anne, "I will arrange something for you later," whereupon Anne quickly walked down to the pram and rowed back to *Moonraker* where, she said, she had work to do.

Sauna was in a small wooden house, painted red, with a large brick chimney out of which poured thick blue smoke from flames heating the torture chamber. I looked at my host carefully. He was a trifle younger but I thought I was as fit as he was.

Sauna, which had been heating for over an hour, was now pronounced ready. We each were given a towel, a basin, a bundle of birch twigs, a cake of soap, and with these we marched in single file like prisoners made to carry the ropes with which they are about to be hung. We turned right into a small dressing-room, where we stripped and then were taken into *sauna* itself. The walls, as I had been warned, were blackened by years of steam and heat, and in one corner was a large concrete tub full of hot water and to one side of it a boiler with a heap of granite stones on top. Under this roared a wood fire which, according to a thermometer on the wall, had sent the temperature up to a hundred degrees centigrade. There were two benches, one above the other. On the uppermost sat our host (where the heat was greatest), at ease and comfortable, but it took me a few minutes to become acclimatized. Sweat poured off my body and the slight singing noise in my head soon vanished. We lathered ourselves with soap, beat ourselves and each other with the bundles of birch twigs whose fragrant leaves (soaked in hot water) filled the room with the smell of a forest shimmering under the noon-day heat: and the tingling of the skin after being beaten was pleasant too.

Our host said, "*Sauna* is more than a way of getting clean. The family take *sauna* together, father, mother, the sons, the daughters and their betrothed, the children; all are equal before God."

He bestirred himself. Even in this darkened room I saw a gleam come into his eye like that of a Spanish priest extolling the virtues of the Inquisition. He said, "Now, gentlemen, a little heat." He scooped a handful of water in a baler from the steaming tub and threw it negligently on to the granite stones. It was like being thrown into Dante's Inferno. I gasped for air, my heart throbbed, my chest ached, my body ran with sweat like lava down the side of a volcano, and when I had a chance to steal a glance at John, he seemed to be in no better shape. I looked at my host, sitting there, relaxed, with a ghost of a smile on his face. He said, "We Finns are naughty people. We say to you, 'Not much heat this time,' but then we think how funny to see the Englishmen retreat to the lower bench and our hands slip as we throw water on the stones." He gave us an appraising glance: he said, "It was hot. You did well."

"It wasn't as bad as I thought it would be," I answered, and at once I saw I had been foolish. The next time I only escaped by putting my head between my knees for a long time. "Relax," said the Finn. "Take it easy: lie down. In a moment we will take a swim and then you will feel good." And he was right. We ran naked down to the water's edge and plunged into Kotka's icy harbour.

I felt like a king and walked confidently to the dressing-room.

"Come back!" shouted our host. "That was only the beginning."

Hours later, or so it seemed to us, we sat drinking beer out of tall glasses, for after *sauna* you must quickly replace the fluid you have lost. The Finn said, "In the centre of Finland, in the heart of the forests and on the shores of the lakes, life is still very primitive, just as it was in the days when Alexis Kivi wrote *The Seven Brothers*. They go to the communal *sauna* on Saturday nights. The young men make jokes. They throw beer and *aquavit* on to the stones and the fumes of alcohol go to their heads with results at which you would be surprised. Yes," he said wistfully, "everything happens in *sauna* that happens in life. Even babies are born there."

As I waited at the quay for Anne to come and fetch me in the dinghy I thought about *sauna* from the medical standpoint. The mechanics of the thing are simple: the great heat lowers the blood pressure through vasodilation, the plunge into cold water (or snow) constricts the blood-vessels, thus raising the pressure as quickly as it had fallen. The fluid lost by sweating is replaced by drinking as soon as *sauna* is over, but I must admit that if I thought my arteries had calcareous plaques on their walls (like fur on the bottom of a kettle) which might at the slightest provocation break away and cause a thrombosis, I should steer a course that would keep me well clear of *sauna*. As I have reason to think they are no worse than age has made them I was glad of the experience and not averse to repeating it. The good thing about *sauna*, it seemed to me, is that it makes people forget the every-day tensions so that they come out of *sauna*, sometimes after several hours, relaxed and with the worries of the day behind them.

Later we were to meet electric *saunas*. As they save the labour of lighting a wood fire they are more usually met with in people's houses and give a drier heat, making it possible for the victim to withstand a yet higher temperature, but for myself, give me the steam *sauna*, in which I received my initiation.

On Saturday morning Captain Lehmuskallio, Captain of Pilots, drove us to his chalet from which Eino Koivistoinen was to collect us by boat to go to Net Island. The little Volkswagen trundled along the bumpy road, birds flew up at the unaccustomed noise, squirrels leapt from branch to branch and a rabbit scuttled across our path, narrowly missing death, for the Captain believed in getting home as fast as he was able. These two seamen have been friends for years: Eino: lanky, deliberate, slow of speech but with an easy turn of phrase; the Captain of Pilots short, quick in his movements, his words tumbling out like notes from a barrel-organ, so that by the time he has finished you are not even half-way there.

We drove down to the water's edge where Eino Koivistoinen was waiting for us in a long flat-bottomed boat like a Thames punt, with an outboard motor attached to the stern. By its side was another with a large American engine. The two captains were like children. "If only you could navigate," said Eino, "I would ask you and Hanna to lunch."

"Navigate!" spluttered the indignant Captain of Pilots, bending over his engine.

"Quick," whispered Eino, "into the boat. I don't think he knows the water has dropped a foot, and I know another way." As he pushed off, Hanna ran down to the quay, but in a moment we were among the reeds, cut off from the world and the wind and the sun, so tall were they. Suddenly Eino put his helm hard over to port and we shot into a narrower deeper channel that wound like a maze towards the distant fiord. We heard the other boat's engine as it roared past the opening into which we had turned. There was a sudden shout . . . then silence. A smile spread over Eino's face. "Our Captain of Pilots has gone aground," he sighed as he made for the open water.

Net Island was almost completely circular. Its diameter could not have been more than thirty yards and on it grew rowan, birch and elm among sand, grass and boulders. On top of the miniature hill stood the house, the castle of which Eino was king. On the quay were the family waiting for us, the Finnish flag waving in the breeze.

They looked so happy standing there. . . . Salme, her youngest boy Eero, her daughter Marjut, who after all was not quite like Miles Smeeton's Polynesian girl. She had the same high cheek-bones, the same poise, but her eyes were blue and her hair like winter's sunlight.

Built of pine the little house was painted a yellowish brown with green shutters and the door handles were grown branches of birch. Inside the wood was untreated, so that when you first went into the living-room it seemed to be full of yellow light as if it lived for ever in the afternoon. A yellow pine table, two benches, bunks along one wall like those in the fo'c's'le of a sailing ship, a parrot, a rocking chair and a wide, hard settee, a room filled with the smell of pine instead of the salty tang of the sea. The Koivistoinens live on Net Island from June till September. After that they use it as a week-end cottage until the fiord freezes over, when they occasionally cross on skis to light fires and keep it warm. The countryside looks bare then, because the reeds have gone, but when spring comes in the middle of May the ice melts and in two weeks they are back. Although there is no running water, no telephone, no electric light and no drainage you cannot call it isolated, because all you have to do is to take the outboard across the water (finding new channels every spring), walk two miles to the nearest road, where a bus runs once or twice a day into Kotka, and bring back the bread which is your staple diet. Water is from the well, lime looks after the earth closet: fish is fetched from the fisherman's house and eggs, milk, cheese and piimää (buttermilk) come from the farmer. What more can man want?

Outside the living-room a veranda ran the short length of the house. There was, of course, the *sauna* and our bedroom which led out of it, with two bunks along one wall, of which John had the upper and Anne and I the lower.... Half-way down the little hill a hut had been built for Marjut and her friends.

We sat round the table drinking coffee, cup after cup, like nectar. A wonderful feeling of peace stole over me. There were no clocks and time had no meaning: and yet how perverse is the human spirit, for Eino now chose to speak of war. "It is strange," he said, "that war brings out so clearly the qualities in man that alone makes him great: as if to compensate for the miseries that are left. 'Britain's Finest Hour,' your Mr Churchill said, and in Finland it was the same. In the end, the Russians annexed Karelia and peasants who had farmed the land for generations were given two weeks to get out or to become Russian citizens. Westwards, along roads, over fields and through forests, carrying their small possessions on barrows, trucks or carts, a hundred and fifty thousand people trekked towards Finland. Winter was almost on them, but before it came shelter had been found for every child, woman and man. Not one remained in Karelia."

After supper the children, with John, went for an expedition in the boat, leaving the three of us talking round the table. Salme had been saying to Anne that she had no idea of what Marjut would do when she left the university. Eino stopped strumming on his guitar. "Aye-ee, Aye-ee," he chuckled, "I know very well what Marjut will do.... She will be a mother, like you."

The day finished with *sauna* and with a resounding Finnish victory. On the second round of the contest, so to speak, there was a howl of delight from Salme as Anne fled to cool off in the water.

Sleep came quickly to us in our wooden bunks, but we woke to a morning of rain. "Do you feel strong?" asked Eino, as we ate sugar bread. "I have arranged that we go to buy fish and fresh buttermilk for lunch."

We landed at the fisherman's quay. Two double-ended boats were drawn up out of the water, and nets stood drying in the sun, arranged, said Anne, like long evening gowns. To the right was the house hidden in trees. The fisherman came out to greet us, showed us *sauna* (pride of place), invited us into his house where his wife, a young woman with a sweet face and a gentle voice, was weaving flax grown on their land into lace curtains, as delicate as a spider's web. The big room contained a table, three upright chairs, a rocking chair, a great wood-burning stove and a tall cylindrical boiler that reached to the ceiling to keep them warm in winter. Fishing did not end when the fiord froze. The fisherman bored holes in the ice and caught the fish underneath.

The fish, like little pike, were put in our boat and we left them with Salme to make fish soup with dill, while Eino filled up with fuel. The farm, where we now were bound, was a little bigger, a little more prosperous, and the room, as you might expect, showed evidence of its advancement: a low modern table with awkward legs that might have come out of any department store in London or New York; and there were other anachronisms which I have at this distance of time forgotten. The farmer himself had the red, jolly face and broad-shouldered look of his cousins in Essex. His wife managed the house, and he and his sister worked the farm. It was difficult to calculate its size, but after much drawing, and interpretation by Eino, we thought it to be about two hundred and fifty acres, a third woodland, a third grazing and a third for wheat and maize: hard work for two of them. In both houses we were entertained to coffee and sweet bread, but the farmer's wife would not sit down at table with us, remaining in the background like the Polynesian women, and that brought to my mind the way nature has of teaching the people with whom she is closest in contact the basic principles of a harmonious life: good manners and cleanliness.

On the way back to Kotka that night Captain Lehmuskallio took us down to his Inspection Ship in which he tours the Pilot Stations under his command. His is not altogether an enviable job, for he has as yet not enough pilots to go round, and in the smaller ports into which bigger and bigger ships are nosing their way the pilots are still fishermen with local knowledge. Handling a fourteen-thousand tonner is a very different matter, the Captain said, from piloting a coaster. The Inspection Ship had been built in the days when steamers still had the rounded sterns of sailing ships and her tall smoke stack rose jauntily above the high central bridge. Below, her appointments were solid and comfortable, built to last a couple of hundred years, but on the bridge, radar, echo-sounder, gyro-compass, direction-finder, all the modern navigational aids, had been poured into her like new wine into an old bottle. She had, nevertheless, a certain dignity of her own, helped, perhaps, by the distinguished visitors who from time to time had voyaged in her: the King and Queen of Denmark, Envoys of States, Marshall Voroshilov. Not until we had signed the Visitor's Book had I imagined that our names would have been in such close proximity with that of the Head of the Soviet Union.

Captain Lehmuskallio dropped us off at the Koivistoinen's flat. It was a malicious evening. Wind hurled sheets of rain against the tall panes of the windows and a grey light filtered through the low clouds that swept across the town from the south-west. Inside, it was warm and dry, and a disinclination to trudge back through the streets along whose gutters ran turgid streams of brownish water stole over me. As if reading my thoughts Anne said, "Let's spend the night here. I'm so tired I could sleep for a week." So we cooked ourselves a simple meal of eggs, dipped into more of Eino's books and listened to Sibelius. We turned in early, but no sooner was I in bed than my mind woke up. It wandered up blind alleys trying to piece together all the impressions that had forced themselves upon it during the last few days: the shriek of the paper mill, the keen executive who could command seven languages, leap to the defence of Mr Charles Morgan and chuckle over Mr Shute's description of the American small town Hazel; the Russian Tsar who liked chopping firewood for the kitchen stove, Hanna Lehmuskallio who spoke English without a trace of accent, looking young and pretty in spite of bearing her husband five strapping sons of whom the oldest was now in Navigation school, the youngest a baby in arms, and whose cake, I suspected, was at this moment responsible for my wakefulness, for it was a "wet cake," richer than anything I have ever eaten. And the Koivistoinens . . . Koivistoinen means in Finnish Little Birchwood. . . . Shade against the noon-tide sun, shelter from the stormy wind, music in its leaves rustling in the summer breeze; not dark and sombre like the pines, not unbending like the oak but resilient.

We slept heavily. The sun came up into the rain-washed sky, the light poured into the sleeping flat, but no one stirred. The key turned in the outer door, footsteps walked through the hall and Salme opened her bedroom door to find two heads on her pillows. Barely stifling her laughter she softly went into the kitchen and through the open door came the smell of coffee.

CHAPTER FIFTEEN

THE Port of Kotka was to be the point of our return. To the east lay the Iron Curtain through which we, as private individuals in a private ship, could not at the moment penetrate, although we could have gone by bus to Leningrad. Our course was now westwards, not by the sea whence we had come, but by the inland channels: the way the coasters go, the galliasses, the small motor ships, the ketches, schooners, tugs and barges which sail these watery highways like lorries on the roads of Britain. This simile is more apt than might at first be imagined, for some of these channels are no wider than a four lane motor road, winding between the shores of close knit, wooded islands. But, in case you should conjure up a picture of ships packed bow to stern like motor cars on the Brighton road or barges on a Rotterdam canal, I must add that this "traffic" amounts to half a dozen coasters, and a yacht, perhaps, to be met with in a day.

These are the trunk roads from which branches leave the parent tree to connect some of the oldest towns in Finland with the sea while other, lesser ones, meander like country lanes up long inlets to end in hamlets with fantastic names. It was to travel these roads, to sail the country lanes to the hamlets and the towns whose buildings and bygone prosperity had their roots in the sea, that we left the town of Kotka one sunny afternoon. We got no farther that day than Svartholm, for the wind which had headed us up the Gulf of Finland was now firmly established in the west. Our anchorage was a small bay whose seaward side was protected by five small islets. Dark pines came down to the water's edge and over its surface eddies of wind drifted like thistledown over a field. There are houses, I believe, on this island, but from where we lay we might have been a hundred miles from the nearest human habitation. That night the wind rose from the west. The birch leaves sighed and I lay awake reflecting on the time it had taken to sail this short distance from Kotka. It was now the height of summer, but already there was a small circle of night, no bigger than a man's hand which, during the next few weeks, would grow at an alarming pace as the short northern summer drew to its close. Our time, if we were to get home before the autumn gales, was limited. We must work to a plan: to see and record something of this coast upon which, for three hundred years, the life of Finland had depended.

Eino Koivistoinen had suggested that we should see Loviisa and the Nordström shipping company, Porvoo, the home of the salt schooners, Helsinki, the capital, Hanko, through which we must pass again, and Turku the old capital at a time when Helsinki was an insignificant village. From there we should go back along the shores of the Gulf of Bothnia, to say goodbye to our friends in Mariehamn.

There might be magic for John in the streets of the cities but Anne wrote in her diary: "Take your dusty towns and let me sleep till the sun shines and the water laps again. It is the skerries that beckon, and the heather, the wild berries, the tang in the air and the song of the birds at evening and at dawning: the wild walk over smooth boulders, the feel of the sand below the toes and the silence that comes at night."

I have little recollection of the next day's sail and even the diary into which she usually packs so much descriptive detail, Anne filled only with notes on towers, beacons, buoys and leading marks, with a single entry: "on our right was a fat island bursting with ramparts and overgrowth," as her one comment on eight miles of sunlit coves, islets, trees and villages which line the long inlet at the head of which stands Loviisa, one of the oldest towns in Finland, so intricate were the channels through which we had come, and I thought again what fine seamen the captains of these coasters must have been to work their unhandy vessels in such waters.

Because we were tired and had had, for one day, our fill of maritime adventure, we anchored on the outskirts, behind the island of Krakholm (the crocus island). From here we looked towards the town, half hidden in trees with green meadows sloping down a hill.

Loviisa, a place of some importance in 1855, had been visited by the Anglo-French fleet (but not by the yacht *Pet*) and it so happened that this coincided with a fire which swept through the town and, fanned by a strong wind, utterly destroyed it. The new Loviisa crouches low on either side of the hill, separated by a ridge of parkland, on which no houses have since been built, for the authorities were determined to save at least half a town should another fire break out.

We had just settled down to an early tea (for Anne had misread the clock by an hour and John, who was permanently hungry, had thought it unnecessary to correct her) when the noise of a powerful engine could be plainly heard, rapidly approaching our secluded anchorage. John put his head out of the hatch. "We have been discovered, skipper," he said. A large high-speed launch came alongside and a young man stepped aboard.

"My name is Nordström," he said. "Why did you hide in such an out of the way place? We might have missed you." He sat down at my side, swallowed a mugful of tea and a glass of whisky to get rid of the taste of the tea. He said, "We have strict instructions from Kotka to take care of you, and I will take you up to the office as soon as you are ready."

The launch drew up at the quay and we were escorted to the offices of the Nordström Shipping Company. The man who had founded this maritime business, whose sons were now so hospitably entertaining us (and whom we never met) had worked before the first war as a stevedore at Valcom, the commerical port for Loviisa, had bought his first small coaster after that war had ended and from this small beginning built up a fleet of thirteen vessels of between five and sixteen thousand tons. What made his family so proud of him was not so much the success of the business as the care with which he looked after the people who now worked for him. "To be poor," he once said, "is the finest education because it gives understanding." And as soon as the company was firmly established he had built houses for his employees which they could buy with money borrowed without interest from the company. His sons and daughters lived in houses round the shores of the fiord, and to one of these we were taken that afternoon. The eldest daughter met us at the doorway of a Georgian-looking house, if you can imagine a Georgian house of wood, took us through the large drawing-room on to a terrace and down through an orchard to the waterside to look over acres of logs that were waiting to be towed to Valcom: then back to what Anne called the "armoury," where battle-axes, sabres, cross-bows and an arquebus hung on the drawing-room walls. As the evening wore on I sensed a growing excitement, or amusement, for which I could find no cause until the door opened and in came an English girl, the wife of one of the sons, who, not having been forewarned, was as surprised to hear us as we were to hear her. At dinner that night I sat next to Marti's English wife and I suddenly wondered how she was making out in her voluntary exile from her own country. When I asked her, she said with a laugh, "Consider Surbiton: then look out of that window at the view."

"But the long hard winters?"

"The white winter (from January to April) brings snow and sparkle but the 'grey' winter is awful. I remember thinking it was no wonder revolutions were started in October. I could quite easily have started one myself. . . . And November is worse. In Finnish it is called Marraaskuu, the 'Dead Month.' Have they told you how, before Christianity came to Finland, the people buried their dead in deep vaults, laying their bodies on mattresses of straw and in November they would take them food and drink 'to strengthen their spirits'?"

She said, "I've got over that now, and our summers are usually so wonderful they make up for the autumn."

"Do you go back to England?" I asked her.

"Oh, yes: but England seems to have changed, or I have. Out here I feel they have a better way of living, a simpler set of values."

"More like England thirty years ago?" I said.

"Well: I can't remember what it was like as long ago as that," she laughed, "but I think that's roughly what I do mean."

Later, when I was watching the lights come up on the other side of the fiord, Marti joined me. "When I was a boy," he said, "I remember seeing the salt schooners beating up to Valcom and on Sundays the longships, painted black [*snipan,* I think he called them] each rowed by four pairs of oars as they came pulling up the fiord from the distant villages, the oarsmen and their passengers dressed in their best black, the men pulling with all their strength to get there first, on their way to Church. But now," he smiled, "they come by outboard."

It was after midnight that Marti's brother took us back to the ship. The wind had gone and a pale moon peeped over the trees. Across the water came the voices of men gossiping in the street, for in summer the Finns waste little time in bed.

Immediately after breakfast Marti came for us, bundled us into his car and drove us round the town. At one time Loviisa had been a frontier town with the Russian border just across the water. Later, when Russia annexed Finland it was a watering place, the residents letting their houses to the Russian nobility as some of our country mansions are let to Americans. Of this older Loviisa, before the fire destroyed it, there is one house left, although how it escaped, for it is in the middle of the town, I cannot think. It is a timbered building, the weatherboards running vertically, which in its time has been an inn, a church, a courthouse, a school and a private dwelling. It is now a restaurant in winter, but in summer the staff move *en block* to the yacht club, where they serve meals at any time of the day or night. Over the brow of the hill we came to the second half of the town, where, on the outskirts, is a settlement of small houses among trees and lawns known as the "Fighter's Village," where the men who were disabled during the war now live. Although Marti said nothing, I rather gathered that his father had had something to do with the founding of this, too.

Marti took us back to his office. He said, "It is a peculiar thing that the shipowner now has far more to do with the problems of the sea than in the old days."

To illustrate this he told me a story which although by no means unusual, bears this out. "Two years ago," Marti began, "we had an exceptionally severe winter. One of our ships arrived at the Elbe from Odessa in the middle of February. There was ice at Brunsbüttel and in Kiel Bay all movement of shipping had been suspended. I re-routed her round the Skaw. She discharged oil at Helsingborg and by that time the Sound was full of ice. I arranged ice-breaker assistance but there were so many ships in trouble that help was not forthcoming. A few days later the pack ice started to move and the master thought it would be safe to leave.

"On Saturday at 13.00 she was hard and fast in the ice south of Drogden tower. I rang up all the ice-breaker offices along the Swedish coast but they were closed for the week-end and the Danish ships were not allowed to operate in Swedish waters. From time to time the master spoke to me over the radio telephone. The ship was slowly but steadily being carried towards the Sandflyten shore by the ice in which she was held fast. The master said, 'The glass is falling and the wind is getting up from the west. All efforts to clear the vessel, by going hard astern and full speed ahead, have failed. I can do nothing more without assistance.'

"It occurred to me, as I sat there waiting for the R.T. set to crackle, that few of the old shipowners would have led such easy lives if they had had to share the anxieties of their sailing ship captains running before Cape Horn gales and in danger of broaching to for days on end.

"The silence between reports was the hardest thing to bear. On Sunday evening the master called me again. He said, 'I have six feet under my keel. All efforts to break out have failed. I will call you again if there is anything fresh to report.'

"On Monday I called the nearest ice-breaker office, but they told me that no help could reach the ship till 13.00 and at 11.30 the Master spoke to me. He said, 'The echo sounder shows no water below the ship and in ten minutes I shall be ashore,' and then his voice rose a note . . . 'It's moving.' The line went dead and for an hour, or perhaps two, I waited, knowing nothing. Then the R.T. crackled into life. I heard the master's voice, as unemotional as if he had been ordering a loaf of bread. He said, 'The ship managed to clear herself from the ice. I am now anchored seven miles to the west of my previous position and await the ice-breaker. She will be here in one hour.'

"So I left the office for the first time for three days and returned home."

CHAPTER SIXTEEN

BETWEEN Loviisa and Porvoo, a distance of twenty miles as the crow flies, are four inlets up all of which we might have sailed to explore the settlements with the fantastic, unpronounceable names which are joined each with the other by forest paths or lanes as tenuous as spider's threads, but for this there was no time and it was towards the sea that we now were heading. As I stood at the bottom of the companionway studying the large-scale charts it looked to me as if some god-like general, when the world was young, had laid out his defence in depth. First, the outer rocks or skerries, worn smooth by gales and ice, then the smaller islets, the "pockets of resistance," and finally the main defences: islands which were small, compact and overlapping. The stunted trees with their backs to the sea, their skeleton branches bent before the onslaught, the wrecks of ships upon their windward coasts, showed at the end of a long winter just how severe the attack had been.

So well, I thought, have the strategists planned their campaign that here only the merest whisper could be heard at the height of battle. But there were gaps in the defences and it was down one of these that we sailed this afternoon from Loviisa, between the island of Kejvsalö and the mainland. Apart from an islet or two in the distance and a few rocks and shoals which extend ten miles to seaward there was nothing between us and the Gulf of Finland, but on this fine afternoon with the wind off shore the water was as smooth as a lake. At the bottom of the fiord we turned almost ninety degrees to starboard and in a moment the whole scene changed.

We found ourselves in the midst of a hundred islands (the main defences) through which we had to beat. The channel was well marked by sparbuoys and beacons, but at one moment it was as wide as the London river and the next a mere gateway between marks. This sort of thing has the stuff of youth, the ship depending for her safety not on any one of the crew, but upon the whole; and as a team we were now in tune. The helmsman concentrated on sailing the ship, one of us worked the sheets, and the third, with one finger on the chart and one eye on the changing scene, was pilot. So exacting was this that our three-hour watches were changed to one. And to add to the excitement a change of weather was in the offing. A dark pall of cloud spread up from the south-west and I for one was glad that we were behind the lines and not to windward of them. It was long past our dinnertime, and ahead lay what looked like an ideal anchorage, a lagoon formed by three large islands and a few small ones into which we could sail through one of two channels. As Anne was at the helm I gave her the choice. She said, "I'll take the narrow one. It's shorter and I think I can lay it without a tack."

She worked her up to windward and then set the ship at it like a hunter at a five-bar gate.

"Keep up to windward," I cried, "Keep up to windward." But no sooner had I said it than the ship ran gently but firmly on to a rock and came to rest on the windward side! We hauled her off stern first, not without difficulty, and lay to our kedge all night as the wind rose and the leaves of the trees rustled and sighed like the silken dresses of women in a ballroom.

Perhaps it was this incident, for no man likes to run his ship on a rock, however gently, or, again, it might have been the wind, storming my defences and keeping me awake, that put me into the obstinate frame of mind which, Anne says, sometimes afflicts me, and which next morning made me determined to face the gale that was now blowing down Pellinki sound. This Sound, five miles long and so narrow that the Finns have drawn a large-scale chart on the back of chart No. 16, runs almost due west, into the teeth of the gale. The strong current set up by the wind, the gusts laying the ship over to the tops of her bulwarks, coming about before the ship had enough way to be certain of answering her helm, made me do a thing I have only once done before—start the engine and "motor beat" (disgusting phrase) until the channel widened.

Now there was more room but much more sea. Half a mile away a black squall came tearing across the water, the clouds not much higher than the trees. Anne suddenly looked up from the chart. She said, "If you want to go on you must do the pilotage yourself. I will have nothing to do with the wrecking of the vessel."

There was a finality, a conclusion in her voice that took me back over the years to a different occasion, and because it was this that made me now run for shelter I will tell you what happened. It must have been twenty years ago. We had set out from Harwich bound for Terschelling. The weather was fine, the wind light from the south-east, but towards evening the glass fell and there was a sunset like the wrath of God. Anne said, "D'you think it might be wise to turn back, before it's too late?"

"Of course not," I told her, reassuringly, "we should get across long before the weather breaks." Suddenly that same note of finality came into her voice as she said, "I'm going back now, at once." The ship was sailing herself and we were standing on the foredeck. I suddenly seized and shook her. "We're nearly half way there," I shouted, "to turn back would be to quit."

Anne goes very pale when she is upset and now there was anger in her voice. She said, "I'm not going to put my ship in danger because you're frightened of being afraid," and she walked quietly aft, took the tiller, gybed the ship all standing and put her on her homeward course.

Next day it blew a full gale from the north-west, which might well have put us on a lee-shore.

Well I was wiser now, so we found shelter behind the island of Björkholmen and sat on the sandy shore beneath the spruce trees.

I was more than half asleep when Anne woke me gently. "The wind's backed, it's time we were off." We had dinner while beating through a rock-strewn channel while peals of thunder exploded overhead and gusts laid the old ship over but not enough for me to go on deck, for I was cook and it was warm and dry below. We raced up the fiord with a fair wind and the sun went down leaving upon the water a trail of blood up the middle of which we strode like an executioner in the French Revolution. The wind died down to a gentle breeze and we slipped past the brow of a little hill on which stood a house with a light in a lower window. A young woman came out and called to us in Swedish, to which we answered in English that we could not understand. She went on calling and calling until we were out of earshot and none of us had any idea of what she was trying to say. The shores closed in upon us, so that the fiord was now no wider than a river on which swift shadows played. The pines stood black against the reddened sky. It was the sort of place where Longfellow might have written "Hiawatha" while his mind rang with the lilt of the Kalevala....

> Sailed away to loftier regions,
> To the land beneath the heavens.

When it became too dark to see the next mark from the last we turned aside and anchored under the lee of an islet.

I woke early next morning. Nothing stirred, nor was there anything to remind me of the sea except the tall sparbuoys following the winding channel far inland, among green pastures and parkland. We broke the anchor out and set sail to wind, with the channel, towards Porvoo where we tied up, more like a horse than a ship, to a couple of bollards beneath the trees. Tall houses stood well back from the river and we walked to the handsome bridge whose span crossed the Porvoonjoki. From the middle of this I looked towards the hill upon which stands the town. At this distance of time the picture which stays in my mind is one of colour: blue sky, fleecy clouds, black-hooded top of the cathedral, sitting like a mother hen above the green in which hid the houses and streets. Down by the waterfront stretched a long line of ochre-red sheds to which, a century ago, schooners brought salt from Portugal. It put me in mind of Chartres, and bears, perhaps, much the same relation to Finland as that city does to France.

We crossed the bridge and climbed the hill and on our way back to the ship came to a quiet square where the Town Hall stood, painted pink and etched in pale blue as though a child had cut it out of cardboard.

Of the next day Anne wrote:

Peter and I buy two small and expensive fish in the market and on our return John has the cabin ready and the dishes washed, so we turn round and motor down river, reefing to a fresh breeze. The wind is soft and we find our way through a narrow channel where a bus is travelling from one island to another on a ferry. It is islands all the way: rocks, reefs, beacons, and tea is taken in a smother of tacking just before we come to Kajholmen, an island owned by N.J.K., the principal yacht club of Helsinki. There is a short bay between two reefs, bespattered with buoys, posts and a jetty arched like a bridge. The island is small, and low where the wind is strongest. Ashore, there is an eating house, sleeping cabins and a *sauna* and a member of the yacht club in good English and a highly varnished folkboat gives us a formal welcome: but from the many yachts which came in during the day no one came to see us nor were we invited to visit them. Inside the long eating house are three tall-backed chairs; one carved like an old man of the sea, one like a woman with full cheeks and long hair and one in the shape of a yet unformed plant. Can these be us? Outside there are stones for tables with smaller ones for seats, a miniature light tower on one point and paths that wind in and out, but it is an island over-lived on and not for discovering. We cook our green fish which are pink inside and go to bed.

We had, indeed, entered another world, of yachts and yachtsmen. That Sunday afternoon, as we approached the outskirts of Helsinki in the company of not less than forty sail, we passed between Sandhamn and the island of Mjölö where a hundred years or more ago, the yacht *Pet*, with which you are now familiar, anchored to watch the bombardment of Sveaborg by the combined fleets in the closing stages of the Crimean War. There is a terrifying lithograph in Mr Hughes' book showing her with her topmast housed and her bowsprit reefed, the seas breaking over her as she lay to two anchors. Not far away are *Hastings* and *Cornwallis* (ships of the line), with their top-gallant masts struck and black smoke pouring out of their funnels as they steam full ahead into the gale to prevent themselves from dragging. Looking at this your fears are immediately aroused that the *Pet* will not survive the night, but there is no need for worry: Mr Hughes is well able to look after himself.

Off the southern end of the island of Valisaari we turned ninety degrees to starboard and for the first time in many days we ran, making towards the scene of the last picture in Mr Hughes' book which shows the *Pet* under heavy fire from the Citadel on Sveaborg, from half a dozen other forts and earthworks and from an old Russian three-decker, as she flies through the quiet water under every stitch of canvas she can muster, a formidable spread by modern standards, on her way to make an unofficial reconnaisance of how the battle is progressing. In the background is Helsinki (little bigger than a village) and behind the *Pet* is the island of Sveaborg in flames. You will be as glad as I was to hear that she suffered no damage and later made her way in safety to Stockholm where she was laid up for the winter. As to the results of the battle, they were entirely inconclusive, which saddened Mr Hughes' martial spirit. He compares the spirit of the Navy (or the men in charge of it) to that of Nelson. He writes, "Now, if we sacrifice this prestige . . . if a notion begins to creep about that British ships are shy of shot, it were better and cheaper for us that these magnificent vessels, and which our authorities seem to love not wisely but too well, were rotting amongst the congers." Which makes me think that Mr Hughes' heart was as sound as his seamanship.

Although our own entry into this harbour lacked the drama that usually accompanied the *Pet*, the steep, rocky sides of the islands between which we had to pass, so close that the ancient walls pressed down upon us, made it seem as if we were passing through a tunnel all the narrower for the magnificent open bay which, as we emerged, confronted us. To the east the shores were lined with green islands, ahead others appeared with houses, while to the north and west were the spires and tall buildings of a crowned by the copper dome of St Nicholas Cathedral. We were bound for the north-east corner of this bay and it was a little like finding your way through a suburb with the narrow waterways taking the place of streets. When we finally came to our destination, helped by a map on the back of the usual envelope, we found it to be a pink house built in the Italian style standing half hidden in trees above a lawn which dipped to the water's edge. At the garden gate we dropped anchor.

CHAPTER SEVENTEEN

THE reason for our being here dated back to before we left England, when Mr Ericsson, in the name of the Sea Bears, offered me the charts of Finnish waters and suggested that we should start our personal discovery of Helsinki from his house. Bad weather now held him prisoner on his island, but while we were talking to his housekeeper a couple came up the drive. They had been sent, they said, to look after us until the Ericssons came back, and would like to drive us round.

It was a Sunday and no day is so unkind for seeing a city, because it then has to rely on its buildings, the layout of its streets and its surroundings, and few can afford to do that. To add to this unfortunate start the sky was overcast, rain was in the air and a bitter wind blew through its empty streets.

I find that I cannot yet accustom myself to the enormous rectangular blocks of concrete with a thousand windows peering at you like artificial eyes, which seem to have been accepted as normal architectural practice, but if you like this sort of thing the modern centre of the town will undoubtedly please you. Not that some of these buildings do not hold the eye: they do. The Olympic stadium whose tower at one corner looks like a giant crankshaft, and the railway station, designed by the late Elial Saarinen, which, for no particular reason, made me think of a marriage between the Crystal Palace and a Moorish temple. No: to my antiquated taste the Great Square, with the University buildings (not unlike the terraces of Regent's Park), the magnificent flight of steps leading up to the Cathedral doors from which the inhabitants, all dressed in their best clothes, once watched the bombardment of Sveaborg, the Cathedral itself, looking to my untutored eye far more Russian than the Greek Orthodox Church, a quarter of a mile away, are infinitely preferable.

But what I have written is only of its bones. For me Helsinki's charm depends more upon nature than upon man. Its almost incomparable harbour, its parks, gardens, woodlands, all set about the city, make it in the summer a pleasant place to live in.

Inside the pink house the Italian style was not carried through, although there were paintings of the Italian scene into which had crept, unofficially as it were, the northern light of Finland. There was a library and a considerable number of archaeological pieces from Rome and Greece, of considerable worth, I suspect, for our host was by inclination first an archaeologist, second a sailor, third an author (his book on unusual anchorages among the islands reminded me of Eric Hiscock's book on south-west Ireland) and last and least, he assured me, a shipowner, which was what brought him in his bread and butter. The night we dined with them they gave us a Finnish meal: three sorts of cold fish marinaded in various spices, followed by a special fish whose name Anne's diary unfortunately failed to record, in a sauce that could only be called exquisite. Cristoffe Ericsson was small and dark. Whenever he came to see us he talked about Bristol Pilot-cutters and ocean voyages and if circumstances had been different there is little doubt that this sort of sailing might have been added to his accomplishments.

On a rainy, windy day we sailed round to the Nylanska Jaktklubbens (familiarly known as the N.J.K.). I have the Englishman's usual aversion to tying up to a quay, preferring to anchor off or to lie on someone else's mooring, but this was an exception: perfectly protected, uncrowded, water laid on and the Club itself, almost a hundred years old, the finest I have ever been in. The dining-room is large with a high raftered roof in dark wood, reminding me of the days when I had dined in Hall. The food is good, the view over the harbour superb, the prices not entirely ruinous and its members more than hospitable.

We had been told that Helsinki would be empty, but we took this to be the sort of thing that was said about London in August and September thirty years ago. The market on the quay fairly teemed with life, and I remember noticing the predominance of young people and the enjoyment in their faces, and I can honestly say that I did not see one bored face in Helsinki, which is more than can be said of any English town. I remember plenty of cross ones, at the price of cabbages (3s. 6d.) or new potatoes at 8s. 6d. a pound when they were first brought in by boat from the islands. Some of the people to whom we had been given introductions were away sailing or staying on their islands, but on our first day there a schoolfriend of my half-Finn friend in England brought his wife over to see our ship. Bertil Gripenberg's father had been Professor of Architecture at Helsinki University, and Bertil, like my friend in England, had followed the same profession.

Bertil said, "I have taken the day off to show you something of Helsinki." So he bundled us into his car, showed us a passing glimpse of the modern architecture of the city (looking much better because the sun was out), some designed by his father and the largest hospital in the city, which was of fine proportions, but here he started to tell me a story that drove sightseeing out of my mind because he told it as a fairy story, which indeed it was. A young friend of his, a Dane, had been staying with them when he crashed his motor cycle and had to be taken to hospital where he fell in love with a nurse.

He was too shy to ask her name or where she lived and when he returned to do this (on Bertil's advice) she had gone and no one knew anything about her, so it looked as if he had lost his princess and after a week or two he returned to Denmark.

A year later he came back. He again stayed with Bertil, but never put in an appearance at the office where he was supposed to be working until one day when he burst into the room looking radiant. "I've found her," he cried, "I've found her at last," and when Bertil asked him what on earth he was talking about, "But that's what I came back for, to look for my girl." He had besieged hospitals, kept a watch on nurses' homes, made friends with students, who took him into the wards disguised as a medical student. They asked him, he said, what she looked like but what could he say except that she was the most lovely girl in the world? To which they replied that there were eight hundred nurses in Helsinki who, in the same circumstances, might answer that description. And then that day he had walked into a coffee-house and there she was sitting in front of him, drinking coffee.

"Well, what was she like?" I asked Bertil.

"Oh, she had fair hair and blue eyes, just like any other Finnish girl," he replied.

The Gripenbergs lived in a street not ten minutes from his office, which is in the centre of the city. There was a row of houses on each side, and at the end was their house. It was built to embrace a view overlooking woods and meadows and an arm of the sea upon which lay his folkboat. Only from the boys' room could any other houses be seen and Bertil had taken the precaution of designing these to please his eye. But if the design was his, the decor was his wife's. She was English born but her mother was half Latvian and her high cheek-bones, her vivacity and her flair for clothes might have made her more at home in Paris than in London. She was, she said, the tidiest person in the world and her house reflected all this in its muted tones, the splendour of a Venetian painting and the meticulous arrangement of wood, glass and fabric, but if Anne and I were let loose in it for a few weeks Bertil might be as astonished as a landscape gardener whose ordered rose beds have beomce a mass of marigolds and meadowsweet.

While we stayed at the Yacht Club there was considerable coming and going, and the paint came off *Moonraker*'s decks as the spike-heels of some of our women guests dug into it. They were charming, and offered to take off their shoes, but it seemed better to repaint the decks than for them to snag their stockings. In the middle of this the British and Americans started to pour planes and troops into Jordan and the papers to talk about a third world war (as they do on the slightest provocation), so I rang up the Military Attaché, whom we had met for a few minutes at Kajholmen and who had asked me to get in touch with him at Helsinki, to ask his advice. He said, "I've just heard from my brother-in-law [high up, I believe, in the military hierarchy] who says he is coming out here for a fortnight's holiday. You'd better come out to lunch with us tomorrow."

It turned out to be a rather hilarious affair, because we found, as so often happens, mutual friends with whom we had stayed in British Columbia and who have since become famous by turning turtle in the neighbourhood of Cape Horn. The Colonel told me the story of how B. made her first solo flight. Before she went up she said to her instructor, "I hate all these instruments and things. I want to fly by instinct, like a bird." When she had successfully landed she saw on the field a friend who had come to watch her performance, and by his side a high-ranking R.A.F. officer whose face was grey and whose limbs were trembling as if with fever. She said, "Don't you think you ought to take him home? He looks so ill."

"Nonsense, B.," retorted her friend. "There's nothing the matter with him. He's just seen you land."

One thing, of course, led to another and we ended the day by watching the Russian ship *Molotov* (her name tactfully changed to *Baltika*) leaving harbour with an English Air-Commodore aboard and with the strains of "Finlandia" echoing down upon us from her crowded decks.

One of our introductions was to the head of a shipyard that specialized in building ice-breakers, and to this yard, one hot summer's morning, we paid a visit. We were met by the Managing Director (not unlike, in manner, our friend at the Kotka paper-mill). He showed us over the drawing office in which there were models of ice-breakers that the firm had been building since 1945. Their cut-away bows tend to make them rise up on the ice and crush it and protect the screws, which the most modern of these vessels keep in front as well as behind. Asked if we should like to see the latest order from the U.S.S.R. we were taken into the yard to see an almost shapeless mass of welded plates, stringers, frames, bulkheads that, within a year, would become the largest ice-breaker in the world next to the atomic ship the Russians themselves were building.

Next to it (I say "it" because at this stage no ship could be said to possess a soul) was another vessel, a successor to the diesel-electric *Oden*. Looked at from forward what struck me first (apart from her forward propellers) was her immense beam and the shape of her hull amidships. At the waterline the plating forms an angle of twenty degrees with the vertical, followed by a marked tumble-home in her topsides, both of which, apparently, make it more difficult for her to be held fast in the ice.

There was a deep groove in her stern, padded with a fender of massive rope into which could be fitted the bows of a ship that could not otherwise be towed. Aboard, the vessel was a jumble of wires, cables, machinery, instruments and men: all the ordered disarray of a ship which very soon will be running her trials. In this ship of a little less than three hundred feet and with a beam of about sixty-three, will live sixty-five officers and men. They may have to work in conditions of the utmost severity, and for long periods without a spell ashore, for her habitat will be the Arctic Ocean.

Everything, it seems to me, has been done to make them as comfortable as possible: the temperature can be varied to within a degree, there are drying-rooms, laundry-rooms, showers, and a *sauna*. The officers and petty-officers have rooms to themselves, and the men share a two-berth cabin and have their food in a self-service cafetaria. I saw for the first time in my life a bridge without a wheel, a system of levers taking its place, and down in the bowels of the ship the enormous diesel engines and the electric motors, one to each screw, upon which her existence depends. A whole room had been devoted to her steering-gear. It was, in a way, the most impressive part of the ship, because it gave me an idea of how vulnerable in such a vessel is her rudder.

As we took our departure the Managing Director stopped for a moment before hurrying back to his office. He said, "Let me give you a tip. Never be lured on to an ice-breaker unless she is surrounded by ice. She would make Neptune himself feel sea-sick."

The day before I was thinking of leaving, Anne said, "You haven't yet been to the Tourist Office. You promised Major Ek in London that you would go and see what they could do for us." So she and I went along and were taken up to the Head of the

Department, who had as steely an eye as major Ek himself.

"I've been wondering when you would come and see me," he said with a tight-lipped smile. "You've been here a week already."

I apologized and told him how short of time we were. He said, "We think the best thing is to show you something of Lapland. You cannot say you've been to Finland if you have never seen the Lapps."

I agreed it would be wonderful, but I was a little hesitant in case it would be more than we could afford. He said, with a charming smile, "It will cost you nothing. You will be guests of the Finnair on the journey and our guests at the Tourist Inn."

"Would you like to leave tomorrow?"

CHAPTER EIGHTEEN

INARI, the village at the south-western corner of Lake Inari, is a hundred and eighty miles north of the Artic Circle. At Helsinki airport we boarded the plane, a machine with two engines, attending the last-minute rites with a certain morbid interest, for this was Anne's and my first experience of being airborne; but so effortless, so smooth was the take-off that it made putting to sea a much more frightening performance. At first there was a bed of cotton-wool clouds below us, with a few of those upright ones, like soldiers on the march, which, they say, can strip the wings off a plane by the force of the up-rushing draught. Then, quite suddenly, the clouds rolled away like a magic carpet, revealing lakes, islands, forests; a tremendous panorama of long thin lakes with slender ridges of forest separating one from the other like the fingers of a many-handed giant. An occasional settlement, the slender chimney of a factory rising incongruously in the middle of a vast green swamp, passed swiftly astern and I remember a road, yellowish brown like a golden thread running from one end of the world to the other, and on that road not a single cart or car as it cut through a dark green forest and skirted the shores of a lake, so remote that it seemed to bring to life the story Miss Paul told in her book, *Green, Gold and Granite*, of the man who lived by the shores of such a lake. One day a friend came to tell him that someone was building a house fifty miles away. Whereupon the man dropped everything he was doing, seized a knife and went forth to slay the intruder.

After two hours we came down at Oulu, where we changed to a smaller plane and now, as we winged our way northwards, the Gulf of Bothnia lay on our port hand, the sun's rays glistening on its furrowed surface, for it was blowing half a gale. Below were the harbours: dull, shallow places strewn with great rafts of timber.

The Head of the Gulf of Bothnia appeared to the north-west, upon which islands were scattered, as bare as boulders in a drying stream: a wild unfriendly coast, dangerous to small vessels in bad weather....

Again we came down; at Rovaniemi on the Arctic Circle. A brand-new town with red roofs and white-painted houses built on the ruins of the old town which had been destroyed (razed to the ground would be a more accurate phrase) by the Germans at the end of the second Finnish war. Here most of our Helsinki passengers left and their places were taken by peasants in long grey dresses under which, judging from their bulk, were innumerable petticoats. The country changed too. The lakes had gone and hundreds of miles of forest met the eye as it searched the horizon, and so clear was this arctic air that I thought I could see to infinity. Smooth-rounded fells rose out of the forest, but it was only near the top that the hills escaped from the throttling trees. For the last time we came down, landing on an airstrip that was little more than a clearing in a forest, with a wooden hut in which we waited to join the country bus for Inari. Full to capacity the bus jolted and swayed to avoid the worst of the pot-holes, but so steep were the banks, so thick the trees, that we caught no more than a glimpse of the country through which we were passing and of the river which ran by the side of the road. We were a strange mixture: a couple of Belgian girls with shrill voices, chewing gum in the fashion of American teen-agers, a party of German hikers, Finns, Swedes, Norwegians and we three English sailors. Most were students who hoped to find shelter in Youth Hostels, Lapp huts or in the tents which they carried on their backs. The bus shot out into a wide clearing. Small houses stood back from the road and on our right was a broad expanse of water ruffled by the cold north wind. Two Lapps strode down the street, their red coats with fur trimmings, their short bow legs, making them look like small Dutch cheeses. The bus stopped outside the sign of the post-horn: Inari.

It was very different to what is must have been in Halliday Sutherland's time when he came here in the middle thirties. Now it is a sophisticated little place with boat trips on the lake, seaplane excursions to Lapp settlements, tours to this and that. The streets swarmed with Lapps in costume, for on Sunday would be held the Summer festival to which came reporters, tourists, photographers by car, bicycle and bus. At the Tourist inn was all that the traveller could wish for: baths, central heating, comfortable rooms, *sauna* and mosquito-netting, and of these the last was by far the most important.

From our room Anne and I looked out on a swiftly-running stream as it splashed, laughing, past boulders, skirted silent pools and filled our room with sound. Beyond were scattered pines, looking a little shop-soiled, but scarcely moving in the wind. Anne muttered, "Might as well be in Scotland." And I, too, was slightly disappointed. The lake, a hundred miles long and very deep, gave no indication of its size, for it was cut up by islands into something very like the archipelago of southern Finland and not half so beautiful; and where were those rolling plains of tundra that I had led myself to expect, or was I thinking of Siberia?

But these trees, thousands of square miles of them stretching as far as the eye could see from an aeroplane without a single break, surely there was something here that would give this place some purpose, and I made up my mind that it was to the forest that I would go. We went: the three of us spending the whole day getting lost and soaked by heavy showers to return that night with blistered feet and myself with a cold which kept me indoors for three days.

It was two nights later that I came down, while the others were still out, to stake a claim for dinner. The inn was packed, and there were no tables vacant. There was one place opposite an American attorney, a man with whom I had already exchanged a few words, but in my present condition I was in no mood to contribute to his admirable thirst for information. And there was a table with a single occupant. He was dark, powerfully-built, but it was his face that arrested me. It was like that of a priest I once met going quietly about his work in a poverty-stricken village on the west coast of Spain. I pulled a chiar out opposite him. I said, "Is this seat taken: may I sit here?"

At once his face lit up. He said, with hardly a trace of accent, "I should be delighted: it will give me a chance of improving my English, and save me from becoming bored with my own company."

Dr Gustaf Saren was the Forestry Research Officer for Northern Finland and at the moment he was engaged on a scheme for growing trees (chiefly birch) right up to the north coast. "There is evidence," he said, "that they grew there once so we can grow them again because"—and here his eyes seemed to smoulder—"if we don't we shall cease to exist. Once there was a saying that we should never run out of trees because we only cut them down on six days of the week and the trees grow for seven, but with greater efficiency much more wood is being exported and with trees you have to plan not five or ten years ahead but a hundred and fifty."

At that moment Anne and John came in and I made the introductions, saying that John might be interested in taking up forestry himself. The good doctor gave him a searching look. He said, "Every summer they send me students from Helsinki University. They stay with me for three months working in the forest, living as I do. Of the eighteen, this year only two will be of some use. In some ways it is a good life but very lonely. It has to be, for it is only by being alone in the forest that you learn the small sounds, the minute details upon which your life depends." For a time we continued our meal in silence. Then I said, "From the way you spoke there seems to be danger in these forests." The doctor smiled. "There is no danger in normal circumstances," he said, "if you are not used to the forest you may get lost as you did the other day, in winter there are bear and perhaps wolves, but usually they run away and if they don't you can shoot them. No: my mind had gone back for a moment to the time when I was in command of a company behind the Russian lines, in Karelia. We were all woodsmen, if we had not been we should not have survived. For weeks our lives depended on our being able to correctly determine the sound of a twig falling on snow, the different note of a bird's call, the silence which may slip with no tangible evidence from normal to sinister. It is wonderful how observant you become when death may lurk behind the next tree."

The meal was nearly finished. Our friend said, "I would be honoured if you would be my guests tonight." To which Anne replied, "We should have been delighted, but we happen to be the guests of the Tourist Association itself." As this seemed to need an explanation she told him the sort of life we led and what we hoped might come out of this expedition. He said, "Do I understand that you go with your husband across the oceans?"

"Of course. If I did not he might not find his way back."

He drank his coffee in silence. He said, "There is one thing about my job that is not good. It is too lonely for a woman to share, especially one that has been brought up in a city. What I need," he said ruefully, "is a wife of wood." Then, with a rather wistful smile, he said, "My little boy, aged five, has been staying with me. I have just seen him off on the plane to Helsinki, but when I go to do my laboratory research at Helsinki in November he will be living with me in my flat, so that for a short time I shall not feel so lonely."

We moved to more comfortable chairs. He said, "I am so sorry that tomorrow I must go for two weeks to inspect my trees because I should have liked to have shown you something of the country."

"Do you go by car?" asked Anne.

"No: for one day by canoe up a river and then by foot."

"You camp out at night?" (The temperature outside our bedroom window was one degree above freezing-point.)

"That depends. Sometimes I pay a visit to one of my Lapp friends, but we drink coffee and talk all night, so it is better to sleep in the forest."

"But you must carry a tremendous load," insisted Anne, thinking of the things she puts into the pram when we are off for a week-end.

"About forty kilos [eighty-eight pounds]," replied the doctor. "Food, sleeping bag, cooking equipment and, most important, a fishing-hook and a change of clothes."

The doctor pulled himself out of his chair. He said, "I will speak to the Forestry Officer here and ask him if he can take you to the old Lapp Church. It is interesting, but a little difficult to find. I will call you in half an hour." He did so and when I lifted the receiver he said, "If you go round to the Forestry Officer's house at nine o'clock on Monday he or his son will be very pleased to take you out." There was a moment's pause. Then he said, "Will you please tell your wife that she has made me very happy tonight, for she has given me hope that one day I shall meet a woman who will share my life as she has shared yours."

Before we went to bed that night I said to John, "Well, what d'you think of forestry as a career, now?"

"It sounds awfully like hard work," he replied.

The Forestry Officer's house was built in a clearing outside the village. We were shown into the living-room; a man's room with comfortable chairs, a dining table of pine with benches on each side as at the Koivistoinen's cottage. We were given coffee out of the traditional coffee-kettle into which the coffee is put first, cold water added and then boiled for eight to ten minutes.

They were very different to look at, the father and son. The father was short and stocky, weatherbeaten like an acorn which has lain for a long time on the ground. He spoke only German, as that was the first language to be taught in the country until after the last war, when English took its place. His son was tall and extraordinarily good-looking in a Scandinavian way and spoke English with an American accent picked up when he was studying engineering at Chicago University: full of vitality and enthusiasm. The difference was so marked that I should have been interested to meet his mother, but she was at Rovaniemi for the summer because, said her son, she longs to travel and by working in the Travel Agency she now lives in the adventures of her clients.

The father, unlike Dr Saren, worked in Lapland throughout the year. "Surely you go away for your holidays," I said.

His son gave a great shout of laughter. He said, "Father spends his holidays fishing on the river."

The first part of our expedition was by launch along the shores of Lake Inari. After that, for me, it was a slow plod (how I hate walking!) along forest paths, skirting small lakes, stumbling over stony tracks through what seemed to me miles of forest. Our guide showed us a grey-green moss, a little like the flower of cauliflower but smelling of mushrooms, upon which reindeer depend solely for their food. He told us how to tell north from south by the colour of the bark of the birch and spruce tree (the bark is lighter to the south). Once he stood quite still for several minutes, smoking a cigarette while mosquitoes, big as elephants, hung on his jacket like grapes on a vine. He said, "I thought I knew my way here, but now I'm not so sure."

"Ought we to go back?" I murmured hopefully.

"No: we have plenty of time and it is light all night."

Soon after this we came to a grove of birch trees, then to a clearing and across the clearing was the church. Its timbers were weathered to a golden brown and it looked very lost in all this wilderness. Inside it was almost like a doll's house with tiny pews and a child-sized pulpit, for the Lapps are extremely short.

"How much more real would yesterday's service at Inari have been if it had been held here," said Anne. "No reporters, or photographers taking flashlight pictures, and so many tourists there was no room for the Lapps."

We had just come out of the church when a herd of reindeer trotted sedately across the clearing. Our guide looked at them through his glasses. He said, "I can't see who they belong to: I can't see their marks."

"But could you distinguish them from here?"

"The Lapps could. They have wonderful sight, and they can tell their own herds from a great distance by the markings on their ears."

He added, "They never steal each other's animals."

We were now homeward bound at a steady and confident pace. John asked, "How do Lapps live in the winter?"

"They shoot elk and deer and bear: but times are changing even up here, and many Lapp children now go to school. Some do well, but, of course, there are not many true Lapps left: about two thousand in Finnish Lapland. The owners of the big herds are rich men and I too have a herd: eight reindeer!"

John said, "Is there any chance of buying a skin?"

"I will find out," said our host, "they cost about eight hundred to a thousand Finnmarks each but you must never buy a pelt that has been cured in summer. It won't last."

Anne said, "Do the young Lapps go south?"

"No. Lapps, even young ones, don't seem happy in towns or cities."

Rain was now slanting down, and a horrible doubt came into my mind that our boatman might have gone home without us.

"Don't worry," said our friend. "In Lapland there is always plenty of time. If you make a date with a Lapp to meet you under a tree on Monday and you don't arrive till Wednesday, he will still be there."

On our way back across the lake we made a slight detour to pass close to Burial Island, once a burial ground for Lapps. In shape it is not unlike Diamond Rock off Martinique, on a much smaller scale. Our friend said, "There is supposed to be a cave there which has a secret passage to the mainland under the water and when the Germans were slaughtering Lapps like cattle many escaped to the island, but no one has ever found the cave, and no Lapp will ever speak of it."

Our short stay came to an end. We left Inari by waterbus for Ivalho, sailing, or driving, past islands which summer visitors rented for fishing and to a "Hermit" who could not have been really lonely, for the waterbus took its passengers each day to have a look at him. Anne got into conversation with a German woman who had travelled down from Utasjoki by post-boat alone with a silent and enigmatic Finn whose engine had broken down, and the passage had been prolonged from eight hours to eighteen. She had slept for a short time on the floor of a Lapp hut with two old women who slept in their peasant clothes and now she was twenty-four hours late and not at all sure that her husband, whom she was to join in some Baltic port, would remember where she was to join him or to leave the ship and wait for her if she wasn't there. Anne asked where she lived.

"In Hamburg. My husband has a living there. He is in the Church."

Both Anne and I had felt she was at first a little shy of talking to us but now she said, "Before the war we lived in East Prussia. My husband was in the army and fought through the Russian campaign almost to the end. I also was fortunate, for I managed to get away before the Russians arrived and I went to West Germany until it was over."

"Do you think you'll ever see your old house again?" I asked.

"Never: but then . . . the war was our fault and it is no use grumbling if we suffer for it."

CHAPTER NINETEEN

ON our return to Helsinki the Crayfish Season and the Junior International Regatta were in full swing, and if it seems a little odd to put fish in front of yachting I must explain that the start of the Crayfish Season has almost the force of a festival. Öle Öker-Blom, whose wife was the eldest Nordström daughter, paid us a visit (eleven people squeezed themselves into *Moonraker*'s cabin that afternoon) and later he took us to dinner at the Club. We were given frilly bibs, water in large glass bowls with which to wash our hands, quantities of beer or schnapps, for, explained our host, you must drink lavishly while eating. A hugh dish of red crayfish, arranged in a pyramid, was then brought in. A special instrument, a silver knife with a prong like an elephant's tusk, was provided with which to open the crayfish's belly and dig the flesh out of the claws. Slit, suck and scrape: while the juice runs out of your mouth and you anxiously await your host's next move. I have a note in my journal that I disposed of fifteen of these creatures, a poor showing by Finnish standards, for my host ate fifty and, unless the Finns were pulling my leg, the record stands at one hundred and forty.

In the main body of the hall two long tables had been arranged at which sat the boys and girls of nine countries, and as I watched them laughing and talking, their faces flushed and excited as each new impression registered itself on their open minds, I thought what a wonderful thing this international gathering was. A chance to glimpse new countries, to sail against helmsmen trained in different methods, in different boats in strange waters and, more important than all this, to meet each other.

It was nearly midnight before Öle Öker-Blom accompanied us aboard. We settled down to yarn over a bottle of whisky and as time went on it seemed to me that here was a man, and in this materialistic world there are not many, who would like to break away for a spell and set out to see the world from the deck of a small boat. He did not look the part, dressed in immaculate city clothes, but I have found adventurous spirits dressed in stranger clothes than this.

He wanted to know how much water we carried, how we kept our watches and was it difficult to learn celestial navigation; and what did it feel like to be out of sight of land for weeks at a time and what did the ocean look like from a foot or two above the water instead of forty, the only height from which he had been able to watch it? Then he shook himself as if he were coming down to earth. He said, "So many questions! You must be tired, but if the opportunity comes I should like to follow in the footsteps of Slocum or Robinson so that I could look back upon my life knowing that I had accomplished something I really wanted to do, just once."

"It may become a habit," I said.

Time pressed. The weather, "this terrible summer" as the Finns called it, showed signs of an improvement. A north-west wind blew offshore, we dropped out buoy and filled on the starboard tack. Helsinki lay behind us and on board were three happy people freed for the moment from the cares of the land, uplifted by the sudden coming to life of the ship, the most joyous thing I know in life, next to love, as she pushed half the waters of Finland in front of her powerful bows, charging through the smooth water like a buffalo through grass. We steered a middle course between the outer skerries and the smaller islands, towards the Porkkala peninsula, coming into sight of the lighthouse for which we had looked so longingly that night when we encountered, as the Press might have put it, "unidentified naval craft." Past Ravos we turned towards the land. Evening was coming on and the breeze was dying. The smooth red rocky sides of Lill Svarto beckoned us and we worked our way to within a few yards of the shore and dropped anchor in four fathoms.

Anne wrote in her diary:

Ashore the island is first of blueberry bushes and crackling twigs beneath the pines. A wild strawberry plant clings below a plateau of rock. We climb and over the top a meadow lies at our feet. Picking wild strawberries at fancy we scatter and I cross the meadow and climb again a pathway of smooth boulder tufted with green and gold lichen and moss, and purple and blue flowers. In the evening sun the grass is plumed with a golden spray. Long square cut blocks of granite from the outline of a house and a field of vegetables lies in a hollow. There are houses building and ruins of others that the Russians destroyed but although a new house has flowers in its windows no one is at home. We eat our strawberries for dinner and thunder cracks like a whip over our heads, the water is studded with rain and the rock shines blue when it is over.

I also wandered among the ruins of those houses which have ceased to exist since the Russians "rented" the Porkkala area until two years ago, and my thoughts turned to Captain Saarinen and of how he had told me that before the war the waters of the Gulf would be sprinkled with the sails of yachts crossing from Tallinn and other Estonian ports to cruise in the archipelago or race against Finnish clubs. From what the Captain said, I pictured them as a gay, laughing race, kind-hearted and gentle but lacking the toughness of spirit that can be so clearly seen in the faces of so many Finns; which explains, perhaps, the fate which overtook them, although it could be pointed out, no doubt, that England, in the distant past, had done as badly, or worse, by some of the people she had conquered.

All next day we beat against a light head-wind, our eyes delighted by bays and inlets, some of which could be seen for miles, others coming into view at a moment's notice and as quickly passing, our bodies warmed by sunshine, our minds preoccupied by overtaking a ketch of similar size to ourselves with six men and one woman on board, a victory only partially damped by hearing that she was the slowest boat in Finland. In the afternoon we left the buoyed channel and ran between two full-bodied islands, Skjämmö and Einsö, turned to starboard and dropped anchor off a boatshed and a dilapidated quay. Masked by a wood of tall birch trees climbing up a hill was a small red house belonging to the mother of our half-Finnish friend whose sketches, beautifully drawn on thick white paper, had been so successful in bringing us here.

Fru Sjöström is English. She is no longer young but she insisted on my rowing her out to our ship. She refused a hand to help her over the bulwarks, stood for a moment fingering our mainsail, looking at its colour, a peculiar shade of pink, bleached by the Caribbean sun from a rich turkey red. "Now I know I'm right," she said. "I saw you sailing down Kattegat at the beginning of June. I said to the Captain, 'That's the boat that is coming to see me in Finland,' at which he had roared with laughter and laid me ten kroner to one that I was wrong. It will give me the greatest pleasure to collect my money from him when I go back."

We gave her a drink (adapting herself to the custom of the country, she drinks her whisky neat) and then she said, "Now you must come ashore and see my house. Cyril designed it but young Bertil thinks he could have done it better."

The house, as I have said, stands on a slope and the rooms smell deliciously of untreated pine. As you stand at the window you look between those tall straight silver birch trees towards the sound, a level grey in the evening light. At one end of the room is a curving staircase, each step cut with a broad end tapering to a narrow and set to alternate, so that if you want to arrive at the top in safety you must start off on the right foot. This architectural quirk, if Cyril will forgive me using this word, fascinated me, although I understand it is by no means new, but it was the only way the staircase could have been put into so small a space. But what gave the room its character, apart from the personality of its owner, was the gallery upstairs with its balustrades leaning outwards, and as I stood looking down into the room below with not a thing in it that jarred the eye, I understood why Fru Sjöström came each year over a thousand miles to live here for the four months of spring, summer and early autumn. I, when I get to her age, would like to do the same.

Fru Sjöström's husband had been a well-known Finnish architect who had designed a church on Suomenlinna (Sveaborg) at the entrance to Helsinki harbour, which is also used as a lighthouse. He was one of Sibelius' closest friends. She said, "In my husband's eyes, Sibelius could do no wrong. He would turn up at one or two o'clock in the morning and to him our house was known as the 'Café Sjöström.' It was through his influence that I went through the Conservatoire in Helsinki and afterwards became a member of the Finnish National Opera Company. I remember I was singing Muzetti in *Bohèmme* and in Act Two, when she is complaining about her shoe being too tight, I, in my exuberance, kicked it off and it sailed through the air to land on the first violin. Thank goodness it wasn't the drum! Sibelius, who happened to be sitting in the front row of the stalls, said it was the best thing in the opera, but his delight, as I later was to find out, was not shared by my Stage Manager."

Two pictures hung on the walls: a painting of a young girl in deep thought by Risaanen and a portrait of Fru Sjöström with great blobs of brilliant reds and blues scattered above the canvas.

She saw me looking at it. "That was done by Akseli Gallen Kallela," she said, "who did the illustrations for the Kalevala. We were giving a party for him and at two o'clock in the morning he suddenly demanded that I should sit for him. After two hours I couldn't keep awake any longer and begged for a half hour's rest, but I was so tired that I did not wake till mid-day. He had gone, of course, but he had left a note. It was quite short. He said he refused to finish my portrait and would never forgive me. He never did."

As we sat over our coffee after dinner that night Fru Sjöström went back to the days which, I think, will stay with her most vividly, not only because music, sculpture, painting and architecture were growing like corn after rain, in a country freed for the first time since the dark days of the Middle Ages, but because life itself hung by a thread; for shortly after Finland had gained her independence civil war had broken out. She was at that time living in a flat in Helsinki and very soon she found that in a civil war no one can remain neutral.

"It was difficult," she said, "for I hadn't the figure for hiding guns. Always their barrels poked out somewhere. Cartridges were easier, but once when I was hurrying along with my milk-can there was a burst of firing in the street and as the bullets ricocheted against the wall I tripped, the lid fell off my can and out rolled a stream of cartridges. There was nothing to do but pop the lid back and carry on and I remember arriving back at the flat, hoping for sympathy, only to find my husband and a friend so busy making their wills that they never even looked up."

While Fru Sjöström had been reminiscing about Sibelius I had remembered another little story told me by a Finn who had known him. He and some of his fellow musicians had met one evening at a café. Finns, my friend had said, were great talkers and once they got into their stride they became oblivious of time. It was well on into the next morning when a well-known conductor, who was sitting next to Sibelius, suddenly remembered that he had to conduct a concert at a town three hours' railway journey from Helsinki. He caught his train, conducted the concert and returned to Helsinki very late that night, but he thought it just worth while to go along to the café before returning home. He found them still deep in conversation: his chair, next to Sibelius, still empty.

He sat down in it. Sibelius turned to him: "You've been a long time in the lavatory," he said.

I woke early next morning. The sun was up, the Sound a mirror in which the ship's inverted image was undisturbed by the faintest tremor, and as I looked around I thought what a pleasant stretch of country Fru Sjöström had chosen to live in. To the west, a broad meadow rose to the brow of a hill upon which stood an imposing building with a small belfry like the ones you see on Victorian school buildings in England. It is, in fact, a barn for livestock belonging to the farm, whose owners live in a humbler mansion. The hay in the meadow had been cut and stacked on short wooden spikes making it look as if a host of beavers had come ashore and settled in their huts. A raft of logs, from which the bark had been peeled, floated in one corner of the bay, shining whitely like the bones of a prehistoric skeleton.

The big white house to which Fru Sjöström and her husband

first came so many years ago still stands above the wood, next to her present one. In those days few of the country people could read or write, and charms were hung on garden gates to keep out evil spirits, and mirrors on cottage porches: so that the devil, on seeing himself face to face, was so alarmed that he immediately fled into the forest.

Domestic help was no problem, however large the establishment, but now, when the village urchin is tomorrow's physicist and the chambermaid's daughter earns more in a week than her mother was paid in a year, the trek to the towns has grown from a trickle to a swollen stream and domestic help has disappeared, even here. Not that that worries Fru Sjöström. She belongs to the same breed as an aunt of mine: so spiritually tough that she could survive anything (except annihilation) and retains an elasticity of mind that makes mine creak like an elderly cartwheel.

CHAPTER TWENTY

WE were under way before breakfast with a fair wind which died as we entered Barösund. Islands were miraged in the lifeless water and for once I told John to start the engine. We motored down this waterway that the Finns regard, in much the same was as I regard the Deben River, as the most lovely in their archipelago. The narrowness of the sound, the small boat quays, the lighthouses with white faces and black, hooded eyes, the discreet houses are, indeed, attractive, but the wild unspoiled beauty that I love so much in Finland has gone, as must happen when man steps in. Round a sharp bend came a galliasse, her decks buried deep in timber, a jib-headed sail hanging limply from her mainmast. Of all the coastal sailing craft, the galliasse is queen. Her varnished hull, bluff bows, great beam and buxom transom, like a countrywoman's buttocks, have proved themselves most suitable for the coastal trade. They, like the Thames barges, are but ghosts of their former selves with their cut-down rig, powerful engines and huge exhausts out of which belch unspeakable diesel fumes. These ships, Cristoffe Ericsson told me, had been designed by a Mr Chapman, a Scot living permanently in Sweden, nearly two hundred years ago. So successful were they, as I have already said, that they were still being built, without alteration in design, up to the beginning of the last war. There is one, I was told, that still works under sail alone: three jibs, a staysail, two enormous topsails and a main boom that sticks out beyond the transom like that of *Pet*.

We got no farther than Buso that day, for the wind, when it came, was as usual ahead. In the island's lee was an attractive bay whose depths were assured by a large-scale sketch in Ericsson's book but getting there was a different matter. One channel was too narrow to beat through, the other seemed to have escaped the attentions of the hydrographer. I put John in the bows, Anne aft with the lead, and we were nearly home when we ran full tilt on to a "stone," as the Finns so aptly call their rocks, hesitated for a dreadful moment and slid off again. Thank goodness I had not taken the topsail off. I don't recollect much about the island except that we picked wild strawberries for dinner and there were more wild flowers than we could name, but I do remember a couple in a small boat beating into this very narrow place, the owner at the helm, his wife at the sheets, and a charming Finnish cat asleep on the middle of the cabin-top taking no notice of the antics of her home, not so much as by one flick of her tail. She refused all invitations to go ashore, spent the time her owners were away in licking herself from truck to keelson until she shone like a man-o'-war on the Queen's Birthday, settled herself down to a sleep from which she did not wake (to the best of my knowledge) until breakfast time, when she disappeared into the cabin to call the crew.

The wind was so light that I decided, half-way through the morning, to leave the inside channels and take to the Gulf of Finland, a decision I soon regretted, for the breeze backed into the south-east bearing upon its wings the mist. We were now among the outer skerries with occasional reefs between. I streamed the log and took some trouble with the various courses to steer and for hours there was nothing but the gentle swish of the ship cutting through the silent sea, and bare shapes of rock-like ghosts of the Never-Never Lands, uninhabitable to man.

Every sixty seconds the two notes of the siren in Hanko bay grew slowly louder and we were just wondering whether we should wait till the mist cleared a little more before attempting the entrance, when the scene unfolded so abruptly that it was as if the safety curtain had risen to expose the stage.

Early next morning the mournful notes of a siren wove themselves in and out of my dreams. I woke up and when I looked out I could not see the length of the ship. The plaintive notes took me back, by some trick of memory, to a day some years ago when Anne and I had sailed into Vancouver City in November and before we had had time to tidy up, the town had been obliterated by fog. There were four foghorns in the vicinity and their sequence had been arranged (or was it just chance?) in a melody so sad, so haunting, that it seemed to weep for the inhumanity of man, like the girl in Mr Bates' book, *Fair Stood the Wind for France*.

Somewhere above my head two men were talking, one low, persuasive and anxious, the other harsh and authoritative, a situation which placed me, for a brief moment, in the role of conspirator, like Carruthers creeping along the wall at Memmert. I must confess that as long as I am safely in harbour I am attached to fog. It muffles noise and invests the meanest streets in mystery, but when I am at sea it makes me behave like a wounded animal creeping into a hole, and more than once I have anchored on a sandbank on the outskirts of the Thames Estuary with a few feet of water under my keel while the hounds of war, those terrible steamers, passed harmlessly by on either hand.

Before we had finished breakfast, footsteps crossed our deck, and down the companion-ladder came Captain Saarinen with a basket of strawberries from his own garden. Over a mug of coffee he asked what route we proposed to take for Turku and when I told him he said, "You are fortunate that I should have come to see you this morning. That route you speak about is no longer recommended and the marks have been removed." He said, shaking with gentle laughter, "If you had tried to find it last night you might have got lost and then I should have come out in my *Isakari* and towed you into harbour as my prize."

It was late afternoon by the time the fog cleared, leaving us four hours to sail twenty-five miles to our next anchorage but long before we could get there a cloud of fog rolled in from the sea and we looked for shelter in a group of islands of which the largest was Gunnarson, dead to windward. A bay full of rocks was our only choice and into this we crept with all the urgency of an innocent trader pursued by a Barbary pirate. By morning all traces of fog had gone. It was a wonderful day: fine-weather clouds marching across the sky, the water an icy blue. Our course lay dead to windward, then through a channel not much wider than the Thames at Richmond with small hamlets in sheltered coves into which we beat just for the fun of the thing.

Between Högsåra and Kasnäs, between Narmarö and Krakholm, between Hamnholm and Purnpaa, the old ship flew with a grand beam wind, her lee rail buried whenever a hard squall blew down the narrow leads between the islands. On she went, across a wide estuary where land was scarce and quite a little sea came tumbling home (although we were now twenty miles from the Gulf of Finland), never for a moment losing our place on the chart or missing leading marks or failing to identify a sparbuoy, for with the ship sailing at seven knots even a Finnish stone could rip the bottom out of her if she hit it on the nose.

Anne and I studied the chart. She said, "By the time we get to Nagu Sundö we shall have had enough," to which both John and I agreed. Anne went below and soon afterwards I took over from John. He showed me where we were. I took a quick look at the islands. I said, "Between that one and the next?"

"Yes," he said.

"Give a haul on the mainsheet, then. Our course is closer to the wind." Together we hauled it in. He looked round.

"*Not between these two*," he shouted, "*between those!*"

But it was too late. We were now faced with two small islets with reefs off each and a shallow patch where there were no soundings but over which we surely had to go. Anne had come up, taken a quick glance at the chart, another at the scene.

"My God," she whispered and walked forward to con us through before she realized that the sun was in our eyes and no dangers under the water could be seen. Hard on the wind, sailing her full to reduce her draught, I watched the islets pass, the little waves breaking on the rocks. As we sailed into deeper water Anne came aft.

"All right?" she asked, and went below to make the tea.

An hour or so later we brought up within a few yards of Nagu Sundö under a cliff. Of our excursion ashore Anne wrote:

> After dinner we climb the blueberry slope to a path soft with sand and pine-needles. It leads to a valley of onions, carrots, marrows in orderly rows and a garden full of children and bright wooden chairs and red tulips under apple trees. The farm is a long yellow building and some young people are playing Badminton. The players gather round us and take us across the island to admire a long curving beach of golden sand. One, a chemical engineer from Turku, explains that this beach is one of the sand ridges that lie diagonally across Finland from the eastern border to Jurmö (near Utö), which was left after the retreat of the ice age.
> It is backed by close-knit trees and moss, and the play things of yesterday lie about, for there is no tide to disturb them. The engineer and his warm brown wife walk with us back to the ship and come aboard. Turku, they tell us, is a big industrial city and by passing under a bridge of twenty metres we can come quickly to Naantali, a town old and asleep. As their children ought already to be in bed they leave early. We see that it is midnight.

The next morning we took our friends' advice and sailed northwards on the wings of our fine wind, so fresh that we no longer needed the topsail, up the broad waters of the Airisto fiord where we turned to the right for Naantali. Round a bend we caught sight of the bridge under which we had to pass. I had never measured it. As we approached with a fine fair wind the mast grew taller and taller and the bridge sank lower and lower. We took down the burgee and Anne and John, standing by the mast, began a low desperate chant, "We shan't make it, we shan't make it," until I was almost unnerved. But for once I put my faith in figures, and we sailed through unscathed, turned to starboard and made fast to a dolphin under the great church whose walls of dark stone and whose black-topped belfry looked as old as time itself. To the west rose a hill from the top of which the view was something I shall always remember. Below, the sheltered town with its two long streets of timbered houses which, in their carefree indifference to being upright or square one with the other, reminded me of an old French town in Provence; to the north the broad led, more lake than fiord, to the east, the dark eternal forest. Freedom and space . . . and I remember Dr Gustav Saren, in one of his more eloquent moments, saying, "My country cannot perish as long as there are men to cut down trees and others to plant them."

We had just started dinner when the clear note of a bugle burst upon the still evening air. With a concerted movement we left the table and stood, our eyes fixed upon the belfry in the church tower whose shutters had been thrown open revealing the figure of a trumpeter. And as the beautiful notes, so exquisitely played, floated down from the tower I recalled to mind the scene in James Jones' book, *From Here to Eternity*, when Prewit blew Taps in the courtyard of the barracks in Honolulu and those hard-bitten men, the thirty-year men, came streaming from the dayrooms: "They stood in the darkness of the porches, listening, feeling suddenly very near the man beside them, who was also a soldier, who also must die. Then, as silent as they had come, they filed back inside with lowered eyes, suddenly ashamed of their emotion, and of seeing a man's naked soul."

The chorale ended. The shutters closed and we, like the enlisted men, were about to file below when the shutters facing the town were flung open and once more the clear notes of the chorale swept across the harbour, more lovely than before because this time we were not caught unawares.

By the time it was over John had gone, running up the steps of the tower to meet the trumpeter coming down. For the last hundred years at eight o'clock each night from April to October the trumpeter plays first to the President of Finland (whose house lies across the water) and then to the people of Naantali.

CHAPTER TWENTY-ONE

AS I grow older I find myself becoming allergic to large towns where pavements reflect the heat or collect rain in shallow pools of ugly water, but Turku was once the capital of Finland, it has a castle, a university, a cathedral. There is a guide-book which displays its charms like a poster advertising a film-star, so there would have been no need for me to enlarge on this had we not come across a little gem of a backwater, like an exquisite water-colour amongst a wall full of rather dull etchings: a canal with boats, bridges and trees on the other side of which rose Turku cathedral which, though lacking the tracery and the stained glass of Canterbury (or Chartres), has a firm defiant look as if its congregation were expected to keep one hand on the prayer book and the other on the sword. Inside, however, there is peace in the high vaulted roof, the large chapels and great nave on to which we looked down from the gallery.

For the rest I remember only that it was a Saturday, the bus steamed in the rain and I was glad to get back to Naantali.

Our wanderings through the two hundred and fifty miles of archipelago from Kotka to the Gulf of Bothnia were almost over, but the last thirty, upon which we now embarked, have an untamedness which makes them hard to forget. Perhaps the weather had something to do with it too: the wind, the rain and the low dark clouds racing over the tree-tops, and the glimpses of village life as we beat down a reed-fringed channel; the swinging bell of a tiny church at Merimasku and three old women in long black dresses slowly making their way up the churchyard path and then the last straight lead to Lypertö, the trees becoming darker and shorter, more widely spaced, feeling the presence of the sea.

To the north of our quiet berth, tucked in behind an islet, was a building that we thought might be a church. It had a tower at least sixty feet high and with some difficulty we found a path leading to it, only to realize, a little late, that we were trespassing on private property. We were about to turn back when an old lady who had been picking wild strawberries at the foot of a rock addressed us first in Swedish and then in German.

Having reached some sort of understanding she led us through an archway into a courtyard round which was built a house of considerable size and charm. Our hostess told us that of all her family of sons, daughters, grandchildren and great-grandchildren (they were as the grains of sand in the Gobi desert) she was the only one who spoke no English, and as it happened that they were at the moment all away from home this was a trifle unfortunate. Her husband had been a surgeon at Turku and had had this house designed by a young architect who had built the outer walls of the living-room, in which we sat, of great tree trunks one on top of the other for the whole of its length. We sat down to coffee and cakes and I wondered how the crew of a Finnish yacht found inadvertently wandering through the grounds of an English country house would have been received.

"But why the tower?" I asked.

"Oh," said the old lady, "my husband always wanted to sleep in a room with a view."

And there she stood beneath the tower waving as we sailed past, for the first time, towards the blue waters of the Gulf of Bothnia. The weather had changed overnight and the sun shone down out of a clear sky. On our starboard hand rose a slender light-tower, black and white, on the island of Isakari, after which Captain Saarinen had called his lifeboat, and to the south-west were the long chain of skerries and rocks that separate the coast of Finland from that of Åland. The day was vibrant with an edge to the wind which was north of west, and we had just completed a narrow turn to windward between nests of islets when a sail, the first for days, hove in sight on the starboard bow: a beamy double-ended ketch with short masts and a cut-down sail-plan flying the Swedish ensign. Her owner was single-handed, stripped to the waist. He had a golden beard and a wide, gentle smile, but I could not see the name of his vessel nor have I any notion of who he was, but both he and his ship looked as if they belonged more to the open ocean than the rock-strewn channel through which they were now sailing.

Our course trended to the south, the sheets were eased and the others went below to read or sleep, leaving me to contemplate a bare skerry where a flock of sheep searched diligently for the coarse grass on which they hoped to feed . . . until they saw me. With one accord they swept across rock and shale like a charge of cavalry making noises that left me in no doubt that they thought I was a rescue ship. After that I had time on my hands and my thoughts wandered back to the single-hander who was now out of sight astern, and to what made people sail alone. There were so many reasons: a desire to prove themselves against man's worst natural enemy, a last desperate bid to escape from the security of the Welfare State, because they could not tolerate another person at such close quarters, and once I met a doctor who refused to jeopardize another's life, so he sailed his ship across the Atlantic on his own.

The long lead down which I had been sailing was coming to an end and as I stood by to call John to come and help me work the ship through the next group of islands I decided that single-handers are a race apart and nothing would induce me to follow their example. Imagine making a landfall in a Polynesian dawn and not being able to go below and wake Anne, knowing that however sound asleep she might be she would at once come up on deck and share my mood.

There are other reasons, too, of which this very evening was to prove an excellent example. We were beating into a bay in which there were no soundings on the chart and a thunderstorm was rapidly approaching. I had just downed the topsail when in one blast the wind rose from Force 3 to Force 7 on the Beaufort scale and veered from south to west. The sails came down at a run, but there was no room to put her into the wind.

"Let go the anchor," I shouted, but the ship sailed on and out snaked the chain like a mamba after its dinner.

"Jump on the bloody thing," I called and rushed forward to add my weight to the others. The three of us fell in a heap, the chain checked, the ship shuddered to a stop.

Single-handed? Never.

Our good weather disappeared with the thunderstorm and next morning a falling glass and a grey pall over the sky gave us a warning of what to expect. My pilot said, "It's going to be a long hard day."

In and out, tack and reach, but never run, we worked our way along the prescribed route for the Åland islands. It meant sailing three sides of a square, first to the south, then west, and north again towards the finest scenery, Edgar Erikson had said, in the whole of Finland. I looked longingly at the chart, for there was a fourth way, one side of the square, but there were no soundings on the chart, not a single mark, beacon or sparbuoy. I said to Anne, "The water should be deep and all we have to do is to count the thirty islands we must pass (and identify); and look how much quicker it would be."

She said, "You're like a small boy who's been told he mustn't but thinks it worth having one more try."

She was right, of course, for the weather came in thick and in the afternoon I managed to get between the wrong pair of islets, only getting back to the proper channel five minutes before my error would have been discovered. Then it started to blow, but by that time we had completed the second side of the square and had entered the Åland islands between Vardö and Österholm and were in sheltered water. The day ended with a sort of rural conjuring trick. We had anchored in a bay on the northern side of Prästö. Not a breath of wind crept into this lonely place and rain fell vertically from the leaden sky. Among the reeds and boulders were half a dozen cows come down for a drink. We rowed ashore and spent an hour among the dripping pines trying to find the farm that owned the cows, without success. By the time we returned two or three others had joined them. Anne said, "Just look at all that milk. In five minutes I could get all we want."

At that moment a motor-boat came round the bend and a man jumped out with a couple of pails, whipped a stool from behind a hedge, picked up our can and before you could say "Hey Presto," it was overflowing with rich creamy milk!

CHAPTER TWENTY-TWO

I woke the next morning thinking that in England this was August Bank Holiday week-end. I pushed myself out of the hatch. The air was as heady as new wine: birds sang, gulls wheeled, clouds chased each other across the sky like lambs across a field and there wasn't a soul or a sail in sight. It was blowing half a gale so we put three reefs in the mainsail, hauled the pram on deck and away we went like a rocket bound for Tensödevig, the first of the inlets which make the north coast of the Åland islands look as if they have been savaged by the jaws of some legendary mastiff.

Across the mouth of this fiord is a "wandering shoal," unmarked, but which we could clearly see as a dirty brown patch against the deep blue sea. We had our hands full after that. The fiord narrowed, its banks hidden by trees bending in the strong breeze. We passed a broken-down quay at the end of a road, an old farmhouse and a sturdy double-ended open boat which followed us up the inlet. She passed us, her owner standing at the helm with his back to us, but when a hundred yards ahead he suddenly turned and gave a shout which was promptly lost in the wind. Another shout . . . and this time there was no mistaking his meaning. He pointed ahead and then to the bottom. A rock: a shoal? But where? With a shrug of his massive shoulders, as if to say that it was now up to us, which indeed it was, he disappeared round a corner. The fisherman's warning left its mark. We were extra careful. John and Anne were up in the bows and I worked the sheets from aft. We sailed into what looked like a broad inland lake and the wind, which had been quite troublesome, now came in little gusts which played with themselves on the placid surface of the water. There was no sign of our friend and the danger must surely now be over.

"*Helm to port!*" yelled John, and as the ship turned on her heel I leaned over the bulwarks. This was no Finnish "stone," but a jagged mass of granite, encumbered with growth like an old man's beard, which leered at us through five feet of limpid water.

And then I made a discovery that made me blush. In Ericsson's little book was a plan of Tensödevig and on that plan was the rock. I had not realized that he had covered the Åland archipelago as well as that of Finland.

On the west bank of the fiord stood a tiny frame house and a little quay to which we rowed in search of food. The owner of the house could speak no English and we could not understand one word of his Swedish, but by signs and drawings our needs were made clear. The fish he would catch in the morning and a friend would be here in an hour who would take John by water to the road which led to Saltvig, no more than five miles away. It was fortunate that John liked walking.

The fisherman and his wife came to coffee and a drink after dinner that night. To me the lack of a common language seems, at first, almost insuperable but Anne has a way with her and soon people are laughing at her sallies in all sorts of improbable tongues and once the ice is broken some sort of interchange of facts is possible, but it remains extremely simple. We returned their call next morning. Young Mrs Jansson removed two beautiful flat loaves from her oven and insisted that we took them with us. These two, with their small son, had been living here for five years. They had built the house, of two rooms, a barn for their three cows; they tilled a field of maize and in another they grew flax. They kept hens, ducks and geese. The first frosts come at the beginning of September, there is ice along the shores of the fiord until the beginning of June, the sun does not rise above the tops of the trees for months on end and their nearest shop is at Saltvig. They have no wireless and no television and they are so contented with their lot that they would not change it for all the tea in China.

"But what do you do in those dark winter days?" asked Anne, although she did not say it quite like that. Our host went to a cupboard and pulled out an assortment of treasures: ash trays, bowls, pipe racks, boxes, all carved from a growth that affects the birch tree.

Like most new growths it is harder than the parent body and the result was a smooth perfectly polished yellow surface. These he sold to the tourist trade and while he was making them his wife worked on rugs and a small tapestry of their little home of which she was enormously proud and was in itself a labour of love. If times became hard the husband could always get a job felling trees, but so far they had managed to be self-supporting.

Months later Anne had a coloured print made from a transparency that she took and sent it to them for Christmas. A letter came back from Olaf written in English, surprising well-written, so he must have added the learning of English to his other winter activities.

We sat under the shade of a silver birch the whole of that hot afternoon, half asleep, drinking in the peace of that lovely place. I doubted the wisdom of wasting such a day, but on the next the weather still held and we raced along the north coast, past the "mountains," smoky green, on a sea that was as blue as the Pacific.

We sailed within a few yards of a deserted pilot station flying a black ball half-way up its forestay (out of control?) and beat down the west coast, coming to an anchor in a bay off the island of Isaksö. So gorge-like had been the channel down which we had just sailed that it was like sailing out of a tunnel into a wide circle of light and a bay bordered by flat fields. Large sheds stood by the waterfront and to one side was a broken-down slipway, the timbers askew, rotting away with age.

While the others walked up to the farm I pottered round the sheds, which were locked. Through dusty windows I could see old capstans, fathoms of thick, rusty wire, blocks which would need a man to lift them and, in the largest shed, what looked like a squaresail-yard that might have come from a topsail schooner or a small barque. This must have been one of the places, I thought, where the islanders had built the fleet of sea-going vessels which was to make their name so famous. It was an ideal place to have chosen, for the shores of this bay are exceptionally steep-to.

Up to two hundred years ago the Ålannings were not a seafaring race. They were farmers and fishermen, living a hand-to-mouth existence while the Baltic trade swept past them; to the east, through the Finnish leads among which we had just sailed and to the west down the Åland Sea into the Baltic. It must have dawned on them that here was a gold mine on their doorstep, ready for the digging. They had no money, no shipwrights and no naval architects, but they knew what a boat should look like, for with them boats took the place of other nations' carts and coaches, and they had plenty of wood. On the beaches of this archipelago, farm-hands, who were born knowing how to use an adze, started to build ketches, schooners and finally barques up to five hundred tons. They manned these ships with farm-hands, victualled them with the produce of the home farm and put to sea to build up amongst their neighbours a reputation as a seafaring race no less than that of the Cayman Islanders in the Americas.

We were now within a day's sail of Mariehamn, but first I wanted to put into the old fishing harbour of Eckerö to see Captain Carl Palmar, who for six years, you may remember, had served with Captain Gustav Erikson. From our rather small-scale chart (there is no other) the place looks full of rocks, but Ingemar (Captain Carl's son) had told us that it was not as bad as it seemed. He drew me a plan and with this in my hand and a fair wind to take the ship in, we approached the entrance with no less faith than Sir Francis Drake when he sailed down his famous channel. In a half circle we swept round the inner perimeter of the bay leaving all rocks to starboard and brought up head to wind in two fathoms, as secure as a ship could be against a hurricane.

Round the shores of the harbour were the sheds of a once profitable industry. Some were falling down, most were empty and when I turned out at four o'clock in the morning to be sure of getting a fish only four small boats came in with their catch. In contrast to all this was Captain Palmar. He must now be around seventy-five years old.

Short, thick-set, shoulders well back, steely blue eyes which could still see a frayed strand in a topgallant bunt-line, he is as agile as a monkey. When he left the sea he was made Instructor in Mathematics at the Nautical School at Mariehamn, and on his reaching the retiring age they asked him to stay on for a year or two. He stayed on for seven, for they could not find his equal.

He rowed out to our ship in a great double-ended black boat that would have broken my back if I had tried to row her, but which, in his powerful hands, was like a plaything. He stepped aboard. He said, "My son told me to expect you. I have been down looking for you for a week." He came below, sat on the Captain's side of the ship and we yarned over a bottle of whisky. He had once spent twenty-eight days beating off the pitch of the Horn and had then given it up and run round the world to Australia, a not infrequent experience, and he told me a story of how he sailed the *Port Caledonia* over the Columbia River bar on the Oregon coast. This was the Captain's second attempt. On the first occasion a tug had put a line aboard, but as they were approaching the bar had slipped the towline and left the *Port Caledonia*, with a south-westerly gale coming on, to her own devices. Captain Carl had got sail on her in time and had ridden the gale out at sea. By the look of the sky and the falling glass another was on its way; it was now or not at all, but there was no tug to be seen and the pilot refused to take the ship in without one. The Captain's patience was exhausted. "Get to hell out of here," he roared. "I'll take her in myself."

Here the Captain gave a little chuckle. He said, "That swell was bad, and once I thought she'd broach to, and that pilot, he said his prayers. But the sea passed safely under our stern and in a few minutes we were in sheltered waters."

It so happens that I have seen a photograph of a four-masted barque being towed over the Columbia River bar. It was taken in good conditions and it was as if that barque was riding the crest of a snow-capped mountain with the tug in a great black valley below.

I steered the conversation round to Captain Gustav Erikson.

"What d'you want to know?" growled the Captain.

I said that to English people interested in the sea the name was a famous one and I wondered whether there was any story that would show what sort of a man he was.

The Captain shook his head. "I sailed with him for six years," he said, "and many people have asked me to talk about him, but I have always refused." In a gentler voice, he said, "I was too close to him for too long to get him in the right perspective, and, besides, if I were to tell you some of the stories about that man, you would not believe me."

The day we left for Mariehamn the wind was fair. The Captain said he would show us a short cut, and you may be sure that *Moonraker*'s crew were on their mettle. As we swept past the entrance the Captain stood at his tiller.

"She's a proper little ship," he said.

The sun shone out of a cloudless sky, and Anne did a week's washing and hung it all up to dry as we ran southwards with the spinnaker set for the first time since arriving in Finland, two months ago. It was a Sunday, and the Club at Mariehamn was crammed with yachts, but we were not in the mood for company and anchored on the other side of the sound.

We had just finished dinner when I heard a boat come alongside and there was Ingemar.

"I hear you met my father," he said. "Did you get what you wanted?"

"Not a word," I replied.

CHAPTER TWENTY-THREE

THE day before we left Mariehamn the Eriksons asked us to lunch at the Nautical Club. Mrs Erikson had been in Sweden when last we were here. She is Dutch: an elegant person who loves driving across Europe, a woman whom you would be more likely to meet in Stockholm or the Hague than in the shady streets of Mariehamn. She gave Anne an appraising look. She said with a laugh, "Edgar has told me so much about you that it almost made me jealous."

The board groaned under homeric dishes of different sorts of fish and meats from which we helped ourselves. I took mine over to the window which overlooked the yards and docks of the *Pommern* and recalled the stories I had heard of these ships taking weeks to beat down the Baltic against the prevailing winds of autumn. Erikson came and stood by my side. He said, "You'd better spend the rest of the day with us at Styrsö. It'll take your mind off those thousand miles of head winds that lie in front of you."

The Eriksons have built themselves a delightful log cabin, painted black with green shutters to the windows, in front of which we sat in cane chairs, warm and relaxed in the sunshine, still full of that excellent lunch, which, something told me, would last me for the rest of the day. In the land-locked sound on to which we looked lay *Moshulu*, Edgar Erikson's stem-head sloop which, his wife said, he never took time off to use, and around us played half a dozen children who were in and out of the water like eels, for the Eriksons had some Dutch friends staying with them.

Suddenly the Dutchman, who had been half asleep, woke up. He said, "When I was driving a truck for the Russian army during the war . . ." The whole party sat up as if someone had put fireworks under their chairs.

The Dutchman had a smooth unwrinkled face, soft brown eyes and a figure that reminded one of the curving sails of his country's fishing boats, and it was difficult to imagine now, that he had spent years in forced labour camps in Germany. As the war had progressed he had been shifted ever farther to the east until he was set free by the advancing Russian army. They gave him, he said, two alternatives. He could go back to France *via* Odessa or he could join the Russian army. He said, "All I wanted to do in those days was to fight Germans, and if I had gone home I was afraid the war would be over, so I became a Russian soldier, driving a truck for the remaining months of the war."

"What was it like?" I asked, spellbound.

"Their shock troops were magnificent. Well led, well disciplined, as mobile as the Americans; and as brave as the British," he added with a little half-smile.

Jan was at the head of a large shipbuilding concern and his English was as idiomatic as mine. He said, "What shattered me were the men that followed after, with their cattle and women all living off the country, for they were given nothing but petrol for their lorries and vodka for their stomachs, and when they had gone it was as if a plague of locusts had settled on a field of corn."

He said, "I got on with them well. And their discipline! You've heard stories, no doubt, of men being shot for some trivial offence like stealing a watch. Well: that's true. I've seen it done."

Not far from the log cabin was the old farm house which Captain Gustav converted for his own use, and it was in this house that he died. His daughter showed us over the orchard of a hundred trees and a square concrete house built out to the edge of the water, where they held their crayfish parties and dived into the water after *sauna*. Fenced off by chains which had once passed through the hawse-pipe of one of the Old Man's sailing ships was a platform where they used to dance through the short summer nights and I sat there thinking what fun these children must have had before the War destroyed it all.

Edgar Erikson drove us back to Mariehamn at twenty knots and stopped to have a last drink aboard. He said, "If the wind is south-west, work the east coast of Gotland where there is less current and plenty of off-shore anchorages for rest and shelter," and with that last piece of seamanlike advice he took his departure, and we heard the roar of his powerful engine long after he had disappeared from sight.

The south-west wind blew freshly as we sailed away, our thoughts still linked with friends that we were now leaving behind, perhaps for ever, and down the narrowing sound our tacks grew shorter, our sheets grew harder and heavier, our hearts fainter. In behind Åskär the water lay calm and still as a pond. "One more night," begged Anne, "and then you can drive both the ship and us to the limit."

But it was a mistake. The wild strawberries had gone, the flowers had faded and a handful of heather only added to the sudden chill in the air as night came down, so much earlier each twenty-four hours that you realized how soon the winter would be here.

While the others slept I listened to the freshening wind in the trees and wondered why it was that after so many years I could not yet set out on a voyage with the same tranquillity as a farmer plods across a moor to collect his sheep.

With a reef in the main we ran out of our snug anchorage and beat round Flotjan Tower for which we had looked so diligently more than two months ago. Now, as then, it marked a turning point, for that tower was our last sign of solid land for five days.

We lived a sort of half-life, speaking in low tones, moving quietly about the ship while she sailed over the smooth sea wreathed in tenuous coils of mist, bathed in drizzle or beset by fog so thick that you could not see the stem from the stern. The wind, if you can call so gentle a breeze by so robust a name, backed and veered, our bows pointing first at the coast of Sweden, then the Gulf of Finland, at Gotland or at Öland, all in turn and at none for long.

By the forth day out, if anyone told me that I was in the Gulf of Bothnia or at the gates of Leningrad I would have been quite prepared to believe them. Fortunately the sun shone, at noon, through haze and I promptly shot him with my sextant. What was even better, he came out again later that afternoon and I was able to fix my position. To my surprise I was not far away from where I had hoped to be and twenty-four hours later, at dusk, we picked up Hallshuck Light on Gotland's northern coast, sailing into Fårösund, which makes the northern tip of Gotland into an island on its own, at dawn.

This is a military area. We were not allowed to take photographs and had to leave in thirty-six hours, which was no hardship, for, to our amazement, the wind went round to the north-west. We sailed on through Fårösund, turned south and the wind followed us round as we sailed down the east coast, past bays and deep inlets till we came in the evening to Ostergarns Holmen, an island with a lighthouse at each end like the breakwater at Plymouth, and inshore was Herrevig, a fishing harbour so new that it was not marked on our chart: a queer place, all boulders and rocks lying about on windswept hills with stone cottages interspersed with a canning factory and a few suburban villas, and not a shop in the place. But it was friendly, as fishing harbours always are. Men from a neighbouring boat brought us fish, another produced eggs from a paper bag. Next morning a northerly breeze blew straight into the narrow harbour entrance driving before it a short, awkward sea.

Just before noon we slipped our stern-line and swung to the wind. Heads popped out, men swung their legs over bulwarks and sauntered over to the breakwater, turning their backs on us but with a glance now and then to see how we were getting on. The topsail was sheeted home, and John started the engine which pushed us out of the tiny opening into the outer harbour where it took fright, choked and stalled. All eyes were now on us and I must admit, as I tacked a fraction late and the bowsprit swung within inches of that harbour wall, that I would have been more than willing to have exchanged the place of actor for that of onlooker. When at last I had time to look back, our audience, feeling perhaps a little cheated, had vanished: only the captain of the Rescue Ship had stayed to give us a friendly wave.

We made our offing, rounded the headland, set the spinnaker and foamed down this rocky coast teeming with coves and offshore anchorages about which Edgar Erikson had told us. The August sun poured down on dry decks, and for the first time this summer we were really warm at sea. By dusk the low pointed end of Gotland was abeam and already the nights were shorter. At noon next day the southern tip of Öland appeared through the haze and I was again astonished at the strength of the current, which in this fine weather, set across the shoals running out to the south.

The wind rose; Force 4, Force 5. If ever I get into serious trouble it will be through carrying too much sail when homeward bound with a fair wind. In the middle of dinner, and with a crack like a whip, the after guy of the spinakker-boom carried away, the jaws broken, the sail thrashing the ship with the boom like a fishwife belabouring her husband on a Saturday night: but John and I belaboured the fishwife, hauled the boom out of the water, sent down the topsail, pulled in a reef, and, as soon as we had repaired the boom, re-set the spinnaker. This was real passage-making weather. The wind held all night and by two o'clock the next afternoon Trelleborg was abeam.

"Two hundred and fifty miles in two days is good going," I said, "let's go and have a look at Sweden." So into Trelleborg we sailed.

That night the weather changed. Rain slanted down across the empty quay and while I was ashore the glass fell another tenth, and now, in case you are unfamiliar with these waters I must explain what we had to do. Trelleborg lies on the south coast of Sweden and at the south-west corner, eight miles to the west of the town, shoals, like an underwater peninsula, extend almost due south for ten miles. All we had to do was to clear these shoals before altering course for the Sound and for Copenhagen. The wind was east, Force 6, visibility poor, the rain heavy.

With a couple of reefs in the main we ran out of the harbour, and I watched the current running on the outer buoy, which I guessed to be one and a half knots, and on the course we steered we should at no time have been within two miles of those shoals.

By the time we were a mile off shore the land had disappeared. After an hour I took over from John. The wind had backed and risen to half a gale: the ship was pressed in the squalls, the seas were steep and hollow, with their crests blown off by the wind. "Come up," I shouted to the others, "We'll have that third reef in now." They cast the halyards off the pins, let the lee topping-lift go free and lowered handsomely on both peak and main, and at that moment there was a cry from Anne, "*Look over there!*"

I peered under the boom. Two hundred yards, or perhaps a trifle more, the seas were a mass of white as they hurled themselves on to the Falsterbo shoals.

"Get up that mains'l," I shouted, but already it was half way there. Sailing a point or two free we plunged through the tops of those seas which might so soon have been pounding the ship to death, but what jolted me even further out of my false complacency was the thought of how long should I have carried on without being aware of the danger towards which I had so rapidly been driven.

It was a wet, exhilarating sail: the wind at near gale force, the tremendous current (it must have been running at four knots) sweeping us to the westwards. For John, this was his first experience of bad weather at sea and I remember the look of mute protest in his eye when, as he was kneeling to put a reef-pennant back in the rope-locker, a sea swept over the lee rail filling the whole of the after part of the ship up to the top of the bulwarks so that, to keep afloat, he appeared to be swimming.

"Good practice," I comforted him, "for the North Sea."

I had often heard of the sudden changes of weather that afflict these inland seas and now, within the hour, the wind dropped and fog obscured everything more than a dozen yards away.

Had we, in fact, cleared the shoals or not? I said we had, Anne thought we hadn't, which reflected our temperaments if not our judgment, but no sooner had she rather pointedly placed the lead line on the bridge-deck than the thin reed of the Falsterbo Lightvessel could be plainly heard at no great distance ahead, and we were lost no longer. Under a cloud of sail we put into Dragör later that evening, a charming little village with a rickety brokendown quay, more like England than Denmark. I rang up Knud Hansen, now safely back from Viana do Castelo. He said, "I am glad you have come. I have a friend here who saw your boat in California but missed seeing you: Mr Gann, the writer."

CHAPTER TWENTY-FOUR

WE met Ernie Gann two nights later at the House on the Hill at Skodsborg. There were other sailors there but Ernie Gann really looked the part. He was broad and short with a rugged-looking face weathered to the colour of his own deck fittings, and I remember Knud raising his glass in the delightful, rather formal way the Danes do on these occasions, saying how glad he was to welcome two sailors who seemed to have been looking for each other in different ports in the world and had now met at his table.

I said how much I had enjoyed reading *Fiddler's Green*, a story based on the lives of the San Francisco fishermen. Ernie Gann gave me a deprecatory grin. He said, "Thanks: but I have never been sure that that book was a commercial success. I spent two years with those fishermen before I acquired enough data to write it."

After we had had coffee I slipped into the garden and looked across the placid Sound to where *Moonraker* and *Sol-Lys*, Knud's famous ship, were lying side by side. The wind, which had been blowing from the west, had dropped and, with a rising glass, I was a little afraid it might go into the east, putting us on a lee-shore. I felt a touch on my arm. "Say, d'you think our friends would notice if we went aboard your ship for a few minutes?" asked Ernie Gann.

"What about tomorrow?" I demurred.

"Tomorrow's no good. We sail at ten."

So we jumped into the pram, and I rowed him out to *Moonraker*, discussed the sort of things sailors talk about when visiting each other's ships, went below, gave him a drink and brought out the Visitor's Book, but before many minutes were out the conversation turned, as it always does, to other ships and men.

"D'you know Dick Rheem of the *Morning Star*?" "Ever come across that guy Thompson who wrote *Fifty South to Fifty South*?" "Yes, I met him in a roadside café near Monterey at breakfast . . ." And so it went on until I glanced with horror at the clock and found we had been away too long. Like children out on the spree we tiptoed across the paving-stones and edged ourselves one by one into the deeper shadows of the drawing-room. Ernie Gann gave me a prodigious wink. We had not yet been missed.

At ten o'clock in the morning we were at Langaline. The last time I had seen the brigantine *Albatross* was on the films, in the *Twilight of the Gods*, being towed out of Honolulu to be burnt to the water's edge, and I was glad indeed that this had been a producer's trick rather than the end of so fine a sailing ship. Ernie Gann worked his vessel with six men forward, a bosun and a mate. He gybed her round in the restricted space of the harbour and headed for the entrance. It must have been some time since a vessel of her size had sailed out of the port without the help of power, but she had a sad look about her, as if she knew that her master was taking her down to Oporto to be sold, like a horse, in the open market.

The wind came from the east. John was spending the day with some young friends in Copenhagen, and Anne and I were to dine at the House on the Hill. As we rowed ashore Anne said, "I'm not sure we ought to go. If it starts to blow we shall never get back."

We were a silent little party. Helga and Masta were tired, Inga was talking quietly with her father, Anne and I were preoccupied.

Through the open windows I could see the branches bending, and my mind went back over the years to when we had been nearly caught off Great Inagua in similar circumstances. At last dinner was over and I excused myself. Anne came with me and we were joined by Knud. He said, "Do not worry, Peter. The holding ground is good. It is blue clay and even if it were to blow hard your ship would not drag. And look, it is only a small wind."

Blue clay? What had I heard about blue clay? And then I remembered a man telling me he had once anchored on this stuff with a C.Q.R. and a large chunk had broken away and the ship had driven ashore.

I said, "I'm sorry, Knud, but there isn't any excuse for leaving your ship with an onshore wind. We'll go back now."

Knud said, "Wait while I change and I'll take you out in the longboat." So we launched the Norwegian *shaefter*, a wonderful double-ended beamy craft, pushed her head into the small waves which rolled hissing on to the sandy shore and pulled out to *Moonraker*.

As I watched Knud at the oars, his sou-wester pulled tightly over his ears, his long legs encased in sea-boots, his glistening oilskins, he looked as much like a Skagen fisherman as one of Anker's paintings.

Knud sniffed the air. He said, "I shall sleep sounder, Peter, if you and Anne are behind the walls of Vidbaeg." Up went the main and jib, out came the anchor and we paid off on the starboard tack.

I saw Knud point to *Sol-Lys*, then drop his arm with a shrug. *Moonie* gathered way and cleared *Sol-Lys*'s bowsprit by several yards. Knud came aft. "In my ship I would not have dared to pay off on that tack," he said. An hour later we were moored in Vidbaeg's harbour and as I listened to the spray coming over the breakwater I too slept more soundly.

Had I known that I should never see Knud alive again, once we had left the Sound, I should not have slept that night . . . While this book was still in the printer's hands I heard that Knud had been lost overboard off Anholt in Kattegat. It was a great shock: not only had I liked him as a man and a fine seaman but he had, I thought, the same approach to the sea as had Conrad. Few men love the sea. Many love their ships for they look upon them as a means to an end in their struggle against their most implacable enemy but to Knud, like Conrad, the sea was a mirror in which a man may search for the truth about himself and find it.

The wind veered to the south-east. Up the Sound we sailed, past Kronberg, into Kattegat, a pause for dinner at Anholt for we were well in advance of our time-table and I had no wish to sail up the Limfiord at night. Before that brave fair wind we sailed swiftly through the night, passed Hals at breakfast, stopped to take breath at Aalborg, sailed past towns and villages, our wind never faltering, a north-east wind in September, a thing I have never experienced. A night at Thyborön: then out into the North Sea, reeling off the miles like running in the North-East Trades. How different to the formidable experiences of the yacht *Pet* in the same season of the year, more than a hundred years ago. The Aurora Borealis, great streaks of red and green, flickered across the sky while a glow like molten metal hung over the northern sky, a display as awe-inspiring as a tropical sunset in the hurricane season. On this night we heard on the wireless that the towns and villages of southern England, not three hundred miles away, were being disturbed by thunder, struck by lightning, deluged by floods: trains ceased to run, cars were abandoned, and in a town not very far from our village there was nine feet of water in the high street and passengers were marooned for some hours in the upper deck of a bus.

"Pity the poor bastards ashore on such a night as this," said John.

Our brave wind faltered and died. We lay like a painted ship with the island of Terschelling just below the horizon and when the breeze came it was from the south-west. In the chill of the morning we ran through the Stortmelk (so called because of its creamy appearance in bad weather and with a contrary tide), closed the edge of the golden sands upon which the early morning sun was shining and turned into the Schulpengat. Brandaris Tower, dark and square, rose behind the sand-dunes from the middle of the village in which it has stood for the last three hundred years. A boat put out and there was David, who was ready, now that his father was no longer in danger, to step aboard and sail with us for England. I cannot count the times I have lain in this harbour listening to the wind whistling through the narrow streets, for this is a windy corner and I was very pleased, that night, to be within its shelter. The people of Terschelling go early to bed and we walked past the little houses lit by the four great beams of Brandaris Light which swept the sky with the rhythm of a giant merry-go-round at a country fair.

The next morning the sun streaming into the sleeping cabin woke me up, but the air was cold. The wind was back in the north.

It was the sort of passage sailors dream about: the breeze abaft the beam, the ship purring along over the tumbling sea and as night spread from east to west lights appeared from trawlers and coasters like lamps in crofter's windows on the Westmorland hills.

The darkness grew more intense. Looms appeared from coastal lights forty, fifty, sixty miles away and as we closed the English coast (still forty miles off) it was like sailing down Piccadilly.

Never before have I seen the loom of the Shipwash Light-vessel forty-six miles away. The breeze held through the early morning, freshened as we ran down the Shipwash channel on the first of a young spring flood, veered to the north-east as we swept past the swirling tide rips nibbling, like a litter of hungry tiger cubs, at the shoals off the West Rocks, raced down the Wallet into the approaches to the River Blackwater: sails in the estuary, a dinghy race off West Mersea, out-of-work tankers swinging idly to their anchors, the cranes, scaffolding and concrete blocks of the Atomic Power Station hurling themselves into the air like the outlines of Fallen Jerusalem: our generation's accepted view of civilization.

This impact was, for us, softened by a tiny episode. Moored off Stansgate was a coaster, painted the usual grey, from whose stern flew the white flag with the blue cross that we had come to know so well.

As we sailed past her to anchor in the lee of Osea island a man came out of the wheelhouse. I saw him stare, fetch a pair of binoculars. I saw him wave and heard his shout. Men came tumbling out of the hatches, lining the decks. I was so moved by this that I quite forgot to memorize her name, which still eludes me, but her port of registry was the town in Finland that we remember best, the port of Kotka.

Back door to Brazil

PETER PYE

THIS BOOK IS DEDICATED BY ANNE PYE

To Jock who so unselfishly stayed with us all the way and helped to make our voyage memorable.

With acknowledgements to those without whom THERE WOULD HAVE BEEN NO BOOK: To all who helped, encouraged and urged me on during the years since Peter's death until, when even the scattered pages of his MSS were assembled and put in order I could do no less than, to quote a Great Man's immortal words "FINISH THE JOB"

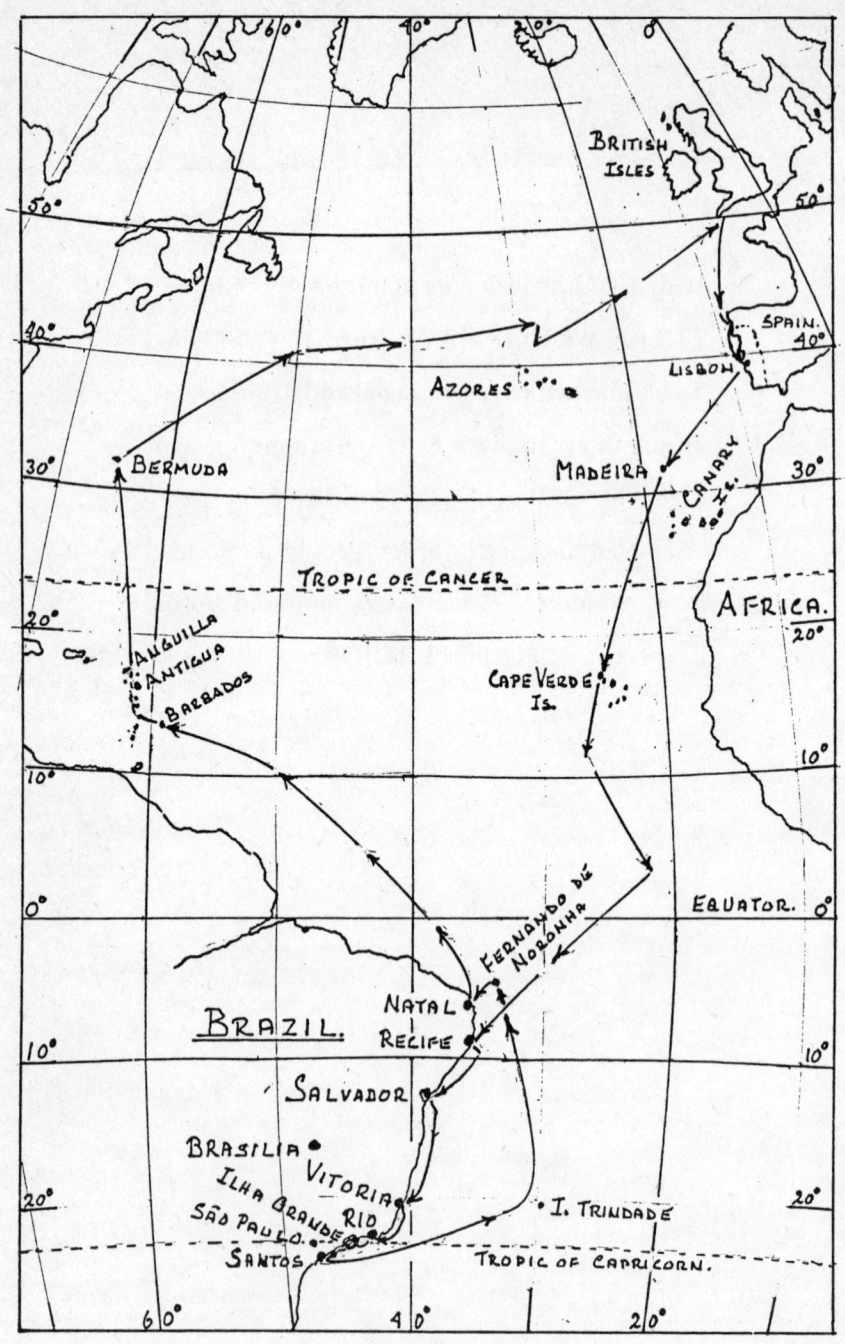

Track Chart of Voyage

CHAPTER ONE

...ure as I remember it was of a dark slab of an ...ts steeply rising valleys leading to a cloud ...ummit, surrounded by a desolation of sea. It ...in and out of my memory for almost as long as I ...

... ago a volcanic crater on this island erupted and mo... ...habitants were brought to England. My wife and I, wand... ...her disconsolately round the Boat Show, came upon a q... ...orner where men were working on a double-ended boat of un...ual construction. They were oblivious of the crowds sauntering by but their Portuguese-looking faces had something of the look of dumb animals away from their natural habitat. One of them paused to lay down a saw and I ventured to ask him whether he would return to the island if the opportunity arose. He replied that he was hoping to go back in a year's time. I said that his island was a place I had always wanted to visit. Now I have none of the hallmarks of a seaman: I am small, not sturdily built, and I was dressed in town clothes. Sparing me no more than a brief glance he turned away but after picking up his saw he came back as if a spark had managed to cross the gap between us. "Are you a sailor?" he asked.

"Not a professional. My wife and I sail our own boat about a bit." He looked at us closely then, and his dark face came alive for a moment. "If you sail to Tristan," he said, "Go in summer. By the middle of March it can be a bad place."

This small incident was another piece in the jig-saw puzzle that we were then engaged in building up. Others were falling into place: Anne's win of one of Ernie's major prizes; a new 8½ horse-power engine from Lister's to replace our forty-year-old Kelvin; an idea planted casually by a friend which grew, as an oak tree does from an acorn, that we should sail our own ship into Rio de Janeiro which he described as the most beautiful harbour in the world; and lastly our meeting with Jock. On all our voyages it has been our practice to take a third hand so that the last fragment of the puzzle fell neatly into place when we were introduced by a friend to this young man.

Jock McLeod was a Highlander who came from Skye and my first thought on seeing him was of his quite remarkable likeness to Prince Philip when the Prince was a young man. He was a soldier who had had to retire through a disability which prevented him from walking more than a mile without pain but did not prevent his sailing. His reason for wanting to come with us was that one day he hoped to make a similar voyage single handed. He was an experienced sailor and like ourselves a member of the Royal Cruising Club.

He drove down to our cottage in Essex and we took him to see *Moonraker*. She is a surprising boat. Apart from a rather elegant sheer and a fine run aft she looks as if there is far too much of her to push through the water for her length (twenty-nine feet) and no one, from outside, would credit the amount of room inside. While we sat in the bare unfurnished cabin and Anne made tea I tried to explain that although we had sailed a considerable distance I was not the sort of man who never made a mistake and that it often seemed to us that our sort of sailing was a constant progression from one crisis to the next, Jock turned to me with a disarming smile. "I spend my life," he said, "Trying to cover up my mistakes."

Back at the cottage we pored over charts and pilot books on the drawing room floor reading each other paragraphs from the *Ocean Passages of the World*, and by the end of the evening we had formed a rough plan. After a month in Scandinavia in the summer to see that we did not get on each others nerves we would leave Fowey in the following spring for Brazil. From there we hoped to return via Montevideo, Tristan da Cunha, St. Helena, Ascension and the Azores. And now, in case you think this seems a long time to be away from medicine, as my colleagues in Brazil later pointed out, I had better explain how it is that I, a semi-retired general practitioner with a private income that would do no more than keep a heavy smoker in cigarettes comes to be setting out on a voyage that could not take less than fourteen months.

Just before the National Health Service came into being I sold my practice, our house and most of our furniture which was a thing I should never have had the courage to do had it not been for Anne's enthusiasm. Nor was this enthusiasm entirely for my benefit. After twenty years in a London suburb the thought of living for weeks at a time at sea in a small boat seemed to her to be almost pleasurable.

During the next twelve years we had made three long voyages and many smaller ones. In the three years between we had given talks, written about our adventures and had done locums for the doctors in our district so that I had become known as the "Spare

Doctor". Looking back, as it were, through the eyes of my more useful colleagues this might seem to be a sort of hit and miss existence but its variety and challenge gave us enormous pleasure, not the least of which was seeing how people lived in the remoter parts of the world. It was a sort of prolongation of Weston Martyr's *£200 Millionaire*, that delightful book which for us had started it all.

By the middle of May we had taken on board half-a-ton of stores and *Moonraker* was ready for sea. Now stocking up for a first voyage needs much thought and care but the more often you do it the easier it becomes for you to know what lockers to fill and what to put in them. On this occasion, however, we had run into unexpected difficulties. The Brazilians had never met anyone who wanted to cruise down their coasts. To come for a race; that was understandable: but to sail from port to port (some of them, they warned me, were a long way from each other), in a small boat; that, they implied was the act of a madman, and a mad woman which was even worse. We paid no less than six visits to the Brazilian Embassy and at last we were told we could go if and when a cruising permit arrived from Rio. Up to date, (and it is now three years since these events took place) it has not reached me.

I do not regret these delays and frustrations for they taught me a useful lesson. Patience and courtesy were more highly valued by the Brazilians than gold.

The start of our voyage followed a familiar pattern for I have never yet had to beat across the Bay of Biscay. We were hard on the wind until we had rounded Ushant where we picked up a north easterly breeze flowing out of a cloudless sky. This slowly strengthened until, as we neared the north-west tip of Spain it was blowing a gale. It was some years since we had come this way and I noticed how age was creeping up like the beginnings of a flood tide. I no longer had to fight to keep awake in the long early watch from one to four nor did I become exasperated by calms, or frustrated by crews who would not carry enough sail, and as we fled down this mountainous coast half hidden in haze the suggestion that we should heave-to off La Coruna for dinner for no better reason than that it would be more comfortable came not from Anne, nor from Jock, but from me. It was the start, I thought, of a new era, perhaps more suitable for our ageing ship than the last.

The gale blew itself out and several days later we sailed up the

Tagus coming to a berth in the Bassin of Bom Successo just east of Belem Castle and almost under the shadow of the memorial recently set up to Prince Henry the Navigator, while across the street stands the Church, which is part of a Monastery and under whose lofty nave seamen have been blessed before the start of historic voyages. It was with one of the most important of these voyages that we were now concerned for, although their navigators did not then know it, it was to be their fleet which was to discover Brazil.

In March of the year 1,500 A.D. thirteen ships began to assemble in the mile-wide river under the leadership of Dom Pedro Cabral, a young man chosen, as was not uncommon in those days, for his powers of leadership more than for his experience as a seaman. There were Neos Redondas (Round Ships with square sails), Caravelas Redondas, square rigged only on their foremasts and the small Caravelas, lateen rigged on all masts, some of them not much more than twice *Moonraker*'s size. All Lisbon had come to see them off to India, via the Cape of Good Hope, and if they returned loaded down with spices and gold then, God willing, Portugal might be relieved from her perpetual state of poverty. After the Blessing of the Fleet the captains with their officers, pilots, scribes, astronomers, soldiers and sailors returned to their ships. "These", wrote Joam de Barros the Portuguese historian, "made the river, with their liveries and blazonry, as gay as a spring garden in full flower. And what of all was the most spirit stirring was to hear the drums, trumpets, tambours, tambourines, the flute and the shepherd's pipe, now for the first time going upon the waters of the ocean; and from that time forward they were taken in every fleet, that the men in so long a voyage could lighten the wearisomeness of the sea."

The fleet crossed the bar on 9th March.

From the experiences of Diaz and de Gama, Cabral and his pilots knew about the doldrums, a belt of squalls and calms between the North-East Trades of the north Atlantic and the South-East Trades of the south Atlantic which may vary from between five hundred miles to fifty in depth, depending on luck, the time of year, or the degree of longitude in which you try to cross them. He decided, almost with second sight, to do so more to the west hoping for better winds. He found them but he did not know, for he had no means of fixing longitude, that the south equatorial current was sweeping him to the west at anything up to seventy miles a day. He crossed the line in good time but once in the south Atlantic the winds were more southerly than he expected so that he was pushed farther and farther away from the west coast of Africa to which he had to get back. Not that he was worried about sea room. The charts of that time showed no land between himself and the Far East so that you can imagine the excitement on board when, on 23rd April, a high mountain was sighted on the starboard bow. Cabral closed the land and finally came to an anchor off a river protected by outlying reefs. Cabral set up a stone cross on a hill and took possession of what he and his men thought must be a large island, in the name of the King of Portugal, calling the "island" Santa Cruz. All this, of course, must have been very tiresome for him because he was bound for India and anxious to be away. Putting two convicts ashore (unknowingly amongst the worst cannabalistic tribes in the world) he weighed anchor and set course for the Cape of Good Hope. Poor Cabral. He lost six of his ships in a great storm and he eventually returned to Portugal thinking how little he had to show for his voyage, when in fact he had discovered a whole new continent and a colony which was to prove more valuable than all the spices and gold in India.

CHAPTER TWO

ALTHOUGH modern aids to navigation have become extremely complicated a small boat sailor still fixes his ship's position when out of sight of land by means of sextant and chronometer. Unlike Cabral he is able to provide himself with accurate charts, pilot charts of the world's winds and the direction and strength of the ocean currents. *Ocean Passges of the World* tells him the quickest way of sailing from A to B and the best seasons in which to do so. All these, however, are but a guide, for winds and currents are almost as unpredictable as the human mind is to a psychiatrist.

From Lisbon to Recife in Brazil we were faced with two long passages in which we might expect fair winds separated by an unpredictable centre like synthetic cream in the middle of a cake. This centre—the doldrum belt—was least difficult to cross during June and July and the instructions for doing so were crystal clear . . .

When a vessel enters the belt having lost the trades (12°N 25°W) (Point A.) she will meet southerly winds and must keep on the starboard tack heading south east until she reaches a point where the 5th parallel crosses the 19th meridian. Then, and then only, may she go about on the port tack to enter the south equatorial current sufficiently far to the east to cross it without fear of being carried past the north-east tip of Brazil and on up to the West Indies. After striving to cross the line in 24°W. she can set course for her destination. These three points at which we had to alter course we labelled A, B and C, marking them on the ocean chart as if they were islands in the Atlantic.

As we sailed down the river Tagus at the respectful distance of four hundred and sixty-two years, trimming our sails, as Cabral had done, to a study north wind, we were very conscious that the same winds and currents which faced him now lay ahead of us. The same north wind which had carried Cabral through the Canary Islands and down into the North-East Trades did the same for us (and we picked them up a hundred miles south of Funchal). (These Trade Winds blow throughout the year almost from the west coast of Africa to the Isthmus of Panama.) This is a sea without fear, cushioned by the high pressure system of the Azores from the gales of the north Atlantic; a sea with the restlessness of youth, the strength of maturity, the wisdom of age.

As day follows day and week is succeeded by week time seems to merge into eternity but whether you like this timelessness is a matter of temperament. I remember, not long after our first Trade Wind passage, receiving a letter from an acquaintance who was thinking of shipping his boat out to the West Indies. I wrote, with intolerable meddlesomeness no doubt that he would be missing an experience which had given me a contentment of mind that I had never known on land. I tried to convey the loneliness of the sea and the sky, the light of the tropic moon on the curving sails, the graceful flights of the flying fish, the dolphin streaking past the hull in flashes of gold and green. Perhaps the rat race had fastened itself on his tail or the thought of thirty days without seeing so much as the smoke of a passing steamer was more than he could contemplate but whatever the reason I have not heard of him from that day to this.

Although a first ocean crossing is a thing which can never be repeated this peace of mind returns to me whenever *Moonraker* sails a Trade Wind route. It returned to me now as we steered a little to the west of south for the Cape Verdes:

> The Sun came up upon the left.
> Out of the sea came he!
> And he shone bright, and on the right,
> Went down into the sea.

On the eleventh day out from Funchal the mountains of Sao Antoa, rising seven thousand feet above the sea, appeared on our starboard bow at dawn. There are eleven islands in this group of which we saw only two. Barren, treeless, utterly remote, this is an archipelago to which Anne and I must some day return. However light the breeze outside, the Trade Wind frustrated by the mountains of these two high islands, roars down the narrow strait between them and it was under the barest rag of sail that we beat into the sheltered harbour of Porto Grande on St. Vincent.

Overlooking the harbour the little red roofed town of Mindelo clings to the mud brown soil, and down by the water's edge the Port Captain sits in his office in a small replica of Belem Castle built by some lonely administrator longing for the pleasures of Lisbon. That day we lunched in a house where a Victorian hat stand stood in the hall with a neat city umbrella hung on a peg and two bags of golf clubs leaned back in the racks. We lunched on English Lamb and green peas and from the windows of the room we could see Mindelo at a glance: the tree lined square (the only trees on the island) the narrow streets, the shacks, not much bigger than sentry boxes where longshore men, fishermen and hangers-on sleep on bare boards or in hammocks and the house were the doctor lives with his family and the more palatial building he had bought for his mistress. In the night the wind howled through a pass in the mountains and over the harbour where the old ragged schooners and ketches on which the island trade depends, snubbed at their chains like prisoners struggling to escape. It would make a good background for a novel by Mr Graham Greene and after three uneasy nights we sailed for the quiet of the open sea.

The wind drove us south under a burning sun until in the early hours of the third day out we were gently dropped on the doorstep of the doldrums like a goat trussed for sacrifice. That calm went on and on. The ship rose and fell on the dull burnished swell and the only sound was the creak of the mainsheet blocks and the slap of the loose footed mains'l as it hit the boom on the roll.

> All in a hot and copper sky,
> The bloody Sun at noon,
> Right above the mast did stand,
> No bigger than the moon.

I found a bit of shade on the foredeck and slept. It must have been an hour later when I woke to find Jock, officially on watch, standing over me, "We have a visitor," he said. Not a cable away was a large grey vessel moving so slowly towards us that there was hardly a chuckle round her forefoot. She was one of those ships that carry passengers as well as cargo and these now lined her starboard side.

"Anything you want?" asked the captain from the wings of the bridge.

"A little wind, Sir." She was now so close that I could see the smiles on the people's faces.

"I'll send it along when I find some", the captain replied. He asked the usual questions: where we were bound, what was our last port and then, after I heard the engine room telegraph ring he shouted

"Do you want me to report you?"

"No, thank you", I replied for I knew of no one interested in my whereabouts who would be likely to read the *Gazette*.

This did not, however, stop him from doing so and in due

course I was reported to myself, Dr. E.A. Pye at "Mizzen Cottage", Steeple in the county of Essex for which, a long time later, I paid two pounds. Not that I grudged it. For the master of a vessel to come four or five miles out of her way to make sure that a small sailing boat was not in trouble shows a chivalry that is in keeping with the oldest traditions of the sea.

Day turned into night. The stars came out, the riding light was hung on the boom gallows and we went below. The lamp above my head burned with a low yellow flame and my mind kept harping on the ocean currents in which this part of the sea abounds. Somehow we had to get out of the weak south westerly stream in which we now rested and into the Guinea current, not more than a hundred miles away, which would help us reach Point B more than five hundred miles to the south east. How simple it was, I thought, to plan a voyage with charts and books and how difficult to put it into action . . . I fell into a hot uneasy sleep when dimly I heard Anne's voice

"Hurry, Peter. A breeze from the NW!"

For twenty-four hours this wind blew, as unexpected as a ticket for a horse in the Irish Sweep. It blew us into the Guinea current which only last night had seemed a million light years away. And once more we were becalmed, but now rain fell from a leaden sky, moisture dropped from the cabin walls, the bread went green, the pineapples rotted as they swung from a beam and the rain hissed as it struck the lifeless sea, drops bouncing off its flat grey surface like bullets off an armoured car. Lower and lower dropped the dun coloured ceiling like that of a room in one of those sinister German Inns I remember reading about as a child in which it slowly closes on the helpless prisoner. But now there was movement. Trails of vapour swept over the top of the mast and across the pock-marked sea a hard line flecked with white advanced towards us. We donned the tops'l and before the yard was stowed in the scuppers the squall struck the vessel.

Under shortened canvas *Moonraker* plunged into the most unpleasant week that any of us could remember. The sea was short and steep, the decks were smothered in spray and down in the cabin, which we now called "the cave", rivers of sweat poured off our bodies if we so much as pumped the Primus or crossed the cabin to take something out of a cupboard. When the clouds broke up we greeted the sun with enthusiasm only to find that here was an even worse enemy. If the wind was light we rigged an awning for the helmsman but when it breezed up the watch had to bear the brunt of the heat as best he or she could. At the end of a three hour watch in the middle of the day I thought I knew what life on the west coast of Africa, only four hundred miles away, could be like.

In order to reach Point B it became necessary to beat. We sailed on the starboard tack by day and let the ship sail herself on the port tack at night. There is a line in Anne's diary which sums it up in a single line. "The whole of living is to stay quite still and not by movement to aggravate oneself into a flame."

22nd July. Point B, if it were an island two thousand feet high would at last be in sight. When we reach it, the ship is put about, the sheets are eased and so susceptible is the human frame to its surroundings that the air immediately seems fresher, the ship has grown to twice the size she was yesterday and Recife is a great deal nearer. Twenty-four hours later we cross the sixty miles of Dead Water between the two currents and enter the south equatorial current.

We were now deep in the South-East Trades. Having read of more than one crossing of this sea in the winter I had expected a rough and gloomy passage but the sun shone and the white cotton wool clouds sailed across the sky as they do in story books of the sea, and the sweat and toil of those past eight days vanished from our minds. We crossed the "Line" on the 24th meridian passing from high summer to the depths of winter without a drop in temperature, and each day the Southern Cross rose higher in the sky. In eight days we sailed a thousand miles. Six hundred miles from land the first frigate bird with its long white tail swooped and dived round the tops'l and we passed, no farther than twenty yards away, two sleeping whales lying side by side as if in bed together. The ocean swell became a short choppy sea as it reached the continental shelf and the Trade Wind clouds built up into great masses of cumulus from the bases of which rain drove over the sea in front of the squally wind.

Before dawn on 1st August a red glow like that from a setting sun behind layers of cloud appeared on the starboard bow: the glare from the city of Recife still fifty miles away. I came up before ten o'clock that morning to take over from Jock but before doing so I climbed to the crosstrees and there, running north and south was the coast line of a continent as new to us as it had been to Cabral.

A landfall should be the consummation of the navigator's art but this was a bad one. Just a line of tree covered hills with no distinctive feature.

"See anything?" called Jock.

"Brazil is there but where Recife has got to I don't know." And then, just as I was about to come down, I saw a church perched on a hill to the south and at the extreme range of my vision four great towers standing in a row, the skyscrapers of Recife. The Brazilian current which, near the coast, turns back on itself to run in a northerly direction, was running much harder than I had allowed for. It took us all that day to overcome that current and late in the afternoon, against the outlines of this modern city which we were at last approaching, my eye caught a glimpse of what looked like the triangular fin of an enormous shark. As it topped a sea it revealed itself as a raft with a long low triangular sail, two men standing aft, one straining at a steering oar, the other nonchalantly threading bait on hooks. Cinnamon brown, in torn shirts and shorts, they approached at a tremendous pace crossing our bows not twenty yards away without so much as a glance in our direction as they disappeared into the murk of an advancing squall to return to the distant past to which their vessel so obviously belonged.

It was almost dark before we reached the harbour breakwaters and started to beat, half-blinded by rain and the strong gusty wind, up the channel which is in fact a river running between a reef a mile-and-a-half long and the city itself. Here were all the ingredients of a modern industrial port: cranes, shutes and tugs covered in a haze of smoke from the funnels of steamers anchored in this narrow place.

As Anne, shivering with cold, bent down with both hands to release the jib sheet below a foot of water she shouted to Jock, "If this is Recife we might just as well have gone to Liverpool."

When the last freighter lay astern and we came opposite a swing bridge which no longer swings, we dropped anchor.

Anne went below to put the cabin straight while Jock and I, soaked to the skin, padded about the decks coiling stiff refractory halyards, beating the sodden mains'l into something of a harbour stow, lashing our sails to the mast hoop, the exact shape, I suddenly thought, of the ones through which I tried to hit a croquet ball more then fifty years ago.

Slamming the hatch behind him Jock followed me down out of the rain-soaked night.

Transformation.

Gone were the drab sea covers and on the polished table laid out like dead mice outside our cat's front door lay treasures lost, now found: a spoon, a broken pencil, a shackle pin and a favourite knife given me many years ago by an ancient Baltic seaman living in North Carolina who had once sailed before the mast in the only seven masted schooner to plough the wastes of the Pacific.

Relaxed, our minds blurred by the startling thought of a whole night in, the first for twenty-two days, we sat down to dinner.

CHAPTER THREE

I woke at six o'clock next morning, slipped on a pair of shorts and went up on deck. Lorries filled with sugar cane rumbled over the iron bridge towards the docks on one side of me: the sea thundered on the reef on the other.

On land the off-white towers of concrete dwarfed the old churches and warehouses on Recife island from which this city started, and in the channel up which we had sailed last night an old schooner, her patched sails gleaming whitely against the dark cloud of a passing squall, beat patiently past a modern freighter while the sails of small trading sloops like those we had seen on our first voyage to the West Indies came winging down the river.

My mind went back to our own immediate problem. Owing to our unusual method of travelling by sail instead of by air our visas for ninety days had expired two days ago so that when we entered the Policia Maritima on the Recife side of the iron bridge I had no idea when we were likely to come out of it. There was also the cruising licence for which we had not waited.

The hours we spent there were so confusing that I shall describe this first meeting with officialdom as Anne wrote it in her diary, for she at least could speak a few words of Portuguese having studied her Hugo while on passage.

She wrote: "The rest of the day is spent with the Maritime Police in a building of peeling yellow stone. Sitting on a wooden bench on the top floor we see men come and go as on a stage. The "Bus Conductor" in full police uniform, his hat pushed back on his head, the Fat Inquisitor who watches us out of the corner of his eye while he reads the paper, the Fatherly One with gentle eyes who tells us how he fishes for 'le sport', the Ardent One with the forward bent stomach and dark eyes who asks admiring questions, learns how we keep our watches and shows *Moonraker* to everyone who passes opening the shutters to do so, and Abrahmo Fazio, owner of a powdered milk factory who came to help us because he is a member of the Yacht Club and was taught English twenty-five years ago by an old English lady who made him sing Three Blind Mice at the end of each lesson. There was the Head Man who, when leaving, offered me his office to use 'as my home', the Customs man who had to write so many papers that it was dark before he could let us go and was sorry for the work we had made him do, the Press who seemed better fed than the others and the doctor's assistant who did the work while Dr. Barbosa manœuvred me into a corner to tell me about his asthma, that cortizone made him giddy, about his singing lessons and his voice which is bass although he speaks on a high light note. . . . And down below the howls of the women arrested last night as they peer out like animals behind the bars of their cells."

With the last papers signed, the last handshakes exchanged, the "Bus Conductor" escorted us down the stone stairs and out to our dinghy. Elegantly he bowed to Anne: "The city," he said, "is yours. Leave your boat here where she is safe." The city was ours. We had found the back door to Brazil.

Our visas had cost us nothing and were valid for a year. And the cruising licence? No one in Recife had ever heard of it.

Three rivers flow through the heart of this city: the bridges which cross them are pleasing to the eye and you will come across other small humpbacked bridges spanning quiet backwaters. On this somewhat slender resemblance Recife is known as the Venice of Brazil.

On hoardings and walls are hugh photographs of politicians enlarged to more than life size and from loudspeakers strung from lamp posts voices bellow to passers by, who seem utterly indifferent, although the elections are only a month away. There are slogans on the walls too, but the main appeal is through sound rather than sight for in this city of a million people, more than five hundred thousand cannot read or write.

To me it was a muddling city in which I got lost every time I went out by myself: the squares looked all alike, as did the churches and the broad main streets and it even took Anne, who has a well developed bump of locality, two days to re-find the padaria (bakery) where we had been interviewed by Television as we bought our bread that first night. It stood on the corner of a tree-lined square and as soon as we entered it the manager came out from behind the counter and shook us warmly by the hand. He had seen himself grouped with us on the T.V. screen since when business had doubled. He gave us a kilo of "raivas", so called because they melt in your mouth so fast that they fill you with rage because you cannot ever eat enough to satisfy you. He plied us with cafezinho, thick black coffee in tiny cups half-filled with sugar, and with talk. He had come out from Italy when he was sixteen and now his own country never entered his thoughts. As he said good-bye he turned to Anne.

"Always buy food in the market. It is the best and cheapest in Brazil but you should get there before eight o'clock."

At that hour the market is a daunting place, the great square packed with all forms of humanity of every sort of colour: well-dressed housewives with servants to carry their purchases, shop-keepers buying in bulk and the rest like ourselves buying a kilo of this and that, but when the stall holders realized that Anne was a stranger with only a smattering of Portuguese their first quesiton was always:

"És Alemăo, Senhora?"

"Nao, Senhor, Sou Ingles." A string of questions would follow with much laughter and many gestures. As she fumbled with the strange currency her purse would be taken out of her hand, the appropriate note extracted and the change given back with the purse. Not once was she given short measure.

Caught in the thrusting gossiping throng a lorry gently panted like an elephant making up its mind whether to trample through the jungle. On the front were painted the words "Sou mais grande que vossi" a truism ignored by mothers and children who exchanged good natured banter with the chocolate coloured driver. We wandered down the aisles of the covered market past meat and poultry stalls, pottery, peasant-made lace, rush baskets, crystals: anything from a clay figurine to a bicycle.

At last, loaded down with potatoes, abacaxi (pineapples at 6d each), oranges, bananas and eggplant, we made our way home past the lorry which had not moved. The driver was helping a stall holder whose pile of water melons had collapsed in front of the wheels.

To the north of Recife, but as closely associated with it as Leith is with Edinburgh, lies the town of Olinda. Four hundred years ago the Portuguese had established a trading post on this natural harbour (the only one in six hundred miles of coastline) where ships could load and unload undisturbed by the scene of the sea. The advantages of this place, however, had not gone unnoticed by the French who attacked it but in insufficient strength to capture it. When news of this attack reached Salvador, four hundred miles to the south, the Governor sent Dom Duarte Quelho to look to its defences. Quelho was a soldier so that, as he sailed up the coast, it was to the hill to the north of Recife, the only hill and therefore easy to defend, that his attention was first drawn.

"O que linda situaçam para funda uma villa," he cried. So a town was built on the slopes of this noble hill with its magnificent palm trees. It became known as Olinda—The Beautiful.

Nor did he neglect the defences of the harbour, building two forts to prevent the recurrence of an attack by the French. Quelho, by the standards of those days, was both energetic and humane, trading nails and geegaws for land, and only driving the Indians out if they were foolish enough to want to hold on to it. Sugar plantations spread out in a broad periphery of up to twenty-five miles from the coast, slaves were dragged out of the stinking holds of ships that now sailed from Portuguese West Africa all the year round. Agricultural machinery, stores, guns, ammunition, tiles and marble for the churches came from Portugal, gold and silver from Peru. But Recife, whose business houses, warehouses and docks, criss-crossed by narrow mean streets were still confined to the small Recife island, remained the back door to its prosperous and growing neighbour in whose houses tycoons and their wives dined too well, if the illustrations of this period are to be believed, off tables groaning under the weight of gold and silver plate. Over a period of not more than twenty-five years Olinda became not only the richest city in Brazil but in the whole of the Portuguese empire.

Her greatness, however, was to be short lived. At the end of the sixteenth century the Dutch invaded at several points along five hundred miles of coastline. It was a private war (Portugal and Holland remaining officially at peace) instigated by the notorious greed of the Amsterdam merchants, and it dragged on for fifty years, each side behaving and fighting as ingloriously as the other. Eventually the invaders were thrown out but not before Olinda was razed to the ground by a fire, a disaster from which she never recovered. By the time the town was rebuilt Recife had overflowed on to the plain and established itself as a growing industrial city. It is now the third largest in the country.

Friends drove us along the mile long road which crosses the swamps flanking the Beribe river to enter this quiet backwater which might well have been a small town in one of the remoter parts of Portugal. Upon the brow of the hill stands the church, with the seminary just below it; these were the only buildings to escape destruction on the night the Dutch burned the town. As I looked down on the narrow empty streets and the decaying buildings I thought how extraordinary it was that the rich of Recife had not moved in lock, stock and barrel out of that noisy city like their predecessors had done when Olinda was first built. My hostess said, "All this land belongs to the church. They will not sell a yard of it to state, industry or to private individuals."

The church itself was empty. Paintings of angels on clouds as round and billowing as the Neos Redondas of Dom Pedro Cabral's fleet decorated the ceiling of the nave but the statuary and ornaments with which these Portuguese churches seem sometimes overcrowded were not for the most part there. It was as if I were in the presence of an old man who had fought his battles, not always with success, but who had learned to accept the future with faith.

On the west side of the hill the slope was more gentle as it dropped away to the plain. At first glance it looked like a sea of rich tropical vegetation but when your eyes became accustomed to the depths of light and shade you saw that it concealed a sort of secret village of tiny mud huts roofed with corrugated iron or thatched with pandannus wherever the ground was flat enough for it to rest on. Each was the centre of a battle against near starvation which the thin care worn mothers and their brood of pot-bellied listless children did not always win.

"They live on black beans," said our hostess, "if they find enough soil to grow them, but if the 'husband' (these people cannot afford the luxury of marriage) finds a job they would add to this a little rice, if there is any."

"Ordre e Progresso," quoted Anne from the words on our Brazilian flag, "seems to have a long way to go."

"It has, these, the peasants, are the forgotten people. There is no basic wage, no schooling for their children and therefore no young to clamour indignantly for a better life, and they have a curious stubborn acceptance which may help them to live but does not call attention to their hardships."

That these people were more fortunate than those living within the city we were soon to find out. The very next morning when I came up to bail out the dinghy before going to market I found it, and its painter, gone. The old ferryman was just passing with a passenger and I called out to him, asking him if he would come alongside. Very fortunately this man spoke perfect English and he kindly offered to come with me to the Maritime Police so that within a few minutes we were being taken down the harbour in the Police launch at ten knots. We searched the reef, the docks, the backwaters on the further side of Recife island: in vain.

The launch then turned upstream towards the red roofs of a village which could be seen from our anchorage. "The captain thinks," said my interpreter, "we may find your boat at the Bad Village. He is going there now." "Why should it be called the Bad Village?" I asked. "Because the boys from there have torn down the lamp posts on the bridge so often that the city can no longer pay to have them put back."

Extensive mud banks narrow the channel near the bridge and the launch nosed her way along the bank with caution. The village lies sheltered from the Trade Wind by a thick belt of trees so that the sun beats down on the flat rocky ground with a glare that hurt the eyes. At first I thought there was no one here at all. The huts, no less poor than those in the village in the woods, were crowded together without shade, their water supply a rusty oil drum filled from the single tap which supplied this large place. My interpreter friend smiled: "You can be sure that we have been anxiously watched for the last ten minutes. The inhabitants have gone to ground."

But at last I saw a dark object on the shore which I identified through glasses as being our dinghy. The launch swung for the bank and when she touched my friend and I jumped from the bows and strolled over to the boat on which a tall lanky youth had rested a proprietary hand. A little to one side stood two old men, their faces half hidden by grey stubble out of which peered two pairs of watchful eyes, ready to see fair play.

"Where did you find this boat?" asked my friend of the boy.

"On the reef. My father and I were fishing."

"Where is your father now?"

"Fishing."

I said, "The dinghy would not have been blown from the ship to the reef. The wind would blow it the other way." The two old men spoke in unison as if rehearsing a part: "Before dawn," they said, "it was blowing off the land."

"Did you know the boat belonged to the Inglesei?"

"Si, Senhor."

"Then why did you not return it to them, or to the Police?"

There followed a long conversation of which I could not understand a single word. My Brazilian friend turned to me; "Do you not think it possible that the knot in the rope became undone?" The rope is not cut." I said I had never known a clove hitch by Jock to undo itself but I could see that he was not convinced. I said, "What do you suggest I do?" He gave an expressive shrug of his shoulders. "Give the boy a conto." (A conto at this time was about 15/-.)

We stuffed some coconut fibre into the hole in the bottom of the boat and carried it down to the water with the help of the boy and the two old men who were now smiling broadly. The boy came too as I had brought no money with me. As the launch turned cautiously my Brazilian friend made a sweeping gesture over the peninsula upon which the favella, as these villages are called in Brazil, stood. "All this," he said, "had been marked down for the city airport (it was indeed so marked on our chart), They had cleared the bush and were about to begin laying down the concrete runway when on a dark night forty families from the destitute streets of Recife crossed the bridge and before morning each family had erected four corner posts on top of which they had laid bits of corrugated iron to make a roof. Now we have a law in this State which says that once a man has established a roof over his head he cannot be turned out. So they had to put the airport somewhere else."

When we got back to *Moonraker* everyone came aboard for a drink. The boy's eyes grew round with wonder at the pictures on the walls, the books and the brightly coloured cushions and the carpet on the floor although heaven knows it is simple and homely enough. Anne showed him the galley where we cooked and our three "dog dishes" out of which we eat at sea and made him laugh by miming a scene of what it was like to eat when the ship was trying to stand on her head. We parted with expressions of mutual esteem and the police took the boy back to the village in their launch. We then rowed our friend to the Pernambuco Yacht Club for which he had set out some three hours ago.

We thanked him for all he had done to help us. "Nada, nada," he said. "Everything has been brought to a satisfactory conclusion. The thief was pleased with his conto, the police were pleased that the Englishman had not made too much fuss, you were pleased that you got back your boat and I am delighted to have made your acquaintance."

CHAPTER FOUR

WE should not have stayed in Recife for so long a time had it not been for our meeting the Professor of Otolaryngology at the University. De Sá has been a Pernambucano name for centuries both in politics and medicine. In the professor's drawing room hangs a portrait of his father, professor of surgery until he died in harness, a man with a dedicated look, dedicated to medicine to which he adhered against the constant appeal of his friends to enter the political scene. The son had little of the look of his father. He was a big man with high cheek bones and a rather flat face as if some Lowland blood had become mixed with his Portuguese ancestry at the time of the Dutch invasion. He wore thick heavy rimmed glasses but when he took them off you were faced with a pair of friendly brown eyes which nevertheless regarded you shrewdly as if weighing up your true potentialities. If I were a student I would expect to have to work for his favours.

The professor had called on us on a Saturday afternoon, bringing his small sloop smartly alongside with the assured manner of the single-handed sailor. A boat that was sailing in company followed his example and soon the professor, an anaesthetist, a psychiatrist and a physician, with a couple of medical students, were sitting in our cabin. The doctors all spoke fluent American, behaving with a boyish enthusiasm which, I remember, became slightly embarrassing when they heard that I had been a general practitioner in a London suburb. "In Brazil," they said in unison, "we are all specialists. Every doctor, surely, knows more about one part of the humam body than another. Which part is yours?" I had, it was true, given anaesthetics at King Edward's Hospital in Ealing but this was before the days of curare and freezing and heart lung pumps and it would be humiliating if subsequent conversation exposed my abysmal ignorance. Thinking back still further, I said, "I did a spell as a doctor in a sanatorium in Switzerland."

"Splendid," they said. "You are a Tisicist." Little did I know the sort of situation that was going to land me up in.

The professor brought his wife along next day. Anne exclaimed delightedly, "But surely, you're English?"

"Indeed I am," replied Joan de Sá. "Didn't Geraldo tell you? How like him. When he goes afloat he forgets everything."

Geraldo de Sá had, like most of the Brazilian medical profession after taking their degrees, worked for some years in the States and it was while he was working at a clinic in Missouri that he met Joan, who was looking after the children of an American family. As he was leaving to take up a junior post at Recife university in ten days he could have wasted very little time for by the end of it he had persuaded this rather shy English girl to come out later and marry him. One must acknowledge that this was a brave thing for Joan to do for the whole structure of Brazilian life is as different to that in England (where the family is now based on the principle of an equal partnership) as rigid Victorianism was to the post-war shuffling in and out of marriage which seems to have spread across the Atlantic from North America to England. Joan, it seemed to Anne, tackled it in the only possible way. She studied Portuguese before she came out, she made no attempt to get in touch with the considerable English colony which I am told still resides in Recife, but made her friends among the wives of her husband's colleagues and had so far forgotten her native tongue that phrases and words paused on her lips as if she was not sure that they would convey the right meaning.

Only once, Joan later told Anne, did she long for her own people around her. It was at a time when her husband was putting in for his full professorship and, as so often happens, not only in Brazil, local politics were dragged into the issue, for the liberal views which he had inherited from his father did not always find favour with those in authority. His professional life was at stake, for Geraldo would never leave Recife to take a post at another university.

Fortunately for him full professorships are awarded in Brazil by a board from the joint universities of Rio and Sao Paulo and Geraldo duly became the youngest full professor in Brazil. Very soon after this he had a coronary.

Even now, although Geraldo had made an excellent recovery, Joan was never free from anxiety when he sailed his little boat off-shore in the summer. "Why doesn't she go with him?" Anne asked. "Because, my love, the wife's place is in the home. Men in Brazil keep their hobbies to themselves."

The de Sás' were on the point of moving into their new house, one of those modern houses you see from time to time in *Homes and Gardens,* with a flat roof sloping back from the front and with the living room rising to the full height of the house with a gallery half way up on to which opened the principal bedrooms.

The ground floor was L-shaped, the horizontal limb being two steps up from the vertical with a marble topped bar where men could sit on stools sipping their drinks while their wives sat more comfortably but on a lower level. Windows reached from floor to ceiling and in the solid parts of the walls tiers of short lengths of piping, like the guns of an old three decker, increased the ventilation. Joan had planted sixteen different varieties of fruit trees, as well as sown a lawn six months before the house was started and in this luxuriant climate the trees will be bearing fruit and the lawn will be green by Christmas time.

At the back of the house were rooms for two servants and a nannie. Joan said, "When I came out here one of the things I looked forward to was help in the house. That is fine but I soon found there were unexpected drawbacks. The girls have no sort of insurance and if they are sick you cannot send them home because the conditions there are quite impossible. So you nurse them, pay their doctor's bills or the hospital: a friend of mine babysits for her maid's illegitimate child when the girl has an evening off."

Because of the de Sás the doors of other doctors' houses were opened to us although few of their wives could speak English. We did our best, not always with success on my part to learn Brazilian manners. On one occasion I remember leaving the men talking in one corner of the room to cross the floor to where my very attractive hostess, one of the few to speak perfect English, was talking to Anne but before I could reach the half-way mark I found my arm firmly gripped by my host who guided me tactfully back to the place I belonged. It is not until dinner is served that the men and women come together and at table husbands and wives sit next to each other.

Our first party, I remember, had been at the Port Doctor's house. The conversation was a mixture of medical shop and sailing (the doctors seemed to be the only people who sailed through the winter), until one of them asked the professor if he had heard that the free milk, something like half a million tins of it sent as a gift from the U.S.A. to help the starving children in the waterless north-east, was appearing in the shops of the towns through which the lorries had passed on their way to their destination. The shops were selling them off at a reduced price and people were buying them like hot cakes.

Geraldo said, "They ought to have put it ashore at Natal, not Rio. The governor of Rio Grande do Norte would have seen that it reached the children."

"But surely," I said, "the government can put a stop to its being sold in the shops?"

"My dear Peter, someone in the government has probably arranged it."

My host, Dr. Barbosa, who had been growing more and more impatient (he could not bear anything that was either unpleasant or sad), now took me by the arm and led me into another room, flinging open a large cupboard door. "There, doctor, have you ever seen anything like that?" I had not. In front of me were one hundred and eighty different brands of whisky. "Where did you get all these?" I asked him. "I have many friends among the sea captains. They know about my little collection and now and then one of them finds a new brand." I could well believe it. I had once heard the professor say that if you did not like Fernando Barbosa there was something the matter with you. And there must be many small ways in which a port doctor can help a ship's captain. Fernando Barbosa was jubilant that evening for he had, he said, just received a free ticket from B.O.A.C. for Hong Kong.

He said, "I meet one of the directors of your airline at the airport. I give him a good dinner and I show him the murals by our artist Ayries. I say to him 'How far will your airline fly me for free?' He asks where I go, I tell him Hong Kong."

"How nice for you," I said, "but why Hong Kong?"

"It is a long way and I have never been there."

His pretty wife who was engaged to him for fifteen years before he married her was not so fortunate. Her husband's undoubted charms were only good for one ticket.

There seemed little doubt among the doctors here, although with usual Brazilian courtesy no one said it in so many words, that American standards of medicine and the methods of teaching, were higher than those in England: but to this one of them would not agree. He was a heart surgeon who had worked at Oxford. He admitted, later, that his views were biased by the concept of free medical advice and free drugs which, he maintained, must be followed by Brazil if the health of the country, and by that he meant the health of the peasants and workers, was to be improved. This led to a heated debate in which the general opinion was that medical fees in Brazil were so scaled down to the ability of the patient to pay what he could afford that state medicine was not necessary.

"You're kidding yourselves," said Geraldo. "How can you afford to pay for a doctor if you earn three thousand cruzeiros a month? As to the peasants living in the interior, most of them die before seeing a doctor at all. No: I agree with our friend from England. Plan your Free Health Service, then teach people how to use it."

Before we parted for the night the heart surgeon asked me whether I would like to watch him operate on a child with a pulmonary stenosis the next day. As I had never seen a heart operation I was delighted.

The hospital (a free hospital for the poor) was a Georgian looking building built in 1847. The wards were small and most of them half empty but each occupied bed had a little family grouped round it for the mother or wife or some close relation is encourged to live in to help nurse the patient, to give confidence and to contribute to the diet of the patient.

The heart surgeon said, "Our worst problem comes not from lack of equipment but of nurses. The ones we get here in the north-east are usually half-literate girls who choose it for its status value."

Inside the cardiological department, however, there was a brisk efficiency and no lack of well-trained staff. The child had been given curare and gas and oxygen and was now being cooled down to 30°C in a bath full of ice. She was then taken into the operating theatre. The surgeon said, "I would prefer to do this with the heart-lung pump but it is so difficult to get syphilitic-free blood in this country that we only use the pump when we must. With this method I have six minutes from the time I open the auricle to the time it must be closed. I hope to do it in five."

Fourteen years have elapsed since I had anything to do with a major operation. I was given an excellent view but I had forgotten what it was like to stand for three hours without moving a muscle.

Things have changed too since I was a student. Surgeons no longer throw splints from one end of long wards to the other just to vent their wrath nor do they any longer suggest to their anaesthetists that the patient is about to jump off the table or to ask with innocent curiosity, "Doctor, is your patient still alive?" But the sense of drama is still there: a tightening of the nerves that even the best actors and actresses feel on an opening night, for there is usually something of an actor in every top ranking surgeon.

At first the operation proceeded through its various stages with impressive smoothness. Then came the incision into the left auricle. Blood poured out of the heart in spite of the freezing, packs were thrust round the heart to keep the field clear, transfusions poured into the patient through veins in her arms and legs. Not a second was lost through hesitation or the misunderstanding of a gesture and in five minutes flat the auricle had been sewn up. The heart went into fibrillation. The usual cardiac rhythm which had been pursuing its even course across the electrocardiographic screen went completely mad, broad undulating bands galloping from end to end like horses jumping fences at Aintree.

A sharp word from the surgeon: an immediate injection. Eyes wary and still behind masked faces. And then an almost inaudible sigh like the dawn wind rustling the leaves of an elm at the first sign of recovery: the shrug of a gown as the surgeon bent to continue the operation.

I went back with the surgeon the next day to see the child. I would not have believed that any child who had been so near to death, even for a very short time, could look so well.

CHAPTER FIVE

THE University of Recife is to be moved nine miles outside the city. Some of the new faculty buildings of red brick and concrete are already finished and would have been in use had there not been a general strike of students throughout Brazil since the beginning of June. Others have been started but the money had run out before the walls were completed so that they stand like victims of some long forgotten battle waiting for the jungle to move in for the final kill. One of these skeletons is the new teaching hospital in which Geraldo hopes to work. Its fate hangs on a decision to be taken by a government department a thousand miles away which has for many years regarded the north-east as a financial millstone round its neck. I tried to visualize this place as it might be in five or even ten years time. A few abandoned buildings like ancient sacrificial stones to forgotten gods? Or a well-knit university campus surrounded by student hostels filled with the young upon whom the fate of the world will depend? It might be either but I trust that it will be the latter.

Some of these students, none of whom could tell us what the strike was about, came to call on us on *Moonraker*. Borrowing an ancient longboat from an obscure part of the harbour they rowed across the swift running tide to sit in our cabin half the night through.

It was students' talk: about the blunders and injustices of old men who were no longer fit to govern; about the greed of the rich and the poverty of the remaining four-fifths of the people who, they said, were only kept from revolt by ignorance, an ignorance they hoped to penetrate by distributing thousands of transistor sets throughout the north-east so that at last the people would know what was happening in the outside world.

From all this talk, interrupted by much harmless fun and laughter, it emerged that Castro of Cuba was the current hero in whose favour they produced facts and figures that we were in no position to challenge; Castro was in favour today, tomorrow they might have another idol; but of their faith in the ultimate emergence of their country to take a leading part in the world we were left in no doubt whatsoever. Of course, if they had the handling of the reins themselves this would be sooner than expected.

It is a compliment to the elderly when the young take trouble to come and talk to them and we enjoyed these evenings. On one occasion, after a heated argument with Jock, who believes in dicipline and the status quo, they swarmed on deck chattering like a lot of monkeys. All at once I saw the lights of the police launch coming up on the port bow and for a moment I wished our volatile young friends had not chosen this moment to depart for they also had seen it and clenching their fists they were yelling "Viva Castro!" "VIVA CASTRO!"

In the light of their deckhouse lamp I could see the captain's face as he headed the launch up-stream and the grin as he recognized our visitors, and I thought how differently might such a small incident have ended in Brazil's mother country.

One Sunday morning the de Sás called for us at the Policia Maritima before eight o'clock in the morning. Joan said, "We thought you'd like to see something of the country away from the sea. We've been meaning to go to Caruaru for some time to buy Vitalino figurines."

The road, once free of the city and its surrounding plain, ran through sugar cane country: small hills and valleys of heavy tropical green fringed by acres of red brown earth where already the cane had been cut. By its side runs the single gauge railway. We passed through an occasional village, the façades of the houses crumbling away to reveal the basic earth walls, the shutters rotting through lack of paint. There was not a single hotel or inn for the traveller but if you were in distress someone would offer shelter of a sort.

Small lakes vied with sluggish streams where women knelt on the banks washing clothes. Any still water, Geraldo pointed out, was likely to be so heavily infected with hook-worm that it would not be safe to put one's little finger into it.

Mansions stood on hills overlooking plantations. The slave houses were empty but the men still had to accept what wages they were given. It was little more than would keep them alive and at work, but for each there was the sun, the Trade Wind which could still be felt this far inland, the patch of land which though not his would not be taken away, the house, of one room or partitioned into two, his woman who worked the land, producing him as well a child a year. Of this brood nature, through disease or lack of food, would remove at least half.

We passed, after twenty-five kilometers, into open country. The road ran like a twisting thread in a carpet of green and brown towards the range of hills now confronting us until we reached the head of a pass eighteen hundred feet above the sea. The air was like wine after the heat of the plain. Geraldo drove the car on to the side of the road from which we could look westwards over fifty or sixty miles of scrub and small trees with no sign of human habitation except for the wisp of smoke from some lonely fazenda hidden in a trough. The ground fell away steeply from where we stood but at no great distance, running parallel to the road, was a hedge of thick green bush. We were scrambling down towards it when Joan stopped us. "That," she said "is called the Devil's Fence. Do you see these green pods? They are extremely fragile and are filled with a milky fluid. If you tried to force your way through the hedge the pods would break and if the stuff got into your eyes it would blind you for ever."

This country must be like the veldt of South Africa. Green bush fading into the wine dark distance with hills like islands rising out of a limitless sea: the sort of country that drives men to the limit of their endurance just to find out what lies beyond their immediate horizon. It would be a long trek. Two thousand miles of forest and river, of swamp and fever lay between us and the Andes, most of it virgin country except for a scattering of Indian tribes who might well still be cannibals.

Geraldo, as if he could read my thoughts, said, "A friend of mine went to practice in a small town, you would call it a village, in the Matto Grosso. He collected money enough to build a small hospital where he could operate on his patients and it became the centre for a very large area. One day he was called in to attend the wife of the principal landowner for an emergency during labour. In this he was successful and on his last visit to his patient he was sent for by the landowner who thanked him for saving his wife's life and that of her baby and praised him for his skill in doing so. He then explained that as he (the doctor) had seen his wife in these most compromising circumstances it would naturally be impossible for him to go on living in the district. My friend said he had never heard of such nonsense and did not the landowner know that this was the twentieth century?"

The landowner regarded him with a stony eye. "I am prepared," he said, "to pay all the expenses incurred in your moving to another district and to pay you compensation for having to do so but if you refuse I will see that you are driven out of this place without a cruzeiro to your name. And if, my dear doctor, I am not at first successful, you have been here long enough to know that I have surer methods of removing you which I do not at the moment wish to employ."

The doctor left the Fazenda a very frightened young man but the size of the gratuity he received was such that he never needed to work again."

Once more we took to the road (always an adventure in Geraldo's old Plymouth as something had gone wrong with the starter) and after another two hours we came over a slight rise to see in front of us, like a mediaeval fortress built on the top of a steep hill, the red roofed town of Caruaru, the largest in the interior of the State of Pernambuco, a state which is itself about the size of England.

Our arrival coincided with the finale of a marathon bicycle race. We had passed the stragglers many miles back, laughing and talking to each other for they had long given up any thoughts of winning; but as we neared the town the pace became hotter. Legs working like pistons, shoulders bent over handlebars, faces glancing neither to right nor left to acknowledge the cheers of their supporters who had come to urge them on. As we toiled up the steep cobbled road, not much faster than the leaders in the race, we met a crowd advancing to welcome the winners led by a girl drummer band banging away with joy and expertise. If I were in the van of that race I might well think it to be worth winning.

As if to assert itself as being something more than the hub of a wilderness this little town, about the size of Henley-on-Thames, is the noisiest I know. From every lamp post, street corner and from every open window (and they were all open) the radio blared at full blast while the people in windows and doorways shouted to their neighbours to make themselves heard over the loudspeakers. It was like being present at some nightmare cocktail party.

We came to the centre of the town and to a small museum dedicated to the work of Joao Vitalino and his disciples. Vitalino was an Indian peasant whose work was discovered by some accident now long forgotten and his figures of peasants with bright beady eyes, with questioning stoical faces, always bearded, always with pipes, men playing accordions, leading donkeys, pounding corn, men with thin tightly drawn in stomachs as if they were permanently short of food, are now sold throughout Brazil at very high prices.

Vitalino himself, whom Geraldo knew, lived in a small shack on the outskirts of the town. When he first started all his figures were painted in bright colours but now they are the natural colour of the red brown clay. Geraldo once asked him why he no longer used paints. "Because no one now gives me the paint," was the laconic reply.

The drive back to Recife was at breakneck speed because Geraldo hoped, although he was too polite to say so, that he would manage to take his boat out for a short sail before dark. I was glad that this was not a summer Sunday in England. The lorries and cars that we passed that day, unless my memory deceives me, could have been counted on the fingers of two hands. You could see them for miles ahead. Dust rising up out of the plain as if a troop of Bedouin were galloping across the desert. Behind one could see nothing but it was not likely that anything would pass Geraldo this afternoon. There were no cross roads: just a few deep-rutted red-earthed tracks wandering into the interior, unmarked, for the most part, or with the name of a fazenda or a village too far away for us to see even the church tower. It must be about a hundred miles from Recife to Caruaru, a mere crack in the coastal crust into the country beyond but all that land which we had seen that day, indeed all the land of Pernambuco, the size of England, belonged to a few Pernambucano families who kept it as tightly in their grip as the earls of England in the time of the Wars of the Roses. Their days, like those of the earls, are nearly over. Already one or two are beginning to sell and others will follow. It suddenly seemed to me to be rather sad. This land which had been theirs by gift from a sovereign four hundred years ago, handed down from generation to generation, fought over, ploughed over, the home of their herds of cattle. Which of us, given the chance, would not have liked to have been born in those days of great landowners as long, that is, as there was no chance of having been born a serf.

CHAPTER SIX

A janguada same con Chico Feverimento,
A janguada volto so.
Com certeza foi la afosa um pe do vento,
A janguada volou so.

DRAWN up on a beach next door to the Praia de Boa Vista, the Copocabana of Recife where some of its wealthiest citizens live, are a cluster of sailing rafts called janguadas, one of which, you may remember, crossed our bows whilst we were approaching the city.

These boats are of the most primitive kind, built of a balsa wood known locally as acaça. Five logs, flattened on their upper surfaces so as to form a platform for the crew to stand on and tapered a little to make some sort of "front end", are through fastened laterally with long spikes of a different wood whose name I no longer recall but which, when it swells, holds the logs in position. The short mast is stepped fairly far for'ard and the triangular sail is clued to the end of a long boom set well above the deck so that the tack of the sail is bowsed down below the spar. When not sailing the boom rests on a tall permanent gallows to which are also attached fishing lines, hooks, bait and a large wicker basket for the fish. A steering oar, a grapnel weighted with a large stone and a wooden dagger plate completes the simple equipment.

Ten years ago there were hundreds of these boats, if you can call them that, between Fortaleza and Bahia but Recife is now the only port where they can be found in any number. There might have been fewer still had not two fishermen from Recife sailed their janguada two thousand miles down the coast to Buenos Aires. The Argentinians, so the story goes, were so impressed with this feat of endurance that they gave the men a motor fishing boat but, after trying this out, the Pernambucanos went back to fishing from their janguada. Like the crew of Kon-Tiki, the nearer they were to the fish the more they caught. The imagination of the Brazilians had also been fired by this voyage. The five cruzeiro note, worth little more than a farthing, has printed upon it one of these rafts under full sail and more than one artist has used the janguada as a symbol to illustrate the war waged by man against the sea.

As one could imagine, there are many tales that are told about these fishermen: most of them are sad but one at least has an amusing side to it.

One fine summer morning during the war two men had sailed their janguada far from the land. The wind had dropped and the sea was like glass. The men were asleep at the foot of the mast to which their sail was roughly brailed. A sudden blast from a siren brought them to their feet to see, at no great distance, the grey hull of a warship. Alarmed for their safety, for the ship was coming straight towards them, they waved their arms and shouted. The destroyer turned full circle and came up alongside. A big man with gold braid on the peak of his cap leaned over the wing of the bridge: from the deck a line of faces looked down upon them. A rope ladder was lowered and they understood from signs that they were being invited aboard but now a breeze had sprung up and they wanted to sail for home. They shook their heads. More shouts, and this time they shouted back in Portuguese. The captain's face grew red with anger, for his ship, as long as she remained stationary, was a sitting duck for a torpedo. He barked an order. Men came down the ladder and before the crew of the janguada had time to defend themselves they were removed to the deck of the destroyer which immediately got under way, leaving the janguada rocking in her fast retreating wake.

In two or three days they came to a strange harbour. Again they were taken before the captain whose language they could not understand. With him was a Brazilian who seemed to be enjoying a joke. He spoke to them in their own language. "Commander X. of the British Royal Navy wishes to offer you his apologies. He mistook you for survivors from a torpedoed vessel and your janguada for a raft. He wishes me to tell you that you will be compensated for the loss of your janguada and I will see that you are taken back to Recife."

Putting his hand on the embarrassed commander's shoulder he said, "I trust, Captain, that next time you see a raft with survivors you will make sure that it is not a janguada."

The beach from which these boats sail is particularly suitable to their needs. A reef, through which there is a narrow pass, lies a cable from the shore and protects the beach from the worst of the swell so that the janguadas can be launched without difficulty and sail close hauled through the pass. Every afternoon, between four and five o'clock they return; running before the Trade Wind through the pass, and as soon as they touch the beach boys and young men come running out of the huts to place logs under the bows and run them up above high water mark.

The janguadas cost little to maintain and are very cheap to build but the men have no protection from the sea and in bad weather they are in danger of being swept overboard. As life becomes more precious, which it always does when conditions become less hard, these boats will disappear as surely as the Thames sailing barge has almost vanished from the east coast of England.

CHAPTER SEVEN

BEFORE leaving England we had been given the name of a shipping agent who might be able to help us with the inevitable paper work with which one is faced when cruising in foreign waters. This agent had his offices on Recife island amongst those of other agents, ship-chandlers, banks and shipping companies. In daytime there was nothing out of the ordinary about this part of the city. Tall houses, some of them very old, look down over narrow streets through which crawls the heavy traffic bound for the docks; but at night, we had been warned, this was not the sort of place where a stranger would linger just to satisfy his curiosity. If Joan de Sá came to collect us in the evening we noticed that she never got out of the car and was not entirely at ease until she had re-crossed the bridge.

Although the agent's office still bore its English name it had been taken over by a Brazilian father and son. It was a busy, salty place where one saw sea captains and ship's officers of every nationality, where the English language predominated for it is still the premier language of the sea. After waiting our turn we were shown into the son's private office. He was a man of about forty, tall with a narrow thin face and dark intelligent eyes which suddenly sparkled with delight if anything amused him. He spoke fluent English without a trace of accent. Hung on the wall behind his desk was a framed caption headed:

THE AGENT

A CAPTAIN is a man who knows a great deal about very little.
He goes on knowing more and more about less and less until he knows everything about nothing.

AN ENGINEER is a man who knows very little about a great deal.
He goes on knowing less and less about more and more until he knows nothing about everything.

AN AGENT, on the other hand, starts off by knowing nearly everything about everything but finishes up knowing nothing about anything. This is due to his close association with captains and engineers.

Senhor Evaldo caught me looking at this. He said, "I keep it there because it amuses my clients. Like too much of the English which is written nowadays on both sides of the Atlantic, it reads nicely but means nothing."

We had come to ask him whether he could arrange for us to take on water. He made a couple of telephone calls before answering our question. He said, "Water, here, is pumped into ships by the ton but I have asked the captain of the crane lighter whether he can let you have some from the two hundred tons he carries. I think I'd better drive you down there. He speaks no English."

We fixed a time with the captain, the following afternoon, and Senhor Evaldo promised to have some cans put on board the lighter so that we could ferry the water across to *Moonraker*.

The following afternoon the cans had not arrived. I rang up and was told that the cans had been used for paraffina and if others could not be found new ones would be made. I wondered how much they would cost to make. Nothing happened next day and the day after that the lighter, but not the cans, was towed out of sight to another part of the harbour.

I rang up my friend. He said, "I shall see that you have water this morning."

An hour or so later I was doing a little painting on the bulwarks when I saw an enormous tug with a great bone in her teeth charging up the harbour. Wondering idly where she might be bound I watched a man come out on the wings of the bridge and switch on the loud hailer.

"Agua," he said.

I tumbled aft, caught the heaving line, pulled aboard a hose the size of an elephant's trunk, while Anne and Jock, with commendable speed, undid the top of one tank, opened the valve on the other and unscrewed the deck plug. With a swoosh that wrenched the hose from my grasp the water roared out of the pipe knocking Jock back into the cabin as if hit by a blow in the face and swamping Anne from head to foot.

"Lentemente, lentemente, por favor!" I cried.

"A PRESSA, A PRESSA!" shouted the crew, their dusky faces wrinkled with glee as the water cascaded over our decks like Niagara Falls in springtime. The great ship was also having her difficulties for the fresh off-shore wind was blowing both vessels athwart the strong ebb tide. She was being beautifully handled but the wing of her bridge became entangled with our crosstrees and the note of laughter altered.... Churning propellers, a spoke or two of the wheel and the huge tug moved forwards, the three of us clinging to the wriggling hose until the skipper leaned over the bridge and said he was off.

"Muito obrigado," I cried.

"Nada, nada," replied the skipper raising his hand. "Boa viagem."

"TE LOG" (so long) shouted the crew.

We went along to see our friend later that day. With tears in his eyes he flung one arm round my shoulders and pumped my hand up and down with the other.

"I watched it all," he cried, "did you not think it funny? The largest tug in Brazil for the smallest ship in the harbour?"

Gone were the memories of the creaking crosstrees, the huge iron topsides of our too-close bedfellow: my half-drowned crew and the ruined paint.

I embraced him with fervour.

Before we left we again called at his office. He handed us a sheaf of papers: crew lists, clearance forms, and introductions to other agents along the coast. I thanked him for all he had done.

"How much do we owe you?" I asked him.

"Nada," he said. "It is nothing."

CHAPTER EIGHT

ON our last evening at Recife the de Sás came to say goodbye. They brought with them a pair of my trousers which had been missing at the cleaners and a large slab of "jerked meat" (thin layers of beef in rolls of fat, already dried and salted so that it keeps for a week) which Geraldo thought might break the monotony of tins.

He had a look at our charts, spreading an enormous hand over a hundred miles of coastline. He said, "From here to Bahia you must do one of two things. Beat down the coast against wind and current: a low, desolate coast with only four powerful lighthouses in four hundred miles and one port which would be safe to use in the winter, Maceio, which is not worth going to anyway. Or, you make a tack out to sea for fifty miles where you will find the winds more favourable so that you can sail with it on your beam to Bahia."

I said we would choose the second.

Geraldo had had a busy and frustrating day and whenever this happened his chain smoking rose to prodigious speeds. It was a subdued little party for it is sad that friendships made while making an ocean voyage have so soon to come to an end and that we, who are on the receiving end, can give so little in return. The wind had come in fresh from the south and moaned round the ship and the thunder of the seas on the reef drowned the noise of traffic. Joan said, "Stay another day and spend the evening with us." I shook my head for I know that if I put off sailing for a day it is so much harder to sail on the next. It was already late when we saw them into their aged Plymouth and watched them drive across the bridge for the last time.

As soon as the tide served we slipped down the river while the seas creamed over the wall like they do at Colon in Panama but once clear of the land the wind steadied and they became longer and kinder. Now the compensation for being close-hauled in *Moonie* is that she will sail herself with the tiller free without ever putting herself about so that on a night like this, with the wind up to Force 6 (another reef had been put in the mains'l), and with frequent rain squalls the crew remain dry below and get a considerable amount of sleep: and should this seem to be an unseamanlike way to sail so close to a strange coast I must explain that this is not like the English Channel where an experienced helmsman should be on watch both by day and by night, and that in five days and five hundred and twenty-seven miles of sailing we saw only five steamers, two of them being small coasters.

Anne was on watch at first light. As I stood at the galley making the porridge, watching Jock beating up the eggs, I suddenly realized that I had forgotten the land: that we might have been at sea for weeks and that this ship, whose size seems never to be constant but to diminish or increase according to the height of the seas, was our only home and the sea our natural element.

Once we had made our offing, a hundred miles instead of the fifty Geraldo suggested, the sheets were eased and the daily runs mounted into the hundred and twenties. On the fourth day out we made our landfall to the north of Bahia hoping to catch a glimpse of the famous Itapoan beach backed by high sand dunes which, when seen in bright moonlight look as if they are covered in snow. The current, however, turning north-eastward near the land had set us towards a low sandy shore with stunted trees and with not so much as a native hut or a canoe drawn up on the beach, a deadly coast with an indrift which has to be experienced to be believed. We stood off-shore but before we turned in I was puzzled by what looked like a great column of fire whose flames were reflected upon the low cloud. It was, we later learned, flaming Penta gas from an oil well which had exploded fourteen years ago. As there seemed to be no way of putting it out, it may one day be shown on the chart to make an excellent, if extravagant, landmark.

So ingrained in my memory was the strength of the set towards this unlit coast that I made too great an offing. Before dawn I came up and after a word with Jock who was muttering that we had probably missed the bay altogether I sat astride the crosstrees looking for Santo Antonio light which was still below the horizon. The ship was running almost dead before the wind so I stayed at my post while the pre-dawn light spread downwards, as it always does, from the western sky while to the east the sea took on that hard steely look which so well reveals its merciless nature. As the light broadened I caught sight of Bahia de todos os Santos, an inland sea held in the arms of a gentle land and looking as fair, with its smooth round hills and tree covered island, as any landfall I yet have made. Thus, over three hundred years of time, must the slave ships have seen it, the first land since Africa, bringing perhaps some momentary gleam of comfort to the slaves before extinguishing it for ever.

The most modern architecture has long since arrived in Bahia so that you enter the bay with the lighthouse close on your starboard hand dwarfed by a thirteen-storied building, with others to match, but if you turn your head to port it seems by that one small movement to put back the clock a hundred years for there is the fishing fleet putting to sea: their great lateen sails full of the free wind, lifting their crude, brightly painted hulls over the now white-crested seas. Just beyond the conspicuous church of Sao Antonio de Barra is a small deep indentation at the base of a cliff. We half drifted in and let go in four fathoms. The members of the Bahia Yacht Club were seated at breakfast.

CHAPTER NINE

THE city of Salvador when approached from the sea looks compact and handsome. It is built in two parts, the lower town belongs to the considerable wharves and the ships alongside them, to the maritime houses, to a small naval school and to the mass of coastal sailing craft packed so tightly together that it would be possible to step from one deck to the next for a hundred yards. To the south of the harbour is a conspicuous church whose interior is decorated in silver brought from Portugal. At one time the waters of the bay lapped the steps leading to its massive doors but the Brazilians reclaimed the land and have built a road between the church and the water now fifteen feet below it. For the benefit of those who have to walk, and in Salvador these are in the overwhelming majority, the Lacerda lift, named after the engineer who designed it, takes people from one town to the other at a cost of less than a penny. At the top of the lift is a terrace where one can sit under umbrellas of many colours, drinking ice-cold Brahma beer, pale as the Danish Pilsner, looking out over the sparkling waters of this inland sea to the blue hills beyond. Saveiros, schooners and lateen-rigged fishing boats go about their lawful occasions without an engine between the lot of them. The terrace lies not far from the site of the original settlement which came to an unfortunate end. The stockade, behind which sheltered a few primitive dwellings, was overrun by Indians who boiled down their victims in pots not so much out of revenge but a genuine preference for human meat to that of other animals. By the middle of the sixteenth century, however, Salvador was properly under way. Helped by the great sugar plantations springing up in the country and round the shores of the bay it prospered both commercially and politically until it became the capital of Brazil, a title it held for more than two hundred years.

To the south of the terrace is the business section. The streets are crowded and small children of all shapes and sizes and colours press you to buy shoelaces, matches, trinkets and even to have your shoes cleaned. It makes progress difficult. The din is such that my mind became a blank and only on entering a large store, just like any other in one of today's cities, did it start to recover. Presently I noticed that the girls behind the counters had stopped work and were examining with discreetly veiled glances our crew.

Anne went over to Jock who was examining some fishing tackle. "Don't look," she said "but I think the girls believe that Prince Philip has come back incognito." One could hardly blame them for the resemblance is striking if you forget the disparity in age and it was some time before it got through to them that this was not the Prince. With small sighs and a hint of tears they drifted disconsolately back to their work.

There is nothing particularly remarkable about this part of the city except for its theatre. Set at the back of a tree-lined square it presents a startling contrast to the colonial houses which surround it. The building was closed indefinitely for on the opening night it had burst into flames, completely gutting the interior.

Between the city and the district of Sao Antonio where *Moonraker* lay are the new university buildings of which those for philosophy, engineering, medicine and technology are already completed. In their ramps, convolutions, curves and columns I found them more stimulating than any other modern architecture I had yet seen but I could not be sure I should like to live within them.

If you walk across the square to the north of the terrace you come to the brow of a hill which overlooks a broken skyline of roofs like the opening shots in Sous Les Toits de Paris. This is Salvador as it used to be. Houses like witches on broomsticks, like bent old women leaning over ivory-handled canes nodding somberly to each other across narrow cobbled streets, fearful lest they be taken away as rubble on trucks. Fortunately they have been saved by the Preservation of Ancient Monuments. This part of the town is hilly and the streets are steep like those in San Francisco. A church or a monastery crowns each summit and near the top of one of the more important streets is a wide-open space, the middle being railed off like a market place. At first glance it looks normal enough. Donkeys and oxen plod up and down the slope, men gather at bars and women at open doors but on the hottest day it sent a chill down my spine for this is the Palino where the slaves were brought to be punished. For this city, devout in its one hundred and sixty-seven churches, became the greatest slave port in the South American continent.

In *The Masters and the Slaves* the sociologist Alberto Feyre (a friend of the Professor de Sá in Recife) writes . . .

Every Brazilian, even the light skinned, fair haired ones, carries about with him on his soul, if not on soul and body alike, the shadow or at least the hall-mark of the aborigine or the negro.

On the inhuman treatment of the slaves he lays Brazil's present troubles: the laziness, the corruption, the lack of a civic conscience. After reading the book however, one feels that one good thing may have arisen from all this misery. Surely the mixing of so much Portuguese blood with that of Negroes and Indians (the masters disported themselves with the young women slaves daily at five o'clock) has had some influence in producing a nation which is the least colour conscious of any that I have yet visited?

Rather than face the extreme heat in the main harbour we stayed at our anchorage off the Yacht Club. We usually managed to get a lift in a Volkswagen with a man who lived in some obscure part of the building. He was a German whose English was limited but whose choice of words made one think he might have been a schoolmaster or a university lecturer. A short active person who seemed unable to cope with small mishaps without becoming moody and irritable. One day he unexpectedly collected us and drove us to the great church of St. Francis of Assisi outside which, at noon of every day, gathers a long queue of people who are given free bread and soup. Our first impression was that the whole of the interior of the church was decorated in gold. To one side of the nave was a large high-ceilinged room, too big for a chapel, in the centre of which stood a black catafalque like a four-poster bed around which shuffled a thin stream of people in deep mourning. Our friend said, "President Vargus shot himself exactly eight years ago. He was the first president to make the people feel that someone in authority cared for them. He had many friends here in the North East and some still think he was murdered for his liberal views." Vargas left a "suicide" letter in which were included these words: '. . . Once again the forces that are co-ordinated by the interests against the people have anew unleashed themselves against me . . . '. This letter's authenticity seems still to be in considerable doubt.

While Jock and Anne were examining the statuary so boldly finished in gold leaf my host suddenly gripped my arm and hurried me through a small door into a court about the size of Nevil's Court at Trinity which in form it closely resembled. The walls were decorated with Portuguese tiles depicting the triumph of virtue over evil. We climbed a staircase, walked through a room in which scrubbed deal tables were set for a meal, into a refectory where the sideboard and a table that ran the whole length of the room were made from jacaranda and polished to the colour of an old meershaum pipe. At the head of the table was a group of monks deep in conversation. My companion hesitated but one of the men looked up and then came forward with outstretched arms as if to welcome a sheep returned to the fold. I stood to one side, a spectator over whose head words flowed like the tranquil waters of a great river and it came to me that I, a stranger, was here as a support, or perhaps as an avenue of escape, for my companion could not have known what form his reception might have taken. I could see that he was deeply moved. After a long time the murmur of discourse ended and he accompanied me once more to the door into the church, where he shook hands with me. "You must forgive me for leaving you now," he said, "some years ago I made a decision that I now believe was a mistake. But I must think carefully. I cannot make the same mistake twice."

More than once I have wondered how he tackled his problems and whether he found contentment.

Before leaving Recife Geraldo de Sá had said he would write to a Dr. Silveiro, a friend in Salvador he would like us to meet. What he did not mention was that Professor Silveiro was President of the World Organization for the Prevention of Tuberculosis so that it was with a slight feeling of dismay that we accepted an invitation to call on him at I.B.I.T. (Brazilian Institute for the Investigation of Tuberculosis). The professor welcomed us with great courtesy and I said how honoured we were that he had spared the time so that we could meet him. He smiled disarmingly. He said "The pleasure is mine not only at meeting a friend of Geraldo's but someone who travels about the world in such an unconventional way. But what interests me, doctor, is that your wife sails with you. Or," he said, turning to Anne, "do you like the sea as much as your husband does?"

"I think the reason for our travelling so unconventionally, as you put it, is very simple. We have our boat, the wind is free and we cannot afford to travel in any other way."

The professor smiled. "An excellent reason," he said, "but one that would not, I assure you, be advanced by any Brazilian wife." He then went on to say that Geraldo had told him I had worked in Switzerland for a short time and that I might be interested in seeing over his unit. He said, "You will probably wonder why we are spending millions on research into a disease which is now so well under control in Europe: but here it is rampant. It is of course a social as well as a medical problem but we are hampered at the moment by the drift from the interior, where tuberculosis is most prevalent, to the cities where it so easily propagated.

Add to this the African fear these people have of every disease and of all doctors, so that patients are half dead before we see them and you will have some idea of what we are up against. However, my new hospital of one hundred and fifty beds, which you must have seen from outside our front door, will be open next year and this will at least ease the situation in Salvador."

There was a knock and the professor rose to his feet. "It is most unfortunate, I have to fly to the States this evening but I have arranged for a colleague to take you round," and he introduced us to a short dynamic and much younger man who had entered the room. "I believe," he said with a smile, "that he also knows something about boats."

I.B.I.T. is one of four such units in the world and the only one in South America. There were four single rooms, luxuriously appointed and looking out on to a courtyard where the long flame coloured petals of the Brasiliera tree bloomed the year round. They were empty, for only very special cases are admitted here. There is an out-patient department, several superbly appointed laboratories, X-ray rooms, an operating theatre and a small very perfectly-designed lecture theatre with seats like the best stalls and every form of equipment for demonstration. It held about fifty people. But what struck me most forcibly was the quiet. No doors could be slammed, rubberized floors prevented heavy footfalls from being heard and even the doctors, technicians and nurses spoke in muted tones. I should have liked to have stayed here myself.

The professor's colleague then very kindly drove us back to the boat. "Tomorrow," he said, "is a festa and I am free. My wife and I will come alongside at ten o'clock. I must warn you I am never late." Punctually at one minute to ten we heard a peculiar horn with two notes like the braying of a donkey so that our doctor friend became known to us privately as Two Tone. They wasted no time transferring us to their vessel and with the help of its powerful engine in under one hour we covered the fourteen miles to the Ilha dos Frades where, in the early sixteenth century a large monastery had been built because "It was as near to Paradise as could be found on earth".

A dark green bluff. A half moon bay with a beach of golden sand. Virgin territory I thought at first until I saw the tree-trunk canoes drawn high up on the beach, their sails set to dry and then deep in the shadow of the forest the darker shapes of low palm thatched huts.

"O Claudio...," shouted Two Tone. "O Clim ei ro." Out of the jungle came Claudio and Climeiro leaping into a canoe as their ancestors might have done when the monastery was first built, but that would have been for a different purpose. In a moment, it seemed, we were transported ashore, a short but to me a perilous journey, and were walking slowly towards an ancient chapel with bronze bell and rusty clapper, the only surviving remnant of the monastery which had been swallowed hook line and sinker by the jungle after it was burnt to the ground by the Dutch. It was a happy day: changing in a cool shuttered room of the chapel, now a rest house, keeping a wary eye open for scorpions, bathing in the limpid water, drying out on the hot sand, eating red snapper caught that morning before dawn and cooked on a flat stone outside Climeiro's house: the murmur of voices, the dark wrinkled faces of the women who wanted nothing out of life but the means to continue it, watching the slanting eyes and high cheek bones of the men as they talked through the afternoon with Two Tone. Later, when we came here ourselves, we learned more about this village. Once if fishing was bad they would have starved but since Two Tone first sailed into this bay they did not. Tins of milk and meat were stored away against the times of no fish in the sea, and the village, which had been in danger of being abandoned more than once, survived. As we left this enchanted place Two Tone said, "In the city I am a man of some importance but here, where I am happiest, I am nobody, accepted by these people as one of themselves."

From that day on we never knew when Two Tone might whisk us away, to a coming out party for his god-daughter, aged fifteen, at her father's house which held a hundred and fifty people without being crowded, to Itapoa where the south Atlantic breaks in isolated splendour on ten miles of curving beach in front of tall sand dunes which when seen in moonlight appear like snow: to an estate belonging to friends of his who happened to be away. That did not stop Two Tone. The overseer was routed out (on a Sunday), a dark handsome man, leather booted and mounted on a superb white horse, to show us over a brickworks fired by wood, (this infuriated Two Tone who said "they ought to use oil") with an ancient clay moulding machine that had to be turned by hand. Twenty men instead of three, perhaps, but what would happen to the other seventeen and why worry if they made enough bricks to keep it a going concern? The fazenda, which Two Tone made the overseer open up, stood in a grove of jacaranda, sapoti, bread-fruit and eucalyptus trees which, though their shade was cool, added to the dark and gloomy interior with its furniture of pure Victoriana and its large marble bath. Two Tone then drove us through a lush countryside of low hills to a State Farm begun as an experiment a year ago. Already it was paying its way, farm lorries taking the produce into the towns to sell at street corners undercutting markets and shops. There was a community centre, a hall, church and school, rows of bungalows with a riot of flowers in each tiny garden, children playing, people exchanging the news of the day, batteries of incubators with large notices "Please Do Not Sound Your Horn", fields of corn, groves of oranges and mangoes, pastures with cattle: but to make the thing pay, knowing only too well that the Brazililan peasant does not take kindly to too much work, the government had imported Japanese labour. The Japanese would not, however, live with the Brazilians and had built their own centre eleven miles away. A long line of identical bungalows as forlorn as the Dead Sea, devoid of flowers (curious for the Japanese), stripped of any sign of human life so that one felt conspicuous and inquisitive walking past shuttered windows and closed doors. At the last house a door opened and a girl came out shutting it quickly behind her. Anne spoke to her in English and was answered in English. She came from the north of Japan, from a remote country district where there was snow and a bitter wind in winter, little food and no chance of getting a good job. She was fortunate to be amongst those chosen to come to Brazil. A young man came out to join her. He explained that all the men were out working but as it was a Sunday and he was a teacher he was at home. As we drove off we speculated whether they were brother and sister. Two Tone said, "If they had been man and wife he would never have allowed her to speak to you alone."

On the way home Two Tone took us to a part of the city where I should never have dared go even in daylight. It lies on the western shore of a sort of inland lake connected to the tidal waters of the bay through a narrow neck at its northern end. Houseboats whose bottoms fall out from time to time drowning their occupants lie against rows of rotting piles on the top of which totter the meanest shacks. Thirty thousand people live here: without drainage, only the stinking mud and the sluggish water, no light or drinking water. It is, perhaps, no worse than parts of New Orleans or Hong Kong but it was the only place we discovered in Brazil, although there may be others, where poverty had bred brutality and viciousness. It was like a cancer which had been allowed to become inoperable and could now only be destroyed by death.

"You would think," said Two Tone, breaking the silence which had lasted until we were nearly home, "these people would band together to help each other. But if one of those shacks becomes vacant it is immediately bought up by someone a little better off and the first thing he does is to put up the rent."

But in all these expeditions the pattern of Two Tone's personality stood out clearly however dark or light the background. Fishermen, tough young dockers, old women frying shreds of meat in olive oil with rice outside their wayside huts would stop what they were doing and talk to him about their problems or themselves, laughing at his most outrageous comments, so patient was his interest in his fellow men.

Two Tone and his wife lived in a long narrow house with a strip of garden at the side. His father, who at the age of thirteen had come out from Portugal with a single gold sovereign and a letter of introduction, lived with them. One night they gave a party for us at which his wife made a charming hostess. It was a hot still night and after dinner we had our coffee in the garden. Two Tone insisted on bringing out his latest toy, a huge radiogram and wireless with a panel of knobs like a telephone exchange by which you could alter the volume of the different orchestral instruments if you felt your musical sense was likely to be greater than that of the composer. It was far too powerful an instrument, as Two Tone rightly pointed out, to be used indoors, so that the garden was just the place for it but I still maintain that the earth beneath my feet vibrated with the shattering waves of sound. On the other side of the garden fence a tall block of flats, some twelve storeys high, had recently been built. Two Tone said that not only did it dwarf his own property but the occupants so far forgot themselves at time as to throw things out of the window into his garden.

If I had been up there that night I should have dropped a bomb on it.

CHAPTER TEN

BAHIA de Todos os Santos is nearly thirty miles deep and twenty in width at its widest point. In it lie some forty-five islands with many coral patches and shoals and in the channels between the islands the tidal streams run strongly. In such a bay shelter for a small boat is as easy, or easier, to find that in the Solent or the Thames Estuary; there are miles of coral sand beaches, settlements nuzzling under hills or along the foreshores of quiet bays. At the head of the inlet are a number of oil rigs whose lights glitter at night like stars on the still water which spreads like the ripples from a stone thrown in to point to every beach in the bay; to some, of course, more than to others.

The wind system inside the bay is as regular as the Trade Wind outside it; starting from the north in the early hours of the morning, backing slowly through east to south during the morning and becoming westerly late in the afternoon before it falls light or dies away altogether at dusk. The wind is free and in Bahia time does not yet mean money so that sail has held its own and on one occasion, on a dancing Bahia day, I counted no less than forty head of commerical sail, saveiros, lateen-sailed traders and two large schooners under way at the same time: a thing I never though I would see again after our first voyage to the West Indies.

The day we sailed away from Salvador was one in which the usual wind pattern had been broken. The sea was calm and up from the south-west came the first small ripples of a swell which grew like mountains out of mole hills until the crash of breakers drowned the noises of the land. And still there was no wind. Jock said, "Hadn't we better get out under power while we can still get the anchor up?" I hesitated, but I have lived too long with an engine that only went when it wanted to so that even though we now have a reliable engine I have made one rule that I break as seldom as possible, I try not to get the ship into such a position where, if a speck of dirt gets into an injector, she will run the risk of becoming a total loss. I said, "We'll wait. The wind won't be long and then we'll have two strings to our bow." It came and under all plain sail we got underway. It did not blow hard but before we were out of sight of land I could see that our berth was completely untenable.

Once away from the city, the oil rigs, the piers for loading tankers and the cement factories which flourish like weeds in one of nature's most beautifully landscaped gardens, you walk straight out of the twentieth century into the past.

On the northern shore of Ilha dos Frades which to this day we remember as Two Tone's Island, is a village where they will still build you a saveiro for £600, a vessel fifty feet in length with a tree as a mast, stepped well forward with convenient branches left upon which to hang peak and main halyard blocks and a small mast forward of that, like a Thames barge's mizzen on which to hang a narrow square sail which can be braced well for'ard by a line to a thin spar raked like a barge's triced up bowsprit. These boats are flat bottomed with a marked rake to their transoms and the whole hull is cargo space except for a tiny cabin aft for two crew. They sail like the wind and this rather primitive but logical sail plan with its long leading luff to the main has remained unchanged for the last two hundred and fifty years. We got to know a shipwright family whose children ranged from a baby in arms to a girl of nineteen. I have a photograph of about half the family, the father seated in a chair with an enormous guitar in his hands, his wife, three daughters and two sons standing beside him, the girls remarkably good looking with light-coloured skins, one of whom would not look out of place walking down a fashionable street in Amsterdam. Indeed all the children in this village have a Dutch look which comes, I suppose, from the occupation of almost the whole of Bahia, with the exception of Salvador, by the Dutch during the fifty years they were on this coast. The well where everyone goes for water is at one end of the long village street, and when I say street I mean nothing more than a deeply-rutted cart track. The water is carried for the most part in empty oil containers and I remember a girl running down the street, one of these things perched on her shoulder, with the water pouring over her from a dozen holes in its sides and bottom, when she arrived at last in front of her house the container was empty. With tears of frustration she threw the can into the middle of the street and disappeared into the dark interior. Suddenly I saw a boy dart into the street, pick up the can as if it were a crock of gold and carry it away triumphantly. We were bound for the shipwrights house and there ahead of us stood the boy, sullen and angry at having his toy taken away watching his father fit wooden pegs into the tin. "Now," said his father, "take this back to Gabriella and tell her if she is careful it will last a bit longer. Tins are valuable, even if they do have holes in them."

From Bom Jesus we sailed back on our tracks looking for somewhere quiet enough to paint the ship. We found it at Itaparica.

The village stands on a narrow peninsula at the north-western end of Itaparica Island, the bay to the south being full of drying sandbanks with a channel between, where, from half ebb to half flood, there is no movement on the water. That, from the chart, was how we read it but as we rounded the old fort and the village, the church, the tiny market place and a dozen saveiros basking in the yellow light of the afternoon came into view we were confronted with a large iron wreck right in the middle of the channel, unbuoyed, and unmarked on our chart, with nothing to tell us on which side to leave it. The wreck had been a Greek steamer which had arrived at Bahia on fire and had been sent round to Itaparica as the place where she could burn herself out with least inconvenience. That was forty years ago. There was no need to buoy her. Everyone knew she was there and a stranger sailing into Itaparica would be an event so unusual that it would not be worth bothering about.

The village of Itaparica can be divided into two parts. The "Resort", a line of summer bungalows and a hotel built round the beach looking over the water to the Ilha dos Frades and the village proper which took no notice of the tourists who in their turn ignored the village altough it was not a hundred yards from the beach where they spent all their time. The life of the village starts in the market which opens at six o'clock in the morning when the first donkeys come trotting along the cobbled coast road from the "radio-active springs" from which water is bottled and is drunk all over the State of Bahia and beyond. It is free to the people of Itaparica if they get it themselves from the springs or they can have it delivered to their houses for 60 cruzeiros a load, four barrels to each donkey, worth 8d of our money. Soon after the donkeys arrive the saveiros sail in on the first of the morning breeze with fruit from the plantations on the island which is more than twenty miles long and where the only communications are by water and by saveiro except for the steamer which leaves the pier at seven in the morning and returns from Salvador at five-thirty in the afternoon. The meat and the fish, if any, come in later, usually at the same time as we did. The hub of this little place, however, is the Hotel Icarai at the apex of the peninsula. We should not have known this had not its proprietor, seeing our ensign, called on us two days later....

The afternoon was a blister of heat and the only human sounds came from women talking in shrill voices as they searched on the drying sands for mussels. The ship was careened as far as possible to the starboard side, Anne and Jock were working on deck and I sat in the pram digging stoppings out of weeping fastenings. Sweat ran over our faces and arms and it would not be difficult for a stranger to realize that fitting out a small boat in the tropics while living aboard might well be a necessity but could hardly be a pleasure. I had been vaguely conscious of an approaching outboard engine but noticed it more when it stopped. A voice said, "Where on earth have you come from?" There was a rather long pause, each of us waiting for the other to speak. Then "From England," said Anne non-committally.

"In this?"

"Yes."

There was, I thought, rather too long a pause. I said, "I'm sorry, but we can't ask you aboard at the moment."

"I don't want to stop you working. I came to ask you to dinner at the Hotel Icarai this evening."

"That would be splendid," said Anne, her spirits reviving at the thought of not having to cook. "What time?"

Having given us a time our friend withdrew and it was not until he had gone that we realized he was no more than a face which had offered a meal for an exhausted and hungry crew.

That night we walked up Itaparica's street where the houses lean towards each other across the narrow road, their balconies reflected by the moonlight on to the peeling walls like rows of prison bars. We walked with more confidence than we felt through the hotel doors into a half circular hall with small tables in the windows and at once a man detached himself from the couple he was talking to and came over. "My name's Sam Millar. It's nice to see you. My wife will be down in a minute. She's just back from Sao Paulo where she's been staying with the children." Even during this short greeting a number of people were waiting respectfully to see him and it became obvious that he was no guest but the owner of the hotel.

Some years before the Millars had come over to Itaparica on a day trip from Salvador whereupon Sam had decided it was the one place he wanted to live. The Hotel Icarai happened to be up for sale and he bought it outright. He knew nothing of a hotelier's life but he so obviously liked his fellow man, a feeling which he combined with a shrewd business head, that success was almost assured. He was a cockney and had come out to join his parents when he was fourteen years old, had fought his way through the business jungle in Rio, and had married a Brazilian girl. Just before we went into dinner his wife joined us. She was petite, wore her clothes with such elegance it was difficult to think of her as a grandmother but at the moment she was finding it hard to adjust herself from the sophistication of her beloved Rio to Itaparica which she described almost with venom as "this one horse village". Indeed, had it not been for Sam's inexhaustible good nature it might have been embarrassing but before it became so she and Anne had, in the way women do with so much more ease than men, established a "rapport" that made Anea forget where she was. While the two women were talking Sam was saying that Anea's dislike of the village had worried him until he had hit on the plan of giving her the management of the hostel as extra pin money. The hostel was close to the hotel and housed some of the workers and technicians at Petrobras, the Brazilian State Oil Company. "It worked like a charm," said Sam. "Anea loves money, has a good business head and it has taken the responsibility of the hostel off my shoulders." And at that moment the door from the kitchens was flung open and a man rushed up to Sam to say he was wanted at once at the hostel where a fight had broken out. "It is terrible," said Anea, her face pale beneath her make up, "these men carry their machetes in their belts and they can split your belly up cutting like a knife through butter. Like zees", she hissed, with such a bloodcurdling gesture that Jock and I had difficulty in controlling our faces. Presently Sam came back looking pleased with himself. I asked him what happened.

"Just a man full of caçaça with a knife. He's back in bed now."

"What d'you do with a man full of caçaça armed with a knife?"

"Simple:" said Sam. "You greet him with a beaming smile, put one arm round his shoulders as if to embrace him and knock him out with a left to the chin."

"What happens if someone gets killed?"

"Nothing: the killer escapes to the bush, changes his name and is never heard of again in these parts."

Before we said goodnight Anea and Sam insisted that we should dine with them every night after we had finished work. It was something to look forward to every day. We were not the only people at their table. I remember a priest who was able to tell me the origin of the name Ilha do Medo—the Island of Fear—it owed its name to a great battle between the Paragassu and Itaparican Indians in which the Paragassu carried off the enemy chief's daughter but were overtaken by the war canoes of the Itaparicans and landed on this tiny island to fight it out. They were slaughtered to the man and if you are brave enough to spend a night there you will see the ghosts of the dead warriors.

I think it must have been that story that started Anea off on Candomblé, the Bahia equivalent of Macumba: rites which slaves brought over from Africa. Over the years these have been integrated to some extent with the Roman Catholic religion so that the negroes (only found in pure strain round Bahia) can worship both God and their own deities as a sort of insurance against all eventualities. It is impossible for a stranger to attend these sessions but I had seen a posy of flowers or a half burnt out candle or a bottle of caçaça by the wayside showing that Candomblé had been this way. A few years ago one of Anea's servants had persuaded her to attend a ceremony in the depths of Itaparica island. There was a big negress there with her two-year-old child, both of them dressed, like the others, in long white garments. The woman had started to whirl round and round, on and on, faster and faster to the rhythmic beat of the clapping hands, the child, held by its feet streaming away from its mother like spray before a storm tossed sea. Suddenly she let go of the child and fell to the ground unconscious. When Anea got to the child, in spite of arms and hands which shot out to restrain her, the child was dead.

When the work on the ship was finsihed the Millars asked us to stay with them for a couple of days to recover. It was during this time that I realized what a large part Sam played in the life of this small community. Peasants, fishermen, masters of saveiros came to ask his advice and although conversations were in Portuguese and I could only guess at most of them, no one seemed to go away unsatisfied. One morning a man came to see him who had a sad and infinitely weary expression on his long thin face. After Sam had sent him off on some small errand he said, "These people are unemployable. You recognized the disease—Chagas Disease? There is a lot of it here. It is carried by a small cockroach with a bright yellow band on its back which bites you while you are asleep, then defecates into the bite and the acid from its excreta sets up an intense irritation so that you scratch it violently, which ensures that the trypanisomes enter your blood stream. In five years you will be dead. You can tell these people at once. They all have that sad expression on their faces as if they know their days are numbered."

We could understand how Anea found it so hard to adjust herself to the life Sam loved. There was a store in the market place, a shop opposite, where bric-à-brac was piled high from floor to ceiling and where we bought a hand painted water carrier for 6d and a small incense carrier that maids take around with them to ward off the bad temper of their mistresses. That was the sum total of the amenities. Anne, who was now trying to stock up, wrote in her diary . . . "Anea takes me about the village in the dark avoiding dogs and dung and uneven cobbles and broken paving for there is no street lighting here. The iron gates into a courtyard are unchained and glossy green leaves grow out of spaces among the stones. The houses are all of one room. There is a cage where Rhode Island Reds live and eggs are promised when laid. Because Betts, whose house remains in darkness, is not speaking to her, Anea has to ask Rosina, whose house is lit up, to ask Betts to make the cake we have asked for."

On our last night two well-dressed young women joined us for dinner. They came from the south and were gay and amusing to talk to. After we had finished they disappeared upstairs with two large suitcases with Anea and Anne. Sam said, "There are no lengths to which people will go these days to sell things. These girls will hint that the goods they are selling are smuggled into the country and therefore can be bought cheap. Like a feather lure to catch a simple minded fish." (Sam is a great fisherman.)

Nevertheless, when Anne showed me what she had bought it seemed to me to be extraordinarily cheap.

It was a wonderful morning when we sailed away from Itaparica; the ship clean and painted, spars shining with new varnish, a new burgee at the truck and her crew refreshed and rested. We sailed west of Ilha dos Frades, passed Bom Jesus where a saveiro was up on the beach being caulked, waved to our shipwright friend wielding a mallet who promptly dropped it to wave back to us. Our only misfortune that morning being the loss of our hand lead through the breaking of the line at the very moment that I was swinging the lead aboard. From Bom Jesus we headed north among a maze of small islands on a falling tide, sands drying out all round us, and when the wind dropped we came to a natural standstill. We put out eighteen fathoms of nylon warp (at the end of five fathoms of three-eights chain) and came to an anchor. Close by was a glorious beach from which to bathe with only the faintest trace of oil and the only sound was that of an adze wielded ashore by a man building a boat. It was a place to stay a long time in.

There was a single row of native huts, incredibly poor; of the sort which are sometimes infested with the cockroaches with the yellow bands of which Sam had spoken so graphically and which can be found only in the very meanest dwellings of the

Itaparicans. We had a glorious afternoon on our beach but before dinner Anne and Jock went ashore on the village side to see whether there was any chance of a fish. When they came back, after a considerable time, Anne said: "D'you mind seeing a patient in the morning?" She and Jock had gone into the hut of a man who was reputed to catch fish to find a young woman bending over a crude sort of wooden cradle in which lay a child who, the mother told her, had been ill for the last three months. The mother had been crying. Not knowing any other way to help (and after hearing there was no doctor within miles) Anne had asked her whether she would like me to see the child in the morning. So it was arranged that she and her husband would bring the child out in their canoe (with the fish).

They paddled out to our ship soon after breakfast dressed in their best clothes and I was glad that I had put mine on too, although these were not the same that I wear to see patients in England. The child was indeed very ill, running a high temperature and with a swollen abdomen containing free fluid. It was emaciated and one felt that its chance of recovery were slight. I learned, with Anne's help, that they had taken it to a clinic on a neighbouring island which advised hospital treatment and told the parents to take the child to Salvador—a twenty-five mile journey by canoe. Although a southerly swell would make this passage impossibly dangerous one felt that it could have been made with care and patience if only they could spare time from fishing, their only means of subsistence.

We tried to convey to them that we knew a doctor in Salvador and that on our return (we hoped to be there that afternoon) we would get in touch with him, try and arrange a bed at the hospital and return within a day or two for the child. They left, pathetically grateful for the small amount of help we could offer and a large tin of Minho (powdered milk) which we told them how to use for they could not read. News of this sort travels quickly and no sooner were we underway than an old man came out in the same dugout, wheezing and coughing with bronchitis and heaven knows what else. After the briefest of examinations I left him with a small bottle of antibiotic tablets hoping that the instructions we had given him were at least partially understood. By this time we were almost ashore but managed to get the ship round in time and proceeded towards Salvador.

I managed to get hold of Two Tone on the telephone that evening. I told him my story and then hung on for some considerable time. He said, "I think it would be better if you were not personally involved in this. I am going up to Ponta Nosses de Senhora on Sunday (in two days time) and I will go on from there and collect the child and bring it back to Salvador." I never knew what happened to the child, except that it arrived safely in hospital.

We were now anxious to continue the voyage as we had stayed here a month instead of the two weeks we had planned and there were all the last minute preparations for a voyage, even if it would only last for a few days. Two Tone was busier than ever and after he had been to tell me how he had brought the child back I never saw him again. Just before we left the Club Manager arranged for two men to clean our copper with coconut husks. They worked hard for an hour by which time she was clean. The charge was 3/6 for each of them.

CHAPTER ELEVEN

THE wind was steady from the east: the sea smooth, the sky empty of all but the smallest clouds sailing towards the land like the white sails of galleons. Inshore was a saveiro bound for the port of Ilheus some forty miles away, the *mise-en-scène* for Jorge Amado's novel which describes the growth of this cocoa town in the 'thirties when it threw off the yoke of the plantation barons who ruled the town and the districts round it with their private armies. We might have gone there had it not been for the *Pilot* which reads as follows: ". . . in fresh onshore winds there are heavy breakers in the entrance when the outgoing stream is running and entrance (and exit) is almost impracticable . . .".

The wind slowly backed into the north-east. Our course for Victoria, five hundred miles to the south, lay parallel to the coast but out of sight of land. The perfect weather, the long easy roll, the passing of the watches induced a timelessness which in itself was a danger for I was well aware that our voyage had to end next summer in England (via Montevideo, Tristan da Cunha, St. Helena, Ascension and the Azores) and I knew how easy it would be to wake up one morning to find that the seasons would prevent our getting home for another year.

On the evening of the second day out we were approachng the long line of reefs which protrude thirty-four miles into the south Atlantic like the Horns Reef into the North Sea. At the end of this reef, on one of four small islets, stands a lighthouse called Abrolhos. The name is derived from "abre olhos" which means "open your eyes". It is a twenty mile light and we picked it up on the starboard bow at eight-fifteen that night. Pecked lines on the chart showing the southern limit of the South-East Trade Winds pass just south of St. Barbara, the islet on which stands the lighthouse, and now the wind, as if reading these lines beyond which it dares not blow, fell away to a gentle breeze while from every point of the compass heavy rain clouds massed above us. "Abre Olhos . . . Abre Olhos." The stillness of the night, the solitary flash now on our beam, the roar of the seas on the miles of reefs, kept the three of us on deck waiting for something, we knew not what, to happen. Down came the tops'l: the genoa was exchanged for the jib. A sudden cold blast caught us aback from the south-west. Round came the sheets, off went the ship, round went the wind,

180 degrees in as many seconds, over came the boom in an almighty gybe (the runners were secured to the shrouds) and down came the rain as it did outside Sadie Thompson's hut in Somerset Maugham's novel. At last the wind seemed to steady in the south-east and Jock and I retired below leaving Anne in charge of the streaming deck and the fast receding reefs.

For three days it rained.

As if to mock us the clouds travelled from the NE, the wind came from the SW, right in our teeth. Once in the middle of a terrific thunderstorm I started to lower the tops'l. The sail took charge streaming out to loo'ard on five fathoms of halyard like a great kite, whipping the top of the mast like a rod with five hundred pounds of fish on it, one moment lit by a brilliant flash the next plunged into total darkness. I shouted for the others who came tumbling out of the cabin like hooded monks from a cell and as the ship came into the wind the tops'l, on its long heavy yard, plummeted like a great wounded bird to where Jock was waiting to catch it before it went through the deck.

The bread went green, moisture dripped from the cabin walls and we cursed the climate, the ship, the wind and each other into a damp sullen stupor.

And then one morning I came up on deck to greet the sun, a following wind and on our beam a great mountain range (the first real mountains we had seen since leaving the Cape Verde Islands), which dwarfed the foothills and the islands in Espiritu Santo Bay. It looked as primeval as it must have done to the first Portuguese who came here: except for two things: a brilliantly white building which we mistook for a luxury hotel and a clutch of steamers, thirteen of them, anchored off an apparently deserted shore. Where the steamers were, we argued, must lie the entrance to the river leading to Vitoria. Light towers and buoys mark the dangers in the entrance but the set of the tide, which runs up to three or even four knots, on to a reef upon which the sea breaks with a snarl like that of a hungry tiger took us by surprise for there is no warning in the *Pilot* of its strength or its danger. If I was to arrive here at night I would lie off until daylight.

Running between islands on the one hand and wooded hills on the other the river winds towards the mountains and the still hidden city. To port, perched Tibetan-like, on its rocky summit stands the Convento de Nossa Senhora de Penha (our luxury hotel), built, stone by stone by the hermit Panus and his followers and finished in 1585. Panus must have been a remarkable man for after the monastery was completed he continued to live in his cave by the beach (now marked by a bronze plaque) so that he could the better help and preach to the settlers who were continually threatened by Indians from the interior and by pirates from the sea.

On a festa, a Saint's Day, on which we happened to visit it, the people flock here in their hundreds, the old, the young and the middle-aged, toiling up the steep rocky hillside after a walk of several miles, dressed in their best clothes but barefooted as is their custom, carrying their most fashionable shoes in their hands until they put them on before entering the chapel to pay homage to God, the Virgin Mary and Panus. In the chapel are three paintings; one of the original landing of the Portuguese, one of the hermit preaching to the fishermen on the beach, his face alight with fervour and devotion, so different, I felt, to that of a priest in a side chapel baptising a baby held in its mother's arms, her face puzzled by his complete indifference to what to her was a very important day. The third picture shows a terrifying assault by a well-armed force in overwhelming numbers before which the settlers are fleeing. But, from out of the clouds, are descending a host of heavenly horsemen and you are left with the impression that the raiders will be driven back into the sea. Now at about this date Sir Thomas Cavendish raided a Portuguese settlement in Espirito Santo bay and was repulsed with heavy losses. There is no mention, however, in Haklyut of a host of heavenly horsemen.

Vitoria has grown since the days of Panus. Tall white buildings come into view, compressed between hills and rivers. At the base of the Sugar Loaf, a small replica of the one in Rio, the flood pours through the narrows and I could no longer hear what the others were trying to tell me above the rumble of lorries and the clanking of trams. A low bridge across the river, not marked on our chart, seemed to be coming too near too fast and a bay on the chart in which Geraldo de Sá had marked the place we should anchor had mysteriously disappeared.

Alarmed by this we beat back through the narrows and came to an anchor in a shallow bay off Ilha das Pombas, the Island of Doves. Near the head of the bay was a large building of noble proportions which we thought might be the Governor's Palace. It had, in fact, been a convent but was now the State Penitentiary for the worst criminals.

The solution to the mystery of the lost bay was solved that night in the Rowing Club of Vitoria. Pointing to our chart they said,

"This land has now been reclaimed from the sea and this cross is now in the middle of a fair ground."

We stayed here for a week under the management, or so it seemed to us, of the British Vice-Consul who, not being a seaman himself, thought that sailing here in a small boat was something to talk about. He talked to the Port Captain who talked to the Governor who granted us an audience in his Palace. The guard saluted as we drove up. Into the great hall of a magnificent mansion, up the stairs to wait in an anteroom where Jock and I eyed each others' jackets and trousers, the best we could produce for the occasion, both of us envying Anne who takes more care of her clothes. The room into which we were ushered was one that, just for once, I should like to dine in with the candle light flickering on the long polished table, on gleaming silver and on the faces of the distinguished guests and the high carved ceiling. I shook myself out of this reverie as the Governor, who had been talking to the Port Captain at the farther end of the room, came over to welcome us. He was long and lean with a quiet studious face like that of a university professor whose knowledge of English, however, was little better than Anne's of Portuguese.

We sat round a small table sipping cups of cafezinho while he told us, with a half-smile, that he was only the Acting Governor, the Governor himself having had to retire six months ago in order to stand for election again. He did, however, express a wish to see our boat. In effect, he said, "Not that I am a sailor, but I hear that yours is an English fishing boat and I am a fisherman."

We imagined that we should have the privilege of entertaining him in an informal way but long before he arrived in a naval pinnace the Press and the Camera men had taken over. I can only hope that *Moonraker*, who is as unused to this sort of thing as we are, conveyed to him something of her former life, fishing off the Eddystone, summer and winter alike, when the decision to make one more cast with the trawl before the weather really broke might bring disaster to her crew.

Although Vitoria depends for her new prosperity on the shipment of iron ore it is also the nearest port to that part of the Minais Gerais in which are found precious and semi-precious stones, so that it was, we were told, the cheapest place to buy them. Anne had set her heart on an aquamarine. We were given the name of a merchant whose office was at the top of a narrow winding staircase. Most of the room was taken up with a massively built table of Jacaranda whose warm rose-red surface was covered with trays of jewels and stones which sparkled in the strong light like a thousand stars. The proprietor welcomed us with smiles and with the rubbing together of hands but he had a look about him that reminded me of a hooded and predatory eagle which has suddenly seen a prey. It made me aware that not one of the three of us could tell an aquamarine from well-cut tinted glass.

Anne found a stone which she liked but at the last moment deferred buying it until after lunch. At lunch the young Brazilian wife of the Chief Engineer at Westerns told us that even she, who knew something about aquamarines, could not always be sure of their quality, but if Anne wished she would accompany us back to the office. Without much hesitation she said that Anne's stone was of poor quality and did not advise us to buy it. By now the merchant was getting a little tired of us. He took a tray out of a different shelf and left us to it. One was found of which our friend approved. I got out a roll of contos and was about to hand it over when Teresinha, who had been examining the stone again, said "Wait a moment, please." She then spoke in very rapid Portuguese to the proprietor and back and forth rolled the words like the waves on a sea shore until Teresinha said to us "I am going to get a friend of mine to have a look at this stone. I will be back in five minutes." After examining the stone with a lens for a considerable time her friend said, "I'm sorry to disappoint you but this is a second-class stone for which you have been asked a first-class price." With something like a snarl of rage the proprietor shooed us down the stairs. I could not blame him. The prey had escaped.

Vitoria, because of its mountainous surroundings, is still short of roads so that in the main the sea looks after the heavy transport and the air carries the passengers. For Brazil the aeroplane arrived at the right time, at the beginning of her industrial expansion. The Brazilian pilots are second to none and recently the government has had to step in to prevent too many of them leaving the country for the U.S.A. where the pay is better. Weather conditions, mountainous country and Brazil's precarious economic position have all combined to make flying by Internal Airways plane an exciting if necessary means of transport as a recent flight by a young friend of ours from Rio to Vitoria in the same bad weather we had just experienced along the coast will show. In poor visibility the captain found himself too far above the runway at Vitorio to land and too near a hill to do anything but throw the aircraft into a near vertical climb. Our friend, sitting at the back of the plane, found himself bombarded by bags, passengers, seats, china, glass, and paper bags full of vomit while all around him the Brazilian temperament let itself go with cries to the Holy Virgin and screams of terror. Inevitably, the plane stalled and now descended as vertically as it had climbed only this time our young friend was not on the receiving end. The pilot cleverly got his aeroplane flying in a more normal manner and flew to Campos where a rival air company had an airstrip. There were no lights on the runway and he overran the airstrip into soft mud from which he failed to extricate it. The passengers had had enough and wandered away to find what accommodation was available. In the morning all but six (but not our friend) returned to Vitoria by bus. The aircraft was dug out of the mud but now the rival company refused to allow them to re-fuel. Threats and bribery overcame this obstacle but the fuel was of a low grade on which only D.C.3s could fly and theirs was a Convair. However, with a greatly reduced load the captain decided to risk it. At the last possible moment the aircraft rose into the air and landed at Vitoria safely.

By taking a "Bonde" (as the trams are called because the money to buy them was by raised bonds floated in the City of London) you can ride on the narrow track through woods and sandhills as it rattles and sways like a ship at sea towards the shores and islands where most of the English colony live. The majority that we met worked for Western Telegraph, as Cable and Wireless is known in South America. Most of them had Brazilian wives who showed us things they thought we as strangers should see: the first attempt we had seen at a community centre, an improvement on the terrible shacks and hovels surrounding it, and a new village for the fishermen; huts dry, well-built but still with no water or lighting. We learned other things too when a young Brazilian wife unthinkingly sat in the back of a car between Anne and myself. Just as her husband was driving off she leapt up with a horrified look and insisted on changing places with me, saying that in Brazil no man or woman must sit in a car between man and wife.

"But surely it doesn't matter with friends?"

"Yes, it does. It is . . . very bad form . . . yes?"

Like so many enterprises that were begun by Britain during its Victorian greatness "Westerns" is beginning to shrink, or perhaps it might be more accurate to say expand by replacing, slowly but at all levels, its personnel with people from the country where it operates: half Brazilians but likely to spend most of their lives in Brazil, I hope that some of the young boys we met would be able to carry on the traditions of this great company. Their hospitality to small boat sailors goes back for many generations and we were no exception. To replace the lead we had lost in Bahia they made us a new one with loving care, stamping on it the name of our ship, the place, the date and the initials of the men who helped to make it.

On the first morning of our stay here we had rowed over to the little quay on Ilhas das Pombas to ask if the boatman could keep an eye on *Moonraker* while we were in town; and while we were talking his wife came running down from the little house to ask us up to coffee. The house overlooked the river. It belonged to the Customs and Excise who also owned the island, and the boatman and his family had been given the house rent free because he was known to be a trustworthy person who would report any illicit happenings to his landlords. The house was as clean as a Polynesian's hut but even more bare, there being a table supported on two packing cases, two benches, a double bed and several hammocks in which seven people slept. There were three rooms, the biggest no longer than our cabin, no windows and no doors. By the time we had seen all this the kettle on the stone oven was boiling and we were given cafezinho, as good as that which we were to have at the Palace, but to our embarrassment our hostess, who looked as if she gave most of her food to her children, produced three small white rolls which they wanted to share with us. As this might easily be the first white bread they had seen for several weeks Anne managed to convince them that we had had an enormous breakfast and could not do justice to them. Looking back over this last paragraph I feel I may have given the impression that this family was poor. On the contrary, it was something of a success story. They had a son attending "navigation school", a daughter of fourteen who was already a beautiful girl, three younger children and they had had three others who had died because there had not been enough food when the husband left the sea to be with his family but could find no work ashore for month after month.

He could, however, both read and write and eventually he was taken on as a boatman ferrying sailors between their ships and the shore.

After two years he had saved enough money to buy a boat so that now the profits were his own and because of his reputation along the waterfront they now had a home of which they could be proud.

They took us over the island, showing us the maize and

mandioca plants struggling up through the dusty shallow soil and the traps which were waiting to be repaired with which they hoped to keep down the rats. There was a banana and a mamáo tree and, as the boatman said, there were plenty of fish in the sea. They promised to pay us a visit but we were away a good deal so that it was unfortunate on the morning of our departure and after the anchor was aweigh, that we saw them rowing out to us.

Anne said, "You can't disappoint them. We must go back."

I said, "If we do that we shall miss the tide."

As we sailed out into the channel Anne said in a frozen voice "I hope it will blow a gale in your teeth."

We made a good ten miles in eight hours. Wet clouds clung to mountain peaks like too tight dresses. We knew those clouds: on the snow covered peaks of the Queen Charlottes, over the hot barren hills round the Gulf of Tehuantepec, they have the same meaning—bad weather. But ahead, not more than fouteen miles away was the Rio Guarapari and a small harbour sheltered from all winds. We had seen it from the land: a charming haven where small dark women with high cheek bones make lace to sell to the tourists, and if we could get there before dark we should at least have made a start. I came on watch, drowsy after an afternoon's sleep to find the ship, becalmed, pitching into lines of short steep waves marching up from the south: and at that moment, from dead ahead, the wind darkened the water. Anne's gale was here.

I put up the helm and in two hours we were back in the lee of our island. In the middle of the night I turned out to let out more chain. Under my Imak jacket and trousers, no longer in good condition, I was soaked to the skin by the rain driven before the southerly gale. Satisfied that the ship was not dragging through the soft mud I returned below thankful that we were not hove-to outside being driven back up this coast down which we had been so long coming. Although the gale blew itself out by the evening the wind remained obstinately in the south. Our little family from Pombas paid us a visit. The children were gay. They all had the most perfect manners and before they left Anne showed them our pressure cooker in which was a sizeable lump of steak. She explained that we were going out to dinner that night with friends and tomorrow it might be bad. It seemed such a pity to waste it. Could they possibly eat it? After many protestations, during which the childrens' eyes became rounder and rounder, they finally accepted.

At six in the morning we were greeting our friend. He returned the pressure cooker looking as it had not looked for the past sixteen years and the muslin which Anne puts over it to keep out the flies had not only been washed but ironed. Our friend hung on his oars and pointed to the north from where a light breeze had sprung up.

"Mucho vento," he said. "Mucho vento do norte."

"Muito bem," we said.

He nodded his head doubtfully. "Mais tarde, vento forte do norte."

Then, seeing that our minds were made up he shook us warmly by the hand. "Boa viagem," he cried "Muito couragem."

"Te log" we shouted.

CHAPTER TWELVE

TO reach Rio de Janeiro a ship must round Cabo Frio, one of the great capes of the world. In the days of sail it was the scourge of ships bound from the south to the east coast ports for the odds were five to one that both wind and current would be against them. It is a bold headland, an island, not unlike Cape Horn, of about the same height, which it resembles when seen from a distance on a sombre day. Though Frio may seem a curious name for so warm a latitude, the cape was so named from a branch of the cold Cape Horn current which at this point turns inshore to give a freshness to this place that is found nowhere else on the coast. From this brief description you can understand that we looked forward, coming as we did from the north, to a fast passage. Having cleared the roads outside the Vitoria river, where eleven ships of seven nations rolled uneasily in the cross swell, *Moonraker* reeled off the miles before a strong wind Force 7 on the Beaufort scale under three reefs, rolling down to Rio. The wind gods, however, had loaded the dice against us. Our good north wind died away and the south-west wind which followed it, bringing rain and poor visibility, delayed our rounding of the cape until the third morning out. At first light we were again utterly becalmed and the roar of breakers at the base of this iron bound shore hung in the air as one continuous sound. My thoughts, however, as I sat at the useless tiller were some five thousand miles away in a house in the Essex countryside where I had met a young Brazilian. His father had died two years ago and at the age of twenty he had been catapulted into the business world of Rio, the only man in the family firm, guided by his mother and his aunt. He had, on that evening in England, already given me useful advice about Brazil but when he spoke of Rio his voice changed like that of a man speaking of someone he loved. He said, "Rio has everything: the most beautiful girls, the finest beaches, the most spectacular scenery. It has something which I cannot describe to you although I might do more justice to it in Portuguese. I guess its how a Frenchman feels when he returns to Paris after a prolonged stay in London." Some weeks later I had a letter from him giving me names of people and places I ought to see on my way south and extending a warm welcome to all of us when we got to Rio. The fact that he had written at all surprised me because I knew by then that he was not expecting to see us, at least not in our own boat. Our friends in Essex, on the morning after the dinner party, had taken him to see *Moonraker* where she was laid up in a mud berth at Cardnell Bros. yard in Maylandsea. One look at her, bereft of rigging and spars and with rust streaking down her sides had been enough. "To sail in such a boat to Rio," he had said "would be impossible."

After seven hours the calm, which had threatened to put off our arrival at Rio for another day, broke. A sea wind from the south, bringing wind and rain, drove the ship at her finest speed, as sightless as her crew who, huddled in the bows, strained their ears for the sound of breakers and their eyes for a glimpse of the Mariocas, two small islets standing like signposts on the way to Rio. A shout. "To starboard. . . . In line with the shrouds." Bare though they may be, to us they were beautiful for now we knew where we were. Eight miles to go. And now, as if at a great distance off, there appeared a glow fine on the starboard bow. In the place of mist came violent squalls of wind and rain hiding the leading lights, keeping us anxiously on our toes. Clouds were down over the mountains and Copocabana beach, whose reflection can be seen on a clear night for a hundred miles to seaward, looked no more exciting than Brighton waterfront seen from the English Channel. As the shores closed in on either hand Anne said, "There's a passage inside Ilha Lage which is a short cut to Botofogo Bay and the Yacht Club." Reading from the *Pilot* she continued, "There are rocks in the channel with three and four fathoms over them and a reef extends south west of the island. This passage must only be attempted with local knowledge." She peered out of the hatch at the short steep seas and the tide sweeping us past bare black rocks. She said, "On a night like this I do not like it."

There was, however, a fresh commanding wind and my eyes were blinded by the shortness of the cut. As I put the helm down I felt for the first time the grip of that tremendous current; and at the moment the wind dropped. In the next we were surrounded by breaking seas and the thunder of the surf on the reef.

"The engine!" I shouted.

I remember Anne's wild scramble for the deck, the chart in hand, Jock's leap for the engine room and my thoughts racing through my head that at the very moment we had reached our goal I had thrown away our ship. Then a hard puff off the land steadied her and she gathered way into the smooth waters of Botofogo Bay. The clouds were lifting. Before my eyes, still clouded with fear, a hole appeared in the sky and, lit by an eerie light from behind, the figure of Christ stood high above us. It was as if a miracle had taken place before our eyes....

We stole quietly into a small cove and anchored in two fathoms off the village of Urca.

Not until the early morning sun came streaming into the cabin did I awake. I went on deck in my pyjamas. It was not the Corcovada with its statue of Christ at the top of a thousand foot precipice which held me there, it was not the famous Sugar Loaf nor the outlines of the city sprawling along the shores nor the islands in Guanabara Bay. It was not the part but the whole; and, like my Brazilian friend, I became, immediately and completely, Rio's slave.

The Rio de Janeiro Yacht Club is as exclusive as the Jockey Club. At its gates is a Porter's Lodge and a chain is kept at waist height across the entrance to keep out all comers who are not known to the gatekeeper or cannot produce passes. Even the wife of the First Secretary of the British Embassy, in a chauffeur driven car and C.D. numberplates, was refused admission on the morning we arrived until an acquaintance happened to come along to vouch for her. But the Brazilians have a special place in their hearts for strangers and soon a less official password caused the chain to be dropped: "The English Yacht...?" "But of course..."

The Clubhouse is a long ranch-style dwelling with a broad terrace outside where you can lunch or dine under the palm trees. There is a dining room for the cooler nights, a reading room, billiard room and a wide covered veranda with easy chairs and tables but enough room for the youth and beauty of Rio to parade, hand in hand, up and down the gangway on Saturday nights. There is a bar, of course, and a coffee bar where cafezinho is served free to members from early morning to late at night. Telephone calls to Rio are also free. Set in the grounds at some distance from the ranch house is a ballroom and a swimming pool. To belong to this club candidates have to buy one million cruzeiros worth of shares which they can sell if they want to resign and the yearly subscription is one hundred contos. Riches alone, however, will not guarantee membership to this distinguished club. Over it presides the Commodore, Senor Cecil Davis, a Brazilian with at least some Celtic blood in his veins and we were made honorary members for the rest of the year.

One of the things we had learned since we had been in Brazil was that the day rarely ended as we thought it would; and this one proved no exception. We had tea that afternoon in a flat ten storeys up from the Praia de Flamenco and through the open windows the noise of Rio was muted to a low mutter of sound. Cars crawled like ants along the boulevard below and as the lights of Rio went up Mary de Salis' husband came into the room. "Charles," said his wife, "D'you know these people have lived in their tiny cabin for six months without a break? I'm driving them up to the Alto tomorrow where they can stay for a few days in the cottage and stretch their legs." Her husband walked over to the window and in the fading light I could see the place we had anchored in the small hours of the morning. "We saw your boat sail out of Urca before breakfast," he said, "From something Phillip told me (Phillip was the friend who had given us this introduction) I thought she was the sort of boat you'd have." So that was why his wife had arrived almost before we had anchored!

We dined out that night in a restaurant where the customer chooses his meat from long spits turning over a charcoal fire and eats it at tables set among tree trunks that ended just below the roof. Charles de Salis had been a schoolmaster, had served in Intelligence and had only joined the Foreign Service when the war ended. He spoke Portuguese as if he loved it and this with his slightly ironic humour and a keen sense of the ridiculous has made him more than usually simpatico to Brazilians.

As we walked back to the flat he told me that a member of the L.C.C. had come out to some conference. He had taken one look at the pot holes in Rio's roads, "These roads," he said "would bankrupt the L.C.C. in a week." "The Cariocas," said Charles de Salis "grow trees in them when they get too big, but last week I heard a man had fallen into one and found another man at the bottom who had been in there a week."

Few cities of over three million inhabitants can boast a forest within forty minutes drive of their centres. The Tijuca forest lies within the arms, but not totally enclosed by, this growing octopus-like city, penetrated by a road up which we sped the next day, twisting, turning, climbing between banks of Shameless Mary (or Busy Lizzie), their pink petals waving lustily in the wake of our passing car. Great trees, three hundred different varieties of them, climbed up the steep hillside so closely woven that the forest looked impenetrable. The Alto de Boa Vista right in the middle of it is strangely hard to find. Not till I had been there half a dozen times did I even think I knew the way and I am sure I could not find it now. The de Salis' cottage stands where the road ends. It is a bungalow with a glorious view of forest and mountain and not a sign or smell of the sea. I was glad of this. After taking in our stores we waved to Mary de Salis as she swung the car down the drive promising she would pick us up in four days time. We felt, as we stood on the lawn looking over the sea of trees bending and lifting like the waves of the ocean tossed by the mountain wind, as if we had been marooned by some tyrant captain in whose promise to send relief we no longer had faith.

At sunset the wind dropped. The birds had gone to bed, the stars were so near that you could reach out your hand to touch them and it was so quiet that we sat on the veranda without speaking, drinking in the peace of this beautiful place.

Some two hundred feet below the cottage was the Sitio to which all the land round about belonged. The house was a low ranch-type building overlooking a lake with ducks and swans on it and several large farm buildings on the far side. Over this ruled Alice Gross, looking after the estate for the owner who lived in Rio. Her husband was managing director of a tobacco company and they had invited us to supper with them one evening. Alan had been too long in this country to have any faith in its quick financial recovery. He thought the only hope was in finding a benevolent dictator who would be strong enough to enforce the laws he made. "There's nothing wrong with the laws on paper. It's just that they don't work. For instance they made a law (to protect the worker) which forbade an employer to sack a man after he had been with him for ten years. So all the employees of nine years standing were sacked on the spot." He was pessimistic on the future of British enterprises in the country. "We never have any difficulty in getting labour. They know we look after them better than their own countrymen do but as soon as they've had a few caçaças they daub the walls with slogans: 'Brazil for the Brazilians. American and British go home.'" He puffed away comfortably at his old churchwarden pipe. "I've been here too long. A cottage in the south of England would suit me."

As we walked up the hill to the cottage in the pouring rain (it had been raining all day) we all agreed that here lived two very kind people. To what lengths their kindness would go we were later to find out.

Faithful to her word Mary de Salis came for us on the fourth day, the one rainless day we had up there, but we were rested and refreshed, eager to plunge into the heart of Rio and find out what she was made of. Before dropping us Mary promised to bring her husband to see the boat in a couple of days time and we presented ourselves at the Porter's Lodge and ran straight into the arms of the press. It was not late but there was no one at the Club to translate and they talked so fast that even Anne was completely bewildered. I thought of our Brazilian friend whom we had not yet had time to contact. I rang him up, apologized for not doing so before and told him what was happening. He said "Where are you speaking from?"

"The Rio de Janeiro Yacht Club."

"You didn't come all the way in that boat?"

"Of course."

"No wonder the Press are after you. I'll be down in ten minutes."

Even in the short time since we had last seen him, less than a year ago, Eduardo looked older and more mature. He handled the interview with expertise, made the Press write down our ages (60, 58, 34), which they seemed to want and tried on their behalf to extract something of interest in the way of a storm or some hair-raising incident but, as we had had no bad weather except a fresh gale in the Bay of Biscay lasting less than twenty-four hours, we could do nothing to help them. When they had gone he wanted to know where we were staying. We showed him *Moonraker* just visible in the light from the city. "This is ridiculous. We cannot put you up at home but at least I can find a hotel where you can stay as my guests." It was some time before we could persuade him that we liked our primitive life aboard. Before he left he asked me whether there was anything else he could do for us. Now amongst our mail was an aviso from the Customs that an Imak jacket sent out to me by a friend from Copenhagen had arrived and that on the payment of nine thousand cruzeiros, more than the jacket was worth, we could take it out. He said, "The Customs at Rio are difficult but it might be worthwhile for me to take you down to the Alfandego in the morning."

When he arrived he was carrying a newspaper under his arm. We all knew what was inside it: a very indifferent photograph of the ship and a worse one of ourselves under the caption:

SEPTUAGENARIANS SAIL BOAT FROM ENGLAND TO RIO.

This was not all: there was a graphic account of how we lay prostrate in the centre of the south Atlantic hurricane (any seaman knows that there are no such storms in these waters) and other exciting adventures which were new to us. In a word it was the sort of story which would raise more than one eyebrow amongst our friends in England if any of them had the misfortune to read it. Eduardo drove us down town to the Alfandego, an old time-worn building in dockland, with a heavy battered open door through which we entered a large hall with a counter running the entire length of the room behind which sat twelve bored men at twelve dusty desks perusing papers that looked as if they had been there unchanged for several years. Eventually one man got up and walked over to where we stood waiting. He took the aviso from our friend's hand, glanced at it and said, "Nine thousand cruzeiros please and one hundred and twenty for the stamp."

Eduardo took the newspaper from under his arm and let it fall open at *Moonraker's* page. "Have you seen this?" he asked.

"Yes," replied the man. "They have courage."

Eduardo pushed us forward. "These are the people," he said. Immediately twelve bored faces broke into twelve rippling smiles like the first tiny waves on a dead pan sea and eleven men rose as one, shaking hands, patting us on the shoulder, congratulating us on our miraculous escape from the hurricane and asking questions which, as you can imagine, were embarrassing to find answers for. And then the head man himself, who sat at a desk in a sort of pulpit-like place well above his inferiors, came down and added his congratulations to theirs. He read the aviso, walked into another department and returned with a parcel. Handing this to me, he said with a smile, "That will be one hundred and twenty cruzeiros for the stamp."

That afternoon Eduardo drove us up to the Corcovada, the Hunchback, upon which, on the edge of a thousand foot precipice, the hundred foot statue of Christ stands. As I looked at the lines of sorrow and compassion which the sculptor had moulded into that face I was reminded of Mary de Salis' comment when we had told her about seeing the statue framed in cloud as we sailed in that night. She said, "I'm afraid he looks down on an awful lot of wickedness." From the foot of the statue Rio looked white and yellow. White for rich, yellow for poor. More than a million people live in favellas without heat, water or light which climb up the mountain sides because there is no room left for them on the flat. Yellow shacks with mud walls, wooden huts with rusty iron roofs, all colours and shapes but yellow as the predominant colour, a dirty smoke-begrimed non-descript yellow rubbing shoulders, it seemed from this height, with large white mansions in elegant gardens, which once housed the cream of the Portuguese nobility. As the sun set behind the mountains in the west darkness rose from the valley. All the lights in the city sprang up at once sparkling like jewels in a surrealist setting. Without comment Eduardo touched me on the arm. "We must be going."

Eduardo's car was (it exists no more) a Rural Willys, a sort of family jeep with plenty of room and comfortable seats. Like most Brazilians he was an expert driver with split-second reactions and a racing instinct: we were not sorry to see that the Rural Willys had a four-wheel drive and a comparatively slow top speed of a hundred and thirty-five kilometers. He drove us back through the Tijuca forest, the car spluttering with loud explosions in the exhaust box whenever he pressed the horn. Round a sharp bend right in the heart of the forest the engine stalled. The battery was dead. We got out. The forest was deathly quiet. Eduardo said, "This could not have happened in a worse place. We must push." We pushed until the sweat ran down our faces and our shirts clung to our backs but we could not push that car over the incline which stood between us and the descending road beyond. Eduardo said, "Get in the car and don't get out. If anyone stops and speaks to you answer him in English at once. I am going for help." He disappeared down a steep path towards two lights which flickered among the trees. "I can't think what he's fussing about," said Jock. "This is a proper road and there must be cars passing all the time." But no cars passed and no one came by on the road. Time dragged by. Just as we were wondering whether we ought to go in search of Eduardo he appeared with a crowd of children and in less than five minutes the car was over the hump and we could if necessary free wheel to the outskirts of the city.

Eduardo gave the children something out of a paper bag which seemed to please them, let go the brake and we were away, the engine starting after we had gone a hundred yards. He said, "Last week two men were robbed in that place. One was shot dead, the other was knifed and lay for several hours before anyone came to help." I wondered about those lonely shacks in the forest. Did anyone hear the shot or the cries of the wounded man? Perhaps, but if you live in the Tijuca forest, it is safer to hear and see nothing. The rest of the drive went off hilariously. As we tore down the dark tunnel of trees the lights and sounds of the city lay at our feet. The rush hour in Rio was not entirely over. Cars were bumper to bumper when again the engine stalled: all Eduardo did was to wave on the car following him who pushed him until the engine started. The next time it stalled it was a bus driver who obliged. After that we turned into less crowded streets down which Eduardo rushed keeping his hand on the horn because the explosions in the exhaust pipe delighted him. It was surprising it did not blow off.

Eduardo's mother had been in the U.S.A. when we arrived but as soon as she returned Eduardo brought her aboard; the first time he had entrusted himself to being rowed out in our pram, strictly on her insistence. She looked more like an elder sister than his mother. Smartly dressed, feminine to the tips of her toes, it was hard to believe that when she had taken over her husband's business, she had widened its scope to avoid duties forced on private enterprise by a failing economy, by driving up to Diamontina in the Minas Gerais where, dressed in jeans and with a revolver always to hand for some of her customers were decidedly tough, she had made her contacts by jeep.

She took us that day to lunch in the city, to a restaurant in the Rua Branco whose tall uniform buildings swamp the old Portuguese churches and buildings like the sea of materialism which is sweeping over the world. After lunch we were taken thirty-five floors up to Eduardo's office which has a magnificent view right out over Guanabara Bay and the ships at anchor awaiting a place at the wharves. Eduardo pointed out a small island which had been in the news a few years ago. It was being overrun by the widow spider whose bite is fatal to man. All efforts to kill them failed so the island was evacuated and the Air force was detailed to drop bombs on the spiders. Unfortunately they bombed the wrong island. After that they called in a scientist. He said "There is no problem. Put two hundred hens on the island. In a week they will have eaten the spiders."

I was looking at some specimens of precious stones in their natural state when Eduardo suddenly turned to me. "I am taking you to Brasilia tomorrow." Anne opened her mouth in astonishment. "That would be wonderful." Then she turned to his mother as if in some doubt. "Will that be all right? Can you spare him . . . ?"

"Of course I can, but nothing would make ME go to Brasilia in that car."

We had seen enough to know what she meant.

CHAPTER THIRTEEN

WE did not, in fact, start for several days. Although we as a generation live in a crisis-ridden age the clouds now looking over the political sea seemed more than usually ominous. As Russian ships approached Cuba and the American navy took up positions to head them off the Brazilian wireless became more and more tense. Programmes were interrupted by frequent announcements, pouring out like an ebb tide through the Portland Firth, few of which we could understand until the words, spoken in an ever rising scale, reached the climax of "TOTAL NUCLEAR WAR!" After this the dry factual programme of the British Overseas Broadcast came as a welcome end to anxious days.

By the time the political scene had recovered the Rural Willys had not. New tyres and a new battery had been installed but the car had to be rewired. Finally, on a Saturday evening, Eduardo said he was calling for us at six o'clock the next morning. We were a motley crew, Eduardo immaculate, the rest of us with kit bags slung round our shoulders carrying bursting duffle bags for neither Anne nor Jock would ever travel without enough to go down a coal mine or to dine in a civic hall. After a closer scrutiny Eduardo said, "You look like the Pau d'Arara." When pressed he said it was a name given to the people of the north-east who came to build Brasilia. And translated it means the Black Crows.

With Anne and myself in the back and Jock in front we roared out along the double track road, the only main road out of Rio, past the unspeakable shanty suburbs out into the country and the foothills where the road divided, to the left for Sao Paulo, to the right for Petropolis (a spa town with an ex-Emperor's Palace, a lake, and a large hotel with silent ballrooms and echoing corridors), and a dull modern town beyond, and for us the road in front: climbing, twisting, buffeted by winds, up the sides of mountains deeply forested, black with clouds while behind the sun shone on the golden valley that led to Rio whose hills now looked like those of ants. Up into clouds, swirling round us in the fierce wind, past three crashes on the road, (round a bend where the concrete parapet had gone and the remains of a lorry that had carried it away far below in the ravine:) over the pass, four thousand feet above sea level, then losing height by the side of a mountain torrent, into rolling country with distant views, broadening out as we fled from the great mountains whose peaks had been hidden in cloud, past rich houses in splendid gardens, shacks by the wayside, the Rural Willys broke into the broad main and only street of Areal where we stopped for a second breakfast. Stalls with bright bananas, leather water bottles, saddles, hats, trays of Jabuticaba like black cherries with fronds to keep them cool, cafes with honky tonks, wireless blaring from open shops and a thin stream of men and women in black moving steadily towards the church, for it was Sunday morning, to which a cracked bell summoned them. As Eduardo summoned us "Forward" was the cry. . . . Now Jock sat behind and I in front: on past small fields with anthills eight feet high, old and grey like the columns of Stonehenge, round hair pin bends and banana plantations ("I turned the car upside down into that one three months ago") Eduardo airily waved his hands, up and down long stretches of straight road, just wide enough for two buses to pass, and with a two hundred and fifty foot drop on each side and long cracks spreading towards the centre from the soft verges, until after several hours we came to our first town, Juiz de Fora which means Judge of the Outside.

A hot dusty town with cobbled streets and a hotel serving the usual steak and farofa and Eduardo petulant and panting to be off. "Anne: why go to Ouro Preto, or Congonhas. They're old."

"But that's why I want to see them. If I must miss something out it would be Belo Horizonte."

"But Belo is new, Anne," he said, "Everything new is exciting: the old is dead."

Up into the hills again, the hills of the Minas Gerias where the Bandeirantes came from Sao Paulo, tough unscrupulous men, thrusting into this unknown country, killing right and left, Indians and Jesuits alike, in their search for gold and precious stones, where men now seek for minerals. Green hills, but of a peculiar shade as if the iron below shows through the thin green covering. Rain. Eduardo silent; battling with the drenched roads, the slithering car, peering through the windscreen across which the wipers no longer move as we speed through this silent empty valley with an occasional glimpse of a distant mine.

A sign post!

"Must we go to Congonhas do Campo?"

"PLEASE."

An irritated turn to the left off the main road, down a red earth lane to the foot of a village perched like a fortress on the brow of a hill. Eduardo brings the Willys to a halt outside a church with a blue door and a terrace overlooking the village street up which toil six oxen pulling an empty cart. It was this we had come to see. We share this view with twelve sculpted figures in stone (the twelve apostles) by Antonio Francisco Lisboa, known throughout Brazil as Aleijadinho (Little Cripple). He was the son of a Portuguese carpenter and a negro slave, who contracted leprosy and lost his hands but went on working with his instruments strapped to his forearms, helped by the softness of the green soapstone of the Minas which hardens on exposure. Even Eduardo was impressed by the beauty of this eighteenth century work in its superb setting, all his petulance silenced by the sheer beauty of Aleijadinho's work.

Back on the road for Ouro Preto (Black Gold). Eduardo is not sure if he had enough petrol, the gauge is low and there is nowhere to buy any. It is dark. No lights of cars, not even a paraffin flare in a shack. Anne and I, together again in the back, no longer peer out of windows for there is nothing to see except a black void to starboard and trees clinging to the steep sides of hills to port. Anne is planning how to make the back of the Willys into a bed for three if we run out of petrol and Jock is asleep. Suddenly, out of this blackness, we see a glitter of yellow lights far below like a cluster of topaz in the bottom of a salad bowl. We glide down a long hill and enter the town. Not without difficulty, for the steep streets are running rivers and Eduardo has never been here before; we find the Pensoa de Chico Rei which Alice Gross has strongly recommended. The door is opened a crack and a dark girl stands in the crack. She is sorry; there is no room. She suggests the Grand Hotel at the top of the town and there with a sigh of relief we start unpacking the car. We have been on the road for thirteen hours.

The hotel is not grand but is adequate. We each have a small suite. A sitting room with a table, two wooden chairs and leading off a small spiral staircase to our bedroom, shower and lavatory. Unlike others we have met on the road, this one works.

The sun was over a mountain ridge when I stood by the window and looked down upon this sleepy forgotten town which is visited, as we were visiting it now, for its past. Like Olinda its shadow has grown smaller. Two hundred years ago it was a harsh and violent place, a base for men seeking their fortune. It was in this town that the first plot was hatched to seize independence from Portugal by a young army lieutenant who became a national hero under the nickname of Tiradontes (The Toothpuller becaue he was reputed to have been a dentist). He was thirty-three years too soon. The plot was discovered, the plotters severely punished and he was hung drawn and quartered and his head hung up for display over the door of a house which later was pointed out to us.

The town itself, within its wide mountain bowl, is built on several lesser hills each of which is topped by a church, thirteen churches in all. In most of them are the works of Aleijedinho for this was where he lived. Now Anne and I are no sightseers and thirteen churches were about ten too many, although we did struggle through four, by which time most of the things I'd seen were forgotten. These, however, I remember: a small wooden statue of Christ on the Cross by Aleijadinho, the most beautiful thing of its sort I have ever seen, a pulpit of soapstone with a scene, perfect in detail, where St. Paul, with a self-deprecatory and faintly ironic look in his eye, stands by the side of a cow with a book in his hand, as if he were doubting the wisdom of trying to teach it to read; and a picture of a blue fine weather sky, pearly gates, a man in a boat sailing out of a cloud, angels with trumpets—space, light, happiness. Eduardo, who graciously came with us, said it was the first picture he had seen that made him want to go to heaven.

At lunch time I rang the proprietress of the Pensao de Chico Rei, and Alice Gross's name worked wonders. She would be delighted to give us dinner that night and I gathered that if she had known our references before, rooms might have been found for us last night. After lunch Eduardo took Jock away to help him with the car while Anne and I spent the afternoon wandering through the streets. I was persuaded to buy a sort of prairie hat, guaranteed waterproof, of which Eduardo strongly disapproved and which I have never dared to wear in England. In the square a large white horse was eating out of a dustbin and an old woman, swathed in jumpers and petticoats and tied with a girdle of twisted string, came to beg from Anne, telling her that she was seventy-four and had been Miss Ouro Preto fifty-six years ago at the age of eighteen. I had wrongly supposed this sort of thing to be a product of the post-war years. We finished up in the Museum of Mineralogy: gobs of gold in black rock, copies of famous diamonds as big as coat buttons, every sort of precious stone including an aquamarine of almost peacock blue that made Anne gaze in wonder. That night we presented ourselves at the Pensaoa de Chico Rei. Chico had been a tribal chief in Ibo (Nigeria) who with his wife, eight children and his entire court had been sold into slavery, and then worked in a mine near Ouro

Preto. He became a diligent and faithful worker and finally bought his "afiranebti" (liberation) and that of his entire family and court. Once a year he used to parade through the streets in full regalia so that he became known as the King of Ouro Preto.

The Pensao was run by a Danish woman married to a Brazilian whose father had been a collector for museums of art. Anything which was too expensive for his clients he kept for himself. Senhora Lily took us up to the drawing room herself. It was a room in red. Red walls, red upholstery, an exquisite table of jacaranda, a wooden cradle, like one that I had seen in a museum in Holland, and a pair of sceptres used by Chico Rei himself in an African dance. The food was excellent and we drank a sort of Brazilian claret known as Trapiche which went well with the meal. The Senhora very kindly asked us to come and see their own private collection at their house. This we had to refuse for Eduardo, having wasted, well—not quite wasted—a whole day was adamant that we should leave soon after dawn.

More trees, more green mountains, mines, steelworks and much more rain but less inconvenient because Eduardo and Jock had got the wipers going. By midday the rain had stopped and the road brought us over the brow of a hill to a general view of Belo Horizonte, a name no longer appropriate. It spread like the arms of a squid into the green surrounding country. From its circular head streets diverged radially so that a building, sixteen stories or more high, would start at a corner like the bow of an enormous liner no more than a few feet thick. We made a grand tour conducted by the enthusiastic Eduardo but the only thing I can remember was a rather dismal lake on the outskirts of the town and a futuristic church in blue and white by the famous Niemeyer with a tower like one of the ventilation columns over the Dartford Tunnel in miniature. The interior reminded me of the church at the university of British Columbia in its simplicity and its cold bare light, but behind the altar, taking up the whole of the wall, was a painting by Portinari of a scene from the life of St. Francis of Assisi. In the original of this work the artist had depicted the Saint with one eye in his chest for which heresy the Roman Catholic Church had excommunicated him. However, after two years in outer darkness Portinari put the eye back in its right place and was received once more into the arms of the Church.

We dined that night in the Restaurant Amizonas at a table by the window looking down from a great height on the busy street below and into the private lives of those on the opposite side at a slightly lower level. Round the walls were murals of local Minas celebrities: Aleijadinho, Tiradentes and a poet, Anchiete, sitting writing in the stern of a lateen-rigged boat while a sailor with a monk-like face buried the anchor with his own hands.

From Belo to Brasilia is a distance of rather less than five hundred miles. The road is good, the traffic limited: about one car or lorry in every hour, if my memory serves me rightly, once the Sao Paulo road has branched off to the left. We had been told that the drive would be dull and monotonous but my first sight of the great Brazilian Plain was one of the things I shall never forget. It was as if you could see half across the world: a world of scrub and small stunted trees, green and brown melting into blue as your eye travelled even further to the west. As the Willys surged over the sweeping rolling plain, cresting the hills, diving into the hollows, it was as if the land were in motion and these hills were the waves of a Brobdingnagian ocean. From time to time, at anything from twenty to sixty miles, we would roar over the brow of a hill to see a tall pole with an "Esso" sign as naked as a gibbet on Dartmoor and a small filling station with concrete facing, a restaurant where coffee was drinkable and food uneatable. Behind would be the "Comfort Station" as the North Americans call them but for us they were not even approachable. Not a single loo worked but this did not deter clients from using them. Anne, I believe, fared a little better but I noticed she always wore her small sea boots. In four hundred miles we passed through no villages and saw only one town in the distance, Tres Marias, where a dam has been built to make a reservoir from the Sao Francisco river and a town has grown up on the edge of it. There is a bridge which cannot be more than five years old crossing this great river and only a fortnight after we got back to Rio the bridge collapsed when two of the big Rio-Brasilia buses were crossing it at the same time. Forty-eight people were drowned. There would be an occasional signpost and a red-rutted road would disappear into the bush but either the place was too far away to see or it was hidden in a dip. There was a fazenda or two with cattle grazing and some fields of corn but what was surprising was the number of isolated huts bordering this lonely road. They did not cluster together but were five or ten miles from each other. Were they hoping for some vast ribbon development so that their land would increase a hundredfold?

Eleven hours after we had left Belo we crested a rise and on the opposite side of a shallow valley rose tall and delicate buildings like the scattered sails of a distant fleet on a wine dark sea.

Eduardo stopped the car. Behind this ethereal city was the blue black cloud of a thunderstorm and at that moment the last rays of the setting sun painted the snow white buildings in a sort of alpenglum. So might a pilgrim have felt when he gazed for the first time on Mecca.

Lights sprang up on curved and slender standards, flittering like diamonds over the darkening hills, tracing roads that are not yet streets and without a single building near them. We drove up the empty eight-lane highway past the incredible beauty of the Square of the Three Powers, the two porcelain-like bowls, one right side up, the other upside down, which form the congressional chambers floodlit from every angle. Here we turned to the right down what may one day be a street of ambassadors but which at the moment is marked by names of countries on short posts staking their claims for the future. We arrived at the Brasilia Palace Hotel, looking, as we approached it, like a mouth organ on legs. The Willys was splashed with red earth from head to foot from the rains of Ouro Preto and I felt like the Willys. But for Eduardo, who has a flair for preserving his appearance, I do not believe we should have gained admittance.

CHAPTER FOURTEEN

A CITY built in a wilderness by the single mindedness of one man, Juscelino Kubitschek; who sacrificed his country's economy, so his compatriots say, for a dream; a city designed by an artist, Oscar Neimeyer, who knew how to harness concrete and glass to clouds and sky giving space, light, movement; a city which H.G. Wells would have chosen for his Air Men to live in. The capital city of the fourth largest country in the world with a population of Newbury in Berkshire. Yet it is a city where no Brazilian I met ever wants to live; to which congressmen fly from Rio under protest to return at the earliest possible moment: a city without a railway, with one main road to the south and one to Belem in the north, now closed: a visionary city only now thrusting up the first flowers—strange glass flowers of man's imaginatioin—through the rich earth, preparing great spaces for men to live in, wide roads for men to drive on before man himself has arrived. A cathedral whose bare concrete ribs, rust red and unlined, form the shape of a crown; the Palace of Dawn, the High Court of Justice, their sides like wings, the two slender blocks of administration, face to face and twenty-five storeys high soaring over the two congressional bowls like the Town of Babel over the City of Babylon.

A memorial to the men who built Brasilia, the Pau d'Arara, brought down from the north-east in trucks, their ragged clothes flapping in the wind, for they were the only people who were tough enough to stand up to the conditions in which they had to work. I am no student of architecture, nor do I like most modern trends but no one could fail to be impressed by the columns, ramps, curves, flares, the proportions of some of these buildings. As to the Memorial to the people of the north-east, it is pure symbolism of gaunt black metal. I thought it magnificent.

At the bus station roads pass under or over each other to avoid the need for traffic lights. Kiosks sell mementos and books of photographs and you can lean over the parapet of the bridge watching peasants with Indian features waiting patiently on benches for a bus to Goiania, or tourists filing slowly into that gently breathing monster, the Interstate Brasilia-Rio bus. There is of course a hard core of living places: offices, hotels, and shops (prices are astronomical to cover the cost of transport), private residences with gardens and flowers and a few scattered houses in what one day may be suburbia. But twenty thousand people set in the middle of the Great Brasilian Plain, five hundred miles from the nearest city could rightly think of themselves as being isolated.

I asked Eduardo if he thought it would survive. He shrugged his shoulders. He said, "If Kubitschek comes back into power it will grow rapidly. He will see to that, even if it ruins the nation. I think it will succeed anyway. A lot has been done since I was here for the inauguration and that is only two years ago."

The Skinners, whom we had met in Rio, very kindly asked us to lunch at the house which, until a more elaborate building has been set up, serves as the British Residency. We were shown into the drawing room where our host and hostess greeted us and then introduced us to a man whom I at once recognized as being a sailor and a member of the Club under whose burgee we sail. He was up here for an International Conference of M.P.s and is the secretary of the World Organization for Peace. He and Eduardo got on well together and we arranged to meet in Rio. After lunch Eduardo said he had to go and service the car and the Skinners took the rest of us down to the lake which has been made by damming a river and on the shores of which there is now a yacht club and a round dozen small boats that can sail on fifty square miles of fresh water. It had been raining heavily and there were many pools on the concrete paving. Suddenly M, who was walking by my side, took a violent lurch to port as his leg disappeared down a hole full of water. How he recovered himself without breaking it I cannot think but it was probably his sailor's instinct for keeping on an even keel. I told him Charles de Salis' story of the man who had been in the pot hole for a week. "If there's anyone down that one," he said with a grin, "he'll be drowned." What worried me about that rather lovely lake and the boats that will be sailing on it is how are they going to keep the water free from hook-worm?

Around Brasilia two satellite towns have sprung up where the workers live: shanty towns whose streets are full of milling crowds of adults and children of every shade of colour and opinion, happy, laughing, alive: where, a few years ago, nothing existed at all except for a few thatched mud huts harbouring the dreaded cockroach with the yellow band that infected the miserable inhabitants with Chaga's disease. And now this... Brasilia MUST succeed. It has passed the point of no return and if it were to fail it would be more than a national disaster: for one day this will be one of the great cities of the world. Its purpose is sound: to open up communications in the interior but it will only grow with speed when people have confidence in it and banks and light industries put money into it.

That may come more quickly than I then thought for as I write this not two years since we were there the population, I am told, has risen to one hundred and fifty thousand.

The Brasilia Palace Hotel, near the Palace of Dawn where the President lives when in residence, is the most comfortable and luxurious hotel I have ever stayed in. The rooms only face south-west, looking over the Brazilian Plain, and breakfast is brought to your room where you have it on the balcony in the warm morning sunlight. It is built on columns and when Anne first saw it she said it was "like a mouth organ on legs". Our room was at one end of the mouth organ and Eduardo's and Jock's at the other. Jock was so impressed at the time it took him to reach our room that he paced it out, making it three hundred yards. Our room would have been quiet had it not been for the Samba band who were playing that night at the final ball for the International Conference of M.P.s, practising in the room next to us before the dance and talking about it afterwards. The second night was quiet but we left at six o'clock the next morning. A bright clear morning with Brasilia ethereal. As we topped the rise of a hill I looked behind me. The city had gone: sunk without a trace in the vast sea of the Great Central Plain. We lunched at Tres Marias on river fish that Eduardo refused to touch because he said it was full of worms and disease. When I said that frying in deep fat made it safe he refused to believe me. We arrived at Belo in time for dinner. Here Eduardo insisted on taking a suite for himself and Jock, and we dined with them in their room. When the meal came up it was cold. Eduardo said, "If I were to have served a meal like that when I was a steward with Brasilian Airways I'd have got the sack." The waiter looked at him with added respect and re-heated it. Our room was two floors below but in our bathroom we could hear every word that Jock said booming down the hot water pipes.

Now Eduardo was in a hurry, he needed new plugs but had to go to four garages as each had only one. Anne and I had again got up at five o'clock but we could have had another three hours sleep and still have been on time. The weather was fine but until we get to the Rio valley there is not more than a mile of straight road at a time, maddening to a racing driver. In the afternoon when the heat was at its worst and Eduardo was beginning to feel the strain we were passed by an Interstate bus, powered by two

Mercedes-Benz engines, with a top speed approximating to our own. This was a challenge he could not resist. Tyres screaming, we raced round hairpin bends up hills downhills until we came out at the top of a long straight gradient with a two hundred and fifty foot drop on each side, soft verges, cracks in the road which made it only just possible to pass in comfort. The needle rose to a hundred and thirty-five kilometers, the car swaying almost on to the verges and over the cracks and now we were level with the back of the bus. There was the bridge at the bottom of the incline and a bend in the road beyond it. Slowly we crept up until I could see the driver's face, as alight with battle as Eduardo's, neck and neck until the bridge became all too near. Then round the corner came a car. Who would give way . . . ? Or neither? With a last regretful look at the driver Eduardo took his foot off the accelerator. I looked round. Anne grinned at me reassuringly. I said, "Jock?" Then "Why, the lucky fellow is asleep."

"I'm not asleep," said Jock. "I did not dare open my eyes."

Over the pass four thousand feet up, down towards the tunnel through a side of a hill out of which smoke eddies as if a train had just gone through. "Fog," I said. In we went, our lights reflected back to us as if from a million invisible mirrors, the roar of the engine reverberating against the tunnel walls so that one was deaf as well as blind. Out into the fog, visibility twenty yards, a grey world for the moon was up, so that I felt I was in an aeroplane slowly losing height in cloud, resigned to the skill of the pilot. When we came to the junction with the Sao Paulo road the fog cleared and from there it was the usual mad Saturday night Rio rush: the savage passing of cars on either side, some unlit, none of them showing signals, until, drained of all ebullience, Eduardo brought the car to a stop in the streets of Rio.

"Shall I drop you at the Yacht Club?"

"No," said Anne. "Come to the Florentino with us. Pizza e limao versh dupla, your favourite dish."

The moon was high and as we sat on the patio the sound of the sad sea waves breaking on the Copacabana beach was the most beautiful music I had heard for days.

CHAPTER FIFTEEN

ALTHOUGH I was almost certain that M. would be too busy, once he got to Rio, to visit *Moonraker*, Eduardo brought him aboard before lunch the next day. Afterwards we drove up to the Alto to call on the de Salis'. We made the introductions. Charles said accusingly "D'you know that H.E. has been trying to get hold of you all day?" M., whose face had fallen like that of a fourth form boy in trouble with his headmaster, made abject apologies; "I'll ring him first thing in the morning."

It was one of Rio's perfect spring days. We sat out on the veranda, Anne telling Mary about Brasilia, which she had not yet seen, the men grouped around M. who was sitting cross legged in one of Mary's more comfortable chairs like a small Buddha, with myself somewhere between the two so that I caught myself listening to each as I do at a cocktail party: ". . . Kubitschek didn't do all that badly for himself. He was a poor man before he became President but at the end of his term he was worth seven million . . .".

". . . My dear, no one EVER stops for an accident. The Police can hold you as material witness for days . . .".

". . . If I had the choice I'd rather live in a Rio favella than a Glasgow tenement . . .".

". . . Now Peter said to Jesus, 'You've been too kind to Brazil. You've given her a perfect climate, all natural resources, wonderful scenery, a sense of humour . . .'. 'Wait a moment,' said Jesus. 'You've not yet seen who I'm sending to govern her' . . .".

When the Grosses came up from the Sitio for tea and I found myself next to Alice, I told her how we had called at the Pensao do Chico Rei but had been refused admittance although when we had dinner the next evening there had been no other guests. She laughed. She said, "Some time ago the wife of a congressman had booked a room for the night. When she came into the drawing room she saw her husband's mistress sitting on the sofa. She opened her handbag, took out a small revolver and shot her. It's made them rather careful who they take in."

We dined that night at the Squirrels restaurant on the edge of the Tijuca forest; silent but alive, if you listened carefully. Full of predatory eyes and the animal lust to kill: a jungle not much less ruthless than our own. We were the only guests in a room full of heavy Victorian furniture and tables with thick red shades over the lamps so that our scampis, fried, Brazilian fashion, in butter, looked like small teak parrel balls. M. must have had quite a session of Eduardo's beloved Rio that day; the Rua Brancho, Copacabana, a church, a favella at his own request, and now the Tijuca forest. So it may have been with an eye on retaliation that he embarked, in a remarkably clear and lucid fashion, on his own subject. With surprising results. Eduardo's cynicism was at its most critical when directed at world statesmanship and it had been his firm belief, during the Cuban crisis, that Nevil Shute's *On the Beach* was developing before his eyes from fiction into fact. Now his imagination was suddenly caught by M.'s account of what was being done and what could be done for world peace. This was no flash in the pan enthusiasm and Eduardo's questions were worthy of the thoughtful answers M. gave to them. It is too long ago to be able to quote him and I suspect that his words might not look so convincing on paper, but the merit of it all was that he dropped into fresh young soil one seed of faith. And who knows what may come of that?

It must have been about this time that I first met Francisco, a Brazilian translation of his name by which he was known to herdsman and a fisherman alike, a name to which he was much attached for it was among the Brazilian people that he was most at home. He was born, as far as I can remember, in the Argentine, had been educated in England and had spent his life in Brazil. Charles, at whose flat I first met him, had spoken of him as the "Cattle King" of Brazil for no one knew more about cattle than he did. On one of his periodical visits to England as a young man he had met a girl who was a consulting interior decorator and had persuaded her to give up a flourishing business, marry him and live in the Matto Grosso. It was the sort of build-up that has the effect of making me extremely nervous but by a chance encounter in the general circulation we found ourselves face to face half way through the evening, a fortunate chance for by that time the good food and wine had smoothed away the worst of my complexes.

Francisco had the sort of figure a cattle man might be expected to have, short and stocky with powerful shoulders and a penetrating eye. When he spoke in Portuguese his sing-song voice was full of music.

We talked long enough for me to realize how free of exaggeration Charles' account had been and I was naturally delighted when he said he would like us to come and stay for a few days at their fazenda.

Blinding rain swept across Rio the day Pamela (Francisco's wife) picked us up at the Yacht Club but the clouds were beginning to lift as we branched off the Sao Paulo road to wind through a deep valley with lakes and rivers and steep pyramidal hills like those you see in parts of China. The rivers were in full spate, yellow-brown from the soil washed away by the rains. Even the lakes looked like soup. By the side of the road a few wretched huts looked as if it would not be long before they too floated away.

Dom Carlos Fazenda lies nine hundred feet up in the hills sixty miles from Rio. From the bottom of the garden you look up over a rolling lawn to the ranch-style house as one looks up an avenue of trees to an English country house. The house, blossom-pink, is new, built on the site of a fazenda which had been there in the days of slavery and Pamela had been given carte blanche to decorate it. They had found old style windows from partly demolished houses and carved "bosses" had been worked in as central pieces of the ceiling. Three old stone steps formed the sides and top of the large fireplace, in which logs were now burning for it was cool in the evening. At one end of this faintly austere, uncluttered room was a painting of a Jangada that I cheerfully would have stolen had I thought I could get away with it. That evening, as we dined by candlelight, I found it hard to imagine Pamela, who is the most chic woman I met in Brazil, coming out as a bride straight from Mayfair to the heart of the Matto Grosso. The nearest village was sixteen miles away. From it there was a train to Sao Paulo twice a week.

Francisco was in a rare mood. Although he would always tell you what you wanted to know he did not often reminisce but tonight he was living in the Matto Grosso looking back as a sailor looks back on his first ocean voyage. "When I brought Pamela out here," he said, "I had a nice little flat at Sao Paulo, which even in those days was the most civilized place in Brazil. We'd been there only a month when I was told to take over a fazenda up country. There was one store, about a mile from the house kept by a man who had been president of one of the big insurance companies until his manipulations of its finances made it necessary for him to disappear into the bush for a time. He was a good chap and helped me out more than once. There was a fight one night in the men's quarters and one of them got his belly ripped up with a machete. A bit of gut sticking out too . . .".

'Darling, really!'

"Well, Peter knows about that. I expect Anne does too. . . . Anyway, we got him to the store and laid him on the counter. My president friend filled him full of brandy and I sewed him up with a cattle needle and boiled string. He made a jolly good recovery."

"What were the people like to work with?" asked Jock.

"Oh, a good bunch on the whole. You had to know their code. If you sacked a man you had to do it without wounding his pride. If you hurt that, you might get a knife stuck in your back."

We sat over our coffee round the log fire and were shown photographs of their first home: flattish rolling country, bush country with rivers and crocodiles and large fish and different sorts of cattle, the Zebu predominating. I said, "D'you make the same sort of treks they do in Australia, lasting for months?"

"Not so often and with smaller herds. Eighty days was the longest I was on. We were bringing several hundred cattle down from the Amazonas to Sao Paulo. The worst job was getting them across rivers where there was pirana. One drop of blood seems to attract these fish like a swarm of locusts and on a long journey most of the cattle get sores or scratches. We'd send one over first and then get the herd across up stream before the fish had finished him. We lost a lot like that, I'm afraid."

Anne and I slept long and deeply in the cool mountain air. I half woke in the early morning thinking I was back in a country vicarage near Cambridge and the grunting of pigs and the shuffling of cattle must be coming from the farm next door. I stumbled out of bed and stood by the window, still less than half awake, staring at queer looking cows with long ears and heavy faces. Those hills might be the uplands of the Lake District but the blue, craggy mountains beyond had a distinctly foreign look. And what was this. I peered through a half open door. No vicarage bedroom I had ever stayed in had its own blue and white bathroom. And with that England vanished five thousand miles below the horizon.

After breakfast Pamela took Anne to see the swimming pool which was filled through the mouth of a stone lion, at least three hundred and fifty years old, which Francisco had picked up from an old ruined fazenda. Anne stood stroking his mane already warmed by the morning sun. She said, "You never said how you liked the Matto Grosso. Did you like it?"

"I loved it. The riding and the country and the people, and after Caroline came along, you haven't met her yet, have you?, I was never lonely." She broke off, laughing: "I shall never forget my first morning. Francisco had gone on ahead and as soon as I got rid of the flat I followed him. It had always been a bachelor establishment and there were three young apprentices living in the house. At the bottom of the garden, about as far as that shed over there, was the usual little house, a three seater. There was no lock on the door. I carved a hand with five fingers out of a piece of wood and painted it red. That evening I said 'When you see the red hand above the door none of you is to come near.' Next morning I went down and stuck the red hand up over the door. Immediately there was a fusilade of shots, all five fingers were neatly shot away and bullets were ricocheting round my head. After that Francisco put a lock on."

When Francisco went visiting he took us with him. In one courtyard an old woman mixed pig food in a huge copper bowl with brass studs round the rim which, Francisco said, would be worth more in the antique shops of Rio that all the rest of her possessions. "They send agents out to look for these things now and I have told her not to sell without my being there to help." Here and there were new small houses for his workers. "It's like getting blood out of a stone. My directors think Brazilian workers need less comfort than my animals." At the moment Francisco was going through an anxious time. The government had pegged the price of meat which promptly disappeared from the markets leaving him with hundreds of extra cattle on his hands to feed until public opinion forced one side or the other to give way.

It was strange to sit down to lamb on a cattle fazenda.

Every morning Francisco collected the mail from their market town, Vassouras, five miles away. Round the central square were peculiar tall palms like those in Josephine Bonaparte's square in Martinique and in the centre a fountain to which all slaves used to go to fetch water for their masters. We had seen at Francisco's house some of the heavy iron cuffs and chains which reduced their stride to a crawl. A hundred years ago this was a thriving town for it was in the middle of coffee country but after the abolition of slavery the fazendas could no longer be run economically and the town drifted into a lethargy from which it has not yet recovered. An occasional lorry rumbles and rattles over the cobbled streets and an old woman with a bundle of washing set on her head like a pumpkin shuffles up the hill keeping close to the walls of the houses, which seem to lean over towards her, to get the last patch of shade from their balconies. Old iron hooks still hang at street corners but the lamps which hung on them have gone.

Francisco collected his mail from the box. "It is easier now," he said. "When I first came here three years ago all the letters were thrown on to the mail room floor and you had to sort out your own. These boxes were put in last year."

On the way home he took us to a fazenda belonging to friends. As we drove in at the gates we were greeted by an old black retainer with a small wrinkled face like a monkey who greeted Francisco like a son he had not seen for years. He said, "The Senhor and Senhora are away in Rio, but go in, go in. Their house is your house as yours is theirs."

The house and its attendant slave houses, where three large horse drawn carriages were kept in spotless order, is more than a hundred and fifty years old. It was surrounded by trees and two well-kept lawns but it had a rather overbearing appearance. Inside, the rooms were long the ceilings high, the walls panelled in dark wood so that you felt you could never get enough light through the windows. The dining room table seated fifty people. In the bathroom was a marble bath weighing at least a ton and plumbing (knowing Brazilian plumbing rather well by now) of which I was deeply suspicious. The owners of this fazenda have two children, now grown up, a son and daughter who have become bitter and implacable enemies. Although I am no psychologist I cannot, having seen the house, be altogether surprised and I shook the gloom of the place off my shoulders as I came out into the hot sunlight.

One rather wet evening Francisco took me down to the end of his garden and through a gap in the hedge we found ourselves looking down on to a track wide enough for a large lorry, with deep trenches on either side for drainage, and overhung by the dripping branches of trees. The track was full of potholes and loose stones and might have its counterpart in England in the approaches to one of the more remote, and not too well kept up, farms. As I was wondering where it went or, indeed, why Francisco had brought us down to see it, he said, "This, until five years ago, was the main Sao-Paulo—Rio road, the most important road in the country. If you embarked on a journey between these cities in the rainy season you would take with you, if you were wise, a pick, a shovel, a plank and if possible a crane in the back of your truck to help other people." This brought home to me, more than anything else I saw in Brazil, the incredible advances made in the past five years in this exciting country.

On the night before we left Francisco suggested that we should sail to Jaguanum in Sepitba Bay, an island like a crouching Jaguar, where they had a cottage. He said, "Denys the fisherman will bring you food from the mainland or catch you fish and his wife will do your washing. Denys and I are like brothers and you as my friend will be like brothers too. If we are free at a weekend while you are there, we should meet again."

"Let's make a plan," suggested Anne. "You two and Mary and Charles come and have supper on *Moonraker* on St. Andrews night. Haggis and Whisky."

"We must invite Eduardo...".

"And the Lamberts...".

"And Caroline...".

"AND...".

I hoped for a fine night without much swell.

After an early breakfast we packed our things into the car, sad to think that we should never see this beautiful house again. Fate, however, was to decree otherwise. Manoel, who was driving us back to Rio, had started the engine when a grin came over Francisco's face. He ran down the steps and put his head inside the car. "I forgot to tell you. I have one claim to fame. I am the only man who has lassooed an escaping dinghy at Burnham-on-Crouch."

CHAPTER SIXTEEN

WHEN we got back to the Yacht Club the Santos-Rio ocean race, the event of the season, had just finished. Over the two hundred mile course the fleet had suffered from too light winds and it was rumoured that one boat had run out of water and the crew had had to wash their teeth in beer. As in North America the racing fleet was accompanied by a naval escort. The Commodore did me the honour to ask me to present a cup to a Bahia yacht which had won her class having had to sail two thousand miles to take part in it. The party was held in the ballroom. The white uniforms and gold braiding of the Brazilian navy and the gay colours of the women's dresses made it a brilliant occasion. Now Brazilian Portuguese is slightly different in pronunciation (and more melodious to me) than that of the mother country and as I listened to the eloquent phrases rolling across the ballroom floor like "the waves of the perilous seas through which these brave little boats had sailed" my eyes filled with tears and I quite forgot, as no doubt the brave owners did, that there had been neither waves nor peril.

But our stay in Rio had lasted a month and it was time to go.

Anne went with Jock and Eduardo to do the final shopping. She records: "The sun beats down like a redhot coal and there is no shade and no seat, only endless stalls of lace and ribbon, plastic toys, oranges, mamao, cabbage, chu-chu and abacaxi. We pick our way and fill our baskets. A small boy with a wooden box on wheels porters it to the car; Jock is invisible under a sack of bread, a bag of biscuits, lemons and jubuticaba. Even Eduardo twirls a small package of cake round his little finger. We search Urca for meat and finally buy it at a Disco store and then go farther west in search of kerosene. The road is up and a man holds a tin flag, green on one side, red on the other. Green if for us. We start to go through when a car comes up against the red. Our man opens his mouth wide in utter surprise and rage, gives a monumental shrug and hurls the tin flag at the car. We return to the Yacht Club to drink long glasses of orange and have lunch with Eduardo, say goodbye to the Commodore, collect photographs from O Cruzeiro and sit exhausted (me), not an ounce left in me for the things I still want so much to do . . . Jock and Peter atow. We have tea, read our letters, stow again more firmly and creep ashore to eat a simple supper while the waiters grin at 'The Ship that does not Sail'. We are embraced by the Gate Porter, whose teeth gleam with gold, but cannot find the launch men and leave their cruzeiros at the gate without much hope that they will get to their proper destination . . .".

We leave at dawn with the first of the ebb taking us out through the same passage which had so frightened us on the way in, but on the ebb and with a leading wind it shows a different face. Out on to a calm blue sea sparkling with sunlight and a dancing southeasterly breeze, out between Cargarras Islands and Ilha Redonda, astonished by the tremendous set towards the reef upon which an ill-fated ship went to her doom not ten years ago, abeam the massif of the Pedra de Gavea and ahead, now coming into view, is the great plain, its northern limit marked by distant hills. Of Rio, just round the corner, there is now no trace, the city might have been a hundred miles away.

The breeze dropped at sunset. The night was dark; no sound from the land nor lights on the sea. *Moonraker* and her crew, except for the watch on deck dozing on the fo'c'sle head (it was me) were asleep.

Twenty miles to the west of where we lay the Restinga broadens and rises to a great blob of land as Chesil beach ends in Portland, but so light was the wind that it was not until the following afternoon that we rounded it and entered Sepitiba Bay. On our port hand was a great wall of mountain, a massif whose peaks rise to over five thousand feet, dark and threatening under storm clouds already gathering, while ahead in bright clear sunlight little dark treed islands sit on the water like currants in a bun. With one exception; on our starboard hand is a larger island like a beast with its head between its paws: Black Jaguar. As we sailed farther into this magnificent place I had the feeling that this was not just another section of a continent but an island in the middle of time. I had the same feeling many years ago when I sighted Hiva Oa in the Marquesas, where nature reigned supreme and allowed those few inhabitants there were to live in her valleys or by her shores so long as they obeyed her laws and not only their own.

We opened up the bay to which we had been directed and sailed in with a fair wind, tying up to the only buoy; we looked around at the pale green water over the shallows, the half moon beach of sand as white as if it had been bleached by centuries of noon-day sun, the painted canoes drawn up under the shade of trees, the dark green forest climbing up the hill, the native huts peeping out from beneath the palms and, at the eastern end, near a tree covered with yellow flowers, our friend's cottage, its veranda discreetly hidden by a screen of feathery bamboo.

Ashore steep stone steps led from the beach to a small balcony with a low rampart like an ancient watch tower. In the fading light I looked over the steel-grey water as a Portuguese soldier might have done three hundred years ago, on guard against an attack by cannibals: and at that moment a long canoe full of small dark men rounded the headland and came towards me. But my fantasy was rudely shattered. It was propelled by, of all things, an outboard motor, given to the men by Francisco.

Three bedrooms (each had been a native hut) opened on a veranda which in turn led into a living room in which was a scrubbed pine table, a bench, several upright garden chairs and, on the right, through an archway, a galley with sink, tap and primus stove. Beyond was a small room with a shower and a lavatory which worked. There were shutters in the bedrooms and the living rooms but no glass in the windows, and the floors throughout were cement. Soon the cottage looked like home: books, papers, letters spread about, typewriter on the table and spars on the veranda ready for sandpapering. Supper was over. Lightning over the mountains, an occasional peal of thunder rolling across the bay, had been going on for some hours without coming any nearer. Down by the water nothing stirred, although the night was so dark that I could hardly see the ship twenty-five yards away, moored to a large rusty buoy.

Under the Aladdin lamp hung on a beam Jock was writing to his mother and Anne was still in the galley. I picked up a book but could not settle to read. I watched a lizard stalking a moth on a rafter. A sound . . . Inside or out? Steam . . .? Escaping from a valve, coming closer? "JOCK! CLOSE THOSE SHUTTERS!" Pandemonium swept through the cottage like fire through a forest of gum trees. Lights blew out, doors opened and slammed, papers soared into the air, chairs fell over as we groped for the shutters, rain stormed through the long thick bamboo screen and I rushed to our bedroom for the sealed beam torch. Soaked to the skin (the temperature had dropped like a stone), we huddled like sheep on the veranda with the beam on the ship as she pitched wildly into the short vicious seas which galloped into the bay like lines of advancing cavalry.

Thoughts flashed through my brain; had we parcelled the nylon warp where it ran through the ringbolt? We had, but it might have shifted. Why hadn't we shackled the chain on to the buoy? Because . . . because and because. It was high water springs and if she went ashore in this. . . . And what weight of concrete did Francisco say he had on the end of that chain? It had sounded all right then . . . But now . . .?

A sheet of lightning lit the nightmare scene: the struggling ship, the angry waves, the storm tossed trees. Thunder shook the earth until it seemed to tremble under our feet and as its echo died away there was a sudden stillness broken only by the surf on the beach and the vertically falling rain. I looked at my watch. What had seemed like an hour had been little more than fifteen minutes.

Beyond the cottage a path winds through the trees to the huts where Denys and his wife live with their brood of children. In front of the hut were rows of tiny pots each with its flowering plant which Nance was always watering. Inside it was dark and cluttered with things that almost hid Francisco's latest present, a gas stove with a bottle gas cylinder which stood idle against a wall. Beside it was a large slab of stone on which a charcoal fire cooked the midday meal, to which Denys would return from mending his nets under the thatched roof of the boat shed with his hand on his tummy or a groan as he limped, for this dark skinned, small boned Brazilian Indian, was at heart a hypochondriac.

He had a long thin face but I thought it sifnificant that Anne, who has the loving gift of being able to make people laugh with her however difficult the language problem, could never do more than make Denys smile a little uncertainly. Not that he did not look after us. When there was fish we shared it and whenever a canoe went into Itacuruça it brought back meat, if there was any, and anything else we asked for. Francisco had said, "Denys and I are like brothers" but that was not quite true. To Denys, Francisco was a god.

We bathed before every meal in the silky waters of the bay and each night we took our coffee on to the balcony to sit without speaking on the stone rampart (our watch tower) overlooking the beach now silent except for the whisper of the surf as it spread, gently like a lover's hand over the sand. Time had no meaning. When we had gazed our fill we collected our coffee cups, stacked them by the sink and went to bed.

CHAPTER SEVENTEEN

ITACURUÇA, five miles across the water from the cottage, is separated from the island of the same name by a narrow channel. A row of small houses, sheds and shacks faces a broad expanse of sand which blows into your eyes and ears and fills your hair with grit. If there is no wind it is stupefyingly hot. But even now, two years after we left it for the last time, I remember it most clearly in rain. Rain pouring off the awning of the Danemarka restaurant like a babbling brook, filling the potholes and churning the furrows of sand in the dirt road into a glorious pudding of clinging mud. It is a long village with one street parallel to and behind the row of houses facing the water. In this street are a couple of bars, a few small shops and a radio hut from which broadcasts are relayed through loudspeakers attached to lamp posts at two hundred yard intervals so that the inhabitants who used to sing to the guitar may now listen without effort to canned music. As there was at this time a major fault in the electricity Itacuruça was quiet by day and dark by night. The main event, the daily arrival of the Rio train, is attended by most of the town in the hope that one day they will see a new face.

We had dropped anchor just east of the little quay to which coasters come to load bananas which are brought in by lorry from the plantations: a quay that is rarely unoccupied for this is a banana town.

No sooner had we given the ship a harbour stow than a man in shirt, shorts, white stockings and a small tyrolean hat which sat awkwardly on his large head came leisurely across the sand and demanded to be brought aboard. This was simple enough but it became more difficult to get him below because his girth was bigger than the entrance to our main hatch. His Scandinavian accent softening his English words, he said, "Take it easy, take it easy. If I can turn round I can slide down the companion way feet first." This he did.

"My name is Carlos. Francisco asked me to see that you had everything you wanted. You will please have dinner with me at the Danemarka tonight as my wife has not yet returned from Rio."

He had been, he told us, a consulting marine engineer in Copenhagen before the war but became convinced in the winter of 1940 that Hitler would invade Denmark. "I did not like that man," he said "so I shipped aboard a freighter belonging to a friend of mine as Chief Engineer. I spent the war at sea."

"But how do you come to be here?" asked Anne.

"I came to Rio after the war and met my wife there. She brought me down here and I have stayed ever since."

He finished his whisky and stood up to go, filling our cabin completely.

"Now you must come with me to visit the Port Captain. In Brazil the smaller the port the greater the self-importance of the Port Captain: Itacuruça is a very small place."

Opposite our anchorage was Carlos' boat yard. Here he picked up his bicycle and his small spotted dog who always sat in the basket on the handlebars and without which he never ventured. We proceeded with slow and measured tread over the sand pausing now and then to speak to passers by for Carlos, through his Armenian wife, is related to nearly everybody. The Port Captain was a dark irritable little man who invited us into his living room and questioned us closely on how long we were staying and where we were going next and for how long. He introduced us to his wife, a blonde young woman with a sharpish face whose eyes wandered more than once in Jock's direction. She came from the Midi and had met her husband while she was in a touring company in Marseilles. She gave us cafezinho and sticky cakes and told us that this was a one horse place and that she was sick to death of it. "If only," she said, "her husband could be moved to Rio . . .". She was, curiously enough, the only person we met in Itacuruça, of which we were to see a great deal more than we then thought, who wanted to be somewhere else.

Before we left they showed us postcards of places where the Captain had been including Kotka, our favourite port in Finland, under snow. As we strolled along the beach Carlos said, "Did you notice that most of those pictures had been bought in Rio?"

The Danemarka, with its tables on the pavement sheltered from the rain which now fell heavily, and its patrons, sitting long after their plates had been cleared as if unwilling to leave the candlelight for the darkness of the street, also had an air of the Midi: a sort of detachment that was more French than Portuguese. Inside, the walls were covered with trophies of the sea: stuffed crabs and sail fish, the tail of a manta ray, iguanas, a crayfish, a python and several baby crocodiles one of which was given to us by the proprietor as a memento. Carlos said he wanted to sail round the world in a catamaran of which he already had the design but as I watched his small lively eyes full of humour as he recounted the life of this intimate community I could not believe he would ever bring himself to leave it.

The only time Carlos ever complained was about his weight. He said, "Even when I was torpedoed I did not lose it. We were six hundred miles west of Ireland and our boat was sailing well with a fine wind when someone opened the provision locker. In it there was nothing but candles. I got so hungry I ate them but after twelve days at sea I only lost twelve pounds." He took his cigar out of his mouth and spat into the road. He said, "I can still taste those candles."

As we rowed out to the ship Jock said, "This is my sort of place. Bit of boat building and a cool beer under the shade of one of those trees. If I were here in my own boat I should be in no hurry to leave."

From the eastern end of Sepitiba Bay to the western end of Bahia de Ilha Grande is a distance of sixty miles, all sheltered water, which is divided into two parts by Ilha Grande itself. The numberless islands, the many fiords and the fact that in all this tortuous shore line there are three towns of which only one, Angra dos Reis, has any claim to being a town at all, makes it a splendid hide out for smuggling at which the Brazilians are past masters. Even grand pianos, a Brazilian once proudly told us, had been smuggled in through these waters. The climate is good in winter, dry with a northerly wind except for a few southerly gales but in the summer it is hot and wet and the winds light and variable; a climate which brings out mosquitos and borachudos in their millions. The mosquitos can be for the most part kept out of the cabin by putting a match to Dorma Bem, a green spiral strip like a large coiled spring which burns slowly all night. Borachudos, small black flies, attack more by day than by night and are utterly resistant to all forms of counter attack.

We left next morning with an easterly wind and sailed for Ilha Grande. It is green and mountainous with deep fiords into one of which we did not go for the grim prison walls repelled us on this lovely day. At least one smuggler baron, who thought himself powerful enough to stand outside the law, languishes within its cells. Once you have passed the narrow channel between the northern end of the island and the mainland the character of the district changes. Mountains are more rugged, thunderstorms more frequent, buoys mark the shoals, beacons are lit, trawlers cross your bows and even a freighter steams slowly up towards Angra dos Reis. You have returned to the twentieth century.

It began to rain. Land lay all around us but was out of sight in the torrential downpour. We motored. Ahead appeared an islet and beyond, a long curving beach with a small stone jetty, our landmark for an appointment made in a Rio flat in which none of us pinned much hope. So sophisticated had our hostess appeared in her own surroundings that we could not see her huddled on deck with the salt spray flying. But then we did not know the Ilha Grande. . . . We dropped anchor, bundling our sodden sails into a heap under the boom: A couple came down the jetty and stood waiting patiently with umbrellas in their hands. We hurried ashore and were escorted, the umbrellas placed firmly over our heads although we already were soaked to the skin, and walked up to the large frame ranch house barely visible in its grove of palm trees. The caretaker had a message for us. "Senhor Cavalcanti telephoned to say that you must stay at the Club as his guests. He hopes to be with you tonight."

To describe this place as a branch of the Rio de Janeiro Yacht Club might give the wrong impression. There were no yachts or yachtsmen and it was so quiet you could have heard the rustle of a snake moving in the grass. We ate a simple meal cooked for us by the caretaker's wife of steak, black beans, cucumber and farofa, followed by Doce de Goiabada, a sweet conserve of guava fruit while the rain drummed down on the roof. It was midnight before our friends arrived, their car covered in mud, their eyes blurred with fatigue for the last twenty-five miles from the Rio-San Paulo road had been little less than a nightmare.

In the morning the rain had stopped. The sky looked exhausted, as well it might. For three days we explored Rabeira Bay, a galaxy of islands set in a fairy sea against a backdrop of theatrical mountains and tumbling waterfalls, and we the spectators and actors both moving from scene to scene, from island to island under the direction of wind and current and the whim of the moment, as we wailed this timeless sea. A ruined hut, a sun dried canoe on a golden beach, an old plantation house, its rotting floors sagging under beds and tables long since forgotten, and green dungeons which echoed to the clank of chains and the shuffle of black feet over damp stones. These and an old wizened man with a sack on his back who had seen our ship in a cove and had walked two miles on the chance of selling a loaf of bread. These are our memories of this enchanted place.

The last dying breath of the afternoon wind found us anchored once more in front of the clubhouse and after dinner we talked, far into the night. Mickey Cavalcanti comes from an old Pernambucan family. He is a doctor of science and an engineer.

He fought with his regiment in Italy. He is an experienced sailor and had just bought a cruising boat but I do not think that his hope that Zuza will go to sea with him will be realized. Maybe there are Brazilian wives who put to sea but if there are we did not meet them, although daughters are beginning to sail with their fathers.

Zuza is Russian. She was born in Latvia but when the Russians took over she and her mother escaped to the West, always on the move as the Russian front swept forwards. For the last six months of the war they lived in Berlin and it was only two weeks before the city fell that they escaped. At Frankfurt, which had just been captured by the Americans, her mother collapsed. Somehow she managed to get her into hospital, but for herself there was nowhere to go. After roaming the streets she applied for a job at the American H.Q. and on the strength of five languages, one being Russian, she got it.

You might think, at first glance, that these experiences had not touched her. She is both gay and engaging and is one of the few women who looks well in a bikini, but under the surface there is a restlessness as if her life, or at least her peace of mind, depended on some internal spring that had to be wound so that she must always move forwards and never have time to look back.

At this distance of time I cannot recall all that we talked about but I do remember that on one occasion politics came into it. I was saying that I did not see how, when the peasants and workers in Brazil had become educated (and by that I meant learning to read and write) some form of communism could be prevented; brought about by the gap between wealth and poverty. Mickey would have none of it. He maintained that the middle class, especially in the cities, was growing rapidly, that the Church still had a firm grip on the minds of the people, and lastly who had ever heard of a communist with a sense of humour? I was still not convinced although I conceded that Brazilian communism might not be Marxist. Mickey, who until now, had been arguing in a light vein suddenly became deadly serious. He said, "Peter, it is most important that the world should know that communism could never come to this country. At the first sign of a sell-out by a president or a revolution it would be stamped under foot immediately. This I KNOW, although I am not at liberty to go into details." As subsequent events have shown, Mickey was right.

On the fourth morning Mickey announced that he would have to leave after lunch but he proposed taking us in to Angra dos Reis to have a look at the little town. The road was stony and full of holes but nothing, nothing at all, Mickey said, to the one down which they had driven on Friday night. It ran past the orderly grounds of a small naval college to the little town where the houses were in unusually good repair, the shops stuffed with the latest electrical gadgets, with wine and whisky, with clothes and toys. Big bells hung in the belfry of the old church (1702) which, however, had been made to share in the general uplift by being painted such a dazzling white that it hurt you physically to so much as glance at it in the sunlight. We found a place, half-restaurant, half-shop, where steaks were grilled on the points of long irons fashioned like swords and we drank Vinho Verde in small brown jugs until we felt at peace with the world. Zuza said, "Mickyzinho, I cannot go back to Rio today. Let me stay one more day."

"Zuza, you know I must be back tomorrow morning."

"Then I shall stay here and come back when I feel like it."

"No: Zuzazinho, if you do that I shan't know when I shall see you again."

"Mickyzinho ... One more day; PLEASE!"

Mickey threw up his hands in despair. "All right, but we must leave early tomorrow."

But when *Moonraker* sailed with the offshore breeze next morning a full two hours later than we had intended her to, Zuza lay sunbathing on the empty beach.

At the north-east end of the Ilha Grande is one of those rare anchorages, safe from a storm from any direction, a bay within a bay reached through a narrow neck of water so that it has the appearance of an inland lake. In the evening the encircling hills cast deep shadows upon its waters so that I was suddenly reminded of the days of my youth when I used to bicycle to the lake at Friday Street in Surrey. Mangroves line the shores except for a patch of yellow sand off which we anchored. On the opposite side of a rocky middle ground (some of the rocks showing above the water) is the village. It is called the Saco do Ceu, the Heavenly Bag. There are no shops nor is there anything to buy but at the northern end of this tiny settlement is a slightly larger house with a thatched palm roof. A man stood in the doorway beckoning us to enter "Uma casa do pobre". The floor was wood instead of the usual mud and two benches and a hammock were the only furnishings. The only other room was entirely occupied by a large bed and on it rested a wooden cradle.

Six (out of eleven) "filhos" blocked the doorway gaping at us in astonishment as the Romans must have stared at the "Angels". To feed this brood the father ran a small plantation with his older sons to help him. In a thatched shed he showed us with great pride a large wooden press, a copper embedded in cement with faggots underneath ready to light and a wooden box fitted over a grated wooden wheel for grinding the mandioca husks. All this, he said, he had made himself. The de-husked and washed grain was then crushed under the press to grind out the poisonous exudate. It is then cooked in boiling water in the copper with frequent stirrings by long wooden instruments like hoes.

Night fell quickly in this bowl-like place and little pairs of lights could be seen fanning out from the village, swaying from side to side (as the men worked their paddles) like glow worms making love.

If you ever go to Ilha Grande you must not fail to visit the Saca do Ceu. But if you do, remember to wrap yourself up in all the clothing you can, even if you half suffocate in the heat, for this is the place, Mickey Cavalcanti says, where the Borachudos finish their assault course training. We thought we were becoming immune but the first pre-dawn light saw us running out of that bay as fast as the light offshore breeze could take us, itching, itching all the way.

Gaily we returned to Itacuruça in time to ask Carlos to dine with us at the Danemarka (his wife was still in Rio). Half way through the meal I pointed over the road to a broken down building with two blue doors with red lettering.

I said to Carlos, "What goes on in there?"

"Pronto Seguro," he said.

"They look as if they have been closed for a long time."

"I've never seem them opened nor anyone go inside."

"Just put there to give the people confidence?"

"You might put it that way."

Later in the evening Carlos, who was in a reflective mood, had been telling us how he had been torpedoed in the Denmark Strait and had been in the water for over an hour before he was rescued, he had only been saved, he supposed, by his fat. "When I got back from that voyage I was told that my wife had been killed by a bomb."

"Oh Carlos . . . how awful for you . . .".

"After that I used to spend what leave I had in Scotland."

"Where, in Scotland?" asked Anne.

"A little place I don't suppose you've heard of; on the border. A village called Coldstream."

"I was born there." she said. "Did you meet my brother, Lex Welsh?"

"Lex . . .! You are Lex's sister? I can't believe it. I used to shoot and fish with Lex and knew him better than anyone else in Britain."

This established, so to speak, a link.

CHAPTER EIGHTEEN

SAINT Andrews, the day of the party, began as a hot windless day. In the morning Pamela arrived at Itacuruça with a big stainless steel pot full of haggis presented by Ken Lambert, manager of the Anglo-Frigerifico meat factory. She was immediately packed into a dugout canoe with a paraffin refrigerator as big as herself with Denys' brother to manage the outboard motor while Francisco, who seemed to be fighting an inner war with himself, jumped into his own motor boat, shoved off into the stream where his engine cut out, and he was carried away by the tide in the opposite direction to his wife to the accompaniment of strange Brazilian oaths. Jock and Anne had long since vanished into the town as completely as if it had been an impenetrable jumble and I was left aboard *Moonraker* without a dinghy. Soon after finishing my lunch, which I ate in mounting rage, Eduardo arrived on the beach followed a little later by Charles, Mary, Caroline and the two unknown young men.

Out of earshot they had to interpret my gestures as best they could and after a little while they too wandered away in various directions.

But this was Brazil. Now that everything had reached an impasse the pieces dropped into place as if drawn by an invisible magnet. Francisco appeared with his engine going full blast and a broad smile on his face, Anne and Jock staggered down to the water's edge with blocks of ice wrapped in sacks destined for the refrigerator if by some miracle it should arrive safely at Jaguanum, and the rest of the party, carrying stores, stood by our dinghy reporting for duty. The Lamberts, with Lancashire accents and warm hearts, relieved us of the ice which they put into their motor cruiser and Francisco removed one of the young men. The rest of us set about sailing *Moonraker* to her destination against a light breeze and a strong current. Charles, Caroline and John Laurensen each took a trick at the helm while the permanant crew served tea, keeping an unobtrusive eye open for rocks.

We arrived off the cottage at sundown and tied up to the buoy. I suppose the people who give a party are the last to know whether it is a success. Here, most of the people knew each other well but after the cheese and goiabada stage and while Anne was busy with the coffee I slipped away in the pram. The water was like glass and the stars looked back into your face as if from a silver mirror. Against the dark forest the ship was reflected in her own pool of light; the long bowsprit, stumpy mast, ratlines, baggywrinkle, the cloud of running gear; one of the last ships of a forgotten era when men loved their boats next to their wives instead of changing them every year like their cars. I had not, however, come to admire my ship but to put into practice the theory, often repeated, that the gauge to the success of a party was the noise which it creates: that a cocktail party must be heard from the front gate, a dinner party from the front door. I rowed away until I could hear ours no more. By that time I was outside the bay. I paddled contentedly back and climbed aboard by the bows. To my surprise I found myself looking down on Francisco who was stretched full length on the fo'c'sle with his head propped on the forsail.

"Where have you been?" he asked. I told him.

"D'you like parties?" he asked.

"This sort of thing is fun," I said cautiously.

"One of the things the bush taught me was to stick to one's own set of values. I found it harder than I thought. People push you around, make you conform. Keep up with the Joneses. That's one advantage of getting old. You realize that Money is barter, not an objective."

I said, "Somerset Maugham wrote 'I would not cross the street to shake hands with a millionaire.'."

In the early hours of the morning dinghys left the ship and if one or two of them put out towards the sea instead of the beach (Francisco rounded them up quickly enough) it all went to show, I hope, that the party had been a success.

The sun was well up when I awoke. A fine breeze blew from the NE. The cottage was waking up and we made a plan to go for a sail in *Moonraker* leaving in an hour's time. Before the hour was up Caroline sailed away in Francisco's catamaran and when we mustered on the beach there was still no sign of Caroline or cat. Francisco had just made up his mind to go and look for her when she rounded the headland and beat into the bay. On the second tack, the cat was going like a bomb, I saw the girl lean forward to cleat the mainsheet before coming about when a dark line swept across the water. In a fraction of a second the weather hull flew up into the air and over she went, the hull appearing in the next moment upside down, for Francisco had earlier removed the float at the top of the mast. There was no sign of Caroline. In less time than it takes to tell Francisco had leapt into a dinghy and with short swift strokes pulled for the scene followed by Anne and myself in our pram. Only Anne could see ahead. She shouted to Francisco, "Caroline's up. She's swimming round the hull."

The cat was anchored to the bottom by her mast, the outboard had gone to the bottom in three fathoms of water, but the hull appeared undamaged. We hauled Caroline into the pram, mortified and slightly shocked, and Anne rowed her ashore to where Pamela was waiting but the girl ran past her into the house. "At such a moment, I suppose," said Anne "the ones you love best are the ones you don't want to see. Let's do something practical." So she and Pamela went aboard to prepare lunch.

The spot where we hoped the engine was lying was marked with a buoy; the mast, not without difficulty, was removed from the hull which was towed to the shore. Here we ran into difficulties. A swell had got up and we could not bail the water out of the hulls before the sea filled them up again. By brute force and weight of numbers we dragged the cat out of the water on rollers only to find that both hulls had been holed by the logs we had used. We broke off for a rather sad little lunch to which Caroline did not come. The loss of one's first command is not a thing to be easily set on one side.

After lunch Eduardo left with Carlos who had unexpectedly arrived in his *Star* and after he had gone Francisco and I went on dragging for the outboard without success until Denys and his brother came out in their canoe with a nylon line and a shark hook. Francisco said, "My bet is that he will have that engine on his hook within an hour." He was right to the minute.

Already the daylight was fading. We said goodbye to Charles and Mary to whom we owed so much, promising to give their love to our mutual friends in England. We rowed them out to the Lambert's boat. We saw Caroline come running down the steps of the cottage jingling keys on a key-ring, to fetch something for her father. She paddled out in the tiny dinghy, retrieved what she wanted, locked the cabin, stepped into the dinghy and over the side went the key-ring. She gave a sharp little cry like a wounded bird. In the next moment Ken Lambert manœuvred his boat alongside. His wife said, "Caroline, my dear, you'd better come with us. We'll wait for your parents at Itacuruça." She called to Anne, "Tell Pamela we've taken Caroline to the mainland."

When Francisco heard of this latest disaster he allowed a faint smile to spread over his features. "I have a spare key-ring which I keep here." Pamela said nothing. In a matter of a few weeks

Caroline would be going to England to start her career in the Foreign service and this was probably the last time the family would be together at Jaguanum. We helped them down with their bags and the outboard engine which Francisco was taking with him. Pamela said, "I haven't locked up, Anne, because I thought you'd be moving in. Goodbye, my dears, I'm afraid today has not been what you might call a stunning success." We listened to the roar of their engine as it slowly faded away. Anne said, "Not tonight. All our things are on board and to take their place so soon would be . . . its difficult to find the right word . . . unbecoming . . . ?"

Utterly exhausted and very weary we rowed to the ship where Anne prepared a chicken which we were to eat with rice. In draining this she let some of it slip through on to the grid we keep on the bridge deck.

"Be careful of that," she said, "You'd better wash it down."

And I forgot.

We had a quiet meal and after washing up I took the basin in one hand and my pipe in the other and with my mind not on the job I slipped on the rice as the ship gave a jerk in the swell. I fell, with the washing up water on top of me, into the cockpit, on to my side. I was in great pain and instructed the others to get me below and strap me up, which is the usual treatment in England, for broken ribs.

The next morning, after a wretched night Anne and Jock wanted to take the ship to Itacuruça but I insisted on being moved ashore. Anne went along to the thatched shed which Francisco had helped to build for the fishermen to keep their canoes out of the sun and enlisted the help of two of them to move me out of the ship into the dinghy and up the steps to the cottage while Denys' brother opened the Lambert's cottage to find a comfortable chair that would support me.

Monday, Tuesday, Wednesday, Thursday. On Tuesday Anne wrote to Mary to tell her what had happened, that I was still in pain and that she was worried. I read the letter and pushed it back into her hand. "You'll have to re-write this. They'll think something dreadful has happened. Say I've broken a couple of ribs and I'll be all right in a few days." We argued but I for once insisted.

The days passed slowly. I sat on the veranda listening to the crickets, to the murmur of the surf on the beach and twice a day, as regular as clockwork, Denys talked Portuguese to Anne who could hardly understand his patois. He was suffering from a stomach complaint and was going to the doctor at Santa Cruz, a day's journey, on Friday.

On Thursday it blew a gale from the NE. Rain slanted through the open cottage, the bamboos bent under the weight of wind. Jock and Anne rowed out to *Moonraker*, lying to her own anchor, and put a line out to the buoy. Before supper I was feeling remarkably off-colour and while the others were out of the room I took my temperature. It was up a little. I started on the penicillin. It was a long evening. The wind howled through the house, the lamp swung on the beam from the draught through the shutters, the lizards (George and Margaret) stalked their evening prey, Jock and Anne sat reading at the table but I noticed that Anne had not turned a page for the last half-hour. She later confessed that she felt she was looking over a precipice into a bottomless void.

The brilliant sunshine woke me up. The 'Can't you read' bird was winging his morning song, water dripped off the rocks and outside hung on drooping leaves as it does in the Lake District. The wind had gone. I made my way to the bathroom, had a wash and a shave and went back to the bedroom shutting the door. I was very tired and got back into bed. Suddenly an agonising pain shot into my right chest and the next moment I was fighting for my breath. When I recovered from my surprise, I tried to work it out. Surely, this must be a spontaneous pneumothorax from a bit of rib having penetrated the pleural lining. First aid? I had no needle big enough to let the air out, nor did I fancy unskilled hands trying to push a needle into my pleural cavity.

At that moment the door opened and Anne came in. She stood, absolutely still, as I have seen her at the helm in some grave nautical crisis, no more than a foot from my bed, her eyes veiled so that I should not see the fear behind them. I said, between breaths, "This started . . . ten minutes ago . . . rib through pleura . . . spontaneous pneumothorax."

She knew about that because, years ago in Boston Road, a man had collapsed with that in our waiting room and she had sat with him until the ambulance arrived to rush him into hospital.

I said, "Get Carlos . . . to ring Charles."

"Is there anything I can do for you? Now . . . ?"

I shook my head.

They discussed Jock taking *Moonraker* to Itacuruça (I heard their voices on the veranda) but Anne turned this down for she could not bear to lose her only line of communication, and then I heard her footsteps running down to the beach. Jock put his head round the door to give me a friendly grin: "Bad show," he said, "Help will be coming. Don't worry."

Presently Anne came back with a dark small woman with long black hair. "Denys' wife would like to see you, just for a moment."

The woman came over to the bedside, took my hands in hers, touched my forehead and went slowly out of the room shaking her head from side to side. Following her Anne suddenly turned and gave me a prodigious wink. It cheered me up no end. There was a pause: then the sound of the big canoe being dragged to the water's edge on rollers and at the end Anne's cry:

"Muchas gracias . . . Te Log . . .".

She came back into the room, her face exhausted. "There was only Denys' brother and I could not make him understand how IMPORTANT it was. He said there was no outboard (Denys had taken that) and when I picked up a paddle he shook his head. So I went along to Denys' wife but she would only help if she saw you herself. Well: we saw what she thought!"

For the next hour or two my battle for air took up most of my time, with Anne sitting quietly beside me, and I remembered that once she had said, after she had married me, that she had put all her eggs into one basket. It seemed to me that the bottom of the basket was rotting away. And yet I realized, not for the first time but never so forcibly, what a happy person she was and that there was one enemy she would never have to fight—self-pity. I said, "If anything goes wrong . . . I want you to promise . . . get someone out . . . to help sail *Moonraker* back to England."

She looked at me "Darling, You're very much alive at the moment. I refuse to believe you can't hold on for a few more hours."

Throughout our lives together Anne has always in the crisis found the right word. It WAS extremely odd that by now I was not a lot worse. And then in a flash of insight that any second year student ought to have had hours ago, I knew what had to be done. I sent Anne for the scissors. Quickly she cut through the plaster bandage and tore it off. I felt to see whether my heart had been displaced by air. It had not.

To clinch the diagnosis the pain slowly spread to both lungs and although that made things rather more difficult pneumonia was a thing I could do something about. I remembered the streptomycin the heart surgeon at Recife had given me. It was a big dose but this was a severe infection. Anne, with Jock's help, gave me the injection, her first, which I never felt. Then we settled down to wait.

Back Door to Brazil

When Denys' brother arrived in Itacuruça he learned that Carlos had gone to Rio. He shuffled round the little town, loathe to return to Jaguanum without doing something more. Then he thought of Senhora Lambert whom he knew to be a trained nurse. He enlisted the help of the Post Office who found the Lambert's number and he got through to their house only to be told that she had left five minutes ago and would not be back before dinner. He tried the Anglo-Frigerifico factory and asked to speak to Senhor Lambert. A voice, recognizing his patois, snapped back at him, "He cannot speak to you. He is busy," and slammed down the receiver. At this stage he might so easily have given up but instead he wandered into a small store with whose owner he was acquainted and told him what was happening on the island. He told him that Carlos was expected back on the five o'clock train. Denys' brother showed him Anne's letter on which she had written VERY URGENT. Although he spoke no more than a word of English the owner of the store recognized its probable meaning. He said, "I will come with you to the station."

The train for once was punctual.

Carlos quickly grasped the contents of Anne's letter. He looked at his watch. At half past five at the latest the embassy staff would have left for the weekend and he knew that it took two-and-a-half hours, if you were lucky, to get through to Rio. I can imagine his ambling along to the Danemarka like a large Kodiac bear, seizing the telephone and shouting into it, in a voice quite unlike his own: "This is Senator X speaking. I must speak to the British Ambassador at once." He got through, he told me, in two-and-a-half minutes.

He spoke to Charles' personal secretary who was on the point of leaving. He read out to her Anne's letter. The de Salis' were dining with friends before going up to the Alto. She said, "He's been worried about the Pyes and left a number in case of emergency. I will give him your message at once."

Charles rang his own doctor who organized a chest surgeon, a doctor, a nurse and an ambulance. The relief expedition was to leave Rio at half past nine; on one condition. Charles and Mary must lead it for to the surgeon Itacuruça and Jaguanum were as remote as the Matto Grosso.

Denys came back from Santa Cruz to the island reassured about his stomach and the day ended, Anne told me, in a wild sunset of crimson, green and gold spreading like a fan from behind the wall of mountains. At ten o'clock a fishing boat steamed into the harbour, a canoe was lowered into the water and a man jumped into it and paddled ashore. This was Denys' brother bringing a note from Carlos saying that help was on its way and that he would bring the doctors over in the Lambert's motor cruiser. With the note were some acromycin tablets of which I took a couple to be getting on with. I leaned back on my pillows and for the first time I slept. I woke with a start. Outside there were strange noises, people giving orders, the shifting of heavy loads. A candle flickered at my bedside throwing its shadowy light over the bare floored room so that I could see that the truckle bed upon which Anne had been lying fully clothed was now empty. The door opened a little and Mary peered round the corner waving a hand at me, asking how I was. I could not find words to express how pleased I was to see her cheerful face.

Charles came in followed by a tall aesthetic looking man, the surgeon I presumed, whose nose wrinkled with displeasure when he saw at once that this was no spontaneous pneumothorax for already my breathing was easier.

He was followed by a nurse and a young doctor who would have made a fine front row forward. They had a look at me, Charles interpreting. I had pneumonia. "In that case could I not remain here and take my antibiotics?"

The great man shook his head. Already I had an effusion and hospital was essential. He had arranged a bed for me at the Strangers Hospital.

The front row forward carried me down to the beach. The moon was high and bathed the half moon beach in a cold clear light so that it was like looking at a black and white print which I can remember today as clearly as I saw it then. My chair was fixed on the centre thwart of a small dinghy and two men rowed me out to the motor cruiser. Just as we reached her topsides I saw the dinghy half-fill and felt it begin to overturn and at the last possible moment a huge black hand seized my chair, with me in it, and held it against the boat's side. The dinghy capsized and the men disappeared. A voice at the back of my neck said, "Do not worry. I am the strongest man in Itacuruça. I can hold you until help comes." This was not long.

Anne, who had been packing our things on *Moonraker*, was the last aboard. I was glad she had missed that little episode. It had been a close shave and she had had enough for one day.

At Itacuruça I was hoisted on to the quay like a sack of potatoes and made as comfortable as possible in a padded upright chair. Mary said, "The road is awful for the first fifteen kilometers. We are going in front so they can't drive too fast."

It was a nightmare ride. Anne and the young doctor sat with me and the nurse sat with the surgeon round whose neck she put her arm. This meant nothing, so Mary told me later, for she had done the same with the front row forward on the way down. It took two-and-a-half hours to cover those fifteen kilometers. From where I was sitting I could see nothing but rows and rows of banana trees and the dust rising from the broken surface of that terrible road. Dawn heralded another day and now I could recognize the fantastic Rio mountains, the Corcovada, the Finger of God, dark against the pale sky. The first pink flush announced the sun as a trumpeter proclaims his king.

Our pace quickened down the Sao Paulo road, into the waking city, sirens screaming, through the early morning streets, near deserted, past a Lodge Gate and up a ramp to stop before a grey stone building at a doorway. The door opened and I was wheeled, by the young doctor, into a lift. Anne made to follow but there was no room. She turned away but not before I saw her face. So might she have looked had she heard the prison gates clang behind me.

CHAPTER NINETEEN

ANNE was, in fact, allowed in to see me for a moment before returning to Praia do Flemenco with Mary and Charles. The pleasant room with its French windows open to the balcony with its view over the city, the splendid bed in which I was comfortable for the first time for six days, the authority and discipline which is felt the moment you enter any well run hospital, did much to reassure her. I said, "Nothing can go wrong now. It's just time, rest and antibiotics."

Nevertheless I prefer to draw a veil over the next thirty-six hours. At the end of that time I emerged from the depths like a storm battered ship entering a landlocked estuary. My recovery started with Charles coming into the room on the Sunday evening. He gave me an anxious glance and then recoiled in laughter.

"What's the matter, Charles?" I asked.

"You look so like the Baker in the Hunting of the Snark."

Anne gave me the mirror from her handbag. Charles was right: the same long ears, the dragged down face, the mournful expression in the eyes.... From that moment on I began to take an interest in my surroundings.

The Strangers Hospital had come about in a rather special way. At the turn of the century yellow fever paralysed the port and city, the hospitals filled with the dying and the cemeteries with the dead. Temporary huts were put up by the English Colony who nursed the sick so devotedly that they were given the land upon which they later built the Strangers. The senior nursing staff are either British or North American and when I was there the Matron and the Sister in Charge of each floor were British. The rest were trained Brazilian nurses.

The hospital is private, there being no public wards and no resident staff. The patient is looked after by his own doctor. Charles' doctor looked after me but he was, pre-eminently, a surgeon and on that first night he called in a Brazilian Physician for a second opinion.

I was washed each morning by a male nurse and given a cold shave by the barber. The food was excellent. From time to time the language difficulty became acute and may in some way have caused the minor crisis over the amount of acromysin I was being given. In Rio, and particularly in the summer when the air is hot and humid, the European dose of antibiotics is doubled but my dose was quadrupled. I hid the extra tablets which I was most unwilling to swallow until Anne arrived to drop them over the balcony into the gutter far below, along with the scampering rats. My Ukranian-born night nurse, who spoke perfect English, was horrified and there were no more excessive doses.

One day when I was free of pain and well on the road to recovery Anne put her head round the door, "Visitors from England! Three guesses who they are."

"I haven't got a clue . . . not . . . no, it couldn't be (my memory slipped back to meeting Tom Worth at Vancouver airport when I thought he was in Sidney, Australia) . . . not Tom and Anne, surely?„

"Right first time."

She ushered them in and with them seemed to come a breath of the wide ocean although they had arrived by air instead of in their own boat. We seemed fated to meet in different parts of the world; in English Harbour, in Papeete in Tahiti where they had come knocking on our hull at five minutes to midnight, but on this occasion they had no idea we were here. They had been lunching with friends when their hostess said, "I suppose you don't know a couple called Anne and Peter Pye?"

Within a few minutes they were on the telephone to Anne. Tom asked whether this set back was likely to alter our plans.

"I'm afraid so," replied Anne, "although to what extent we shan't know until Peter is well enough to sail again."

All too soon Anne took them away promising they would return next day before flying on to Argentina, but Tom came back. He said, "I hear you are still thinking of Tristan da Cunha."

"Tom! Has Anne been getting at you?"

"No: it's just this. I think you as a doctor ought to consider whether a long sea passage down to the edge of the Roaring Forties, to an island where you probably won't be able to land, is the right sort of convalescence for you as a patient."

When Tom left England seemed further away than ever and I felt very forlorn. I had no idea what expenses I should have to meet except that the ambulance would cost not less than a hundred thousand cruzeiros and when I asked my doctor when I should be able to leave the answer seemed to vary from day to day. Looking back on this I can see what a thoroughly tiresome patient I must have been. Nor was I happy about the ship. Jock had been up the day before and had told me the decks were leaking and he could do nothing to repair the rubberized compound with which they had been treated because of the climate. Torrential rain was followed by the intense heat of the vertical sun making the decks steam like a boiling kettle. I said, rather gloomily, that she might have to lie there for some time. "Don't worry," he said, "I'm happy at Itacuruça and I don't mind how long I stay."

Like a genie appearing by magic in answer to a beggar's prayer Charles arrived unexpectedly early the very next morning. The British Legion, of which Alan Gross was the treasurer, had the right, in certain circumstances, to a free bed at the Strangers Hospital. He said, "Alan thinks you fit the bill, so you don't have to worry about the expense of your room. And, by the way, Anne asked me to tell you that Alice rang. They were going away for Christmas but they changed their minds and have asked you to go and stay with them."

I found it hard to express my thoughts. During the last few weeks we had accepted so much from so many. I have always felt that it is what you put into life that is important but once more it seemed that our balance was more in the red than ever.

A few days later my doctor asked me whether I felt well enough to continue my convalescence at the de Salis' flat. "We'll have you X-rayed in two weeks. Take it easy. You've lost fourteen pounds since you've been in so don't expect to feel fit the moment you're out."

He was about to leave when the door opened and Anne came in. She looked worried. "Doctor," she cried. "Has there been some sort of an accident? The whole floor looks like a first-aid post and all are women with dressings on their faces." He laughed: "Those," he said, "are the wives whose husbands have given them a face lift for a Christmas present, waiting to go home."

Charles sent the Embassy car, with Anne in it, to collect me the following day. I left by the same door through which I had come but, thanks to all the staff, in very different heart.

When I first saw Charles and Mary's flat I thought I might have been in Paris. The long silk curtains, the quilted hangings, the small elegant well-padded chairs were so unusual in Brazil where the heat makes you long for bareness and for as much air round yourself as you can arrange for but the flat belonged to the only woman ambassador in the Brazilian Foreign Service, at present in Costa Rica. There was a small elegant library which Charles sometimes used for his liaisons with Brazilian contacts, three bedrooms and a bathroom in which the water heater had been known to explode, with disastrous consequences, if carelessly used.

Outside the living room was a weather-proof balcony from which you could look down on to a pattern of car roof tops as they advanced in stop-go rushes at the changing of the lights like an army of well-trained beetles. Beyond were the blue waters of Guanabara Bay and the narrows through which steamed the freighters to and from the South Atlantic ocean. It was a pleasant place to live in with one disturbing feature: a large painting by a Brazilian artist, Josephine Petersen, of an allegorical cat, as big as a leopard with cruel green eyes: it sat with its tail curled round itself against a livid jungle and distant mountains. I found myself looking at it again and again, against my better judgement, trying to discover what was in her mind when portraying that remarkable animal.

To help her run the flat Mary had the services of Eugenia and Joanna. Eugenia was so small that she almost might have been a San Blas Indian. She may officially have been a Roman Catholic but if the surface was scratched she was as primitive and pagan as Josephine Petersen's cat. Joanna was a larger woman, uncertain in temper but an excellent worker, of whom Eugenia was intensely jealous. At one time both women had lived in but Eugenia had ousted her rival who now came by the day. One afternoon while I was having my afternoon rest and when Mary was shopping an uproar broke out. Shrieks rent the air, Eugenia fled to her room and bolted herself in while Joanna hammered on the door with her fists calling down curses upon Eugenia's head. I got there when Anne had the situation in hand. She had asked Joanna to go and make tea for us and then knocked on the door.

"Eugenia," she called.

"E Senhora so?"

"Si, Si, Eugenia."

A head put itself round the door. "She has put a curse on me" she whispered. "Already I feel the knife in my heart." Then she bolted the door and refused to come out until Mary came back. Eugenia, however, was essentially practical. When warned by Mary that she might not be able to replace Joanna she decided that an armed truce would be preferable to doing twice the work. It gave me an insight into what life might be like in a Rio favella.

On Christmas Eve Eduardo drove us up to the Sitio Baixo which, you may remember, lies in a valley some two hundred feet below Charles and Mary's cottage. This was the June of the Northern summer and the gardens were a riot of colour. After the heavy stale odour of Rio it was like living in the Haute Savoie, and it had the stillness of a forest in the afternoon. The house was low and L-shaped: the foot of the L being the kitchen and the servant's quarters where "Edith" lived with her child and where Alice did most of the cooking. At the other end of the house was a large open room with a bar in one corner from which you looked out over the lake to the forest climbing up the hill on the other side of the valley. It was in this room that the four of us sat before dinner sipping cool beer or any other drink that took our fancy.

Each day I walked a little further, climbed a little higher and in Alice I had a wonderful example of almost inexhaustible energy. She ran the house and the farm, whose buildings we glimpsed through the luxuriant trees, she looked after the farm workers' families, went to the clinic three times a week to give injections to the poor of Rio's favellas and was a collector of things for good causes. In six months time Alan would be retiring and already had bought a cottage in Dorset. One evening we had been talking, if I remember rightly, about the emergence in England of a half-educated disatisfied and bored young community to which violence seemed to be the only outlet. "In Brazil," said Alan, "it's the other end of the social scale that gets into trouble. The rich men's sons; because the parents are too lazy to discipline their children at home. If they are caught their fathers pay hush money to the police to prevent the poor little dears from being sent to prison."

"There was a case that came up a year or two ago. A girl threw herself out of a top floor flat in Copocabana trying to escape from being raped by three young men. The ringleader was the son of an ex-chief of police so nothing was done until he was safely smuggled out of the country. The girl's father, however, went to the press which in Brazil is as free as ours in Britain. They took it up in a big way and the young man had to be returned to stand trial. He was found guilty and sent to prison. About six months later the press managed to get a reporter into the prison to interview him. His 'cell' was found to be a comfortable flat with a sofa on which to entertain his girl friends at night and a television set to amuse him by day. That story really set Rio humming."

"I imagine that might happen in any Latin American city."

"No doubt. I'm tired of the lot of 'em. It will be a pleasure to live once more in a country where the people are more or less law abiding and the politicians are, by and large, honest."

"You wouldn't like living there at the moment," said his wife who was reading a letter from home. "It's covered in snow and ice, the trains won't run because diesel engines don't like the cold;

power cuts prevent you from heating your house, pipes are frozen and theres no electricity to cook by."

"Personally," she said, "I would rather put up with a spot of corruption and stay in a warmer climate."

Towards the end of our stay Anne and I were out for a last stroll before going to bed when we heard the beating of drums. We slipped through a gate in the wall and down a path which led to two rows of huts facing each other across a muddy lane. The lane was packed with people, their eyes rivetted on a group of semi-African faces which shone, under gold paper crowns, in the chinks of light from behind the closed door of a wooden hut. The beating of the drums, the shrill notes of the demanding repetitive refrain made me see myself as a spy looking down on a secret rite; we stood undetected until a wandering eye discovered us. The effect was electric. Every face turned towards us in a sullen unwavering stare. We made to leave but at that moment Alice came hurrying down the path. "Donna Alicia," they shouted, "Donna Alicia!" She spoke to them in rapid Portuguese, talking to them in their own patois. They looked back at us and now their faces were friendly and welcoming. Drums rose to a crescendo and the door of the hut opened. An old woman stood on the threshold, the candle-lit room behind her, and at the far end, on a packing case covered in cloth, stood a crib and a manger. The woman bent to receive a standard from a girl dressed in white, and beckoned the party to enter her house. The door closed.

"The Folia dos Reis," said Alice as we walked back to the house. "It is a ceremony in which the banner of Christ is carried to the house of selected people in the country districts of Brazil. They must play till the door is opened and they are invited to be given refreshment. The timing is important. If the door is opened too soon or if they are kept waiting too late they do not visit that house again. I was told tonight that they would be coming to us in three days time. They do not as a rule visit the houses of foreigners. I wish you could be with us then."

These little ceremonies continue from Christmas to Twelfth night.

I left the Alto a different man. Alice took us down to the Strangers in her ancient Ford Prefect to which she was deeply attached, and my X-rays showed that my lungs were now clear. We then took a taxi to the Praia de Flamenco where we found Eduardo waiting to say goodbye to us as he had to go to Sao Paulo and we should be gone before he got back. He looked at us with grave concern. Ever since he had sailed in *Moonraker* he had lost what little faith he had in our ability to sail safely back to England. "Why don't you behave like normal people?" he asked. "Why not sell the old boat and fly back to England?"

"But we like it, Eduardo," cried Anne. "The wind is free and takes us about the world without fuss and noise. If I had to travel any other way I would rather stay at home."

On our last evening in Rio Charles and Mary took us along to meet Josephine Petersen and her husband who was a professional pianist. Their flat, as one could imagine after seeing that painting, was not entirely conventional. It was a big room but made considerably smaller by two grand pianos, while from the ceiling hung, on fine threads, strange black shapes which revolved in the invisible air currents reminding me of the shadow films I had seen at the Academy Cinema before the war. From the walls cats, with their backs to tropical forests and lava mountains glared, simpered or just stared in such a way that had I been alone I should have run unashamedly away. I am negative about cats, while liking our own, but the effect of this room on Mr. Paul Gallico would be most interesting to observe. Next to their living room is a small museum in two parts: in the first are shelves and cases crammed with painted clay figurines (including some by Vitalino), shrunken human skulls, stone axes, red and black lizards, a pre-Columbus pot, tough and shiny like hide, and photographs by Orlando Villa Boas, of a group of Indians adorning the heads of their enemies (whom they had just eaten) with the feathers of tropical birds. Villa Boas goes unarmed into the interior with medicines for the Indians. Each time he sets out to penetrate still deeper into unknown territory they do not expect to see him come back alive. In the next room was Mr. Petersen's library; first editions of books on Brazilian and Portuguese history, rare manuscripts including the diary of a Jesuit priest at the time of the Jesuit expulsion. Just to hold the book in my hand and look through the thick parchment pages of neat upright handwriting seemed to link the past with the present. The order to expel the Jesuits was carried out with ruthlessness and dispatch and all their documents were destroyed so that this work alone must be of immense value.

The Petersens have a house at Terezopolis, close to the mountain known as the Finger of God, a long slender pinnacle pointing to the sky. Their next door neighbour, with whom they are on excellent terms, keeps a shop. Recently he had shot his brother for having an affair with his wife. "He now sits behind the counter with a revolver to his hand waiting for her to come back. He is quite blind but is confident that he will recognize her footsteps once she had entered the shop." The Petersens asked us to go up with them to Terezopolis for the weekend but I said we had arranged to rejoin the ship at Itacuruça. I saw Anne's face relax. I do not think she had been convinced that the shopkeeper could be relied upon to recognize his wife's footsteps from those of others.

CHAPTER TWENTY

I had been looking forward to seeing by day the road along which I had been driven in the ambulance by night, but the engineers had recently run the grader over the rutted surface and it was, in fact, excessively dull, the car crawling along the immense flat plain like a beetle crossing a runway. At one point Mickey had to take the car down into a steep gulley: the bridge which spanned it had collapsed.

We drove into the sun-baked little town in the early afternoon and were met by Carlos and Jock who took Mickey and Zuza to a cafe to cool off with pints of Brahma beer. Anne and I loaded our gear into the dinghy and rowed out to *Moonraker*. From bow to stern and from the bottom of the keel to within an inch or two of the waterline a magnificent tropical garden, like Bahamian coral seen through a glass-bottomed boat, clung to the copper. Aloft she was ship-shape and Bristol fashion but the deck, as Jock had warned me, was in a shocking condition. There would be plenty of work to do on this when we reached a more reasonable climate. I slid back the hatch. On settees and cushions, on the cabin walls, was a fine blue mould and from the galley rose a curious smell which we traced to six dozen eggs, some of which had burst and others which had split; their contents trickling into the cardboard containers. It was obvious that Jock had been concerned with boatswain's work and had only been below to open hatches and skylights when the weather permitted.

Mattresses, books and cushions went up on deck, eggs went over the side and for a couple of hours the two of us worked without exchanging a word. At the end of that time we came face to face as the last things were put back into place.

Anne murmured, "Will Jock come back with us, or will he stay here?"

"I don't honestly know."

There was little opportunity to discuss the situation with Jock when we met ashore. Hoping to do so later I said, "Are you sleeping aboard?"

"I don't think so. Not tonight."

"Then we'll meet for breakfast tomorrow and make a start on cleaning the copper at slack water."

I had a word with Carlos who agreed to make me a nine foot oar with a hard wood scraper screwed to one side of the blade and he suggested we should lash a small empty oil container to the other side of the blade to keep the scraper pressed hard against the hull.

Dinner that night at the Danemarka was the first of our Despedidas. In Brazil, when a person or family goes abroad each of their friends gives them a Despedida, or Farewell Party, so that by the time they leave they can hardly stagger to ship or aircraft. This dulls their sense of loss at leaving their country. Mickey and Zuza insisted on giving this because when they left next day it would be for them as if we had already left the country. I must confess I was hardly in a party mood. I was exhausted after my efforts aboard and I was worried at the possibility of Jock deciding to stay at Itacuruça. Before long I realized that Carlos had something on his mind too. In his quiet voice he suggested I was not yet fit to put to sea and why did we not stay in Itacuruça until the autumn when the winds would be more favourable to make up the east coast? I replied that we should like to do so but there was so much we still wanted to see in Brazil.

"Itacuruça IS BRAZIL."

In a confidential voice he added, "I do not think Jock is prepared to leave us just yet. Nor do we want to lose him. Think it over."

The conversation became more general and Carlos did not return to the subject of our departure. Helped by his gentle wit and by Mickey and Zuza who had fallen in love with Itacuruça I began to recover. Zuza, at her most outrageous, was giving Carlos a dramatic account of her room at the hotel where she had nothing to help her make up her face except a fifteen watt bulb and a small cracked mirror. Carlos, his small eyes twinkling, reassured her. "The hotel belongs to my mother-in-law and I will see they provide you with a candle."

The Port Captain and his wife strolled by and stopped for a drink, his wife sitting down beside me. "How heartless of you to even think of taking Jockey (they had put a diminutive on his name as they do to all they like) away from us so soon," she cried. "On New Year's Eve he saved my life!"

"What happened on New Year's Eve?" I asked her.

"There was a dance at the Pavilion. There was lots and lots of caçaça and some of the men became quarrelsome. One of them insulted my husband who aimed a blow at him but hit me instead. Toute de suite un grand fracas!" she cried. "Some went for my husband thinking he was trying to kill me, others for the man. Suddenly he drew a revolver pointing it at me. I screamed and at that moment Jock, who had left the hall a few minutes before, rushed in, seized the man from behind, kicked away the revolver as it fell from his hand and threw him out of the window."

"Oh la la!" she cried, "It was magnificent!"

It was midnight before Anne and I rowed the short distance back to the ship. "I would have given a good deal to live like Jock" she said, "in this little town. But why hasn't he learned more Portuguese?"

"Because Carlos speaks English," I replied. "No one really matters to Jock except Carlos. Not even Maria Guadeloupe, whose English, by the way, has improved considerably."

Before I turned out the lamp above our heads Anne said, "Pamela has asked us to go up to Vassouras. Jock told me before dinner. Don't you think a few more days would help you?"

"We can't delay any longer."

Another cloudless day broke over Itacuruça. I sheltered under my wide-brimmed Recife hat and the flimsiest shirt I could find and while Jock did the scrubbing I held the dinghy. The sun beat down mercilessly. After one side was finished Anne begged me to let her take my place. When we were half way along the other side I wished I had accepted. I went ashore to see Carlos about the oar. He looked at me closely. He said, "It is not for me to tell you how to look after yourself but I do know this climate. If you insist on working in the sun you'll soon be back in the Strangers Hospital in Rio."

When I left him, instead of returning to *Moonraker* I walked to the Danemarka and picked up the telephone. Presently Pamela's voice answered me. I said, "Jock tells me you very kindly asked Anne and me to stay a few days. Is the offer still open?"

"Of course. When would you like to come?"

"I've been rather stupid this morning, working in the sun."

"As soon as Manoel comes back with Francisco I'll send him down. He should be with you about four o'clock."

My Anne was very angry. Angry that I had had to find out for myself that I wasn't fit to work, angry that my first step forward should end in a long step backwards; but all this passed over my head like a summer's gale over a field of young corn. I was reminded of the negro in Hawaii whose job it was to sort bad pineapples from good. On being asked if he liked his job he shook his head. He said, "It's nothing but decisions, decisions, decisions from morning to night." The time had come when I too refused to make another.

We stayed away for five days. The cool air at night, the wide view of uplands, of forest and distant mountains; sitting outside on the patio in the evening listening to Mozart and Beethoven, the lowing of the cattle . . . I would not have believed that in so short a time I should feel so different a man: like David, ready for Goliath.

We were met by a deputation who gathered round our dinghy on the sand in a half circle. Carlos, the Port Captain's wife, pretty Maria Guadaloupe and a crowd of nephews, nieces, and hangers-on. Carlos made a little speech saying he hoped we would stay with them for another two months until I restored to good health. Near to Carlos stood Jock.

I felt at a disadvantage for I could not disclose my fear that in two months Jock would be as unwilling to leave as the ship would be incapable. I thanked them for all they had done for us, for taking Jock to their hearts and into their homes, told them none of us wanted to leave but we were a long way from England and that there was still much in Brazil that we wanted to see.

I said, "We sail in the morning."

Feet shuffled in the sand and all eyes were turned on Jock. He looked at them for a long time as if he was trying to store their faces in his memory. He said, "I have been happier here than at any other place. One day I shall come back to you all in my own ship." Then he joined Anne and me and we rowed out to *Moonraker*.

During the afternoon Carlos came aboard with an invitation from Donna Selma, his mother-in-law, who wished to give a Despedida for us that evening. Nothing could have pleased us more. Anne wrote in her diary . . . "We walked past the Danemarka to a gate in a wall through a small courtyard into a room which, stripped of the teeming life inside it, was full of down at heel furniture and peeling walls. In a chair sat Donna Selma, eighty years of age, doing fine lace work on tiny garments without using glasses. She is tall with a mop of white hair, paper-white skin and a flattened yet shapely nose. She is thickly built for her height and wears a pale grey dress. Her eyes are on the present but are sad with the past. It is said that her husband, a wealthy industrialist in Rio, lost his fortune (and his life) in the Wall Street crash. She now runs the Banana Agency in Itacuruça.

Vicky (Carlos' wife) appears to have done the cooking. Soup, fried and marinated fish (Cavallo) and peeled shell fish served with lemon. Rice, beans and a banana docé follow, with cafezinho. Maria is there, a nephew and a girl friend: We are nine and two small grandchildren. We are waited upon by a small black girl in pigtails. She is deaf, with bright dark eyes.

Before we go we look at charts with Carlos and fade one by one away into the night with sprigs of jasmine. We push off while a gathering group sings Auld Lang Syne to us and the full moon . . ."

There was one call to be made before continuing our voyage to the west: to Jaguanum to thank Denys and his relations for answering our call for help. We sailed in at midday and tied up once more to the red conical buoy. I had forgotten how beautiful it was. The pale green water sighing as it crept up the coral sand, the white deserted beach, the tree with the yellow flowers on it, Franciso's cottage half hidden behind its bamboo screen; just as it had looked when I last saw it in the light of the moon instead of the sun.

Anne went off to discuss with Denys' wife the sort of Despedida the people would like. This, it would seem was a dance. She thought one of the men had an accordion.

By nine o'clock rows of cold meat sandwiches, biscuits and cheese, flagons of wine and small delicacies which Anne had brought from Rio were ready on Francisco's pine table. The islanders came up two by two, the girls with flowers in their hair, the men shy and bashful but the red wine and the moon coming up over the trees soon got them going. But there was the same curious flatness about this little scene as we had noticed in other Portuguese islands in the Western Ocean: the shuffling feet on the stone floor, the level rhythm of the singing and the tunes to which they danced, the flat Indian features, and I wondered whether the party had in some way misfired. It was only many months later when we met Francisco in England that we were told they still remembered that particular Despedida. It was well after midnight when the party broke up and for some time after that we heard the sound of the harsh peasant singing coming from Denys' hut.

But for Anne this bay was too full of memories. Twice she woke, bathed in sweat having dreamed of a man in white twisting and leaping over the water and later of three black crouching figures carrying a weighted sack down to the water.

We awoke late to a hot windless day of which Jock and I took advantage by cleaning most of the rest of the growth off the copper with Carlos' excellent tool. We had almost finished when Gabriel came alongside in his dugout. "Would the Senhora please come back with him?"

In half-an-hour she was back.

"Two of the fishermen are ill. Also Denys' wife."

"Nothing to do with our party, I hope."

"I don't think so. Would you see them?"

So I took my stethoscope and some boxes of tablets. It was nothing: a mild attack of La Grippe for which I was able to prescribe; but, as I rowed back I wondered why Gabriel had first called for Anne isntead of for me. Was it fear of "The Doctor?"; was it because they communicated more easily with her (but this had happened in countries where I spoke the language better than she) or was it some quality, a sort of simplicity, which she has and which I have not, that these rather primitive people were able to recognize and appreciate?

It is about fifty miles from Jaguanum to Parati in the southwest corner of Bahia de Ilha Grande. A good day's sail but, as you must have gathered, this is a difficult place to sail in. If there is wind in the eastern half there is often none in the west, if it blows in the morning it is calm in the afternoon. So when at dawn I woke to find a breeze from the east I turned out the crew and we breakfasted underway. As I had expected we lost our breeze once we had passed the northern tip of Ilha Grande itself and lay becalmed until a wind came in from the sea in the late afternoon. Parati was now out of reach before dark but there was an island to windward, which shall be nameless, and from the chart this appeared to be uninhabited. When, however, we anchored behind a reef we found that this was by no means so. Three trawlers shared our berth and a number of huts could be seen amongst the trees. To our surprise, for this had never happened before, we found a hardly veiled hostility. Our overtures were rebuffed, and when we passed the huts the women standing in the doorways turned their backs on us. We followed a path which ran parallel to the coast about a hundred feet above the water until it dipped into a bay where a waterfall had made a channel for itself through the sand like a tiny river. By the side of the waterfall was an elaborate hut of considerable size and a rock garden irrigated by half-boughs of trees which carried water from the fall to all parts of the little estate. It was so delightful that in spite of the poor light, for it was well hidden, Anne took out her camera to photograph it. In a moment a woman rushed out of the door.

"Senhora! Nao, nao. Es interdito a fotografar, por favor!"

We beat a retreat.

Back on board I noticed we were being closely watched by one of the trawlers and presently a boat put off with five men in her and came alongside. I asked them aboard, showed them below and gave them a drink. Their captain, a young man with an unusually fair skin and the sort of wrist watch that tells you the day of the week as well as the time, spoke a few words of English with a rough American accent. He wanted to know why we were here rather than enjoying the delights of Rio or Santos, how long had we been in the district and when we were going and where. All these questions we answered but Anne thought she would take turn.

"Do you live here, Senhor Capitaine?"

"Si, Senhora."

"In the house by the beach and the waterfall?"

"Si, Senhora," he answered, his face looking puzzled.

"It is a pretty house," she said to him. "So pretty I wanted to photograph it but I'm afraid your wife was angry with me for trying to do so.."

His eyes hardened. "We do not like strangers taking photographs."

While we had been talking something had been knocking at the door of my mind but I could not pin it down. When they got up to go, however, I realized what it was. These five men had come off a trawler in from the sea. Not one of them smelt of fish.

In the night I was wakened by the sound of diesels. All three boats were leaving the anchorage without a navigation or deck light amongst them. In the morning one of them came back.

With a fair wind we slipped out from behind the reef under sail and ran down the coast. A little later I was altering the trim of the spinnaker sheet when I happened to glance over the side and to my astonishment we seemed to be passing through a sort of minefield of wooden cases upon which was clearly inscribed a world famous name. Each was moored about two or three feet below the surface. I was about to shout to Jock who would naturally have been interested, for it was a famous Scottish name, when I saw our trawler of last night coming up astern with a great bone in her teeth, her master with his glasses glued on our vessel. I immediately engrossed myself with the set of the sails, giving him, when he was almost close enough to toss a biscuit aboard, what I hoped was an innocent wave to which he hardly replied. Twice he encircled our ship as if he could not make up his mind what to do with us and I was reminded of the schooner of a distinctly raffish appearance which had tried, some years ago, to entice us into a Cuban port.

Then, as now, no other sail had been visible on the horizon.

At least our friend seemed to be satisfied that we had not poached upon, or perhaps not even seen, his preserves and he dropped astern.

I went aft to explain to an infuriated Jock what it was all about.

"Shall we come back tonight and relieve him of some of his plunder?"

I thought not.

Parati lies at the base of a valley whose precipitous sides rise to jagged mountain peaks often hidden in storm clouds which add to its wild and isolated appearance. The inhabitants claim that it is the second oldest town in Brazil but Salvador and Ouro Preto seem to have established their priority. For transport Parati relies on the horse and the mule. There is a track over the mountains which, in fine weather can be negotiated by a jeep but we were told that only one car had ever reached the town and it had been in no fit state to start back.

In the shops hang magnificent leather saddles, leather bags for the rider to carry his luggage in, silver spurs, whips and embroidered coats for the horses which wait patiently outside the shops for their masters to reappear before setting off down the stony uneven street at a sharp staccato trot.

The ancient cathedral faces the water, buttressed by scaffolding. Above the altar rise tier upon tier of yellow and red wax flowers. The interior is cool and white. In one niche the mother of Christ is life size with a young Portuguese face and ringlets. Tears run down her cheeks and in her hands is a baby's garment. Behind her and to the side are effegies of Christ taken from the cross, mutilated by nails and thorns. The story is brought straight into the home of any Portuguese family.

Along the northern edge of the town a river ebbs and flows between banks of coarse grass and as we explore the muddy path there is a thunder of hoofs and horsemen gallop over the narrow humpback bridge like a Sheriff and his Posse in a Western.

There was a shop which was reputed to have carvings of canoes and ships but when we tracked it down, next to the bank, it was shut. We went into the bank to enquire whether it would be open later. The bank clerk, or it may have been the manager, then gave us a bottle of caçaça as a "Lembrança de Parati" and said he would go next door and rout the old man out. "He likes a sleep after his lunch."

Leaving the door of the bank wide open he went round to the

back of the old man's house and presently a rosy apple cheeked face peered at us round the door of the shop. We apologized for disturbing his siesta. He brushed this aside and ushered us into the dark musty shop. He had no models of canoes for the man who made them had died but we bought a round rice sieve made from pandanus which now hangs on a wall in our cottage.

Three months ago in Angra dos Reis we had been told to contact Sebastiao the Slave who had a fund of stories about the last days of that era. We should find him quite easily, they said, in the market square or in one of the rum shops which abound in this little town.

Sebastiao the Slave, however, had died five years ago.

It takes a long time for news to seep out of Parati.

This should have been our last night in this district but the wind, as so often happened, decreed otherwise, leaving us becalmed off the opening of one of the long inlets in which this end of the district abounds. Here we lay for the moment out of the tide until Jock, technically on watch but in fact half asleep under the shade of the useless sails, suddenly called down, "We have a visitor."

A wizened little man clung to our rubbing strake pointing to the bottom of his canoe in which lay fish, eggs and fruit. He and Anne then bargained leisurely and amicably until reaching a price which meant we bought at a cheaper rate than at the market and he was saved the long journey to the town. So intent were we upon our business that we failed to see a breeze coming out of the inlet until the ship started to move through the water. Our little man nimbly jimped aboard, tied his canoe up with what looked like a ragged bit of string, took the helm and said, "I will sail you to my home."

Looking slightly put out at thus losing my command I went below to look at the large scale chart and saw that the bay was free of dangers.

In the meantime our friend had Jock and Anne well under control, working the sheets like a well-trained ocean-racing crew as he tacked up the ever narrowing fiord. Off the only dwelling in the inlet he brought the ship into the wind and Jock went for'ard to drop the anchor watched by the man's eleven children and his wife (in the unlikely event that he had ever had the money to pay the priest to marry her).

They lived a carefree nomadic life. If their tiny crops of maize and beans failed through a winter of drought or were washed out of the shallow soil by summer rains they moved their house to more fertile land. If they wanted money he sold fish at Parati. When we told them we should be leaving for England from Santos our host fetched his guitar and his wife an old tin lid piled high with mangoes, song after song they sang while we ate sitting on the sand. Vesticlo de Bolero. The smallest of all Despedidas.

CHAPTER TWENTY-ONE

IT was two months since I had put to sea. I weighed less than eight stone, and whenever I hauled on a halyard I felt like Atlas holding up the world.

The day was cloudy with threatening rain, the sea lumpy with a persistent south-westerly swell over which the ship ploughed her way like an elderly cart horse at the end of a long day.

Exhausted by the movement of this less than moderate sea the one hundred and thirty miles between Ilha Grande and Santos seemed like crossing the Pacific Ocean. The wind came from every point of the compass and varied between Force 0 and 2 on the Beaufort scale. The coast was black and uncompromising, a rock bound shore with off-lying islets backed by mountains continuously hidden in thunderclouds. At intervals of from thirty to forty miles a village, each with its own small church tower, rose out of the jungle like an island in a lush green sea.

We sailed into the Canal de San Sebastiao to avoid going round the island of that name. The cut is narrow in the centre with steep hills on either hand. As a short cut it was a mistake for the wind funnelled through it right in our teeth and drove the water before it. I remember a horseman watching us watching him as we gained a few feet on either tack until he suddenly must have realized what a time waster this was. He put spurs on his horse and galloped away into a banana plantation. Late that afternoon we dropped anchor off Ilhabella, a tiny fishing village where we ate our meal in a hut overhanging the water listening to the handbells ringing the return of each small canoe. But the magic of the Ilha Grande is gone. A new road connects the little town across the water to Santos and Sao Paulo and soon Ilhabella will be gobbled up.

The rest of the passage, less than sixty miles, took us more than forty hours. Anne writes in her diary . . .

"The sun is shining and there is a genoa breeze. The hills of Santos are in sight. They grow clearer and by evening we are approaching. At ten o'clock at night when I am again on watch tall rectangular buildings are irregularly spaced and the lights in windows, red, pink, blue and gold, look like many-coloured crystals. Ahead is Moela Island and into the dark tunnel between it and the land the ship is running with me at the helm, straining my eyes, blinded by the revolving light from the light tower, watching for the black outlines of rocks. The sound of a small engine comes towards us. A motor yacht: her green and red lights like eyes set too close together, squinting. She passes and I see the dark lumps of islets to port and hear the snarl of surf curling round their bases. We round the long Manduba Point and make into the bay before Santos that has no name. We have chosen it from the chart: it seems to have a small beach and a pier. As we approach cries echo out of houses of the wooden slopes and a road curves down to the beach. Anchoring and leaving the mains'l up to lessen the rolling we brew cocoa and go below to sleep...".

Daylight showed many mysterious shapes spread around the beach and it was obvious that this was a hush hush place into which we had no right to penetrate. We hauled up our nylon warp, broke out the anchor and fled before the first of the offshore breeze.

Ahead rose the tall modern buildings of Santos, Recife-like, on our port hand in contrast to the low flat mangrove swamps to starboard. With a fair wind we entered the channel between the islands of Sao Vicente and Amaro, past the old Portuguese fort and, with the last of the flood turned into the third river on the right up a well buoyed channel to the Santos Yacht Club.

Our slow passage had convinced me that we must slip *Moonraker* before putting to sea again but when I enquired at the office I was told that it would be at least ten days, and perhaps three weeks before this could be done. Sunk in gloom and wilting in the great heat of this oven like place we retired to cool off on the veranda with long drinks. Presently a man whose face was vaguely familiar (I am bad at putting names to faces) stopped at our table. He was the Vice-Commodore of the Club and had met us at Rio. He said, "I am told you want to slip your boat. My own yacht was to be hauled tomorrow but I will be honoured if you would take my place." He would not take "No" for an answer.

Later that afternoon the foreman of the shipyard run by the Club came to examine *Moonraker*'s underwater body so that the cradle could be adjusted to take her. The water was like a black soup and smelt like the harbour of a Spanish town off whose main drain we had once inadvertently berthed. Our foreman, short and thick set with the shoulders of a bull and the laughing face of a Tahitian, held his nose and plunged into the turbid water, feeling along the run and the turn of the bilge with his hands. After several submersions he professed himself satisfied and walked off the staging shaking himself like a dog.

So, after a year of voyaging *Moonraker* came out of the water.

Club members gathered round for they had never seen a boat of *Moonraker*'s underwater shape but Brazilian good manners were equal to the occasion and she was adjudged a fine sea boat. Not content with this generous appreciation they armed themselves with brushes and a thing that looked like a long handled garden hose and attacked the jellied growth along the bottom of the keel which had resisted all our efforts with Carlos' scraper. Round the bows, however, there were several small holes in the copper. Although no toredo worm will work its way through tarred felt this may easily be torn away to leave the wood underneath vulnerable. After a long search a narrow sheet of copper was found out of which we cut a dozen patches. It was woefully thin but better than nothing.

Moonraker's re-entry into the water was not exactly the treatment I would have prescribed for a boat of her age. To ensure her reaching deep enough water she had to be launched at a run down the concrete ramp. It was like being in a tram that had suddenly taken to the cobbled streets and I was terrified that the carriage would slew to one side and the ship would fall over on to her bilges.

The next morning I went to the office to pay for the slipping and for the copper which I had been told "costs more than gold". The Secretary said, "The Club would be honoured if you would accept any slight services it has been able to give you as a present." Such is the calibre of Brazilian hospitality to the stranger.

For the last few weeks Anne had been writing to friends of friends, whom we had never met, explaining why we had not yet arrived in Santos. Now, Irma Dinwiddy was coming to take us to their home on the outskirts of Sao Paulo. She is a Romanian whose father was Professor of History at Budapest in Hungary. She spoke Romanian, German, Hungarian, Russian, French, Italian, Spanish, Portuguese and English fluently. Later she told us that while she and her husband were courting they spoke English but she wrote to him in German and he to her in French because in these languages they could best express their emotions.

It now began to rain with tropical ferocity and the cobbled streets of the older part of Santos were half under water. Irma Dinwiddy drove round the old city square (there was no place to park) while Jock cashed a cheque at the bank. Conversation did not at once flow easily. Irma was shy, uneasy perhaps that we should want to talk about nautical adventures in which she could have no possible interest while Anne and I were a little nervous that we might be involved in considerable social activity, for Sao Paulo has the reputation of being the most sophisticated city in Brazil. As we crossed the bridge from Sao Vicente island to the mainland Irma put our minds at rest. She said, "George and I thought you might like a few quiet days to start with so we have arranged nothing until the end of the week."

"Bless you," said Anne. "It's just what Peter needs but please don't let us be a nuisance. In any case we ought to get back to the boat next week."

A new road now snakes its way up the Sierra. Irma said, "I had hoped to take you up the old road which is much more exciting but in this rain it is not safe."

As we reached the top the rain ceased and she drew into the side of the road so that we could look back on the way we had come. The rivers, the islands, the channels and the city itself were laid out like a small-scale model in an architect's office. "It was here that the first of the Bandeirantes came," Irma said, "the first serious step towards finding what lay behind the coastal range. Whenever I look down from this place I can picture them struggling up the mountain side, their flag in the van, their long muskets slung on their shoulders, their pack horses slipping and stumbling on the treacherous rock. And their women. . . . There must have been women because it is a law of survival that women must follow their men."

"One would, I suppose, want to sing the praises of such men but in fact those who came from Sao Vicente were the most rapacious and cruel of all the early adventurers. When they had scaled these mountains they found, as you will see for yourselves, a great plateau with three large rivers flowing into the interior. They built themselves a boat and set off down the river known as Rio Tiete and when they came to unnavigable rapids they hauled this boat for twenty kilometers over the land to rejoin the river lower down. I will show you the memorial they have put up to commemorate this feat tomorrow. They made slaves of the Indians they captured and at a later date they even slew their Jesuit countrymen for trying to Christianise and protect these tribes. And yet . . . they were patient and prudent. They would settle down in some fertile valley, grow corn and egg plant and forofa and beans, hunt wild pig and boar, sometimes for a year at a time, until their stocks were sufficient to move on once again. That was, of course, how Sao Paulo came into being. It grew from a settlement founded by Jesuits on the feast day of St. Paul."

"Where did they finish up?" I asked.

"Always they travelled north and west. Into the Minais Gerais and the Matto Grosso and northwards to the Diamentina district. If there had been no Kimberly mines the Diamentina would have been the greatest diamond producing territory in the world.

"They found gold as well, in fact it was probably the rumour of gold that started them off but it was never found in great quantity and the veins were superficial. As you know, semi-precious and precious stones are much more common."

We were now driving along the plateau between artificial lakes which had been cleverly made by damming the three large rivers so that they turned back on themselves. Just as we were coming to the suburbs of Sao Paulo Irma suddenly took a sharp turn to the right. "We've just time," she said, "to show you that boat. I would like you to see it while the story of the Bandeirantes is still in your mind."

It was most impressive. There was movement and a sense of striving in the figures as they put their shoulders to the great boat and there was a striking resemblance to the Memorial to Prince Henry the Navigator which overlooks the Tagus so that for a moment I wondered whether the same artist had executed both works. On looking more closely I thought this probably was not so. At the bows of the boat stands a stately horse with an up-curving mane carrying his rider upright astride him. Surely the horse, and his rider, should be pulling their weight and yet I had the impression that the boat was pushing the horse.

Irma said, "The Paulistas call this 'VAI OU NAO VAI. TO GO OR NOT TO GO': for in spite of all the efforts of the men nothing ever moves!"

Irma's house, when we finally came to it, looked out on a main thoroughfare which bore more than a slight resemblance to the North Circular Road. It was of one storey, the rooms were light and uncluttered and it was deliciously cool for we were still some fifteen hundred feet above sea level. Nearly all the pictures on the walls were painted by Irma.

I could find that house to this day, coming from Sao Paulo. It lies on the right hand side about a mile past a Statue to Borbo Gato, a Bandeirante who, I suppose, was instrumental in the founding of the city: a brutish, dull fellow holding his gun like a walking stick with his great hand firmly grasping the muzzle. It seemed at the time to be a realistic piece of sculpture which fitted Irma's description of the Bandeirantes like a glove, but later, when I heard his story, I felt differently about him.

Left in charge of an Emerald District by his superior, Dias, who had to return to Rio, he was suddenly ordered to hand over the entire territory to a Spaniard, an arrogant and contemptuous hidalgo, sent out by the King of Portugal. In loyalty to Dias he at first refused to do this but in the end he suggested, to avoid bloodshed, a conference to which neither party should bring arms. Unfortunately the two men became extremely excited and one of Gato's men, who had brought his sword concealed under his jacket and who feared for his leader's person, now drew his sword and slew the King's Emissary. Knowing that he would be held responsible Borda Gato fled to the bush were he lived among the Indians for some years. His lips thickened, his body swelled, his hair matted and his features became those of a savage. During his exile his longing to see once more his wife and their children became so unbearable that he eventually set off for the long journey back to Sao Paulo. At last he presented himself before his house without realizing, for he had no mirror, that he had changed beyond recognition. His wife opened the door to him herself. Overcome by her beauty he tried to embrace her but she gave a wild shriek which brought out the soldiery. They beat him up in front of her and then drove him back into the bush.

CHAPTER TWENTY-TWO

GEORGE Dinwiddy is technical advisor to all J. & P. Coats' plant in Brazil and at the moment there was a strike at the factory. The Government had decreed that the workers should have a "thirteenth month bonus" but as the firm had been paying the equivalent of such a bonus they merely substituted the Government's gesture for their own and the men were therefore no better off. They walked out.

George came home that night tired and depressed. For him and his boss all this meant long hours of wrangling with labour leaders, decisions which might or might not be understood six thousand miles away in Glasgow.

"Communism" was often on people's lips. It seemed odd to me that Sao Paulo, where more rich men live than in any other city in Brazil, was the one place where that word was mentioned as an active menace. Perhaps if you are very rich you easily may be frightened of losing your riches. I kept out of these discussions for I find it difficult to blame men for trying to get higher wages when they can hardly keep warm in winter or buy enough food for their children at any time. I am sure Irma felt the same but she had been brought up behind the iron curtain and the word "communist" had much the same effect, I imagine, as the name Mao on a Republican minded general in the U.S.A. armed forces.

The strike persisted. It made me look at the people we saw in the streets and for the first time I saw discontent on many faces. It must be something to do with "progress". On our last day here the men went back to the factory defeated. I was glad for George.

The Paulistas call their city the Birmingham of Brazil: technically, perhaps a compliment but architecturally, and even more, climatically, an insult. As we looked down from one of the glassy slopes of the main thoroughfare with its sense of breadth and the sun lighting the tall yellow buildings which seem to give it a cohesive instead of an asymmetrical appearance I could see the footbridge called the Viaducto de Cha (The Bridge of Tea). Only fourteen years ago this bridge had joined one part of a tea growing estate to the other and now it is almost in the heart of Sao Paulo. On every side the city spreads outwards invading the country like some neoplastic adventurer and in the centre it grows upwards. You can almost feel the stitches giving as the unweildy giant bursts open another seam. Near the Trianon a small tract of forest has been preserved as the Bandeirantes knew it when they first came here. Lianas hang from the trees and the undergrowth is so thick that if you left the narrow paths which intersect it no sunlight would ever reach you. No one ventures there at night but even in broad daylight I felt when I came out that I had been transported by magic carpet straight from the Amazonas to Ealing Broadway.

It was in one of the flats overlooking the Viaducto de Cha that I met an elderly doctor, now retired, who came out to Brazil long before the second war. He had taken his degrees in Dublin, "House" jobs in English hospitals and locums round the countryside. He had fallen in love with the daughter of one of his principals and was anxious to settle down. He found an assistantship with a view to partnership at Swindon which he hoped would bring him in about £1,500 a year but a few days before signing the agreement he was introduced to a Rail Man from Brazil (all the top Rail Men were British in those days) who was on the look out for a doctor at £400 a year and all found. "The rest is up to you," said the R.M. "If you make good the sky's the limit."

He wrote to his fiancée and asked whether she would take the risk and go out with him. She wired back, "Will leave you if you stay in Swindon."

The Doctor said, "While I was doing the Railway job I learned Portuguese and took my Brazilian degrees. I found I had some dexterity as a surgeon and very little in the way of opposition. I came to Sao Paulo when it was just starting to grow and not long afterwards I was doing brain surgery."

His eyes still had a touch of youth in them as he smiled at me mischievously. "My wife and I think as you two must do. That life should be lived at the maximum point of insecurity. Then you may get some fun out of it."

Poor Irma! She worked so hard trying to keep us together in those busy streets. Jock would stop and gaze upwards at a building as high as a mountain while Anne would dart into a shop after a baucho horn. Shopping is a nightmare to me unless there is something I know I want and my contribution was to keep open the communications, not always easy as it was as difficult to park a car as it is in London.

The day we went to the Art Museum Jock was not with us because paintings mean little to him but Anne was there lost in contemplation of the Poor Fisherman by Gauguin whose pictures always make me want to go back to Tahiti; Irma took me over almost at once to where three large canvasses were displayed on an otherwise empty wall. They were by Candido Portinari (now most lamentably dead of lead poisoning), the man who had painted, and then repainted the wall behind the altar in that curious church at Belo Horizonte designed by Neimeyer. Irma left me and I sat on a bench looking at them for a very long time. All three were painted against a background of a dead flat plain: stony, bare, colourless. Each depicted a scene in the lives of the north-easters, those forgotten people, forgotten unless they are wanted for work which no one else will do, who die of thirst if they cannot buy water at 25 cruzeiros a litre or of starvation if there is no rain at all and their thin crops fail. Portinari's figures are bone, muscle and sinew. Feet and hands, legs and arms are large and anatomical but I know of no other man who can put so much feeling into the sole of a foot. The centre picture is the most dramatic. Two men are carrying a hammock slung on poles in which lies the body of a dead man. He was too poor to be buried in a coffin and even the hammock will be retrieved at the last for hammocks cost something to make. Kneeling on the ground as the men pass by is his woman: her feet splayed, her arms extended upwards and outwards in the ultimate gesture of despair. Tears from her hidden face fall like stones to the ground.

The painting is called Enterro na Redo.

On our way home an idea began to germinate in my mind. If I was not fit to go home by Tristan da Cunha, if the winds were southerly instead of northerly, then why not sail to the real northeast whose nearest port would be Natal. As if reading my thoughts Irma said, "You ought to see that country. You could stay with friends of ours at Natal and they would arrange for you to go up to the Cotton Farm, right in the heart of the north-east.

But by that time my thoughts had taken another diversion. If we went to Natal, why not go by way of Fernando do Noronho? Ever since Tovarich da Silva the heart surgeon in Recife had said it was the most lovely island he had ever seen it had been at the back of my mind.

George and Irma had arranged a party that night and it so happened that the Brisith Consul-General was among the guests. I asked him what chances we had of getting permission to visit Fernando. He was pessimistic. Althouth the American missile men had gone the Brazilian army had a post there and they were, he thought, sensitive to strangers. "If you like," he said, "I will make some enquiries." I begged him not to. Whenever we have gone to out of the way places where our welcome might be doubtful I have found that the role of an ignorant fool is safer than that of a wilful intruder.

For the moment Fernando do Noronho was shelved.

As a result of this party, and of Irma's delicate engineering of chances that she took care we did not miss, we were invited to spend the day (and the night but this was not possible) at Fazenda Sao Bento which was run by a congressman, the Presidente do Union Democratico Nacionale. "It is not as a politician that I want you to meet him. He makes coffee pay and as that is one of our major exports (Irma always used the word 'our' when talking about Brazil) this is an important thing."

We left early in the morning. The road led through open rolling country, then through Eucalyptus forests and fields of milho and coffee plantations, the older trees bunched like fat green sheep sheltering from a storm: through two towns, Itaparati and Ampora, each with its small central square ablaze with flowers and always smiling friendly faces. On the far side of Ampora we turned off onto a dirt road and came to a gate from which the road descended into a valley with a small stream at the bottom and a cluster of houses. On a low hill and sheltered among trees stood a house with the same pink wash as the one we knew so well at Vassouras.

At first I thought we had come to the wrong place. Surely this must be a hotel packed to bursting point with summer visitors? People diving off a board into a swimming pool at the side of a purple cloud of bougainvillea, people shouting, arguing, laughing, talking. I was quite wrong, of course. Of this great crowd, I learned later, there were not more than twelve guests including ourselves. The rest were family.

Irma introduced us to our host and his wife who immediately took us off to change so that we could have a bathe before lunch, followed by caçaça in coconut milk which is one of the most refreshing of drinks.

The house is only sixty-six years old, built on the site of the original, and much larger coffee fazenda when the size of the estate depended upon the number of attendant slaves. Not that this house was inconsiderable. The dining room alone could not have been less than forty feet and beyond that, at a slightly higher level, a sun room had been added. My host said, "Until a few years ago it was always assumed that as soon as the meal was over the women retired into the kitchens: but now this won't do. The younger generation want somewhere to talk and play together, so I had to build THAT on."

We sat down to lunch, some fifty strong, under an enormous picture of the Last Supper, the grandchildren having already been served. My neighbour on my right was my host's sister, half-a-generation younger. She had been educated in England but the fall of the cruzeiro had prevented her from sending her own children to school there. "We are very much pro-Britain in this family, especially since my brother took a number of 'deputados' to England at the invitation of the House of Commons: a system of Government he admires although he does not think it could be made to work over here."

Looking smilingly round the table she changed the subject:

"To a stranger I imagine we are rather difficult to 'take'. There are so many of us and we make so much noise."

"On the contrary," I told her. "In the short time I have been here you have made us so welcome that I feel we are almost one of the family."

"Counting cousins and grandchildren," she confessed, "there must be at least seventy-five of us. Every Thursday, in Sao Paulo, we have a family gathering in one of each others houses and it is not often that we sit down to dinner less than fifty at the table. My sister says you can hear us a mile away."

I could well believe it.

After lunch my host told me that he had some matters to discuss with one of his guests and that he would be unable to show us around the estate himself. "My sister, the one you were talking to at lunch, will take you round. She knows more about it than I do myself."

To the north of the house were several small hills covered with the same thick bush-like trees that we had seen on our way up here.

"This is a small estate," said our guide, "typical of the kind that are now no longer paying their way and are being sold up throughout the country. The reason for this is labour. Each crop, each tree, must be hand-picked and there may be as many as three crops between May and July. On a fazenda of this size each crop takes about twenty days to gather and after that it is maintenance work only. So the men drift away to the towns and larger farms where their jobs are more secure. My brother has shown how this can be prevented by keeping pigs and cattle and growing fruit so that we have our own permanent labour force of eighty men who live with their families in the village you passed on your way up to the house. They have their own school where the children are taught in the mornings and where evening classes are held for workers who want to improve their technical knowledge. All this is paid for out of the profits of the estate."

The coffee trees, each tree having four roots, are four-and-a-half feet high, spaced at intervals of six feet. The trees, at this season, are thick with green coffee beans. The seed is laid on the ground under cover and protected by hollow cylinders of wood and at the end of a year they are transplanted, four plants to every six feet of ground. They are then thinned out again to their adult spacing. Each tree yields up to nine pounds of coffee in the two or three yearly crops. The beans are then sent down a shute to be washed and then dried in a cement courtyard before being packed into bags.

We returned via the orchards of Bourbon mangoes, lemon and orange trees and vines to the piggeries. Never had I seen such cleanliness since being shown over Austen Levi's show farm on Eleuthera island but here they have even managed to get rid of the flies by an ingenious method of putting cow dung on a grating over water. The flies settle on the dung, the larvae burrow through the dung and fall into the water where they drown.

Twelve thousand hens, some cows and cattle, complete the activities of this model farm. When I told my hostess how much I admired the care and effort which had gone into the planning of such a venture, she replied, "People come from all parts of the country to see this place but my husband and I are left with the impression that they have no intention of involving themselves in such hard work and responsibility."

It was dusk before we left. My host said, "I'm sorry Irma has to take you back to Sao Paulo tonight. She tells me you are about to set out on a long voyage so I have taken the liberty of putting a small present for you in the back of her car."

Twelve dozen eggs!

On the way home Irma said, "One of my younger friends married into that family. To begin with she had been frightened by the very size of it but after a little while she told me she thought they had given her everything she had wanted from life: love, tolerance and companionship."

On our last night at Sao Paulo we dined with a Brazilian who owned a plastics factory. He was an amateur seaman of an unsual calibre to be met with in this country. He owned a Sparkman and Stevens yawl and had installed, among a great many other things, a record player on gimbals so that he could listen to Mussorgsky's *A Night on a Bare Mountain* in a howling gale and Mozart's piano concertos on quiet moonlight nights. He was planning to leave in a few weeks bound for the Ilha Trinidada, where E.F. Knight had spent a hideous night among all those giant land crabs when he sailed there in the *Falcon*: this would be a voyage of over two thousand miles by the time he returned to his moorings in Santos.

He also castigated us for not spending another year in this country so that we could see something of the Interior and when we told him the many obstacles which made this impossible he shrugged his shoulders. He said, "Then I had better tell you the story, which, to my mind, shows the Brazilian scene in a nutshell."

It was a simple story: a man died and was met by St. Peter at the Gates where he was told that his record on earth was such that he could not be admitted to heaven but must go down to hell. When he got there he found a vast barren plain, like the Brazilian northeast, upon which stood great enclosures with the names of the countries to which they belonged written on the outside walls. Thinking that the U.S.A., being the most modern, would also be the least uncomfortable, he tried it first. Inside there was a wailing and gnashing of teeth and when he asked why they were so miserable they replied that he would be too if, like them, he was boiled in oil from eight till twelve, frozen stiff from two till six and had to listen to the Devil talking to him about his sins till ten o'clock at night. Thinking this would be little fun he visited all the other countries in that neighbourhood but found them to be just as uninviting. So he walked out into the middle of the plain and in the distance he saw a very different sort of enclosure. Its walls were breaking down and the name of the country to which it belonged had long been obliterated, but from within its walls came the sound of laughter and singing. He entered and immediately he was surrounded by happy men and women and was kissed by the girls and embraced by the men. He said, "Why is it all so different here? What goes on?" They answered him, "The same as everywhere else: boiled in oil from eight till ten, frozen stiff from two till six and the Devil comes along and talks to us about our sins until ten o'clock at night. BUT, my friend, THIS IS BRAZIL! We have no more oil. The refrigeration has broken down years ago and no one bothers to mend it and the Devil comes late on the job and as soon as he has had his work ticket punched he goes off back home."

CHAPTER TWENTY-THREE

WE were now faced with a voyage of several weeks: homeward bound but by which route? By Tristan da Cunha, St. Helena, Ascension and the Azores, or by Natal and the West Indies? Our route could not be finally determined until the first seven or eight hundred miles were behind us. Nor was it merely a question of winds. For the first time in *Moonraker*'s wanderings skipper and crew were divided.

There is an entry somewhere in Anne's diary which reads: "My small piece of boat—my third—would now turn towards that haunting bay of Bahia to recapture something of Brazil. Jock's I suppose, would head back for Itacuruça and heaven knows where Peter's would go: towards one of those abominable islands in the middle of nowhere?"

She was worried about me, of course, as to whether I was fit enough to go at all, for she knew what the layman finds it so hard to understand that even if you never change sail—which you probably do about three times in the twenty-four hours—your muscles would still be fully occupied in the simple act of living on the high seas. To tell the truth I was not unworried myself.

It was high summer in these southern latitudes and along the coast from Santos to Natal the winds, according to the *Pilot Charts* should be north-easterly: nearly two thousand miles of adverse winds against the prevailing current. But, said the local pundits, if we were to make a long board out into the South Atlantic these winds might come from a more southerly quarter because there seemed to have been a change in the meteorological cycle.

Such problems were very much in my mind when Irma drove us back to Santos which we entered, as we had left it, in rain. The air was like the inside of an oven, the ship was damp, it was getting dark and the mosquitoes, baulked of this particular prey for the last ten days, were already launching a full-scale attack. Irma helped us unload the stores we had brought from Sao Paulo, insisted on helping us stow them and shared our meal of an old tin of steak and kidney pudding, originally brought out from England, before leaving to spend the night with a friend in Guaruja. She was back next morning sitting contentedly on a bunk sewing cushion covers or washing out glass jars as to the manner born. When she had gone our plastics friend turned up:

a stroke of good fortune because he immediately took us off to the Santos market which was a long way away. When Anne apologised for taking two hours to choose fruit for a month at sea he replied, "I have learned more than I shall ever remember and I shall put to sea in better order for this experience." After this flowery tribute he introduced us to the Port Captain where we sat drinking cafezinho in a large room with a bizarre lighting effect of harlequin squares thrown across our faces from the stained-glass windows.

The Captain said he was being driven crazy (he spoke fluent American) by strikes and lockouts and wished he was back at sea. There was a photograph of a handsome young man whose likeness to the Captain was unmistakable. I said, "Does your son follow your profession?"

"No: my son wants more than can be got from the sea. Already at the age of 22 he earns more than I do after twenty-five years service."

"But would you change with him, Captain?"

"When I am on my bridge I would not. I think," he added reflectively, "I would not anyway. The other day a man came to my house selling fruits. They were good fruits and I gave him a large order. When I ask him how many cruzeiros, he say 'You will not remember me Captain but I was shipmates with you ten years ago. These are for old times sake.' No, doctor, there is more to this world than money."

By chance the Port Captain knew the Commandant at Fernando do Noronho. He immediately sat down and wrote a letter which he handed me to give to the Commandant. "With that," he said, "I am sure you will be able to land." He added a warning. "If a swell comes in from the north-west you must leave at once."

We were to sail on 3rd February, our wedding anniversary, but, since our return to Santos, Anne had felt jaded with the heat and worried by the approaching voyage so I promised her one night of peace at Bertioga, a place she had chosen from the chart where, our plastics friend said, there was nothing.

At the last moment Irma and George—looking young and gay since the ending of the strike—came down to see us off bringing with them a bottle of champagne in which to drink our health and for us to drink theirs. A crowd had collected at the Yacht Club and as we gybed all standing into the river, narrowly missing the mud, a burst of firing (into the air, not at us) was followed by shouts of "Boa Viagem . . . Chegado seguro . . .". Shouts calling to mind those from the schooners in the Cape Verdes.

Not two hundred and fifty yards from all this frivolity a police launch was recovering the body of a young boy who had been drowned when his dugout canoe had capsized. A reminder that the sea was like a predatory beast of the jungle waiting for the brief but fatal moment of inattention by the unsuspecting victim.

Our own moment of inattention followed quickly. The sky to windward had been building up to a wall of darkness, a prelude to the usual afternoon thunderstorm from which, while we had been there, no more than a moderate breeze had sprung. On a broad reach, and with every stitch of canvas set, we sailed out into the bay when I noticed some low detached cloud behaving in an odd way as if it were being torn apart from the central mass. Heralded by a blinding flash and a thunder clap, wind and rain swept across the bay and the old ship took the bit between her teeth and plunged like a frightened horse towards the sea. The gear held—we should have been in a sorry state if it hadn't—and the ship was soon under control. I don't suppose the storm lasted more than half-an-hour but when I looked aft the dinghy was full of rainwater and the painter almost frayed through by the added weight.

It was dark by the time we arrived off Bertioga, watched by the eye of the old fort which must have seen some strange things in its long life and by the yellow lights from huts among the palm trees, their reflections marking the drying pools on the long sand spit running out from the north bank at low water. It was more my sort of place than Anne's because she is a woman of the plains and the sea and Bertioga lies under the shadow of the high sierra. On the south shore, so ran the instructions from our friend, we should come to a beach upon which were drawn up three dugout canoes: at least they were there ten years ago. Our sealed beam torch picked up the canoes looking as if they had not been moved since he had last seen them and, still following his instructions, close west of them we anchored.

Monkeys chattered in the trees.

That short storm had shown up one or two defects. The forehatch leaked and water was coming in through the deck on to our tinned fruit shelf. And while I stood there in the cool and the silence of the early morning the word "water" rang a bell in my waiting mind. I went below and looked at the water gauge which is not in an easy place to read. To my utter astonishment (we had drawn nothing off) eighteen gallons had been lost since Santos. If we hadn't put in here we might have soon been in the same predicament as the yacht that left Oahu for Tahiti without a drop in her tanks: each of her crew having left the filling of them to another.

The cause was a faulty cock on a valve on top of the tank. By the time this was put right, the watertanks filled from a cottage near the canoes, the forehatch made less of a sieve and the deck caulked (a poor job, like stopping a tooth with the decay still left underneath) it was late enough to warrant another night in harbour. Our last act was to post some letters. The Post Office was shut but a woman who lived opposite said that when it opened (tomorrow or the next day) she would do so for us. Leaving a larger cruzeiro note than was strictly required we handed them over without complete confidence that they would reach their destination.

We made a slow start but by dusk we were close, rather too close through an unexpected eddy of the ocean current, to Alcatraz island with its overhanging cliffs white with guano and its solitary light, unwatched; a creepy place at the best of times and at the moment downright sinister, for two thunderstorms were converging upon it. By some freak each went up one side leaving Alcatraz, and us, dry, but down the cliffs rushed the wind like an express train and we were off, heading east south-easterly towards our unknown destination. By dawn land was out of sight and the voyage had begun.

I must confess I find it hard to write, at this juncture, about an ocean voyage. One sea is very much like another, although each has its own characteristics, and if you keep north of the 40th parallel in the Southern Ocean and out of the high northern latitudes in winter you should be able to avoid those troubles which make good books for seamen to read. I still find it a little odd, however, that I am happier at sea than in any other place, or so I think when I am not here, but I like the small world of our twenty-nine foot boat with its self-imposed disciplines, the regular meals, the watches—no one ever late on these—the necessary vigilance without which no ship is safe, the reading of the signs from sky and waves (no forecasts to frighten us, thank God) and the feeling that you alone are responsible and there is no one to get you out of trouble except yourselves.

No one in their senses would read a ship's log for pleasure, unless it was his own. The columns of courses sailed, directions and strengths, of winds, currents, barometer readings, miles recorded on the patent log, change of sail entered under "Remarks"; but I have a fair memory and some of my old logs take me back to some lonely sea, to a stormy night hove-to in a gale, or to a quiet evening with the ship slipping over the rolling sea when the Trade Wind falls light. But I suspect that my memory becomes soothed with time. I will tell anyone who cares to listen that I can work out a sight in four minutes but if you ask Anne she will tell you an hour. The gap is not quite so wide as it looks. She takes it from the time I come up with the stop watch to put in her hand telling her to run the ship off or gybe or tack so that the sun will not be hidden behind the mains'l. There may well be two or three sights and readings of the chronometer watch before the plot will have been drawn on Mr. Baker's chart and the ship's position marked on the ocean chart. You will see, therefore, that I give the more pleasing, optimistic figure and Anne the more realistic, with a little added for extra caution.

This caution is not carried into her writing. Her diary, if it were printable, might be a best seller. She writes down not only actions and events but her thoughts. When I recall that she once said, "Do you think it is easy for me to live for months at a time with two men in my bedroom?" I realize, as you will that this diary is more than a record. It is a safety valve for her emotions. No one has ever seen it except myself and it is disconcerting to be the subject of occasional unguarded comment (this, by the way, is not reversible) but these comments do contain from time to time uncomfortable grains of truth which, after an initial period for recovery, I try to absorb for the future; so you would find her account of the voyage and mine were seen as it were through a different pair of glasses.

This is the only voyage upon which I look back with something less than pleasure. It had its moments, of course, as on a night to the east of Cabo Frio, for that perfidious cape which it took the Crowes four days to round in *Lang Syne* towards the finish of their world voyage, was now safely behind us. It was a night as near to perfection as a man can expect. The wind was fresh and a long swell rolled up as if from the depths of the southern ocean and the moon, sailing through the rents in the swiftly moving clouds transformed the crests of the seas into sprays of molten silver. With a reef in the main and the working jib the ship was sailing her fastest and on such a night I would barter my life for that of the *Flying Dutchman*.

But the next ten days were different. The wind backed towards the east and the ship came hard on the wind heeling her to her greatest angle so that stirring the porridge or handling the presure cooker became a demanding effort instead of a chore to be taken in my stride. Water poured through the perished rubber with which we had caulked the forehatch so that whoever went to the heads on the port tack came out as swiftly as possible before they died of drowning. Even the cabin was no longer sea-proof and as she crashed into a larger than usual sea a dollop of water would pour through the closed skylights on to the victim below.

The thermometer remained fixed at eighty.

In the middle of preparing a meal or in the afternoon watch below would come a cry from the deck, "A reef in the main and the second jib. All Hands!" and up we would go through the hatch to be greeted by a slice of the South Atlantic which had mistaken us for a half-tide rock, and to wrestle with the sodden canvas. Each shift of wind meant bringing the ship about to use the most favourable tack to make our easting. "Easting" became my obsession and more than once, out of breath and frustrated by may lack of strength I would catch Anne's glance in which exasperation seemed to be tempered with a trace of fear.

On the 14th day out from Santos we came suddenly on to the Victoria bank some two hundred and seventy miles east from Cabo Thome. It was as if the long ocean swells were a pack of hounds which, in full pursuit over rolling country, suddenly lost their scent and ran hither and thither losing their sense of direction and ignoring the rules of the chase.

A check on my reckoning. I went below to look at the chart over which Anne was at that moment bending.

She said, pointing with the end of a pencil, "I suppose, from the change in the motion, that we are here?"

"If we eased sheets we could run for Bahia. The air there is good and a rest would help you."

A great rage filled me as if she were robbing me of a fortune. With an effort I made my self speak in a near normal tone. I said, "Listen: we have nearly made our easting. In another two days we will be able to square away for Fernando."

"And what happens if the wind backs into the north-east?"

In defiance I said, "We go to Tristan."

"You're mad," she said.

We pressed on. Up tops'l, down tops'l. In reef, out reef, until Jock helping me to change a sail on the foredeck suddenly explained. "Round and round the deck and up and down the mast. I feel like a monkey in a cage."

We were saved by the South-East Trades. They came at a higher latitude than we had any right to expect and in an hour the ship was almost upright and the whole picture changed. The daily runs crept well over the hundred mark and Fernando no longer seemed unattainable.

As we swung up the east coast three hundred miles off shore Brazil prepared for Carnival. In Rio and Salvador, in Recife and in every town, village and hamlet work would stop for four days and four nights, young men and girls pour into the streets to dance and sing until they drop with fatigue and recover to start again.

The endless repetitive refrains, the ironic, lampooning songs came through from our wireless flooding the decks with sound while Anne and Jock, so it seemed to me, sat with their backs to me in protest at my not putting into Recife. But I had my offing and nothing would make me lose it.

On the evening of the twentieth day out I reckoned we were seventy miles from Fernando do Noronho. I had sailed to the east to counteract the strong south equatorial current. The sky was overcast with low cloud. The sea was smooth.

At ten o'clock Anne called me to see the loom of a light: not a nautical loom which spreads fan-shaped from below but a quick tubular sort of flash like that of an aerial beacon. The sequence was a flash every ten seconds. On the large scale chart of the island there was a beacon with a flash of that sequence. It bore some 20 degrees on the port bow and I altered course to keep it fine on the bowsprit end.

It was a very long way off.

When Jock took over from Anne he also saw and timed the light. Two hours later it disappeared but at dawn the island lay dead ahead. It is one of the more dramatic landfalls, with several hills of moderate height and a remarkable mountain with an overhanging top called Pico which reminds one of those around Rio. It lies on the route between Europe and Bahia or Rio, but no ship ever calls there. The bright green water over the shallows, the black volcanic rocks, were a welcome sight after twenty-one days at sea but when we approached the bay to the west of the fort where we had been told to anchor there was far too much swell and we beat back to the wide Bahia de Sao Antonio protected on three sides by reefs and islets. The sun poured down on to a sandy beach upon which the sea broke with a low mutter which did nothing to encourage us to go ashore in our dinghy.

Nothing stirred: but in the afternoon Jock reported an ambulance making rather heavy weather over what must be a very indifferent track. But why an ambulance?

A heavy boat was pulled down the beach and three men got in

while three others waited patiently for the right moment to shove them off. They came alongside.

Speaking hesitant English an officer addressed me courteously. "My name is Captain Durado. I am the army doctor here and the Commandant has asked me to enquire if you need fresh food or water."

"We don't need anything," I said "but fresh food is always nice. Won't you come on board and have a drink?"

He shook his head. "I don't think . . ."

At this point I handed him the personal letter from the Port Captain to the Commandant. "I also am an English doctor." This seemed to turn the balance of the scales in our favour. He came below for a drink and said he was certain that the Commandant would allow us ashore and, after all this time at sea, would we like to stretch our legs for an hour or so? We would.

We landed, not entirely dry, and the doctor drove us in the ambulance (it was the most comfortable vehicle on the island) to the foot of a hill up which we climbed. We had a fine view over the northern end and could see the surf ringing every rock and beach; and yet the South Atlantic looked like a mill pond.

At the top of the hill was a tall iron structure, the aerial beacon. I told the doctor we had seen the loom of this aerial beacon from sixty miles away last night.

He looked at me in utter astonishment.

He said, "But, doctor, this light has not been working for two years!"

CHAPTER TWENTY-FOUR

THERE is a romance about single islands thrusting up out of the middle of an ocean that I find quite irresistible and Fernando is no exception. The grass is greener, the contours fairer, the inhabitants more welcoming. This is a personal thing which I cannot expect others who see it from the bridge of some passenger ship to share: to them it might well appear as a rather dull lump of land, apart from the remarkable Pico.

It was discovered in the year 1600 A.D. and was given to Don Fernando de Noronho by the King of Portugal: a minor gift to a minor favourite in the hope that he would occupy it to prevent anyone else from grabbing it. It was later seized by the Dutch while they were trying to establish themselves along the Pernambuco coast but they were driven off by rats which, records Mr. Southey in his *History of Brazil*, had very short front legs. Their bodies trailed along the ground so that instead of running they hopped like fleas.

When the Portuguese returned they found the rats, turned cannibal, had through their own destructiveness destroyed themselves; a lesson which the human race might profit from.

More recently the island has been drawn into the sphere of "World Defence". The Americans put two hundred scientists here tracking missiles but, owing to the improvements in the missiles, only four remain and the Brazilian army now occupy their quarters. It was here that Dr. Durado brought us in the ambulance next morning to have a brief word with the Commandant who stamped our passports and told us to collect them in the evening.

In life, I thought, as I sat in the cafeteria, things never turn out as you expect. Here we were on a "desert island" where no tourists ever come, which is often inaccessible and only known to its own people as a place for political prisoners and convicts, drinking Nescafé in an air-conditioned room with checkered tablecloths and tubular chairs like a clean edition of a Transport Drive-in, while next door a month of *Moonraker*'s none too salubrious washing was being churned around amongst a battery of shining washing machines, to be returned to us neatly pressed and ironed.

In contrast the village lies in a hollow close west of the old fort.

Two streets of tumbledown houses saved from an utter tawdriness by the brilliant flowers of the flamboyant trees and the flowers planted in decrepit tins outside each of the little houses. It was a village in a wood: the hot deserted streets ringed by a thousand trees their leaves rustling and sighing in the South-East Trades: a village dead to the world after four hectic days and nights of Carnival: a church with crumbling walls and bolted doors, a school which would open tomorrow for the autumn term, a hospital whose patients had miraculously recovered four days ago and where Dr. Durado had produced three hundred babies in the last three years, a Governors' Palace, a relic of bygone splendour upon whose echoing walls were hung paintings of the first Portuguese landing in Bahia Sueste, the ships lying off while longboats transferred reluctant colonists to terra firma. In the old prison the rank and file of the army now live in what once were prisoners' cells.

As the island is only five miles long by one-and-a-half broad it did not take long to encompass it. The ground is fertile but little cultivated, the peasants growing only enough to feed the fifteen hundred inhabitants. Here, as in the village, there was nothing to be bought after carnival.

Bahia Sueste had been marked on our chart as a possible anchorage if the wind had come from the north-west. There were no soundings and from our vantage point the sea broke almost entirely across the narrow entrance. It might be possible, after sounding in the dinghy, to bring a vessel of *Moonraker*'s draft into the circular bay inside but it looked very shallow indeed at its inner end.

It is a lonely place. Wild horses roam over the open country and "geeps" graze in the undergrowth. They have long ears and are a cross between a sheep and a goat. Driving from here to have lunch with the Americans we passed the end of the airstrip. Across it, in orderly lines like rows of tin soldiers were hundreds of oil drums filled with stones. The doctor told us that for the past few months French trawlers had been fishing round the Ilha das Rocas (Brazil claims these rocks as her own) some eight miles to the west of Fernando. Not only had the Frenchmen been poaching but they had failed to throw back the breeding type of lobster into the sea. Tempers had become very short, there had been incidents and Brazil had sent first a gunboat and then a frigate to protect her interests. Now, it was rumoured, France was sending a cruiser to protect hers. The airstrip had been put out of action to prevent a landing by aircraft from the cruiser.

Although all this seemed a little Victorian, a storm in a small teacup, the islanders felt themselves to be very much in the middle of the cup.

I said to the doctor, "Suppose they do make a landing?"

He looked at me with one eye half closed.

He said, "We ask them to dinner and give them lobster."

The Americans lived in two caravans with a large living room added and a sort of look-out, under a spreading pandanus thatched umbrella with table and chairs beneath, from which they could admire a view that compares favourably with most as long as there is no objection to rather a lot of sea.

These men were on a three-year contract allowing them a fairly generous amount of local leave which they spend in Recife and a month each year at home with their families. Seven films were flown in every fortnight from the U.S.A. with steaks, bread, milk, fruit, ice cream, liquor, vegetables and salads. They had all mod. cons.: a washing machine, deep freeze and a girl to "do" for them from Natal.

They gave us an excellent lunch, hugh steaks with French fry, lettuce, tomatoes, apple pie, ice cream and milk from the fridge. They also offered us a dozen grapefruit and when I protested that we could not rob them of their supplies one of them said, "You'll be doing us a favour. They sent these god damned things instead of the canned juices we asked for, and who wants the trouble of eating grapefruit?" Well . . . we did.

One extrovert and three introverts cut off from their local surroundings, isolated by the Great American Way of Life from learning the language and talking to the people who would surely have taken them fishing. Not that they were insensitive: quite the reverse. I had the feeling during that lunch that here might be the ingredients for some author to construct a play in the Strindbergian mode.

On the drive back the doctor stopped and introduced us to a woman walking along the road carrying her child. This was his wife whom Anne described in her diary as "gay as a Flamboyant, radiant with living". Durado had been a pupil of Geraldo de Sá and was hoping soon to meet him. He was leaving the island as soon as his relief came on Saturday. "But," said the doctor, "my relief has been arriving on Saturday for the last six months so I have little hope that he will come this time. Fernando de Noronho is not exactly a sought-after post."

By the time we got back to the Commandant's Office the light was going and we were told the swell was building up. On the way to our end of the island Durado stopped to pick up two men. He said, "One of these men knows more about boat work than anyone on the island." He had, he told us, been a convict in the prison settlement but one day he escaped and rowed (there were no sails in the boat he found) to Natal, two hundred and ten miles away. There he was immediately re-arrested and sent back to the island. The same thing happened a year later and once again, after a few days at liberty he was caught and sent back to Fernando.

Again he escaped but this time he rowed three hundred and fifty miles to Recife. He was arrested and hauled before the Governor of the State who looked at him with the utmost severity.

He said, "You have escaped too often."

"Si, Senhor."

"You have, however, shown considerable initiative in rowing a small boat from Fernando de Noronho to Recife and I will give you a free pardon. I am also prepared to pay your air fare to any town in Brazil."

"Graças a Deus, Senhor. Mil graças!"

"Where would you like to go?" asked the Governor.

"Back to Fernando de Noronho," was the immediate reply.

The heavy boat was pulled up beyond the reach of the surf and while we waited for more helping hands Anne spoke in slow Portuguese to the man whose prowess had won him his freedom. Suddenly she turned to me.

"Did you ever find that chart of Natal?" I shook my head.

With the doctor's help she asked him if he could show us what the entrance looked like. Seizing a bit of wood he drew on the wet sand the coastline, the lighthouse, the reef, the gap, a cable-and-a-half wide through which we should have to sail. He put a cross to one side of the entrance. "Here, a reef. Very dangerous because the current sets you on to it. You understand," he added with naive simplicity, "I know it better than my own hand."

We said goodbye to our kind Brazilian doctor who loaded in the new rolls of bread he had persuaded the village baker to make for us, and the loot from the American camp. The boat was pulled down the beach into the water and we got in. Two men on each side standing up to their waists in water, the two oarsmen on the two front thwarts. I kept my eyes on the land thinking how fortunate we had been to be able to land at all and all we wanted now was that our good luck should hold.

Suddenly there was a cry. "Vamos . . .! A pressa, a pressa . . .!" The heavy boat was thrust forward, the men bent to their oars.

Then, as the first sea rose ahead of us we almost lost way, the bows rose up like the head of a rearing horse, the sea curling over as we reached the top but only a few gallons came into the boat and then we were in deeper water. The doctor had told me that the last two days were the first for three weeks in which a boat could have go through the surf.

We spent an uneasy night. The wind was still offshore but *Moonraker* rolled from side to side groaning and muttering as if she were a patient delirious with fever and I could understand why no yachtsman had ever landed there. More than once Anne and I looked out and each time the roar of the breakers grew louder. When day came, a fresh cheerful day much to our surprise for we had imagined sinister things in that lonely place, we hove up the anchor and set sail to a spanking breeze that took us to the Natal river in some forty-three hours. I would not have liked to have rowed it.

Everything was just as our friend had sketched it on the sand and the sea broke over the dangerous reef but we had a leading wind and we did not even open the engine room doors. The morning was perfect. Along the shore are dunes which resemble those to the north of Imuiden on the Dutch coast giving a sandy feeling to this country, but the village at the entrance has a Moorish look. We swept up the river on the strong flood tide and there was the city perched on a hill on the left bank. It was the first time, in a place of this size, that there were no towering blocks of flats which Mr. J.I.M. Stewart so rightly described as looking like cigar boxes stood up on their sides, and of which we had become rather tired.

The wind dropped as we came under the lee of the town and the tide swept us past an old Brazilian steamer and two fishing quays. Realising we would soon be swept under the railway bridge we dropped anchor, stowed the canvas and got the dinghy off the deck. Presently Anne, using the glasses, said, "There's someone waving to us from a quay. He seems to want us to go there."

Jock went down to start the engine which had not been looked at since we had motored out of Bertioga in a flat calm, twenty-four days before. With all his considerable strength he could not turn it an inch. Water must have got in through the exhaust plug. After a long time the two of us managed to get it moving in a grinding sort of way. "I think," said Jock, "if Anne pulls the decompressors forward when I say and you advance the throttle I may get her to start."

There was a loud explosion.

"That," said Jock, breaking a stunned silence, "is that. This is where we call in an expert."

Anne, who I don't suppose has put her head in the engine room since the thing was put in two years before, was having a look round.

"It looks all right," she said, "don't you think it may have blown all the water out? Try once more."

I know nothing about engines but I do know Anne and I would have been willing to bet a million dollars, if I had them to spare, that that engine would start on the next swing. It did.

CHAPTER TWENTY-FIVE

IT was a Sunday. Above the tarred boards of the fish quay the air quivered as if tortured by the heat. A young man who must surely have some connection with the three Scottish fishing boats with tattered ensigns nailed to their mastheads as if in defiance of their new surroundings, leaned down to shake hands. "We'd given you up. We thought you'd gone home a different way. I'd some work to do in the office and saw your sails coming up the river. I thought it must be you so I rang the Wallaces and Douglas is coming to pick you up in half an hour."

"Lock up the ship. The people here are so poor you can't blame 'em for pinching anything but we have a nightwatchman for our own boats so he can look out for yours when you're not here."

"By the way, if you want anything done, sailmaking or shipwright work, we can do it."

He wouldn't come aboard. "I'll see you later. You want to clear up and I've work to do."

The Wallaces lived in a long low bungalow hidden from the road by trees, some three miles out of town. It was an open house with the Trade Wind blowing through the rooms by day and by night, and from the wide veranda you looked out on a large circular lawn which reminded me of a house in England. Only one line of sand dunes separated it from the sea. It was a quiet house, the sort of house where there is time for reflection rather than the pulsating pressure-driven retreat to which the chief executive returns to entertain all the important people without whom he feels lost and faintly inadequate.

Douglas was large boned, a big man with eyes full of gentle humour; his wife tall and dark, rather pale as if the heat and the white glare of the sun had drained something out of her, and a smile which spread over her face like the promise of a fine day. They had a son, Ian, aged six.

Now that the most troublesome part of the voyage was over, or so I hoped, it was inevitable that some sort of reaction would set in so that I found myself half dozing in the long chair into which I had been put after lunch. With a conscious effort I said, "I think it's time . . .", when Diana, interrupting me, turned to Anne and said "A siesta would be good for all of us. I'll show you to your rooms. Yours has a bathroom which Jock can share."

"But I've brought no things," murmured Anne, "and besides

we can't...".

"We wouldn't dream of letting you stay in that furnace of a harbour," said Diana, "Besides, we've been looking forward to this since Irma wrote to us. We'll get your things from the boat when it gets a bit cooler. Come along. Peter's half asleep already."

That evening we talked about going to the cotton farm. The rains, Douglas explained, had just started in the Interior and if they were heavy the road might be impassable for days at a time. "For eleven months of the year it's as dry as the desert, in March it is flooded. This is March. I think you should go as soon as possible. Charles comes to town tomorrow. He manages the farm and you'd better go back with him on Wednesday. When you've seen as much as you want, come back to us."

On Wednesday we left after an early lunch, driving along a paved road through plantations, fields, pastures and a number of villages which became smaller and more battered until it seemed little short of a miracle that people could live here without abandoning hope.

"These," said Charles, "are the lucky ones for if they run out of water it can be brought to them. Further to the west it has to be searched for."

The paving ended. Red-brown, the road pointed as straight as a compass course across the broad flat plain. Portinari's country. A world of cactus, thorn and stone. Great boulders strewn about as if a race of giants had amused themselves by throwing pebbles. There was, however, a difference. Only the cactus, black and as tall as telegraph poles remained as Portinari painted them. The scrub, the thorn, was green, a young vivid green as the withered bushes lapped up the rain falling intermittently from a lowering sky. The bush now came right up to the road, thick and impenetrable as the Devil's Fence. Out of it flashed a streak of bright yellow jolting the speeding car. We stopped. A long wild cat, as big as a full grown fox with a head like a small puma, lay dead at our feet. The driver opened the boot and flung it inside. Meat for his family and a pelt to sell.

Slowly the scene was changing. Small dark hills, more stony than the plain, rose like islands from a pale green sea and as the car breasted the top of a ridge we came in sight of a village.

"That," said Charles, "is Larges. The only town on our route."

"Town, did you say?"

"Well: it's a town to us."

We drove into a red-brown square with not a single blade of grass, a trackless waste dominated by a white-washed church as ugly as a Unitarian chapel, ringed by houses whose fronts were not too dilapidated: as empty of any mortal moving thing as if they had fled from the threat of war.

"There's a place here where we can buy a drink," said Charles surprisingly.

It was, I remember in the left-hand corner, a wine shop with benches and a table or two. As we stood with drinks in our hands, Charles chatting with the proprietor, the square came to life. A man crossed from the other side, a horseman trotted up leaving his steed outside untethered, the rider hesitating before entering as if he had no wish to intrude; but one by one the place filled up. Small-boned men with not a grain of fat between the lot of them but fit and tough, their faces like the leather of their saddles, for this, like Parati, was a horse town. The rough sing-song voices flowed over my head although one or two of the men, with impeccable manners, tried to engage me in conversation. I think Charles must have told them something about us because I caught several astonished glances levelled at Anne. There was no other woman there. In Larges, said Charles later, women were very much kept in their place.

Rain came down in torrents, turning the dust covered square to mud. Charles, anxious to be off, asked what the road was like between here and the Fazenda Sao Miguel.

"Mala . . . mala . . .," they said with one voice, but "mala" was a word I imagine that was much in use in this place.

As we drove out of the town I said to Charles, "How comes Larges to be here at all, in the middle of the wilderness?"

"It's a centre for a large area, you know. Several hundred square miles. There are a few small fazendas: cattle . . .".

"Cattle in this country?"

"Zebu; originally imported from India. They're incredibly tough. They have to be to survive."

"But what about water?"

"There may be a well with a deep spring below it. I know they've built a dam somewhere. They can count on that being filled up most years at this time."

Heavy storms swept across the sky from the north-east making it almost impossible to see through the windscreen wipers however hard they worked but in the intervals one felt that one could see for hundreds of miles. A mountain, whose summit resembled the well risen crust of a steak and kidney pie, could now be seen ahead and to the left.

"Cabugi," said Charles. "It's a landmark for fifty miles around."

We live on the other side."

Mile after mile the road dipped into what last week would have been dry river beds but were now running streams. Each time we got across with a few inches to spare and after fording a stream where the engine nearly stalled Charles said "One more river to cross and we're safe."

In less than half-an-hour it stretched across our path. It looked deep but the driver knew his ground. In low gear we crawled safely through the rushing stream with the water over the floorboards but the bank on the other side was a different matter. It was now dark. We got out of the car and walked up to the top. The surface was little better than liquid mud. The rain had stopped but a fresh wind blew over the plain. A silent wind not stirring the bush over which it passed so that if anything prowled you might hear it, Anne thought, for she remembered the cat in the boot.

We set to work with our hands: stones, earth, rubble in two tracks up the rise while Anne spread brushwood over the rest of the slope. It took, I suppose, an hour. The driver got in, started the engine, got the wheels gripping and opened her out. Halfway up she skidded almost broadside on but we lent our weight and once more the wheels took. In another moment she was over the top.

In silence, for all of us were feeling a little tired, we drove on through the black night until suddenly I saw a light. It was like sighting a ship in the middle of a very lonely ocean. A notice board announced Fazenda Sao Miguel and we turned off on to a well made track leading to a miniature village with school, church, hall and neat little houses for the workers and their families, until we came to the upper guest house where we were to sleep: an ornate bungalow with Grecian pillars supporting the roof of the veranda and a view of Cabugi from our bedroom window. The sky had cleared. The boulders looked bleached in the moonlight, like the bones of dead whales on the shores of some dark forgotten sea.

Charles said, "I expect you'd like a shower. When you're ready for dinner lift the receiver and you'll be through to me. I'll come and fetch you. The going, in the dark, is rough."

From a wrought iron gate large blocks of stone paving led between argaroba trees and feathery climbing plants to where our hostess was waiting to welcome us with long cool drinks and garden chairs.

Having an undisciplined imagination which often wanders beyond recall, and with the American camp at Fernando de Noronho fresh in my memory I had thought this might be the sort of place where tensions could stir the pen of a Somerset Maugham so that it was a surprise and a relief to find myself chatting with a young woman who showed a crisp practicality and a not over-analytical mind: far too busy looking after four children to brood over how lonely she might have been without them. To remind us of home she had gone to considerable trouble to produce an English meal for us.

Although we were there only for a few days I feel quite sure that if I had asked them whether they wanted a change of scene the answer would have been "no". Charles liked his job and was virtually his own master and the only complaint I heard from his wife was that she had so little time to help with the personal difficulties which beset this small community. They had made friends with some of the Brazilian families in the nearer fazendas and once a month they received half-a-dozen films, of the 1920 period, and most of the horror variety which often caused more merriment than their producers could have foreseen.

This is an experimental farm seeking to grow cotton in the most economic way and to study the spacing of plants and the effects of insecticides when sprayed or dusted. The cotton fields were in flower. The bushes, the size of currant bushes, shared the fields with crops of milho and beans, and carnauba wax plants with long thick spikes and fan-shaped leaves which soon will no longer be grown, for synthetic wax has almost replaced it. The cotton plants were shaded by groves of argaroba trees which keep their foliage all the year round and at twelve years reach the size of a small elm. Locally they are known as "Nibby's" trees after the chief executive who first transplanted them from southern Brazil against the advice of all the botanical experts. From the seed grown on the farm they gave two hundred tons a year to local farmers free and bought back the cotton. For a time they could not understand why it varied so much in quality until it was discovered that some of the farmers were mixing it with native cotton which yielded an extra crop and therefore more money!

In the Ginning factory the cotton, like wisps of thistledown, is separated from the seeds. The cotton is sent to Sao Paulo and the seeds to the factory at Natal to be made into cattle cake and oil. It is quite a complicated process, the finest cotton being "rolled" and the not-so-fine sawn but whatever the process the air in the factory was thick with dust. The workers wore masks but often enough these were no better than a pad across the mouth and nose which was soon torn off in the stifling heat. Some of the men I saw wore nothing. With the basic requirements of the tubercle bacillus ready to hand: great heat, under nourishment, infected milk, overcrowding in small insufficiently ventilated houses, it was no wonder they had a high percentage of losses. Even with efficient masks which were available if only the men would use them, I doubt whether the incidence of tubercle could be properly controlled.

As we were about to leave the factory a large lorry with two drivers drove up to be loaded with cotton for Sao Paulo, some fifteen hundred miles away. One of the men had a smattering of English and I asked him how long he expected the journey to take.

"Sixteen to twenty days in the season of the rains," was the reply.

Only two days less than *Moonraker*!

The cotton farm, like the Fazenda Sao Bento in the State of Sao Paulo, did not limit itself to one product nor confine its experiments to plants. Zebus were being crossed with Friesians in the hope that they could improve the yield of milk without lowering the ability of the Zebu to survive, but the Friesian bull, I thought, was not having a very enjoyable time. He looked so tired and bored that he could hardly stand on his four legs. Perhaps it was the heat.

On our tour of the stockyard we were accompanied by a crowd of children of all ages who giggled and laughed at these funny looking strangers, but standing a little apart was a tall older girl with delicate bone structure and the unconscious graceful movements of a ballet dancer. Her large dark eyes were fixed with interest on Anne who, seeing this, went up to speak to her. Later she said to Margaret, "Surely she's a very exceptional child?"

"I agree. Her teacher says she has never had anyone like her in the school; but what can one do? Her family are amongst the poorest and the only hope would be to send her to a private school in Natal. I have, however, a Brazilian friend who might be interested and the next time she comes I shall arrange that she has a chance to speak to the child. It will have to be a delicate operation for this woman would do nothing unless the child strikes some chord in her own imagination."

"It's a grim thought, don't you think," said Anne, "that the whole of this girl's life hangs on another person's whim?"

"That's the way it goes, in this country."

Charles, in trying to improve the lot of his peasants and workers within the limits of the firm's financial commitments and at the same time adding a little colour to their drab lives, has had an up-hill job. For so many years these have been the Forgotten People and was it likely, they must have asked themselves, that foreigners, with profits to make, were more likely to help them than their own countrymen? And yet, one by one or two by two they were beginning to use the village hall, the only one I saw in a Brazilian village, for dancing to the record player or the wireless, and Margaret had ambitious plans for a play now that her family were approaching the age when they would be leaving for school in England.

There was one luxury, Margaret said, that she didn't know how she had ever done without: a swimming pool. It had been built this year and now, however busy they were they always had a dip before lunch and dinner. Over our pre-prandial bathe that night Charles said "Tomorrow we'll take you to Fernando Pedrosa. The town takes its name from the local landowner. It's bigger than Larges and we have friends living the other side whom we should like you to meet."

As it had been raining solidly for the past twelve hours the main road was flooded and we had to make a detour of some miles driving, as I believe they do in the Australian bush country, over trackless ground known only to the initiated. Fernando Pedrosa is just an ordinary little town with a covered market open on Sunday but the sun was now shining and it had a holiday air for there was no doubt in the minds of the people that the rains had come to stay and this would not be one of those terrible occasions in which no rain came for twenty-three months on end.

We could not, however, meet Charles and Margaret's Brazilian friends because between them and us flowed what looked like a sizeable river. Boys and girls, young men and women, were larking and swimming, washing their clothes, while on each bank, facing each other like armies drawn up for battle, were lorries looking down on the stream in the middle of which was one of their confederates, firmly and irretrievably stuck. This not only provided amusement for the onlookers but pleasure for the truck driver's family who were accompanying him. Mother and children, fully dressed, were swimming in the river and the lorry was already hung with washing drying in the blazing sun. By our side was a donkey, with full saddlebags, whose rider was strung with knapsacks as he was going for a long journey. He said, "This is the quickest transport," whereupon he gave the animal a flick of his whip and it waded past the lorry towards the opposite bank.

The driver of one of the lorries on our side had temporarily abandoned his vehicle. I should like to have met him for on the front he had painted in white letters:

"AMOR TODOS TEEM   MAR POUCOS SABEM   ALL CAN LOVE   FEW KNOW HOW TO LOVE"

It would add, don't you think, to the culture of the British race if our lorry drivers followed the example of their Brazilian brothers?

Charles, after his bathe that evening, looked at the sky. He said, "There's been a shift of wind. Tonight it'll be fine but tomorrow we shall have bad weather. I think, if you want to get back to Natal with any certainty I should go tomorrow."

After dinner we strolled down to the third of the resident houses on the estate. It had been empty for some years because Charles said he could manage without an assistant but I do not think this was purely to save his company money for it was obvious such a near and only neighbour might create a problem, just such a Maugham situation as I had been imagining when I approached the wrought iron gate of Charles' house that first evening.

CHAPTER TWENTY-SIX

CHARLES' weather forecast proved accurate. Rain held off until we got to Natal but the driver, we heard later, caught between two swollen rivers on his way home had to spend the night in the car.

Douglas carried us off to the Mill next morning so that we could see what happened to the seeds arriving from the farm. The mill was only three years old, very up to date and with far less dust in the air than at the Ginnery. The men were also different: more alert and of better physique. The seeds poured down a shute on to wire mesh trays which shiggled and shoggled separating the last of the fluff and dirt from the seed before passing into huge compressors like inverted cones where the oil was crushed out of the de-husked seed to be mixed with solvents and refined before stored in tanks ready for shipment. The crushed seed, drained of oil, now appeared as a grey dung-like material—cattle cake. There was also a by-product, a gooey, khaki coloured stuff which was made into soap and sold to the workers at the Mill and the Ginnery. It was, of course, much more complicated than this but I am not good at remembering a mass of data. Nor am I entirely at my ease when watching men oiling moving parts, opening manholes or lifting heavy weights from one place to another for it reminds me of important men a long time ago being shown around a laboratory in which I was working as a student, their faces blank and impersonal so that I felt I was no more than a microbe under my own microscope.

From the Mill we accompanied Douglas back to his air-conditioned office at the top of a tall building from which you could see the convolutions of the river winding like the coils of a snake towards the sea. At the moment Douglas was contemplating it with disfavour. "Ship's captains don't like this place," he said. "The dockyard is obsolete, the depths are insufficient for any but smaller vessels and they never know when a strike will hold them up so if I want a ship I have a fight to get her. Now my storage tanks are full to the last gallon and if the ship, which ought to have been here a week ago, does not dock on this tide I shall have to close the factory. As we work on a twenty-four hour basis there are quite a lot of men who will go hungry."

At that moment the telephone rang. We watched Douglas' face relax as he listened to the other end.

"Right," he said "you can start loading at once."

The ship had arrived while we had been at the Mill.

A year ago there had been a crisis or another sort. Letters from this office were not getting through to headquarters in Glasgow. The postmaster disclaimed all knowledge or responsibility and then Douglas remembered there had been a new messenger boy.

"I had him up in the office. He'd handed the letters over to be weighed, bought the stamps and posted them in the right box. 'What time d'you post them?' I asked."

"In the afternoon."

"The afternoon? They should go in the morning."

"It's cheaper in the afternoon."

"The man behind the counter in the afternoon had been charging him less for the stamps than the man in the morning. The boy had made his point."

After making enquiries Douglas was told that this was a new man who had not checked on what he thought was the postage for Britain. The sorting office, finding the letters were insufficiently stamped, had thrown them on the floor where they had mounted into a considerable pile. If, said the postmaster, Senhor Wallace would have them collected and restamped he would see they were sent on their way.

A few weeks later the postmaster left his office at the usual time and was later found dead, stabbed in the back by a knife, not far from the office. A new man, said Douglas, proved to be more efficient.

There was a saying that no one came to Natal if they could keep away from it and from our first few sorties into its rather dirty streets and the market where the fruit was not very good and the meat looked stringy, and the shops, some of them long and narrow and dark, which made me think of pawnbrokers in the east end of London, we could understand their attitude but as the days went by and we came to recognize familiar faces in the streets and to know the men and women in the market stalls we had the feeling, in this town of a hundred thousand people, that we belonged. And you would have thought that a foreign yacht fitting out at a busy fish quay would have got in the way but instead of angry looks there was only laughter and gossip and if a man met Anne struggling with a heavy load (she is a lot stronger than she looks) he would invariably give her a hand.

After we came back from the farm our days fell into a pattern. We worked on the ship all day until Douglas called for us at half-past five. Occasionally Diana would look in for a cup of tea and take Anne off to do some shopping and on these expeditions she always brought Neil and his friend Alfonso. Alfonso was eight years old. He lived beyond the gates of the house in one of a few pitiful shacks and Neil had met him when he had been exploring which he was forbidden to do.

Neil very quickly became attached to this dark little boy with the wrinkled old-mannish face and Diana, who may have felt a little guilty that her boy had so few friends to play with, told him to bring Alfonso home. After a few days she went to see the mother and explained that Alfonso could spend as much of the day as he liked at the house returning to his home at night. The family were delighted. It would be one less mouth to feed and his brothers and sisters rejoiced in his good fortune without envy. Instead of two small maize patties, a cup of rice water and, if he was fotunate, a slice of bread for supper he had three good meals a day but his bones were small and rickety and it was only now that he was beginning to fill out. He was still smaller than Neil who was two years younger.

Six months ago Neil started school in Natal in the mornings. He seemed to make no friends and one day he asked his mother why Alfonso should not come to school with him. It was a question to which neither Douglas nor Diana had yet found an answer. If they sent him to this school they would have to see the thing through to the end but what would happen if Douglas was sent to Europe or South Africa at a few months notice? It was a question that was not made more easy to solve by Alfonso's obvious intelligence.

Since we started work on the boat we had seen quite a lot of the young man who had first welcomed us; his name was John. He had had *Moonraker*'s topsides painted while we had been up at the farm, the deck over the tin locker caulked and some patches sewn on to our ageing foresail. It became his habit to drop in for a drink in the early evening and at times he would tell us about his problems not because he wanted advice but it helped to clear his mind. He had come out with his wife and child to manage a lobster concern into which a large British company had poured some capital. "You'd think," he said one evening, "in a town like this they'd welcome any new venture that would give employment and bring money into the place. Lobsters are plentiful, we get a good price for the tails in the States where they are all the rage. The men like these Scottish fishing boats but everywhere on the waterfront we are looked on with suspicion as foreigners, and the fishermen are jealous of competition. So I am confronted on all sides with red tape and if I call on the Port Captain he is either out or too busy to see me. To crown it all, there's a conference of the three main shareholders at the end of the week. My boss from the firm, my boss the Sicilian American, my boss the Brazilian lawyer. Each wants to run this show a different way and if it wasn't for the help and advice I've had from Douglas I would pack the job in."

We caught a glimpse of the smooth Brazilian lawyer and were introduced to the Sicilian American, an elderly, immensely rich man who, Diana discovered to her astonishment, could neither read nor write. He was accompanied by his wife, a tall gaunt woman with agate eyes.

We were able, in a catalystic way, to make John's path a little smoother. It came about in a roundabout way, at a party given by the Wallaces in which they had asked, amongst a great many others, John and his wife, the Port Captain and the Head of Television. I felt immediately drawn to the Port Captain, a young dynamic seaman whose head was full of improvements for the port, but in the middle of the party Anne, Jock and I were whisked away, all quite unexpectedly by the Television Man to the Philosopher's Hall to take part in a sort of In Town Tonight show in which questions and answers had to be translated. Afterwards we were introduced to the Governor and his family.

Douglas said to me the next morning. "The Governor and the Port Captain have expressed an interest in your boat. Would you like to invite them aboard?"

"We should be most honoured."

"Would you also invite John?"

It was to be a very informal party but one to which I was looking forward for the Governor was deeply concerned with the growing poverty in the town where an industrial worker was paid 350 cruzeiros a day, the equivalent in England to about 5/-, while the price of food was soaring. The other day he had marched into the market with a platoon of soldiers at his back and I could see that thrust-forward chin like that of the Spaniard striding up the hall in the film of La Kermesse Heroique, and the sudden hush in the busy square as he seized the slate on the nearest meat stall, wiping it clean and chalking up the new price, 460 cruzeiros a kilo.

Leaving the soldiers to see that his commands were obeyed, he walked out. On the next day and the day after that there was no meat to be had and everyone thought the Governor would have to climb down but on the day after that supplies were being sent to the market and sold at 460 cruzeiros a kilo.

The Governor came aboard with an escort of elegant young men. He had small dark eyes which seemed to snap as they glanced from face to face when making a point. He did not stay very long but on his way ashore he visited the ice plant where the lobster tails awaited their air passage to the U.S.A.

The Port Captain lingered. There is an aura about the cabin of a small sea going ship that no layman could be expected to understand. It smells of the sea and brings back to the seaman a sound of the wind so that problems to do with the sea which might prove insuperable on land become settled in a very short time. After the Captain had left John came back. "This may have been more help to me than you might think," he said. "Thank you for asking me."

"Don't thank me," I said with a grin, "Thank Douglas."

Next day the stores began to arrive and on one occasion when Jock was handing me a carton of tins the ship sheered and I dropped the lot into the muddy water followed by a dozen dark touzled heads diving like pelicans after fish from the quay. They retrieved a dozen tins before they realized that here was a gift from the gods.

"Amanha," they said, "talvez," with a shrug. But half-an-hour after we left the ship I would be willing to bet there would not be a tin on the bottom.

As Douglas was anxious that we should take some jerk meat on our next voyage he and Diana took us that evening to a café in a dark narrow street down by the water where they served it cooked in oil. As I recalled only too well the jerk meat we had tried on passage from Recife to Bahia I could not say I was looking forward to this but it was delicious, just like fresh steak done to a turn.

This tiny place, without a sign or a light outside, with half-a-dozen iron tables and some chairs and benches was known to people from Rio and Sao Paulo who, when they came to Natal, eat here instead of at the Grand Hotel. Although Anne was told how to cook it one could hardly expect a chef who was on his way to becoming famous to give away his secrets so that I felt that this jerk meat might easily suffer the same fate as that from Recife. We stowed it away as the chef had instructed us, in layers of sawdust.

There was nothing more to be done.

Although the most awkward part of our voyage lay behind us there were still six thousand miles to sail between Natal and

Fowey by way of the West Indies, with the possibility of bad weather once we were north of the 45th parallel in the north Atlantic.

On the way up from Santos the ship had been making more water, four times as much water, as usual. *Moonraker*, you may remember, is copper sheathed over iron fastenings, a galvanic experiment so successful that its dangers had been shelved from my mind for many years but since she had been lying in the sheltered waters of the harbour, when she should have been making nothing at all, Jock or I had had to pump fifteen strokes every day to clear the bilges, and my fears returned.

Apart from one small seep for'ard we could find no leak but there are five tons of iron ballast between the mast and the after end of the cabin sole and without taking it out we could not see what was going on beneath it. This was not an impossible task but if we discovered a leak we could still do nothing about it for there was no slip on which a boat of *Moonraker*'s size could be hauled out. Anne alone would not take it seriously. She maintained that the climate of South Brazil was such that it would make any boat leak and as soon as we reached a more temperate zone the hull would take up. Jock and I thought the chances against her being right this time were fifty to one.

The last fresh food and fruit came aboard, the last goodbyes were said. Our lines were cast off and we slipped down to the Officers Club where we anchored for the night.

The tide served at ten next morning. At half-past nine, as we were hauling the dinghy on deck, we heard a call from the shore and there were our friends on the float off the Club. We sailed up to them. The ship gave a final curtsey a few feet away from where they stood and then turned on her heel with the first of the ebb. I gave a last backwards look at the town on the hill, the valley, the river and our friends. The ship rounded the first bend and the last visual link between them and us broke.

CHAPTER TWENTY-SEVEN

AS the last night on the Brazilian coast dipped below the horizon I realized with a sense of shock that the meat of the voyage was over.

This, then, was the place to end the book but now that I am writing about it I have begun to have second thoughts. We were not in one of B.O.A.C.'s aircraft or even a Blue Star liner but in our own small boat crawling over the ocean as a snail crawls over the land with its possessions on its back; an insignificant unit but our own. This is not only a story about Brazil but about us and I must end where we began.

If you could read Anne's diary you would not recognize it. Gone were the tensions for I was now rested well. It was a record of meals and watches, of winds, sunsets, the shape of clouds, a ship's lights seen at night and of her first wash; "I seize the opportunity," she wrote, "to have a bath for the first time since we left port. The daily bath is lovely but the first wash in a mugful of water after eight salty days is really a thing to savour."

I remember the day because we had that morning picked up the winter North-East Trades, the most beautiful of all winds in the world. It was, to our humid-ridden lungs, as if we were standing on Dengie marshes looking out over the North Sea on a bright spring morning.

In the next six days we sailed eight hundred and forty-six miles; the roar of the bow wave as it creamed up to the stemhead, the frothing bubbling sea, all bark and no bite, to which her stern rose more than a thousand times a day, the watch anxiously regarding the log at the end of each three hour spell in case the reading fell below the twenty miles on the clock. Then the incredible thing happened. *Moonraker* who had been making as much, if no more, water than she had been in Natal suddenly, on this day in which her noon to noon run was no less than one hundred and forty-eight miles, took five strokes of the pump to clear the bilges and from then on remained the dry ship to which we were so used. Anne did not even remark upon it.

On the fifteenth day we sighted South Point light on Barbados, nineteen hundred and twenty miles from Natal. We had no charts of Carlyle Bay (our charts would be waiting for us there) so we hove to for daylight. It was as well. The place was crowded with yachts and in our old solitary berth was an oil tanker tied hand, foot and tail with a huge pipe connecting her to oil tanks ashore. To the north was a new deep water harbour and there were no flying fishermen setting out in the early morning like clouds of butterflies.

The island, which always seems to me to be a small slice of England come to roost in a tropic sea, appears to be on the point of bursting with prosperity but if you lie to your anchor in some quiet bay on the leeward coast you can still see the charm of Barbados as we saw it thirteen years ago, when we first came here.

There was a holiday spirit about our cruise up the windward islands for this was home ground and it was fun sailing Jock into all the places we had been to before so that a month passed before we entered English Harbour.

If you asked the average off-shore cruising man to which place his ambition would take him, given the time, nine times out of ten the answer would be English Harbour.

He might find it a little difficult to locate for the faces of the old brown cliffs seem to present an unbroken line but if he kept up to windward until he had identified the Pillars of Hercules and the old fort now cleared of undergrowth and the dark trees on Charlotte point rustling and swaying in the freshening morning breeze he would suddenly see the opening and, with a man aloft to con the ship in, sail into sudden quiet water as blue as a Swiss lake with a dazzling white coral beach on his starboard hand and the winding channel leading to Nelson's dockyard looking much as it must have done at that time, so well have the Friends of English Harbour restored this national monument. He would be faced by a forest of masts, the masts of schooners and ketches, the charter fleet equipped with big engines and radio and electronic equipment which enables them to safely convey their rich American guests all the way to Grenada and back and allow them to keep in hourly touch with Wall Street if they so wish. He would then, if he is wise, anchor in Commissioner's Bay saving two dollars fifty American money a day, and avoid the rats which, when we were last here, used to scamper round our decks at night.

It was thirteen years and one month since we first sailed in here. Vernon and Emmie Nicholson then lived in the Paymasters House and their schooner *Mollyhawk* was the only resident yacht. Now their charter business has grown to such proportions that if all the vessels taking part are in together there is hardly room to turn.

The buildings then were falling down, some were roofless, and at night the guard at the guardhouse gates kept strangers away so that on a moonlight night, strolling across the dusty sward, one could pause for a moment and people this silent place with ghosts of the ships and men that lived, drank and died when Nelson lived in the Admiral's House. Anne used to write her letters there. Sometimes I would find her with her head on her hands staring out to sea while the shadows lengthened and the waters of the channel darkened.

The old boards creaked under our feet and as we left a small cloud of dust rose into the lifeless air. Now the Admiral's House, much restored, is a museum which also houses a retired commander who is in charge and has a violet curtained bathroom.

The guardhouse had gone and out of its ashes rises, Phoenix like, the Admiral's Inn. A friend of ours, a fellow member of the Royal Cruising Club, happened to be visiting Antigua on business and had come over to look down on English Harbour and found himself looking down on *Moonraker*. As he was unable to dine aboard with us we dined with him at the inn. It was something of a gala evening with a steel band playing Calypso and a tall very black negro gave a thrilling exhibition dance that was half-Charleston and half-Hula. Afterwards he came up to speak to us. "I remember yo'," he cried. "Yo' was here eleven years ago at Christmas and I played to yo' in the Death of Hector band. Remember?"

"Of course I remember," answered Anne, "and when I asked why you called your band Death of Hector, you said, 'Page 88.' "

"That' right, m'am. Page 88 in the history book."

As we sat outside and the band played and the girls and boys danced the Twist and the moon shone down on masts and spars and on the great anchor and the guns driven into the ground for bollards I could see the sailors dancing the Hornpipe on the very square upon which more slender and sophisticated feet now tread the modern equivalent.

I glanced up and caught Anne's eye. I do not think that she or I will enter English Harbour again.

Our last port of call was Anguilla, our favourite in the West Indies. It is off the tourist-ridden route and is still a home for commercial sail where schooners and cutters carry on their trade without engines. It lives on its salt industry and boat building and Sandy Ground, its only sheltered anchorage, has the most beautiful shades of colouring of any bay in the world that I have seen. If you have no car and want to visit the bakery, the Commissioner, the Public Health and the Court of Justice it would be a two-day walk.

There is a family living here whose grandfather came out from England nearly a hundred years ago. At one time they owned a fleet of schooners and a herd of sheep on Dog Island but the last two schooners were lost in hurricane Donna and the sheep have been stolen or died. The mother, a charming old lady, had died two years ago and the only daughter who can still get about ran down to the quay in wild excitement to welcome us, although the last and only time she had seen *Moonraker* was in 1950. She took us into the house, now badly in need of repair, where we met her sister and one brother both crippled with the same nervous disease and surrounded by rocking chairs and Victorian bric-a-brac with the same pictures of Highland cattle and religious texts in frames on the walls which we remembered from our former visit.

The much younger brother who might have restored the family fotunes had taken to the bottle.

Because it seemed cruel to leave we stayed more days than we had intended. When we finally rowed back to *Moonraker* for the last time leaving the sisters on the quay (the crippled one having by some miracle managed to get down there) Anne, much moved, said, "Forget what I said about coming back to the West Indies. I'm very glad we did."

Bermuda lies just over eight hundred miles almost due north of Anguilla but there was one incident at the end of that passage which showed that a little luck is necessary when sailing boats across oceans.

Now whenever I leave on a passage I always check the index error of the sextant. I checked it on leaving Anguilla. On the sixth day out with Bermuda only a hundred miles ahead I took a meridian sight as usual in the morning and in the afternoon took another to check it. When the position was worked out there was a thirty mile error to the east. Either I or the sextant or the compass had gone mad.

"Check the index error," chanted my crew at me in unison, and finally I did. Since the morning sight there had been an error of fifteen minutes. If the silver had started peeling off the glass (the cause of the error) three days after leaving Bermuda with two thousand and seven hundred miles still to go we should have had to go back to the days of dead reckoning.

We sailed from Bermuda in June. At first it was summer sailing on a summer sea but once we were north of the 40th parallel it grew colder and the wind piped up, moulding us, as nothing else will, into an efficient wordless team. At the end of two weeks we had sailed one thousand four hundred and fifty miles and as this should be the slowest part of the ocean I was looking forward to a fast passage. On this day the whole sky was covered with high streaks of cloud, some straight, some with curly ends, moving from west to east, and the barometer, which had been exceptionally high, was steadily falling.

Jock said, "But that's upper air, Peter. Nothing to do with us."

"That's what they say," I agreed, "but I've often seen it when there's a change of weather coming."

In the afternoon the sun peered through a thin film of cloud with an enormous halo round it. Of all warnings of bad weather in the higher latitudes this is the most reliable. But when another day and night passed, still with a falling glass and a light southwesterly wind Jock said, "If there's been any bad weather it's gone somewhere else."

That night it rained and the wind backed to south but by the morning it had cleared and the glass was steady. At noon the next day the wind switched, in a few minutes, into the north and it became very much colder. This must be the cold front. During the afternoon and evening the wind rose steadily and the glass as slowly fell. Dusk came early and I was reminded of the seaman's warning.

> Last night the sun went pale to bed
> The moon in haloes hid her head ...

At ten o'clock Anne took the helm while Jock and I pulled down the third reef and checked that everything was properly lashed on deck for I was convinced by the tight feeling inside me that this was going to be something unusually unpleasant.

At ten o'clock in the morning on that fifth day of July Jock called me. Water dripped off his oilskins, his face, his beard, onto the cabin sole.

"It's a filthy night," he said. "Bloody cold." and I looked at him with sudden curiosity for in the eighteen months we had been together that was the only time he had used that word. I had a gusty, squally watch with a vicious cross sea building up over a long ominous swell rolling down from the NE. It was daylight when I called Anne.

A freighter, some two miles away had turned 90 degrees from her course and was making towards us and by the time Anne was at the helm she was on our port quarter with her engines stopped and the officer of the watch studying us through his glasses while I studied her.

None of us raised a hand for this was no courtesy call. It was a big ship making sure, before the advent of bad weather, that a small one needed no assistance.

Before going below I took a last look to windward. A high smooth bank of cloud was etched with vivid green and small bands of black scud swept down from the NNE like brigands on the prowl. I put in the wash boards and slammed the hatch in disgust. I was out the moment my head touched the pillow.

Watch succeeded watch until the wind flew into the NE in the middle of a squall and the grey sullen sea suddenly became as white as snow driven over a winter landscape, the wind at fifty knots. We hove to, pulled down the fourth reef, set the reefed staysail, took off the jib, lashed the helm hard down, wedged two terylene sails to windward between the dinghy and the cabin top, and went below out of the cold.

Anne said, "After all that I'd better bake a scone loaf for tea." The work had made us hungry. "Where's the second half?" asked Jock having had his share of the first.

"I've put it away," Anne told him. "You may be glad of it tomorrow."

The wind rose until it howled round the ship like Dr. Zhivago's wolves on the Siberian steppes. Exhausted by the events of the past twenty-four hours we dozed. As the ship struggled through the night a figure would rise from one bunk or another to make its stealthy way aft peering through the perspex board onto a world of rain and spray and sea so intimately mixed that it was hard to believe that we were still afloat.

At dawn the wind dropped: from Force 10 to Force 8 and while I was assembling the things for breakfast a sudden shaft of sunlight shone through the galley porthole. I threw on a jacket and hood, pulled back the hatch. Out of the thin driving mist came wall upon towering wall of water like mountains and valleys in perpetual motion, each crested ridge caught in the pale beams of momentary sun. I felt as if I had suddenly been transferred to the nave of some lofty cathedral whose size and beauty robbed me of the power of movement and at that moment a rogue sea burst over the ship and water came pouring down the hatch.

Morning and evening Jock and I, clothed from head to foot in sea boots, oilskins and hoods, cautiously toured the decks as a houseman makes his rounds of the wards at night in case one of his patients should die. Each terylene lanyard holding the shrouds, the nip of the halyards, signs of chafe: the things a seaman watches to safeguard his ship. At noon we pumped her out, twelve strokes of the pump.

No ship, no old ship, is dry in these conditions. In spite of the sails lashed between the dinghy and the cabin top spray would be forced through both of them, through the closed skylights and pour like a cold water shower onto Anne's bunk but Anne is an old campaigner and is not easily caught out. She had provided herself with a plastic shower curtain and kept dry beneath. She would then struggle out of her bunk, throw the pool of water on to the floor and mop it up without comment.

This gale, with two intermissions, lasted five days although it never again approached the ferocity of that first night and on the fifth day it blew itself out.

I have a photograph of Anne and Jock, Anne standing in the hatch, Jock by the rigging, both of them looking to windward, their faces pale as if they had been prisoners in solitary confinement; showing a relief after tension to which neither of them yesterday would admit.

After two days of sunshine and light breezes the wind strengthened to gale force, this time from the west. After our last encounter this was almost a joyous affair for it was a fair wind but it was distinctly strenuous for it rose unobtrusively as a thief climbs into a house at night, the wind rising a note each time we put in a reef so that we had to pull in another until there were no more to tie down. It was a wild scene. The long seas, their grey backs mottled like tiger skins, the ship foaming along under her tiny rag of sail dark to the head with spray, Anne and Jock huddled round me waiting for me to give the next command. Anne's voice in my ear: "Take it in now, while there's time.·", a note that held such urgency compelling me to action.

"Right," I said, "Mains'l down and we'll set the spinnaker for'ard of the forestay sheeted to the pinrails."

Much later I remember crawling about the cabin floor pouring cocoa into mugs. It was three o'clock in the morning, still Anne's watch but Jock had taken one look at her and in a fatherly voice told her to go below. When I joined her she said, "I'm too tired to sleep. I'll make some cocoa to warm us all up." and it was then, looking at her face which seemed to have shrunk round two large eyes which regarded me gravely that I realized how desperately tired she was. Not be be wondered at, I suddenly thought, for in her sixtieth year she would have sailed, by the time we reached

Fowey, eight thousand miles in the last five months.

We picked up the Bishop Rock at the end of four days of fog, rounded the Lizard with its siren blowing right over our heads and sailed into Fowey with every stitch of canvas we could set before the light fair wind.

We had not, as we had thought, entered unobserved.

On a balcony belonging to one of the old grey stone houses overlooking the harbour two elderly women were enjoying the afternoon sun which was just strong enough to penetrate the summer haze.

Suddenly one of them stood up. "Look," she cried, pointing to *Moonraker* coming in through the entrance, "She looks just like the *Victory*."

A compliment as charming as it was inaccurate.